PARADIGM WARS

PARADIGM WARS
Worldviews for a New Age

MARK WOODHOUSE

Frog, Ltd.
Berkeley, California

Paradigm Wars: Worldviews for a New Age

Published by Frog, Ltd.

Frog, Ltd. Books are distributed by
North Atlantic Books
P.O. Box 12327
Berkeley, CA 94712

Cover illustration by Ruth Terrill
Printed in the United States of America

Library of Congress Cataloging-in-Publication Data
Woodhouse, Mark B.
    Paradigm wars: worldviews for a New Age / Mark B. Woodhouse.
      p.   cm.
    Includes bibliographical references and index.
    ISBN 1-883319-42-0
    1. Parapsychology and science.   2. Science—Philosophy.
  I. Title.
  BF1045.S33W66   1995
  140—dc20   95-50946
                                              CIP

1 2 3 4 5 6 7 8 9 / 99 98 97 96

For my children
Alejandra and Erik
Comrades, starseeds, and future leaders
in times of great transformation

Acknowledgments

Permission to quote from the following sources is gratefully acknowledged: Strawberry Hill Press, Portland, Oregon, for Thomas Bearden's *Excalibur Briefing* (second edition, revised and expanded), copyright by Thomas Bearden, 1980, 1988; Heldrof Publications for Christina and Stanislav Grof's "Spiritual Emergency," *ReVision*, vol. 8, no. 2, (1986), reprinted with permission of the Helen Dwight Reid Educational Foundation; *New Age Journal* for Ken and Treya Wilber's "Do We Make Ourselves Sick?" (September, 1988).

Many individuals assisted in the birthing of this work. Tricia McCannon, Janet Quinn, Cannon Garber, Harriet Wall, and my students at Georgia State University, especially Isadora Vaderos, David Perlman, Pat Rich, Kirk Hutchins, Robert Flanders, Helgi Hardarson, Jerry Zerbach, Lori Feig-Sandoval, Kenny Smith, Jeffrey Tucker, and Jenni Jordan, who have provided inspiration, critical feedback, and moral support. John and Rebecca Montague provided friendship and a place to write at a critical time in my life. Susan Palmer gave effective editorial assistance, and Cybèle Tomlinson provided editing and production services. Ayelet Maida provided the book and cover designs, and Ruth Terrill created a cover illustration. And Priscilla Omega provided financial assistance essential to continuing the project.

From my parents, Johnny and Alice Woodhouse, as well as from MacBride Panton, Bill Torvund, Tom Kenyon, Peter and Marianne Kelly, Joann Marnie, Ken Ring, Lorelei Robbins, Tracy Schmidt, Etel DeLoach, and especially Nancy McCary (who *never* lost faith!) I have learned much, both intellectually and personally, that has informed the evolution of the project. Ken Wilber's compelling and extensive treatment of the spectrum of consciousness has exerted a profound influence on my thinking, even though he would not necessarily agree with certain directions I have taken.

A special word of acknowledgment is due my friend and teacher, Jackie Woods. Not only has her work "behind the scenes" positively changed planetary history, her discerning and empowering guidance has also profoundly changed *my* history—and with it, the evolution of this book.

I am indebted to Fred Mills for permission to publish as an appendix the results of his extensive research on sacred geometry, field theory, and the "Face on Mars." He will publish separately the full justification for his conclusions together with extensive applications.

Robert Almeder, Stephen Braude, Huston Smith, Jonathan Lee, Dan Peterson, Linda Kurtz, Jack Crittenden, David Griffin, John White, and Michael Zimmerman have commented on various portions and saved me from errors of fact, logic, or interpretation. Richard Grossinger, senior editor at North Atlantic Books, provided a critical overview that led to further revisions. In a work of this magnitude, however, the opportunity for error is great, and I must claim responsibility for those that remain.

Various interdimensional beings, especially Pheadrea, Pheobus, Michael, Gabriel, Hilarion, Raphael, Maitreya, and Sananda have provided teaching, guidance, friendship, healing, and protection. In the academic world, to acknowledge such alignment is considered vacuously self-serving at best. I suspect that the times in which we live will repay a similar compliment for opposite reasons.

My children, Erik and Alejandra, unselfishly pursued other activities on countless weekends when I disappeared in order to write. In their own unwitting fashion, they both encouraged me to keep the faith and provided miniature test cases for various ideas. The vicissitudes of their father's journey never diminished the boundless love in which they are held.

Finally, I owe an enormous debt to countless pioneering spirits in the current quest for a larger integrative vision, many of whom I regrettably could not include in this project. Their published works have inspired both my professional and personal growth. More importantly, they have established an intellectual and cultural legitimacy without which a book such as this would, in the words of David Hume, "fall stillborn from the presses."

Mark Woodhouse
Lakemont, Georgia

Table of Contents

Introduction

In 1980 I attended a major conference in New York City sponsored by the Sufi Order on the topic "New Dimensions of Consciousness." It carried major addresses by luminaries such as David Spangler, Fritjof Capra, Karl Pribram, Jean Huston, and Pir Vilayet Khan on the meeting of science and spirituality and the transformation of culture. A number of factors had already predisposed me to look beyond the constraints of mainstream philosophy. But this conference was the catalyst that caused me to turn my attention away from the issues most philosophers found important and to focus instead on the challenges of an emerging New Paradigm. A lot more was blowing in the wind, I felt, than hot air and laments about the sorry state of things. I began publishing articles in *ReVision*, rather than in *Philosophical Studies*, and I started attending workshops on healing, rather than on epistemology.

As I plunged into a period of intense personal growth work and (what I shall henceforth refer to as) "New Paradigm" exploration, it became evident that 1980 was a profound turning point in my life. While continuing to teach and write at a major state university, my path led me—as if by divinely orchestrated synchronicity—to feminist debates, free energy conferences, extraterrestrial channelings, kundalini awakenings, holistic health centers, alternative schools, Native American power spots, Buddhist ashrams, spiritually based psychotherapy, and essential briefings by former intelligence officers—to name but a few! Needless to say, these are not the kinds of topics one hears discussed in university classes. This exposure, plus the inspiration and personal guidance of some extraordinarily gifted individuals, continued to nurture my growth.

It became evident how much we are living in times of enormous challenge and transformation. However, I felt conflicted over whether we would merely stumble through this period in a piecemeal fashion, sampling the disconnected agendas of, say, psychic development, holistic health, Greenpeace, and the New World Order, or whether a new and integrated worldview would emerge from this cultural mélange. *Paradigm Wars* is the result of that intellectual and personal journey (which is still very much in progress). A new worldview *is* emerging, and many are knee-deep in some very messy transition dynamics.

The shift from old to new promises to be comparable in scope and confusion to the shift from the medieval mind-set to the Enlightenment. Major paradigm wars, I think, will transform our most cherished institutions. In many areas the conflicts have been underway for several decades. And, as with most major cultural transitions, things will probably become worse before they get better.

From where are we coming and to where are we headed? What are the principal challenges fueling the current shift? Many paradigms inform Western history, for example, the Judeo-Christian and Cartesian-Newtonian. There is no single perspective that we can identify as *the* Western worldview. However, I identify most of the important principles associated with the idea of a Western worldview. From these principles I distill the metaphors of fragmentation, reductionism, competition, hierarchical control, and fear that have shaped Western intellectual and cultural history.

While I do not aim for an exhaustive presentation in this regard, these metaphors are the ones most at risk today. For they have led us to crises of such magnitude that we can survive only by abandoning the ways of thinking and behaving that have brought us to the brink. In Chapter One I briefly describe ten transformational challenges in areas such as health, education, paranormal phenomena, science, religion, and the environment. In subsequent chapters, I argue that the most promising responses are supported by the inclusivist metaphors of integration, balance, (multidimensional) wholeness, mutually empowering cooperation, and love.

I have drawn many examples for *Paradigm Wars* from writers and issues that will be more recognizable to North American readers. This is mainly because the America appears destined to play a leadership role in the evolution and application of New Paradigm thought. Here is where much of the action is, although other countries are ahead of us in specific arenas, such as health and environmental concerns. Still, most of the ideas I take up are relevant for Western culture in general and, in a number of instances, for Eastern cultures, too. Developing a worldview that will nurture sustainable and empowering ways of relating to the planet and with each other is certainly not just an American agenda. It is a global one.

From my perspective as an academic, I see contradictions, hope, and chaos in the current paradigm wars. I have written this book partly because the New Paradigm spectrum is full of philosophical confusion. For example, some writers argue the virtues of literal reincarnation. Others reject this interpretation but affirm some *therapeutic* value in "past-life regressions." Another group urges that the empirical case for reincarnation is based on pseudoscientific thinking. Still others chime in with the observation that, according to Buddhism, there isn't any "self" to reincarnate anyway. A final group dismisses reincarnation on the grounds that it promotes social injustice. To one degree or another, defenders of these divergent points of view are all participants in the New Paradigm dialogue. What is one to believe when the philosophical terrain is such a bloody mess?

New Paradigm thinking is a process, not a unified structure waiting to drop into place. It involves loosely knit family resemblances emerging across our personal, social, and professional agendas in response to many challenges. It carries all the pain, confusion, collapse, and rebirth that have attended other shifts in worldview. Accordingly, *Paradigm Wars* clarifies important issues and maps significant territory. However, I do not merely describe positions. I evaluate them and give reasons for preferring one over others. In some areas I propose new ways of thinking about long-standing problems.

Paradigm Wars offers a vision of the "big picture." Few books make such an attempt, and those that do differ markedly from this project. Can we really integrate the diverse concerns of ecofeminism, holistic health, alternative education, the New Physics, spiritual pathways, and extraterrestrial contact into a coherent worldview? I endeavor to show how these and other transformational agendas reflect deep structural similarities that tie key elements of the big picture together.

Two master paradigms, Systems Holism and the Perennial Wisdom, have arisen (or rearisen) in response to the need for an integrative vision. The Perennial Wisdom is not, of course, a "new" worldview; it has endured in one form or another for thousands of years. However, it will seem new to those steeped in the traditions of mainstream religion, science, and social thought. Throughout the book I compare the kinds of solutions that these outlooks offer. In most cases, I find that the Perennial Philosophy (as I also call it) presents the most adequate framework for addressing current crises. Only a worldview that incorporates a multilevel conception of reality, with both seen and unseen dimensions, will prove adequate for the task. Systems Holism makes important contributions, especially in stressing the interconnectedness of all things. In my opinion, however, it does not go far enough.

In a project such as this, the result must be a temporary plateau of partial answers subject to further revisioning. One must inevitably sacrifice some depth for breadth. However, I have emphasized those *fundamental* issues around which much of the rest of the debate revolves. In certain respects, *Paradigm Wars* is a survey. But it covers some of the most important parts of the terrain, namely, those that invite heated controversy and fuel paradigm wars.

Here are some examples. Is Matthew Fox too hard on the New Age? How could six world-class clairvoyants correctly see a future that never comes to pass? Is systems theory weak on spiritual concerns? Is there such a thing as "feminine" energy? Is everything really just "energy and vibrations"? What happens when a reincarnationist joins the abortion debate? Does taking care of the environment merely to save ourselves go far enough? What could account for a government cover-up on UFOs? Is the New World Order simply another version of Old Paradigm thinking? These are but a small fraction of the paradigm wars shaping the horizons of a "Rising Culture" (a phrase I have borrowed from Fritjof Capra).

Commentators on earlier drafts have noted a tension between sections that appeal more to academic audiences, on the one hand, and parts that appeal more to popular audiences, on the other. Indeed, several commercial publishing houses suggested that I submit *Paradigm Wars* to academic presses at the same time academic presses were suggesting that I submit it to commercial publishers. For some, this divergence is a defect. However, since I have intentionally sought to produce a book that appeals *both* to academics and to a more discerning readership in popular culture, this defect is better seen as a virtue.

Academics generally have great difficulty embracing any book that takes seriously such topics as spiritual healing, ecofeminism, and extraterrestrial intelligence. The current direction of history, however, suggests that soon they will have to do so. I have attempted to organize the debates around key trigger points in ways that will make the emerging terrain easier to navigate. By the same token, I believe that the first wave of information is behind us. Intellectually curious readers are looking for something more advanced than *E.T. 101*, as delightful as that little primer is.

Paradigm Wars aims, accordingly, for what might be described as the less rigorous end of academic scholarship and the more discerning New Age/ New Paradigm readership of popular culture. It can serve both as a textbook for college courses and as companion reading for personal exploration. This middle ground represents a huge market that university presses and trade publishers tend to overlook, because their sights usually are set respectively on the upper end of intellectual respectability and the mid-to-lower end of popular culture. Besides, ever since James Redfield proved that a best-seller could be half action-adventure story and half transformational philosophy, all bets should be hedged regarding what type of publication will strike a resonant chord.

Several friendly critics have suggested that the title of *Paradigm Wars* carries too many negative connotations; we should be stressing peace and conflict resolution, rather than war! I wholeheartedly agree. Many individuals are building bridges, rather than tearing them down. However, there are profound disagreements around current paradigm conflicts that affect personal identities, careers, and paychecks—not just the abstract truth of belief systems. For those involved in attempting to radically change the status quo, or to defend it, "wars" is not too strong a term. The transition to a new worldview is never entirely peaceful, despite our efforts to make it so.

While it addresses a number of social issues, such as abortion, education, and the environment, *Paradigm Wars* tilts more toward science, philosophy, and spirituality. This reflects my belief that transformational challenges are powerfully shaped by fundamental assumptions regarding human nature and reality as well as by our participation in levels of reality that penetrate and transcend the purely physical. It also reflects the limitations of space. No author can do justice to all deserving agendas in a single volume.

This emphasis does not imply that, once we clarify our worldview(s), our transformational challenges will take care of themselves. A sustainable culture will not emerge unless we individually and collectively *make* it happen. Books about paradigm shifts are merely guides for a larger evolutionary impulse with which many individuals are coming into alignment— often in surprisingly synchronistic ways!

There are two master agendas for our time. One is the inner goal of exploring and *transforming consciousness*. The other is the outer goal of creating a *sustainable global culture*. Everything else is secondary. Each agenda complements the other, and neither will be accomplished without the other. As individuals, we may identify more with one agenda than the other. As a global community, we can achieve both. I hope that *Paradigm Wars* will be a useful companion along your path!

CHAPTER ONE

Worldviews in Transition

We are on the verge of the new age, a whole new world. Human consciousness, our mutual awareness, is going to make a quantum leap. Everything will change. You will never be the same.
　　　　　　　　　　　　　　　Paul Williams, *Das Energi*

Imagine a yogi, a teacher, a physicist, a social visionary, a physician, a parapsychologist, a theologian, a feminist, a psychotherapist, and an ecologist engaged in dialogue. Boundaries between their disciplines are suspended as they explore remarkable parallels and unsuspected connections that link fast-breaking developments on the frontiers of research. Some connections invite comparison with an ancient wisdom. Others seem to form a basis for a major evolutionary change comparable to the emergence of the Enlightenment from the Middle Ages.

Under discussion are topics relating to the "meeting of science and spirit," the "interconnectedness of all things," the "transformation of consciousness," the "decline of patriarchy," the importance of "living as if the Earth really mattered," and even the "end of Western civilization as we know it." Ideas that used to be considered false or even crazy are now explored as vital ingredients in our survival! Beginning in the sixties and exploding into the nineties, thousands of such dialogues have been undertaken on local, national, and international levels. They cover a dizzying spectrum of topics.

Here are a few examples: science and ancient wisdom, creativity, expanded human potential, varieties of meditation, healing, near-death experience, holistic health, noncompetitive models of education, altered states of consciousness, subtle energies, peace, world hunger, therapeutic touch, ecological consciousness, vegetarianism, extraterrestrial encounters, the women's movement, channeling, globally sustainable culture, psychotronics, the hospice movement, dream symbols, yoga, free energy devices, Tibetan medicine, spiritual arts, applied kinesiology, East-West interfaces, New Physics, mobilizing intuitive faculties, recovering Native American traditions, the end of the Cold War, Green politics, letting go of fear, New Biology, earth changes, learning through both sides of the brain, "shadow" sides and encounters with darkness, decentralist social agendas, steady-state economics, intimacy versus security in relationships, etc.

These far-ranging dialogues and agendas are nurtured by hundreds of institutes, organizations, journals, newsletters, and countless pioneering authors who are creating new genres for libraries and bookstores to contemplate. A massive grass roots movement is evident if we include both issue-oriented groups, such as Greenpeace or the National Organization for Women, and those whose personal lives have been transformed positively through an encounter with, say, meditation, political action, or a healing crisis.

A dramatic ripple effect is not only changing beliefs but also changing lives. We increasingly hear or read of individuals: seeking to get in touch with their latent feminine or masculine aspects; fighting cancer through nutrition and visualization rather than chemotherapy; becoming more present-centered after a near-death experience; leaving the corporate world to adopt a life-style of voluntary simplicity; working out a painful divorce cooperatively; developing their creative intuition in order to render better business decisions; or seeing a psychic to explore personal growth issues.

Marilyn Ferguson, whose *Aquarian Conspiracy* is mandatory reading for anyone concerned with social and personal change, describes this grass roots movement as a powerful fifth column in-the-making:

> Broader than reform, deeper than revolution, this benign conspiracy for a new human agenda has triggered the most rapid cultural realignment in history...It is a new mind—the ascendance of a startling worldview that gathers into its framework breakthrough science and insights from earliest recorded thought. The Aquarian Conspirators...are school teachers and office workers, famous scientists, government officials and lawmakers, artists and millionaires, taxi drivers and celebrities, leaders in medicine, education, law, psychology.[1]

Other writers have expressed a similar sense of powerful cultural realignment, among them Patricia Aburdene and John Naisbitt, authors of *Megatrends 2000*, and historian Theodore White. In White's view, "a new culture is struggling to be born." It is only in retrospect that historians "may be able to sum up all these stirrings and their effects in an epigraphic zeitgeist, or spirit of the times."[2]

Mark Satin, author of *New Options for America*, not only has seen the road ahead but also has helped get us moving in that direction. For him, a "Second American Experiment" already is underway. We are beginning to move beyond assumptions that have limited our conception of what is possible. Instead of seeking new answers for old questions, we are asking new questions.

And the answers often have a more spiritually based ring to them. In *Spiritual Politics*, which Patricia Aburdene describes as "the first articulate, in-depth application of ancient spiritual wisdom to today's political events," Corinne McLaughlin and Gordon Davidson seek to transform the world from the inside out:

> Our aim is to shift the focus of political dialogue from the outer level of physical forms and activities to the inner, causal realm of consciousness. "Consciousness precedes being—not the other way around," noted former Czech President Vaclav Havel in his 1990 address to the U.S. Congress. The human mind is not simply a reflection of prevailing social structures—it creates form. The interplay of human and Divine thought creates all personal and social reality.[3]

James Redfield, author of *The Celestine Prophecy*, views these shifting visions not as hype or fad, but as a "positive psychological contagion" expressing a global spiritual realignment:

> For half a century now, a new consciousness has been entering the human world, a new awareness that can only be called transcendent, spiritual...We know that life is really about a spiritual unfolding that is personal and enchanting and magical—an unfolding that no philosophy or religion has yet fully clarified...We know, [too,] that once we do understand what is happening, how to turn on this growth and keep it on, the human world will take a quantum leap into a whole new way of life, one that all of history has been struggling to achieve.[4]

With these and other writers I concur that a new worldview and, indeed, a new world are in the making. That is the thesis of this book. But what is this emerging perspective indigenous to Satin's "Second American Experiment" or Ferguson's "Aquarian Conspiracy"—this spiritual unfolding that, according to Redfield, "no philosophy or religion has yet fully clarified"? Where did it come from and where might it take us? What is causing the shift? Does the need for change automatically mean there will be change? Are we wishfully projecting more than is really there?

To claim that an old worldview is dying and a new one is emerging requires, first of all, that we clarify what we mean by "worldview" and "paradigm shift." Only then will we be in a position to identify the old worldview, the causes of its decay, and the kind of vision that promises to replace it. A lot of information will have to be organized along the way. But taken a step at a time, the journey will prove less formidable and the destination will become progressively more clear.

WORLDVIEWS AND PARADIGM SHIFTS

A common point of reference in discussions about crisis and transformation is Thomas Kuhn's thesis that science progresses through paradigm shifts. Paradigms are models or conceptual frameworks which give a unified perspective over a range of experiences. Their usefulness is tied to their capacity to explain and to help us understand why events occur as they do. Without them our experience would lack structure and significance. Futurist Joel Barker defines a paradigm broadly as "any set of rules or regulations that describes boundaries and tells us what to do to be successful within those boundaries."[5]

Paradigms may be comparatively narrow as, for example, the behavior modification approach to learning. Or they may be very broad as with the Newtonian/Cartesian paradigm, which at one time was believed capable of explaining everything in the physical universe (including human behavior). While the term is most often linked to scientific contexts, art, religion, and social thought have their paradigms, too. To change major paradigms in any of these arenas is to change our definition of what is possible.

When cases accumulate that cannot be explained by a prevailing paradigm, sometimes a refinement of that model is all that is required; this is the normal course of science. But when refinements fail to work and unexplainable cases continue to exert intellectual or practical pressure, the framework itself must be abandoned and a new one found to replace it. A well-known illustration of a major paradigm shift is the move from Newtonian concepts of space, time, and matter to Einsteinian relativity theory. Sometimes the shift is brief and clean. Usually, it's both theoretically and politically messy, as was the case with the theory of evolution.

Kuhn stressed that major paradigms are embedded in a larger social context along with the habits, expectations, and reputations of leading thinkers. Sixty years earlier, William James had noted that the tension between fact and theory is magnified by "the extreme slowness with which the ordinary academic and critical mind acknowledges facts to exist which present themselves as wild facts, with no stall or pigeonhole, or as facts which threaten to break up the accepted system."[6] Major new ideas tend first to be condemned as ridiculous, then dismissed as trivial, until finally they are accepted as truth.

Unfortunately, some writers interpret Kuhn's proposal more liberally than he envisioned. His views are sometimes described in ways which suggest that the mere existence of paradigm shifts prepares a place for all types of extraordinary and otherwise unsupported proposals. His description of paradigm shifts as "nonlinear" is taken to mean in some quarters that an idea need not have much connection with history, evidence, or even rationality! Calling new ideas part of a "paradigm shift" tends to direct attention away from the need for critical scrutiny.

In any event, more than a mere paradigm shift appears to be at stake. From the opening dialogue, it's clear that changes in our entire worldview are being explored. Ferguson's Aquarian conspirators are emerging from all over the occupational and disciplinary map. They are everywhere. All one has to do is mention a few key words at a social gathering, then see who comes out of the closet. Little will be left unchanged in some radical fashion. For it's not just a new model in physics, or the decline of family values, or even a new health care system that is at stake. Rather, a whole new worldview appears to be at hand. Some further exploration of the nature of worldviews and their dynamics is therefore called for.

To begin with, a worldview is broader than a paradigm. It is a master-perspective involving paradigms from different disciplines, one of which typically dominates, informs, and spills over into the others. For example, a Newtonian paradigm in science involves a narrow cluster of beliefs about space, time, matter, and the laws of motion, a so-called "mechanical" view of the behavior of objects.

A Newtonian worldview, on the other hand, involves a whole network of interdisciplinary assumptions that reflects the basic kind of thinking that Newton and his successors adopted. For example, a Newtonian worldview involves a mechanistic approach to questions of health (the biomedical model), genetics (the double helix), economics (capitalism), and psychopathology (Freudian analysis), to mention a few areas.

This distinction suggests that if we are witnessing a fundamental shift in worldview, we should begin to see it exemplified to a considerable extent across disciplinary and occupational lines. People of diverse backgrounds beginning to talk about new paradigms may be indicative of something big in-the-making. But a worldview requires *functional* roots. Lecturing in the ivory towers of academia is not sufficient. The principles learned there, or from books and conferences, must carry over into public policy and private practice.

A worldview typically is not an *ingredient* in the questions we put to nature and society. Rather, it prescribes practical limitations upon thought itself, a subtle master guide which steers us in certain directions and away from others. Special paradigms within its scope, e.g., Christian theism or the chemical theory of bonding, determine what types of questions can or ought to be asked and the range of answers to consider.

The more narrowly focused a particular paradigm, the more easily it can be examined. The broader and more fundamental it is, the less likely it is to be called into question. One typically doesn't question the fundamental principles of a whole discipline or larger worldview. When you work under one set of filters, the existence of others always seems dubious!

Not until many people in different contexts begin to act and think by means of the newer set of rules can we say that the "shift" has taken place or is well under way. The fact that there is so much talk about critical agendas in our time indicates that a new perspective is not fully rooted, because too much is still unclear and controversial.

A worldview is not merely a set of related propositions about the nature of the physical universe or of society. It also incorporates rules about what types of things can be known and, more importantly, how they can be known. For example, a widely held assumption of science is that "To be is to be measurable." According to this assumption, literal out-of-body experiences are rejected, because science appears unable to measure them. Such rules for knowing are disseminated through the educational system of a culture. They are assumed to be the surest roads to truth until better ones come along.

This poses an interesting challenge for commentators who want to make a place both for science and for phenomena that do not fit into current scientific models of reality. To do so, they may suggest that: scientific method gives us only a very limited view of reality; objectivity is merely another name for a consensus of subjective opinions; there are multiple realities each with its own possibilities for knowing; there are other sources of knowledge such as personal intuition and meditation; and facts cannot always be clearly distinguished from theories which overlay them. We will explore some of these suggestions in later chapters.

A worldview is internally glued together by common values that weave their way through economics, religion, social mores, personal life-styles, and even science itself. For example, Newtonian thought provided a friendly atmosphere for the emergence of Darwinian views on evolution, which in turn gave rise to the Social Darwinism of the late nineteenth century. This in turn reinforced and was supported by the puritan work ethic, a tailor-made marriage for a rising capitalist economy. The message was this: Competition is good and if you don't succeed you probably didn't deserve to. A new worldview carries distinctive values that stand in contrast to the values of its predecessor.

Root philosophical assumptions and metaphors underlie all worldviews. These are illustrated by prevailing models and theories of the time. For example, a philosophical assumption of science is that every event has a material cause. This assumption is closely related to the root metaphor of the machine, which at one time gave us an image for understanding people, whole societies, and even the universe itself.

Root metaphors, while retaining much of their original spirit and intent, do not mean the same thing in all contexts. It's useful to look instead for resemblances within, say, the humanities, the sciences, or the arts. But that is part of their beauty and their function. Part of their meaning is tied to particular contexts while another floats freely, awaiting further illustration. Every worldview exhibits root ideas which are embedded in, yet transcend, its science, religion, or social structure.

This flexibility poses a two-fold challenge: to identify those root beliefs which underwrote the old culture and to identify those which appear to characterize the coming age and relate them to the first set. Complicating this project is the fact that new worldviews cannot be completely differentiated from older beliefs that feed them. The Judeo-Christian paradigm, for example, wove its way through several major periods in Western history with substantial modifications along the way. The same is true for Euclidean geometry and patriarchal social systems. The idea of God was substantially "mechanized" by Newton, Leibniz, and Jefferson, among others. But the core notion of God was around long before.

Another difficulty with clearly identifying older historical periods is that one's interpretation of history is influenced by current interests and social perspectives. We can interpret the past five hundred years according to several perspectives: as reflecting the rise of scientific materialism, for example, or as class struggle, or as the evolution of consciousness. In retrospect, we can identify key ideas from an earlier period and contrast them with current history. But clear-cut boundaries are rare.

Much attention has been given to describing the weaknesses of older paradigms and to establishing some distance between "them" and "us." This is especially true of the Newtonian worldview, which turns out to be the culprit in most everyone's book. There are good reasons for that judgment. But this decaying perspective is not and never was the tightly structured, monolithic prison it is portrayed to be. Since the plausibility of a new paradigm is often reinforced by stressing the weakness of the older paradigm it's supposed to replace, it is worth reminding ourselves that boundaries are hard to draw in practice. Older ways of thinking tend to creep into some of the most leading-edge proposals.

To understand what fuels the shift from one worldview to the next, it will help to distinguish between *intellectual* structures (scientific theories, religious beliefs, political ideologies, etc.) and *institutional* structures (family, church, political parties, schools, etc.). Institutional structures implement intellectual structures; schools, for example, are supposed to pass on the values and ideas of the culture which they serve. Both types of structure are subject to routine fluctuation and evolution as new knowledge and changing conditions require.

A stable period is characterized as one in which most new discoveries and circumstances are accommodated over time by the prevailing institutions without a need for radical modification. Or if there is such a need, it occurs only in more isolated pockets. The rate and quality of change, of course, will vary within a given culture and also between cultures. A major transition between relatively stable periods is brought on by the fundamental failure of prevailing structures to accommodate changing circumstances.

When the gap becomes too great, the old structure must either undergo a radical internal change—"revolution" is Kuhn's depiction of this in science—or else it will go into a state of decline, dragging other elements of the culture with it. *When major gaps between structure and circumstance begin to appear across a wide cultural spectrum, the makings of a transition to a new worldview are in place.* This is not to say that a transition will take place. The decline of the Roman Empire represents a worst-case scenario. It is to say only that conditions are ripe for dramatic change.

The pressures for change are never uniform. In the transition from the High Middle Ages to a modern worldview (roughly A.D. 1450 to 1650) major changes were evident in art, trade and commerce, social structure, and philosophy. But it was the decline of church dominance, accompanied by the emergence of religious pluralism and the rise of science, that led the way. Between the advances of science and the emergence of "heretics" like Calvin and Luther, the Church inevitably lost ground. One clue that a major cultural revolution is under way is that the structural changes evident in a few areas also exhibit parallels in other, seemingly unrelated, areas.

When we find ourselves in the middle of major cultural change, it's difficult to draw definite lines between old and new structures. This is because they overlap. The new has already begun before the old is washed away. How much change is necessary before we say that an old idea or institution has evolved into a new one? Is Christianity today still essentially the same religion it was three hundred years ago, or is it a new religion?

Every culture must address what seem like great crises. In America, the social fabric seemed to be coming apart in the sixties; the thirties before that, and so on. The mere existence of a crisis does not itself mean that a whole new perspective is in-the-making. Usually there are important changes but not enough to describe the situation as one of worldviews in transition. When we are in the middle of some perceived crisis, we seldom know with much certainty what the end result will be. Some will read great significance into certain trends, while others will view them as minor fluctuations. This is to be expected.

Will holistic medicine replace the biomedical model or simply be absorbed into it? Will meditation routinely be taught to sixth graders? Will parapsychology become part of an educational core curriculum? Will women find true equality? Will we come to respect the environment as Native Americans do? Will the profit motive be transformed by the need for social responsibility? Will we come to see ourselves as part of a "higher consciousness"? Will earthquakes bring on great disasters? We just don't know until after the transitions have been made.

In times of crisis and great change, religious, scientific, and social visionaries rise to point to a new way. They always are met by defenders of the status quo. The less extreme proponents are more likely to transform each other. The current "New Paradigm dialogue," as I shall call it, has not resulted in a fully developed worldview waiting to replace the ruins of traditional perspectives. Rather, it is being defined and worked out in the very clash with mainstream thought. It is for historians of the twenty-first century to determine in retrospect whether this dialogue was merely a fluctuation within a long-term trend or the beginnings of a new long-term trend!

Naturally, I would not have written this book if I did not believe that we are in the early stages of a radically new long-term trend. In times of great change, however, humble respect for the potential differences between what one believes will happen and what eventually does happen is always appropriate.

GUIDING PRINCIPLES OF WESTERN CULTURE

Every move toward something is a move away from something else. Which leads us to ask: If a new worldview is coming, what is it supposed to replace? Clarity is important here, since many proposals are defended just by contrasting them with earlier ways of thinking. We must begin to understand what a new culture is supposed to be by understanding what it rejects. Fritjof Capra, among many others, has made a persuasive case that the Cartesian-Newtonian paradigm together with its social implications is the central model being replaced by new modes of thought which he describes as "holistic" and "systems-oriented."[7]

Merely being against Descartes and Newton, however, is not enough to align one with a holistic worldview. Scientific materialism has been one of the most successful master paradigms of the last four hundred years, especially when we take into account the influence of Marx, Darwin, and Freud, each of whom in his own way extended its influence. Still, it's easy to overstate the case and make this perspective a kind of monolithic grab bag into which one inserts all that a new culture would reject. Depending upon how broadly or narrowly one defines a Cartesian-Newtonian paradigm, it even could be inconsistent. For Descartes was a mind-body dualist, and the followers of Newton were typically materialists.

Many ideas pushed under the umbrella of a Newtonian-Cartesian worldview originated well before the rise of modern science. Euclidean space, patriarchy, mind-body dualism, atomism, Judeo-Christian theology and moral outlooks, and dominion over nature did not begin with Newton and Descartes. There has also been plenty of opposition to mechanistic ways of thinking all along, not only from major philosophical figures such as Kant, Hegel, and Whitehead, but also from within science itself.

In brief, there is no such thing as *the* Western worldview. However, it is possible to describe major guiding principles of Western thought from which we can construct any number of distinctive paradigms. Some of these principles typify mechanistic ideals in science and some do not. Many in fact are found in both Western and Eastern cultures at different stages of development. It is not always necessary to label particular paradigms for examination. However, it is important that we at least identify the particular principles or root metaphors that are most at risk. Here is a sampling:

From (Newtonian) science

1. The objects of our universe are composed of small fundamental units. Depending upon the historical period, they may be termed "corpuscles," "atoms," or (currently) "quarks."
2. Material atoms were originally assumed to be hard, indestructible, indivisible, colorless entities that have no intrinsic connection to any other atom. Even sharing electrons does not affect the intrinsic quality of any atom per se.
3. All change is fundamentally of position or of motion. Other kinds of change are reducible to change in motion or position. For example, a change of texture from cold and hard to soft and smooth involves only a spatial rearrangement of interacting fundamental units. The laws governing such change are the basis of mechanistic science.
4. Fundamental units do not possess information about the larger wholes of which they are a part. Levels of existence (molecules, cells, tissues, organs, persons, etc.) thus tend to be viewed autonomously, rather than as reflecting principles operative at other levels.
5. Complex wholes and their properties are less real than their constituents. For example, consciousness is assumed to be *reducible* to neural-chemical processes. (The whole is not greater than the sum of its parts.)
6. Cause and effect are both distinguishable and distinct. Causes always precede their effects in linear order.
7. To be is to be in a certain fixed place in an absolute (container-like) space and in an absolute (linear) time. Space is intrinsically three-dimensional. Time is independent of physical change.
8. Space and time happen to contain various objects and events but, in principle, could exist without them. Physical space would still exist, even without matter or energy.
9. All events are in principle predictable, if we had the time and resources to determine the causes. There is no genuine

(contracausal) freedom, i.e., the ability to have chosen otherwise. Whatever does happen had to happen!

10. With increased predictability, our belief in creativity and chance events ought to decrease. Creative advance is an illusion based upon our inability to predict. A new species of animal, for example, was already "in the cards." The events we term accidental merely reflect our ignorance of all the factors which brought them about.

11. There is no overarching purpose in nature. Nature is merely the hurrying about of material stuff.

12. Energy is not separate from matter and is viewed as a derivative property of matter.

13. Sensory experience and reason are the only means to knowledge. Beliefs about an afterlife, for example, are based upon faith and are irrational.

14. Nature is objectively and impartially "out there," waiting to yield its secrets to minds free of bias and uncritically held assumptions. The result of scientific investigation is a consensus reality.

15. Higher and more complex levels of organization are seen as emerging from lower levels of organization. For example, animals have evolved from one-celled organisms, religion from personal need, and mind from matter. Where possible, always explain (reduce) the higher in terms of the lower.

16. Physics is the science which all other sciences (or near-sciences) should attempt to be like.

From religion (Judeo-Christian tradition)

1. According to most Western traditions, there *is* genuine freedom which is traceable to the workings of a nonphysical mind or spirit (created by God) that controls the mechanical workings of the body. We are influenced by heredity and environment but are not totally controlled by them.

2. The purpose of the material universe is to reflect the power and intelligence of God. The purpose of human existence is to glorify God and ideally to align oneself with God's will and return His love.

3. God is conceived as an all-powerful, wise, good, male deity who created the world and in various ways interacts with it, e.g., by answering prayers.

4. To be a "religious" person is basically to live one's life in accordance with a set of rules that one believes has come from a transcendental authority.
5. We are separate from God, although we can be very close at times.
6. Our historical epoch reflects a continuing struggle between good and evil, light and darkness. Evil is a force in its own right. Good will win out.

From (patriarchal) ethical, social, and political thought

1. Men are (or ought to be) stronger, more intelligent and rational, competitive, goal-oriented, in control, and generally "superior." Women are weaker, less rational, more emotional, less linear or goal-oriented, and otherwise generally "inferior."
2. Continuous economic growth is both possible and desirable. Such progress is seen as cumulative and incremental. Where we are, on the whole, is better than where we have been. Both capitalism and socialism, for example, assume the goal of growth.
3. Facts and values are very different. The former are objective; the latter, subjective or relative. Morality is the attempt to bridge the gap between what is perceived to be the case and what *ought* to be the case. Various standards and rules are proposed to do this, and the virtuous person is taken to be one who accepts his or her moral obligations.
4. Power and authority are most effectively implemented in hierarchical relationships that distinguish between those who control and those who are controlled. Power means "power over." This implementation occurs broadly, for example, with Church dominance in the Middle Ages, or narrowly, as in doctor-patient relationships in modern times.
5. The corollary of hierarchical implementation of power is its *centralized* concentration, especially in areas relating to the military and to economics. Controlling surplus value from others' labor, whether as feudal lord, private owner, or state manager, is the way to go.
6. Laws and moral codes are (and should be) constraints upon human nature innately inclined toward degeneracy and undisciplined survival. Competition to survive, succeed, and even dominate is natural.

7. Democratic forms of government are preferable to feudal aristocracies, because they allow a greater number of people a voice in pursuing what they *take* to be their interests. However, they are not intrinsically empowering. (Don't let the people gain too much power!)
8. We should work for the triumph of good over evil. ("Good" is usually defined circularly as "whatever right-thinking people take to be the common interest.")
9. Humans have certain natural rights. How many are recognized depends on when and where one lives. We used to have a right to smoke most anywhere we pleased. Now we have a right not to be exposed to smoke.
10. Education consists largely in getting the student to master the same body of facts that the instructor has mastered earlier. The student learns how to conform to the instructor's objective expectations. Education has less to do with learning how to learn for long-term growth than with performing some approved function upon completion of the process.

From (dualistic) psychology, metaphysics, and common sense

1. The best ways to motivate people are by appealing to their self-interest or by playing upon their guilt or fears.
2. Alternatives to almost every area of thought and endeavor are polarized and guided by the law of the excluded middle ("either-or" thinking). For example, "we" versus "they," church versus state, private versus public life, minds versus bodies, liberals versus conservatives, reductionism versus emergentism, religious believers versus atheists, etc. We live in duality.
3. Whether we decay in the grave (materialism) or go to heaven or hell (dualism), we basically have only one life to live.
4. Nature exists essentially to serve the interests of humans. God gave man dominion over the plants and animals. Nature essentially doesn't care what we do to it.
5. Personal relationships, especially love relations, are sanctioned by security, compatibility, and dependence. For example, the woman is supposed to nurture her husband in a marriage relation, while he ideally provides her economic security. Love is essentially meeting different needs. Unconditional love is a luxury that few can afford or deserve.

6. We are basically separate and alone in a universe which, with the possible exception of God, doesn't care. We look for connections in relationships and institutions, but the unconscious fear that we might lose them and the struggle to maintain them are a part of the human condition that we should just accept.

7. In all probability we are the only intelligent species in the universe, and certainly the most advanced. There are no extraterrestrials. But if there were, they would not be interested in us.

8. Conforming to others' expectations is the best way to get ahead and find happiness. Adapting to the status quo is preferable to creating something new, unless our creations are "preauthorized." Those who rock the boat and question too much are potentially dangerous or crazy.

9. When bad things happen—especially to good people—it's usually either a matter of "rotten luck" or it is somebody else's responsibility. They have been victimized.

10. Reader's choice!

This tentative list contains assumptions we're moving away from for different reasons and at very different rates. Many readers already will have rejected most of these beliefs. The list certainly is not complete. However, it does include the basic ideas from twenty-five hundred years of Western culture that have come progressively under critical scrutiny in the twentieth century. There are several root metaphors which weave their way through the entire list.

The first is "fragmentation," the idea that wherever divisions or distinctions are possible, it is both natural and/or desirable to make them. They may be between objects, people, classes, ideas, hierarchies, natural processes—anything at all. In most cases we learn the distinctions at such an early age, and our culture reinforces them so consistently, that it does not occur to us that reality could be any other way. We suffer from the illusion that the distinctions and names we invent within a language automatically have perfect counterparts in the real world. Along with the habit of dividing things is the closely related assumption that objects are essentially unchanged and completely understandable in isolation from their contexts.

A second cluster of root metaphors involves "reductionism" (the simplest parts of something are the most real) and "localization" (to be is to be in a certain measurable place at a certain place in time). While these ideas are closely related, they are not the same thing. Usually, the more we can reduce some phenomenon, the more we are localizing its specific elements or causes. For instance, if we think of values as socialized expressions of approval, and expressions of approval as reflecting states of consciousness, and consciousness as neurochemistry in action, then values become progressively more localizable. We might think of values as nothing more than brain states.

A third cluster involves the metaphors of "hierarchy" (which can involve relations of complexity, of power, or both) and "control" (the exercise of physical, psychological, or institutional power). Once fragmentation occurs, it is natural to give certain parts or levels priority over others. Thus it may be claimed that "Reason should take precedence over intuition" or that "Progress and social order depend upon certain people having control over others (doctors over patients, managers over workers, etc.)." Patriarchy is perhaps *the* classic example of hierarchical control.

A final cluster involves "competition" and "fear." The fear I refer to is typically not something we are aware of. It hangs in the background fueling insecurity, guilt, the need to judge others, and refusals to look openly at new ways of thinking and acting. Fear and fragmentation lead naturally to competition. According to this mind-set, there are only so many resources to spread around, so we had best position ourselves to capitalize upon scarcity. And if some people must lose that others may win, that's just "life."

Those who believe that these root metaphors have reached the end of their usefulness are working to implement a complementary perspective involving *interrelatedness, integration/balance, holism/emergence, love,* and *mutually empowering cooperation.* Naturally, the old metaphors will not simply disappear from the scene in their totality; aspects will be integrated into the newer ways of thinking and being. For example, all competition is not bad; it can be put to good uses. Rather, it is the kind of competition that destroys hope and self-esteem—that validates "losing" in, say, the classroom—that needs to be replaced. Competition in a game of tennis is not the issue.

Any shift from fragmentation to wholeness or from competition to mutually empowering cooperation will not happen automatically. Something has to drive the process. In the case of an entire worldview, this process requires the broad spectrum of transformative challenges described in the following section.

TEN TRANSFORMATIONAL CHALLENGES

In order to make the case for a shift in worldviews, a number of issues need to be addressed. First, we must give some indication of the growing gaps between prevailing thought and the changing circumstances that challenge them. We must show how traditional structures are not accommodating these challenges and how the old ways of dealing with problems are not working. Next, we must show that the challenges cover a broad spectrum of culture. Finally, we must show that the challenges and the kinds of responses they evoke exhibit certain deep-structure parallels. In other words, we need to do more than merely describe different worldviews. We need to explain the reasons for making the shift from the old to the new.

The challenges I will discuss are familiar to most readers, although in some instances I develop them in different ways. Each challenge merits a book-length treatment and has been discussed by many other writers. However, if we wish to understand how fragmentation, hierarchical control, or fear are actually pushing us to a cultural turning point, then a review of some of the most important challenges is called for.

The environment. Inherent in both early Greek and Judeo-Christian thought is the belief that nature is capable of sustaining abuse without human populations suffering major catastrophic consequences. With isolated exceptions, most animal, plant, and mineral kingdoms have been viewed as "simply there" to be enjoyed, ignored, controlled, or abused as we saw fit. A clearer case of both fragmentation and imbalance would be hard to find. Considerable pressures against this assumption are now becoming very evident.

It is a familiar litany. Sulphur expelled into the air as industrial waste returns to earth elsewhere as acid rain. This has already destroyed a third of the Black Forest in West Germany. Pollution is the principal culprit in many regions of the eastern United States where forests are in decline. Arthur Johnson of the University of Pennsylvania states: "This widespread synchronous growth decline has never been reported before...If the trend continues, we are facing the ecological disaster of the century."[8] Despite its comprehensive ban fourteen years ago, fresh concentrations of DDT keep showing up in Texas, California, and other western states.

Chlorofluorocarbons (CFCs) and radiation emissions from industry reduce the protective layer of ozone surrounding the earth. The Environmental Protection Agency (EPA) has estimated that at 1990 CFC growth rates, ozone depletion would lead by the year 2075 to an additional forty million cases of skin cancer and eight-hundred thousand American deaths plus immune system disorders and crop, forest, and animal damage.[9] As of 1994 the rate of ozone depletion appears to have significantly lessened. The long-term trend, however, is still not clear.

Even as "acceptable" emission levels (per car) are being reduced, lead levels in certain population areas continue to rise. Nonbiodegradable fertilizers and pesticides continue to sink deeper into the ground, in some cases toward major aquifer systems—the ones, that is, with much water left. In 1991 the Ogallala Aquifer that stretches from South Dakota to Texas was in some places two hundred feet below normal.

Toxic waste disposal currently far outstrips decontamination efforts. A quarter of the world's population does not have safe drinking water, and more arable land is lost each year than is reclaimed. An ounce of plutonium can kill millions of people, and hundreds of pounds now appear to be missing or unaccounted for. Development continues to destroy delicately balanced ecosystems, sometimes in ways that threaten to pay us back in years to come, as in, for example, the erosion of topsoil. Farmers along the Mississippi River are still losing four tons of topsoil for every ton of grain they produce.

In his *State of the World* reports for 1990, Lester Brown predicted a decreasing global capacity to produce enough food to keep up with population growth. The culprits: erosion, deforestation, and pollution, the effects of which are magnified by aberrations in the weather. Amazon rain forests receive much attention, but deforestation is a worldwide trend often necessitated by the needs of human survival.

Everyone agrees that environmental destruction is a problem. But fuzzy logic pervades government thinking in these matters. On the one hand, we declare the Cold War over, while spending hundreds of billions of dollars on defense for eventualities that have a decreasing probability of occurring. On the other, the EPA demands "clear proof" that toxic waste disposal sites are responsible for increased cancer rates in a community before it reacts decisively.

A broad spectrum of environmentally oriented groups both in the United States and abroad have sought to reverse traditional attitudes and raise our consciousness to a more enlightened overarching perspective. Many are attracted to James Lovelock's "Gaia" model of the biosphere: "The entire range of living matter on earth, from whales to viruses, and from oaks to algae, could be regarded as constituting a single living entity capable of manipulating the earth's atmosphere to suit its overall needs and endowed with faculties and powers far beyond its constituent parts."[10]

We must see ourselves as an interconnected part of nature and live in balanced harmony with it. Our mutual needs can be met by taking or destroying far less than we do beginning, if not yesterday, then now! The earth is a living organism, and much of humanity is approaching the status of unwanted guest. The environment is perhaps our greatest *global* transformative challenge. And there are signs that the tide is turning. On April 22, Earth Day 1990 produced demonstrations of over 100 million people in 133 countries—all demanding that their governments make global cleanup *the* priority for the decade.

Still to be answered: Will the level of our response be effective in time? There is still no comprehensive plan to deal with toxic waste. Will raised awareness translate into comparably raised levels of action after the public relations blitz? How can we minimize the hardships resulting from economic realignments and reduce the power of a simplistic mind-set which aligns jobs against health and ecology? Finally, will Third World countries be able to act merely on the encouragement and token financial support from the industrialized world? While we worry about recycling, they often have little or nothing to recycle.

Education. Much has been written about the crisis in education. This often consists of documenting the decline in quality as measured by various task forces, e.g., the presidential commission report "A Nation at Risk." The issues are familiar: declining SAT scores, grade inflation, social promotions, declining per capita expenditures for education, violence, low standards of reading, writing, computation, and thinking, teacher burnout, student dropout rates, and an almost barbaric insensitivity to cultures other than one's own. We are beginning to see some countertrends in the form of increased graduation standards, possible reversals in SAT scores, merit pay for better teaching, and multicultural classroom television programming.

It is vitally necessary, of course, that we improve students' basic skills. But even if this challenge is met successfully, there looms another basic crisis whose long-term consequences are difficult to predict. Calling it a crisis depends partly upon what you assume the purpose of education to be. Most students tend to see education as job preparation. A recent Association of American Colleges report concludes that "the curriculum has given way to a marketplace philosophy. It is a supermarket where students are shoppers and professors are merchants of learning."[11] The governors National Conference on Education also shared this attitude. Most seemed to think that the crisis consists in "losing our *competitive edge*." Translation: We are losing out to the Japanese and Germans.

Our standing in world markets ought to be a national concern. But something more subtle is happening on the educational scene. Our concept of what it means to be educated is increasingly tied to the ability to say or do the appropriate thing at the appropriate skill level, especially to prospective employers. The problem is that after we have trained Johnny to communicate according to the rules, he still doesn't have much to say—except what his culture, his books, and his teachers have told him to say. Even when skills are raised, we are often left with students fundamentally unaffected by the curriculum.

This is a far more difficult issue to address head-on. We typically teach students to accept rather than to question, to memorize rather than to create, and in general to make the right kind of "moves" in response to complex issues—all on an assembly line basis. As Theodore Sizer, former dean of Harvard's Graduate School of Education, observes, "the structure is getting in the way of children's learning."[12] President Bush's (followed by President Clinton's) self-described "revolutionary" proposals for nationally standardized testing and greater freedom in choosing schools were not designed to move this structure out of the way.

We are fostering in our students an ability to move across the surface of things, where each autonomous section of the curriculum carries its own rules of the game. Johnny is taught to deal in simple facts, formulas, platitudes, and clichés. He is often out of touch with himself and with the deeper threads of culture. When he graduates from high school or college, he will unthinkingly continue to perpetuate many of the very attitudes and ways of thinking that have led us to our current cultural crises.

Computer literacy will help him get a job, but this will only postpone a larger challenge. For the problem is not just one of more smoothly transmitted information. Rather, it is one of more appropriately evoking the transformative power of information. This is less likely to happen in a system that places a premium on linear, analytical thinking, often to the total exclusion of intuition or feeling. It is less likely to happen in a system that teaches Johnny how to say acceptable things but without being connected to what he is saying or to whom he is speaking. It is less likely to happen in an educational system built upon a model of passive learning, where both facts and values move only one way, from the teacher to the student. Finally, it is less likely to happen in a system which places a premium on competition between winners and losers.

Fragmentation is perhaps most easily seen in the rise of specialization in college or university course work. Core curricula require that students have so many hours in this or that area—like, for example, the humanities or natural sciences—but the individual courses are typically taught as if they had no connection to any general curriculum outside their own focus. C. P. Snow's famous "Two Cultures" (the sciences and humanities) is the most obvious split in the curriculum, but universities are amalgamations of many cultures.

Most introductory courses are taught as if the student needs to be prepared to specialize in that particular discipline. As Allan Bloom, author of *The Closing of the American Mind*, observes: "These great universities—which can split the atom, find cures for the most terrible diseases, conduct surveys of whole populations and produce massive dictionaries of lost languages—cannot generate a modest program of general education for undergraduate students. This is a parable for our times."[13]

Bloom's conservatism strikes a raw nerve with many academics who view his proposals as out of touch with current reality. Still, his perception of a growing lack of curricular coherence is well-founded. For at its core are a growing number of teachers at all levels who have concluded that because the past two hundred years of American history (and especially education!) have been an exercise in racism, sexism, and classism, their job is to set things straight.

It's not so much their conclusion, but their means of dealing with it—often through intellectual and moral intimidation—that has caught many of their colleagues without an effective response. Free speech is still defended, of course, but only so far as it is politically correct. If you question the establishment of an African-American studies program, for example, you might find yourself labeled a racist but in a slightly underhanded and less confrontational manner. For in typical institutions of higher learning both here and around the world, one's political agendas need to be dressed in the appropriate intellectual jargon. In his incisive essay "Upside Down in the Groves of Academe," William Henry asks us to:

> Imagine places where it is considered racist to speak of the rights of individuals when they conflict with the community's prevailing opinion...Where it is sexist to order a Domino's pizza because the chain's chairman donates money to an anti-abortion group...Imagine a literature

> class that equates Shakespeare and novelist Alice Walker,
> not as artists but as fragments of sociology…Finally,
> imagine a society in which some of the teachers reject the
> very ideas of rationality, logic, and dialogue as the corner-
> stone assumptions of learning—even when discussing
> science.[14]

Fueling these agendas and the ensuing curriculum wars is a fundamental assumption which parades under a variety of labels, such as "post modernism" or "deconstructionism." The assumption is that an objective *evaluation* of competing points of view is impossible since all points of view are to some extent biased by race, gender, and culture. All that's left to do is to *describe* different perspectives, including those formerly considered inconsequential, and attempt to counterbalance past biases—which might entail leaving Plato and Shakespeare out of the curriculum altogether.

Under this scenario, defending your position often amounts to little more than pinning a label on the other person's position. As Leon Botstein, president of Bard College, has observed: "Nobody wants to listen to the other side. On many campuses, you really have a culture of forbidden questions." And why are they forbidden? Certainly not for lack of answers! It's because most academics haven't a clue about how to resolve the seething conflicts of values and ideological assumptions those answers seem destined to harbor. So the tough questions often are not asked and intellectual fragmentation becomes further entrenched.

Social fragmentation. All cultures undergo a continuous balancing act between the concerns of social cohesion, on the one hand, and diverse religious, economic, political, and ethnic interests, on the other. While there is always some fragmentation, in the past few decades aspects of social fragmentation have reached new highs in America and in other parts of the world, such as Bosnia, Russia, and the Sudan. Whether or not this constitutes a crisis may depend upon how one's special interests are faring, but it is a trend that most would agree cannot continue indefinitely.

It's a familiar picture. The two-party political system is losing much of its power, with more voters acting independently of the labels they may wear. The interests of the elderly, mainly in the areas of Medicare and Social Security, increasingly are pitted against those of younger generations in fundamental ways. Crime on the whole runs higher than at other times in our history. Violence is becoming a way of life in ways, and at younger ages, than traditionally thought possible. Whole new industries are being born whose main purpose is to protect one segment of the population from another. (I would venture to guess that ten percent of the paperwork in this country is related to the desire to prevent oneself, or one's group, from being sued.) Drug abuse eats at the social fabric in an unprecedented fashion.

Even when official unemployment figures are down, real unemployment appears to be up because the government doesn't count certain classes of individuals, such as those who out of despair have just abandoned the search for a job. Meanwhile, newsrooms progressively straddle a disappearing line between truth and public relations.

One-issue politics is running rampant. *The* issue is taken to be advancing the cause of the poor, farmers, women, African-Americans, senior citizens, teachers, fundamentalist Christians, developers, environmentalists, the AMA, national defense, abortion, the NRA, and so on. Every group demands certain rights, with little rational dialogue about how they may clash with someone else's rights. Meanwhile, almost everyone wants the government to do more and tax less. And to help lead us through this mélange, we have a new Speaker of the House, Newt Gingrich, who is arguably the most adversarial, "divide and conquer" politician to hold that position in more than a century.

There are several reasons why increasing social fragmentation is so frightening. To begin with, the stakes are at an all-time high. These include long-term environmental destruction, the end of family farming, new conceptions of the nature and role of women in society, religious and racial intolerance, and the fundamental reorientation of health care delivery—all of which are fueling the paradigm wars in the nineties!

Behind these concerns is a creeping relativism that calls into question the ability of reason and good will to evaluate fairly the narrow agendas of special interest groups. In academia, this is the spirit of post-modernism. In society at large, it's power politics. Thus, it is argued that men cannot relate appropriately to the issue of abortion because they are men or that artistic criticism of black literature by white critics is bound to miss the point and is racist by definition! Or that the Supreme Court, in order to be fair, should contain representatives of all major political, gender, religious, and ethnic orientations.

Our responses to specific challenges, such as the cost of energy, environmental preservation, food production, or insurance rates, are bound up with our responses to other issues in an endless network. The destruction of Amazon rain forests, for example, is directly linked to the consumption of meat in this country, because more land is needed there in order to raise more cattle for export to America. We are desperately in need of an over-arching vision with which we can deal concurrently with these challenges—some way to bridge the widening gap between cultural islands and conflicting agendas. We seem determined instead to play out the logic of fragmentation and control to the end. Congress seems incapable of passing needed legislation when it conflicts with the desire to get reelected. Our options seem to be power politics or nothing!

And why do political pressure and public relations gambits seem to work better than reason and good will? Because for the most part they play to our fears of what will happen if we don't get on board. The lesson ought to be coming into focus. If we are losing a framework of rationality and shared values within which to work out our issues, then psychological manipula-tion—no matter how well it is disguised—will only validate our fears, increase fragmentation, and in the end justify someone's draconian methods of dealing with the problems. Social fragmentation will decline only when we directly address and overcome our deepest fears and insecurities. When fear is unmasked, human bonding with fewer bound-aries will flourish.

Nowhere is the self-defeating logic of fear-based power politics more evident than in the arms race. The ultimate outcome of a social mind-set which pits "us" against "them" on a global scale was, until quite recently, assumed to be a nuclear war which everyone loses and nobody wins. We have stockpiled enough nuclear arms to destroy the world seven times over. So it was not totally reassuring when the United States and Soviet Russia agreed to work toward reducing them by half or when the Bush adminis-tration announced that no more nuclear warheads would be built.

Despite the end of the Cold War and the rise of semipopular democra-cies in Eastern Europe and in the former Soviet Union, the governments of the world (including Russia and the U.S.) collectively are still spending over a million dollars a minute on armaments of one kind or another. In Yugoslavia, the Serbs have demonstrated not only a willingness to use them against the Bosnians, but also a racist mind-set reminiscent of the worst atrocities of World War II.

Nuclear explosions or exchanges have almost occurred by accident on six occasions.[15] Through nuclear power and bomb production, leakage, and testing, radioactive substances have become embedded in the entire ecosystem. Children growing up in the United States today now have six to eight times more Strontium-90 in their bones than their parents.[16] The full extent of this leakage probably still is not appreciated.

One response to the stockpiling of arms in particular and to socio-political fragmentation in general is found in Green Politics, and in the type of thinking associated with it, both in Europe and elsewhere. In certain respects the Greens are a paradigm of what Ferguson described in America as the "radical center." They take as their point of departure the fact that we find ourselves in a complex global crisis that impacts upon our health, environment, quality of life, work, social relationships, and even survival. To solve one, we must address others—on a global scale.

Traditional politicians, both liberal and conservative, simply shift these issues around in light of short-term monetary considerations or techno-logical fixes. Government experts approach these issues on a piecemeal basis. Greenish thinking individuals see them as part of an interconnected whole. In ways that transcend both Left and Right, they support economic decentralization, gender equality, ecological balance, phasing out nuclear power, nonviolence, cooperative (not monolithic) world order, and cultural pluralism.[17]

In *Spiritual Politics*, Corine McLaughlin and Gordon Davidson have compiled a virtual encyclopedia of effective alternative social visions and methods that can take us beyond the politics of fragmentation. By applying principles of both the Perennial Philosophy and systems thinking (which I will describe in Chapter Three), by showing how negative events on the world scene reflect our own inner dynamics, and by explaining how these dynamics can be constructively changed, McLaughlin and Davidson present one of the most compelling transformational visions in decades. Most of what we need to know in order to overcome the dead-end constric-tions of social fragmentation is contained in this book.

The women's movement. Perhaps nowhere are challenges to the guiding assumptions of Western culture more politically focused than in the wo-men's movement. As feminists frequently point out, the transformational issues we now face, both nationally and globally, are the offspring of patri-archal thinking. Transcending all national, religious, and ethnic barriers, it is men who have given us war, fragmented social and political agendas, and caused environmental decay, endless competition, and the subjugation of women.

Patriarchy is slowly but successfully being challenged. In religion, politics, business, and the home, women are assuming, or struggling to assume, positions of greater authority and equality. This birthing process has produced confusion, anger, and fear for both men and women. Debates over the ERA, for example, were only the tip of the iceberg. For many men, the changes have taken place too quickly. For many women, it is not nearly fast enough, especially in light of the historical injustices women have suffered.

There are almost as many schools of feminist thought as there are major religious traditions. Women as a group (and the men who support them) are by no means unified in what they ultimately want or how best to achieve it. Some are trying to beat men at their own game within the system. Some are attempting to transform adversarial relationships in business, law, education, and families into more constructive win-win scenarios. And some have become separatists, preferring to have as little interaction as possible with men. However these agendas work out, a fundamental realignment of gender roles is becoming a fact of life.

What is often overlooked about this revolution, especially by men, is that the women's movement is more than a demand for equal rights. Freedom from oppression is just the first step. Women do not want equality just to become more like men, although some have had to do this for strategic reasons. Beyond equal rights, they want empowerment so that, as women, they can make their distinctive contributions to culture. Another few thousand years of modified patriarchal agendas (war, competition, fear, institutionalized hierarchies) under different labels is not their goal; rather, their goal is to birth a new way of being in *relationship* with ourselves, each other, the planet, and our gods and goddesses.[18]

Transformed relationships will reflect caring and nurturance, feeling and creation, and mutual respect and empowerment. In these transitional times, it remains to be seen what lasting changes the shift from controlling to empowering relationships will produce. However, they are certain to be both numerous and profound. New roles for women in the military, clergy, and business, feminist critiques of patriarchy, debates over abortion, and the rise of women's groups such as NOW are only the beginning.

Economics. The history of economic thought, from Adam Smith to Alan Greenspan, is a quagmire of interrelated and questionable assumptions. Smith's "Invisible Hand" of rising material prosperity has not trickled down to the lower economic classes as equitably or as widely as predicted. And the market place is neither as competitive nor as free as economists like to assume; all participants in market transactions have nothing close to equal and complete access to the relevant information.

Government intervention has proved unsuccessful in avoiding the cycles of "boom and bust" by managing such variables as taxes, interest rates, and money supply. In their quest for scientifically rigorous models which quantify all variables in order to predict future trends, economists conveniently set aside many qualitative factors that bear upon our well-being. Fritjof Capra describes this blindness as follows:

> The Keynesian model concentrates on the domestic economy, dissociating it from the global economic network and disregarding international economic agreements; it neglects the overwhelming political power of the multinational corporations, pays no attention to political conditions, and ignores the social and environmental costs of economic activities. At best it can provide a set of possible scenarios but cannot make specific predictions. Like most of Cartesian economic thought, it has outlived its usefulness.[19]

Underlying the preceding failures and most economic philosophies is the belief that long-term undifferentiated economic growth is both desirable and necessary. Accompanying this belief is the further assumption that the competition fueled by self-interest among individuals, corporations, and countries is a necessary stimulus to this growth. Since most everyone wants to participate in rising material prosperity, it is only natural that they should find themselves in adversarial relations.

Growth is defended as the best means of improving material standards, yet competition typically requires both winners and losers; it tends to work in such a way that the rich get richer and the poor become worse off. The obsession with economic growth transcends most major economic philosophies. Both capitalist and socialist economies, for example, are fundamentally committed to growth, but countries in either economic camp seldom question where such growth may ultimately lead. They just know they want it.

Two critical factors, labor and natural resources, fit into the growth scenario of classical economic thought. To promote growth, labor and industry must become more productive. To accomplish this, labor initially must be mobilized by a class of managers who have the knowledge to organize its direction and the capital to underwrite the means of production. At a comparatively early point in this mobilization, labor begins to produce more than it consumes.

The resulting surplus value, as it is called, then typically begins to accumulate in the hands of the managers and investors who control the means of production. Apart from the cycles of labor unrest and alienation that this scenario generates, the net result after several hundred years is that in America eighty percent of the wealth is owned by approximately five percent of the population. And this imbalance is reflected in the United States' position vis-à-vis the rest of the world. With six percent of the world's population, it controls at least twenty-five percent of the planet's wealth. How long can such imbalances be sustained?

The transformative challenge is not simply one of redistributing wealth to the poor, but rather how all people in the lower end of the spectrum (the other ninety-five percent) can begin to participate in both the decisions and rewards that affect production and standards of living. In theory, rising material wealth is supposed to "trickle down" to poorer working classes in the form of more and better-paying jobs. In practice, managers are always looking for cheaper labor pools. Unions help raise wages only up to the point where the company moves its facilities to a country where people will work for less.

In theory, capitalism is supposed to make us more equal on a long-term rising tide of prosperity. In practice, not only do economic growth and equality not necessarily go together, they also may be incompatible, in view of our declining natural resources. This decline requires ever-greater amounts of capital to invest, which can be returned to the investors only by maintaining *inequality*. As *The Wall Street Journal* pointed out some time ago ("Growth and Ethics," August 5, 1975), industrial countries must choose between growth or greater equality, because inequality is necessary to create capital! This is, of course, not what the average person has been taught to expect in a market-driven economy.

At the international level, the gap between rich and poor continues to grow wider. The world has approximately one hundred and fifty-seven billionaires, but one hundred million people are homeless, living on sidewalks, in garbage dumps, and under bridges. Special weight loss programs are a five billion dollar industry, while the world's poorest four hundred million people are so undernourished they suffer mental retardation, stunted growth, or death.

The other side of economic growth involves the discovery and translation of natural resources into useful goods and services. Here, a dark side raises its disturbing head in the form of conspicuous consumption far beyond our needs and our ability to sustain. Coupled with overpopulation and declining natural resources on a global scale, such localized over-consumption only accelerates the competition for scarce goods and promotes entropy.

In a closed system, changes in mass/energy proceed in one direction—from heat to cold, from available to less available energy, from order to disorder. The deficit can be made up by infusions of energy from outside the system, but that simply increases the drain on another system. For every increase in order or material complexity, there are correspondingly greater depletions of energy in the environment. For everything there is an entropic price, and the end product will always represent less than the total amount of energy used to produce it. Energy is always lost in production.

Energy can, however, be lost in greater or lesser amounts, depending upon how efficient the process is. The food chain provides a graphic illustration. At most stages, eighty percent of the matter consumed by a predator is lost as heat energy, leaving that much less to pass on to the next stage. Controversial futurist Jeremy Rifkind offers the following example.[20] Approximately three hundred trout are required to support one person for a year. Those trout in turn must consume the equivalent of ninety thousand frogs, which must consume the equivalent of twenty-seven million grasshoppers. The grasshoppers in turn would require one thousand tons of grass. All this for one human!

By fueling economic growth in the United States, consumption accelerates entropy through institutionalized inefficiencies. The amount of grain required to produce an average steak for one person would be sufficient to feed five people instead. More grain and less meat would retard entropy. With six percent of the world's population, we consume a third of the world's energy. Swedes and Germans have standards of living comparable to ours, yet their per capita consumption of energy is only half of ours. If everyone in the world lived according to average standards of prosperity in this country, the world's known natural resources would be used up in twenty-five years!

Economics exists because there is not enough money or resources to satisfy the *perceived* needs of those who count themselves part of the system. As Stephen Goldstein of Nova University points out, we have simply become so accustomed to having money that we cannot imagine doing without many apparent necessities of life—like tortilla chips, marshmallows, and potato chips (upon which we spent six billion dollars in 1991); pornography (eight billion dollars); toilet articles and cosmetics (sixty-two billion dollars); and children's toys (fifteen billion dollars, when we could read to them for free).

The same logic that fuels countertrends in health care and the environment is also applicable to this depressing picture of personal spending habits. Health care will break the bank unless we take better care of ourselves to begin with. Landfills will consume us unless we, as individuals, start recycling more at home. Goldstein's observations are part of a small but growing trend; ask not what others should do for us, but what we can do for ourselves. It's time to redirect our personal spending habits.

The picture is bleak, yet the germs of a counterrevolution are in-the-offing. A generation of new economists is developing models which incorporate global, ecological, noncompetitive, and selective growth perspectives.[21] They stress decentralization, voluntary simplicity, quality of life (rather than material prosperity), and production of what is actually needed, rather than what we have been conditioned to want.

Margrit Kennedy's *Interest and Inflation Free Money* takes aim at some mistaken assumptions found in free market economies, such as the beliefs that we only pay interest if we borrow money and that inflation is an integral part of market economics. Of greater significance, however, is her explanation of how we can create a neutral exchange medium that requires neither interest nor inflation but that surprisingly works for everybody, including those who currently profit the most from interest rates and inflation.

Hazel Henderson's *Creating Alternative Futures: The End of Economics, The Politics of the Solar Age,* and *Paradigms in Progress* are indispensable guides to implementing a sustainable culture by questioning the foundations of economics itself. We do not have to assume, for example, that greed is good (or at least "OK"), that economic growth is desirable, and that the inevitable price of such growth is depletion of our natural resources and a permanent underclass. Significantly, Henderson's alternative visions and critiques are neither capitalist nor Marxist in their orientation. Rather, they redefine the very ground on which we thought we were standing.

Herman Daly's *Steady-State Economics* is a veritable bible for those who oppose growth in favor of an economy in which stocks of wealth and people are continually renewed even though neither is growing. His recent joint effort with philosopher John Cobb, *For the Common Good: Redirecting the Economy toward Community, the Environment, and a*

Sustainable Future, contains many proposals for restructuring traditional economic institutions. These institutions, such as the banking industry, are the chief obstacles to a just and sustainable culture.

Here are four of Daly's more revolutionary proposals. First, stop counting the consumption of natural capital as income. When country A ships too much of its timber or its fish to country B, this helps A's balance of payments and, other things being equal, A's economy improves—but only for a while. For when more is taken than can be replenished, country A's economy begins to suffer. Natural capital, such as fish or petroleum, is currently counted as foreign exchange income. Daly proposes that we more realistically count these exchanges as capital transfers between countries. Such a policy, he believes, would steer banks away from investing in unsustainable development.

Second, Daly argues that labor and income should be taxed less, whereas the flow of energy and materials from the earth, through the economy, and back in the form of waste, should be taxed more. His reasoning is disarming. Why tax at a higher rate what we want more of, such as income, and at a lesser rate what we want less of, e.g., solid waste and pollution. Daly is not against taxes per se but favors a radically different tax base.

Third, we should maximize the productivity of natural capital and invest in increasing it. In their search for efficient investment strategies, bankers seek for the most limiting factors, typically labor and man-made capital (money), that hold back production. Then they find a way to improve or coax more from these factors—like building more sawmills to produce more timber. But these days the limiting factors are often in the natural resources sector. We don't need more fishing boats; we need more fish. It will pay us, therefore, to invest heavily in expanding our replenishable resource base.

Finally, we should move away from the ideology of ever-expanding free trade and capital movements across national boundaries and more toward national production for internal markets.

> The royal road to development...is thought to be the unrelenting conquest of each nation's market by all other nations...It is necessary to remind ourselves that the World Bank exists to serve the interests of its members, which are nation states. It has no charter to serve the cosmopolitan vision [NAFTA, GATT, etc.] of converting relatively independent national economies into one tightly integrated

world economic network, upon which the weakened
nations depend even for base survival.[22]

Will idealistic proposals for dramatic economic reform actually work?
A small but growing body of criticism, as yet only a dark cloud on the
horizon, holds out little hope until we are willing to confront the sources
of hidden economic and financial control.[23] The international banking
system and multinational corporations—key elements in the widely pro-
phesied move toward a global economy—at a certain level are sources of
control in themselves. Up to a point, their workings are open to public
scrutiny. In the background, however, may lie deeper sources of control
limited to perhaps no more than several dozen individuals and their most
trusted associates, not all of whom are necessarily American.

This control may be so pervasive and powerful, so hidden behind
veneers of respectability, that huge profits are made in both war and peace
and in both economic upturns and downturns. According to this scenario,
war and negative economic cycles are engineered for the benefit of a
comparative few—not, of course, with complete predictability, but enough
to maintain and expand the power base of those in control. This hidden
base of power and the international banking system through which it
operates thrive on debt—whether consumer, corporate, or national. Our
national debt is projected to surpass 6.5 trillion dollars before 1999, at
which point it will be greater than the gross national product. Virtually no
economist will predict the dire consequences of such a state of affairs. And
despite recent attempts to balance the budget, Congress appears unable to
deal constructively with the unprecedented transformational challenge that
this debt structure has created.

And what of the banking system itself? Most citizens believe that the
Federal Reserve, which critically affects the financial health of this
country, is owned by or is a branch of the United States government. In
fact, it is a private corporation whose chairman is appointed by the President but whose shares can be owned, very indirectly, by foreign interests
like the Bank of England.

The literature of conspiracy is voluminous, even if restricted to banking
and finance. Professor Carroll Quigley's respected study, *Tragedy and Hope*,
which links American foreign policy to the power of an "international
financial coterie," is important reading for serious students. Pat Robertson's
more recent *The New World Order* ambitiously links the Illuminati,
Freemasons, European banking interests, the Federal Reserve, Council on
Foreign Relations, and assorted political figures to an end-times scenario

familiar to conservative Christians. Critics argue that anti-Semitism lies festering just below the surface of many of his claims.

I draw attention to Robertson's book, not out of sympathy for his religious and political causes, but because it is accessible and moderately comprehensive in summarizing through extensive citations the case that others in addition to Quigley have made in this arena, notably two older works: Nesta Webster's *Secret Societies and Subversive Movements* (1924) and Eustace Mullins's *Secrets of the Federal Reserve* (1954). Michael Lind's extensive critical review, "Rev. Robertson's Grand International Conspiracy Theory," (*New York Review*, February 2, 1995) and subsequent elaboration on April 20 provide both a useful overview of major threads of conspiracy theory and an effective counterbalance to some of Robertson's more speculative claims.

What readers who look deeper into this long-standing debate may find troubling is that too much energy is often devoted to showing that someone is anti-Christian, anti-Semitic, or paranoid, or influenced by someone they should not be. By contrast, the issue of whether there actually exists hidden economic manipulation at the levels claimed is not given the attention it deserves. Economic conspiracy theorists may not have produced a smoking gun, but there is clearly a great deal of smoke around this issue. And pinning labels on the opposition is not the way to clear the air.

Religion. It is widely assumed that being religious means that one believes in a transcendent God from which certain moral rules follow (such as the Ten Commandments); one should attempt to live one's life in accordance with those beliefs and rules; as a result one should gain, especially in hard times, an emotional stability and satisfaction not typically enjoyed by the atheist or agnostic.

The challenges to this conception come from varied sources. They include the emergence of existentialism, the demythologizing movement, the social activism of the sixties, the rise of scientism as its own religion, the encounter with Eastern religions, paranormal spiritual experiences, and secular humanism. Through it all, a number of overarching questions have assumed increasing significance. What is the purpose of religion? What is left for religion to be or to do?

The challenge can be mapped out as a trilemma in response to each of the above three components. Regarding the first component, factual claims about what the universe is like or what God wants have progressively given ground to modern science. Literal accounts of scripture have been progressively harder to defend, and many theologians now recommend not even attempting to do so.

And what of the second function of religion, that of translating one's beliefs into action? It has become apparent that any worthwhile activity done in the name of religion, such as helping the poor, also can be done in the name of something else.

Finally, with respect to the search for security and happiness, other institutions increasingly have taken over functions that used to be found primarily in a religious setting. These include exponential increases in psychotherapy, support groups, and various networks devoted to specific causes. Many ministers, priests, and rabbis have acknowledged the increased importance of this side of their work as they go back to school for advanced training in counseling. And so far as the promises of an afterlife are concerned, many individuals have found support for their beliefs outside of organized religion.

So what is left of a truly distinctive nature for religion to do? One response is to promote genuine spirituality. Actually, this has been a minority function all along, but it is now moving closer to the mainstream. Briefly, the message is this: Look within and (paradoxically) find yourself "in" God. One does not merely have to believe in things transcendent, but can experience dimensions of love, power, and understanding that unite us and transform daily living. One can do good not out of obligation, but because it's a natural expression of enlightened consciousness. On this view, the priest, pastor, or rabbi is less a guardian of the flock, more a facilitator of the expansion of consciousness.

In its lead story for November 28, 1994, *Newsweek* took note of the fact that "whether it's middle age, or the coming millennium, or a bad case of the blues, many Americans are on a quest for spiritual meaning." This includes everything from pilgrimages to the Great Pyramid and Native American "power spots" to taking up meditation and visiting spiritual healers.

In their desire to explain this search in purely social and psychological terms, however, both academic and media establishments have overlooked the possibility that people *are* essentially spirits yearning to break free of cultural and religious constraints. They have overlooked the possibility that people have visions of angels because angels are actually intervening in their lives, that they may be having transcendental experiences because there are transcendental realms to access, and that some sacred places derive their power not just from the need for ritual, but from an invisible spiritual energy that actually occupies those places. As we shall see in later chapters, there is more to this possibility than mid-life crises and millennium fever.

Personal identity. Psychological health obviously means many things to many people. This is evidenced by the many schools of psychotherapy: Gestalt, transactional, Freudian, Jungian, rational-emotive, etc. Let us assume, however, that minimum psychological health involves the ability to: *adapt* to changing circumstances in ways that are consistent with primary emotional needs (love, security, etc.); *integrate* the results of the needs/circumstances interface into a coherent and stable self-image; and *grow* beyond levels of maturity required merely for social survival or economic success: that is, to actualize latent capacities for joy and meaningful life projects. Satisfying these conditions is always a challenge, no matter what the historical period. But over the last few decades, the stakes have been raised.

To begin with, the media gives us access to powerful and conflicting information, often while we are still children. Violence, sex, humor, fantasy, religion, and conflicting points of view about why the world is in such a sorry state are found lumped together on television any night of the week.

A wide range of job possibilities, life-styles, and moral and social values, plus assorted role models unfortunately do not come with criteria to sort it all out. The advice of parents, religious leaders, peers, and teachers generates confusion as often as clarity. The television message tells us: "This is your brain on drugs." But little is done to address the causes of why teens turn to drugs in the first place. How far would Alcoholics Anonymous have gone with the message "Just say No"?

Social fragmentation gets built into personal identity. "Do whatever makes you happy" may be well-intentioned, but is useless advice when one doesn't know in which direction to move. Many traditional roles and values (the status of women, human sexuality, work and leisure, self-sacrifice and patriotism, cultural pluralism, and the place of individual rights) have been in a state of fundamental flux over the past several decades.

The ethical precepts and social codes emerging out of this mélange are often on a collision course. Shifting relationships, AIDS, the drive to succeed, and fears that most everything we eat will turn out to be carcinogenic are but a few of the patterns that drive stress levels to new highs. The net result is that we have many fragmented and not altogether happy personalities walking around.

In addition to these socially adaptive pressures, a special challenge has arisen in the past few decades that is certainly unprecedented in American history and perhaps also in Western civilization. This challenge pertains to the encounter with the paranormal. Increased belief in such things as ESP is itself a major part of the picture. This is evidenced in a variety of polls conducted throughout the eighties. In 1981, twenty-three percent of the population believed in reincarnation; sixty-seven percent of teenagers believed in angels. Forty-six percent believed in life on other planets. Sixty-seven percent of widows believed they had had direct contact with the dead. And forty-three percent thought they had had an unusual spiritual experience. Overall, the figures have not looked like this before.[24]

The list of types of paranormal encounters is extensive and growing. Near-death experiences, visions of deceased relatives, apparent hauntings, precognitive dreams, spontaneous out-of-body ventures, kundalini awakenings, and spontaneous memories of past lives present extraordinary difficulties for integration. The situation has become so critical that spiritual emergency networks have arisen to assist in dealing with transpersonal crises that mainstream psychiatry and psychotherapy either ignore or explain away.

A third challenge to personal identity has been amply documented and developed in the literature of psychology and sociology over the past forty years. This is the sense of angst, meaninglessness, spiritual dis-ease, or a growing sense that behind one's socialized exterior there may be nothing holding it all together. Personal growth appears pointless or unattainable. Alienation and mere survival are the orders of the day, especially among teenagers.

Such feelings give rise to a whole range of nonspecific psychological disorders which, once again, mainstream psychiatry and psychotherapy have been unable to deal with effectively on a large scale. One may have integrated many roles and appear to be very much in control yet still be plagued by feelings of being a "fake," of wanting fulfillment over and above success, of wanting spiritual contentment rather than religious salvation, and of fearing that if one lost control, the whole show would come apart. What does one *do* about such feelings?

Karl Marx's alienated man, Jean-Paul Sartre's unauthentic man, Vance Packard's organization man, Viktor Frankl's meaningless man, Erich Fromm's marketing man, and Pauline Clance's imposter woman all represent unhealthy and often unconscious adaptations to stressful circumstances. It is a familiar story. People identify with parts of themselves to the exclusion of other parts begging to be set free. They are so heavily involved with their external worlds that they are afraid to explore their inner worlds—perhaps because they sense there would be nothing to see!

We move to other roles when our usual ones are challenged, postponing the need for internal transformation. What is behind the persona? Where is one's fundamental identity to be found? What is the most lasting and fulfilling anchoring point around which to build one's life? Viktor Frankl draws our attention to the fact that at a major American university, of sixty students who had attempted suicide, eighty-five percent reported that life was meaningless. But of those, fully ninety-three percent were "actively engaged socially, were performing well academically, and were on good terms with their family groups…Ever more people today have…no meaning to live for."[25]

The transformational challenge we face is one of developing a more comprehensive paradigm of human nature and more effective therapeutic interventions. This paradigm must provide ways to overcome effectively the emotional scarring and negative programming that destroy one's self-image. It should suggest ways to meet rising pressures for adaptation and integration. It should also help us to integrate and to properly understand psychic encounters and emergencies. Finally, it should help put us in touch with deeper levels of ourselves where creativity, empowerment, and joy lie in waiting.

Science. With some notable exceptions, Western science has been guided by the assumption that to exist is to be in a certain measurable place in space and time and that the interactions between objects occur along pathways that are spatio-temporally continuous. Together with the further assumption that the interactions themselves are guided solely by the forces of attraction and repulsion, this outlook forms the basis of a mechanistic philosophy of nature. A veritable landslide of phenomena which do not conform to this model are making paradigm shifts progressively more likely on a number of scientific fronts. Indeed, physics since Einstein's early discoveries already has experienced such a shift, which still has not been filtered through the educational system.

Some strange phenomena have found a new theoretical home, some are looking for a home, and some await judgment as to whether they deserve a home. Consider the following developments in physics alone: relativity theory, virtual particles and vacuum-state fluctuations, annihilation experiments, electron jumps, Bell's theorem, and the uncertainty principle.

These have caused fundamental changes in our beliefs about the uni-directionality of time, the vacuousness of space, the "substance" of physical objects, the spatial continuity of particle movement, the necessity of local causation, and the knowability of an objective world.[26] Scalar weapons systems, so-called "free energy" devices, and antigravitational technology represent further deep challenges to the thinking of mainstream physicists.

In chemistry, work on dissipative structures far from equilibrium has resulted in a reinterpretation of the Second Law of Thermodynamics, in particular the assumption that time is linear and reversible. In biology, the failure of promises to explain the self-organizing properties of living systems is a standing challenge which some argue cannot be met.

The failure of neuropsychology to explain memory storage and retrieval by various localization strategies (i.e., by finding "engrams" correspond-ing to memory content) is just short of embarrassing. In medical science, acupuncture continues to be an anomaly. Kirlian photography, especially of phantom limb phenomena, still awaits a secure theoretical interpreta-tion. The same challenge exists for explaining how, under extreme con-ditions, chickens appear capable of transmuting potassium into calcium.[27]

Reports of paranormal phenomena and altered states of consciousness fill volumes in the collective challenge to mainstream scientific thought. The evidence for telepathy, clairvoyance, precognition, and psychokinesis to varying degrees remains controversial, yet strong enough to justify the search for suitable explanatory models. For example, how is it possible to "see" a future that, according to common sense, does not exist? Or is that future already fixed? In out-of-body experiences, how is it possible to "see" without physical eyes?

If meditation can reduce hypertension, if yogis can alter oxygen consumption at will, and if guided imagery sometimes can assist in the re-duction of cancerous tumors, what revisions are necessary in the all-too-fragmented distinction between mind and body? If a spiritual counselor can look into your past and within an hour uncover some forgotten and deeply repressed childhood trauma, what are the implications for psycho-analysis?[28]

Both our science and our root metaphysical assumptions about human nature stand to undergo dramatic transformation. The ideal of dividing the world into isolated units responding to linear causal forces is already becoming a more limited paradigm within an overarching conceptual framework which stresses deep structural and dynamic relationships across space/time.

A widely discussed example of such modeling is the holographic (or holonomic) paradigm developed by Karl Pribram, David Bohm, Paul Pietsch and others.[29] Pribram, for example, argues that the brain stores information holographically, i.e., by virtue of complex interference patterns generated from vibrating fields of energy. There are significant differences in various holographic models. But all borrow from the critical insight that holography allows us to understand how a part of something can reflect properties and encode information from the whole.

Health. It is often assumed that health is the absence of disease, that disease is essentially something that attacks a person and, apart from following rudimentary rules of sanitation and nutrition, one's primary line of defense after the attack consists of placing oneself in the care of a physician who has the special tools and knowledge to repair the body and repel the invader.

These assumptions are part of what has come to be called the "biomedical model" of disease and health care. It is so pervasive in medical education that questioning it in any fundamental way can be interpreted as an act of heresy. It has proved its usefulness in many ways, especially in the reduction and eradication of infectious disease and in the repair of physically damaged bodies. And it will continue to do so.

However, there are increasing challenges to the biomedical model.[30] One is the rise in our population of degenerative and chronic diseases, such as cancer, arthritis, and diabetes. Many such diseases are now seen as a function of multiple variables, some of which may be in the environment, some in a patient's body (not especially in any one place), and some "in the mind." Instead of simple and linear cause-effect models, we are beginning to think in terms of the disposition of a *total* complex system in explaining health and disease.

We are placing more emphasis upon maintaining optimum health in the first place, rather than merely curing the patient during a health crisis. More individuals are demanding greater responsibility in managing their own health—ideally in partnership with their physicians, but if not, then in collaboration with informal health networks. Associations and health centers that promote holistic, noninvasive models and procedures are clearly on the rise and present some of the best evidence for a paradigm shift in-the-making. Homeopathy, spiritual healing, and bodywork may carry negative connotations for the AMA, but not for the rising tide of a new culture.

Economics is another transformative force. Simply paying for health care is a challenge that already has reached crisis proportions. This fact impinges on the physician/patient relationship in a variety of ways. When the physician is tacitly given primary responsibility for effecting a cure and patients come to expect ever more in this regard, the likelihood of more diagnostic tests and increased malpractice insurance rates is assured.

Alienation between physician and patient is often the result, with issues involving informed consent further muddying the waters. The net result over the longer run is that if we cannot afford to become sick, we are more likely to assume a greater responsibility for our own health. And models which stress invasive procedures to "fix the machine" will move toward preventing illness and disease in the first place.

Extraterrestrial cultures. For the past few thousand years, we have assumed that we are the only intelligent species in the physical universe. To be sure, we have wondered about life elsewhere in the universe. And there have been isolated pockets of civilization where the idea of contact with beings from "elsewhere" seems to have played some role in the belief systems and evolution of those outposts. But in the absence of overwhelming evidence to the contrary, we have proceeded on the assumption that we are alone in the universe.

More recently, a new twist has been added to traditional thinking about extraterrestrial cultures. Astronomer Carl Sagan, for example, has calculated that there may be as many as several million planets with conditions suitable for sustaining the evolution of sentient species. But if some of these planets do support advanced extraterrestrial cultures, he quickly adds, there is no reason to assume that they have made contact with us, or that they could make physical contact (given the distances involved), or (even if they could) that they would want to interact with such a warring and technologically inferior species as ourselves.

This three-part assumption is about to become massively unglued. Indeed, for the past few decades, it already has begun to become unglued. Whether on the basis of over a million UFO sightings both here and abroad (thousands of which have been carefully researched) or through investigative reports of UFO crashes, confessions of retired military officers, initiation of friendly contacts by groups such as CSETI, or alien abductions, it has become clear that major governments have covered up both what they know and their own involvement in this arena. One unanswered question is why. The other is how we will handle public contact with extraterrestrial cultures in the very near future.

It would be difficult to imagine a clearer challenge to the foundations of any worldview than that posed by such contact. The laws of physics, the origins of our religious beliefs, and the way we structure relationships would all be nakedly exposed and potentially at risk in the event of such an encounter. How could they travel faster than light? What do they want from us? Do they believe in God? Are they peaceful? Do they have families? Where do they come from?

While some investigators have developed preliminary answers to these questions, a complete account will obviously have to come from representatives of alien cultures. Chapter Fourteen explores not only why I believe a cover-up has been perpetuated, but also why the answers to these and related questions are coming sooner than we might think. The truth about extraterrestrials is not just "out there." It's far more complex than most imagine. And our human-centered universe is about to be turned inside out!

In summary, then, ten transformative challenges are pushing deep-seated assumptions involving fragmentation, hierarchical control, reductionism, fear, competition, and our place in the universe to historical turning points. These assumptions are being challenged by those which incorporate wholeness, balance, emergence, mutual empowerment, the power of love, and galactic membership. Following is an outline which organizes the overall structure of this shift. The information presented is indicative only of the types of changes we face. The particular examples I've chosen will not always be the most important to the individual reader. In most instances, the types of responses outlined here will be explored in greater detail in later chapters.

A SUMMARY OF TRANSFORMATIVE CHALLENGES AND RESPONSES

1. Environment
   Area assumptions: Nature exists essentially for our dominion, can receive abuse indefinitely, and doesn't care what we do to it; higher vs. lower life forms.
   Challenges: Massive deforestation, ozone depletion, loss of arable land, toxic pollution of water and land, over-population; rethinking our claims of superiority over animals.

Responses: EPA, the "Greens" in Europe, Greenpeace; interest in Native American attitudes; GAIA thesis; recycling technologies; search for alternative energy sources.

2. Education

   Area assumptions: Learning is essentially memorization. Education is job preparation. School is for learning to transmit what authorities value; right brain emphasized.

   Challenges: Students becoming robots; loss of creative edge on the international scene; functional and cultural illiteracy; violence, drugs, higher dropout rate, teacher burnout.

   Responses: Experimentation with psychotechnologies and non-competitive learning and social formats; recognition of the power of self-image; educating the whole child.

3. Society

   Area assumptions: Society *is* ideally united by certain common interests, best governed by controlling hierarchies. Some wars are inevitable. Common good inevitably conflicts with personal freedom.

   Challenges: Rise of one-issue politics; decline of common working values; appeals to the "common good" not working; terrorism and violence increasing; arms race; fragmentation found everywhere.

   Responses: Increased use of conflict-resolution strategies; win-win attitudes that transcend political left and right; intentional communities; overcoming fear and working on self-esteem issues.

4. Patriarchy

   Area assumptions: Men should be in control. God is male. Competition with resulting "losers" is natural. Women are the weaker gender.

   Challenges: Women demanding equal pay, equal rights, and equal responsibility; systems of rigid control losing ground; feminist critiques of patriarcy.

   Responses: Textbooks rewritten to include the contributions of women; support groups for changing roles; new roles in business, home, clergy, and military.

5. Economics

   Area assumptions: Infinite expansion is possible, desirable, and necessary. Competition necessarily fuels progress, and entropy can be overcome.

Challenges: Fossil fuel depletion, increased competition for scarce resources; labor alienation; global implications for local decisions.

Responses: Search for alternate energy sources; greater labor participation in management; decentralization and steady-state economics.

6. Religion

Area assumptions: To be religious is to believe in a supreme being, live more or less according to "His" teachings, and derive a measure of emotional satisfaction.

Challenges: Successful rise of science, demythologizing movement, secular humanism, Eastern religions, pluralism, personal growth and support groups, feminist theology.

Responses: Increased spiritual seeking; focus on heart energy, transforming consciousness (not just believing); interest in prophetic visions and healing; millennium watch.

7. Personal identity

Area assumptions: A healthy self is a socialized self, a persona that simply adapts to and integrates the roles and values given to it.

Challenges: Powerful inconsistent demands for adaptation and integration; psychic encounters; alienation and quest for deeper personal meaning.

Responses: Meditation, personal growth and support groups; new psychotechnologies (guided imagery); emotional release work; Twelve Step programs.

8. Science

Area assumptions: Everything real should fit models which stress objectivity, materiality, localization, and quantification.

Challenges: Quantum mechanics, Bell's theorem, life fields, equipotentiality, psychic phenomena, transpersonal states of consciousness.

Responses: New Physics, humanistic and transpersonal psychology, holographic paradigm, systems theory, holism.

9. Health

Area assumptions: Health is simply not being sick. Abuse the machine until it breaks down, then fix the causes with surgery or drugs. Doctor always knows best.

Challenges: Medical care not affordable; chronic and degenerative disease on the rise; dissatisfaction with invasive technologies; patient and doctor alienation.

Responses: Holistic health movement; concern with whole person; individual responsibility for health; search for alternative remedies; emphasis on prevention; disease as metaphor.

10. Extraterrestrials

Area assumptions: We are alone. If ETs did exist, distance would all but rule out visitations. We would not interest them anyway.

Challenges: Massive sightings; investigations of landings and crashes; leaked information and disinformation; films of UFOs; alien abductions.

Responses: Demands to end government secrecy; expanding UFO organizations; help for abductees; attempts to initiate friendly contact.

ARE CURRENT CHALLENGES GREATER THAN IN TIMES PAST?

Whenever some commentators point to the prospects of great cultural change, others arise to downplay the perceived implications of that change. They point out that cultural change, even major change, is more or less an ongoing fact of life. Why invoke a whole change in worldview when our current challenges are probably no greater than in times past? After all, we have survived Darwin, Marx, the death of God movement, and World War II!

When viewed piecemeal, it can seem that a given challenge is no greater than many crises we've survived in the past. We can fail to see the forest for the trees. But when we begin to view the challenges collectively, the picture changes dramatically. For example, recent threats of even limited nuclear war and radiation poisoning, the destruction of our environment on a planetary scale, concern over women's rights, fascination with ESP, the social costs of drug addiction, and an explosion of interest in UFOs have never been greater in the past four hundred years—if not the past four thousand years! As Joseph Campbell observed shortly before his death: "There are certain periods when the [more or less ongoing] transformation [of culture] is quite special and extremely radical. And ours is certainly one of those periods."[31] In its manifesto, "At the Crossroads," the Communications Era Task Force (a cross section of researchers and citizens from every specialty and walk of life) addresses the problem as follows:

The shift through which we are living is unique in two critical ways. First, it is taking place within the lifetime of those alive today. Our previous patterns of behavior are no longer effective. For the first time, human beings must deliberately search for new ways to understand the world if it, and we, are to survive. Second, since the beginning of history, people have given their loyalty to their own group and feared or distrusted outsiders. Today, our power has become so great that the violence which results from the mutual fear can end in total destruction. We must therefore eliminate the "win-lose" patterns which have dominated our thinking and action and replace them with win-win styles.[32]

In certain respects, we simply do not know how profound the various transformative challenges we face will be. Surely they are of unequal strength. Technological advances, for example, may fuel another economic renaissance and support conspicuous consumption for the indefinite future. Or they may not. Shall we gamble or mend our ways? Only after we have come through these transitional times will we be in a position to rank the severity of the challenges we have faced.

The interconnected nature of these challenges strongly suggests that we will not be able to successfully meet some without also addressing others. This fact alone means that we are facing a cultural turning point of tremendous magnitude. In every challenge we have surveyed, there are interlocking clusters of assumptions brought to the surface. For example, the kind of thinking that makes men think they can win a war is closely related to the kind of thinking that keeps women down, destroys the environment, and dismisses subjective phenomena which are not explained by science.

To take a different example, we cannot deal effectively with racism or sexism until we have both rethought our economic assumptions and confronted what Jung termed our "shadow" sides. *Each transformative challenge gains strength by virtue of being connected with others.* To successfully deal with one, we must take into account others. The probability of a shift in worldview is directly proportional to the extent we acknowledge that we are *not* dealing with isolated trends.

Of course, even massively interconnected challenges do not guarantee a shift in worldview. And even if the outlines of a new worldview were clear and its case made, there is no automatic progression to a culture which lives by it. I have merely described some of the kinds of responses now in evidence. The root metaphor of hierarchy might take hold in new ways while retaining some of its old affiliations. Challenges to male domination, for example, could be followed by female domination: same game, new players. Were this to happen on a significant scale, we would not have a new worldview, but merely a newer version of the old one.

I don't believe this will happen. But nobody can predict with great accuracy how much of the original root metaphors will be whittled away or how much change is necessary to force the abandonment of the original ideas altogether. Many large corporations are training their managers to be less controlling and more inclusivist in their decision-making, which is a major shift in thinking. But they are doing so primarily to maintain their profit margins, which is business as usual. The responses to transformative challenges are nearly always mixed. We simply have to live through the process with as much clarity and courage as we can muster.

Defenders of traditional ways of thinking are still very much in power and don't care for such inclusivist win-win thinking, especially when it affects their agendas. With our transformational challenges so inextricably linked, however, it's vitally important that we move toward a worldview built upon this newer kind of thinking. The critical question is less a matter of who is in control now, but rather which way the winds are blowing. I hope the answer will be clear by the end of this book.

CHAPTER TWO

Critical Questions for the New Age

Until now, I have avoided associating any of the ideas or transformative challenges under discussion with the phrase "New Age."
This phrase means many things, both positive and negative, to
many people. Until ready to deal directly with the issues these meanings
attract, we are better advised to set the phrase aside. The New Age label
functions as a floating reference point in discussions of the broadest
possible subject matter in both mainstream and counterculture circles. And
whether you are for or against it, the territory usually is slippery.

My purpose in this chapter is three-fold: to clarify different senses of the
New Age in order to develop a more coherent sense of what it's all about;
to defend the New Age against superficial criticisms; and to explain what
I think are its main shortcomings. Throughout, I shall stress that it's not
so much what New Agers believe that sets them apart from other movements (although that is certainly an important part of the picture), but
rather how they come by their beliefs and promote them in the public
arena.

THE NEW AGE SLIPPERY SLOPE

One path through New Age territory narrowly focuses upon the most sen-
sational and naive pronouncements that New Agers make. Crystals, UFOs,
and channeling easily raise the New Age specter. It's not just crystals per se
that create a stir, but what New Agers claim about them—like "Wear this
gemstone around your neck to enhance your prosperity consciousness."
Critics find such prescriptions easy prey. By contrast, a broad, flexible
approach views the New Age label as a place marker for various responses
to current transformative challenges. For example, New Agers are as
critical of patriarchy as feminists are, but for quite different reasons.

As we proceed, it will become clear that the New Age label cannot be easily distinguished from a wide variety of viewpoints. As just noted, what ultimately makes one a New Ager has less to do with what one believes than with how one came to those beliefs and how they are integrated into a worldview. Both Buddhists and New Agers, for example, believe in reincarnation, but Buddhists are not nearly as interested in specific past lives.

My concern throughout the book is with the search for a more comprehensive master paradigm, not with a label. Like most commentators, I am sympathetic to some ideas that attract the New Age label and skeptical about others. Unlike most commentators, however, I don't run from the label in all contexts. Instead, I make a decision about its potential value *in a certain context* and proceed accordingly.

I have been called a defender of New Age ideas on radio talk shows about healing, for example, and a critic of New Age thought because I believe that most prosperity seminars are hopelessly naive. When there is lack of clarity about an issue, we should tie down specific details of the discussion, not pin a label on someone and run. What one means by "New Age" is likely to change from one context to the next in this period of great change.

Why is there so much confusion and controversy about the New Age? The answer becomes evident when we survey its multiple meanings. "New Age" can refer to: psychic things, like ESP, reincarnation, and Edgar Cayce; Satan's undercover work in the final days before the Second Coming; a period of world peace and harmony or the Age of Aquarius; new techniques for emotional release and actualizing human potential; dissatisfied people looking for new meaning in life; hippies trying to make a comeback; the interconnectedness of all things; the need to give up traditional assumptions in politics and education; holistic health and alternatives to allopathic medicine; adopting a creative, nonjudgmental lifestyle; new frontiers of physics and consciousness; honoring the Earth Mother; understanding what "Christ consciousness" is all about; looking for new paradigms to put it all together; trying to change history (like the Harmonic Convergence) just by thinking; organic gardening and sustainable agriculture; pyramid power; space music; etc.

This list barely scratches the surface. But it helps explain why many have trouble with the New Age label. In fact, the range of meanings is so large that even New Agers themselves often identify with certain areas while remaining oblivious to others. People who think that the New Age is about awakening psychic potential, for example, are surprised when they hear of Mark Satin's book, *New Age Politics*, which came out in 1978. Their first tendency is to think that it has something to do with "psychic warfare." The simple truth is that we can select any particular item from the above list and call it New Age—or something else! Both defenders and critics do this all the time.

In 1988 *Omni* magazine asked twelve leading commentators for a definition of "New Age."[1] Is it a movement? A concept? A twenty-first century religion? An old worldview with a new label? The answer was "yes" to all of these, but a lot more, too. While most commentators held out some hope of what the New Age could be, there were strong threads of skepticism in evidence—some from rather surprising sources.

Abbie Hoffman saw it as out of touch with street-level issues such as hunger and poverty. Richard Bach saw it as an "amorphous thing" which affects people in irrational ways; he eschewed the label. Ken Wilber did not see any global spiritual transformation for at least several hundred years. And Marilyn Ferguson thought of yuppies caught up in a false spirituality while missing extraordinary opportunities for social transformation. She preferred instead to think in terms of a "shift in cultural values" which would ideally bring us closer to caring and sharing.

Carl Raschke, the author of a study on the origins of the New Age movement, offers a sweeping dismissal:

> The New Age Movement is a codification of the idealistic fervor, religious experimentation, anti-intellectualism, millennialism and self immersion of the 1960's counter-culture, and it reflects, in part, a generational mid-life crisis. The 60's generation has come up against the limits of opportunity and human mortality, and in the New Age movement it is seeking an innocence and immortality that is beyond human grasp.[2]

Raschke's exercise in reductionism and character assassination is almost useless for understanding the meaning of the New Age. Yet this kind of reduce-things-to-their-deviant-origins approach typifies much criticism of the New Age. At a recent American Academy of Religion meeting, for example, it was argued that the New Age Movement represents a response to the socio-spiritual crisis of the sixties that *parallels* the Pentecostal/Charismatic revival.[3] For some, this will appear as guilt by association. But let me address Raschke's line of thinking in a more detailed fashion.

To begin, very little has been codified about the New Age as evidenced by the many different things it can mean to different people. (If it had been, I would not have to write this chapter.)

For every individual who fits some aspect of Raschke's description, there are another five who don't and yet still adopt the New Age label. For example, what about New Age teenagers with very "straight" parents who escaped the sixties?

Raschke simply assumes the answers to some important questions (as do most criticisms of the New Age). For example, we are told that immortality is beyond our grasp. Don't we require a major analysis of arguments for survival of death in order to establish that?

Mid-life crises send people in all kinds of directions. That in itself doesn't tell us anything about the worthiness of the newer life-style. Why is it a *defect* if one gets divorced at forty-five and takes up meditation with the (New Age) music of Kitaro in the background?

Elizabeth Clare Prophet's community, which reportedly combines armed preparation for Armageddon with channeled sermons from angels, would probably qualify for inclusion in Raschke's narrow description of the New Age. Certainly there are the trappings of self-immersion. But Prophet's community is an extreme example with elements that many New Agers question or reject.

For virtually every new movement in history, there will always be some parallels with earlier movements. Every movement begins somewhere! However, that does not detract from the uniqueness of each. Transcendentalism, gender equality, honoring the Earth, and psychic experiences have long been a part of different agendas. But that observation in itself does not begin to capture their current evolution or the ways they are now coming together. The New Age isn't any one idea or agreed-upon set of agendas. Any attempt to reduce it to a ready-made set of categories consequently will fail.

All major cultural realignments and shifts in worldview carry great confusion, lack of personal integration, and the usual fringe elements. This was true with the Reformation and the Enlightenment, and it is true with our current cultural crises. It's no more a special problem for the New Age than it was for the birth of America.

It is easy for critics to focus on isolated elements within a larger cultural realignment that are simplistic, make for good press, and play upon latent fears of too much change in too little time. These considerations typically represent no more than the tip of the iceberg. But this tip nonetheless gets a questionable label—in this case "New Age." Soon the label begins to command attention. Meanwhile the revolution continues, with or without the critics. This happened with Jesus, Galileo, Darwin, and Marx. Why should it be different now?

It makes for interesting press to label meditation and visualization groups as "cults," holistic health practices as "pseudoscientific," and New Agers as crystal gazers looking for the prophet of the week. A story about Ronald Reagan consulting an astrologer makes far better press than, say, a story about a quiet revolution where thousands around the country each week gather in private homes to discuss Gerald Jampolsky's *Love is Letting Go of Fear* or John Bradshaw's *Homecoming*. In fact, more than ninety percent of the subscribers to the periodical, *New Age*, are college graduates. They are three times likelier to travel abroad and four times likelier to be politically active than the average citizen—a far cry from the stereotype of self-immersion used by the media to fan the flames of fear and ignorance.

NEW AGE VERSUS NEW PARADIGM

No single definition can capture the essence of the New Age, either as a movement or as a set of principles. To demand one or to assume that only one definition is correct is as fruitless or misleading as requiring a single definition of religion, science, or art. However, there are a number of considerations that can shape our understanding of the New Age.

The New Age label and some of its synonyms might very well disappear from the scene. If so, we wouldn't have to worry about defining it. For example, many New Age beliefs and practices are being assimilated into the mainstream. *Publisher's Weekly* already has declared the New Age dead—not because it fizzled, but because it is losing its identity vis-à-vis the mainstream. There are millions of professionals who may have at one time rejected the New Age label but who now incorporate many of its ideals and practices in their lives, without associating them with any particular label.

Another reason why the New Age label may disappear is that some of its more distinctive aspects may be subsumed under other specialized labels. At a typical New Age trade show, many dealers have put distance between themselves and the New Age label. They are burned out on their own hype and stung by relentless criticism from the press.

So they practice what the U.S. government already has perfected: put a new twist on some idea and call it by another name. For example, it may be urged that a certain process is not New Age visualization; rather, it's "integral" visualization. Many competent and sincere individuals, especially with transformational agendas, have chosen to avoid the confusion that comes with trying to explain why their ideas or products are or are not New Age. Some call themselves "futurists," much to the chagrin of other futurists who reject the New Age label but actually adopt many New Age ideas under different names.

Let me, then, clarify *my* use of three labels used throughout the rest of the book.

New Age: A primary, though not exclusive, concern with some combination of channeling, reincarnation, extraterrestrials, esoteric aspects of holistic health (psychic healing, herbs, etc.), and self-improvement (obtained through rebirthing, affirmations, etc.). This is not an altogether fair description, since New Agers have other interests. Moreover, these topics in themselves have long been a concern to researchers outside the New Age community (like UFOlogists and parapsychologists). However, this is the "popular" sense of the term.

New Paradigm dialogue: An ongoing discussion and exploration of the full range of cross-disciplinary, leading-edge, personal and social transformational agendas. This can include sophisticated exploration of any of the above areas but additionally covers serious spiritual practices, the New Physics, New Biology, New Economics, transpersonal psychology and parapsychology, education, the environment, new health models (e.g., those stemming from psychoneuroimmunology), feminism, the restructuring of personal and social relationships, decentralist political agendas, peace and global responsibility—in brief, those developments underwritten by the search for wholeness, balance, mutually empowering cooperation, and love.

Rising Culture: I have borrowed this phrase from Fritjof Capra. It refers to all persons, trends, and cultural institutions whose actions and perspectives are informed by the New Paradigm dialogue and to some extent by New Age agendas. At this level, we are not so much concerned with defining what holistic health is, for example, as with the cultural dynamics pushing us in that direction. We are concerned with awareness in action, e.g., with why more people are integrating holistic health practices into their lives. Most people in the Rising Culture have interests in both popular New Age topics and in the New Paradigm dialogue. Examples would be an ecofeminist who consults a psychic or a Greenpeace representative who uses Bach Flower Essences.

In short, the (popular) New Age is both more restricted than the New Paradigm dialogue in the breadth of its vision and less sophisticated in articulating that vision. But the two are sometimes closely related under the umbrella of a Rising Culture.

I cannot stress too much the importance of clarifying specific ideas and agendas whenever any of these phrases surfaces—especially "New Age." If one is talking to a specific group, such as Baptists or physicians, I suggest setting the jargon aside and using terms these groups can relate to. Be aware of the unique demands of shifting contexts. The more one retains general labels, the more likely one is to introduce confusion and controversy from other parts of the cultural map. It's impossible to know whether one is for or against the New Age until one knows what the phrase means.

When an academic colleague asks me what I think about all that "New Age stuff," this is one way I respond: There are two master agendas for our time. One is the inner goal of exploring and positively *transforming consciousness*. The other is the outer goal of creating a *sustainable global culture*. Everything else is secondary. Each agenda complements the other and neither will be accomplished without the other. As individuals, we will naturally be inclined to invest more of our energy in one agenda than in the other. As a global community, however, we can complete both under as many labels—"New Age" or otherwise—as we like.

But can we blend so many diverse goals and outright disagreements both within and between New Age and New Paradigm communities? How do we get reincarnationists and those interested in sustainable agriculture together? Or feminists and homeopaths? The answer is: We don't have to, although nothing rules out one person being involved in all four areas. There isn't any single definition that all parties will agree on.

In fact, there doesn't have to be an all-purpose definition in the first place. All we need are some overlapping goals at a theoretical level and a sufficient number of *bridge* movements at a social level. The emergence of a new worldview is never a monolithic, prearranged affair in which we all pledge mutual respect and agreement before we jump in, so to speak.

Certain topics by their very nature lend themselves to bridging the spectrum. The New Physics carries themes, such as the emphasis upon complementary interrelationships, which are applicable to a wide range of issues. The women's movement, with both its political and spiritual wings, is a dynamic, bridging force in its own right. The holistic health movement brings together scientists and spiritual healers. Agriculture brings together farmers and experts in psychotronics. Personal growth brings clinical psychotherapists both to spiritual retreats and to channelings with Lazaris. Environmental concerns bring together political leaders and Native Americans. There is no end to the possible connections.

No matter where one is in the spectrum of a Rising Culture, there are as many bridges as there are primary agendas. This isn't surprising, since bridge-building and networking are high on everyone's list. This is partly why I prefer to look for deep structural themes that connect and cross-fertilize particular agendas at any point in the spectrum—themes that include ideas and practices which seem to have little to do with one another.

Where are these convergences? If you find yourself moving away from ideas or institutions involving fragmentation, reductionism, oppressive forms of hierarchical control, competition, or fear and toward those of wholeness, integration, mutually empowering cooperation, and love, then you are more in the Rising Culture than out of it. If you are seriously concerned about the need for healing on multiple fronts (mind, body, spirit, society, environment) and are doing something about it, then you are in the Rising Culture, no matter what you call it.

This means that the women's movement, the environmental movement, peace and nuclear disarmament groups, human rights groups, the New Physics, the New Economics, the holistic health movement, the human potential movement, psychic exploration and integration groups, spiritually based religion, holistically oriented scientists, visionary artists, and New Age musicians all occupy a legitimate piece of the total picture, both philosophically and sociologically. For anyone who takes the time to review the titles in the Bantam New Age Series or the lead articles in, say, *East West Journal*, this is evident.

However, bridge movements may not appeal to those who are philo-sophically opposed to certain pieces of the New Age (or New Paradigm) pie. They simply do not buy into the "one big happy family" theme. Let us remember, though, that Marxists, Darwinians, and Freudians were not members of one big happy philosophical family either. Yet all three schools of thought emerged from the prevailing Cartesian-Newtonian worldview. Family membership is not an all-or-nothing proposition; it is a matter of degree. You can disagree about certain aspects of holistic health practices and agree with others. There only have to be more convergences than divergences. Here are some of the convergences.

Striving after wholeness:
Spiritual practices that reconnect us to higher dimensions
Women's groups (most women having been oppressed for ages)
Living on the planet as one species
Searching for paradigms to connect spirituality and science
Holistic health (making a place for emotional/spiritual concerns)

Striving for balance and integration:
Holistic health concerns (body-mind-spirit integration, etc.)
Sustainable culture issues (e.g., eating only what we need)
Dealing with psychic and spiritual emergencies
Teachers and parents becoming copartners in growth, learning
Social responsibilities of business, networking

Striving after empowerment (self and others) and cooperation:
Peace group
Self-help networking groups, human potential
Human rights groups, animal rights groups
Meditation groups (connecting with the Source)
Teaching children how to learn, not merely what to learn

Exploring unconditional love/compassion:
Coming to see ourselves as giving/receiving links in a whole
Helping the Earth Mother
Holistic health concerns
Service groups (Habitat for Humanity, Mother Theresa, etc.)
Personal growth

Exploring nonlocality:
In transcendental states of consciousness
In field effects of group meditation
In the implications of Bell's theorem
In remote viewing
In healing at a distance

Some practices appear under several categories precisely because the practices that go with them are interlocked. Meditation, for example, is relevant to all five agendas. It can lead to better grades, a healthier body and mind, a greater capacity for giving and receiving unconditional love, and mystical union with the Divine Source. It helps overcome the constraints of ego, which in turn lessens the need for control, the tendency to destroy the environment, and (for men) the tendency to "keep women in their places." Spiritual teachers, feminists, environmentalists, and holistic health groups can all get together on this one. In fact, they all might be found at a meeting of the World Futurist Society.

The connections and parallels among the many agendas of an emerging worldview are direct and obvious. Clusters on one side of the map may be only indirectly linked to those on the other side. For example, one normally does not talk about celestial mechanics and Social Darwinism in the same context, but both figure prominently in a Cartesian-Newtonian perspective.

Similarly, the duality of waves and particles has nothing to do with the duality of masculine and feminine consciousness. Yet each may be viewed as expressing a *dynamic interaction between complementary opposites,* a principle that figures heavily in New Paradigm discussion as well as "Old Age" Taoism. We seldom find clear beginnings, boundaries, or ends. Worldviews and their subparadigms spill over into each other often in ways that create more confusion than clarity.

Groups with distinctive fundamental agendas often do not care for single umbrella labels, be it New Age or something else, partly because they are not interested in being subsumed under a larger movement and partly because they are concerned about the company they would be keeping. Feminists, for example, are typically not interested in the metaphysical implications of Bell's theorem or how homeopathy possibly could work. They are interested in rectifying the imbalances of patriarchal oppression. Then again, they might be persuaded to support research on homeopathy, since homeopathy is rejected out of hand by the AMA, and the AMA is very patriarchal. Strange alliances are the order of the day in times of great transition.

Labels carry much perceived inconsistency in such times. However, it is people more than words that make for change. Quantum mechanics, Green politics, Taoist spirituality, and feminism might not seem to go together. But as some readers are aware, they fit nicely in the evolution of a perspective that Fritjof Capra, Charlene Spretnek, and others have persuasively nurtured. John Denver, Ted Turner, and Jane Fonda don't like the company they would be keeping under the New Age label. So they describe themselves as futurists with special concerns about world peace and the environment.

This is a reasonable way to shape one's public identity, with several qualifications. On the one hand, nobody has the market cornered on peace and the environment. New Agers legitimately resent being typecast as naive and uncaring. On the other hand, Denver, Turner, and Fonda in *other* ways are very New Age. Do we need to call ourselves Christians in order to do Christian work? Not really. What we do need to do is place less faith in labels and look to the *actual* agendas, convergences, and assumptions behind them.

The last thing to expect during a period of major cultural change is for members of all the different leading edges of that shift to buy into the special interests and models of others. It took the early Christian Church centuries to decide where it stood on the question of reincarnation. The worldview of a Rising Culture attracts many labels precisely because it's not a monolithic, fully articulated body of truth, capable of subsuming all agendas and subsidiary paradigms at once. The most that we can perceive now are the outlines of a convergence which may or may not reach fruition. This is all anyone caught between worldviews in transition can affirm with confidence.

ARE NEW AGE TRENDS HEALTHY?

How could trends which seek to overcome fragmentation, hierarchical control, or fear be unhealthy? If we adopt a broad interpretation of the New Age, the question is all but unanswerable—sort of like "Is religion healthy?" If we take a narrow interpretation, then we must look at specific practices that attract the New Age label. Such a piecemeal approach would give us some answers regarding what we should abandon or pursue. But it would not allow us to reject all the practices and ideas connected with the label. Let us explore three widely discussed criticisms relating to health practices, religious cults, and social responsibility respectively.

When traditionally oriented health care providers think of New Age, they typically think of holistic or "alternative" health care practices. And when they conceive of these practices, a potpourri of possibilities comes to mind—chiropractic, herbs and nutrition regimens, psychic healers, reflexologists, quacks with strange machines, and so on. Many physicians take the position that most of these practices do not work, some appear to work because of a strong placebo effect, and a minority may actually help under certain conditions.

However, with few (if any) controlled studies, we don't know what really works. And if we don't know what works, then most physicians feel they cannot responsibly prescribe these practices. Only experimentally supported interventions are clinically or morally justified, according to this line of thought. Patients *might* receive some benefit in pursuing these alternative remedies but in doing so, they are on their own. Unfortunately, many patients lack the critical skills necessary to make informed scientific evaluations of holistic practices. Therefore, such practices should be discouraged, banned, or brought under the control of those who are licensed to practice medicine—in the interest of "public safety." Such is the reasoning from the FDA, the AMA, and other governing bodies.

While variations of this thinking are fairly common, they do not capture what is allegedly unhealthy about these practices. In the mind of the traditional physician, such practices are unhealthy when there *is* an approved course of treatment but the patient is encouraged to attempt some combination of alternative therapies which lack experimental support. For instance, chemotherapy is approved for certain forms of cancer; macrobiotics and visualization are not. It is therefore dangerous and irresponsible to encourage or allow people to pursue the latter when the former is available.

It is not my purpose here to comment on the effectiveness of particular modes of therapy. Nor is it to comment on the self-serving logic of the National Institutes of Health which, until quite recently, had refused to fund significant research into alternative therapies and then determined that, sure enough, there is not sufficient research to justify funding them. Rather, my purpose is to show that the number of cases potentially affected by the above line of reasoning is so small that concerns about public safety ought to evaporate. The critical question is: "Dangerous as compared to what?"

Alternative practices on average are less dangerous than traditional therapies. Anything can be overdone; 100,000 units of Vitamin A each day is toxic. But actual vitamin overdosages are extremely rare. More than sixty percent of all illnesses will either self-correct or not progress if left untreated. So how can treating them with alternatives be more irresponsible than with approved drugs?

Most alternative practices are directed to the two areas where traditional medicine falls short: prevention and treatment of chronic or degenerative conditions. Arthritis, for example, has no cure—only symptom relief—and thus easily attracts experimentation with alternative remedies. If you don't make unsubstantiated claims for having *the* cure, what's wrong with suggesting alternative remedies where others have proven ineffective?

If you take the time to read the literature of holistic therapies and talk to the practitioners, three things become evident: virtually none attempt to lure clients away from their physicians; only a relatively few make specific claims to be more effective than traditional approaches (e.g., chiropractic treatment of slipped discs); and the great majority prefer to work in *complementary* ways with mainstream health care providers. For example, a combination of spiritual healing, niacin, guar gum, visualization, vitamin E, radical reduction in fat intake, and exercise may significantly reduce the need for bypass surgery.

Most alternative practices presuppose that an illness has already been diagnosed in some approved manner, so the prospects of misdiagnosis are correspondingly reduced. In spite of this, every so often a horror story surfaces about a chiropractor or a "psychic surgeon" misdiagnosing, say, a liver malfunction when neither is licensed or trained to do so.

The critical question is whether misdiagnosis, with actual harm to the patient, occurs any more in alternative practices than in the practice of mainstream medicine, which has its own share of horror stories. In those cases where traditional medicine appears unable to diagnose some unusual symptoms, how can we reasonably object to seeking the services of an applied kinesiologist or clairvoyant healer to shed some additional light on the problem?

The actual number of cases where attempting some alternative therapy would be dangerous is quite small. These would be situations where the individual faces a serious health problem for which there is a clearly established method of diagnosis and treatment with a strong likelihood of positive results; where attempting alternatives in conjunction with approved procedures would in itself produce negative results or reduce the effectiveness of the approved procedures; or where the alternatives are recommended by holistic practitioners who prey upon clients unaware of the benefits of the approved procedures.

This last condition sometimes occurs, for example, in the case of a faith healer who takes a person's money for bypass surgery and claims the person is healed, when in fact he or she will die of a heart attack without surgery in a few months. But the relevant question here is whether holistic practitioners as a group are any more unscrupulous than physicians.

There are, after all, the matters of too much unnecessary surgery, malpractice, and misprescription of drugs (especially to the elderly) in traditional medical practice. No doubt some mainstream health professionals fail to live up to the highest standards of their field. For every alternative practitioner who has made a mistake you will also find a physician who has made his or her share. The holistic health movement harbors no more dangers or irresponsible behavior than does traditional medicine. Many would argue that it harbors far fewer.

After all the discussion about who is best qualified to act in whose interests, there is the simple constitutional question of one's right to implement the therapy of preference. If I determine I want to fight my cancer by some means other than chemotherapy (whose virtues are sometimes overstated anyway), then presumably I have the right to do so. I might improve with either choice. Or I might die. But having the right to be wrong in one's own case is part of what living in America is supposed to mean. If the government has a clear obligation in this regard, it is to insist upon informed consent across the board—the pros and cons of all treatments, "approved" and "alternative."

Thus far, the response to this challenge at both national and local levels is not encouraging. It consists, on the one hand, of affirming people's rights to explore alternatives, while on the other hand, campaigning or attempting to legislate against those alternatives on the grounds that, in many cases, their implementation amounts to "practicing medicine without a license." At the state level, we have seen some relatively isolated skirmishes. Authorities in Georgia, for example, have gone after electro-meridian therapists and midwives who are not also licensed nurses. We are bearing witness to some major paradigm wars over these issues.

The irony is that the first major hospital in America to open its doors to "full spectrum" practice—the best of traditional and alternative health modalities—is going to be flooded with admission requests from all over the country. And the insurance industry, known more for its pragmatism than for its principles, will be watching carefully. Metropolitan Life, for example, has funded a pilot program for testing less expensive alternatives to bypass surgery. I suspect the insurance industry will play an important role in the paradigm wars over health and healing.

Is the New Age a kind of "upscale cult" with potentially destructive underpinnings?[4] By no stretch of the imagination does the New Age fit the definition of a cult. It stresses maximum personal freedom and responsibility and is so broadly based that a central dogma to which everyone subscribes is out of the question. To be sure, many New Agers practice some form of meditation or visualization. But meditation is a far cry from mind control. And it is mind control that we associate with cults. New Agers visualizing peace are no more cultist than Democrats praying for peace.

There are, of course, individuals in any general movement whose motives are questionable and whose capacity for self-delusion adversely affects those around them. But this is no more a special problem for the New Age than it is for Christianity, the AMA, or feminists.

Those who see sinister motives behind New Age developments often have a vested interest in preserving their own traditional outlooks. This causes them to focus on relatively narrow areas where their beliefs may be affected. To a Christian fundamentalist, the New Age label typically refers to the ways Satan is deceiving us in the final days before the Second Coming. For example, he is convincing people who have near-death experiences that there is no heaven or hell but rather a comparatively pleasant afterlife for everybody. Of course, for someone who sees Satan everywhere, even in miraculous healings by non-Christians, there is little possibility of constructive dialogue.

The Spiritual Counterfeits Project in Berkeley, California has emerged largely in response to the "darker" implications of New Age thinking for the Judeo-Christian tradition. Especially troubling, in their view, is the idea of seeing God in all of us (even bad people), which they mistakenly equate with each New Ager claiming that he or she is God. This is nothing less than reducing God to the level of the personal (and sinful) ego. I have yet to meet any New Ager who claims that God is just the sum total of our finite egos. Behind this criticism is a powerful confusion between reductive pantheism, on the one hand, and a spiritually based pan*en*theism on the other. I will explore this distinction in greater detail in Chapter Thirteen.

More liberal thinkers in the Church take issue with the New Age for what appear to be closely related reasons. Well known priest and activist Daniel Berrigan sees the whole movement as "just the death of the reality of God in one's life and the degradation of the human being who yields to it."[5] This is because, in his view, New Age thinking vindicates ego, appetite, and self-worship. There are, of course, plenty of New Age gatherings around the country with no explicit spiritual focus, just as there are meetings of Democrats and Republicans where loyalty to one's country is not the primary agenda.

However, for anyone who takes the time to visit a New Age gathering with an explicit spiritual focus, such as a Light Group praying for the planet (by no means the only type of spiritual focus), Berrigan's observation is roughly equivalent to reducing the Christian Church to snake-handling. It is as out of touch with the spirit and actual practices of the New Age as Vice

President Spiro Agnew's denunciations of peace demonstrations in the late sixties (of which Berrigan was a leader).

And what about this "spiritual focus"? Does it translate into socially responsible action? Or do New Age trends betray a fundamental lack of social responsibility? Perhaps nowhere does this issue come into clearer focus than with the Harmonic Convergence, held in August of 1987. This typifies the kind of event and thinking that critics find objectionable. So let us explore the matter in more detail.

The issue is not that comparatively large groups of people got together to pray, meditate, visualize peace, and generally celebrate a critical turn in what they believe to be the governing energies in this part of the galaxy. In one way or another people have been doing this for centuries—and for the strangest of reasons, too!

Rather, the issue is that so many people who claim to be 100 percent for peace, love, the environment, and the end of oppression, injustice, war, and poverty, have the naiveté or audacity to believe that these goals will pretty much happen by themselves because they are "scheduled" to do so in keeping with the Aquarian Age or that collective consciousness raising by a large number of people in itself will be instrumental in bringing these goals into reality. In choosing between means and ends, New Agers are simply confused. Hungry people do not get fed with words and intentions. Martin Luther King did not effect a revolution simply by visualizing racial harmony in a Birmingham jail. This, then, is the charge. Let me attempt a response.

To begin, this is an area where terminology again becomes critical. Feminists, Greenpeace, the Association of Charismatic Healers, and Physicians for Social Responsibility are all *doing* something about their professed beliefs. And all in their own ways are part of the Rising Culture. If we take the broad view of the New Age label and include all who should be included, then the charge largely self-destructs. But of course critics want to pin the label on a relatively narrow constituency—those interested in psychic growth, crystal healings, channeling, astrology, and the like. This is roughly equivalent to labeling the Republican Party as racist because fifteen percent of its congressional representatives did not vote for a certain piece of civil rights legislation.

With this initial clarification, the next step is to concede that many New Agers ought to aim for a greater balance between thought and action, intention and deed. By comparison, however, this is not a large concession. Physicians, large corporations, and mainstream religions should all be more demonstrative in the expression of their social responsibilities, too! Who shall cast the first stone? Why pick on Shirley MacLaine, rather than Donald Trump, for not mobilizing action for the homeless? Part of the answer is simple: it makes for great press.

Which brings us to what neither the press nor anyone else has done much research on. Nobody has any accurate information on how many New Agers, in or out of the closet, wear other hats that speak to pressing social concerns. I suspect that there are a good number who, let us say, work through *A Course in Miracles,* try to heal themselves with macrobiotics or wear crystals, but who also contribute to their favorite charities, volunteer at soup kitchens, or take in battered women. There are more than a few dissertations in sociology to be written on exactly what New Agers do with their time.

Mainstream thinking about social issues assumes that to make things better we need to change our environment and mobilize our physical energies. Put real food into real mouths. I never met a person remotely connected to the New Age label who didn't support such an approach. But New Age people want, perhaps first and foremost in this arena, to *change consciousness,* that is, to work from the inside out.

Should we spend a million dollars on more teachers, courses, or equipment to reduce the high school dropout rate or on a "New Age-ish" program to revitalize the self-image of struggling teens? Or some combination of both? It is difficult to say what will work best for a given problem over the long run. But reasonable and well-meaning people on both sides of the question can agree to differ on these kinds of issues.

Most people who wear the New Age label believe that consciousness is very much like a universal field of energy in which we participate. More specifically, they believe that focused attention in one part of the field can set up reverberations in other distant parts of the field—areas beyond their bodies, or even their vision. So if a hundred experienced meditators, for example, set up a strong "love vibration" in an area that doesn't have much love to go around, then we should look for behavioral changes in the environment that temporarily reflect that shift in energies. Those who practice transcendental meditation have made just that claim and offered research to support it.[6]

Such claims of course do not fit the paradigms of mainstream science and for this reason are likely to be rejected out-of-hand. However, the hypothesis of "conscious field action" does admit of empirical verification or falsification. It can be put to the test. It may be a strange idea, but it is not a flaky one. Given sufficient research, this is something we could have a clear answer to in ten years. The history of science harbors far stranger ideas.

CRITICISMS OF THE POPULAR NEW AGE MIND-SET

Many critics of New Age thought fail to appreciate the surface indications of deeper structural change, or simply beg the issue against a different way of looking at things. However, there are legitimate criticisms to be made, far more than I can summarize in a single section. For now, I will set aside questions about the *truth* of certain themes that we will look at more closely in subsequent chapters. For example, I won't discuss here whether reincarnation is a defensible belief or whether our attitudes can make us physically sick. I will describe instead some of the most important shortcomings of the New Age *mind-set* as it is reflected in popular culture.

To begin with, far more is promised than delivered in typical workshops, tapes, and conferences; the goals are oversold at a level well beyond the parameters of normal advertising. Consider all the ways that we see the phrase "In this workshop, you will..." completed. You will, for example, experience past lives, open your "third eye," discover your potential as a healer, learn techniques of affirmation that will enable you to open any blocks, get in touch with your higher self, discover the god-consciousness within all of us, reprogram your subconscious, etc.

I don't deny that these things can happen and sometimes do. Some people are ripe for a sudden transformative change. But such changes do not happen to the degree that the promoters would have us believe. The workshops may be interesting; that is a different matter. But genuine transformation takes time, work, and patience. New Agers both crave and claim more immediate results.

Much claimed success in New Age workshops is based on stretched interpretations. For example, the image of a Roman Centurion during meditation may be interpreted as one of your past lives, tingling in your hands as the awakening of your healing potential, breaking through an ego-barrier as a direct experience of transpersonal consciousness, running a stop sign as the universe "trying to give you a message," and so forth. These correlations could be significant. But the interpretations don't logically follow from such limited bases. Minimal data tend to be maximally interpreted.

Failure to achieve certain goals is typically your fault, not the responsibility of the healer, teacher, or guide who held those goals out to you—a somewhat broader version of what has come to be called "New Age shame." Thus if you do not attract money after a "prosperity" workshop, it must be because you have a hidden fear of success. If you are not healed, it is because you blocked the process. If your relationships keep falling apart after several weekend "intensives," it must be your karma. These explanations could be appropriate in some circumstances. But they are often overworked to the point where anyone can set himself up in business and explain away all failure as the "client's issue." This is too easy. Responsibility for success and failure needs to be shared.

Most New Agers are undereducated about scientific matters. They tend to make claims that reveal only a superficial understanding of complex scientific ideas. Here are some examples: Bell's theorem has shown that we are all one. Studies at Duke University have proven ESP. The Simontons showed that we can visualize cancer away. Quantum mechanics shows that we create reality. Relativity theory demonstrates that time is an illusion. Since acupuncture works, *ch'i* energy must exist. Physics indicates that the mystics have been right all along. The Mayan calendar predicted the Harmonic Convergence. Government studies have shown that Therapeutic Touch really works.

There is no problem with being scientifically untutored per se. But if you are, there is a problem with then claiming scientific proof for your favorite New Age belief. The *most* charitable interpretation of all of the above claims is simply "maybe." A number are straightforwardly false.

How many times have we heard: "If you sincerely believe it, then it's true for you." The problem with this platitude is that it straddles a dilemma. On the one hand, it can be so vacuous as to apply to anybody. Naturally, if you believe something then *you* think it's true, regardless of whether there is evidence for the belief; you're already committed.

On the other hand, there is the often unstated meaning that if something is true for you, then it is as true as it needs to be—that evidence and other beliefs, even criticisms, don't need to be taken into account. New Agers often have great difficulty accepting the possibility that their beliefs could be mistaken. This prompts them to deal with rational criticism by appealing to the following: "Well, that is just *your* point of view," or "I appreciate the fact that you have chosen to believe that way," or even "That merely reflects your particular level of evolutionary understanding." The irony of these appeals is that they are often used to justify radically inconsistent beliefs *within* the New Age community, such as "Crystals heal" versus "Crystals don't heal."

The New Age desperately needs a set of principles to enhance the prospects of working through the contradictions. Disagreement is to be expected in the transition to a new worldview, a point that I will stress repeatedly. But what is the average reader to make of the following contradictions? "I could have freely chosen otherwise" versus "All things are in Divine Order." "Some people have literal out-of-body experiences" versus "People who have OBEs are only tuning in to the collective unconscious." "Evil exists" versus "Evil is simply in the minds of those who allow it to exist." "God is in all things" versus "We are each God." So it goes.

There is much psychological and spiritual naiveté in the New Age which is difficult to pin down other than through example. For instance, we hear proclamations about the value of unconditional love coming from those whose hearts still harbor fear. We see holism embraced at wellness centers but all-too-familiar patterns of specialization and competition guiding what transpires there. Too much is often made of what psychics predict for one's personal life, without understanding the dynamics which make for success or failure.

To continue, "proof" often is offered for New Age themes which are little more than appeals to the already converted. For example, the proof that you chose to have an automobile accident is that you had the accident. This can also be cited as proof that Mercury is in retrograde (even though as many bad things can happen to you when Mercury is not in retrograde). Whole karmic patterns allegedly are lifted through rebirthing in a tub of warm water. Or channeled personalities automatically may be assumed to be who or what they say they are. Affirmations are held out as a panacea without considering the need to deal with unconscious counter programming or the question of how sincere one is in doing the affirmations. Evil is not taken seriously, presumably because "it's all in your mind." In short, too much is readily accepted without the benefit of serious critical reflection.

A closely related point, but deserving separate attention, is the fact that New Agers often have not done the deep transformational work on themselves that they think they have. They claim that "All things are in divine order" when faced with struggle and disappointment. In many instances, this is a mental belief they have formed. But in their hearts they still feel victimized. If their lives are not working very well, they validate their own denial by repeating affirmations. They talk about their issues in insightful ways—setting limits, honoring the inner child, releasing fear, etc.—but simply don't walk their talk.

When this discrepancy is pointed out, they prove very adept at converting it into *your* issue. They may act vaguely perplexed, for example, about your "tendency to judge them." All too quickly, then, the discussion may become centered on your judgment issue, rather than on their lack of self-discernment. And unless you are careful, their control drama wins the day—sometimes with nobody the wiser!

The last, and perhaps most frustrating, defect of the typical New Age mind-set is found in endless games of one-up-manship. The following examples speak for themselves. "Of course, I've been working on ascension to the fifth dimension for some time now." "Then I called in Archangel Michael to help out." "I'm working with the new psychotronic crystal generator; it heals everything." "I'm taking so-and-so's workshop, since he's studied with three different spiritual masters."

Self-promotion, of course, is a fact of life. With a change of terminology, each of the preceding examples has parallels in business or the academic world. It's just that the New Age seems to bring out the worst in some of its defenders. It is a breeding ground for quick answers, with little to back them up. Small wonder. All one has to do is claim that his or her "spirit guides" have confirmed the reality of a certain situation and it's as good as God speaking to Moses. If somebody else's guides have told them differently, the stakes are quickly raised. After all, how could a self-proclaimed member of the legions of Metatron be mistaken?

This type of thinking also happens outside of New Age contexts. But the New Age provides an unusually large number of trump cards with which the average person can quickly gain a perceived advantage. It is almost as if the first person to make the claim automatically has the high ground and other New Agers, lacking a clear way to dispute the original claim ("How dare you suggest my guides are wrong!"), tend to go along unless they have a personal stake in the outcome. The New Age makes it too easy for self-importance to win out over genuine discernment and balanced inquiry.

WHAT'S NEW ABOUT THE NEW AGE?

It has become popular to assert that very little, if anything, is really "new" about the New Age. But this is an impossible claim to make until some critical distinctions are made. Of special importance is the distinction between the *ideas* which characterize an emerging perspective, on the one hand, and the actual grass roots *trends* it fuels, on the other. The idea of reincarnation is one thing. The question of how many people integrate this idea into their lives is quite another.

Critics make several questionable moves here. First, they interpret the ideas on a narrow basis. Thus the New Age may be identified mainly with belief in, say, astrology and channeling. They then point out that these ideas have been around for a long time, which is true enough in the case of astrology or channeling. Religion professor Randall Balmer expresses the familiar academic dismissal on this topic:

> It strikes me as no accident whatsoever that the 1980s spawned two religions that appealed to self-interest: the God-will-make-you-rich-and-happy pablum of the tele-vangelists and the I-can-do-this-on-my-own spirituality of the New Agers. Both elevated individuality over commu-nity, self-aggrandizement over altruism, eclecticism over orthodoxy. Is there anything novel about that? Hardly. Recent research into the religious life of colonial America has shown that the earliest settlers also consulted astrologi-cal charts...The so-called New Age religions were only the most recent example of this durable strain of spiritual eclecticism.[7]

Ken Wilber has suggested that the origins of the New Age movement are in American transcendentalism, e.g., Whitman, Thoreau, and Emerson.[8] To a limited extent this may be true, *if* one takes the connection between the personal and transpersonal as *the* definitive New Age agenda. But even if one did make this assumption, the average New Ager is more likely to explore this idea within the context of Hinduism's identity of Brahman with Atman (a very old idea) or of contemporary transpersonal psychology than by reading Whitman or Thoreau.

Some New Age ideas, for all practical purposes, are brand new—like the proposed coming shift of the Earth's vibrational matrix from "third" to "fourth" density, a change which, in addition to affecting everyone's behav-ior, will presumably make it easier for extraterrestrials to interact with us. Who in five thousand years of recorded history has predicted this? Individual novelty aside, however, the critical question is whether the par-ticular *combination* of all New Age practices has found a more powerful expression at any point in Western culture. Honoring the Earth Mother, for example, is an emerging New Age theme which also happens to be found in Native American culture (as well as others). It's not new. But linking it to the women's movement, reincarnation, and emotional release work is not something that has been done before.

Besides, many New Age ideas and practices have emerged in substantially revised form from their historical roots. For example, past lives are not supposed to be directly accessible in classical Hinduism, whereas they are in the New Age. So it is not altogether cricket to suggest that New Age ideas have "been there all along."

Critics of New Age thought often fail to address its impact at the grass roots level. When in the history of Western culture have so many people believed in reincarnation? When in the past two thousand years has gender equality been such a major agenda item? Or have peace groups united against war? Or meditation been so widely practiced? Or so many people consciously worked on their personal growth? Or condemned the damage we are doing to the environment? Or investigated UFO phenomena? At the level of implementation, plenty is new!

How might we rank the various submovements? A map of the leading edge of the entire New Paradigm dialogue would have some ragged edges. The times and rates of change are quite varied. Major conceptual changes in the New Physics were in place by the mid-1930s. Spiritualism started in the 1850s. Human potential and holistic health movements got under way in the 1960s, and the environmental and women's movements were established by the mid-1970s. Education has yet to evidence large-scale fundamental change. We should not expect uniform evolution of the various wings of any mass movement—New Age or otherwise.

A comprehensive sociological analysis of the actual impact of New Age ideas and trends in American culture has yet to be produced. Carl Raschke, the vocal critic we examined earlier, described the New Age movement in 1986 as "the most powerful social force in the country today."[9] And that is just the narrow version. As of this writing (1995), it is not difficult to find a broad version of New Age thinking spilling over into, or emerging spontaneously within, most every area of contemporary culture. Unfortunately, many academics, who are charged not only with transmitting but also with extending the leading edge of culture, don't have a clue about the magnitude of the shifts on the horizon.

Of course, the Rising Culture is still a minority phenomenon. Capitalism, materialism, patriarchy, theism, fear, and allopathic medicine are still the prevailing paradigms of thought and action. Republicans, Democrats, and most Independents keep trotting out variations of the same worn-out ideas. The critical question, however, is not where the ships are now, but which way the winds are blowing. Are holistic health practices still on the rise? Is belief in reincarnation growing every year? Is the government cover-up on UFOs about to become unglued? Are more people choosing to let go of fear?

Will things get better? Or will they become worse? The New Age is often criticized as having a naive "peaches and cream" view of the future. Just tune your crystals and wait for the Age of Aquarius, as the stereotype prescribes. So far as faith in the future is concerned, New Agers divide up like most any other group. Some are optimistic, some are pessimistic, and some believe things have to get worse before they can get better.

Certainly the prospects for war, greed, oppression, economic collapse, and environmental catastrophe of one type or another are strong. There are no clear crystal balls for the nineties (or beyond) in such matters. The average New Ager affirms only what enlightened people of many persuasions are affirming—that the future hangs precariously upon how much individual and collective responsibility we are willing to assume, here and now. New Age speculations about what will happen in the next ten years are no more or less credible than those offered by politicians, farmers, or the National Weather Center.

Behind the current deep-seated uneasiness about the state of the world are the most ancient of urges: the quest for unity and wholeness and a growing desire to live in greater harmony with our physical environment, with each other, with our bodies and minds, and with our spiritual roots. This quest appears to be moving us toward a massive transformation of consciousness and the creation of a globally sustainable culture associated with many different labels. We may not succeed in this venture, at least in the way that New Agers envision. However, the prospects will be enhanced in a small way if we pay less attention to labels and more to what is actually happening!

CHAPTER THREE

The Search for a Master Paradigm: Systems Holism and the Perennial Philosophy

We have surveyed various challenges fueling the quest for a more adequate worldview and some of the responses these challenges invite. But we have not explored the shape of a new worldview per se. Indeed, I have given only a general indication of the overall scope and direction that such a vision might take. It is one thing, for example, to describe the conflicting demands of fragmentation and wholeness in the areas of health or the environment, quite another to develop a vision of what "wholeness" is all about.

There is much confusion in popular New Age versions of wholeness. There are also so many agendas under the New Age umbrella that it's easy to criticize its weaknesses and overlook its strengths. Like a sitting duck, the New Age invites the mainstream media, such as *Time*, to portray New Agers in ways that make the most outrageous copy, e.g., as pseudoscientific metaphysicians cashing in on the "crystal craze."[1]

But at another level, something quite different and more profound is taking place. Many thousands of intellectually and activist-oriented leaders have been exploring the leading edges of a New Paradigm in-the-making. They do not care for labels, because they question the company and the restrictions that labels can bring. Just as I honored the spirit of New Age concerns in the preceding chapter, I will honor the sensitivities of New Paradigm thinkers with a more resonant terminology.

Popular New Age thought, as portrayed in the media, is both a smaller and more superficial slice of the larger quest for a more adequate worldview. New Paradigm thinkers are not necessarily opposed to New Age ideas. However, they approach them with a probing mind, open to more interpretations than the typical New Ager has patience for. The New Ager asks, for example, "Who was I in a past life?" The new scientist, by contrast, asks "What do apparent regressions to past lives actually show?" The New Ager insists that she creates her reality. The New Paradigm philosopher responds: "Perhaps, but not before we clarify what we mean by 'create.'"

Which philosophical, spiritual, and scientific approaches contribute to the New Paradigm dialogue? The situation at a theoretical level can be as confusing as it is at the popular level. For example, each of the following schools in some way finds a place in New Paradigm literature:

1. Advaita Vedanta
2. Mahayana Buddism
3. Gnosticism
4. Theosophy
5. Sufism
6. Taoism
7. Hermetic thought
8. Systems theory
9. New Thought
10. New Biology
11. Transpersonal psychology
12. Idealism
13. Process philosophy
14. Chaos theory
15. Kabbalism
16. Zen
17. Holism
18. Archetypal psychology
19. New Physics
20. Organicism
21. Ecofeminism
22. Sustainable culture

These schools converge in clusters of current concerns, which are grouped in the lists below. However, you won't find all of your favorite writers; the names included are intended merely as a representative sampling. No cluster stands in isolation. Each overlaps with and is informed by others. Only in a few special situations have I placed an individual in two clusters. Most contributors do not see themselves as part of one big happy family. They reflect important divergences of opinion. However, I believe that this chart will convey a strong sense of the family resemblances that promise to inform a Rising Culture for the twenty-first century.

REPRESENTATIVE NEW PARADIGM CLUSTERS

Perennial Philosophy, Spirituality	Parapsychology, Consciousness Studies	Physics/Cosmology, Allied Sciences
Ken Wilber	Edith Fiore	Harold Burr
Huston Smith	Robert Morris	Bruce Lipton
Mircia Eliade	Charles Tart	Roger Penrose
Alan Watts	Lawrence LeShan	David Bohm
Aldous Huxley	Charles Honorton	Thomas Bearden
Pir Vilayet Khan	Kenneth Ring	Itzhak Bentov
Lama Govinda	Karlis Osis	Ilya Prigogine
Swami Muktananda	J.B. Rhine	Lyall Watson
Sogyal Rinpoche	Elmer Green	Karl Pribram
Matthew Fox	Stanley Krippner	Gregory Bateson
W.T. Stace	Russell Targ	Rupert Sheldrake
Jacob Needleman	Robert Jahn	Ervin Laszlo
Adin Steinsaltz	Jeffery Mishlove	Henry Margenau
Sri Aurobindo	Michael Harner	Paul Davies
Teilhard de Chardin	William Roll	James Lovelock
Rumi	Stephen Schwartz	Marcel Vogel
Frithjof Schuon	William Braud	Robert Becker

UFO/Alien Search, Government Cover-Up	Metaphysics, Esoteric Studies	Human Potential, Self-Help
Raymond Fowler	Rosicrucians	Gerald Jampolsky
John Mack	Theosophists	Jackie Woods
Stanton Friedman	Barbara Marciniak	Jean Houston
Timothy Good	Jane Roberts	Elisabeth Kubler-Ross
Steven Greer	Norma Milanovich	Course in Miracles
Linda Howe	Gurdjieff	George Leonard
Bruce Maccabee	Alice Bailey	John Bradshaw
Donald Schmitt	Dane Rudhyar	Abraham Maslow
Budd Hopkins	Pat Rodegast	Carl Jung
Bill Cooper	Jach Pursel	Michael Murphy
Jim Keith	Rudolf Steiner	Scott Peck
Richard Hoagland	Ken Carey	James Redfield
Jacques Valle	J.J. Hurtak	Stanislav Grof
Whitley Strieber	Drunvalo Melchizedek	Wayne Dyer
Zecharia Sitchin	Brad Steiger	Ken Keyes

REPRESENTATIVE NEW PARADIGM CLUSTERS

**Energy Medicine,
Holistic Health**
Bernard Siegel
Bernard Grad
Norman Shealy
Olga Worrall
Richard Gerber
Carl Simonton
Robert Jaffe
Barbara Brennen
Larry Dossey
Daniel Benor
Louise Hay
Rosalind Bruyere
Janet Quinn
Gaston Naessens
Norman Cousins
Wallace Black Elk
Deepak Chopra

**Education, Environment,
Economics**
Arne Naess
Theodore Roszak
Herman Daly
Chris Griscom
Maria Montessori
Marilyn Waring
John Cobb
Thomas Berry
Susan Meeker-Lowry
Lester Brown
Lynn Schroeder
Mary Ellen Sweeney
Cathy Hainer
Hazel Henderson
Joseph Pearce
Machaelle Wright
Robert Theobald

**Paradigms/Trends,
Commentary/Criticism**
Marilyn Ferguson
Ken Wilber
Fritjof Capra
Willis Harman
Arthur Koestler
David Spangler
John White
John Naisbitt
Michael Grosso
William I. Thompson
Mark Satin
Robert Theobald
Buckminster Fuller
David Griffin
Barbara Hubbard

**Feminism,
Women's Studies**
Charlene Spretnak
Carol Christ
Betty Friedan
Simone de Beauvoir
Gloria Steinham
Riane Eisler
Mary Daly
Sally McFague
Starhawk
Michael Foucault
Andrea Dworkin
Anne Wilson Schaef
Carol Gilligen
Angela Davis
Jean Shinoda Bolen

How might we usefully organize so many points of view? All of the writers included in this chart in some way contribute to one of two master paradigms. Neither paradigm is in fact new. One I shall call "Systems Holism." This perspective punctuates the history of philosophy, biology, and the social sciences since the publication of Immanuel Kant's *Critique of Judgment* in 1790. The other perspective is the "Perennial Philosophy," which includes major spiritual and philosophical traditions from both East and West dating back perhaps as far as 3000 B.C.

Both Systems Holism and the Perennial Philosophy inform the quest for a more adequate worldview. Both paradigms overlap to a considerable degree and each complements the other at certain junctures. Some of the ideas we normally associate with Buddhism, for example, could be included within either Systems Holism or the Perennial Wisdom. Similarly, most thinkers listed above are associated with one of these perspectives. Spiritually oriented ecofeminists, for example, readily fit under the Perennial Philosophy, whereas their more politically oriented sisters tend to fall under the scope of Systems Holism. In Chapter Eight I will explain why.

While Systems Holism and the Perennial Philosophy complement each other, they are not identical paradigms. Depending upon how broadly or narrowly they are interpreted, they may harbor irreconcilable differences. Leaders from each perspective disagree on a number of issues. For example, Fritjof Capra (a systems theorist) and Ken Wilber (a perennialist) do not always see eye to eye. The purpose of this chapter is to describe briefly the history, key ideas, and potential shortcomings of each perspective. In later chapters, I shall explain why the Perennial Philosophy, supplemented at key points by systems thinking, is the most viable foundation for the coming age.

SYSTEMS HOLISM

Systems Holism is a blend of traditional holistic philosophies of science and contemporary systems theory. The term "holism" is rooted in the Greek *holos* meaning whole or complete. It was coined by Jan Smuts in his *Holism and Evolution* (1926). Historically, biology has proved to be the richest discipline for holistically inclined scientists. However, at various times sociology, philosophy, and popular culture have extended and elaborated upon the meanings we attach to the term.

Holistic points of view are found in at least half a dozen major schools of thought in the nineteenth and twentieth centuries. It's possible to interpret the term so broadly that all but strict Cartesians or mechanists would be included, or so narrowly that only a small band of biologists would qualify. Still, the term appears destined to remain with us. So we will use it to identify a common core of understanding to anchor further discussion.

Holism in biology. The title of "first holist" in modern times should go to Immanuel Kant, who forcefully argued that the mechanistic explanations of physics could not explain the teleological properties of living organisms. By "teleological" he meant the capacity of plants and animals for self-organizing and self-perpetuating behavior designed to reach and maintain a completed product. He described this process as a nonlinear one, exhibiting multiple feedback loops to the state of the organism at a given time. For example, we say that a tree is both the cause and effect of itself, because it develops itself "by means of a material which is its own product."[2]

Since mechanistic explanations attempt to account for change by nothing more than forces of attraction and repulsion acting on primary units, they are systematically linear in scope. Feedback or self-regulating processes are not part of mechanistic explanations. In arguing that biology isn't reducible to physics, Kant proposed a theme adopted by future holists and systems theorists.

From this point a tradition developed in German and French biology that is appropriately labeled "teleological mechanism." Proponents of this tradition urged that while a progressively refined mechanical understanding of the interactions of the parts of an organism is obtainable, emergent properties of the organism, viewed as a living (whole) *form*, had to be accepted as given and could not be deduced either from a knowledge of the parts themselves or from a knowledge of the laws acting upon the parts.

Under a variety of labels, such as "vitalism" and "organicism," this tradition continued through the turn of the century in the work of Stephane Leduc and Hans Driesch, later in the work of Charles Sherrington and C.H. Waddington, and more recently in the contributions of Paul Weiss, Rupert Sheldrake, and Humberto Maturana.[3]

The concerns of this tradition vary considerably. But in general its defenders believe that mechanistic explanations are not adequate to account for the following phenomena in biology: the spontaneous emergence of new life forms (or component systems within systems, such as the eye); morphogenesis, the development of characteristic and specific form in living organisms (Why do chimps and humans appear to differ so much if their genetic codes are practically identical?); the maintenance of structure despite continuous and sometimes massive change of content, as in limb regeneration; and the reciprocal interaction of whole organisms and their constituent parts, i.e., the fact that wholes (such as trees) both emerge from their parts (seeds) and influence the activity of those parts—which brings us full circle to Kant's initial insight.

Holism in social science. Holistic approaches also are found in history, sociology, and anthropology, where it is urged that social processes and institutions cannot be understood as mere aggregates of their constituents. A knowledge of individual personalities, for example, does not provide laws for predicting the behavior of a group composed of those persons. A holistic perspective is sometimes labeled as "functionalism" in social anthropology which, according to Bronislaw Malinowski, is the

> ...explanation of facts by the part they play within the integral system of each culture, by the manner they are related to each other within the system, and by the manner in which this system is related to the physical surrounding...Every civilization, every custom, material object, idea and belief (is) an indispensable part within a working whole.[4]

Holism in current philosophy. The importance of conceptual relationships and irreducibility is stressed in much recent philosophical analysis of the nature of truth, scientific knowledge, and consciousness. Some philosophers who work in an analytic or linguistic tradition specifically label their views as "holistic."

Several themes have emerged from work on linguistic holism. One is the thesis that what we mean by what we say, on the one hand, and how we go about determining its truth, on the other, depend upon specific contexts. Meaning and truth reflect integrated patterns of thought and action—what Wittgenstein described as "forms of life" and Willard Quine as the "web of belief." For example, the language of religion (talk about God, salvation, etc.) cannot be fully understood, or its truth claims evaluated, merely in terms of the language of science, empirical verification. To speak of truth in religion isn't the same as speaking of truth in science; neither is reducible to the other.

In cognitive science and the philosophy of mind, holists point out that what we mean by such psychological terms as "depression," "belief," or "thought," appears to have no intrinsic connection to the properties of brain states; we understand what it means to be depressed, for example, independently of what we eventually discover to be the physiological *causes* of depression.

Thus, any attempt to reduce the mind to the brain—since it involves different categories of interpretation and levels of explanation—is not the kind of project that could succeed *or* fail after sufficient investigation. For in the view of some holists, this project is incoherent at the outset, not unlike trying to construct a triangle with sound! This does not mean that they are spiritualists who see the mind as a "ghost in the machine." It means that they view the mind-brain connection as a hierarchy of interconnected levels no one of which is reducible to the others. They are typically described as "nonreductive materialists" who have coined a fancy word — "supervenience"—to convey what is unique about the mind.

Another holistically oriented theme in current philosophy is that beliefs about reality must be assessed, not by how well they correspond to an independent and objective world, but by their connection with other beliefs that make up linguistic and social systems. In its extreme form, this thesis holds that even simple factual beliefs like "The sky is blue" are only relatively true within certain linguistic and social contexts. We cannot get outside of all belief systems in order to judge objectively the correspondence of each to the world. Therefore, we must fall back upon logical consistency and overall usefulness in examining and changing them.

There is no "most fundamental point" which conclusively anchors certain beliefs to the (real) world. Different conceptual frameworks may be *tentatively* anchored over certain areas of experience. For example, we used to label people with multiple personality disorder as "possessed." Now we don't. Still, all conceptual frameworks are subject to potentially dramatic changes. Indeed, some psychiatrists are now taking a second look at the idea of spirit possession and its possible relation to personality disorders.

Linguistic/social holism is a welcome development after the excesses of earlier reductionist philosophies, such as Logical Positivism. But how far should we ride this slippery slope, when the end appears to be a series of question marks about truth, essential meaning, and the idea of a real external world? How far, indeed, when its extreme form prescribes that no values can be logically defended as superior to others, since they only reflect different ways of thinking and acting that advance our interests?

What is left for philosophy to do at the outer reaches of this slippery slope? Apparently, only *conversation* ("Let's keep talking in spite of our relative points of view") and *play* ("But keep it as creative and interesting as possible"). Yet neither of these agendas prevails at meetings of the American Philosophical Association, where defeating your opponent is still a time-honored road to truth. Reflecting upon such schizophrenia ("There is no truth, but let's keep looking anyway!"), Huston Smith concludes that "it really isn't surprising to find philosophers closing shop."[5] Of course, philosophers have not really closed shop. Much interesting and relevant work continues to be done. It's just that relativistic types of philosophy that attract the holistic label appear to lead to dead ends.

Holism in popular culture. At the level of popular culture, I have seen "holism" associated with claims that synthesis is preferable to analysis; that people ought to be open-minded; that religions are essentially the same; that a certain group (psychics, environmentalists, etc.) represents the true spirit of holism; and even that a holistic lighting system (usually meaning full-spectrum lighting) is preferable to one which is not. It's no wonder that many people see the term as a prescription for vagueness.

The most consistent use of the term in popular culture is its association with the holistic health movement. This movement stresses themes such as the irreducibility of mind and spirit to brain chemistry and the importance of *relationships* between these levels. Critics often equate holistic health practices with a certain set of nontraditional therapeutic *techniques*, such as acupuncture. The core of the movement, however, is not so much a set of techniques as an approach to maintaining health and preventing disease.

It stresses self-empowering behaviors, such as meditation and a balanced life-style, and more egalitarian partnerships between patients and their health care providers. Most importantly, it views health and disease as a function of many interrelated factors on multiple levels, both inside and outside of the patient—factors which need to be seen as a whole. Hence the label "holistic" medicine. Such an approach also illustrates contemporary systems theory.

Systems theory. Under the label of "general systems theory" the spirit of holism has had a major impact across disciplinary lines. While its roots are traceable to A.A. Bogdanov's publication in 1912 of his *Tektology* (The General Science of Organization), Ludwig von Bertalanffy is generally credited with being its founder. Many scientists and philosophers have embraced a systems approach to their cross-disciplinary investigations.

This group includes philosopher Mario Bunge, physicist Fritjof Capra, physical chemist and Nobel Laureate Ilya Prigogine, chaos theorist James Gleick, evolutionary thinkers Erich Jantsch and Ervin Laszlo, biologists Paul Weiss and Gregory Bateson, futurist Buckminster Fuller, psychologist Charles Tart, intellectual historian Arthur Koestler, and living-systems theorist J.G. Miller, in addition of course to Bertalanffy himself.[6]

These writers are major players in the quest for a more adequate vision of the world. They contribute converging perspectives to the master model I am describing as Systems Holism. Some systems theorists, most notably Bunge, are metaphysically conservative. They are antireductionist only up to the point of what they can see or measure. Others, such as Tart, are quite liberal.

Systems theory incorporates much which has attracted the label of holism and adds its own special emphasis. It stresses the interaction of ordered hierarchies (molecule/cell, family member/family unit, etc.) and views seemingly fixed structures as reflecting underlying processes whose patterns cross disciplinary lines. For example, Prigogine's model of a dissipative structure in physical chemistry has been fruitfully applied to social systems and even traffic patterns. Fractal mathematics and chaos theory, which describe the sometimes precarious emergence of order through random fluctuations, is a specialized form of systems thinking. This is effectively brought out in James Gleick's provocative synthesis, *Chaos: Making a New Science.*[7]

Bateson illustrates systems thinking by discovering similar patterns of organization at work in the emergence of both mind and nature. He observes, for example, that in both mental and ecological processes, the effects of these processes may be regarded as transforms or coded versions of events which precede them. Philosophers and scientists who work in the area of artificial intelligence are, in effect, systems theorists because of their efforts to model patterns of human thinking in computer technology. Airline reservations programs are straightforward applications of systems engineering.

Capra draws strong parallels between systems thinking and bootstrap theory in particle physics. Bootstrap thinking suggests that there are no basic particles out of which objects are composed, since the *being* of all particles is tied to their *becoming;* it is tied to their dynamic interaction with other particles. In his words, the bootstrap philosophy "emphasizes relationships rather than isolated entities and, like the systems view, perceives these relationships as being inherently dynamic. Systems thinking is process thinking; form becomes associated with process, interrelation with interaction, and opposites are unified through oscillation."[8]

Of course, process thinking is not limited to systems thinking. And Capra's strongly Taoist reading of systems theory is not necessarily one that all systems theorists share. Still, most versions of systems thinking do emphasize the creative interplay of integrating and polarizing tendencies in nature, rather than the mere mechanical rearrangement of parts. This vision also is found in Lao Tzu's *Tao Te Ching*, Hegel's *Phenomenology of Spirit*, Bergson's *Creative Evolution*, and Koestler's *Janus*. Koestler even labels the key element of his system the "holon," an entity which (representing all objects) is continuously poised between the polarizing tendencies integration and differentiation.[9]

One of the most powerful applications of systems thinking on the current scene is found in family systems therapy. Many clinical psychologists find that useful interventions for one member of a family (especially a teenager) often require that other members of the family become involved. For example, parents often unconsciously project their issues through their children and then fail to understand why their children "have problems." Therapists often discover that a patient struggling with issues of denial, guilt, control, victimization, and inability to establish or respect boundaries has parents or siblings with similar problems.

Systems Holism is the integration of two strains of thought: systems theory and holism. I have sketched its central themes in the following list. These principles are not the only ones of interest, but they are the most relevant candidates for inclusion in a master paradigm.

Emergent properties and higher order systems are not reducible to simpler individual parts or to lower-order systems. For example, water is not a mere extension of the properties of oxygen and hydrogen. The interaction between parts of any system gives rise to qualitatively different properties at the level of the whole system. The natural world is structured hierarchically. Higher-order systems, such as a redwood forest, are not reducible to lower-order systems, such as patterns of biochemical organization, even though their evolution is traceable to less complex patterns.

Parts and wholes are equally real. That wholes are more than the sums of their parts does not give them any type of metaphysical or functional superiority. Neither could exist without the other. Any account which stresses one to the exclusion of the other is misleading. Holism cannot be the opposite of atomism but must include it. The condition of the whole is affected by the condition of its parts, and the condition of the parts is affected by the disposition of the whole. Thus, the health of a country is affected by its ecosystem, and the actions of a country affects its ecosystems. Put differently, *each thing is both a whole and a part of a larger whole, so reality is without foundation in just wholes or just parts.*

All things are interconnected within their respective levels. The dividing line between one system and another is always provisional. Networks of relationships and causal interactions cross all boundaries. Growing recognition of this principle, for example, underlies the growing current emphasis upon cooperative networking in preference to hierarchical relations of power and authority. The quantum interconnectedness of distant particles, per Bell's theorem, is becoming the classic example of radical intralevel or "horizontal" relations. But the relationship between jobs and the environment is a more socially relevant illustration.

Nature creatively advances into an open future. Novel situations and processes are more or less continuously emerging from the past (even though they may not be recognized as such). As Erwin Schroedinger once put it: "The universe happens only once." Stated differently, no two situations (objects, events, etc.) are ever exactly identical. In open systems, there are exceptions to entropic decay. The future is both open and impossible to completely predict. In the view of some writers, this allows for human freedom. We are not mere pawns of social and biological programming.

Change is all-pervasive. Systems Holism is process-oriented. Everything is in a continuous process of change. Inert objects, even rocks, are best viewed as matrices of activity. Their being is their becoming. Their stable form is a reflection of the repetition of their underlying patterns of organization. Matter is energy in process. There are no underlying and unknowable substances which support collections of empirical properties, and no spiritual entities which guide biological processes. Cause and effect are best viewed as "slices" of continuous transformation.

Feedback loops can transform a system. What goes into a system is not always the best predictor for what will come out. Any result which can directly or indirectly produce a change in the system from which it came, thus leading to a different result, is described as a (nonlinear) feedback loop. A thermostat is an elementary example of this process. However, in more complex open systems, such as humans, the feedback loops trigger higher order "rules of transformation" that influence events within the system. One such rule might be "Survive at any cost" which, if activated by feedback from a threatening environment, can produce major biochemical and/or psychological changes within a person. The transformational power of feedback loops also fuels decentralist agendas in economics, education, and social planning. Systems theory is often defined as the attempt to identify and apply such transformational rules.

Change reflects the interplay of complementary opposites, resulting in states of relative balance or imbalance. The complementary opposites may be labeled, for example, as Yin-Yang, positive and negative, or the forces of integration and of differentiation. Systems Holism does not uniformly stress this theme, although it figures prominently in certain areas of the Rising Culture, for example, the interaction of masculine and feminine perspectives and agendas. This bipolar fluctuation, as it is sometimes called, leads to imbalance, e.g., patriarchy, which in turn becomes a stimulus for redirection over time spans ranging from seconds to eons. Too much imbalance triggers a drive for balance. The price for achieving a more or less stable balance between extremes is often a fundamental transformation of the whole system. We live in duality. Our choice is to manage it constructively or destructively.

Concepts and theories derive their meaning from their usefulness and social contexts, not just from whether they refer to an objective reality. The languages of various disciplines and spheres of life (art, religious experience, science, etc.) carry their autonomous meanings. They are not reducible to each other, and their appropriate use does not depend upon our ability to prove their truth claims. Languages help us model the world in different ways, but there is no absolute way of thinking which alone mirrors the real world and upon which others are dependent. Words do not derive their meaning from what they refer to, but from how they are used. And how they are used depends upon many things other than what the world is (really) like.

Later in this chapter, I will describe additional themes which are of interest to holistically inclined writers but which are more appropriately included under a perennialist label. The current series merely captures what I take to be the core of systems and holistic thinking. Each principle permeates a wide spectrum of literature, and collectively they reinforce each other. Naturally, holists and systems thinkers have not officially voted on their articles of faith. So this list of common principles must be tentative.

THE TAO OF HOLISM: A DEFENSE OF FRITJOF CAPRA

In his review of *The Turning Point*, noted Harvard paleontologist Stephen J. Gould raises five objections to Capra's call for a systems and holistically oriented master paradigm.[10] Gould is an eminent representative of mainstream science who, in rejecting crude reductionist methodologies, is sympathetic to Capra's concerns. With certain qualifications, he is himself comfortable with the label of holist. Yet he does not see Capra's vision as a cure-all. Gould's review (1983) is somewhat dated. However, since Capra is a leader in the search for a more adequate worldview and Gould's criticisms (typical of much of the current scientific community) bear directly upon the prospects of this search, an extended reply is in order.

To begin with, Gould argues that Systems Holism is not rigorously developed and that Capra merely cites selected quotations from his heroes in various disciplines. To be sure, the reality of Systems Holism as a working paradigm has not caught up with Capra's Taoist vision of it. But Gould does not address the guiding assumption of Capra's quest, namely, that our transformative challenges *justify* the search for a new paradigm. If he had, he would surely be less demanding in his wish for a completed product.

What can we fairly expect of a new paradigm during its birthing stages? Compare our situation to what we would face during the birth of the Cartesian-Newtonian paradigm. We would be told in general terms that knowledge is power (Bacon), that objects are best understood by breaking them into their basic parts (Descartes), and that the interactions between objects can best be understood mechanistically (Newton, Galileo). Some major accomplishments, such as Newton's three laws of motion, supported these claims.

But what we now call the Cartesian-Newtonian paradigm had yet to be applied to anything but tangible moving objects or to make itself felt for a hundred years in all but small circles of learned persons. It was vigorously attacked not only by medieval defenders of the faith, but also by qualified philosophers and scientists from a variety of theoretical perspectives. It was underwritten by a great deal of faith in its potential, which was only gradually realized. In 1650 we would be forced to take a giant leap of faith if asked whether the Cartesian-Newtonian worldview would dominate our culture three hundred years later. The situation regarding the search for a holistic paradigm is similar today. We may legitimately have faith in its potential without laying claim to its completion.

Gould also claims that Capra fails to distinguish between meaningful and superficial similarities in nature. Gould asks, why interpret wave/particle dualities in physics, left and right cerebral specializations, and masculine/feminine attributes as reflecting any underlying unity in nature? These may appear to be similar structures. But apart from contrasting paired opposites, is there any basis for seeing in them a deep level of reality?

Gould is raising the classical problem of whether nature ever can be understood as having an objective form apart from the culturally slanted structures we impose upon it. He apparently thinks not. However, this confronts him with the same difficulty that he attributes to Capra. How can Gould's own stance be any less a reflection of cultural bias? Each scientist can support his or her model by urging its *usefulness* over the competition. For instance, does it better serve human needs and interests? Capra argues that the Cartesian paradigm has *lost* much of its usefulness. But a similar debate over whether his own vision will prove to be the more useful at this stage of our evolution must necessarily be incomplete.

There is a more fundamental response to Gould. Any claim to provide a cross-disciplinary paradigm involves more basic categories than those found within a single discipline. This is how we are able to bridge the gaps among disciplines. At a fundamental level, certain root metaphors and assumptions are found in diverse fields. Their meaning is not exhausted by the particular disciplines where they are found, although they are partially captured by each.

For example, dividing things into elementary parts and seeing people as "machines" are transdisciplinary metaphors which do not necessarily have a common meaning in every discipline where they are found. Cars, people, and planets are quite different kinds of machines. Similarly, fragmentation, hierarchy, and patterns of control can assume varied meanings across disciplines yet not lose their usefulness as root metaphors.

Gould seems to think that if the meaning of a pattern of organization is not the same from one area to the next, then we are imposing our own cultural biases in claiming a natural similarity. But root metaphors never have identical meanings across disciplines. They could not have and still inform an entire worldview. This is as true of the machine metaphor as it is of the integrated systems metaphor of Yin and Yang that Capra prefers.

To be sure, male-female dynamics are not the same as wave-particle dynamics. However, these polarities *can* be seen as reflecting the interaction of complementary opposites. You don't have to see them that way, of course. But then you don't have to see them as reflecting a Cartesian paradigm either. It doesn't work to charge the other person with reading his (Taoist) biases into nature while assuming one's own are more neutral.

Gould continues his criticism by suggesting that, in making the interconnectedness of atomic particles the basis for interpreting other levels of reality, Capra is committing the ultimate reductionist fallacy. As physics goes, so goes the rest of nature—whether Cartesian or holist. In Capra's words: "Here, at the level of particles, the notion of separate parts breaks down. The subatomic particles—and therefore, ultimately, all parts of the universe—cannot be understood as isolated entities but must be defined through their interrelations."[11] Gould argues, on the other hand, that hierarchical autonomy means precisely that we shall not find the same unities at every level of nature. Unity at the quantum level, for example, could translate into disunity at the level of human evolution.

The issue isn't clear. Certainly Capra is not a classical reductionist, and Gould himself is sympathetic to some form of holism. Every author will reflect the roots of his own training: in this case, Capra from physics, and Gould from biology. We have no objective means of labeling one superior to the other. Whether or not we find unity at all levels of nature depends upon what we mean by "unity." Gould sees much struggle within lower animal species, as Darwin predicts, and much struggle between social classes, as Marx predicts. But this can also be seen within an overall context of unity which balances out competing factions. Checks and balances are built into the evolutionary spiral.

The larger context of *The Turning Point* strongly suggests a different reading of Capra's words. This is that physics is a good place to find a specific example of the root metaphor of *interconnectedness* and that this metaphor also happens to be found in other levels of nature. We *can* find parallels at other levels that we find in physics. The hermetic maxim "As above, so below" may turn out to be an article of faith, but it is one which both holists and Cartesians subscribe to. They see certain root principles (interrelatedness and atomism, respectively) at work both up and down and across the spectrum of nature. It remains to be seen if Capra and others can make a stronger case for parallel unities that underlie apparent disunities at other levels of the evolutionary spectrum.

Those committed to a traditional Cartesian-Newtonian paradigm enjoy substantial power. In the scientific arena, for example, they still control the purse strings for awarding research grants and for major government and private foundations. Whether in science, religion, business or politics, holism is still a minority perspective. What, asks Gould, makes Capra or similarly-inclined writers believe that because holism *should* be promoted it therefore *will* be promoted? Where is the motivation for turning this vision, especially Capra's peaceful Taoist version of it, into a political reality? Defenders of the old way are not going to let it slip away without a fight. Capra seems either to be merely promoting his personal preferences ("Conflict should be minimized in times of social transition") or else just indulging in wishful thinking.

Is Capra politically naive? Hardly! All parties are agreed that the clash of paradigms already is under way. The conflict is all around us. It pits environmentalists against developers, the women's movement against defenders of patriarchy, Marxist-leaning Catholic priests against a monolithic hierarchy, the Committee for the Scientific Investigation of Claims of the Paranormal (of which Gould is a member) against believers in psychic phenomena, holistically oriented health professionals against defenders of the biomedical model, and so on.

Is Capra aware that holism is a minority position? Yes, and he has stated so repeatedly. Do Capra and other writers *hope* that a holistic paradigm will prevail? Surely, they do. But hope or personal preference is not the issue. The defensibility of Systems Holism is. And Capra claims only to have made a case for it, not *proven* it.

Capra does not claim that a holistic paradigm will prevail, but only that forces are now at work which make that eventuality both more desirable and likely. Many factors can postpone its emergence or indefinitely derail it. The probabilities for and against the emergence of a holistic worldview are matters over which learned persons may disagree. Who would have bet on the triumph of Christianity fifty years after Jesus' death or on the worldwide spread of Marxism just before the Russian revolution? No paradigm shift ever takes place without leaps of faith by those who lead the charge. Interestingly, Gould does not make a prediction or place a bet in this regard. He suggests only that if such a thing were to happen, the process would be very rough. I can't imagine Capra disagreeing with that.

Finally, in addressing the desire for social and natural harmony, Gould charges Capra with injecting too much of his own Taoist bias into nature. With Capra, Gould understands nature as a hierarchy of interdependent levels, each coherent in itself, but linked by ties of feedback to other levels. Does Systems Holism imply harmony? In Capra's words:

> The systems view of health can be applied to different system levels, with the corresponding levels of health mutually interconnected. In particular we can discern three interdependent levels of health—individual, social, and ecological. What is unhealthy for the individual is generally also unhealthy for the society and for the embedding ecosystem.[12]

Gould observes that harmony does not follow from the mere concept of hierarchical systems. "Advantages to individuals at one level may or may not yield benefits to individuals at adjacent levels…Holism does not imply necessary harmony; conflicts among legitimate demands of different levels are as much a part of the hierarchical model as confluence."[13]

To illustrate Gould's point, consider the fate of people over fifty-five in England suffering from kidney failure. National policy requires that they not be given dialysis and that preference be given to those younger. The system cannot support free dialysis for everyone. This is presumably good for the collective system because it contributes to overall economic survival, but of course it is unfortunate for certain individuals.

This is a difficult issue to assess, largely because "harmony" and its correlates such as "mutual cooperation" are value-laden and often emotionally charged terms dependent upon specific contexts for their meaning. Moreover, it is always possible in the context of a specific debate to argue that apparent harmony or disharmony at a certain level really isn't that way when viewed from another level.

In the case above, it may be pointed out that for some people to die in order for a greater number to live is "more harmonious" than the reverse. Or it may be that the feedback from public health policy to the individual level actually causes people to lead healthier lives, knowing that they are on their own after age fifty-five. The result could be that the policy self-destructs over the long run, because everyone takes better care of his/her kidneys at a younger age. A larger harmony can be served at the expense of a smaller disharmony.

Systems Holism does not imply that everyone obtains what they wish. It does imply that, by virtue of the interdependence of levels, harmony maximized at one level is more likely to be reflected at other (lower) levels. Reduction of institutionalized competition, for example, can benefit individuals falling under its scope. A basic premise of *The Turning Point* is that evolutionary advance to a greater harmony can be purchased only at the expense of some disunity. As every Taoist knows, certain stages of evolution are more painful than others. Capra simply urges us to consider how painful we wish our turning point to be. War, pollution, oppression, and disease are not inevitable.

THE CENTRAL CHALLENGE FOR SYSTEMS HOLISM

Having defended Systems Holism from certain objections, I want to develop a critical challenge for this type of approach. I dub this challenge the "problem of vertical depth." Actually, this is not one problem but a cluster of related issues that focus around a single theme. These issues relate to the existence of paranormal and transpersonal phenomena, to the nature of form that underlies material and evolutionary processes, and to the relationship between so-called "higher" and "lower" levels of reality.

Most holists work with a vision of reality that consists essentially of three levels. Each of these levels may be subdivided according to the interests of the scientists who make them their special domain. We may characterize them as the level of gross mass/energy (the domain of physics and chemistry, ranging from the four forces of electromagnetism, gravity, strong nuclear, and weak nuclear forces to minerals and rocks); the level of living things (the domain of biology, ranging from one-celled organisms to humans); and finally the realm of mind or consciousness (the domain of certain schools of psychology, philosophy, and religion).

Systems holists have much to say about the structuring of these levels and present a coherent revision of that structure which stands in sharp contrast to sciences still dominated by more mechanistic approaches. They insist that these levels are irreducible, that they are synergistically connected, that their internal processes are informed by the dynamic interaction of complementary opposites, that these processes are often self-regulating and nonlinear, and that systems themselves cannot be understood in isolation from other systems. Systems thinkers typically emphasize wholeness over fragmentation, balance and equality over hierarchical control, and cooperation over competition—all desperately needed agendas for a Rising Culture.

Systems holists also make frequent references to higher and lower levels of organization. They do have a vertical depth chart. The critical question, however, is *how far the vertical depth chart extends*. Are there levels of reality beyond those just described? Must all that is real fit within these three levels of matter, life, and ordinary consciousness? What is the relationship between upper and lower ends of the depth chart, however broadly or narrowly it may be conceived? Several considerations suggest that more vertical depth is required.

Paranormal experiences, for example, invite us to reflect upon a wide range of phenomena that transcend normal physical and ego boundaries. These include phenomena such as ESP, psychokinesis, out-of-body experiences, poltergeists, and mediumship. Also included are aspects of transpersonal phenomena related to hypnotic regression, psychic death and rebirth, the encounter with archetypal images (perhaps from a collective unconscious), and mystical experiences in which the ego is temporarily transcended or merged with a higher consciousness. There is not always a sharp division between parapsychological and transpersonal experiences.

These experiences challenge Systems Holism, because they do not easily fit within the three levels of reality just described. For example, where could we fit "floating out of one's body" or "merging with the One"? Conservative systems thinkers restrict their explorations to standard physical and social phenomena. They view paranormal experiences as dissociative hallucinations or self-deceptions. By contrast, more liberal systems holists, such as Capra, Tart, and Koestler, do not dismiss them out of hand.

In a chapter from *The Turning Point* titled "Journeys Beyond Space and Time," Capra encourages the development of what he terms the "New Psychology" and cites with approval the transpersonally oriented paradigms of Ken Wilber and Stanislav Grof. How is it philosophically possible for Capra to do this? The answer is that he sees transpersonal psychology as fully consistent with a systems approach to human nature. The psyche is best viewed as a complex self-organizing system of multiple levels which is intricately embedded in a larger matrix of biological and social systems. A mystical experience is thus seen as a kind of temporary, ultimate integration into the largest system of all—the universe!

As readers of Capra are aware, this theme is also stressed consistently in *The Tao of Physics*, where both Eastern mysticism, especially of a Buddhist variety, and particle physics are interpreted as complementary aspects of an overarching paradigm. Capra even sees Jung's archetypes in the collective unconscious as essentially conforming to a systems approach. In his words: "Although they are relatively distinct, these universal forms are embedded in a web of relationships, in which each archetype, ultimately, involves all the others."[14]

Systems Holism can be applied to parapsychological and transpersonal phenomena because of its neutrality. Like mathematics, we could use it to characterize relationships between fairies or within bee colonies without committing ourselves to the reality or unreality of either. Capra and like-minded writers are usually careful to describe certain features of normal *or* altered consciousness as features *of that state of consciousness* without discussing the related metaphysical issues. One can simply describe the dynamics of mystical experience from a systems perspective and never have to question whether God, or an Infinite Consciousness, or Brahman, etc., actually exists.

Here is an acid test. As most readers are aware, increasing numbers of people are reporting out-of-body experiences. Now it is well and good to call for an expanded model of human consciousness which allows for these and other types of paranormal experiences—a model which acknowledges the reality of the experiences. *But the reality of an experience is not necessarily an experience of reality.* Either people can leave their bodies or they cannot. Either Robert Monroe, for example, actually left his body as described in his *Journeys out of the Body* or he suffered one of the grandest projective hallucinations of this century. What shall it be? Systems Holism does not address in any consistent fashion whether there are other levels of reality beyond those disclosed to ordinary human consciousness.

Since Systems Holism is metaphysically neutral in principle, it should be possible to expand it to higher levels of reality. If one were independently convinced (for reasons to be discussed in later chapters) of the existence of higher transpersonal levels of reality, then one might fruitfully apply systems thinking to the web of relationships found there. But Capra is not convinced. He sees such levels essentially as extensions of lower-level systems. In his words: "Concepts like 'subtle bodies' [spirits] or 'subtle energies' should not be taken to refer to underlying substances but as metaphors describing the dynamic patterns of self-organization."[15] Again we must ask, however, organizations of what?

Certainly there are other writers attracted to the investigation of psychic and transpersonal experiences, on the one hand, and to the development of a systems or holistic paradigm, on the other.[16] A notable example is Arthur Koestler, who devoted part of his professional life trying to convince his contemporaries to take paranormal phenomena more seriously and trying to develop a comprehensive systems model.[17] But seldom in his voluminous writings is there more than a suggestion that there are *actual* higher domains.

Perhaps the most notable exception to the charge of lacking vertical depth is found in the writings of Charles Tart. Tart is well known for his call for the development of "state-specific" sciences (knowledge derived from altered states of consciousness). He is a pioneer in the application of a systems approach to both normal and altered states of consciousness and an authority on various forms of psychic phenomena.

However, a close reading of his philosophical orientation, "The Systems Approach to Consciousness," reveals a strong functionalist leaning.[18] He describes how various structures, functions, or subsystems of the mind/brain act on information to transform it, and how discrete states of consciousness are stabilized by positive and negative feedback.

Passages in his pioneering work, *States of Consciousness*, strongly point toward the Perennial Philosophy. Certainly one can apply systems or holistic thinking to a perennialist worldview. However, while a systems approach is compatible with the idea of higher levels of reality, it does not logically imply anything about the independent reality of those levels. Nor do descriptions of altered states of consciousness. To repeat: A real altered state is not necessarily consciousness of the real. Tart comes close, especially in *Transpersonal Psychologies* and more recently in *Waking Up*, but he seems not to embrace a full-blown perennialism. Or if he does, he is the lone exception in the systems camp.

Systems thinking is essentially an exploration of the dynamic relationships among *components* of systems and their subsystems, not about the reality of the different levels of a hierarchy. This is not a criticism of any particular thinker in this tradition. Rather, it's a comment on the inherent limitation of systems thinking, as liberating as it has been in many other ways.

Another aspect of vertical depth involves the status of form. This topic is as old as Plato. In medieval times and in current philosophical circles, it is often termed the "problem of universals." For example, do the laws of nature exist independently of the phenomena they govern and of their mathematical formulation? Shall we say that Galileo's law of falling bodies ($R=\frac{1}{2}gt^2$) is merely an abbreviated *description* of falling bodies? Or do falling bodies obey some hidden principle that exists without or with material objects?

The general issue is this: What holds an open, self-organizing, and self-regulating system, such as a tree, together in a distinctive evolving form when its content undergoes continuous change? Stated differently, are visible patterns of organization in open systems guided by invisible forms or principles? Or are those forms merely emergent properties of organized content? Gleick's *Chaos* beautifully illustrates both the universality of form in nature and its precarious relationship with content. Most holists do not address this question at all.

Ilya Prigogine's model of dissipative structures is a good case in point, since it is widely considered to be a paradigm case of a systems approach.[19] Prigogine and his collaborators demonstrated how certain open chemical systems, when pushed to a level of activity that threatens their internal structure with imminent disorder (say, under extreme heat), will spontaneously reorganize themselves into a more complex order that requires more energy to sustain.

It is as if the molecules simultaneously "remember" a more sophisticated arrangement that allows them to remain integrated, rather than randomly disperse. Why do they do this, rather than succumb to the pull of entropy? How is it possible for order to emerge so consistently from certain types of chaos?

This issue is especially troublesome in biology where self-regulation and morphogenesis suggestive of "prearranged ends" have long been a mystery. Why, asked Hans Driesch in the early part of the century, when we halve the blastomeres of frog embryos do we still obtain whole frogs, rather than half frogs? How, asks Rupert Sheldrake in the early 1980s when genetics appears still unable to account for morphogenesis, are we to account for the consistent evolution of form (of humans, chimps, salamanders, etc.)? Genetics tells us what kind of material will be needed, how much will be needed, and even when it will be needed, but it provides little clue as to the form of the final product.

Hans Driesch embraced vitalism, the theory that organisms were guided by nonphysical forms embedded in their structure. Rupert Sheldrake has proposed nonphysical "morphogenetic fields" outside the space-time locations of the organisms whose development they influence. Both scientists are antireductionists and sympathetic with Systems Holism—as far as it goes.

Sheldrake's theory in particular, however, signals the need to expand this paradigm to levels of existence which are not fully captured by the mere content of living systems alone. With other levels of organization, such as quantum mechanical systems or ego dynamics, the problem is the same. What holds the content together? (We shall explore in greater detail Prigogine's and Sheldrake's views on this question in Chapter Eight.)

A closely related challenge to Systems Holism invites us to ask in which direction the vertical depth chart is formed. Which end, so to speak, enjoys a greater priority? Do higher levels come from lower ones or vice versa? The gap between the lowest level of matter, on the one hand, and the highest level of human consciousness, on the other, is characterized by increasing levels of complexity. Human consciousness is typically viewed as the complex outcome of simpler processes at a lower level of order, precisely what evolutionary theory prescribes. For holists, the irreducibility of consciousness to physics is essentially the irreducibility of the complex to the simple. Human consciousness is basically an extension of something more primitive.

A growing body of literature suggests that the priorities may be just the reverse—that consciousness is primary and the brain (or materiality) is derivative. For example, the literature from psychical research, including survival studies and out-of-body experiences, suggests that the brain/body is at least no more foundational than is consciousness—that consciousness does not grow out of the body but inhabits it from a preexisting condition. Distinguished neuroscientists, such as Wilder Penfield and Sir John Eccles, have argued that the brain is not so much the seat of consciousness as the vehicle for the expression of consciousness. Synapses in the brain show a remarkable similarity, both in their structure and in the manner in which a nerve impulse is transmitted across them. This is contrary to what we would expect in attempting to explain the emergence of different conscious experiences. "A comparison of the specific micro-neural situations in which consciousness does and does not arise suggests that the brain functions not as a generator of consciousness, but rather as a two-way transmitter and detector."[20]

Furthermore, some evolutionary biologists have argued that evolutionary advances make considerably more sense if conjoined with the hypothesis of pre-existing parameters (perhaps even externally imposed) to which biological structures conform.[21] Sudden changes within a species are not so problematic. For they can be explained in terms of sudden environmental change, perhaps of a cataclysmic nature. More puzzling is the jump from one whole species to another, when the combined genetic mutations necessary to accomplish this defy rational probability.

Perennialism reverses the "bottom-up" priority of Systems Holism and mainstream science in general. It suggests that complexity appears at the physical level by virtue of being partly guided by archetypes or laws at a non-physical level. To paraphrase Huston Smith, the Perennial Philosophy derives "less from more," whereas Systems Holism seeks to derive "more from less."[22]

Systems thinking has made powerful contributions in many areas of our culture, from computer technology to an enhanced awareness of ecological dynamics. The question of vertical depth, however, remains its central challenge. Should we attempt to derive higher levels from lower levels—to squeeze intelligence, meaning, and value from the interactions of material particles? Or should we adopt a perennialist vision in which lower derives from higher, less from more? Is the transpersonal an extension of the personal, as systems thinkers are prone to see things? Or is the personal simply a limited perspective within a preexistent transpersonal domain, as perennialists suggest?

It seems no accident that the film *Mindwalk*, which Capra wrote based upon *The Turning Point*, includes a poet, a politician, and a physicist—but not a spiritual adept. Apart from a single reference to Hindu cosmology, the "crisis of perception" about which Capra writes so passionately and persuasively (the need to shift from seeing ourselves as parts of machines to aspects of an interconnected whole) was portrayed in the film as if spiritual concerns were not relevant. This omission reflects a shortcoming in systems thinking which ultimately may limit the alternatives available for navigating the complex waters of our current cultural crises. To understand why is one of the purposes of this book and requires a clear description of the principles that inform the perennialist's vision.

THE PERENNIAL PHILOSOPHY

The phrase "Perennial Philosophy" was first coined by the German philosopher Leibniz and later resurrected by Aldous Huxley, who defined it as follows: "The metaphysic that recognizes a divine Reality substantial to the world of things and lives and minds; the psychology that finds in the soul something similar to, or even identical with, divine Reality; [and] the ethic that places man's final end in the knowledge of the immanent and transcendent Ground of all being."[23]

Perennialism encompasses two relatively independent traditions whose main principles converge. One tradition springs from the experiences of both Eastern and Western mystics and spiritual leaders, supplemented at times with substantial philosophical insight and argument. The other tradition, which I shall term the "Occult Wisdom," centers around the teachings of psychically gifted individuals or groups whose connection with recognized religious traditions is marginal. Both traditions stress the existence of irreducible and interpenetrating dimensions beyond the physical, a Godhead, spiritual evolution, and the interconnectedness of all things.

Dating back as far as 3000 B.C., the Perennial Philosophy was first distilled in the East from the contemplative experiences of Indian forest-dwellers (the original yogis), partially systematized in the *Upanishads*, and later refined by sages such as Patanjali in the *Yoga Sutras* and Shankara in his *Crest Jewel of Wisdom*. Along the way it underwent independent confirmation and development in various schools of Buddhism, especially as reflected in the *Lankavatara Sutra*. Sri Ramakrishna, Sri Aurobindo in *The Life Divine*, Ramana Maharshi, and Lama Govinda in his *Foundations of Tibetan Buddhism*, among others, bring the Perennial Philosophy's "Eastern connection" into modern times.

In Western mystical and philosophical literature, the Perennial Wisdom is fueled by a broad spectrum of outlooks. Among them are Plato's classic *Republic*, kabbalistic thought in the *Zohar*, Plotinus' *Enneads*, Meister Eckhart's *Sermons*, and the Sufi mystic Rumi's *Mathnawi*. Spinoza in *Ethics* and Hegel in his *Phenomenology of Mind* indirectly lend their insight and dialectical skills to the cause. The tradition is carried forth into the twentieth century by William James's *The Varieties of Religious Experience*, Teilhard de Chardin's *Phenomenon of Man*, Huston Smith's *Forgotten Truth* and *Beyond the Post-Modern Mind*, Huxley's *Perennial Philosophy*, Ken Wilber's *The Spectrum of Consciousness* and *Sex, Ecology, Spirituality*, and Frithjof Schuon's *The Transcendent Unity of Religions*.

Paralleling the development of the mystical/philosophical wing of the Perennial tradition, and in some cases feeding directly into it, is a loosely knit confederation of esoteric schools and systems of thought.[24] These date back to ancient Egyptian mystery schools and to the mythical god-sage Hermes Trismegistus, whose dictum "As above, so below" appears in work of the most divergent spectrum of writers imaginable.

In Greece, occult teachings are traceable to Pythagoras, who viewed the world as composed of numbers and ratios. The briefest survey of the field since that time would include Gnosticism and Kabbalism, Emmanuel Swedenborg (who claimed to move about in a concurrent world of spirits), The Order of the Golden Dawn, and the Rosicrucians, who first emerged during the Renaissance. In the nineteenth and twentieth centuries, Christian Science, Spiritualism, the Theosophical Society, and Alice Bailey have contributed to perennialist thinking. Individuals too numerous and varied to list, for example, Gurdjieff and William Blake, fit loosely into a perennialist outlook while resisting further categorization. And, of course, no survey would be complete without mentioning various shamanic traditions, from aboriginal to Native American.

This brief historical overview requires several qualifications. To begin with, it should be stressed that the core metaphysical and ethical teachings of occult wisdom are *not* the same as the specialized prophetic arts or practices labeled "occult" in popular usage. I refer here to astrology, numerology, majik, alchemy, and in the extreme, voodoo, witchcraft, or black magic. Opinion regarding the legitimacy of these practices varies widely. I will therefore set them aside in order to concentrate on more foundational matters.

Nevertheless, I am including certain themes in the perennial tradition that some readers may find controversial. These include reincarnation and various psychic or spiritual gifts, such as the power to heal. By including these ideas under the general umbrella of perennialism, I am departing from established practice. For example, the great Catholic mystic, Meister Eckhart, does not subscribe to reincarnation, and spiritual healing is not exactly Huston Smith's strong suit.

There is good reason for the historical divergence of perennialism and occultism. Spiritually oriented perennialists are more directly concerned with the transformation of consciousness than with psychic powers. Even the Buddha refused to speculate about reincarnation! With notable exceptions, occult traditions stress group membership, personal psychic skills, and semisecret teachings, which are only marginally relevant to the goal of spiritual transformation.

Still, practical differences should not prevent our acknowledging theoretical convergences. For example, the concept of spiritual hierarchies or planes of existence extending beyond the natural world is clearly a part of both occult and spiritual traditions. Both fall within the scope of the Perennial Philosophy, even though the phrase is usually reserved for the spiritual/mystic wing.

The mixing of traditions is especially evident in the Theosophical Society, which stresses the *proper* unfolding of psychic abilities, the universal truths of great religious traditions, and the brother and sisterhood of persons everywhere. Through its conferences and publishing house, it has sponsored representatives not only of spiritual and occult traditions, but also of other wings of the New Paradigm dialogue, like alternative medicine. The same is true of the Sufi Order in the West, a contemplatively based derivation from Islam.

The core ideas of perennialism are not restricted to spiritual or occult schools. As Arthur Lovejoy brings out in his classic study, *The Great Chain of Being*: "The conception of the universe as...ranging in hierarchical order from the meagerest kinds of existents...through every possible grade up to the *ens perfectissimum*...has, in one form or another, been the dominant official philosophy of the larger part of civilized mankind through most of its history."[25] With the rise of modern science, the idea of a Great Chain fell upon hard times. Only the lower part of the chain (matter, motion, and the four forces of nature) survived in scientific thought.

Over the past few decades interest in the Perennial Wisdom has undergone a renaissance. This has been brought on by the encounter with Eastern religions, the human potential movement (especially transpersonal psychology), a more liberal exploration of psychic phenomena, the excesses of blind technology, dramatic new developments in science, and perhaps most of all, by the widely felt personal need for transcendence and regeneration.

The core of the Perennial Wisdom is essentially intact and lends itself to expansion and refinement in ways that take into account the insights of a particular historical period. It can incorporate elements from many other schools of thought, including Systems Holism, even though this inclusion is not always made explicit. For example, contemporary discoveries in particle physics tend not to surprise the spiritual adept who has explored higher dimensions of consciousness. The relevance of perennialism for science, theology, and even social policy is being increasingly explored on the current scene.[26]

All eight themes described earlier as constituting the core of Systems Holism are consistent with the Perennial Philosophy, even though perennialists would want to qualify them in certain ways. The Perennial Wisdom itself, however, goes beyond these eight themes—sometimes in ways that systems theorists would accept, and sometimes in ways they would not. What follows is my own creative and at times independently argued interpretation with which, of course, not all perennialists would agree.

The "stuff" of reality is nonmaterial. While there is diversity of opinion within the Perennial Wisdom concerning what reality is made of, there is substantial agreement that it is not fundamentally physical. Our physical world is an extension of a more primitive type of stuff, such as held by idealism ("Everything is a projection of consciousness") or neutral monism

("Matter and mind arise out of a neutral, transcendent ground beyond all description").

At the highest level of reality, all things are (nondually) one. The idea of nonduality in part means that the world of distinct things emerges from an infinite spiritual source. Objects that appear distinct at one level are connected in their being at higher levels. This conveys more than the belief that all things are interrelated. It is, rather, that all things are (nondually) one at a certain level and progressively differentiated at other levels. Our individual and collective evolution is toward integrated "wholes," in which higher levels gradually transform the elements of lower ones. This process involves integrating spirit into both mind and body. The highest level of integration, the Ultimate State of Consciousness, transcends simple monism. Nondual means neither "oneness" (which implies otherness) nor "unity" (which implies one and many). It means One-without-a-Second, beyond all conceptualization.

Domains exist beyond ordinary consciousness. At levels beyond ordinary consciousness are other domains variously labeled according to different spiritual traditions. They are sometimes called "subtle," "causal," and "ultimate" dimensions. Subtle and causal domains are divided into subplanes, each of which carry distinctive frequencies and types of interaction. These domains are occupied by various beings described as more and less evolved to the degree they manifest (or fail to manifest) love, wisdom, and selfless action. This means anything from deceased relatives to archangels. Local consensus reality is but a small part of the total spectrum of energy-consciousness.

All domains interpenetrate. Each level in a total hierarchical system encompasses the levels below it, yet is transcended and encompassed by levels above it. The total system is not one of masters and subjects, but rather of dimensional penetration. For example, consciousness literally permeates our physical body; it is more akin to a field in which our body is sustained, not a spiritual lump occupying a section of our heads. Hierarchical interpenetration is asymmetrical, thus allowing us to say that God is in all things, but all things are not equally aware of their divinity. Without this principle, perennialism would be open to a variety of objections stemming from its inability to effectively relate different levels of the Great Chain. This kind of hierarchical arrangement invites us to envisage "higher" as more inclusive or less limited, not as exhibiting more control over elements of "lower" levels. To integrate higher levels into one's psyche is to be empowered to create, not to oppress others.

Everything has a vibrational signature. The underlying mechanism of change is vibration. The basic energy-consciousness of the universe vibrates in an infinitely varied spectrum of frequencies and patterns, thus giving rise to different levels of reality. Even rocks vibrate. Motion through space, alteration in mood, change of atmosphere, and sudden clairvoyant vision all reflect underlying vibrational shifts. However, this does not imply that consciousness is nothing but vibrating energy.

Involution informs evolution. The overall direction of history is from the One to the Many and back to the One—from unity to diversity and back to unity. Paralleling this is the evolution from spiritual levels to levels of discrete matter, leading ultimately back to our spiritual origins. The evolution of physical form on this planet is made possible by a prior "involution" of intelligence. Simple species evolve into complex ones because the outlines of the complex were already partly in place, thus allowing for unpredictable creative advance within an overall set of parameters.

Invisible forms or archetypes underlie tangible patterns of order and self-organization. Change is typically not chaotic; dogs do not turn into cats, the laws of chemical bonding remain intact, and history exhibits coherent patterns. Behind all physical change are forms which provide an intelligible structure for content. They may be termed (Jungian) archetypes, thought forms, Platonic forms, ideas in the mind of God, or (Whiteheadian) Eternal Objects. Without them, even temporary order would be an accident. They underwrite the phenomena of self-organization in living systems, such as self-regulation, morphogenesis, and self-transcendence. Forms themselves may change, but on different levels and at different rates from the physical processes which conform to them.

The highest good is unconditional love together with the wisdom and joy it brings. The capacity for unconditional love is at the core of every person's being. It is the universal, affective connecting principle of all discrete forms of existence. It underlies the urge for community, harmony, resonance, and union. Its opposite is not hatred, but ego, selfishness, and isolation brought on by fear. Love is found by letting go of fear. Love radiates light. Fear attracts darkness. Put differently, as we ascend the Great Chain of Being, we approach the source of goodness. Toward the end of the journey and the integration of a nondual perspective, we discover not only that the good was with us all along, but also that the distinction between good and evil is transcended.

Conscious or unconscious intention ultimately leads to manifestation. The manifestation of conscious or unconscious intent is a restricted version of the broader Law of Effect. Every event, no matter at what level or how small, carries consequences (which we may not acknowledge). Thus, the state of our consciousness is reflected in our bodies, our relationships, and our physical environment. For example, a powerful group meditation that temporarily integrates—and thus activates—our connection to higher levels in the Great Chain of Being can produce interesting effects in the physical environment. This theme also underlies the popular idea that we attract situations in order to mirror what can assist us in our evolution. Power increases as we ascend the Great Chain, but it is the power to create or to influence. It is not the power of institutional hierarchical control for selfish ends.

Consciousness is multidimensional. Ways of knowing are relative to the development of consciousness, that is, to the level(s) of the total hierarchy in which consciousness operates. Thus, whether we see persons as fundamentally distinct or as connected by higher bands of consciousness, whether we can see the future, or whether we operate primarily out of intuition rather than intellect depends on which bands in the total spectrum of consciousness we work out of or can temporarily access. Multidimensional perspectivism is not the same principle as conceptual relativity described earlier. Generally speaking, the more evolved our consciousness is within the vertical hierarchy of the Great Chain, the more inclusive our perspective is on the horizontal spectrum of social and intellectual practices.

Time is the leading edge of eternity. Time is neither the simple passage of physical events (as scientists often assume), nor an independent river apart from physical change, nor a fixed continuum (as mystics have often urged). It is, rather, a hybrid concept which logically presupposes both a changeless domain and the experience of flux. Static or dynamic conceptions of time are themselves but reflections of different levels of understanding within the Great Chain of Being. Time is neither movement nor eternity, but is (as Plato suggests) the moving image of eternity.

Spiritual discernment must ultimately supplant moral relativism and absolutism. Both absolutist (rule-bound) and relativist theories of morality fail as adequate accounts, though each captures a critical element of a comprehensive theory. This theory may be termed "relative objectivism" according to which, when an individual faces a moral decision, there is a choice which s/he should make even though others may not agree. On this view an act is right not merely because a person decides that it is, since one can fail to do what is right for oneself. Perennialists are generally absolutists about certain rules, such as "Practice nonviolence," but relativists about the infinite variety of particular circumstances through which those rules are filtered.

Morality is a function of psychology. Doing good comes from being good, and the latter comes from a gradual awakening to the power of love combined with clearly seeing into the nature of particular circumstances. Perennialist moral theory is buttressed by an underlying reincarnationist metaphysics; the goal is growth on all levels, and the standard of value for particular actions is how much they contribute to or detract from that goal. It stipulates only one unconditional personal right: the freedom to decide what one will create out of his or her situation. All other rights are conditional.

We reincarnate through countless lives. Perhaps no other doctrine so clearly distinguishes the Perennial Philosophy from Systems Holism (not to mention mainstream Western culture) as reincarnation. Each of us has lived numerous other lives, carries karmic issues from the past, and incarnates for the purpose of psychological and spiritual growth—not merely to repay debts or to be punished for misdeeds. The doctrine of reincarnation does not generate any special insensitivity to issues of social justice.

I have described the Perennial Wisdom in ways that complement Systems Holism at just those points where Systems Holism seems to need support. The Perennial Wisdom offers much greater vertical depth than does Systems Holism. Of course, greater vertical depth is a virtue only if there are reasons to believe in the existence of additional dimensions. We will explore those reasons in later chapters.

Systems Holism complements the Perennial Wisdom in a quite different way, namely, by emphasizing themes that are already implicit within that Wisdom. For example, perennialists would agree with systems thinkers that personal (and community) health is a function of many interdependent factors, that nature is structured according to levels or hierarchies, and that global environmental and economic concerns are increasingly interconnected. But systems thinkers have done more to raise our consciousness about these topics and to develop constructive proposals for dealing with them.

The Perennial Wisdom tends to include and then go beyond Systems Holism, whereas Systems Holism tends to *exclude* some key features of the Perennial Wisdom. This does not mean that systems thinkers have nothing useful to say about the more speculative elements of the Perennial Philosophy. Some systems thinkers clearly have a deep interest in perennialist themes, such as the importance of unconditional love. But being inspired by Lama Govinda or Alice Bailey is not the same as adopting a master paradigm in which the richness of their teachings might comfortably fit. Out-of-body experiences, divine love, and reincarnation, for example, are generally not part of the mind-set of systems thinkers.

If you lean toward systems thinking, you can remain neutral about such metaphysical issues and stick to describing interactions in your area of interest. For example, if you were interested in transpersonal phenomena, then you would explore them as interesting experiences but not get caught up in debates over their objective reality. If your client believed that she had an out-of-body experience, you would treat her experience as real for *her*. However, you would typically not attempt to determine whether she actually got out of her body.

On the other hand, you might want to confront questions like "Do mystics actually experience higher domains of reality?" In this case, you would have two options. You could take the conservative road and restrict your reality grid mainly to the lower levels of the Great Chain—physics, biology, and the social sciences. You would thus tend to interpret mystical experiences as projective hallucinations triggered perhaps by unusual brain chemistry. Many systems thinkers take this conservative route.

Or you could take a liberal route and adopt a full-blown perennialist metaphysics, with its expanded reality grid, yet still incorporate systems thinking as a useful method for understanding the dynamics in the upper levels of the Great Chain. I adopt this more liberal perspective. Together with most New Paradigm thinkers, I urge that we incorporate the insights of Systems Holism for such areas as the environment, the economy, and a desperately needed sense of global community. Yet the global crises we are confronting require that we move beyond systems thinking toward the more multidimensional perennialism—and ultimately toward oneness.

The key term here is "multidimensional." For I am not suggesting that perennialists and systems thinkers have territorial rights on upper and lower ends of the Great Chain of Being. After all, holistic health practitioners frequently invoke the unity of mind, body, and spirit. However, it is not always clear what they mean. They might mean, for example, that spiritual concerns ("What will happen to me when I die?") are related in some interesting way to physical health. This is systems thinking. Or they might mean that there really exists a nonphysical spirit which affects the health of the physical body. That's perennialist thinking.

Some holists are perennialists and some (who lean toward systems thinking) are not. But all perennialists are holists and for the most part are open to the contributions of systems thinking. Perennialism is not more inclusive merely because its levels are greater in number or higher in the chain. Rather, its inclusiveness derives from the fact that higher levels penetrate lower levels in ways that affect the patterns of organization found there.

At the usual levels of systems thinking, like exploring the relations between diet and cancer, perennialists hold that something more subtle is going on behind the scenes. In the case of cancer, this "something more" could be a sense of spiritual despair. Liberal systems thinkers are comfortable talking about deeper levels of consciousness; they might even assign spiritual despair to a special category in their flow charts. What they fail to do, however, is acknowledge its place, much less the place of departed spirits, in externally real dimensions.

In summary, whether we are dealing with a personal crisis or a cultural turning point, the transformational journey is nurtured not only by systems thinking ("All things are dynamically interconnected") but also by the less tangible, though equally real, dimensions of the perennialist's Great Chain of Being. In the following chapters, we will explore different reasons why this is so.

CHAPTER FOUR

Paranormal Perspectives on Reality

At the core of any worldview are clusters of assumptions and beliefs about the nature of reality. Thus, it may be asserted that reality is material, that all things have a purpose, that consciousness is in everything, that evil exists (or does not exist), that values are as real as facts, that extraterrestrials are monitoring us, that love is at the very center of our being, or that Mother Earth really cares what happens to her children. The list is virtually limitless, whether we're dealing with an old paradigm or a new one.

But how do we *know* what is real? What makes one belief more reasonable than others? The fact that some spiritual teacher says it is? That someone has directly experienced its truth? That it is scientifically demonstrated? Or that it simply "feels" right? These questions are seldom asked when the subject matter is not controversial. But since most topics in the New Paradigm dialogue are controversial, consideration of why we should accept or reject them should never be too far away.

There is nothing like a good paradigm war to bring one's assumptions to the surface! In the case of paranormal phenomena—events which defy the laws of physics and experiences which transcend normal ways of knowing—the paradigm wars are well under way. Following a brief examination of some current battles over different ways of knowing, we will explore some key claims and criticisms associated with mysticism, channeling, and reincarnation. Whatever one's final opinions about these topics may be, I hope to show how they lend themselves to rational examination and belief.

HOW OUGHT WE TO CONNECT
WHAT WE BELIEVE WITH WHAT IS REAL?

Just believing something is not enough to make it so. So how should we bridge the gap from personal opinion to rational belief? With paranormal experiences, justifying our opinions is especially tricky, for the experiences themselves are often of a questionable nature, and the explanations offered on their behalf are typically part of a paradigm war!

Between skepticism and certainty. Unfortunately, the world does not divide up neatly between those beliefs that are clearly true, on the one hand, and absolutely false, on the other. We have examples of both extremes, but most of our beliefs occupy a spectrum of reasonableness, reflecting varying degrees of reliability. They are either more probable or less probable.

It is often urged that, since there is no clear "proof" for a certain view, then we are not justified in taking any particular action regarding it. For example, there is no proof of UFOs (they haven't landed on the White House lawn), no proof that ozone depletion leads to increased likelihood of skin cancer (we'll have to wait years to find out), no proof that there was a conspiracy to kill President Kennedy. And with no proof, everyone can believe what they like. Such strategies miss the point and mislead the average person. For virtually no claim ever gets conclusively proven. The evidence for our beliefs simply ranges from very strong to very weak.

Here is a spectrum of beliefs with varying degrees of reliability, ranging from the least likely to the most probable. Most beliefs in the larger New Paradigm dialogue, including many of a paranormal variety, fall between the extremes represented on this list. They possess some degree of reasonableness and are neither obviously false nor self-evidently true, even though their critics and defenders would like us to believe otherwise.

1. Nothing is knowable (extreme self-refuting skepticism).
2. Life is a dream.
3. Some Nazis were controlled by extraterrestrials.
4. The earth is flat.
5. Creationism is true.
6. Cancer can be visualized away.
7. Everybody is psychic.
8. There is a fifth force in nature.
9. Darwin's views on evolution are only partly correct.
10. String theory will unify the four forces of nature.
11. Unknown plant species exist.
12. Alaska has a lower mean temperature than Italy.
13. Germs are implicated in contagious diseases.
14. Bell's theorem is mathematically proven.
15. The page you are reading contains print.

16. At least one thing exists (absolute certainty).

Not all readers, of course, will rank these claims in the same order. Some, for example, might rank "Cancer can be visualized away" ahead of "String theory will unify the four forces of nature." But what should move us up or down the rankings is an appeal to evidence and critical reflection. And evidence comes by degrees, not with 100 percent certainty!

Is an idea really true or just true for you? One of the most exasperating claims encountered in New Age circles is that an idea is true just because it's true for the person who believes it. Of course, there are trivial bits of information that everyone can agree on, like "The Earth exists" or "Bill Clinton took office in 1993." But when it comes to controversial ideas in science, metaphysics, or spirituality, it may be claimed that all points of view are equally true or false. It just depends on what each individual chooses to believe.

The extreme version of this line of thinking is that truth is just what you decide to believe; the determining factor is whether they are *your* beliefs. You can base them on careful analysis of the evidence or you can base them simply upon how well they fit your prejudices. Such thinking is closely related to conceptual relativism—the idea that truth is always relative to a particular conceptual framework, whether Newtonian physics, the Hopi worldview, or the esoteric teachings of Alice Bailey. According to this thesis, since there is no way to get outside all of our conceptual frameworks to judge impartially their individual truth value, relativism is the best we can hope for.

Critics have extensively batted this view around, both pro and con.[1] Unfortunately, many commentators in the New Paradigm dialogue adopt some version of it without thinking about the consequences. For example, most New Paradigm writers are convinced that Systems Holism is a better representation of reality than, say, scientific materialism. They believe that "All things are interconnected" is truer than "All things are isolated." But how can they do this if all conceptual frameworks are equally correct representations of reality?

Perhaps they don't mean equally correct, but rather, just partially correct. For if we mean by conceptual relativity something like "partial truth," there is a way around the issue. This is to interpret conflicting belief systems, say, shamanism and behaviorism, as containing different degrees of truth that need to be integrated within a larger master paradigm. This approach still requires us to take into account the *evidence* for shamanistic and behavioristic ideas and to find some more adequate than others.

So far, so good. But we still have not considered the stronger version of conceptual relativity. The stronger version is that whatever one person sincerely chooses to believe is just as true as anyone else's belief. This proposal is better labeled "conceptual egalitarianism," because it's about everyone's *right* to believe what they wish. Few would quibble with this. But rights are not the issue. We have a right to believe falsely, too! The trick is being able to make the distinction between truth and falsity based upon evidence, not just what feels right.

Another interpretation of "I've chosen to believe this theory" is simply "I'm willing to accept responsibility for the consequences of this belief." This might mean, for example, that someone is prepared to go to Hell if his belief in reincarnation is mistaken. However, such a move would still leave the question of truth unanswered. The fact that our beliefs may have personal consequences which we are prepared to accept does not in itself tell us whether they are true or false.

Approaching one's competition with a blind intellectual egalitarianism eliminates the need to develop rational justifications. Too often, New Agers don't know how to argue or to produce a rational defense. They cite an authority and recommend following the dictates of our own inner guidance. This usually produces the effect of *seeming* to convert mere belief into true belief just by uttering the magical words "It's true for me." After all, it could be true for you, too!

There is yet another interpretation of "It's true for me" which steps around the need to present evidence. "It's true for her," for example, sometimes means that she *needs* to believe something at this point in her development. Whether others can prove what she believes is irrelevant, since the belief serves her needs in some hidden way, such as forcing her to look at the need to be in control. She can abandon her beliefs only after she has felt the implications of having lived with them.

However, when we return from the question of what people need to believe to the question of whether what they believe is actually true, the relativist faces a problem of consistency. For no relativist acts as if he genuinely believes that all moral, metaphysical, and scientific theories are equally correct. Why would anyone who claims to believe in conceptual relativism attempt to show that negative emotions contribute to physical disease, for example? Why study it, write about it, or establish healing centers based upon its premise, if the New Age version of conceptual relativism requires only that one sincerely believe the idea in order to make it true?

Some people talk like relativists when critics turn up the heat ("Your criticisms are just reflecting your point of view") but act like absolutists when it comes to promoting their own causes. The popular New Age mindset is especially prone to this shift. If you call New Agers unscientific, they tend to respond: "Only by *your* standards." But if you ask, for example, what the Harmonic Convergence really accomplished, the sermon you get sounds like the absolute truth. Those who value consistency between words and deeds won't get trapped in this dilemma.

A checklist of reality criteria. Few issues in the New Paradigm dialogue are as controversial as those involving paranormal or transpersonal experiences. It's important, therefore, to develop a checklist of reality criteria that draws upon such experiences for its examples. My strategy is to show that paranormal events, of which I shall use out-of-body experiences as a case in point, lend themselves to many of the same criteria of reality as normal events. The reality of paranormal events, with a few qualifications, can be determined by an appeal to the same criteria with which we would judge anything real (or unreal).

1. Do we have an identifiable, problematic, and recurring phenomenon that requires some explanation in the first place? For example, there have to be a sufficient number of reported out-of-body experiences or reports of skin cancer in order for questions like "Can people actually leave their bodies?" and "Is ozone depletion a genuine cause of increased skin cancer?" to earn much interest. If reports about such things continue to grow, the reality question is eventually forced upon us. One UFO is not a problem. Several hundred would be.

2. Do the reports, whether from normal or paranormal domains, come from people who are reasonably intelligent, sincere, free of bias, not on mind-altering drugs, and who possess some expertise relevant to the reports they make?

3. Are the experiences upon which the reports are based veridical? "Veridical" means nonillusory, genuine, or truthful. Are the experiences in every relevant way indistinguishable from those we would otherwise characterize as being of something "objectively real" (like looking at one's hand)? For example, many people have dreamed about being out of their bodies and recognized it as

such—a dream. Others have claimed to leave their bodies while they were not dreaming. It was, for them, as "real" as looking at their hand. They knew how to draw a distinction between a veridical and an illusory experience.

4. Are the reports confirmable? The importance of this criterion cannot be stressed too much. Without it, we would have neither physical nor spiritual science. We must be prepared to spell out a method or practice whereby other people can be put in the position of confirming or disconfirming the view in question. Thus, there should be methods explaining how to meditate or leave one's body for those who have not learned to do so naturally, just as there must be agreed upon strategies for measuring correlations between ultraviolet radiation and skin cancer.

5. Do the reports of a certain type of paranormal phenomena fit one explanation better than others? Any experience can be explained in many different ways. Some of those explanations, however, are more adequate than others. Every aspect of a phenomenon in need of an explanation should receive one, leaving the fewest number of loose ends possible. For example, an explanation of OBEs that accounts for the apparent ability to acquire information from distant places as well as for the sense of "being detached from one's body" would be preferable to one which accounts for only the sense of physical detachment.

6. Do competing explanations have to be stretched to the point where they become as unlikely as the phenomena they explain? For the individual who returns from an OBE with information regarding events on the other side of the world subsequently confirmed by news broadcasts, it stretches matters to suppose that he or she had accidentally hallucinated the representation of those events.

7. Does the purported explanation have useful applications to other related phenomena? The goal of explanation, whether in scientific, paranormal, or spiritual contexts, is to account for more with less. An explanation dreamed up for a narrowly defined series of events, but which could not be applied to other phenomena, would stand little chance of being integrated into a common understanding of the world. An adequate explanation of OBEs, for example, might ultimately relate to a wide range of concerns in Jungian psychology, near-death experiences, reincarnation, neurobiology, personality typing, and the meaning of life.

8. Is the explanation falsifiable? Is it framed in such a way as to permit the possibility of evidence to the contrary? The danger in applying this criterion is that in fundamental clashes of paradigms, each side will tend to accuse the other of holding nonfalsifiable theories. Each side in such clashes should be held to the same standard.

9. Are there additional predictions which follow from the explanation of the phenomena? There is a difference between establishing a good fit between an explanation and what it explains, on the one hand, and deriving additional implications from that explanation, on the other. For example, a certain explanation of OBEs might predict that someday we shall be able to take pictures of human-like forms leaving and approaching physical bodies, given the development of appropriate technology. If this prediction were confirmed, it would lend more weight to the hypothesis that people can leave their bodies.

10. Does the explanation help to make a positive difference in our values, general worldview, and quality of life? Science is not value-free. And there is no reason to suppose that paranormal sciences and spiritual practices are value-free. The ways we approach the question "What is real?" are ultimately shaped by underlying values and attitudes about life. One of the reasons the Newtonian scheme of mechanistic science has held on so long is that it underwrote the development of modern technology which has helped to improve the quality of life. Of course, it has also contributed to a fragmented worldview and indifference to the environment. But either way, science is not value-free.

In summary, these are the considerations we would want to take into account in reviewing beliefs about the paranormal: a recurring, identifiable phenomenon; overall reliability of reports; veridicality of relevant experiences; confirmability; coherence of phenomena within a larger paradigm; inability of competing paradigms to reasonably explain the phenomena; applicability of the explanation to other related phenomena; falsifiability; capacity to generate further test implications; capacity to make a positive difference in promoting shared values and goals.

These are the main criteria by which we would attempt to answer the question "What is real?" in normal science and, appropriately modified, the criteria by which we can approach the same question in the parasciences. The difference between how they are used in mainstream science and how they are used in parapsychology, transpersonal psychology, and spiritual practices depends on how narrowly or broadly we interpret experience. I have adopted the broad interpretation to show how the same criteria can be applied across domains.

PERSPECTIVISM: THE MYSTIC AND THE PHYSICIST

In few places is the interface between the normal and the paranormal more interesting than where the mystic and the physicist share their striking perspectives on reality. Lawrence LeShan (*The Medium, the Mystic, and the Physicist*) and Fritjof Capra (*The Tao of Physics*) thrust the parallels between certain types of mystical experience and physics into the limelight in the early and mid-seventies.

But earlier writers, among them philosopher Alfred North Whitehead and physicist Werner Heisenberg, also were aware of these parallels—especially those involving Eastern mysticism—well before the seventies. The Vedanta Society even published a short tract in the fifties entitled *Advaita Vedanta and Modern Physics*. For anyone interested in the mystical leanings of the great physicists of the twentieth century in their own words, Ken Wilber's collection of essays, *Quantum Questions*, is a good place to start.

Some individuals have inferred from these writings that modern physics, meaning quantum mechanics and relativity theory, corroborates the perennial vision of mystics. In its crudest form still encountered in popular New Age gatherings, the inference is this: If physics paints a picture that looks something like Buddhism, then Buddhism must be true!

Superficially, the case is strong. Capra never claimed that either discipline proved the other, only that there were striking parallels to be noted. However, his book is laced with quotations which make it appear that the physicist and the Eastern mystic are talking about the *same thing from different perspectives*. Compare, for example, the following passages from Sri Aurobindo, a Hindu philosopher/sage, and Capra, the physicist, respectively:

> The material object becomes…something different from what we now see, not a separate object on the background or in the environment of the rest of nature but an indivisible part and even in a subtle way an expression of the unity of all that we see.

> Quantum theory forces us to see the universe not as a

collection of physical objects, but rather as a complicated web of relations between the various parts of a unified whole… All (physical) particles are dynamically composed of one another in a self-consistent way, and in this sense can be said to "contain" one another. In [this theory], the emphasis is upon the interaction, or "interpenetration," of all particles.[2]

There are many ideas involving materiality, causality, space, and time, where the mystic *could* use the words of the physicist and vice versa. The parallels are certainly there. The Eastern mystic and the Western physicist stress the energetic nature of physical objects, the unity of opposites, creative advance, a primordial ground from which all things emerge and, most importantly, the interconnectedness of all things.

But are they really talking about the same reality from different perspectives? Is it the case that the mystic in an altered state of consciousness is looking at the very same quantum interconnectedness that the physicist, from his perspective of ordinary consciousness, infers from his experiments? Wilber has incisively probed this question from a perennialist perspective.

According to the Perennial Wisdom (described in Chapter Three), there are approximately seven major levels of reality constituting a Great Chain of Being. They range from the lowest level of gross mass-energy up through living things, normal states of consciousness, higher states of consciousness (often labeled "subtle" and "causal" domains), and finally the Ultimate Ground of All Being (Nirguna Brahman or Consciousness-as-such). Furthermore, each domain in this hierarchy is said to interpenetrate its lower neighbors, yet also transcend them. The higher contains the lower but is not reducible to it.

According to Wilber, physics is concerned primarily with the lowest level in the scale, the domain of matter and energy. We can jazz up this domain with discussions of fields of energy and N-dimensional spaces. But when all is said and done, the physicist does not presume to be describing levels about God, causal bodies or souls, consciousness or even life energy itself.

So when the physicist speaks of the interconnection of all things, she is merely placing into a new and more proper perspective the strong inter-relations between all objects and processes *within a certain level*. We may, if we wish, view this as the discovery of strong horizontal connectedness. In contrast, when the mystic speaks of interpenetration, it is not only with acknowledgment of the quantum interconnections of the first level; it is also an expression of the vertical interpenetration of higher domains down through lower levels, which is quite a different matter altogether. From this it follows that:

> Physics and mysticism are not two different approaches to the same reality. They are different approaches to two quite different levels of reality, the latter of which transcends but includes the former...Physics and mysticism are not complementary [i.e., mutually exclusive approaches to one interaction], because an individual can be at one time and in the same act, a physicist and a mystic...Physics and mysticism are no more mutually exclusive approaches to one reality than are, say, botany and mathematics.[3]

Much depends here upon what we mean by "same reality" and "different perspective." There is a broad and largely useless sense of "perspective" that permeates much New Paradigm discussion. According to this sense, something is said to be true within a certain perspective where "perspective" means simply "point of view." Of course, anything one chooses to believe is true, according to one's point of view. In this broad sense, perspectivism is often the trump card we see pulled out in order to *make* a certain belief true. It is one of the most overworked words anywhere.

There is, however, a narrower and more relevant sense for understanding Wilber's concerns. In this sense a perspective defines the provisional limits of what a person can directly experience. Within these limits there are typically many points of view involving sometimes multiple and overlapping conceptual frameworks. A tree, for example, can be viewed in its relation to an ecosystem as lumber for homes, as a living system, as a collection of atoms and molecules, and so on. Furthermore, some cultures may have many words for trees and others virtually none. And some may value trees, while others do not.

But if we were to bring individuals together representing all the points of view just described and ask them to look at some trees, they would all "see" trees with trunks and green leaves, even though they would describe their experiences in different ways or in different languages. From those who treasure their lumber value, for example, we would expect less attention to be paid to their leaves or aesthetic value.

However, for all people with normal vision, the raw sense data would be approximately the same. Perspectivism in the broad sense—that is, the diversity of culture-bound *interpretations* of common bands of experience—is a fact of life. But it is perspectivism in the narrow sense that concerns us here. All of the individuals just described share a common *experiential* perspective; they all directly perceive pretty much the same tree. The fact that communication occurs across diverse cultures assumes participation in a common perceptual and auditory reality.

But suppose that this common experiential perspective is altered. Suppose that some (rare) individuals saw colored energy patterns *around* the trees and sometimes saw vortexes of colored energy when they looked directly at the trees. They can see the same trees you and I perceive, but they can also see something else which you and I cannot see. They have two (or more) perceptual perspectives, whereas we have but one. Such is the case with the yogi, the shaman, the clairvoyant, the mystic. And this is perspectivism in the more specialized sense of the term, the sense at issue in discussions about mysticism and physics.

One way of illustrating the idea of radically shifting perceptual perspectives is through an analogy familiar to every school child. Recall what happens when we place a section of leaf under a powerful microscope. First we see just the green leaf. Then as we adjust the power, the picture becomes a greenish blur. Then the arterial network comes into focus, followed by a picture of collections of cells. As we continue to turn up the power, we move down through atomic and subatomic levels. Were it possible to go beyond quarks, we would see literally no thing.

For convenience, let us say that there are seven major levels of reality of this leaf corresponding to seven major perspective levels built into the microscope. Each perspective and its corresponding reality is, of course, quite different. For individuals locked into a certain level we would expect to see different interpretations of physical objects, but they would be appropriate to that level. Communication *within* levels of reality would become the order of the day. Communication between levels, however, would be more difficult, because what people see at different levels is itself so radically different. Those who can move between levels—who can radically shift their experiential perspective suggested by the analogy of the microscope—would be at an advantage because they can see more.

How should we interpret the claim that physics and mysticism are different approaches (perspectives) to different realities? Reality, for the highly evolved mystic, involves higher levels permeating the lower ones. However, the mystic *can* focus upon just the lower level and "see" the same leaf that the ordinary person or physicist does. But he can also alter consciousness in such a way that he can see the atoms that the physicist only can make indirect inferences about. Indeed, some mystics and clairvoyants have reported doing just this.

So long as we distinguish between the lowest level and all others above it, then Wilber's claim that mysticism and physics are about different realities is perfectly straightforward. He reminds us of other levels about which physicists have little interest and no information. On the other hand, a part of the real is still real, and it is perfectly legitimate to inquire into what both the physicist and the mystic see when they focus upon just the bottom level. The mystic or clairvoyant who sees quantum interconnections when he looks at a leaf is using a different approach to the *same* reality as the physicist who performs experiments and makes inferences about those connections.

Of course, the mystic sees both the leaf and quantum interconnections as reflecting higher levels of reality. He may see quarks as God-energy or as Brahman, for example. But Capra never denied that and, from what I can tell, no other serious commentator on physics/mysticism parallels has either. The mystic's *whole* reality is not the same as the physicist's *partial* reality; in that sense they are concerned with different realities. As Wilber notes: "When the mystic looks at a bird on wing over a cascading stream and says 'They are perfectly one,' he does not mean that if we got a super microscope out and examined the situation we would see bird and stream exchanging mesons in a unitary fashion."[4]

True, but Wilber's case would have been better served had he said that the mystic does not *merely* mean we would see such an exchange. By definition the mystic's vision must include quantum connections and a whole lot more! So far as perspectivism is concerned, nothing keeps the mystic or clairvoyant from looking at the bird and stream and observing the quantum exchange Wilber describes. Of course, he can then proceed to access other higher dimensions which the physicist never dreamed of! The answer to the question "Do mysticism and physics represent different approaches to the same reality?" is both affirmative and negative, depending on what is meant by "different perspective" and "same reality."

WHY CSICOP IS LOSING THE WAR

CSICOP is the acronym for the Committee for the Scientific Investigation of Claims of the Paranormal. Its membership is worldwide and includes professionals from virtually every area of rational inquiry. Its leadership is (or has been) supported by such luminaries as B.F. Skinner, Carl Sagan,

Isaac Asimov, Stephan Jay Gould, Nobel laureate Murray Gell-Mann, and magician James Randi, among many others with impressive academic and professional credentials.

Through its principal publication, *The Skeptical Inquirer*, national conferences, and support of skeptical networks, it seeks to help stem the flow of irrationalism. Irrationalism is taken to include belief in anything from ESP to astrology, UFOs, creationism, Bigfoot, channeling, crystals, homeopathy—even exaggerated claims for biorhythms, applied kinesiology, and meditation.

CSICOP has the usual concerns about pseudoscience and the need for evidence. But there is something of a moral mission as well. For when a Gallup Youth Survey finds that seventy-four percent of teenagers believe in angels, fifty-eight percent in astrology, fifty percent in ESP, and twenty-nine percent in witchcraft, one reasonably might have some fears about the leadership of the next generation.[5]

As one sympathetic to the claims of the transpersonal and paranormal, I am probably in a very small minority of individuals who support the general mission of CSICOP and do not dismiss it as cavalierly as it dismisses the paranormal. I have subscribed to *The Skeptical Inquirer* for more than a decade, required my students to read certain lead articles, and attended CSICOP national conferences. When James Randi attempted to expose a fraudulent faith healer, I assisted by seeking the participation of local medical doctors. Even if we do not agree with many of its specific conclusions, there is much to be learned from the *Inquirer's* critiques. The committee's work helps keep us honest, even if we may not always care for its conclusions or style of delivery.

Which brings us to the darker side of the equation. Its skepticism is not always balanced. There is a fair amount of guilt by association and ad hominem argumentation that permeates many of the articles. If you believe in certain crazy things, the implication is that you probably believe in other crazy things (like ESP *and* Bigfoot) because you have lost your power of reason and your appreciation for scientific method. A fair amount of space is devoted to examining weak, more easily refutable claims of the paranormal. The general tone of many articles and letters to the editor is extraordinarily cavalier and condescending. Sometimes it is humorous.

The editors want the facts to fit their theories every bit as much as the pseudoscientists they criticize. Thus, when CSICOP's own statistical analysis of astrological correlations appeared to offer limited empirical support for astrology, they secured another statistician whose analysis was more in keeping with their own views. This led to charges of a cover-up from within the organization.[6] Only skeptical articles are published. And serious critiques of those articles by nationally prominent scholars appear to be discouraged or even rejected out of hand. A neutral spectator at a CSICOP conference would find as many true believers preaching to the already converted as he would at a national New Age conference.

My purpose in drawing attention to CSICOP is not to take sides on any particular issue regarding the paranormal. Nor is it to discuss charges of poor experimental design, lack of repeatability, and the alleged impossibility of paranormal phenomena. Leading independent experts, such as Harvard psychologist Robert Rosenthal, have found the quality of parapsychological research to be very high.[7] Rather, I am concerned with several deeper assumptions which guide the skeptical critique of the paranormal and help us to understand why CSICOP is losing its self-proclaimed war.

Extraordinary claims require extraordinary evidence. This assumption permeates all skeptical thinking about the paranormal. Left unqualified, of course, it is perfectly reasonable. Many parapsychologists have sought to live up to its spirit by attempting to produce extraordinary evidence. In the hands of the skeptic, however, this assumption can become a tool for the systematic exclusion of the paranormal.

The logic works like this. No matter how well-designed one's experiments, how far one has gone to rule out fraud, how many replications have been made, or how certain one is about a particular experience, claims involving the paranormal are so radically extraordinary that the evidence can never tip the balance. Skeptics deny such a strong bias, but in practice this is the way it works out on a case-by-case basis.

Why is requiring extraordinary evidence for extraordinary claims losing its applicability in the paranormal arena? Because increasing numbers of people—not dropouts, New Age yuppies, or wasted hippies— but mainstream, balanced, educated, and realistic individuals *just don't find major areas of the paranormal that extraordinary in the first place.* Hence, the level of evidence required is correspondingly lower than what the skeptic prescribes.

To take a simple example, many people do not find the idea of advanced civilizations in the universe—some of which might be surveying our planet—that improbable. They may consider this unlikely enough to require a careful look at the claims of UFO encounters (from pilots, for example) but not so unlikely as to require an entire fleet to land in Harvard

Square before consenting to believe. The same goes for out-of-body experiences or precognitive dreams.

This is one reason why CSICOP is losing the war. One of its main weapons is a principle which, while abstractly true, is progressively less relevant for the paranormal in the minds of average people and the rising generation of scientists. Of course, it will always be applicable to outlandish claims such as "Harry Truman was secretly married to three other women." We would require extraordinary evidence for this. But in many areas of the paranormal, the demand for extraordinary evidence does not impress us as strongly as it used to, because such phenomena, while unusual, do not strike us as extraordinary. Insistence that we not believe strange things until they have met higher than normal standards of evidence is turning into a mere expression of hope that we will find the paranormal as improbable as the skeptic does.

Paranormal experiences don't count for anything unless they can be repeated under laboratory conditions. This assumption is not just another demand for extraordinarily high standards of evidence. Rather, it expresses the belief that individual paranormal experiences don't count as evidence for anything until they have been put through the ringer of average scientific investigation. Those who hold this view tend to overlook the fact that there isn't any such thing as an average scientific investigation; there are many methods appropriate to difference types of science. Unique events in the history of the world, such as the formation of distinctive geological strata, cannot be repeated at all.

Few would suggest that we abandon standards of critical rationality as applied to the paranormal. There are any number of standing scandals in parapsychology that signal the need for continuing caution. But such an assumption tends to overlook grass roots trends of landslide proportions. These trends include the personal experiences of millions of people not likely to hallucinate, on the one hand, but not able to repeat their experiences at will under laboratory conditions, on the other. Consider, for example, the person who consults a spiritual healer for degenerating lumbar discs and now finds herself free of pain and not in need of expensive surgery; or who has a precognitive dream about his daughter's boating accident which actually comes to pass; or who finds herself floating out of her body during meditation; or who, with other passengers, sees a UFO at very close range for several minutes.

I am not suggesting that spontaneous paranormal experiences automatically prove the claims they lead to. I am suggesting, however, that when they occur with increasing frequency across diverse segments of the population and in ways which lend themselves to the application of the criteria of reality described earlier, then to explain them away *always* as the result of chance or self-delusion is to purchase a ticket to progressive irrelevance. Skeptics in general and CSICOP in particular will have to do better than this.

How do we know the moon exists? Because we can look and see. How do we know that people have auras? Because more and more people appear capable of seeing them. We don't have to reach total agreement with such beliefs. We just have to come close enough so that the lines between the normal and the paranormal become blurred. Perhaps three percent of the population see auras now. But if thirty percent see them ten years from now, the skeptic will have to go to such extraordinary lengths to explain them away that even ordinary perception, in theory, would be called into question.

Behind skeptical thinking about the paranormal are some assumptions about the way science works (or ought to work) carried over from the days of Logical Positivism. According to this view, science is value-free; truth is objective; reality is what fits a particular set of tests and measurements; and there is a single method for science according to which all claims, including those of the paranormal, must be verified.

Contemporary philosophy of science has shown this view to be very limited. Science can be *made* to conform to any number of reality grids; it is not the sole arbiter of which ones we might reasonably adopt. Given the current trends in spontaneous paranormal experiences, my guess is that within ten years it will seem quite reasonable to adopt standards of evidence at the outset that move us in the direction of an expanded picture of reality. Skeptics, especially of a humanistic orientation, would prefer to see science driving culture in all but the arts, but they fail to appreciate the many ways culture drives science. This is the second reason CSICOP is losing the war. True science is open-ended; *scientism* is not.

What do correlations show? There is another line of argument skeptics like to pursue in virtually every area of the paranormal. It consists of correlating a paranormal phenomenon with some natural state of affairs in a way that appears to reduce the "para" to the "normal." It's as if one were to say: "Ah, now we have the proper scientific explanation for these puzzling claims people have been making."

In the case of healing, the phenomena will often be correlated with alleged placebo effects. In the case of UFO sightings, the correlations will be with weather balloons, swamp gas, or unusual temperature/pressure inversions. With out-of-body experiences, the ideal clincher correlation is assumed to involve neurochemical events in one's brain. Finally, in the case of precognitive dreams, it will be urged that dreams that come true can be correlated with sensory cues that the subconscious blended together.

In these examples "correlated with" typically means "explained by." But when we ask what type of explanation, it usually turns out to be either a proposed *causal* connection (that still leaves unaddressed the question of the "reality" of the paranormal effect), or an ad hoc theory with few, if any, additional predictions.

It doesn't take much imagination to apply this line of thinking to any area of the transpersonal. Thus, by virtue of a few superficial analogies of *some* types of mystical experience with *some* types of schizophrenia, "union with the One" will tend to be correlated with—and thereby explained away as—a suppressed need to escape from reality and return to the womb. Such correlation arguments can go on forever.

Correlations do contribute to our understanding of the paranormal but do not in themselves explain the phenomena. They show only that if the phenomena occurred as reported, they were positively correlated with some natural state of affairs. If the correlations are very strong, they might suggest a relation of cause and effect, e.g., that paranormal experience of Type A can be induced by chemical of Type B in one's brain.

Suppose that certain neurochemical triggers were discovered in unusual quantities during the time people have OBEs. The skeptical explanation would be: "Now we know that people who think they are leaving their bodies are actually just suffering too much Type B chemical in their brains." But such a line of reasoning proves little. It does not tell us that people really do not leave their bodies. It merely says that if they do, there is a certain type of neurochemical process that expedites the experience.

A favorite strategy of skeptics is to assume that OBEs (as well as many other types of paranormal experiences) can be positively correlated with deviant personality traits that generate dissociative hallucinations of which OBEs are a subclass. Yet attempts to corroborate this hypothesis have not produced significant results. For example, absorption and hysteroid tendencies, psychoticism, death anxiety, narcissism, defensive style, and negative self-image have all failed to correlate significantly with OBEs. For the most part, OBEs fall entirely outside any recognized type of depersonalization syndrome.[8] The majority occur with otherwise normal people.

It's reasonable to assume that some people are predisposed to have an OBE. For example, a woman recalling instances of physical abuse as a child may turn OBEs into a temporary escape mechanism that can be triggered in a therapy session. In such circumstances she has good reason not to want to identify with her body. But the fact that OBEs can serve as a defense mechanism tells us absolutely nothing about whether people actually leave their bodies when the mechanism is triggered.

In summary, that certain neurochemical processes or psychological dispositions might be correlated with a paranormal experience doesn't prove that the objects of these experiences are purely subjective or all in the mind. It simply tells us that there may be a causal connection. Correlation with the normal doesn't automatically take the "para" out of paranormal; rather, it helps us begin to integrate the paranormal with the normal. It will take more than merely producing such correlations for CSICOP to win the war.

WHO'S IN THE CHANNEL?

Much information about reality is being delivered these days through channels (also called mediums). A channel either in trance or consciously makes his or her body and voice available to spirits from another dimension so that they can speak or write directly to us. The question, of course, is whether we have any reason to believe that channels themselves are legitimate. What is especially frustrating is that much contemporary discussion of channeling disregards the hundred years of critical analysis already on the books.

The picture is considerably different today. It used to be that you could get a message from your deceased grandmother through your local spiritualist minister for a freewill donation. Now, for several hundred dollars you can spend the weekend listening to an archangel or ascended master deliver metaphysical sermons. In virtual disbelief that so many people could be attracted to this practice, critics reach for the most handy explanations, often involving greed and gullibility.

One thing is clear. No matter what the final explanation of channeling turns out to be, it will have to be multifaceted. For every group of channelers to whom certain explanations might apply, there are many others to whom they do not apply. Thus I propose to set aside explanations involving appeals to money, fame, or power, because they are irrelevant to whether genuine channeling takes place. Doctors and attorneys, for example, also have been known to enjoy money, power, or fame! Many channelers have honest personalities, simple lifestyles, modest possessions, and interesting things to say. Hollywood gets the attention, but there are class acts off Broadway, too.

The main question before us is not whether there are *some* channelers engaged in fraudulent activities for questionable motives: there surely are. Nor is it whether we can prove that personalities expressed through a channel are really who they say they are, for we cannot. Rather, the question is whether information is given to a channel from a source other than the channel's own subconscious.

The most useful way of approaching this question is to examine the various alternative explanations of channeling. Of course, anyone convinced of the truth of materialism and of the preposterous nature of channeling will probably raise the standards of evidence so high that no arguments could be persuasive. I hope to show that there are many good reasons for being cautious about channeling but no good reasons for setting it entirely aside. A review of these reasons should help to clarify one of the major paradigm wars of our time.

Is trance channeling self-hypnosis? Much current channeling is telepathic, in that the channel may simply close his or her eyes in a relaxed state of awareness and receive information from his or her "guides." However, in this section we are concerned with the classic trance in which the channel enters a profoundly altered state of consciousness and remains essentially unaware of, or stands aside from, the transmission. There are at least three reasons why trance channeling cannot be explained merely as a special form of self-induced hypnosis.

To begin, the hypnosis explanation is simply not relevant to some aspects of a channeling session like, for example, demonstration of skills or presentation of information not possessed by the medium. Hypnosis may help to induce a certain personality, but it does not explain why that personality is clairvoyant or can speak a language, however haltingly, that the channeler does not know.

Hypnosis is a method for achieving a certain altered state of consciousness. It is a means. In itself, it doesn't tell us whether the personality now in charge is a fragmented or dissociated aspect of the channel's own mind or whether the trance state was necessary to allow an external personality to temporarily move in. In fact, the channeled personality's moving in could be the cause of the medium losing consciousness rather than the effect of hypnosis. We just don't know. Merely associating a puzzling phenomenon (channeling) with a less puzzling one (hypnosis) doesn't answer our questions about the reality of the channeled personality anymore than controversies over today's headlines are resolved by a lecture on how newspapers are printed.

Finally, we would expect mediums to be especially sensitive to hypnotic suggestion for other purposes (like quitting smoking). Some are and some are not. There is little evidence for a strong connection in this regard. It's possible to hypnotize ordinary people and cause them to believe that they are channels. But this doesn't mean that they can do all the things that channeled personalities do. Nor does it prove that regular channeled personalities are temporary fictional entities any more than a magician's producing psychokinetic phenomena proves that there are no (real) psychokinetic phenomena.

Are channeled entities multiple personalities? There is no doubt that "multiples" from a repressed side of a person's personality sometimes appear to be completely other than the person. Some appear to be friends; others, enemies. Some claim to be distinct while others do not. Some are aware of other personalities inhabiting the same body and some are not. Some take names (and then change them!), while others refuse to give names at all. Some commit crimes and then let others take the rap, so to speak. Some are associated with a striking difference in physical appearance, such as different eye color. It has also been shown that different multiples generate distinct brain wave patterns and electrical skin potentials, which integrated personalities acting out other roles do not exhibit. These are but a few aspects of the fascinating and troubled world of the multiple personality.

There are sometimes strong similarities between multiple personality disorder and channeled personalities. Both a multiple personality (or "alter") and a channeled personality can differ radically from the dominant personality of the person who channels or who has MPD. Some multiples talk as if they are little more than attached spirits. For example, they may complain that if another personality comes in, they will have to leave! Some multiples seem very wise relative to the intelligence of the person's ordinary dominant personality and may cater to the perceived need of the questioner to receive information from a real spirit guide. Some multiples may need to be induced through an altered state of consciousness, just as channeled personalities are induced by the medium entering an altered state. Finally, some multiples and channeled personalities may demonstrate skills quite different from those of their host.

In short, a person with MPD can seem like a channeled personality, and a channeled personality (especially of average quality) can seem like nothing more than a dissociated aspect of the channel. The capacity for self-deception through dissociation should not be underestimated. In *All in the Mind*, Ian Wilson shows how such self-deception could be involved with a variety of alleged paranormal abilities.

Philosopher Stephen Braude, author of *First-Person Plural* and perhaps the most knowledgeable commentator on paranormal aspects of multiple personality, has argued that attempts to link the existence of discarnate entities to similarities or dissimilarities between the multiple personalities of the channel and alleged spirit guides are probably doomed to failure. This is due to the fact that objective personality assessments in such contexts—where one personality begins and another ends—are extremely difficult to come by.

On the other hand, psychic researcher Scott Rogo has argued that some multiple personality cases are actually better explained as instances of temporary spirit possession. Some multiples have actually been exorcised as if they were externally attached spirits who became attached during a time of extreme vulnerability of their host. The same surface behaviors may lend themselves to quite different interpretations. Clinical psychologists and psychiatrists knowledgeable about dissociative disorders, channeling, and possession phenomena are sometimes hard put to decide which category they are dealing with. Therapeutic interventions are correspondingly risky, as Nicolas Spanos explains in *Hypnosis, Demonic Possession and Multiple Personality: Strategic Enactments and Disavowals of Responsibility for Actions*.

One of the most tested mediums in history, Eileen Garrett, expressed some ambivalence about her two spirit controls, Abdul and Uvani, each of whom agreed to extensive psychological analysis in order to examine their claims to be separate consciousnesses. Psychologist Lawrence LeShan suggested that Garrett subconsciously invented the personalities for purposes of her channeling, whereas Carl Jung thought that Garrett somehow had access to the far reaches of her own subconscious as well as to the collective unconscious.

The dissimilarities in many cases pose a major block to any explanation of channeling based solely upon multiple personality disorder. To begin, a majority of multiples have experienced severe psychological trauma in their youth (rape, abandonment, etc.) whereas the majority of channels have not. Moreover, channelers typically do not evoke classical multiple personalities, nor do they show indications of dissociation on standard tests or upon scrutiny by experts hidden in the audience—no more, that is, than any other arbitrarily chosen group.

Trance channelers typically control the time and circumstance of their sessions, whereas multiples can manifest at some very inopportune times. A trance channel can simply decide not to channel anymore. People with MPD do not have that option. (If they did, it would not be labeled a disorder.) Major alters are often interspersed with dozens of minor fragment personalities, whereas the entities evoked in trance channeling are typically more consistent, more fully developed, and far fewer in number.

Spirit guides typically admit to having past lives and frequently lecture their audience about some aspect of them. For the typical multiple, existence begins within the lifespan of the person with MPD. Furthermore, channelers *experience* the comings and goings of their spirit guides in quite different ways than people with MPD experience a change from one aspect of themselves to another. Multiples may manifest concurrently, whereas spirit guides do not.

Finally, in rare instances what appears to be a single spirit personality may give related messages through two or more channelers unknown to each other. (This is termed "cross-correspondence" in psychical research.) We might explain cross-correspondence as alter personalities from different people telepathically communicating with each other. But such an explanation is more bizarre than the phenomenon it is intended to explain. On the whole, the dissimilarities between trance channeling and multiple personality disorder outweigh the similarities.[9]

What does paranormally derived information show? Psychical researchers long have been convinced of the existence of occasional high quality mediumship in which the information given appears to be of a distinctly paranormal variety.[10] For example, a person totally unknown to the medium may be given facts about his or her past, future, character, friends, or deceased relatives. Unlearned skills occasionally may be demonstrated, such as speaking in a foreign language. In rare instances, verifiable information not formerly available to any person on the planet is forthcoming.

Does this demonstrate that the medium (or channel) is temporarily inhabited by a discarnate being? Not necessarily. It could be that the medium's own telepathic and clairvoyant powers are accessed unconsciously during a trance and then projected through an alter ego. In this interpretation, channeling would be a paranormal process but not one which demonstrates life after death. Highly regarded investigators have come to just this conclusion. J.B. Rhine, for example, was never able to convince himself that paranormal information from a spirit guide could not be explained more simply as a projection of the medium's own (unconscious) powers of telepathy, clairvoyance, or precognition.

This interpretation is called the super psi hypothesis. Its proponents argue that no matter how much the paranormal information appears to be coming from a separate discarnate personality, it can be explained as the result of some combination of the medium's own psychic abilities. As such, it serves as an umbrella of faith that its proponents claim is simpler than the hypothesis of personal survival.

Super psi nicely fits some cases. It's plausible, for example, to assume that the channeler might unconsciously—but telepathically—derive information from the person obtaining the reading and then simply feed it back to them. However, there are other cases for which this hypothesis does not fit well at all. For example, we would have to assume that the medium can: unconsciously scan the planet for clairvoyant information uniquely relevant to the client; telepathically scan the minds of friends of the client all heretofore unknown to the medium; describe in detail the appearance of deceased relatives in spirit whom the client never saw and who were later so described by other skeptical relatives; suddenly assume literary polish, scientific knowledge, or philosophical wisdom out of proportion to his or her education; or demonstrate unlearned skills such as speaking a foreign language. To suppose that the medium can perform some combination of these skills on demand pushes the super psi hypothesis well beyond its claim of simplicity.

Consider the case of Mrs. Leonora Piper, the wife of a prominent Boston physician as well as one of America's most studied mediums around the turn of the century. Mrs. Piper had several different control personalities during her life as a medium. One calling himself George Pellew surfaced in March of 1892, claiming to have been killed several weeks earlier. With the exception of a reading—or "sitting" as they were called then—five years earlier, he and Mrs. Piper had never met. However, he was casually known to Richard Hodgson, a prominent member of the American Society for Psychical Research who happened to be investigating Mrs. Piper's mediumship at that time.

Hodgson was not aware that Pellew had died several weeks earlier, so was naturally astonished when Pellew's personality surfaced through Mrs. Piper. Not only did the channeled personality correspond to that of the original George Pellew, according to Hodgson, but it later was successful in identifying and commenting on Pellew's personal possessions, which Hodgson later obtained for purposes of testing.

More significantly, the channeled Pellew personality was introduced to 150 different individuals, with Mrs. Piper in trance, and successfully identified just those thirty people known to the living George Pellew. He even changed the topics and style of conversation with each of his different former friends and expressed a remarkable knowledge of their personal lives and concerns. And he provided extensive information, later verified, not currently known to any person in the room.

Hodgson was one of the most skeptical members of the Society for Psychical Research, famous for his role in debunking the mediumship of Madame Blavatsky. Yet on the basis of his fifteen-year study of Mrs. Piper, especially the Pellew material, he found himself unable to account for her mediumship in terms of telepathy or clairvoyance, and he progressively leaned towards the spiritualist belief in personal survival.

Do channels merely access our collective unconscious? Channeling these days often has little direct connection with the personal histories of those in attendance. It is undertaken instead for the purpose of conveying higher teachings. Some of these teachings are higher, while others are less inspiring. But on most everyone's "higher" list would be the teachings of Lazaris (Jach Pursel), Emmanuel (Pat Rodegast), Jesus (*A Course in Miracles*), Raphael, Michael, and others (Ken Carey).

One might cite works from dozens of other sources, such as Jane Roberts, J. Z. Knight, and Ruth Montgomery, each of which makes its own distinctive type of contribution. My higher list is relatively short only because of the degree of gentle humor, inspiration, profundity, and, most importantly, transformative power of the teachings. The critical difference between Roberts's (original) "Seth" and Pursel's "Lazaris" is the difference between conveying information, on the one hand, and providing tools for personal transformation, on the other. Both information and transformation are important. But for the nineties, the information is mostly in place. Acting on it is the critical imperative.

Do these teachings merely reflect the capacity of some exceptional individuals to tap into a vast unconscious reservoir of archetypes and wisdom upon which our daily life floats—the collective unconscious? A comprehensive account of channeling phenomena would have to acknowledge the ability of some mediums to access this reservoir.

Psychologist Ronald Klimo examined a biological version of this idea—complete with holographic encoding in our collective gene pool—as a plausible explanation of some forms of channeling. Increased interest in channeling, he suggests, may even reflect some deeply rooted evolutionary mechanism which will help us through times of transformative challenge and expand the frontiers of consciousness.[11]

Jungian explanations are at their best where universal patterns of feeling and behavior are involved. The encounter with evil, the yearning for love, the possibilities of self-deception, the interplay of the masculine and the feminine, the unity-in-diversity of various symbols, and the desire for transcendence and growth are all part of the Jungian interpretation of culture, personality, and dreams. They are certainly applicable to some forms of channeling.

The channeler's periodic archetypal experiences, however, still leave much to be explained. The mere existence of the collective unconscious does not explain, for example, why channeling takes place at all or the distinctness of the personalities involved. Nor does it account for paranormally derived information or paranormal events in the room, such as perceptions of colored lights, spontaneous healings, or unusual noises. Nor does it account for the experiences reported by some mediums of leaving their bodies. Archetypes are universal forms, not particular moving objects.

Channeled personalities themselves often speak of the importance of the collective unconscious. But they do not claim to be a mere temporary reflection of it, except in the harmless sense that we are all part of a universal spectrum of energy or consciousness. Within that spectrum, we still have separate identities. A broadly framed Jungian paradigm easily can allow for both the collective unconscious and discarnate personalities.

Is channeling merely an expression of one's higher self? It has become fashionable in some circles to claim that much, if not all, channeling merely reflects the capacity of certain individuals to get in touch with their higher selves. Higher selves are usually taken to be nonphysical repositories of wisdom and knowledge concerning our origin and development. They also have more direct access to information from other levels of reality. Aspects of our higher selves incarnate over many lives, typically forgetting where they came from, while a central core remains discarnate (or at least not physically affected by worldly events)—learning, growing, and directing traffic, as I once heard it put. To propose that all channeling is a case of accessing one's higher self makes the phenomenon seem more legitimate. This is because everyone has a higher self and everyone to some degree can learn to access that aspect of themselves. It's as if to say: "Channeling is nothing weird; it's just your higher self speaking, not some other discarnate entity." From the skeptic's point of view, of course, a higher self is just as problematic as any other nonphysical entity; both are unconfirmed and essentially superfluous. So this explanation of channeling carries weight only for those who attach some probability to the existence of a higher self in the first place.

For those who do share that perspective, several issues present themselves. In a trance state, for example, how is it possible to determine that it is one's own higher self, rather than some other entity, which has "taken over"? After all, we are given to believe that there are many spirits out there who have messages. Not all of them are beyond pretending to be whomever they need to be for a chance to reach the folks back home.

By whatever criteria we propose to address that question, the fact still remains that the higher self explanation of channeling is at best incomplete. Some channels experience their higher selves some of the time, but not all channels have this experience. And it is quite unlike the experience many channels have of leaving their bodies and/or allowing themselves to be temporarily taken over by something they perceive as being clearly outside themselves. The higher self explanation also does not account for telepathic channeling where the channel remains fully conscious and essentially reports information given by an entity perceived to have a different form, personality, and message.

Finally, the higher self explanation does not address obvious differences of personalities and transmissions. The megalomania associated with the claim that one's higher self *is* Jesus Christ, Archangel Michael, or Saint Germaine would undermine the purpose of channeling in the first place. Almost nobody would believe you!

The question of filtering. Cutting across the preceding explanations of channeling are mannerisms, personality traits, phrasing, and connections to sources of information which are more suggestive of the channel's own life than of any discarnate entity. Skeptics play up these comparisons for all they are worth. And even strong believers often wonder how much the message may reflect the channel's own unconscious tendencies.

Channeled personalities themselves sometimes complain of the "limited vibrational windows" or vocabularies of their hosts that distort what they have to say. Moreover, psychological analysis of a few channeled personalities (e.g., with word association tests) suggests that they may be the *complements* of the host personality—fitting together like broken halves of a cookie. Finally, their accents often turn out to be a blend of different dialects or else not connected to the time period or culture from which they allegedly come.

It must be conceded that sometimes the mannerisms, accents, character traits, and philosophical teachings are so reflective of what a depth analysis of the medium would show that the separate entity hypothesis loses ground. In other cases, the similarities are not clear. In those cases, if we have reasons for supposing that the channeled personality might be a separate entity (e.g., possessing technical information unknown to the medium), then a reasonable explanation for such similarities would be the existence of a filtering effect.

If anyone (discarnate or embodied!) were forced to temporarily express his thoughts and personality exclusively through another person of a radically different character and intellect, it is natural to suppose that the information and style of delivery would reflect peculiarities of the medium through which it came. Biblical translators, for example, face this problem every day. It requires us to make judgment calls. Some channels are clearer than others. However, such facts of life do not require us to dismiss the existence of the originators of the message.

Critics tend to expect that the trance channel's behavior should conform to the identity of the channeled personality. But the hypothesis of discarnate possession actually predicts just the opposite. If you asked a channeled personality who claimed to have lived in eighteenth-century France to speak in French, but the medium's own neurolinguistic programming did not include French, we would expect a faltering performance at best. Why suppose that the channeled personality either should or could instantaneously override all the host's delivery mechanisms? Channeled personalities are not omniscient or all-powerful.

So when the filtering effect appears rather strong, with whom are we speaking in the better cases of trance channeling? A separate discarnate being or some aspect of the channel's own creative unconscious? Alan Vaughn has proposed that the answer is seldom clear-cut. When Uvani was asked how he controlled Mrs. Garrett, he replied that he worked on a "split of the underconsciousness" and added that he could make this split into a figment personality not only for his ideas but also for other entities. "This seems to mean that the medium is splitting off part of the unconscious into a separate entity, which in turn is manipulated by an outside agency."[12]

This explanation opens up a number of possibilities. For one, the originating consciousness needn't be completely in the medium's body. In fact, one (living) person might telepathically channel through a personality fragment of a medium without the medium's necessarily knowing where the information is coming from. Then, too, an evolved discarnate consciousness might be capable of simultaneously projecting aspects of itself into different channels, where each aspect would undergo further blending.

It is not clear whether this hypothesis explains all forms of channeling. However, it does avoid what Whitehead termed the "fallacy of simple location." And it fits the complexities of mediumistic phenomena better than the hypotheses of simple bodily possession or of super psi.

Channeling and OBEs: a test case. At bottom, there are two closely related concerns about channeling. One is the linchpin of the skeptical agenda: Are there reasons for believing in any discarnate beings, whether channeled or not? The other is a perennial issue for psychical researchers: By what criteria, if any, can we conclude that some channeled personalities are not mere fictions of the medium's own unconscious? One way of answering the first question may help shed some light on the second.

If people can get out of their bodies either temporarily or for a longer period of time (between lives!), there is no reason in principle why they cannot get back in either their own or someone else's for a short stay. And if they can do this, there is no reason why they could not speak through another's body and hence no reason why channeling should be so terribly problematic. The skeptic's concern ought to be with the very possibility of survival in the first place, rather than with channeling per se. For if you grant the former, the latter is more plausible.

But is it? Here, distinguishing the channeled personality from the medium's own unconscious becomes paramount. To this end, psychical researchers have conducted numerous evaluations of paranormal knowledge claims and psychological analyses of mediums. However, this approach seems destined to force us in the end to make educated guesses about what is transpiring inside the mind of the medium. It's like trying to build a case on circumstantial evidence. Sometimes the evidence is strong. Sometimes it's not.

Why not, then, go for direct verification, at least as an adjunct to other paths of exploration? The widely respected healer and clairvoyant, Etel DeLoach, once told me that *she* knew that Arthur Ford, the well-known trance medium, was legitimate because she saw his principal guide when he (Ford) was in trance. Interestingly, she saw the guide (in spirit form) standing next to Ford, not in his body. (This fits Vaughn's theory of blending.) She saw him leaving and she saw him coming.

If we could obtain strongly converging and independent descriptions from three gifted clairvoyants whose presences were unknown to the medium in trance, this would constitute additional evidence for the separate entity hypothesis. It would simultaneously address the skeptic's objection that, since discarnate existence is unproven, classical channeling is a bogus activity.

Super psi proponents would have a field day with making the existence of a separate personality depend upon the perceptions of clairvoyants. How would we know, for example, that the three clairvoyants were not linked telepathically? Such a move is possible but hardly natural. Why would the clairvoyants unconsciously project very similar images to the same place at the same time if they didn't know each other or have reason to believe that other clairvoyants were in the area?

Varieties of channeling. I have not described every type or explanation of channeling. Clearly, however, the phenomenon is so varied and complex that no single explanation will ever be adequate. Following is a comprehensive summary of possible interpretations. In brief, channeling may involve:

1. intentional fabrication (simple fraud);
2. unintended, sincere fabrication (near-fraud);
3. conscious expression of paranormal information from no single identified source (straight "reading" that some psychics may describe as channeling);
4. deeply relaxed nontrance movement of information from the channel's own subconscious (perhaps provocative, but little or no paranormal content);
5. deeply relaxed nontrance movement of information from the channel's higher self (typically wiser, more open-ended, with higher paranormal content at times);
6. conscious, telepathic channeling of information from an identified source (usually a spirit guide with whom the channel conducts a silent exchange);

7. trance state, simple possession by a spirit control, usually without recall by the channel (what the average person believes channeling is supposed to be);

8. trance state, spirit guide telepathic/psychokinetic control of a partly or wholly manufactured unconscious personality or possibly one of the channel's own past-life personalities (the channel may experience this as a partial possession in which s/he moves over or moves out, observes the process, and retains some inner control over it);

9. trance state emergence of an alter personality from the medium's own unconscious possessing apparent telepathic or clairvoyant powers (super psi), with or without recall;

10. reconfiguration of channel's own energy field, allowing more or less permanent connection of channel's consciousness with angelic consciousness, making trance states unnecessary. To the channel, it may not be clear where his/her consciousness ends and the other begins.

We may never know for certain what is going on behind the scenes with channeling phenomena. What we can know, however, is whether useful information is forthcoming.

Is the message the most significant factor? Many individuals have grown weary of the concern with evidence and with how we can ever really know if spirit guides are who they say they are. Indeed, Ramtha, Emmanuel, and Mafu all have waived aside these proof questions. Instead, they invite us to reflect on the message and the teachings we are given. Is the message workable? Is it essentially consistent with other channeled works? Will it help us grow spiritually and emotionally?

If the answer to these questions is yes, then the reasoning often goes: "Who cares what or who is behind the channeling?" Much the same approach, it should be noted, is taken by many biblical scholars: "We will never know if Jesus really was the Son of God, but we can learn from his teachings and profit from one of the great 'cultural documents' of civilization." If one were a Christian, for example, it would be useful to ask whether one's religious beliefs would survive if it were discovered that Jesus was a mere mortal and then to apply the same line of reasoning to the channeled personalities, of, say, Saint Germaine and Ramtha!

So long as we are given something which can be put to the test, such as practical methods to overcome fear or guilt, there is little difference between paying Jach Pursel *cum* "Lazaris" $250 for a weekend workshop or paying a well-known psychologist with a Ph.D. who might charge even more for similar instruction in self-empowerment. The reality question ("Is Lazaris really Lazaris?") may be set aside. However, when the claims turn to straight historical information such as whether Atlantis ever existed, we should pursue the reality question in more depth.

TAKING REINCARNATION SERIOUSLY

It would be difficult to imagine a more controversial topic than reincarnation. Were reincarnation to replace the two main paradigms of Western culture in this arena—materialism versus Heaven or Hell—the theoretical and practical implications would be staggering. New visions of human potential, the meaning of life, and the unfolding of history would all accompany such a shift. Indeed, such visions already have made considerable inroads.

There are various ways to understand the significance of reincarnation. For some people, it is already built into their way of thinking. They refer as freely to their karmic issues as Baptists do to the consequences of sin. These individuals often carry a New Age label or a close variant. On the other hand, it may be just a part of their Buddhist or Hindu outlook on life with no further popular associations.

Then there are those for whom the idea of reincarnation has interesting possibilities, perhaps for psychotherapy, and who see it as worthy of further investigation. These individuals typically reject the New Age label but are comfortable participants in the larger New Paradigm dialogue. They don't view reincarnation as necessarily in or out of any coming worldview.

Next, there are those whose commitments to environmental causes, gender equality, and economic reconstruction rule out otherworldly issues, including reincarnation. They are working for a new world in which reincarnation plays no part. Some feminists, for example, view reincarnation not only as irrelevant but also as downright detrimental to the causes of social justice.

There are also scientifically minded skeptics whose concerns overlap somewhat with the last group but whose overall picture of things is considerably different. They do not see a shift in worldviews coming and, even if they did, would not make reincarnation a part of it. This is because the idea has no empirical support or scientific respectability. It thrives only where people are gullible and are looking for ways to rationalize their questionable lot in life.

Religiously oriented critics offer yet another view. Moderate to liberal Christians and Jews tend to view reincarnation as not taking evil seriously and as generally undermining the importance of moral and social reform, which are so much a part of their traditions. On the other hand, conservative to moderate Christians and Jews tend to view reincarnation as just plain wrong, because it conflicts with already established beliefs.

Reincarnation is neither a distinctively modern nor Eastern idea. The doctrine of rebirth can be found in many cultures throughout the world, dating from the dawn of history. It is found, for example, in cultures of early Africa, Australia, assorted Pacific islands, selected native American groups, and ancient Europe, in addition to India and Tibet where it has been more traditionally located. In addition to being a part of Buddhism and Hinduism, it was also taught in the early (Gnostic) Christian Church, in sects of Judaism related to Kabbalistic thought, in Taoism, in Egyptian and Persian religions, in classical Greek schools, and even in the Sufi sect of Islam.

Indeed, it was such a powerful idea in early Christianity that Constantine the Great had references to it deleted from Christian writings in A.D. 325. The Second Council of Constantinople indirectly declared it a heresy in A.D. 553 by condemning the teachings of the early church father, Origen, regarding the preexistence of the soul. However, in one form or another, it has been kept alive in the West through various nontraditional schools.

Reincarnation has had a powerful influence in the art, literature, religion, philosophy, and psychology of many cultures throughout history.[13] Even a short list of major Western thinkers attracted to the idea of reincarnation helps to dispel the notion that it is merely a "quaint" belief held by backward people seeking a way to justify their miserable lot in life. Among these thinkers are Plato, Plotinus, Origen, Kant, Fichte, Schopenhauer, Renouvier, Paracelsus, Kepler, Goethe, Fechner, Swedenborg, C.D. Broad, Tesla, Edison, and Henry Ford.

On the current scene, the millions of people who have undergone some form of paranormal experience (such as a near-death experience) often lean toward belief in some form of reincarnation, even though these experiences in themselves tell us little about the probability of rebirth. Recent polls show that as much as twenty-five percent of the American public is sympathetic to reincarnation. The figure is higher for Britain.

The fact that CSICOP views reincarnation as a continuing candidate for debunking testifies to its growing influence in educated, literate, middle-class circles. Several years ago, a Methodist minister took my Eastern

religions course mainly for the reason that—as he put it only half-jok-
ingly—he would be out of a job if he didn't have something useful to say
to his parishioners about "reincarnation and those other strange ideas."

Major shifts in social perception sooner or later make themselves felt in
the paradigm shifts of science and philosophy. When we get to the point
where reincarnation does not strike many people as terribly strange or
improbable, then the standards of evidence themselves will undergo an
adjustment to allow greater consideration of the wide range of reasons
offered for the idea. Regressions to past lives are problematic only if one
begins with the assumption that there aren't any past lives. Skeptics regret
this increased exploration when it comes to the paranormal; they fear
where it can lead. But science is not value-free. Social trends affect intellectual inquiry and intellectual inquiry affects social trends. Increased
personal exploration of the paranormal can work for you or against you,
depending upon where you stand.

MISCONCEPTIONS OF REINCARNATION

Standing in the way of a greater acceptability of reincarnation are a
variety of stock objections. I will review them in fairly rapid fashion, since
most do not require an extended response. We will analyze a few in more
detail later. My purpose is not to prove the truth of reincarnation. Proof in
such fundamental matters is not possible. However, I hope to remove a
sufficient number of objections and misconceptions and to describe the
main types of evidence, such that belief in reincarnation will appear at least
reasonable.

Do we reincarnate in lower forms of life? A popular misconception of
rebirth is that if we don't behave, we will be sent back as lower life, either
plant or animal. Many Hindus still believe this, perhaps failing to appreciate that such retrogression is contrary to the purpose of reincarnation.
Nobody is ever sent back anywhere; the choice is ours for the making.
Moreover, no purpose would be served by doing so; the kinds of lessons we
now need to address could typically not be addressed in plant or animal
form.

It is possible and, for some reincarnationists, probable that we began our
evolutionary journey not as the intelligent souls we now are but as sparks
of divinity, back with rocks, plants, and other animals, perhaps billions of
years ago. But this is not to say that we will ever return to those origins. It
is also possible that we originated in other star systems on a level of

consciousness different from plants or animals; however, incarnations as animals may have been necessary to gain some elementary lessons in surviving in a material world.

Stan Grof, a leading authority on the therapeutic implications of LSD, has observed that in certain uses of LSD, memories of animal origins (or at least special associations with the animal kingdom) can be coaxed to the surface. However, he interprets these memories as archetypes rather than as direct evidence for reincarnation, and he leaves open the possibility that they might be the result of genetic transmission.[14]

There are places in the world where the idea of regressive reincarnation is popular. But this version seems generally restricted to poorer and uneducated classes of people whose religious beliefs tend strongly toward polytheism and anthropomorphism. There are also Christians who believe the Devil will get you if you don't obey your parents. But this hardly captures mainstream Christian thinking on the topic of an afterlife.

In rare cases, one might choose to come back in the form of an animal—maybe a dog or a dolphin—where the possibility of confronting a single major lesson exists. Dogs are, for the most part, unconditionally loving. If one is having difficulty experiencing what unconditional love is like, a carefully selected dog's life might be the answer. But there must be a self-chosen agenda that fits the lesson with the animal. Normally, the opportunities are greater in a human body.

Is punishment the primary purpose of reincarnation? The short answer to this question is "No." Most modern reincarnationists would even go a step further and insist that punishment is never a purpose of reincarnation. For punishment implies a punisher, whether another person or a God. And this is not the way karma works.

In its simplest form, the law of karma states that everything one does in this life or any other has some effect, however big or small. And the interconnected nature of all life on all levels means that one is on the receiving end of many of those effects. Karma is neutral in itself and built into the very fabric of things. If its effects are undesirable, this is not because one is being punished. Rather, one is being reminded, perhaps even stimulated, to take steps to correct the imbalances which have led to those effects in the first place.

It is said that karma is inexorable. But this should never be taken as the justification for any particular course of action. One might kill or steal in this life. But this is not necessarily because the people affected by such actions themselves killed or stole from you in some earlier life. Such simplistic eye-for-an-eye views of justice are marginally legitimate. Sometimes your eye as payment for the loss of mine might be the best way to handle a situation. But according to the doctrine of reincarnation, karma works in infinitely varied and complex ways throughout the universe. Retribution is but a small part of the larger pie. One might be born blind, for example, because she saw too many horrible crimes committed in the preceding life.

The overriding purpose of reincarnation, then, is not punishment for misdeeds but personal and spiritual growth toward a state which is either at one with, or qualitatively in perfect harmony with, the Source from which all things came. Karma is the mechanism through which this comes about. In cultures which value competition, materialism, and hierarchical relationships, it's hard for this goal to take root. For if your mind-set is one of winners and losers and you currently find yourself in the losing end of a situation, it's difficult to perceive that situation as offering opportunities for personal growth.

Paradoxical as it may seem, reincarnationist thought actually nurtures the growth of win-win perspectives. We all must learn to grow together. This is not to suggest that we should underwrite a social "win-win" philosophy with a reincarnationist metaphysics. It is to suggest, however, that these ways of thinking are natural allies.

Where do all the souls come from? The population of the earth today is roughly equivalent to the total of all the people who have lived on the planet. In order to have enough souls to go around on the current scene, it does not require a degree in mathematics to conclude that, for the numbers to balance out, we must assume that each person on the planet has had only one past life here. But of course the doctrine of reincarnation holds that we have had multiple lives on this planet. It looks like a fewer number of souls are occupying a larger number of bodies. How can we explain the shortfall?

There are any number of ways to make the equation balance. One might, for example, suppose that more souls were created along the way to account for expanding populations in the future. Or simply that we began with an excess number of souls. Or possibly that there is evolutionary migration from, say, whales and dolphins to humans. The clearest explanation requires merely that we abandon the assumption that we are the only populated planet in the universe. In Vedic traditions, for instance, there are believed to be many other civilized worlds in the universe from which sentient beings may "transcarnate."[15]

Does reincarnation foster irresponsibility? Those whose main commitments are to moral and social problems often see reincarnation as a systematic escape from responsibility. When faced with hard decisions, reincarnationists are tempted to opt for the easier path, or no path at all, and to justify the decision with the appeal that "It's my karma." Or when faced with others' disease, poverty, or misfortune, it is also too easy to dismiss such circumstances as being due to karma.

Some feminists have an especially poignant version of this objection. It is that men attracted to the idea of reincarnation will use the dodge of their male karma to continue to put women down. As one feminist friend put it: "I wouldn't believe in reincarnation, even if it were true!"

Such misperceptions invite several responses. All types of philosophies can and have been used to justify irresponsible action. You can hide out in Marxism, astrology, secular humanism, or even classical theism whenever the going gets rough ("After all, God told me to do it!"). Or you can use these philosophies to foster constructive change and even courageous vulnerability in decision making. The same can be said for reincarnation.

The issue here is accepting responsibility for one's actions, not the particular "isms" through which one works. "It's my karma," when used to excuse one's attitudes or actions, is merely the cosmic version of "It's the way I was brought up," used for the same purpose. Both foster a lack of personal integrity. The last person to point a finger at reincarnationism ought to be the social scientist who views human action as a function of heredity and (mostly) environment. Freedom is stressed far more in reincarnational thinking than in scientific determinism.

As regards the feminist critique, there is nothing about the theory of reincarnation per se which fosters patriarchy and oppression of women. There is a popular tendency to equate male energy with male bodies and female energy with female bodies. However, the picture is far more complex than this.

For practical purposes every man has had lives as a woman—and suffered accordingly!—and every woman has been a man and indulged in male excesses. Men will be incomplete until they bring themselves into greater balance with their female sides. The same holds for women, in reverse. The whole process is a necessary stage for both sexes in our spiritual evolution—an opportunity for growth and integration, not a mechanism for placing blame and guilt.

Why don't we remember past lives? The great majority of people have no recall of any past life. At first this seems like a thorn in the side of the reincarnationist. But it is mitigated by several considerations. To begin, most of us do not remember much of our present lives either. Major places, trips, educational experiences, yes. But these do not constitute more than, say, five percent of the total of everything that has happened in one's life. Why should it be so strange, therefore, that we do not remember an obscure life which took place several hundred or even several thousand years ago?

More to the point, however, is the fact that a small minority of people *do* appear to remember sections of their past lives, sometimes spontaneously, sometimes under hypnosis. These memories are not just fleeting abstract ideas ("Was I a carpenter or was I a thief?"). Rather, they often take the form of full-blown images carrying significant emotional weight. At times, certain experiences appear to be literally relived. They are as clear, powerful, and potentially verifiable as a memory from this life might be.

Why don't we remember events from our past lives if reincarnation is real? The answer comes in two parts. First, most people could not handle such recall. Without an integrated personality and some preparation, the temptation would be to repress such memories or else be overwhelmed by them. Such memories do not fit our current worldview, although that situation appears to be changing. Even for metaphysically and spiritually evolved people, major recall of past lives would make getting on in this life very difficult. Who needs it?

If expanded to a level that would satisfy the skeptic, past-life recall would undermine the very purpose of reincarnation. For an important part of growth is being on one's own and applying the lessons from the past to novel situations. It is learning, for example, to love others (and oneself) naturally, not because one recalls having failed in this regard in two dozen past lives and has concluded that more loving behavior is called for. There is a point to open book tests. But most would agree that the lessons haven't been mastered until you can get on without the book.

Critics point out that too many people who believe in reincarnation claim to have been Cleopatra or Napoleon. Isn't reincarnation, therefore, just a fictional stage upon which some people choose to build up their alter-egos? Such wishful thinking undoubtedly occurs. But serious students of reincarnation do not indulge it. For example, Helen Wambach has shown that when average people are regressed to certain periods of history, they turn out to be the kinds of people, in roughly the same percentages, that historians ascribe to that period. For the period around A.D. 1400, for example, almost everyone regresses to membership in a lower class, not to princes and knights.[16]

Do reincarnationists take evil seriously? Closely related to the question of whether reincarnationism fosters irresponsibility is a deeper issue concerning evil itself. I will reserve for the last chapter a discussion of the most extreme interpretations of evil and focus for the moment upon the tragedies and suffering that are a part of the human condition.

At a common sense level, reincarnationists are just as concerned as any other group about poverty, hunger, and disease. But at an interpretive level ("What is the encounter with evil all about?"), they part company with standard Judeo-Christian thinking. For example, most Christian attempts to rationalize evil with God's power and perfection assume at the outset that the problem is one of *moral* seriousness. So we hear a lot about guilt and grace, the misuse of free will, being tested in this life, being judged worthy or unworthy for the next life, and so on.

To the reincarnationist, the encounter with evil is more a matter of the utmost *psychological* (evolutionary) seriousness. So we are likely to hear more about how well a person reacts to a tragedy, what potential lessons there were, what was learned, which blocks were overcome, and so forth. This is not to suggest that Christian theology is oblivious to the concerns of personal growth; many churches stress this element. But it typically places growth in a moral framework. Reincarnation does not.

Consider the case of a child born blind. The only halfway plausible explanation of such a situation from a Judeo-Christian perspective is that God is attempting to turn others' hearts toward the Good. (Surely we do not want to say the child is being punished for misdeeds, for there have not been any!) However, this explanation harbors a patent unfairness. Why arbitrarily pick on an innocent child to help others learn their lessons? In mainstream Judeo-Christian thought, God permitting atrocities upon the innocent often is explained as part of the mystery of His ways.

Of course, we might take the materialist approach and explain the blindness simply as a poor roll of the genetic dice. But the initial horror remains, especially for the parents. There is no reason to assume that the materialist (or humanist) takes evil either more or less seriously than the Christian *or* the reincarnationist.

Basically, the reincarnationist is charged with not taking evil seriously because she rejects this all-or-nothing stage which the theist and the materialist rely on. You either rot in the grave, go to Hell, or make it to Heaven. Reincarnationists take evil seriously but provide a different interpretation of its significance. The child born blind came in knowing that its blindness would pose a major obstacle but chose this life nonetheless for the opportunities it would afford. Nobody *does* anything to the child.

Moreover, a life of blindness is less tragic when viewed in the context of a thousand lives with sight. This does not mean the reincarnationist is less empathetic toward either the child or the parents. But it is far more likely to be a constructive empathy, helping all parties concerned through a difficult time, because it springs from a larger evolutionary perspective. It is far less likely to cloak mere pity for a child who has lost the one and only chance to see. If there is a real objection here, it should be an honest critique of the metaphysics of rebirth, not the charge that reincarnationists don't take human suffering seriously.

VARIETIES OF EVIDENCE FOR REINCARNATION

Many individuals accept or reject reincarnation based upon what the doctrine appears to mean, quite independently of arguments advanced for or against its truth. We have just reviewed some questions and misconceptions relating to how we ought to understand the idea. In this section, I want to look at the question of evidence. My approach, however, will differ from the standard reviews of past-life stories. This is partly because there are already a number of good critical summaries in print and partly because I wish to draw attention to more fundamental issues regarding what should count as evidence.

What would count for a strong empirical case? In more than thirty years of painstaking research with thousands of cases, limited verification, and cautious conclusions, psychiatrist Ian Stevenson of the University of Virginia has established a reputation as one of the most respected writers in the field of modern reincarnation research. In his classic *Twenty Cases Suggestive of Reincarnation*, and his more recent *Unlearned Language* and *Children Who Remember Past Lives*, he never claims to have proved the hypothesis of reincarnation.[17] He does show, however, that it's reasonable to believe. For his better cases cannot be explained by existing scientific models without assuming additional hypotheses even stranger than the idea of reincarnation they are supposed to replace.

Stevenson's case studies include children who spontaneously remember and identify friends, parents, and places from an immediately previous lifetime; others who speak haltingly in languages they never learned in this life; telltale physical markings in this life resembling wounds ostensibly received in an earlier life; independent verification of sudden shifts in personality indicative of an earlier life. In the thousands of cases that have come to his attention, Stevenson is often his own strongest critic. He carefully records interviews, double-checks translations, checks legal records, and weeds out a majority of cases that can best be explained along more natural lines.

Stevenson is not without his critics, especially on the topic of what counts as speaking an unlearned language.[18] Nor is he the only serious scholar involved in the paradigm war over reincarnation which is beginning to spill over into academic departments. For example, it has pitted Robert Almeder, a nationally distinguished philosopher of science, against Paul Edwards, general editor of the *Encyclopedia of Philosophy*. Almeder's recent book, *Death and Personal Survival: The Evidence for Life After Death*, contains perhaps the most formidable point-for-point defense of reincarnation against a wide range of criticisms.[19]

Both Stevenson and Almeder draw attention to the conditions that ideally must be met in order to produce the strongest arguments. These are the conditions which, if satisfied, would demonstrate the need for a major paradigm shift. As more case studies are presented, they can be judged according to how well they meet these conditions. According to Almeder, in order to provide the strongest evidence for reincarnation from a scientific standpoint, we would require a person who:

1. possesses a substantial number of verified memories not explainable by clairvoyance, telepathy, or cryptomnesia (false memory);
2. demonstrates a complicated skill (such as speaking a foreign language or playing an instrument) that could not have been learned in his or her present life;
3. possesses birthmarks corresponding to wounds received in the remembered life, and the occurrence of the wounds in the previous life is independently verified;
4. makes memory claims that are not much diminished with age and do not need to be induced under hypnotic trance;
5. recognizes the past personality as continuous with his or her present personality, rather than as a substitute for the present

personality, and who maintains the sense of personal continuity with the past personality over a long period of time;

6. has a clear and distinctive identification with the past personality that cannot be explained by the influence of parents or other people;

7. manifests predictable emotional responses to specific events and people remembered in the past life;

8. is recognized and accepted as the past person reincarnated by many extant family members or friends who have nothing to gain by the recognition and acceptance of the past personality.[20]

Each of these conditions has been met individually, and a number of cases have satisfied multiple conditions. But no one case clearly satisfies all conditions. In some instances we appear to be close, but the conjunction of all eight conditions appears to represent an ideal limit which may never be realized. For this reason, Stevenson has concluded that at this time we do not have a scientific demonstration of reincarnation.

There is a difference, however, between what can be conclusively demonstrated, on the one hand, and what is reasonable to believe on the other. So far as truth is concerned, the world (including science) turns as much upon the latter as upon the former. Almeder's work shows that, when normal standards of rationality are applied to the corpus of reincarnation research and to the critical arguments bearing upon it, reincarnation is as reasonable a view as its competitors. We have cases of verified past-life memories, of people whose past-life identification cannot be explained by parental or cultural influence, and of some individuals conversant with a foreign vocabulary they did not learn in this life.

Suppose that your son suddenly began speaking in an ancient language in his sleep and carried on as if he were a person from that culture and period of time. Suppose, furthermore, that he did this on repeated occasions. Would it be a fair test to awaken him and require that he consciously speak a fluent version of this language in order to justify the belief that he was temporarily accessing a prior existence? We have a hard enough time just remembering our dreams. Critics have a way of asking for more, while at the same time failing to explain adequately the data we do have.

What do hypnotic regressions to past lives show? The answer to this question depends upon what we are looking for. As evidence for lives in the distant past that bears directly on the truth of reincarnation, hypnotic regressions typically show very little. The only exception would be a regression to a period in which the subject spoke a language appropriate to that time and place, one which ideally is not now spoken or with which the subject has had no contact.

However, regressions do provide substantial evidence for the belief that our ordinary waking consciousness floats on a vast unconscious reservoir of information, conflicts, desires, archetypes, fears, and personality fragments. This reservoir *may* be our own subconscious, our collective unconscious, our past lives, or some combination of these that is perpetually in flux. From a scientific standpoint, much of the data from regressions can be made to fit any of these models of consciousness. (From a paranormal standpoint, there is the additional possibility that some of the past-life personalities are faked or distorted by discarnate spirits taking advantage of a subject's vulnerability.)

The practice of regressing a subject to a past life is not a new one. As far back as 1904 Albert de Rochas used "magnetic passes" to induce his clients both backward and forward in time. In the majority of cases, there is little information that can be verified or that could not be accounted for by unconscious fabrication and exposure to books on world history.

The therapist's direct or even unintentional suggestions to the client in a trance state can evoke fictional, though seemingly real, stories built around the suggestion. One critic of past-life regressions, Edwin Zolik, put the idea to a test in the following way.[21] After hypnotizing his subjects, he instructed them to remember previous existences which in a later waking state they claimed to know nothing about. He then rehypnotized the subjects and asked them to remember the sources they had used in constructing their past lives. These sources turned out to be experiences from their present lives plus stories they had been exposed to. Some could even recall pages from books they had forgotten they ever read.

This does not demonstrate the falsity of reincarnation. However, it does show that if one has actual past lives, memories of those lives can be partly or wholly confused with reconstructive fantasies from one's present life. For this reason, Stevenson prefers direct conscious recall of a recent life for purposes of verification.

Many of Stevenson's best cases are with children. Yet, as everyone knows, children often fantasize and daydream. Could this explain some of his better cases with this age group? Stevenson responds as follows:

> Psychoses of any kind are extremely rare in children; delusional false identification with another person seems even rarer. I have discussed this question with two child

psychiatrists, one specially expert in childhood schizophrenia. Neither had ever heard of a case in which a child claimed to be someone else. Children do occasionally identify briefly in play with other people or animals, and some psychotic children have identified themselves with machines. But I have not discovered a case in the literature of psychiatry of prolonged claims to another identity on the part of children outside the cases [of ostensive recall of past lives] under discussion.[22]

Do subjects regressed to past lives suffer from cryptomnesia (false memory)? Proponents of the cryptomnesia explanation fail to explain why a review under hypnosis of one's present life may fail to identify the cause of the emotional pain or dysfunction which sent the client to the hypnotherapist in the first place. If it is assumed that the trauma could only have occurred in one's present life, then how can we explain the fact that the trauma is discovered in the context of another life, especially when the patient does not believe in past lives? Even without hypnotic regression, cryptomnesia fails to account for the fact that Stevenson's children begin their recall at a very young age—as young as two years—well before they have a sufficient store of experiences or information with which to construct complex illusory memories.[23]

There are two approaches to the study of reincarnation. One method develops a few well-researched cases and then attempts to show that no theory explains them as well as reincarnation does. The other method derives significant predictions from the assumption of reincarnation and applies them to large numbers of regression cases. One approach tries to show that a theory follows from certain ideal data, the other that, all things considered, the data best fit the theory. The former approach is Stevenson's, the latter Helen Wambach's.

Wambach's extensive work with regressions described in her *Reliving Past Lives: The Evidence Under Hypnosis*, lies between the concerns of scientific proof, on the one hand, and the transformational concerns of past-life therapy, on the other. She reasons as follows. If reincarnation were real, then for every thousand regressions to a certain place or time period in history, a predictable percentage should assume male or female identities, occupy certain professions, be subject to certain diseases, grow certain crops, migrate in a certain direction, or provide information about climate conditions generally available only to historians of the period.

These percentages generally held up in Wambach's research. It would be unreasonable to suppose, for example, that 100 people out of the group accidentally know that a certain type of brown wheat is the staple crop of the period and area or that certain rivers had been flooding good farmland. Some evidence for reincarnation thereby is provided in this group approach. Individual identities or emotional reactions are largely irrelevant in this type of research. It's the convergence of numbers which counts.

In collaboration with hypnotherapist Chet Snow, Wambach also "progressed" several hundred individuals into specific times in the future— 2000, 2100, and 2300—where there again emerged fascinating convergences of opinion regarding what life is like in those periods. The results are described in Snow's book, *Mass Dreams of the Future*. In 2100, for example, there appear to be far fewer people on the planet. Of course, with any prediction we must wait and see what happens. But the convergence of accounts, whether in the past or future, suggests that Wambach's and Snow's workshops were not merely exercises in fantasy construction.

A third approach to the topic of past-life regression sets the entire question of verification aside. This approach concentrates instead upon the practical issue of whether regressions to past lives can be therapeutically beneficial. It stipulates that we should proceed *as if* some current symptoms might have a basis in a past life if no good explanations can be found from this life.

There can be no doubt that past-life *therapy*, in certain circumstances and under appropriate guidance, works. Denial in this life may be linked to traumas in earlier lives (as well as in earlier childhood); fear of the marketplace in this life to having been sold as a slave in an earlier one; inexplicable pains in this life to wounds or dismemberment in earlier lives. The list is limitless. Many people have received help by accessing issues in ostensible past lives and *dealing* with them.

Wambach's work provides good examples of this process. Another excellent introduction to the field is Roger Woolger's *Other Lives, Other Selves: A Jungian Psychotherapist Discovers Past Lives*.[24] Woolger's work is especially significant because it explains why he does not believe that archetypal psychology is capable of accounting for certain past-life phenomena. The Jungian technique of active imagination, he notes, can generate therapeutic memories. But it does not explain how one can be overcome by the pain and suffering of certain relived experiences. Nor does it account for why releasing the trauma associated with those experiences sometimes results in the sudden and dramatic disappearance of chronic physical symptoms.

But what about truth? Is pragmatism always the best response when the therapist is asked if she believes in reincarnation? Obviously, we don't have to know whether reincarnation is true in order to determine if acting on the assumption of its truth can have beneficial consequences. But doesn't the fact that it works provide us with another reason for believing that the idea may be true?

Writers who adopt the pragmatic interpretation of past-life phenomena may be tempted to fall into an either-or trap. They assume, on the one hand, that we have hard-core science with its underlying materialism and direct verification. On the other, we have the hypothesis of reincarnation, which cannot be directly verified but nevertheless works in certain circumstances.

The problem with this dichotomy is that many mainstream scientific ideas also are adopted on pragmatic grounds. Electrons revolving around their atomic nuclei, space-time warps, the punctuated evolution of species, memory storage, and dissipative social structures all involve spatial metaphors dressed up as scientific models which meet two essential conditions. They account for certain phenomena better than other models. And they lead to fruitful and interesting research programs. In other words, they work!

A physicist friend once remarked that he could write a text on electricity without assuming that electricity exists. In fact, he said, physicists don't know what electricity really is. It may well be merely a convenient construct which helps us link certain phenomena together in mathematically predictable ways.

In summary, the fact that certain theories of nature work better than others is itself a reason for believing that they are closer to the truth than their competitors—no matter how strange they are. Insofar as reincarnation lends itself to the accumulation of different types of evidence (Stevenson, Wambach, Woolger, etc.), there seems little reason to hold it to a different standard. This is not to suggest that past-life regressions have reached scientific respectability; the whole field is still in its infancy. Reincarnation is no stranger an idea than evolution was to the average person in 1870. As scientific hypotheses in their infancy, both would seem strange and lacking in theoretical and empirical support.

It might be argued that, after all, evolution has for the most part come to be accepted because it *is* true—at least in its fundamental form. Let us wait and see, however, where reincarnation research is in twenty years. Standing in the middle of some massive paradigm shifts—between world-views in transition—we are hardly in a position to close the books.

This is essentially the position of Brian Weiss, a Yale-educated psychiatrist who, in his best-selling *Many Lives, Many Masters* and more recent *Through Time into Healing*, moved from medical school materialism to a more open worldview including reincarnation and the value of past-life therapy.[25] His transformation was triggered by regressions with a deeply troubled patient during his tenure as chairman of the department of psychiatry at Mt. Sinai Hospital in Miami.

A recognized expert in psychopharmacology and substance abuse, Weiss knew the tricks the brain is capable of. Yet in addition to the past-life component of the regressions, he also found himself talking to spirit guides acting through his patient. He tried to remain open. He tried to explain it all away. In the end it was not verification of the patient's stories but rather the transformation of her personality which changed his outlook.

One of the more unusual outcomes of the whole process was that no governing medical boards sought to revoke his license (on the grounds that a psychiatrist who talks to spirits is incompetent). Nor did Mt. Sinai request his resignation. Twenty years ago, it would have gone the other way.

Weiss's evolution from the medical model is one of many paths leading thoughtful people toward some version of a reincarnational worldview. For example, Gary Zukav, author of *Dancing Wu Li Masters*, has made the journey from the New Physics to a reincarnational perspective in his more recent book, *The Seat of the Soul*, which in some respects picks up where Weiss leaves off. Such developments are not paradigm shifts in themselves. But in retrospect they will be viewed as important parts of such shifts.

Paranormal explanations of past-life phenomena. Explaining the nearly impossible (reincarnation) by appealing to the completely unproven (psychic ability) won't impress the skeptic who rejects all paranormal phenomena. Yet some parapsychologists, uncomfortable with the idea of life after death, have developed just such explanations. Let us see how.

Regarding recall of information from past lives, some researchers have argued that the best cases can be explained as retroclairvoyance plus the subconscious identification with the person whose identity is recalled.[26] Exactly where the information comes from and how the people involved come to have such narrowly focused information are left largely unaccounted for. But such a hypothesis does discount reincarnation.

This explanation is plausible for some situations. But it falls short of covering the most interesting cases. It does not account for the tremendous amount of detail provided by the subjects about their former surroundings and verified by (former) parents still living there. It does not account for the fact that because clairvoyance is a *general* ability, the subjects involved are not generally clairvoyant and seem to possess the ability only in the case of past-life recall. Nor does it explain how such an excellent job of impersonation is possible, such that even former parents could not tell the difference, nor why the clairvoyance and impersonation just happened to come together in the way they did.

Finally, the hypothesis of clairvoyance plus subconscious impersonation does not explain how it is possible for the subject to speak in another tongue which was not learned in this life. Clairvoyance is knowing *that* something is the case. A skill such as speaking another language is knowing *how* to do something. The two are quite different.

A number of past-life therapists concede that *somebody's* past life may be accessed in regression, but not necessarily the client's. For all we know, the client may unconsciously tap into an appropriate archetypal experience of the collective unconscious merely as a way of crying out for help and establishing a defense mechanism. Hidden traumas may trigger a wide range of dissociative phenomena.

Given the vague quality of the average regression, it's understandable how this interpretation should arise. And given that the goal is helping the patient—not determining the truth or falsity of reincarnation—this interpretation probably will continue to surface. For it typically does not matter who you (really) were in some past life in order to get on with constructive therapy.

There is a logical danger, however, of converting the limitations of the average methods of regression into a metaphysical dogma such as: "Since we cannot tell who is who, there may not be any former lives at all." Such a view does not take into account verification of memories in the better cases, the demonstration of unlearned skills, or the prospects of additional (paranormal) verification to be discussed shortly.

Besides, if I recall and relive my experience of being in a blazing fire as powerfully as if I were currently ablaze, why should we not conclude that it was "me" in a former life? This is what we do in our present lives when we recall having been in a fire twenty years earlier, even if there was nobody there to verify our experience. Should we also suppose that most experiences we recall from this life are really someone else's? Shouldn't we address the difficulty of determining past-life identities rather than sweep this problem under a metaphysical rug that questions the existence of past lives in the first place?

Alchemical hypnotherapy is a comparatively small development in past-life work which promises major contributions both to the goals of personal transformation and verification. It's main principles and techniques are described in David Quigley's book of the same name.[27] In addition to going after emotional blocks and information from past lives, the distinctive feature of alchemical hypnotherapy is to bring a particular skill forward— assuming it once existed—for integration into one's current store of abilities or character traits. After all, why should human potential be restricted to this lifetime?

But Quigley warns us against the quick fix. One does not return from a single session with a shopping list fully actualized. But if, for example, you really want to learn a language rapidly, appear to have been blocked in your current efforts to do so, and, moreover, knew that particular language in a past life, then alchemical techniques can predispose you toward a rapid achievement of your goal beyond what ordinary hypnosis would afford. Quigley himself learned piano this way. Success in a few such ventures naturally could be explained in a variety of ways. However, if this technique were successfully applied to thousands of individuals, it would support belief in actual reincarnation, as opposed to mere paranormal explanations of past-life recall.

The many lives of Alan Lee. This monograph of the same title by Ormond McGill and Irvin Mordes, published by the National Guild of Hypnotists, describes the most remarkable series of regressions ever recorded.[28] The regressions were performed on Alan Lee at the Maryland Psychiatric Research Center. Seven physicians and researchers oversaw the procedures and signed affidavits to that effect.

Alan Lee is a Caucasian male born May 4, 1942. He never completed schooling beyond the tenth grade and never learned languages other than English. When regressed to sixteen of his ostensible past lives, he wrote and spoke in the language appropriate to the place and time. Half the languages are no longer taught. Language skills were checked for authenticity, where possible. In deep trance, Lee also provided a translation into English.

"Between lives," his blood pressure dropped from 120/80 to 60/30, and his pulse decreased to twenty beats per minute. Normally, this would cause severe shock. Despite repetitions of this cycle, Lee experienced no harmful effects. Variations in writing style alone were strongly symptomatic of different personalities.

In his regressed state, he wrote and/or spoke with little hesitation in American English, rural English, ancient English, Italian, Cherokee (Tehalagic), Norman French, idiomatic Latin, classical Greek, Hebrew, Egyptian hieroglyphic, Egyptian demonic, Egyptian heretic, Atlantean, Lemurean, and Uranian. Of course, no independent checks on the last three languages are possible. However, linguists might find them mildly interesting. The audiotapes and written samples are a matter of record.

If the record withstands analysis, the case of Alan Lee promises to become a classic in reincarnation research. And if the idea of reincarnation continues to make both the theoretical and practical headway that this chapter suggests, Lee's ability will seem unusual but not extraordinary, the best efforts of CSICOP notwithstanding.

CHAPTER FIVE

Energy Monism I:
Consciousness and the New Physics

N ew Paradigm exploration covers vastly different areas, ranging from health and the New Physics to spirituality and the environ-ment, areas that sometimes seem to have little to do with one another. In reality, however, these explorations are often connected by underlying principles drawn from either Systems Holism or the Perennial Philosophy described in Chapter Three. Four of these principles form a package around the ideas of energy and consciousness, which we will explore over the next few chapters.

1. All things are of a common stuff, energy/consciousness, neither aspect of which is reducible to the other.
2. Matter is (compressed) energy.
3. The universal mechanism of change (via energy) is vibration; the universal principle of order (via consciousness) is intelligence.
4. The physical and the nonphysical are not separate domains but are instead continuous with one another.

What is the cosmos made of? I propose that the stuff of reality is not just energy, as some New Age and New Paradigm defenders assume. Nor is it just consciousness, as those with perennialist leanings would urge. Rather, it is the unity of both. Neither is reducible to the other, and each is an aspect of the other. I call this position Energy Monism, not out of a belief that everything is energy, but because this is the closest descriptive title for my view that is still fairly easy to remember and pronounce. (The fuller description would be a "double-aspected transcendental monism of energy-consciousness." The meaning of this mouthful will become clearer in the next few chapters. However, I shall retain the simpler "Energy Monism.")

In order to show how consciousness and energy are integrated aspects of each other, we need to lay a proper foundation. Here is how we will proceed. In this chapter, I will first explore the topic of consciousness it-self and review the strengths and weaknesses of what different philosophers and scientists have had to say about it. That way we'll know what we have to integrate with energy and what pitfalls to be aware of. We will also look at the concepts of matter and energy. In a brief overview of the New Physics, I will focus special attention on the claim that matter *is* energy. A concluding section on the vibratory dynamics of energy will help round out the picture. We'll then be in a better position to integrate elements of both energy and consciousness into the concept of energy-consciousness in the following chapter. (I refer interested readers to a recent [1994] monograph of the Institute of Noetic Sciences [copublished with the Fetzer Institute] entitled *The Scientific Exploration of Consciousness* in which Willis Harman and Christian de Quincey describe a theory of consciousness that in important respects parallels and extends the vision developed in this and other chapters.)

OLD AND NEW PARADIGMS OF CONSCIOUSNESS

To appreciate New Paradigm thinking about consciousness, a comparison with some older perspectives is useful. Not everything about traditional views is to be discarded, and newer approaches are not always the solutions they may appear to be. Some of the following distinctions and descriptions may seem a bit technical. However, they are necessary for understanding both the paradigm wars being waged around the limits of human poten-tial and the practical applications to be discussed in later chapters.

Dualism, Materialism, and Systems Holism. Consciousness is typically understood to be the seat of emotions, sensations, memories, images, thoughts, personality traits, free will, and the self. Various schools empha-size different aspects to the exclusion of others. Some believe in free will, for example, while others do not. Some subscribe to the notion of a substantial ego (or "I"), while others declare this to be an illusion. How-ever, this list fairly describes the range of standard possibilities (excluding paranormal and transcendental states) that define the territory.

But what is consciousness actually made of? Traditionally, it is assumed to be either a nonphysical "ghost in the machine" or else the very same thing as our brain (part of the "machine" itself). Either consciousness is something other than the brain, as dualism holds, or it is identical with the biochemical processes that make up our brain and nervous system, as materialism holds. Either our minds interact with our bodies and can carry on (at least for a while) without our bodies (dualism), or the only inter-action is between brains and bodies, and the death of the body *is* the end of the mind (materialism).

Why suppose, however, that the mind is other than the brain in the first place? Historically, dualism is associated with religious belief in God, the doctrine of a soul, and an afterlife. Indeed, critics often attempt to make dualism depend upon religious belief. As religious belief falls upon hard times, it's then assumed that the idea of a separate mind must also be discarded. They both get put in the basket of faith and superstition. Yet there are reasons for distinguishing consciousness from the brain that have nothing to do with religion.

These reasons revolve around the axiom that for two things to be literally one and the same they must possess identical properties. Triangles and circles, for example, are different objects because they have essentially different properties. Dualists assert that minds have different properties from bodies and are thus a different *kind* of thing. Here are some of their leading candidates for properties which differentiate consciousness from the brain.

Knowledge of one's own conscious states is private, whereas knowledge of one's brain states, in principle, is public. I have direct, noninferential knowledge of my pain. I know it "from the inside" in a way that puts me in the best position to know if I am in pain and what the pain feels like. Others may draw upon their knowledge of my general physical condition, my brain states, or what I tell them in order to infer whether I am in pain and, if so, what the pain may be like. But they are not directly in touch with it. I do not have to justify on the basis of evidence whether I am in pain; indeed, it would make no sense to do so. If asked about my pain, however, other people would have to rely upon evidence. Doctors might observe the brain state associated with my pain. But only one person can directly inspect my pain, namely, me!

Moreover, their observations of my brain states could be mistaken. My awareness that I am thinking the number ten, on the other hand, could never be mistaken. Private knowledge (from the inside) versus public knowledge (from the outside) is one way to distinguish the mental from the physical.

Also, certain states of consciousness—as directly experienced—have no location in space, whereas brain processes have specific locations and paths. For example, we don't experience a thought or a feeling of depression at any particular place in our heads or, for that matter, in our bodies. If you think you do, try picking out the place! Try pointing, for example, to where you are experiencing the thought of the Pythagorean theorem.

This thought may be correlated with certain brain states that we can point to. But when a scientist examines neural states under a microscope, he will see only the biochemical structures, not the Pythagorean theorem. We can divide neural states or even individual neurons in half, but we cannot split a thought in half! Lack of spatial location offers a second criterion of consciousness. States of consciousness are systematically invisible to an outsider and hence lack spatial location. Physical states, including energetic fluctuations, are visible.

A third differentiating characteristic is intentionality. A typical mental state such as believing, doubting, hoping, or fearing is about something. To be conscious is to be conscious *of* something. Yet ordinary physical objects or processes are not about anything. A lamp, for example, is not about my turning it on. It's just either on or off.

Here is a different example. Suppose I believe that your aunt is in the living room, but I don't know that your aunt's name is Mary Smith. I don't know that Mary Smith and your aunt are one and the same person. Therefore, I don't believe that Mary Smith is the person present. However, I do believe your aunt is there, because I see her and you have identified her as your aunt. In this situation, my brain has a certain image which I can represent in two different ways, either as your aunt or as Mary Smith (if I were told her name). The content of the image is the same (because it's the same person), although I can intend that content in either of two ways. Some philosophers and psychologists believe that intentionality is the most definitive characteristic of the mental and that, if a case is to be made for dualism, this is the place to do it.[1]

Transpersonal psychology and psychical research contain rich examples which suggest that consciousness is something broader and more complex than the average person assumes. Transcendent mystical experience where normal ego barriers dissolve is one example, apparitions or ghosts, another. If people can survive the death of their bodies, or even leave their bodies for brief periods, it would follow that consciousness is something other than the brain.

In summary, there are various characteristics of consciousness that appear not to be properties of the brain and that seem to support dualism. However, these features do not so much demonstrate the existence of a nonphysical mind as they do the limits of scientific materialism. The privacy of personal experience, for example, does not prove the mind to be spiritual; it only shows that the mind is not necessarily a physical thing. It shows that there is an aspect of consciousness that scientific materialism may not be able to explain. That aspect may reflect a halfway point between the physical and the nonphysical—something more than matter, but less than spirit.

Moreover, dualism has its own problems. How could something non-spatial (the "mind") occupy a place in a body? And how does something nonphysical interact with something that is physical? Descartes suggested that interaction takes place through the pineal gland, but never explained how. Contemporary dualists have proposed a different location in the brain which is neurally activated during acts of will. Even if this proposal were correct, it would establish only a correlation of the mental with the physical. And this correlation would not explain how interaction between the physical and the nonphysical is possible.

Provisionally, then, neither traditional dualism nor materialism appear very attractive. What about a contemporary mediating approach such as Systems Holism? This includes research from the fields of artificial intelligence, cognitive psychology, philosophy of mind, and quantum physics. The work of neuroscientist E. Roy John typifies this perspective:

> Consciousness is a process in which information about multiple individual modalities of sensation and perception is combined into a unified, multidimensional representation of the state of the system and its environment and is integrated with information about memories and the needs of the organism, generating emotional reactions and programs of behavior to adjust the organism to its environment. Consciousness is third-order information.
>
> At the same time that consciousness is the product of an integration of preconscious sensations and perceptions structured in the light of previous experience and reflecting emotional state, drive level, and behavioral plans, feedback from consciousness to those more fundamental levels must take place. Memories are activated, attention is focused, perceptions influenced, emotions aroused, drive priorities altered, and plans of behavior revised as a result of this feedback, producing a continuous reorganization of basic processes.[2]

These passages illustrate an important point about how systems thinking under a variety of labels (functionalism, neural net theory, etc.) approaches consciousness. This approach has two virtues. First of all, it tells us what consciousness is by describing what it does. Consciousness is information processing. How it does this is to be explained through detailed scientific research.

Systems theory also represents an improvement over simple dualism or materialism, because it applies to levels of pure experience or to levels of brain chemistry without getting bogged down in the metaphysical question of whether the experiences are physical or nonphysical. As we saw explained in Chapter Three, most systems thinkers adopt an expanded view of the brain/mind continuum in which the properties at one level of information processing in the brain are not reducible to properties at a lower level of complexity. Systems holists are neither dualists nor materialists in the classical sense.

However, in the final analysis, the systems approach to consciousness suffers from a serious shortcoming. It tells us that consciousness is best understood in terms of nested levels of information processing, and that the events between these levels are radically interconnected. By implication, it suggests that the differences between levels is one of degree. But it does not address the radical difference between the highest level in a material (neural) hierarchy and conscious experiences as they appear to the person "from the inside." It does not explain the gap between my felt depression, on the one hand, and perceivable neurochemical events correlated with that depression, on the other.

This is the gap described earlier in terms of privacy, nonspatiality, and intentionality. Once we cross this gap, we are no longer speaking of material properties, complex or not. In fact, the best a systems analysis of consciousness or of neural networks can achieve is a correlation between the two levels of analysis.

Roy John may be perfectly correct in his assessment of what needs to take place in the brain in order to experience oneself as a conscious, embodied person. But a description of the physical conditions of consciousness, even if complete, is not a description of conscious states themselves. It never could be, because "knowledge from the inside" is not reducible to "knowledge from the outside." If it were, there would be no difference between one's inner and outer worlds and hence no way to distinguish where one's own mind ends and another's begins.

We can build many different theories of mind around the fact that my depression is correlated with a certain pattern of neural firings. Correlations in themselves, however, do not necessitate any particular theory of mind—dualist, materialist, or systems-theoretical. All three schools are aware of the correlations and of the gap between them. But they do not successfully explain the gap or bridge it. What we require is a fresh vision that would take into account the strengths of all three theories and avoid their shortcomings.

At first glance, Danah Zohar's integration in *The Quantum Self* of quantum physics with the neurosciences and with how consciousness appears from the inside seems a promising step in this direction. One of her main concerns is with the very gap just described. How can so many seemingly independent brain states give rise to an integrated and unitary field of awareness? How do millions of neurons make for one field of perception? She proposes that consciousness is a strong type of vibrational phase coherence between neurons:

> I suggest that the electrical firing that constantly takes place across neuron boundaries whenever the brain is stimulated might be providing the energy required to jiggle molecules in the cell walls, causing them to emit photons. By way of such signals, the molecules in any given cell wall, and in thousands of nearby ones, could communicate with each other in a "dance" that begins to synchronize their...photon emissions. At a critical frequency they would all jiggle as one, going into a Bose-Einstein condensed phase. The many dancers would become one dancer, possessing one identity.
>
> At that crucial point...the movements of the synchronized molecules within neuron cell walls (or photons emitted by them) would take on quantum mechanical properties— uniformity, frictionlessness (and hence persistence in time), and unbroken wholeness. In this manner they would generate a unified field of the sort required to produce the ground state of consciousness. The phase shift, then, is the moment when "an experience" is born.[3]

Zohar's proposal has much to recommend it. It moves us toward a vibrational paradigm, accounts for various analogies between consciousness and quantum realities, and engages in some philosophical analysis of the issues.

However, it suffers from several shortcomings. Her theory does not explain the apprehension of meaning, the privacy of experience, the emergence of sensory qualities (odor, color, etc.), or the fact that certain experiences appear to have no particular location in our brains.

While Zohar describes her view as holistic, its depth chart is reductive. Although it attributes some degree of consciousness to other animals and even plants, it excludes the possibility of consciousness outside a brain implied by out-of-body experiences. For Zohar, such experiences are phase entanglements of photon emissions between cell walls—nothing more.

Zohar's theory takes us as far as we can go toward a microdescription of the interface of consciousness with physical reality. Wave particle duality may play a critical role at this interface, with waves in some way connected with the emergence of consciousness and particles connected to the construction of matter. But this interface implicitly appeals to correlations of two sides, the inner with the outer. It does not demonstrate the identity of consciousness with phased waves. Why propose that phase entanglements produce ground states of consciousness rather than that consciousness produces the corresponding phase entanglements? The gap between physical energy, on the one hand, and conscious intention, on the other, undermines her attempt to explain consciousness from the bottom up.

Consciousness is a transpersonal field that subsumes its various contents and capacities. Many traditional explanations of consciousness assume that it is just the sum total of its various capacities and contents. Once we have fully explained memory, perception, emotion, belief, self-awareness, thought, and so on, there is nothing left to explain. We would have fully captured what it means to be a conscious human being. According to this point of view, awareness itself is just a higher order integration of the preceding capacities.

From a transpersonal perspective, this account requires modification in several respects. On the one hand, awareness per se—the sense contrasted with being asleep or unconscious—is not reducible to other types or states of consciousness. To be awake and aware is *presupposed* by sensing, believing, denying, thinking, feeling, etc., whereas none of these are presupposed by awareness. To think is to be conscious, for example, but to be conscious is not necessarily to think.

Intentionality plays a key role here. For as soon as we understand that there exists not just thinking but awareness of thinking, not just feeling but awareness of feeling, etc., it becomes clear that awareness is not reducible to a collection of contents or states of awareness. In this basic sense, consciousness is a transcendental field presupposed by its objects, not simply an object or a series of states within that field.

Moreover, this field does not necessarily end at the edge of our skin. At a certain level, it may stretch at least several feet beyond this border. And it may shade off into other levels, to the collective unconscious or to mystical (egoless and contentless) states of consciousness. The brain does not so much produce consciousness as serve as a localized vehicle for its transmission. Personal consciousness, according to this view, would be one of many local perspectives within larger bands of transpersonal awareness.

Consciousness is not just a mirror of consensus reality, but is the source of manifestation of a spectrum of realities. Many people assume that only one reality exists: the three-dimensional tangible world of common sense, which is independent of consciousness. By contrast, paranormalists, transpersonalists, and spiritual adepts invite us to explore a spectrum of realities or dimensions, both higher and lower than our consensus version, and none of which is independent of consciousness. New Paradigm explorations lean heavily toward adopting a multidimensional perspective of which our three-dimensional version is but one subset.

Recent philosophical explorations have shown that consciousness is more active and creative in constructing our experiences and relating to our environment than common sense assumes.[4] However, these analyses typically don't take seriously the possibility that we may create all types of effects that in traditional thinking are assumed to be nonexistent, accidental, or unrelated to consciousness. (Some of these capacities have been described earlier, while others will be explored in later chapters.)

For example, consciousness may: alter physical events at a distance (psychokinesis); create health or disease in one's body; create independent "thought forms" that influence an area; exhibit control over the involuntary nervous system; leave and come back to a body; attract good or bad spirits; telepathically access information at a distance; "see" things others cannot see; send or receive energy from other levels in the Great Chain; and create happiness and joy through its own transformation, etc.

Summing up our discussion, then, an ideal New Paradigm of consciousness would: incorporate the strengths of dualism, materialism, and systems theory; avoid their shortcomings; connect the personal with the trans-personal; and account for the creative power of consciousness, especially as it relates to paranormal experiences. It would also explain the relationship of consciousness to energy. For just as some writers make consciousness the very stuff of reality, others insist that this stuff is energy.

THE NEW PHYSICS

The view that energy is the stuff of reality has received considerable support from the New Physics. However, neither the New Physics nor the conclusions drawn from it are as clear as many enthusiasts assume. Some writers have mistakenly concluded, for example, that consciousness is just a type of energy. Before addressing this issue, however, let me describe what I hope to accomplish in this section.

My first goal is to introduce the uninitiated reader to the main ideas of the New Physics, especially those which have drawn the attention of New Paradigm thinkers. More than just asserting conclusions, however, I will clarify and describe (or develop) the reasons that have led physicists in this direction. Secondly, I will describe some different interpretations that may be given to developments in the New Physics and then argue in favor of my own perennialist interpretation, where that seems appropriate. Finally, I will stress throughout the reasons that justify the transition from "Matter is the fundamental reality" to "Energy is the fundamental reality."

New Paradigm thinking connects with the New Physics at six critical junctures, which we will explore in separate subsections: quantum field interpretations of $E=mc^2$; the unification of the four forces in nature; the dynamic interaction of quantum phenomena; the problematic nature of underlying quantum realities (sometimes described as the "measurement problem"); wave-particle duality; and scalar electromagnetics.

The primacy of energy over matter. Einstein's equation that energy is equivalent to an object's mass times the square of the speed of light is usually interpreted to mean that mass and energy are convertible into each other. From the nineteenth-century conception of matter as fundamental and autonomous, this represented an advance in thinking. Matter and energy came to be understood as extensions or aspects of each other—as coequal realities. There are well-defined procedures for calculating the amount of energy in a given amount of mass and for converting that matter into energy (or the reverse). Nuclear reactions are the most familiar example of this process.

From a metaphysical standpoint, however, matter and energy are not coequal. Energy is the primary underlying reality and matter its derivative state. Any conversion from matter to energy is simply a conversion from one compressed state of field energy to another. This view is supported by a variety of considerations.

First is an "old physics" consideration which I dub the argument from divisibility. Atoms are divisible into their constituent primary particles: electrons, protons, and neutrons. Beneath this level of abstraction are even more primary levels of distinctive particles. Finally, there are perhaps the most fundamental units, quarks, which come with such esoteric properties as "charm" and "balance." However, quarks are purely energetic. They are not solid units but are more akin to energetic packets. When we inquire into the nature of energy, we find more energy, not material particles. As physicist David Bohm has observed, matter is "simply gravitationally trapped light."[5]

Next is a theoretical argument, a version of which was first proposed by the philosopher-mathematician Gottfreid Leibniz. If matter were not already compressed energy, then we could not conceive of converting it to energy in spontaneous radioactive decay or explain how it could be created from kinetic energy in particle collision experiments. The reason is that the classical properties of matter (strict localizability, solidity, and inertness) are logically incompatible with energy particle/fields.[6]

We can conceive how matter might be a compressed section of field energy, a part within a larger whole. But we cannot conceive how a field is a literal extension of a material substance—a whole derived from one of its parts—without giving up our conception of a classical material particle in the first place. A special version of this argument appeals to the creation of virtual particles in so-called empty space. This is possible only if empty space (sometimes called vacuum space) is an underlying field of potential energy.

A third argument for the priority of energy over matter appeals to the general theory of relativity and to quantum field theory. According to the general theory, space, gravity, and matter are continuous with each other. That is, material objects are but curvatures of the gravitational field which in turn *is* coextensive with space itself. In Einstein's words: "We may therefore regard matter as being constituted by the regions of space in which the field is extremely intense…There is no place in this new kind of physics both for the field and matter, for the field is the only reality."[7] Herman Weyl summarizes the same type of thinking in the quantum domain:

A material particle such as an electron is merely a small domain of the electrical field within which the field strength assumes enormously high values...Such an energy knot, which by no means is clearly delineated against the remaining field, propagates through empty space like a water wave against the surface of a lake.[8]

The forces of nature. Physics acknowledges four fundamental forces in nature. In no particular order of significance, they are: gravity, which operates over long distances and for practical purposes on larger objects, such as rockets and planets; electromagnetic, which similarly operates over long distances but on scales which bridge the gap between visible domains (e.g., color) and invisible domains (e.g., gamma rays, electrical charges); weak nuclear, which is the basis of radioactive beta decay and which operates over extremely short distances, no greater than the diameter of the atom; and strong nuclear, which holds the nuclei of atoms (protons and neutrons) together and which operates over comparably short distances. In theory, everything that happens in nature in some way involves these forces, although in practice we do not take them equally into account. New Paradigm thinking, especially of a perennialist bent, suggests that these are not the only forces in nature; they just happen to be the only ones currently recognized by physics. For example, there may be a fifth force (bioenergy), to be explored in Chapter Six and levels of energy well beyond that. According to this perspective, after the unification of the four forces is accomplished, there are further levels in a Great Chain of Energy to be discovered and integrated.

Quantum field theories already have enjoyed considerable success in unifying the four forces. The prototype of this approach is quantum electrodynamics, which views electric and magnetic forces as arising from the emission and absorption of exchange particles or photons. Many physicists believe that the other three forces can be explained along similar lines, with each involving its own distinctive exchange particles. Thus, gravity would be mediated by "gravitons" (considered speculative in most circles). These approaches are labeled "gauge" theories. All tend to view the exchange of particles as involving disturbances or compressions of underlying field energy.

The unification of electromagnetic and weak nuclear forces has been accomplished. And there is a strong probability that the process can be extended to include strong nuclear forces. Some speculative field theories include gravity, but here the conceptual difficulties loom large. This is because the general theory of relativity views space, matter, and gravity as aspects of a single continuous field, whereas the other three forces involve the exchange of apparently discrete particles.

Whenever the claims of continuity involving field energy conflict with claims of discontinuity involving particles (which may seem to appear from out of nothing), a New Physics paradigm guided by perennialist thinking will attempt to show how continuity wins out at a deeper level. This interpretation does not deny discontinuity per se. Rather, it suggests that we interpret discontinuities as local phenomena within a larger context of field energy.

This strategy is illustrated in three recent discoveries with a direct bearing on the project of grand unification: the principle of *spontaneously broken symmetry*, which locates deep parallels within the mathematics of the four forces sufficient to account for their origin from a common source; the principle of *supersymmetry*, which appears capable of mathematically unifying both matter and energy into a single field; and *superstring theories*, which in their most simplified form view all interactions as reflections of superposed, multidimensional, vibrating lines of force.

As physicist Paul Davies explains in *Superforce*, much is still in flux with these proposals, and they may not withstand critical scrutiny. Physicists are not in a position to predict with much accuracy what will ultimately become of superstring theories. Still, some do believe that these principles can be integrated in a grand superstring theory that unifies the four forces and completes Einstein's historic quest for the unified field.[9]

In bringing these views to the reader's attention, I am not suggesting which particular theory will prevail. Rather, I am stressing the kind of thinking that informs unified field theories, namely, the thinking which interprets discontinuity as an aspect of more fundamental underlying continuities. The universe is wholeness moving within itself.

The interconnectedness of quantum events. New Paradigm thinking is also informed by a growing acknowledgment of the dynamic interconnections of quantum phenomena. Quantum nets exist both locally, when one particle is transformed into another, and nonlocally, when a change in one particle is instantaneously correlated with a change in a distant particle, as described by Bell's theorem.

Particles do not merely collide with each other. They mutually transform each other. They have no separate identity, although some exist longer than others. They are not so much "things" as webs of relationships. "Quantum theory forces us to see the universe not as a collection of physical objects, but rather as a complicated web of relations between the various parts of a unified whole."[10] According to David Bohm: "We have reversed the usual classical notion that the independent 'elementary parts' of the world are the fundamental reality...Rather, we say that inseparable quantum interconnectedness of the whole universe is the fundamental reality."[11]

Physicists agree upon the dynamic interconnections of subatomic particles. But how should we interpret this interconnectedness? In describing a web of relations between particles represented by the standard Feynmann diagram (Figure 1), we may be tempted to isolate the "web" from the underlying field(s) which sustain(s) it.

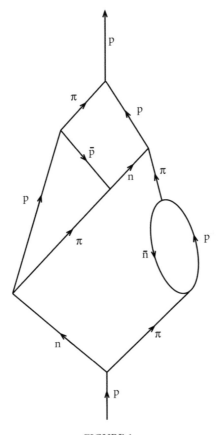

FIGURE 1.
A Network of Virtual Particle Interactions, recreated
from Kenneth Ford's *The World of Elementary Particles*

A perennialist paradigm of undivided wholeness interprets this model in two distinctive ways. First, the parts of a unified whole are seen as expressions of a single underlying field energy, sometimes described as the vacuum state. Quantum interactions are simply interactions of the field with itself. The field is continuous with itself and with the compressions (which we term particles) within it.

Moreover, particle interactions are interpreted as causal connections only from a certain level of abstraction. From the most fundamental level, they turn out to be *transformations* of the underlying field energy. In other words, the Feynmann diagrams do not so much represent certain particles producing local effects as they suggest that causes are continuous with their effects. What we call "the cause" and "the effect" are but temporary aspects of a less tangible underlying field. Physicist Walter Thirring describes this vision as follows: "The field exists always and everywhere; it can never be removed. It is the carrier of all material phenomena. It is the 'void' out of which the proton creates the pi-mesons. Being and fading of particles are merely forms of motion of the field."[12]

The measurement problem. Much has been made of how the very act of measurement itself changes the nature of what is being measured in quantum experiments. As a consequence, it has been urged that we must give up the notion of an objective reality out there awaiting our passive description. Unobserved quantum reality is essentially a probability wave which expresses the likelihood of seeing a particle in a certain place.

The problem is not that the particle may be here or there. As a particle, it isn't in any particular place at all prior to its measurement. Its determining factors—spin, size, velocity, and location—each have multiple values according to a sliding probability wave. Measurement is said to "collapse the wave packet" by virtue of ruling out all of the possible values (all of the tendencies to exist in a certain state and place) other than those describing where it is actually measured.

It's as if physical reality in itself were an amorphous field of quantum waves which, when observed, take on a determinate nature. The shift from "wavelike" to "particle-like" is one way of casting the problem of measurement. In daily life it seems that objects are what they are, independently of our measuring them. At the quantum level, however, this appears not to be the case. So how should we think of reality in order to allow for the radical transformation from indefiniteness to definiteness, that is, from probability waves to actual particles?

In *Quantum Reality* physicist Nick Herbert describes eight reactions to the measurement problem. They range from denying that there is a knowable reality behind our quantum measurements (the view of pioneer Niels Bohr), to proposing that there must be hidden variables which, when discovered, would translate quantum indeterminateness to quantum determinism (the view of Einstein), to urging that human consciousness itself creates reality in the very act of measurement. This last position is the view of Nobel Laureate Eugene Wigner and also of physicist Amit Goswami, whose recent book, *The Self-Aware Universe (how consciousness creates the material world)*, is one of the clearest expositions available. Other physicists, such as John Wheeler, have dealt with the measurement problem by postulating an exponentially increasing number of branching universes or "many worlds" where all possibilities on the initial probability wave become actualized.

For those interested in the finer points of the New Physics, each of the eight reactions Herbert describes is worth further exploration. However, it is the claim that "we create our own realities," which mainly connects the measurement problem to the larger New Paradigm dialogue. So I will probe this interpretation further. Wigner summarizes his position as follows: "It is not possible to formulate the laws of quantum mechanics in a fully consistent way without reference to consciousness...Consciousness is an ultimate reality."[13]

This passage is correct as far as it goes. At some point, reference must be made to the choice and intent of the experimenter to measure quantum reactions in one way rather than another, for the material properties of a particle will in part be determined by that choice. However, we cannot logically derive idealism ("Consciousness is the stuff of everything") from the fact that our knowledge of the properties of a particle is dependent upon our decision to measure it in a certain way.

Moreover, from the fact that the experimenter is an integral participant—not just an observer in the process—it does not follow that normal physical objects are created by consciousness. If it did, we would be hard-pressed to explain how the world existed before there were *any* sentient species, much less humans, upon it.

Wigner observes that consciousness is an ultimate reality, something presumably not reducible to states of a brain. This is also a fundamental tenet of the Perennial Philosophy. But the consciousness in perennialism is more like a universal field out of which progressively more dense and particulate levels of reality are precipitated, including matter itself. Normal physical levels of reality are sustained by or nested in higher levels of the Great Chain of Being. But this process has little to do with the intentions of individual minds.

Do we create our own realities? Surely, and in many ways. We wage war, affect our immune systems with negative emotions, and sabotage relationships with those we claim to love. We may even bend forks with the power of conscious intent alone, which is certainly one of our more interesting creations of reality. However, none of this depends upon what happens in a physics laboratory. The materialization of atomic particles from a probability wave is hardly sufficient to explain the entire spectrum of creation. Those exploring the topic of creating our own realities are advised not to seek proof for this idea in the New Physics. Quantum measurement only *illustrates* the critical role that consciousness plays in a limited domain.

What kind of interpretation does New Paradigm thought suggest for the measurement problem? Systems thinkers are more likely to restrict their discussions to measurable relationships between observable particles. This is Bohr's position and the view of most mainstream physicists who adopt his Copenhagen interpretation, as it has come to be called. Perennialists, on the other hand, are more comfortable with the idea of invisible domains of quantum potentials, virtual particles, and vacuum space (which is actually full of energy). Furthermore, these domains exist prior to the act of measurement. They are the underlying reality from which determinate particles are coaxed.

The fact that physicists cannot directly know these realms, as Bohr lamented, does not mean that they don't exist; indeed, they must exist if we are to avoid the consequence of having to suppose that quantum phenomena simply appear from out of nothing. From a perennialist perspective, all levels in the Great Chain of Being, whether determinate or indeterminate, visible or invisible, are real. Quantum measurement is simply the transduction of a process from one level to another, involving a radical transformation of that which is measured along the way.

Quantum interconnectedness within a level has considerable practical significance, since to change any aspect of a quantum measurement may produce quite different results. Metaphysically, however, it tells us only that no matter where particles appear, they are connected to other quantum processes in a seamless web that bridges the gap from experimenter to measurement and object. This perspective is consistent with perennialism, but is more likely to be stressed in Systems Holism.

Waves and particles. My vision of perennialism is partial to fields, waves, and interference patterns. It interprets particles as derivative from fields and frequencies. Yet there is a wide range of experimental evidence for making the properties of particles as fundamental as those of waves. For example, a beam of light aimed at a metal surface will cause a discharge of electrons from that surface.

If light were essentially wavelike, we could not account for the fact that differently colored light beams, which carry higher and lower energy charges, cause changes in the velocity of the escaping electrons. Hence, light must have some of the properties of particles. The electrons could not have been "bumped" except by other particle-like things, in this case photons. Here is the corpuscular vision, according to Herbert:

> If we look at the world with fine probes, it breaks up into little dots; you don't see the whole anymore, but an array of what printers call "process dots." And that's the way the universe is too. You may look closer and closer, trying to get down to the ultimate substance, but it breaks up into little dots—quantum jumps. The world is made of particles.[14]

The perennialist vision stands in marked contrast. The ultimate substance of which Herbert writes, for example, is field energy itself, not discrete particles. *This interpretation does not deny any experimental evidence for particles or for wave-particle duality.* I am proposing a thesis about what particles are like, not about whether they exist. We obviously live in a sea of particle interactions. However, all arguments for the existence of particles or particle-like properties are consistent with understanding those particles to be compressions of field energy or the function of complex interference patterns. That we can measure something apparently as discrete as a quantum of energy—a "process dot," conforming to Planck's constant—is simply to say that it is the smallest localizable expression of a field. It should not surprise us that the world appears to divide up into discrete entities, since it is of the very nature of measurement to make quantitative differentiations. As Heisenberg reminds us, we measure nature only insofar as it conforms to our method of questioning.

The distinction among several particles in a given region is at bottom the distinction among several visible places within underlying fields where the action is. Radiation energy is put out in the form of apparently discontinuous quanta because waves in any medium reflect distinct oscillation and interference patterns. Even electrons, wrote Schroedinger, "have no real existence" because they essentially "are standing waves." We may even conceptualize seemingly discrete particles as three-dimensional slices of higher order geometrical forms that govern the whirling energy patterns we describe as "spin" and "angular momentum." This line of thinking has been developed in different ways by John Wheeler, Fred Wolf, Walter Russell, and, more recently, by Kostas Lambrakis.[15]

In summary, the perennialist vision of wholeness as applied to physics proceeds from the fact that it is possible to derive discontinuous functions from a continuum, but it is impossible to construct a continuum from a series of discontinuities. We can derive particles from interacting waves or compressed energy, but not waves from particles. We can divide a line into segments, but the sum total of those segments never constitutes a continuum.

Scalar electromagnetics. The origins of scalar electromagnetics go back to James Clerk-Maxwell's synthesis of electricity and magnetism and to subsequent discoveries by Nikola Tesla and E.T. Whittaker around the turn of the century. Many physicists since then have unwittingly added pieces to an emerging picture, among them Richard Feynmann, Brian Josephson, and David Bohm. Only in the last decade or so, however, have the pieces come together in a full-blown coherent theoretical framework that is consistent with relevant experimental data, complete with the necessary mathematical formalism and workable in heretofore unimaginable ways.

Still, you won't find this theory in mainstream textbooks. It represents a reconceptualization of the foundations of physics, and scientific revolutions are never openly embraced by defenders of the status quo. The difficulty is compounded by the fact that scalar electromagnetics may have profound implications for national security. Demonstrations of its workability may fall under the umbrella of classified research. What follows is only the barest summary, but it should stimulate interest in a type of physics we'll be hearing a great deal more about in the twenty-first century.

According to Thomas Bearden, a pioneer in its development, the key is a proper understanding of what happens when electromagnetic (EM) force fields fight themselves to a mutual cancellation, which forms a vector of zero. If this is done in a nonlinear medium (modulator), the summing and multiplying EM vector forces can be locked together and remain as a potential EM system infolded within the EM zero vector. We now have, in effect, a gravitational system. By varying the frequencies in phase of these infolded EM components, we vary the local energy density of the vacuum.

We can create a powerful gravitational wave with EM forces that are approximately 1042 times as strong as the normal weak G-force.

Classical EM theory tells us that when electromagnetic fields cancel each other to form a zero vector, there is no electromagnetism left. However, this overlooks the space-time-vacuum stress of the summed forces and the resulting gravitational implications. Quantum mechanics paints a different picture. Electromagnetic forces are not the primary causes of movement or electrical activity, but rather the effects of underlying potentials. When there is no measured EM force in a zero vector, the potentials still exist. More importantly, when these "forceless potentials" interfere—even at a distance—real EM effects can be demonstrated. This is termed the Aharonov-Bohm Effect, which violates ordinary mechanics and EM theory but has been demonstrated to the satisfaction of most physicists.

This suggests that EM and gravitational forces are exfolded and infolded aspects of each other. We can create gravity waves through the appropriate phase conjugation of EM forces, and electromagnetic energy is an expression of the underlying stresses of electrogravitational potentials of the vacuum. Of course, we normally create electricity through the phasing of magnetic rotors. But according to Bearden, these generators are actually just squeezing the excess stress from an underlying sea of vacuum state potentials and giving it a linear direction through various circuits.

The force of repulsion between two electrons in free space is roughly 1042 times stronger than the gravitational force of their attraction. By "strangling" these forces of repulsion—i.e., by canceling them out through appropriate (though variable) phase modulation—we literally create a field of gravitational potential. However, to unlock the potential of this field, it must interact with another such field. Actual gravitational effects are thus two steps removed from the point of origination.

The theoretical (and practical) results of this transduction are nothing short of astounding. According to the general theory of relativity, space-time, mass, and gravity are continuous; however, scalar physics shows us that we can bend local space-time itself—something Einstein said never could be done! In fact, we can do it in a laboratory; we don't need objects of great mass and distance (like neutron stars) to demonstrate the phenomenon. But this is only the beginning:

> By locking opposing EM waves together, we may easily construct purely scalar electrogravitational waves and beams. In such cases, amazing new phenomena are

encountered: (1) One can increase or decrease the mass and inertia of an object; (2) One can produce a unilateral force in and on each and every nucleon in a body, thus accomplishing the long-sought "anti-gravity"; (3) A unilateral force drive—a "space drive"—can be constructed; (4) transmutation of elements becomes fairly simply done, with minuscule energy; (5) effects at a distance—such as cold explosions or hot explosions—can be accomplished; (6) negative energy and negative time effects can be demonstrated and utilized; (7) Newton's third law can be manipulated and violated at will; (8) Negative entropy effects can be created and utilized; and (9) Direct energy extraction from the vacuum can be accomplished, [thus making possible so-called "free energy" machines]...We have a new physics in the offing—one that is eminently practical and easily engineered by any modern electromagnetics laboratory.[16]

Those who follow developments in the New Physics are typically interested in its implications for other fields and for the larger New Paradigm dialogue. But direct practical applications are seldom spelled out in the detail that Bearden spells out the implications of his vision. Given the applications just listed, we are but a few steps away from equally staggering possibilities for engineering positive solutions for disease, pollution, and the destructive potential of earthquakes!

In some cases the relevant technology for these challenges may already exist. Whether it reaches the light of day, however, may depend upon factors not directly related to its merit. A major scientific revolution that promises to fuel a transition between worldviews is not altogether a neutral political process. Anyone controlling such a powerful technology from behind the scenes would be unlikely to share it willingly for the benefit of humankind.

FROM MECHANISTIC SCIENCE TO VIBRATORY SCIENCE

Discussions of the New Physics in particular and the search for a more adequate worldview in general nearly always point to the inadequacies of mechanistic science. Nowhere is this more evident than with the emergence of vibration both as a powerful root metaphor and as a concrete model of explanation. Matter is energy and energy vibrates! Some preliminary spade work will help to clarify what is involved in this transition. We need to do more than just condemn mechanistic science and wrap ourselves in good vibrations—as the popular New Age mind-set prescribes.

There are eight elements involved in mechanistic explanation. Some elements assume a greater priority depending upon the context. Mechanistic explanation in general assumes that whatever exists must be at a specific place over a precise period of time. To be is to be localizable.

The elements are as follows. First, there must be a physical object or collection of such objects. Second, the objects must occupy places or trajectories in space. Third, if moving, they must exhibit acceleration, deceleration, or uniform speed. Fourth, the objects have a certain mass. Fifth, they also possess size and shape (tiny spheres if they are classical atoms). Sixth, they exhibit spatial patterning with respect to each other. Seventh, movement toward or away from other objects is understood to be a function of the *forces* (mass times acceleration) between them or operating on them from a larger framework.

Finally, mechanistic explanations are linear. This means that objects move only *one way* through time; there are no feedback loops to change critical values, and the future state of the system is completely predictable from a knowledge of the current state, plus the laws which govern that state. In short, a mechanistic explanation is one which explains the current physical state of a system by reference to the physical forces and objects which caused it to be the way it is.

Mechanistic explanation works perfectly well for many objects. It enables us to pinpoint the destinations of rockets or to predict the location of a planet fifty years from now. It has helped make substantial inroads to most every scientific arena, from plate tectonics to thermodynamics (via the kinetic theory of heat), the double helix, cerebral lateralization, and the early Bohr-Rutherford model of the atom.

But mechanistic science represents an ideal of explanation which has achieved complete success in only a few areas. Even in Newton's time, the wave theory of light posed a small dark cloud on the horizon of mechanical explanation. Quantum mechanics and the general theory of relativity are usually interpreted as having "sealed the lid" not on Newtonian mechanics per se but on the Newtonian ideal of providing mechanistic explanations for all of nature. It has become clear that there are many processes in the natural world (not to mention the social domain) which do not fit the ideal of mechanistic explanation.

What has survived, however, is the spirit of mechanistic science and the ideal of localizability, both of which have proven fruitful in various research programs. Models of disease communication ("germ travel"), genetic engineering ("Remove a gene here, put it there"), subatomic structures ("Quarks are the basic 'building blocks' of matter"), memory retention ("For each stored piece of information, there must be an 'engram'"), and even crime prevention ("Put more police officers in high crime areas") contain localizationist assumptions, even where mechanistic vocabulary has disappeared.

What would a vibratory paradigm look like? How might we describe its key features? Here are some proposals:

1. Instead of material things, we would think in terms of fields of compressed energy and quantum potentials. This is not to deny that physical objects exist; it is to reinterpret their nature.
2. Instead of things moving through empty space, we would think in terms of vibrations or waves extended over a field.
3. For speed, we would substitute frequency in cycles per second.
4. For mass, we would substitute vibratory density (which is a function of frequency, amplitude, and interfering wave forms).
5. Size and shape would be understood as reflecting critical shifts in vibratory density within a field ("Mass ends here and curves around there").
6. Force, according to this way of thinking, is reflected in vibratory density with special attention paid to changes in amplitude. Normally, increased amplitude—the distance from the top to the bottom of the wave cycle—connotes increased power. Superposition results when the amplitude of two intersecting and identically matched waves is doubled.
7. Instead of changes in phenomena being caused by changes in the spatial configuration of discrete underlying things, interactions between things would reflect deeper underlying resonance, harmony, or interference patterns.
8. Finally, instead of linear push-pull cause and effect relationships, causality itself would be interpreted as reflecting the transformations of underlying fields. Scalar electromagnetics, for example, connects objects which otherwise appear distinct and unrelated.

The above proposals are speculative, of course, and for practical purposes the language of mechanistic science may remain with us. After all, it's easier to think of a moving billiard ball as a solid, independent object, rather than as compressed wave forms. But a trend toward vibratory modeling nonetheless seems very much in evidence.

Such modeling is not new in Western thought. Pythagoras, Philon of Alexandria, Hippocrates, Kepler, and even Francis Bacon (the "Father of Empiricism"), not to mention many nineteenth- and twentieth-century thinkers, have all found this way of thinking attractive. But for a variety of reasons it never reached the preeminence that mechanistic thinking did in furthering the goals of prediction and control. With some solid accomplishments behind it (the physics of sound and light, magnetic resonance imaging, holography, etc.), vibrational science stands where mechanistic science stood in, say, 1800.

As the case grows, frequency modeling may be applied to those areas which already have yielded only partially mechanistic explanations. In such cases, already existing laws would be theoretically reinterpreted as describing limited subsets within a larger master paradigm—in other words, what Einstein did with Newton. For example, the double helix may turn out to reflect a deeper harmonic structuring of field energy.

Only time can tell which way the scales will tip. But under a variety of labels, vibratory modeling is enjoying increased interest and investigation. Every object, no matter how small or large, every process or event, and every field or discernible type of energy, vibrates and carries distinctive vibratory signatures. To be more precise, things don't vibrate. They *are* expressions of vibratory denseness. In the next century, this may well seem a natural way of thinking. Mechanistic science then will be seen as a phase in the evolution of consciousness.

The technical vocabulary for a vibratory paradigm has been in place for some time. For example, when the frequency patterns from one system approximate those from another system—"phase locking" is the technical phrase—then resonance is achieved. All things have a fundamental *resonance* vibration. When external energies begin to duplicate this vibration, this vibration increases in intensity. If the external energy is sufficiently powerful, the physical structure of a thing may be damaged or destroyed, as in the case of a singer who cracks a crystal glass. When the patterns are noncomplementary, that is, when they distort the existing configuration, *dissonance* results.

When resonance is induced, that is, when the approximate or implicit rhythm of one system is brought into exact complementarity with an original pulsating system, *entrainment* is the result. When two or more systems interact in such a way as to produce a third system, an *interference* pattern is established. This is common, for example, in the production of overtones in music or in the production of holograms in optics. But as we saw with scalar electromagnetics, appropriately phased interference patterns can result in real gravitational effects, too.

APPLICATIONS FROM THE FIELD

The vocabulary of vibrations, resonance, harmony and the like has many applications in the physics of sound. However, as K.C. Cole points out in *Sympathetic Vibrations*, such ideas also have progressively agreed-upon applications in other contexts, including the sudden click of understanding (phase-locking between a mind and some idea) or in feelings between two people which appear in perfect resonance, each being a virtual extension of the other.[17]

Vibrational modeling is based partly on empirical fact and partly upon metaphors with potential applications in contexts outside science. However, science still provides the most abundant supply of ready examples. For instance, perceiving a yellow object involves the dye molecules in our eyes vibrating in the neighborhood of 100,000 times per second. Hearing involves frequency reception ranging from 18–22,000 cycles per second. At room temperature, atoms vibrate at 10^{14} times per second, whereas their nuclei vibrate at 10^{22} cycles per second. Our entire planet is immersed in a sea of gravitational and magnetic oscillations, among them extra low frequency waves (ELFs), some of which vibrate in the same range as alpha waves in the brain, 8–12 times per second.

George Leonard has observed that no culture, from the most primitive to the most complex, is without music and dance.[18] We find music in New Guinea, where tribal chieftains produce complex overtones from a jew's harp made of a living beetle. We find it in monasteries and ashrams in the chanting of Gregorian melodies and the sacred mantra OM. We find it in the piano concertos of Mozart, who viewed himself as a translator of divine activity into a universally intelligible medium. Pythagoras proposed that a rock is nothing more than frozen music.

None of the above would be possible if we were not of the very essence of music, i.e., rhythmic vibrations of energy. We make and respond to music because we are music. Donald Hicks, a chemist at Georgia State University, has even plotted the internal vibrational "swings" of standard molecules, such as water, methane, and carbon dioxide and correlated these swings with their macro counterparts in popular dancing. "In our forms of dance, we are subconsciously trying to initiate the ceaseless vibrations and rotations of the unseen molecules occurring throughout the universe."[19]

Vibrating energy itself does not account for our world. It is the harmonic interactions, the locking of phases, and complex interference patterns which give rise to different levels of reality and to experiences within those levels. (Consciousness will provide other important ingredients, such as intelligible forms around which energy takes shape.) Each vibratory phase is capable of interacting with others of a particular complexity and frequency but not with others outside that range, a fact powerfully illustrated in the chemical theory of bonding. Joseph Needham captures the classical Chinese vision of this interplay at a cosmic level:

> Ch'i condensed in palpable matter was not particulate in any important sense, but individual objects acted and reacted with all other objects in the world…in a wave-like or vibratory manner dependent, in the last resort, on the rhythmic alternation at all levels of the two fundamental forces, the Yin and the Yang. Individual objects thus had their intrinsic rhythms. And these were integrated…into the general pattern of the harmony of the world.[20]

This cosmic vision can be translated into a seemingly inexhaustible number of concrete examples. Two heart muscle cells pulsating to different rhythms will automatically start beating simultaneously when moved into close proximity to each other, thus illustrating the phenomenon of entrainment. Lyall Watson has noted that animal behavior often moves in synchro-similarity to the phases of the moon, the alternations of light and dark, and the fluctuations of geomagnetic fields.[21]

William Condon has demonstrated that in simple forms of human communication, the listener's body will move in a predictable pattern simultaneously with the speaker's utterance.[22] In microanalyses of films, he showed that the reaction we normally believe to be caused by the reception of the words actually begins before the sounds reach the listener's ears. Speech is an aspect of the dance, not the cause of it!

Finally, many writers, such as philosopher Henri Bergson and neuro-scientist Karl Pribram, have argued that our perception of solid objects is made possible by phase-locking structures of our brains. Change the rate of vibration inside and we change our perception of the world outside. As psychologist Ralph Metzner notes: "We live in a consensual reality and the consensus is a function of perceptual resonance."[23]

More than half a century ago, Jagadis Bose demonstrated that plant growth proceeds in rhythmic pulses. Each pulse exhibits a rapid uplift and then a slower partial recoil of about one quarter of the distance gained.[24] Numerous other studies have shown that assorted harmonic sound waves can positively or negatively affect the growth, flowering, fruiting, and seed yields of plants. Mary Measures and Pearl Weinberger discovered, for example, that wheat yields increased the most when stimulated by frequencies of 5,000 Hz.[25] Marigolds, petunias, and daisies all showed accelerated growth when exposed to nearby rhythmic footwork of Indian dancers performing the ancient Bharata-Natyam without musical accompaniment.

The science of radionics is built upon the fact that living things or parts of living things emit distinctive vibratory signatures.

> Each individual, organism, or material radiates and absorbs energy via a unique wave field which exhibits certain geometrical, frequency, and radiation-type characteristics. This is an extended force field that exists around all forms of matter whether animate or inanimate…The more complex the material, the more complex the wave form. Living things, like humans, emit a complex wave spectrum of which parts are associated with the various organs and systems of the body.[26]

In principle, this makes it possible to diagnose a particular type of organic disease by reference to its distinctive wave configuration as well as its biochemical profile. And there are texts with suggested healing frequencies for just about every organ or disease one could imagine. Modern day magnetic resonance imaging (MRI) generates an enhanced interference pattern from the magnetic field and molecular energy pattern of the area under examination.

Treatment of kidney stones with "sonic blasts" is another contemporary application of the vibrational paradigm that informs radionics and its variant, psychotronics. In fact, there is today a veritable explosion of instruments and procedures for treating diseases with various frequencies.[27] Many show clinical promise, although they lack experimental confirmation.

The atomic and molecular structure of objects typically exhibits distinctive wave patterns. This is evident, for example, in spectroscopic analyses of primary elements and chemical compounds. It is also evidenced in cymatics, the study of the relations of matter and waveforms. Here, distinctive wave patterns in metals and other elements are brought to the surface in a medium of liquid or powder by subjecting them to assorted frequencies. As the pitch is changed and pulsed through the elements, waveforms in the liquid or powder also change.[28]

Johannes Kepler believed that the celestial spheres exhibit a deep structural harmony. A number of his calculations, for example, have even been converted into twentieth century musical analogs.[29] Joachim-Ernst Berendt, author of *The World is Sound*, has more recently explored a version of this theme by connecting the planets (and Sun and Moon) with distinctive sounds, colors, and even psychological states.

Following Hans Kayser and Guy Murchie, Berendt sees the octave as a primordial symbol of unity throughout nature.

> The earth has a rotation period of…23 hr, 56 min, and 4 seconds, totaling 86,164 seconds. If one takes the reciprocal value, that is, divides 1 by this number, a frequency of 0.00001160577 (an inaudible G) is obtained. Though this G is below the hearing range (which starts at about 16 Hz), transposing it by 24 octaves will create an audible G.[30]

Were we to transpose it up by 65 octaves, we would arrive at a wavelength of 700.16 nanometers, which on the color spectrum is orange-red. He then suggests that meditating on the Earth's primordial G tone and visualizing orange-red in turn can bring up issues relating to the need to ground oneself. Similar transpositions are possible with all of the planets. The primary tone of Saturn, for example, is D and its primary color is blue. In this and many other ways, vibratory modeling can play an important role in reconnecting fragmented patterns of thought *and* experience. Vibrations can heal and make whole, in both fact and theory.

CHAPTER SIX

Energy Monism II: Beyond Dualism and Materialism

In the preceding chapter we explored several features of consciousness, together with three philosophies of mind. Next, we looked at energy and its role in the New Physics and in vibratory modeling. It is time now to pay the piper and integrate them in a fashion that moves beyond the traditional dualism of matter and mind. This will provide a way to integrate the general concerns of science (energy) and spirituality (consciousness). It will also help us to understand the paradoxical aspects of several test cases: bioenergy, Kirlian photography, and out-of-body experiences.

First, a word about terminology. Materialism stipulates that all things are some form of mass-energy. As such, it's one type of qualitative monism. It stipulates that everything is composed of a single kind of stuff: matter. Idealism, which stipulates that all things are some form of consciousness, is another type of qualitative monism. Both are opposed to dualism, which stipulates that reality contains two fundamentally different types of things: mind and body, or more generally, the physical and the nonphysical.

A third type of qualitative unity has been claimed by a school known as neutral monism. On this view reality is neither material nor spiritual. It simply is what it is, primitive and indefinable being. Bertrand Russell's "neutral particulars" (from which he attempted to construct both mind and matter), the Void of Buddhism, Nirguna Brahman, the Tao, and Spinoza's Infinite Substance all reflect the desire to get beyond any kind of fundamental dualism.

The highest level of reality in the Perennial Philosophy is neither mental nor material, neither subject nor object. It is a ground that transcends all such categories. Physicist David Bohm's description of the "super-implicate order" as a transcendental ground from which the distinctions of the "explicate" order arise also suggests a neutral monism.[1]

My theory of Energy Monism rejects dualism and finds both idealism and materialism equally one-sided. It views energy and consciousness as dual aspects of a neutral ground which, in its primordial nature (i.e., prior to all creation), transcends all such aspects. However, insofar as we live in a world of form, and we find communication both possible and desirable, we may take the stuff of reality to be the unity of energy-consciousness. Explaining and then illustrating how they are unified is the purpose of this chapter.

THE ENERGY-CONSCIOUSNESS UNDERLYING ALL THINGS

Integrating energy and consciousness is a difficult task, one undermined by the tendency to fall back into dualistic ways of thinking. Still, the potential rewards justify the undertaking. Following are nine considerations that address this task.

Neither consciousness nor energy is reducible to the other, although each is reflected in the other. Thus, I am not proposing that energy is (really) just consciousness or that consciousness is (really) just energy. Neither's full nature is captured by assuming that it is a subset of the other.

"Energy" and "consciousness" are the two most frequently encountered terms in New Paradigm discussions of the nature of reality. Thus we hear of the play of consciousness, the power of consciousness, and transcendental states of consciousness, along with energy fields, systems of energy, and healing energy, to mention a few. In scientific contexts, this distinction sometimes is drawn in terms of energy and *information* (rather than consciousness). In the view I am proposing, consciousness is the seat of meaningful or intelligent patterns of information which are expressed energetically over space and time. Consciousness is thus a broader category not reducible to information or to energy.

Many commentators use "energy" and "consciousness" interchangeably in certain contexts. Strictly speaking, however, they are not equivalent terms. To observe brain-wave energy on a monitor, for example, is not to observe a person's thoughts or feelings. If it were, we would not have to ask that person what she's thinking. The most that high-amplitude alpha waves might tell us in this regard is that the subject is probably not thinking at all.

Energy and consciousness are interconnected aspects of a Great Chain of Being. However, either may assume a primary or a peripheral significance depending on the context of discussion or the level of perception. For example, in the context of plant physiology it is appropriate to speak just in terms of energy, because the properties by which we identify changes in plant metabolism are more abundant.

This does not mean that plants or minerals are without consciousness. It does mean that, from our perspective of ordinary waking consciousness, the properties that would suggest attributing consciousness to them are less abundant. An evolved and enlightened consciousness, however, permits mystics and clairvoyants to experience plants and even rocks as conscious (not, of course, as humans are). Turning our perspective in the other direction up the Great Chain away from ordinary experience, we usually think in terms of transcendental states of consciousness, not transcendental states of energy.

Our tendency to reserve energy for the lower levels of the spectrum, to think of rocks as compressed energy not possessing any consciousness, is a function of ordinary awareness. The same sages who from an enlightened perspective identify with consciousness at the lower end also see energy at the upper levels, because they interpret energy and consciousness as aspects of each other. Swami Muktananda, for example, describes consciousness as shakti and shakti as energy.[2] This complementary sliding scale vision of matters is represented in the following figure.

Consciousness is the "inside" of energy. Energy is the "outside" of consciousness. Inside and outside are reciprocal aspects.

Reality *is* energy-consciousness.

Minerals are conscious but, from *our* perspective, appear more as solid and inert forms of energy.

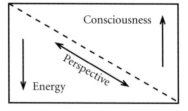

Transcendent states have energetic aspects but, from *our* perspective, appear more as states of consciousness.

Perspective determines whether a state appears to be more physical or more conscious as we move up or down the diagonal. At midpoint, the "natural" metaphysics would be Dualism.

FIGURE 1.

In the ancient school of Samkhya Yoga, the two terms are distinguished yet connected. For example, the term *chitishakti* is translated as consciousness and the term *pranashakti* is translated as energy. This suggests a double-aspect theory. Shakti is the basic stuff of the Great Chain and it expresses itself consciously, in one aspect, and energetically, in another. This is how I think we should begin to think about the mind-body connection.

I began by proposing that energy-consciousness is the stuff of reality, but now seem to be saying that Shakti is the basic stuff. However, Shakti is not some third thing behind energy-consciousness. Our tendency to project an even more fundamental stuff behind the scenes is in part a reflection of our lack of direct experience of the higher levels of the Great Chain, where there are phenomena quite unlike those of ordinary waking consciousness. A different level is not necessarily a different kind of stuff.

We cannot push the reality question beyond energy-consciousness. For the Ultimate Ground of our being, the highest level of the Great Chain, the Source of all things seen and unseen, is itself beyond form, distinction, description, and name. It is what it is. Beyond energy-consciousness there is literally no thing to say, no words in any language, that point to anything in particular. Insofar as we live in duality, there is energy-consciousness. Insofar as we transcend duality, there is an absolute ground of no*thing*ness.

Energy and consciousness share each other's properties. This is another reason to unify them. For example, consciousness expresses itself energetically through intentional movement, and energy may express itself consciously through intelligent patterns of self-organization in biological systems. Moreover, both energy and consciousness satisfy the same textbook definition as the "power to produce change." Finally, both are most adequately understood as underlying fields which may express themselves in particulate form as thoughts, sensations, etc., in the case of consciousness, or as electrons and photons in the case of quantum field theory.

"Energy" and "consciousness" are comparatively neutral terms, given the many areas where they can be applied. They are more flexible across traditional boundaries. Thus, there are many references to both physical and nonphysical energies in New Paradigm discussions. The term is not just reserved for one domain or the other. Similarly, we may speak of the enlightened consciousness of an adept or of the more limited consciousness of a dog.

The comparisons of spirit and matter, or mind and body, at least as they are normally interpreted, do not lend themselves to such cross-category flexibility. The limitless ways that different frequencies, densities, and interference patterns manifest also permit us to draw distinctions of degree up and down the Great Chain. The distinction between mind and body, which tends to be all or nothing, does not. Energy-consciousness is not dualism under a new label.

Perennialism favors consciousness, while Systems Holism favors energy.
When all is said and done, proponents of the more spiritually based Perennial Wisdom give the edge to consciousness. The Great Chain of Being becomes the Great Chain of Consciousness. They are happy to see consciousness projected down to the lower levels but do not want to see energy projected upward from ordinary physical contexts. However, nothing in my proposal suggests that we do this. It does not imply, for example, that the soul is merely electromagnetic energy. That is simply to fall back into an old inverted dualistic way of thinking.

On the other hand, systems-oriented models typically give the edge to energy. Thus, it is urged: "If we must have a Great Chain of Being, let's at least make it the Great Chain of Energy." This has the ring of being more scientific, but projects a lack of understanding that inverts the priorities, mistaking the whole for one of its parts. Energy in the context of physics is not the proper place to begin. Physical energy is a slice of a much larger spectrum. The "energy" in energy-consciousness is no more physical than it is nonphysical.

That this philosophical divergence even can take root is a good reason for adopting the unity of energy-consciousness. In proper holistic fashion, it both allows for yet transcends the "spirit" camps and the (physical) "energy" camps. The drawback of each interpretation becomes the strength of the other. To make consciousness primordial captures our inward sense of subjectivity, our sense of what it is to be a feeling, thinking being. On the other hand, to make energy the prime category captures more of our sense of objectivity as, for example, when we measure electrical fields or see auras out in the world.

I propose, therefore, that consciousness is the inner subjective aspect of energy and that energy, whether in physical forms or in forms not currently recognized by physics, is the outward objective aspect of consciousness. Subjectivity and objectivity are logical complements. To label one thing subjective implies a reference to other things that are objective. Any attempt to reduce one category to the other would be logically inconsistent. It follows that if subjectivity and objectivity are logically complementary, and consciousness and energy are their respective reflections, then consciousness and energy are complementary aspects of each other.

As noted in the earlier diagram, it's useful to think of consciousness as the "inside" of energy and energy as the "outside" of consciousness. But inside and outside are correlative aspects of the same thing, not two names for two distinct types of things. As Alan Watts would remind us, you can't have one without the other.[3] The same is true, I think, of energy and consciousness. The ground of our being expresses itself both energetically and consciously in greater and lesser complementary proportions relative to one's individual perspective.

This proposal is more than a metaphor. It's a primordial fact of the cosmos. Everywhere we look for consciousness outside of ourselves, from the lowest to the highest level of creation, we shall always come up short. The best we can hope for is energetic (or even material) expressions of consciousness. We wouldn't be any closer to finding consciousness in a spirit world. For even as spirits we would still perceive each other as energetic forms. We would not be any closer to perceiving others' thoughts or feelings.

The privacy of experience (knowledge from the inside) is not reducible to visible manifestations of energy (knowledge from the outside). A clairvoyant may see my anger reflected in my aura. And for convenience, he may speak of "seeing my anger." But what he sees is not what I am feeling. I am feeling anger. He is seeing an energetic expression of it, perhaps in the form of a reddish field around my head. To be sure, we can correlate insides with outsides, we can correlate the feeling of anger with states of my brain and even of my aura. But establishing a correlation is not the same as demonstrating an identity.

It is as if the entire physical and energetic universe were gradually parceled on the outsides of a series of concentric spheres. Each time we think we have penetrated a sphere and discovered its conscious interiority, we stumble upon the exterior of another sphere. We may experience things there that we never dreamed possible, but we still have not captured the interiority of consciousness.

The irony is that we *are* the insides of the spheres. We are consciousness looking for itself, trying to give itself an identity by what it can objectify. We are on the inside looking out, suffering from the illusion of identifying with what we find, but suspecting there may be something more. So we take up the search again by seeming to look for ourselves on the inside of things but from an outside perspective. Our search is based upon the reciprocal perspective of what makes it possible in the first place. As long as we live within the duality of insides and outsides, we are doomed to fail. However, our struggle in time will bring us closer to the realization that we are both sides, straddling, as it were, a duality that was only relative, never absolute!

The New Paradigm dialogue is nurturing a convergence of science and spirituality. At a social level, this is true enough. We have quantum physicists taking a serious look at mysticism and the possibility of a divine intelligence holding the whole show together. And we have spiritual adepts allowing their meditation states or healing powers to be examined in the laboratory. But it is seldom explained how this convergence is possible. Metaphysics needs to hang on something more substantive than expressions of good will.

My proposal regarding interiority and exteriority provides a needed model of convergence. Science explores how energy works; spiritual practices nurture the evolution of consciousness. No matter what level we work on, in addition to the contrast between "higher" and "lower," there is the contrast between "inner" and "outer" to take into account.

This fact is forgotten in certain discussions of consciousness and the New Physics. In particular, there is sometimes the tendency to explain states of consciousness merely by reference to distinctive patterns of energetic vibration and even to define whole dimensions of reality merely in terms of higher and lower vibrations. Recall, for example, Danah Zohar's attempt to explain the ground state of basic awareness in terms of phase entanglements between jiggling photons. What she succeeded in doing was draw our attention to an interesting correlation between two aspects of one impasse, the inner and the outer, but not to two distinct things.

An adequate account of the stuff of reality—what everything is made of—must have both vertical (higher to lower) and horizontal (inner to outer) depth charts. To seek to understand consciousness as if the main problem were only one of fitting it into the appropriate levels of an energetic spectrum—that is, to think of "inner" as being merely a certain level on an "outer" plane of energy—is to make a monumental mistake. Higher states of consciousness are outwardly reflected in higher states of energy. However, consciousness is not just energy.

Where does Energy Monism stand in relation to traditional schools?
First of all, it is not just an expanded materialism because materialism by
its very nature is restricted to the surface aspects of things, even if those
surfaces are inside other things, like atoms in our heads. Nor is it a form
of idealism which is similarly restricted to explaining the outside energetic
or material aspects of reality solely by reference to inner states of consciousness.

Finally, Energy Monism is not dualism because I have not posited two
separate things which interact with each other. Outsides and insides—the
twin features of energy-consciousness—do not interact with each other as
separate things anymore than the front and back sides of this page, or the
surface tension and boiling point of water, interact with each other. Yet a
change introduced in one aspect may be reflected in the other. This is
because they already are aspects of one and the same underlying substance.

THE PHYSICAL/NONPHYSICAL CONTINUUM: BIOENERGY

The classical dualism of mind and body is sometimes changed into the
categories of physical and nonphysical energies. By calling auras, subtle
bodies, and healing forces "nonphysical energies," a certain scientific
respectability may be achieved. J.B. Rhine, for example, once labeled parapsychology the "science of nonphysical reality." But the price for this
conversion is high. For it overlooks both the privacy of experience and the
intentionality of consciousness, and then proceeds as if the only important
question were one of how to interpret the outer worlds of energy. Instead
of an inner world and an outer world, we are given two kinds of outer
worlds—one the object of mainstream science (physical energy), the other
the object of esoteric science (nonphysical energy).

This leads to all types of confusion, mostly by scientists who commit the
same kind of reductive fallacy as their mechanistic predecessors, but at a
different level. It is the kind of thinking that leads a physicist interested in
ESP to conjecture that thoughts are telepathically transported by means of
"psi-trons." Or that spiritual healing is just the direction of bioenergy
pulsating at 7.8 Hz. It mistakenly assumes the correlation of a certain
conscious state with a certain energetic state to be evidence for two kinds
of energetic states, one physical the other nonphysical.

The distinction between physical and nonphysical energies is a popular
one in New Paradigm circles. But what does it amount to? Do we really
have dualism all over again? Or can the perennialist paradigm of Energy
Monism bridge the apparent gap between the two domains?

To begin with, distinctions between physical and nonphysical energies are distinctions of degree, not of principle. There are no real gaps between them, although there are gaps in our understanding of how different levels of energy may be related. Moreover, there are not just two levels of energy, the physical and the nonphysical, but a whole spectrum of levels distinguished by their frequencies, waveforms, and resonances.

Some levels are not acknowledged by physics, although they could fall under the scope of an expanded scientific paradigm. As Carl Jung observes:

> The moment when physics touches on the "untrodden, untreadable regions" and...when psychology too touches on an impenetrable darkness—then the intermediate realm of subtle bodies comes to life again, and the physical and the psychic are once more blended in an indissoluble unity.[4]

The credibility of any perspective is linked to how it helps solve problems in specific contexts. To increase its credibility, therefore, I want to apply this perspective to the controversial topics of bioenergy, Kirlian photography, and out-of-body experiences. I want to show how the physical and the psychic are part of Jung's "indissoluble unity."

Some of the most interesting candidates for filling in the gap between the physical and the psychic are so-called life energies. This is because of their similarities to electromagnetism.[5] If a case can be made for something to connect the physical with the nonphysical, this is a good place to start.

The concept of life energy has a long history in both Eastern and Western culture. In recent times, the idea gained currency in the writings of Carlos Castaneda through the Yaqui shaman Don Juan.

> Tentacles come out of a man's body which are apparent to any sorcerer who sees. Sorcerers act toward people in accordance to the way they see their tentacles. Weak persons have very short, almost invisible fibers; strong persons have bright, long ones...You can tell from the fibers if a person is healthy, or if he is sick, or if he is mean, or kind or treacherous.[6]

In ancient Greece, Hippocrates speculated that invisible emanations might be an aspect of a natural healing force found in all organisms and perhaps in the very air they breathe. That life-promoting energy might be conveyed through breath is part of the ancient yogic doctrine of *prana*.

Prana is a universal energy reflected in the human aura and controlled through specific breathing exercises. It is mediated by heat, light, and electricity and is believed to be a link between our spiritual (specifically astral) and physical bodies.

Similar attributes apply to the ancient Chinese doctrine of ch'i. Ch'i is a vast sea of energy in which we are all immersed and which penetrates every cell of our bodies. It flows along invisible meridian lines in the human body. When the flow is obstructed or weakened, disease and lack of vitality is the result. The flow can be reactivated by stimulating acupuncture points which have been correlated with areas of distinctive electrical activity. However, ch'i is not electricity itself. Neural activity may be said to be a reflection of ch'i, but ch'i is not reducible to the transfer of electrical charges.[7]

Returning to sixteenth-century Western culture, the ideas of prana or ch'i seem to find expression in the writings of Paracelsus, a Swiss army surgeon, discoverer of the sympathetic nervous system, and pioneer in the use of anesthesia. Paracelsus held that an invisible fluidlike substance termed the *archaeus* permeates all parts of the body and provides it the nutriment for strength and health. In principle, the archaeus could be affected by the use of magnetic forces. Furthermore, all things are immersed in what he termed the *liquor vitae*, a vital force (or nerve fluid) directly connected to the archaeus. This force "was not enclosed in man, but radiated within and around him like a luminous sphere and it may have been made to act at a distance."[8] This sounds very much like the interaction of prana and the individual human aura!

In the eighteenth century, Anton Mesmer, the discoverer of hypnosis and a pioneer in magnetic healing, set forth his theory of animal magnetism. In a frontal challenge to existing medical theory, he held that "everything in the universe is contiguous by means of a universal fluid in which all bodies are immersed."[9] He felt that this substance could be accumulated, stored, transferred, and generally manipulated through the hands for purposes of healing and diagnosis.

German industrialist and chemist, Karl von Reichenbach, conducted an exploration of magnetic-like energies for thirty years. He labeled the primary life force "odyle."

> Odic force is a universal property of all matter. Its distribution in time and space is variable and unequal. It fills the universe and cannot be eliminated or isolated (making it almost impossible to measure). It flows from such sources

> as heat, friction, sound, electromagnetism, light, planetary
> bodies, chemical actions, and the organic activity of plants
> and animals, especially man. This force is polar. Negative
> odyle gives a sensation of coolness and is pleasant, whereas
> positive odyle gives a sensation of heat and is uncomfort-
> able.[10]

Wilhelm Reich, a physician and student of Freud, came to similar conclusions in his concept of orgone energy which he viewed as a universal, massless substance that mediated other forms of energy and could be controlled for purposes of improving both physical and emotional well-being. Despite the fact that his ideas concerning structural integration and bioenergetics have found their way into contemporary psychotherapy and bodywork, the medical and scientific establishments ridiculed his concept of orgone energy.

Robert Miller continued the exploration of bioenergy in his studies with the famous healer, Olga Worrall. He demonstrated (among other things) that healing energy can alter the surface tension of water in precisely measurable ways. He termed this energy "para-electricity."[11] Continuing her studies begun at UCLA, pioneering physiologist Valerie Hunt not only documented the existence of bioenergetic fields using computer enhancement, motion picture film, and space-age electromagnetic recording devices, she also demonstrated how changes in the field around shamans, healers, and psychics frequently correlated with changes in their altered states of consciousness. In some studies, she transduced subaudible sounds radiating from the field.[12]

Some of the most well-documented work on life energies comes from the Yale laboratories of Harold Saxon Burr, whose L-fields are described in his pioneering work *Fields of Life*. Burr showed that all living things are electrodynamic systems. Each organism responds to electrical fields and possesses distinctive electromagnetic signatures. These patterns are the L-fields, which are correlated with health and disease, emotions, pain, and hypnosis. Shifts in the L-field can have predictive value where the symptoms of a certain disease, such as cancer, are not yet manifest.[13]

One of the most revolutionary current explanations of bioenergy holds that electrical flow within the body underlies all biological processes, especially in the fluctuation from health to disease and back again. Swedish physician Bjorn Nordenstrom (former chair of the Nobel Selection Committee for Medicine) discovered an electrical network in the body (not the nervous system) that is as critical to well-being as the very flow of blood.

In Nordenstrom's view, "the circuits are switched on by injury, an infection, or a tumor, or even by the normal activity of the body's organs; voltages build and fluctuate; electric currents course through arteries and veins and across capillary walls."[14] This electric flow is foundational in restoring the body to health, which he views as a state of optimum balance between positive and negative polarities. His successful treatment of malignant tumors relies directly upon reestablishing electric flow with the aid of positively and negatively charged probes.

In a parallel vein, Robert Becker's pioneering work *The Body Electric* is a bible of theoretically sound and practical information on electromagnetism and biological processes.[15] A pioneer in the field of biological regeneration, Becker draws inspiration from earlier writers on life energies but translates their ideas into the language of electricity. In his discussion of the tiny currents passing between cells, he sheds new light on self-regulation and healing, evolution, acupuncture, and cancer. As these currents go, so go the health and well-being of the person.

All of the energies described in this brief historical overview are not the same. Becker's tiny electron currents, for example, are not identical with ch'i energy. Yet there is a convergence of properties. In some respects, ch'i manifests electrically and bioelectric currents function like ch'i in the maintenance of life processes. We may think of ch'i as the upper end of the bioenergetic spectrum and bioelectric currents as the lower end. To summarize:

1. There exists a fundamental life-sustaining and promoting energy which pervades our life space.
2. This energy is fluid, more or less continuously in motion, not uniformly distributed, and subject to greater or lesser densities.
3. It is invisible and pervades our individual bodies and minds; we can swim in and through it, but never out of it.
4. It expresses itself through bipolar oscillation, whether understood as expansion-contraction, Yin and Yang, or positive and negative.
5. It is mediated by the particular conditions of an organism, such as emotional states, physical disease, and varied external conditions, such as smog or radiation. It is especially affected by electricity or magnetism. It may even manifest as tiny electric current.
6. It has been visible to psychically sensitive individuals across all cultural boundaries throughout recorded history but is seen

typically in its mediated state, such as the individual human aura. For those who cannot "see" it, it is indirectly measurable as electrical or magnetic energy in the immediate vicinity.

7. It can be controlled to some extent by electromagnetic fields or by healers who have learned to sense some of its manifestations.

8. In summary, bioenergy is a fifth force in nature with multiple empirical or experiential effects, depending upon circumstances. However, it is not reducible to any collection of effects.

It's tempting to split bioenergies into physical and nonphysical components. We might call ch'i nonphysical and bioelectricity physical. The tendency to put things into fixed categories is hard to resist. Still, there is no difference of principle within the physical-to-nonphysical continuum. Rather, there are differences of degree, depending upon the frequencies and phase entanglements of the particular level of energy. Radio waves and the visible spectrum of light have very different properties; for example, one can go through walls and the other cannot. Yet they are different levels of an underlying electromagnetic spectrum. The differences between ch'i and bioelectric energy certainly appear to be no greater. Both are life energies just as radio waves and light are electromagnetic energies.

Is healing energy physical or nonphysical? By now, it should be clear that the question assumes a false dichotomy. Healing energies may originate from levels within the Great Chain of Being now thought of as nonphysical. But the fact that healers can produce real physical effects, and can experience tingling, hot spots, and other differences during their practice means that they are functioning as transducers of energy from one level to another.

I will address the question of whether healing really works in Chapter Eleven. But the idea of spiritual healers functioning as transducers between dimensions or levels of energy-consciousness shouldn't strike us as any more strange than telephones converting electrical impulses into intelligible sounds. In both cases we are dealing with differences of degree.

WHAT DO KIRLIAN PHOTOGRAPHS REPRESENT?

Kirlian photography was first developed by a Russian engineer, Semyon Kirlian, in 1939, although it was not seriously investigated in America until the early seventies. It is technically defined as "the transformation of non-electrical properties of the photographed subject into electrical ones via the motion of a field in which the controlled transfer of a charge from an object to a photographic film takes place."[16] By placing the object (typically a leaf or a fingertip) over a charged plate, it's possible to photograph what appear to be auric emanations of energy around the object.

What are Kirlian photographs pictures of? There are three schools of thought regarding this question. A nonphysical interpretation maintains that the emanations pictured are auras, instances of spiritual or psychic energies. In popular esoteric literature (an oxymoronic phrase), this view has gained some currency. But most scientific researchers don't accept it.

A physical interpretation is that the fields pictured are merely reflections of ionized gases or the cold emission of electrons brought about by high voltage. Many critics hold that Kirlian photography can be explained by known physical principles.

Finally, a pragmatic interpretation suggests that the question of what Kirlian images actually represent may be unanswerable and is less important than the practical value they have in diagnosing disease. All parties are agreed that there is some diagnostic value. However, they differ over how far that value extends and what correlations between images and illnesses actually demonstrate. How should we interpret the fact that lung cancer, for example, may appear as a red blotch on a photograph of the energy around one's hand?

Kirlian diagnostic technology holds great promise that should be integrated into holistic health centers. But we shouldn't hide behind pragmatism. There is still the philosophical question: What *are* Kirlian images really of? Before exploring the prospects for a mediating view, let's review some of the strengths and weaknesses of physical and nonphysical interpretations.

The strongest argument for a physical interpretation is that Kirlian photographs have been demonstrated to vary significantly with approximately twenty-five different physical variables.[17] Among these are: voltage, amperage, type of current, temperature, humidity, pressure of the object on the photographic plate, the color dyes used (green, red, yellow) in the film, electrical potentials of the skin, and moisture content of the skin. Furthermore, purely material objects (such as a coin) show similar coronal discharges to those of living things.

Moreover, it has been demonstrated that in a vacuum no coronal flares are present, thus suggesting that a contiguous physical medium (air) is a critical ingredient in the total perceived effect. Finally, it is known that at least some states of the organism, such as stress, are causally connected with moisture content and electrical potentials in the skin, thus providing a link to varied Kirlian pictures. There is thus a strong case for the physical interpretation.

On the other hand, there are a number of phenomena that the physicalist interpretation does not account for and that lend support to a nonphysical interpretation. Healers, for example, have demonstrated distinctively colored and shaped coronal patterns not observed in nonhealers. Olga Worrall once healed a scratch on a plant which had manifested a large red blotch on the Kirlian image and which disappeared after the treatment. Worrall did not touch the plant, but worked only in the area of its energy field.[18]

To continue, the diagnostic capabilities of Kirlian photography cry out for more than a pragmatic interpretation. For example, regarding the detection of cancer, one prominent researcher writes: "By analyzing the energy and also geometry characteristics of the high-frequency discharge channels, and comparing these characteristics with those of normal (noncancer) images, the Kirlian method allows us to judge not only how far the metastases have spread, but also the dynamics of malignancy."[19] The coronas of nonliving things, by contrast, do not change.

Additionally, pneumonia, gastroenteritis, acute schizophrenia, and manic depression have lent themselves to correlations with distinctive Kirlian images, presumably even when moisture levels in the skin did not vary significantly. Why should a brain tumor representationally appear several centimeters from a subject's fingertip? In addition to providing a strong challenge for localizationist assumptions, such studies suggest that information about the body is perhaps holographically encoded in field energy associated with the body.

Which brings us to the strongest argument for a nonphysical interpretation, the appearance of phantom blueprints, i.e., the energetic double of an entire leaf. If such an image appears in the absence of the leaf itself, even if only for five seconds, then presumably all the relevant physical variables are removed from the resulting explanations! Still, might not the leaf be giving off some type of electrical energy that could account for the perceived form? Even if true, this would only explain where the stuff for the phantom came from, not why it takes such an intricate and detailed form, right down to the veins!

Pursuing this line of investigation, researchers inserted a copper plate between the leaf and the electrical field, then removed the leaf. Still the phantom was photographed![20] This suggests that the field energy associated with living things may be a more fundamental level of existence, an energy *to* which living things conform. A reasonable case can be made for something other than a purely physical interpretation of Kirlian phenomena.

Such philosophical standoffs are a breeding ground for the perennialist perspective I am suggesting in the theory of Energy Monism. Clearly, each side has a case and neither appears capable of explaining away all the evidence for the other's position. My integration of the strengths and avoidance of the weaknesses of both physical and nonphysical interpretations is as follows:

1. Closely related to electromagnetism is a fifth force in nature: bioenergy. Such energy has some properties similar to electricity. For example, it is invisible, fluid, vibrational, and may be blocked.
2. It can affect electromagnetic fields and produce seemingly electrical effects. In particular, it can be electrically "coaxed to the surface."
3. Kirlian photographs are not of purely electrical fields and not of purely nonphysical fields. They are of (what we now think of as) nonphysical fields mediated by strong electrical fields. The result is literally an interference pattern of an unusual variety.
4. What we see as auras on the plates do not literally exist in nature apart from their being photographed. But something like them does—something capable of being transduced into a different frequency domain. A physical effect can be produced from something that is only semiphysical, that is, something that approximates electromagnetic energy. When the aura reflects (is correlated with) a mental state, such as anger, the image on the photograph is not of the anger, but rather, of the *energetic representation* of the anger.
5. The difference between life energy and electrical energy is no greater than the difference between X-rays and radio waves, which are each segments of an electromagnetic continuum. We are dealing with differences of degree, not of principle. The idea of transduction between domains poses no more of a conceptual puzzle than the conversion of quantum energy (light) into electrical energy.
6. That Kirlian images don't appear in a vacuum no more disproves the existence of an auric field than it does the existence of God. It tells us that, under certain circumstances, one of the necessary conditions for producing a visible image is missing. Similarly, it

should not be surprising that other physical variables affect the transduction process.

7. In summary, we are not forced to choose between physical and nonphysical interpretations. We can integrate the essential elements of both interpretations along the lines just described.

OUT-OF-BODY EXPERIENCES AND THE MIND-BODY CONNECTION

One of the most interesting challenges for Energy Monism is to resolve the apparent stalemate between dualists and materialists concerning out-of-body experiences (OBEs). On the surface of it, clear evidence for OBEs would appear to be the strongest possible evidence of dualism. If a person could leave his or her body and view it from a distance, this would strongly imply the existence of two irreducible aspects of human nature—physical bodies and the nonphysical minds which inhabit them.[21]

On the other hand, if materialism is true, there is no mind or soul available for departure in the first place. Materialists believe that the experience of leaving one's body is really just a dissociative hallucination brought on by an unusual brain state.

Now I am neither a dualist nor a materialist. And only with certain qualifications do I own the label of systems holist. Yet I believe that, in appropriate circumstances, people can leave their bodies for short periods of time and return. I believe that OBEs are not only real experiences, but also experiences *of* reality in the minimal sense which implies detachment of one's consciousness from one's body. However, this does not in itself endorse any particular version of the ensuing travelogue.

How is it possible, then, for one who is not a traditional dualist to entertain such an objectivist view about OBEs? The perennialist modeling reflected in my theory of Energy Monism offers a way to overcome the limitations of both dualism and materialism. To assume that dualism and materialism are the only possible explanations of OBEs parallels the same mistaken assumption that "nonphysical aura" and "coronal discharge" are the only viable interpretations of Kirlian photographs. Both assumptions lead to a stalemate. Perennialism allows us to view dualism and materialism as partial truths in search of the connection provided by the Great Chain of Being.

Before explaining how, a few remarks on the nature of the evidence for OBEs are in order. After all, if OBEs are just dissociative hallucinations, then further explanations by the dualist, materialist, or perennialist are beside the point.

It is worth stressing, first of all, that we are nowhere near providing a psychological or neurological explanation of OBEs.[22] There is a tendency in mainstream science, especially medicine and academic psychology, to interpret OBEs as a kind of dissociative hallucination. If one looks under the subheadings of depersonalization or dissociative phenomena in the *Diagnostic and Statistical Manual IV*, however, the symptoms described are not those described in typical out-of-body experiences. For example, schizophrenics may suffer a loss of boundary awareness involving parts of their bodies.

By contrast, OBE subjects typically report a clear sense of moving up and away from their bodies, seeing their bodies from a different point in space, moving along a trajectory, perceiving or hearing elements of a physically removed environment (such as a friend's home, several blocks away), and returning to their bodies—sometimes slowly, sometimes rapidly. This is not schizophrenia in any of its forms.

Most people who have OBEs are quite normal to begin with. For example, self-absorption and hysteriod tendencies, psychoticism, death anxiety, narcissism, defensive style, and negative self-image have all been shown *not* to correlate significantly with OBEs. In short, not only has psychology failed to provide a good description for OBEs that does not assume a dissociative or troubled consciousness, but apart from associating them with the all-purpose category of stress, it has also failed to provide a satisfactory explanation for why they happen in the first place. All kinds of people experience them for all kinds of reasons.

Neuroscientists are especially prone to locate OBEs in some particular area of the brain. Here is one such account.

> There is clear evidence that within the temporal lobe are neuronal connections that, when electrically stimulated, produce OBEs...The temporal lobe is connected by serotonergic neurons to the midbrain dorsal raphe, and especially the hippocampus. The hippocampus is the central processing area of the brain, and is the area of the brain most associated with a sense of soul or consciousness. Psychological stresses and psychoactive agents have a neurochemical affect in this area of the brain, mediated by serotonin.
>
> Our model hypothesizes that [such stresses and agents] could trigger OBEs and psychical hallucinations by

disinhibiting target axons in the temporal lobe, from the
level of the hippocampus...Such genetically determined
areas in our brains may well serve as a natural defense
mechanism against stressful situations, such as childbirth
or trauma, both of which have been reported to cause
OBEs.[23]

Whatever one makes of this type of modeling, and whether or not sero-
tonin is the key neurotransmitter, its relevance for explaining OBEs is
severely limited by several considerations. In the first place, temporal lobe
stimulation can produce a variety of dissociative reactions regarding one's
sense of spatial location. However, there is no statistically significant
correlation between reports of such induced reactions, on the one hand,
and reports of OBEs, on the other. "I didn't know where my body was," "I
felt lost in space," or "I didn't know where my body ended," for example,
are not descriptions of the typical OBE. They typically omit any reference
to the role of intention in moving about, which is a key feature of many
OBEs.

Secondly, neurological explanations suffer from the correlational fallacy
described in Chapter Four. If you want to know what's happening in a
person's brain when she's having an out-of-body experience, talk to a brain
researcher. But brain chemistry per se does not tell us whether people
actually leave their bodies; it just correlates the experience of doing so with
a certain state of the brain. Such correlations do not support the claim that
because the triggers of an OBE are in the brain, the OBE itself also must be
in the brain.

Finally, both neurological and psychological explanations of OBEs typically fail to account for the capacity of some subjects to present empirically
verifiable information relating to the time when they were allegedly hallucinating. This is also a feature of some near-death experiences (NDEs).[24]
However, since a discussion of OBEs as an aspect of NDEs is clouded by
other physical variables, such as anesthesia, oxygen deprivation, and endor-
phin release, I have restricted the territory to pure OBEs not triggered by
cardiac arrest or associated with near-death experiences.

The question of whether people actually can leave their bodies must be
answered by determining if a test subject can deliver the goods under
laboratory conditions. Here is one example of a test for intentional out-of-
body projection developed by Karlis Osis and Donna McCormick in a pioneering study with Alex Tanous. In this experiment, Tanous was monitored
in one room, asked to project himself to a room at the other end of the

building, perceive a series of randomly generated images, and return with the information. The sequence of images were independently recorded, but not known to the researchers until after the experiment was completed.

Several features of this experiment distinguish it from clairvoyance (or remote viewing). First of all, the target (a temporary pattern of four colors and five line drawings) was projected into virtual space inside a box by means of a complex series of mirrors and filters. A clairvoyant who accessed this box from a distance, without actually being there, would have seen only a collage of lines and mirrors. The images were designed to take shape as optical illusions only from the visual perspective of someone whose point of view was at the appropriate angle *next to the box*. Therefore, Tanous's projected aspect would have to be next to the box in order to make a correct call.

Moreover, a special strain gauge capable of measuring very small movements or vibrations was attached to the box to record fluctuations during Tanous's ventures. The average activation level of the gauge over all eight sampling periods showed a significantly higher degree of activation when correct hits occurred. Tanous not only brought back information; in 197 trials conducted over twenty sessions, he correctly identified the target 114 times. He also appeared to have caused small movements in the strain gauge near where he was sent.

Critics (even those sympathetic to the paranormal) differ in their interpretations of this experiment.[25] Some parapsychologists, for example, believe that gathering information and creating small physical disturbances at a distance does not constitute any stronger evidence for literal out-of-body ventures than it does for (in-the-body) remote viewing plus psychokinesis. Indeed, some remote viewers describe their experience as if they were actually at the site being viewed, typically from above. However, they do not report moving along a trajectory to the site. The internal experience of remote viewing differs from out-of-body ventures. The fairest conclusion one might draw from OBE and RV research is that it's possible to gather information about a distant island either by remote-viewing it or by visiting it out of one's body.

My goal in this brief excursion is not to offer proof of OBEs, but rather to indicate why belief in out-of-body projection is rational. It is also to provide evidence for my claim that examining their unusual brain states is not the way to determine whether people can project out of their bodies. Having done that, let us return to the question of why OBEs are better explained by perennialist modeling than by either dualism or materialism.

If something leaves the body during an OBE, what could it be? Here is the information around which we have to build a coherent theory.

1. What leaves is conscious: it can think, feel, and perceive. This suggests that, if one can "see" without one's physical eyes, the source of visual perception may be other than one's physical eyes. Physical eyes would filter various frequencies, creating a sense of solidity in material objects otherwise missing when one is out of one's body.

2. Out-of-body experiencers sometimes report that they can see parts of themselves or other discarnate individuals; they have shape and some color. They are best described as "energetic doubles." Some see themselves as small spheres of light.

3. This means that whatever leaves has both conscious and energetic aspects. It is conscious from the inside, energetic from the outside. This reflects a fundamental difference of perspective.

4. No matter how they appear, OBE experiencers always occupy space in the sense of exhibiting dimensional boundaries; they are localizable. To see one's body on the bed is by definition to see it from a point in space.

5. Moreover, they maintain spatio-temporal continuity. They move away from and back to their bodies without loss of consciousness or of perceptual continuity. With practice, they can move effortlessly on a trajectory (which may be through walls) on the basis of their intention.

6. They sometimes appear able to produce physical effects from a distance.

Does this body of information conform to classical dualism, the dualism of Descartes and the Judeo-Christian tradition? In one important respect it does. It implies that people are not reducible to their physical bodies and might get on without them—at least for a while! It is useful to label this capacity *functional* dualism, which tells us something about what minds can do that brains cannot. However, it does not tell us what minds are made of; it doesn't tell us, for example, whether minds are physical or nonphysical. It just says that, whatever minds are, they can temporarily detach themselves from their bodies.

Which brings us to the fact that the information we have on OBEs is fundamentally incompatible with classical dualism. Classical dualism stipulates that the mind is nonspatial and nonphysical. It makes a metaphysical claim about what the mind is essentially made of, namely, nonphysical stuff. OBEs, however, imply that minds are spatial in the sense of having location. Anything that has location and energetic aspects falls within the purview of an expanded scientific paradigm. If it is invisible today, it awaits only the appropriate technology to confirm its existence tomorrow. What leaves the body is hypothetical only in the sense that germs were hypothetical before the invention of the microscope. Energetic doubles are no more "nonphysical" than were X-rays in 1800.

Energetic doubles represent a fifth force in nature, bioenergy, that current physics is not especially well-equipped to confirm. They represent potential extensions of our current understanding of physical energy and the four known forces. Classical metaphysical dualism holds that the stuff of the mind is forever beyond the reach of science, because it occupies a different dimension altogether. It is therefore fundamentally inconsistent with those aspects of OBEs which fall within the scope of an expanded scientific paradigm.

Perhaps one day we shall have the technology to produce clear pictures of people leaving their bodies.[26] But such a development, if it occurs, should not surprise us. This is because whatever leaves possesses all that something needs to possess—energy, form, and location—in order to be detected and visually represented. A picture of an energetic double is not a picture of the interior of consciousness per se. The dualist is correct about the privacy of experience. What might be pictured, however, is an energetic representation of consciousness. Naturally, the dualist and the materialist will cry foul in this portrayal of matters. The materialist will insist that there isn't anything (save the body) to take a picture of. The dualist will insist that whatever leaves the body forever belongs to the realm of spirit, not to the realm of science, and certainly not to the portfolio of the etheric photographer! The philosophical result of OBE research is that classical dualism and materialism are each profoundly correct in one respect, and profoundly mistaken in another respect. The strength of one is the weakness of the other. Each contains a partial truth, neither the whole truth.

Energy Monism profits from the ashes of this dialectic. It incorporates the strengths of dualism and materialism regarding OBEs yet avoids their weaknesses. With the dualist and against the materialist, it makes a place for out-of-body ventures. But with the materialist and against the dualist, it interprets OBEs as lending themselves, at least in part, to an expanded spectrum of energies detectable in theory by future technology. Against both positions, it insists that the differences between the physical and the nonphysical, or mind and body, are differences of degree, not of principle.

In the Great Chain of Being, the physical is not the same as the non-physical, but it is continuous with it. The fundamental fallacy of both dualism and materialism consists in projecting limitations of perspective on to a spectrum of energy-consciousness greater than either school has dared to imagine. Swami Rama's vision beautifully describes this spectrum.

> The universe is a dance of energies which vibrate at many frequencies. They ebb and flow, merge and part, form ripples, tides, currents, eddies, and whirlpools. They become units of all sizes, from atoms to stars, individual souls to cosmic beings...As rays, streaks, streams, rivers, oceans of light, they flow into each other and separate again, changing frequencies—and changing frequencies, they become suns, galaxies, spaces, airs, winds, fires, liquids, solids. They become the bodies of human beings into which the energy called consciousness comes and is embodied.

> Of all the flowing energies in the universe, consciousness is the most dominant, the one from which all the others proceed and into which they all merge. The ancient texts are fond of the phrase, "from consciousness down to the solid earth," for all this is a single matrix, a tantra, of energy, and within it are myriads of matrices, woven and interwoven. The human being is one such matrix of energies—ebbing, flowing, dancing at frequencies ranging from those of solid bones all the way to the subtlest waves of consciousness.[27]

CHAPTER SEVEN

The One-in-the-Many

One of the fundamental anchoring points of all New Paradigm explorations is the claim that everything is interconnected. However, this is not the simple idea it seems to be. It can mean quite different things, for example, to the mystic or the environmentalist. In this chapter, we will explore different types of connecting relations and their implications for a New Paradigm, with special reference to the following areas.

1. Mysticism: Is there a transcendental core that connects all major spiritual traditions?
2. Holography: Is holographic modeling the key for understanding how everything is interconnected?
3. The Great Chain: What are the major levels in the Great Chain of Being? How are they unified and differentiated?
4. Interpenetration: How does dimensional overlapping differ from other unifying relationships? Does its hierarchical structure imply power over (thus, fragmentation) or empowerment (thus, integration)?
5. Bell's theorem: If we assume that an independent universe exists, Bell's theorem suggests that distant events can be instantaneously connected. What are the implications of this theorem for a new worldview?

These topics both fuel the quest for a New Paradigm and provide a stage for the competing claims of Systems Holism and the Perennial Philosophy. They also provide strong challenges to the mechanistic principle that, in order to exist, something must be strictly localizable in space and time. The first challenge to this principle that we will explore comes from mysticism.

THE MYSTIC'S MESSAGE: OF ONENESS AND NONDUALITY

There is one type of stuff in the universe with two aspects: energy-consciousness. This is one variety of monism. An altogether different type of monism involves structure, which is the focus of this chapter. Structural monism is found in major spiritual traditions from both the East and the West and throughout most of recorded history. Its most neutral version is this: There exists an eternal, infinite, primordial source from which all things both seen and unseen emerge, are sustained, and to which (by some accounts) return. Nirguna Brahman, Tao, the One, the Absolute, and the Supreme Godhead are only verbal placemarkers for this nondual source which, properly interpreted, transcends monism itself.

In the *Chandogya Upanishad*, for example, *Tat tvam asi* ("That thou art") affirms the identity of Atman, the individual soul/consciousness, with Brahman, the universal consciousness. The *Upanishads* teach that the entire universe is a manifestation of Brahman. The Rising Culture certainly has not adopted classical Hinduism as its official cosmology. But if there is a single philosophical thread that links the spiritually and metaphysically oriented wings of the New Paradigm dialogue, it's the belief that all things are interconnected.

The question of meaning. What does this mean? Each thing in the universe obviously has some relation to other things. However, "That thou art" implies something stronger than mere relatedness. It implies identity or numerical sameness: things which appear distinct in space and time are in reality one and the same. They are one, not many. "We are all one" is more fundamental than "We are all interconnected."

But now we seem to have a contradiction. For to affirm that all things are one, not many, amounts to claiming that what is, isn't. It self-destructs in its very formulation. We have to assume that all things are not one just to get off the ground and affirm that they are. Critics easily exploit this implication as one more instance of mystical mumbo jumbo.

One way around this difficulty has been suggested by philosopher W.T. Stace, physicist Arthur Eddington, and by misinterpretations of the Hindu doctrine of maya.[1] It proposes that we treat the world of distinct people and things as an illusion, as something unreal. Reality, on the other hand, is held out to be the underlying domain of absolute unity and changelessness.

This proposal falls into the trap of either/or thinking. If reality is one, then unreality must be many—so the thinking goes. The strategy fails because it does not coherently connect the two domains. How could the real give rise to the unreal? Or if it did, would it be real in the first place? Such questions may seem like philosophical nit-picking, but they have closely related analogs. For example, how could a perfectly good God create a world with any potential evil in it and, if so, would it be God in the first place?

Ken Wilber and Eliot Deutsch have defended a more workable alternative.[2] It consists of drawing provisional distinctions between interpenetrating levels of being and refusing to label one as the "real" to be contrasted to all the others which are not. This perennialist proposal requires that we embrace all levels as partial manifestations of a single unqualified source. Rocks, chairs, people, and even angels are real by virtue of their being expressions of the Godhead. Of course, the fact that we are connected to the Godhead does not mean that we have *integrated* this connection into our lives.

Maya is sometimes understood as "illusion." However, this does not imply that the distinct things we perceive out there do not exist. Maya is a veil of ignorance cast over the world such that we come to believe that individual objects and events are the only real things in the universe. The tree, as we experience it, is really there and not a projective hallucination. However, maya challenges us to expand the levels and perspectives from which we experience the tree. The tree is real *as* we experience it, but that is not the only way it exists. Maya is essentially limitation, not illusion. Only when limitations are taken as ultimately real are they illusory.

The idea of hierarchical interpenetration enables us to connect different levels of reality in a very profound manner. It stipulates that higher levels enfold and permeate lower levels and are thus more inclusive. Since inclusiveness admits of progressive differentiation, so do levels of the Great Chain of Being. Each level possesses characteristics that others do not, and hence are relatively distinct. Yet all are permeated by the highest level, the Source of all things.

This Source emanates levels from itself, but is not reducible to any of them. It contains all things within itself, yet goes beyond them. This is the doctrine of pan*en*theism, not pantheism. With panentheism, God is both transcendent and immanent. Pantheism, by comparison, stipulates that God *is* totally immanent but not transcendent. God is nature and nature is God, with nothing left over. Panentheism stresses that God is not just "in" all things, like a single huge ghost occupying many machines, but that the things themselves—rocks, people, or angels—are qualitative variations of a transcendent Source.

To affirm that reality is one, or One-in-Many, or whatever way we wish to express the idea of a fundamental unity, is to take up an implied residence outside that totality. It is to fall into the trap of duality. To describe it as "One" seems to leave us with the question "One as opposed to what?" Some higher perspective yet? This will not do, since we already are part of the totality embraced by the One. Nowhere is left to go. And quite literally nothing is left to say.

The problem is not just one of limited vocabulary. Rather, it's that any word bestows some type of existence upon the One we seek to name. And once existence is implied, so is nonexistence. The great sages have made clear that the highest state, undifferentiated Truth, is indescribable and transcends the very distinction between the One and the Many. The highest level is one of nonduality. The One is a condition of the many, not one among the many.

For this reason, Tao is characterized as both nameless and without form. The word "Tao" functions as a placemarker that refers to no thing in particular. In Christianity, the term "God" normally connotes a being, supreme among all other beings. In this sense, God is one among many. The term "Godhead," however, implies an Infinite Ground, the One-with-out-a-Second. In this sense, the Godhead is not one among many, but a nondual condition of drawing the very distinction between the One and the Many. Theologians speak of God. Mystics express the Godhead in their daily lives.[3]

Still, verbal approximations are possible, even if filled with metaphor and analogy. Some models are more adequate than others, and a monistic vision is closer to the truth than an atomistic one. Despite critics' warnings, phrasing such as "Toward the One" (from the Sufi mystic Pir Vilayet Khan) does not necessarily commit us to the duality implied by "One as opposed to something outside itself." The reason is that the term "One" is ambiguous. On the one hand, it can mean "one as opposed to two (or more)." On the other, it could mean "infinite ground of all that is" or "One-without-a-Second." There is no metaphysical duality implied in the latter phrases.

It is evident that, to define panentheism, we imply a duality of one and many, or unity and diversity. This is the highest level at which things take shape, so to speak. Beyond this, however, is the indescribable state of consciousness—metaphorically signaled as the clear light of the void—in which all distinctions are dissolved.

This ultimate nonduality, the condition of nondistinction, does not negate panentheism. It simply suggests that panentheism itself is the most direct offspring, the first point of manifestation, of absolute, formless being. Paradoxically, then, the Absolute is both conditioned (as the world of many things) and unconditioned (as the world of no thing)! Thus, in panentheism, the One becomes many, yet remains One-without-a-Second. But how is this possible? How can infinite formless being manifest in finite or bounded ways and remain infinite? The answer comes in two parts.

First, the Infinite One-without-a-Second cannot exhaust the fullness of its being in the process of creation. There is, by definition, plenty left over. Even the entire physical universe, if subtracted out of our picture of reality, could not deplete an infinite spectrum of being.

Second, the Infinite One must retain continuity with its finite manifestations; there can be no gaps of nonbeing between them. In other words, what appear as discontinuities to ordinary perception will be viewed as progressively continuous with each other at higher levels of the Great Chain accessible to the mystic. Discontinuity reflects limitations unconsciously projected onto continuity from the fragmented perspective of dualistic awareness. The One and the Many are already integrated, but our subject-object awareness is not integrated with that integration, so to speak.

By satisfying these two conditions, we can avoid the contradiction implied in deriving the finite from the infinite, the limited from the unlimited. Figure 1 below is the wrong way to do it; there is nothing left over to connect the many as one. Figure 2 is a better way to represent the process. For in an infinite line with two or more waves, the difference between one line and two waves is merely one of perspective.[4] One need not encounter a contradiction in trying to understand how plurality is

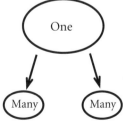

FIGURE 1.

One line, two waves
(which are not other than the line)

FIGURE 2.

grounded in the One-without-a-Second—of how many things emerge from the formless radiance of no thing!

The idea that we are all one at the highest level, each being unique expressions of a divine source, holds out great spiritual and moral promise. Yet it is also an idea where both liberal and conservative commentators find common cause in seeking to undermine it. As social activist Abbie Hoffman once put it: "If you think me and Ollie North [implicated in the Iran scandal] are one then you better get another massage…because you are irrelevant."[5] That is, you have collapsed any basis for meaningful social and political action.

On the other hand, conservative Christians see this idea as "spiritually counterfeit" because it reverses the true relationship between God and man.[6] It allegedly makes God an extension of the ego, sanctifies our own limitations, appears not to take evil seriously, and undermines any kind of religious platform or plan of action whatsoever. After all, if you are God, what's left to do?

I submit, to the contrary, that it would be one of the most constructive revolutions in history if personalities as diverse as Oliver North and, for good measure, former Panamanian dictator Manuel Noriega were to see each other "as one"—linked by a common core of spirit which has little to do with surface differences of politics, religion, and ego. This is not likely, but it is certainly not irrelevant!

This is not to suggest that differences are not really differences at the level in which they appear. My political preferences are not yours and your moral character is not anyone else's. New Paradigm thinking does not attempt to merge black and white or good and evil into an amorphous third category. The "oneness" in question is to be found at an entirely different level of which critics appear to be oblivious.

As to the charge of ego gratification, it is mistakenly assumed that if we are all God, then there is nothing left for us to do or to be. But nothing could be further from the spiritual horizons of the perennialist or the New Paradigm explorer. The correct interpretation of "oneness" here is that each of us is but a finite multidimensional expression of infinite Divine Being. Even if humans did not exist, there are infinite ways for the Divine to express itself.

Concerning the suspicion that there is nothing left to do except to express one's counterfeit pride, the truth is actually the reverse. What is left to do is to collapse the gap between theory and practice, get on with our spiritual evolution, and progressively integrate ourselves within the Great

Chain of Being. Given that most people tend to identify with their perceived limitations, there is a great deal left to do!

Spiritual traditions exist in order to impart practical techniques and moral guidelines for personal transformation that will take us back to the ground of our being. In aligning ourselves with our true nature, we can more naturally experience unconditional love for all creation, heal ourselves and the planet, and see energies and dimensions normally denied to those who identify exclusively with their physical bodies. This is what the "good news" of conservative Christianity should be about.

What is the basis of this good news, this cross-cultural vision the great sages bring? How can we know it? Common sense tells us that our three-dimensional world of separate objects and local processes is the only reality. Immanuel Kant even went so far as to offer logical proof that our mind/brains are hard-wired in such a way as to limit the kinds of things that *could* be known within this domain of ordinary consciousness. Speculation about God, freedom, and immortality outside our three-dimensional reality, he argued, results in logical contradictions.[7]

However, Kant did not demonstrate that our hard-wiring is the only one available. He showed only that, if we are confined to these structures of consciousness (cause and effect, duration through time, distinctness, etc.), our reality must conform to these filters. He did not demonstrate the impossibility of transcending these structures of consciousness that William James so eloquently described more than a hundred years later: "Our normal waking consciousness, rational consciousness as we call it, is but one special type of consciousness, whilst all about it, parted from it by the filmiest of screens, there lie potential forms of consciousness entirely different."[8]

Is it possible to pierce these "filmiest of screens" that separate our ordinary waking consciousness from other forms all around us? Enter the mystic not only with an affirmative answer, but also with a program for doing so. From history, cultural anthropology, classical mystical literature, and firsthand accounts, it is evident that many individuals have pierced the veil of ordinary waking consciousness and experienced themselves, their world, or their God in a radically different manner. One of the most authentic contemporary personal accounts of mystical experience is Norman Paulson's *The Christ Consciousness*. A student of Paramhansa Yogananda, Paulson explored a variety of spiritual dimensions, including ultimately both the Divine Mother and Divine Father aspects of the I AM THAT I AM.

There are important differences among mystical traditions. However, all agree that there are dimensions which transcend limitations of space and time, overcome ego barriers, and connect with our consensus reality. Within such perspectives, all things appear as aspects of a single inter-connected whole. As the great Catholic mystic Meister Eckhart observes:

> Here (in the mystical experience) all blades of grass, wood, and stone, all things are One…When is a man in mere understanding? When he sees one thing separated from another. When is he above mere understanding? When he sees all in all, then a man stands above mere understand-ing.[9]

Even the Void of Buddhism is not a mere nothing, but is more akin to a field of possibilities which, while appearing empty—that is, without form or distinction—gives rise to the world of form. Form is emptiness and emptiness is form; the two are dynamically complementary. In the words of the Chinese sage Chang Tsai: "When one knows that the Great Void is full of ch'i, one realizes that there is no such thing as nothingness."[10] The *Avatamsaka Sutra*, traditionally attributed to the Buddha, describes how the world appears in an enlightened consciousness in which "the solid lines of individuality melt away and the feeling of finiteness no longer oppresses us."[11]

W. T. Stace observes that when we transcend the constraints of ordinary waking consciousness, we find a central core of all introvertive mystical traditions:

> The most important, the central characteristic in which all fully developed mystical experiences agree, and which in the last analysis is definitive of them and serves to mark them off from other types of experiences, is that they in-volve that apprehension of an ultimate nonsensuous unity in all things, a one-ness or One to which neither the senses nor the reason can penetrate. In other words, it entirely transcends our sensory intellectual consciousness.[12]

The question of truth. Such claims to a higher knowledge have not gone unchallenged. One type of challenge questions their truth. Another doubts their intelligibility. And a third questions whether, as Stace believes, they are universally the same. Philosopher A.J. Ayer combines the first two:

We do not deny *a priori* that the mystic is able to discover truths by his own special methods. We wait to hear what are the propositions which embody his discoveries in order to see whether they are verifiable or confuted by our empirical observations. But the mystic, so far from producing propositions which are verified, is unable to produce any intelligible propositions at all.[13]

In two articles, "Eye to Eye" and "The Problem of Proof," Ken Wilber has critiqued the scientism that leads to such cavalier dismissals.[14] A modified version of his critique goes like this. Assume that we have two groups. Group A contains the mystics, a very distinct minority compared to Group B, which contains all the scientific and philosophical defenders of ordinary waking consciousness.

The mystics in Group A claim to know things through direct experience and the awakening of special faculties (the eye of contemplation, the sixth and seventh chakras), which challenge ordinary consciousness. Considerable effort has gone into the development of these higher faculties. They have verified their claims via the methods, perspectives, and practices appropriate to their disciplines. There are, of course, differences of interpretation. But when contrasted with simple common sense, they exhibit a substantial convergence.

Group B also has achieved convergence of belief. There remain differences of opinion here, too, but also general agreement over the guiding parameters of science and common sense. Since this is the majority tradition, educational systems insure that it remains the majority. The programming is usually so powerful that one need only describe the mystics from Group A as "touched in the head" if someone appears to take them seriously. The conversation then quickly moves to other topics.

Each group has met three conditions of verification: instrumental injunction ("If you want to *know* this, *do* this"); intuitive apprehension, an immediate experience of the domain addressed by the injunction; and communal confirmation, checking of results with those who have completed the first two stages. Variations of this process are found in science, daily living, psychic development, and higher spiritual practices the world over. Scientists check their students in laboratories. Gurus check their students in ashrams.

In light of the similarities and differences between the two groups, how should we interpret Ayer's dismissal of mystical truths? Very simply, it represents a colossal instance of question-begging. It amounts to Group B insisting that Group A conform to the verification procedures appropriate to one level in the Great Chain (the material/sensory). Group A responds: "If you want to see what reality is like from our perspective, then here are the procedures to follow. By the very nature of the case, however, our knowledge is not obtainable by the procedures followed on your level."

Still, Group B is insistent: "Your claims ought to be testable by our empirical observations, since if they are not, how do you know you are not hallucinating?" The response from Group A is decisive: "By the same three criteria that determine whether someone in your group is hallucinating. The fact that your Group B has more members is not a reason to assume that we cannot apply these criteria as impartially to our experience. Your assumption that if our truths are not your truths they cannot be truths at all—when our domain is as verifiable as yours—arbitrarily tilts the debate in your favor!"

The question of intelligibility. At this point a different type of philosophical critique surfaces.[15] It begins with the correct assumption that, in order to determine the truth or falsity of a belief, the belief must make cognitive sense. It must be intelligible. We must be able to understand *what* is being asserted or denied to begin with. I cannot know, for example, whether I've killed a grock until I know what a grock is.

The same goes for mystical language, which presents for our inspection all types of claims about "feeling at one with plants and animals," "merging with God," "transcending space and time," "discovering the illusory nature of the self," and so on. What does it all mean? If we cannot deal with the question of intelligibility, then we cannot say whether mystical claims are true or false.

The problem is that in order to understand something we aren't familiar with, we must connect it with something we do understand. We must define our terms and relate our experiences. But the radically transcendent nature of mystical experience leaves us with little to connect it with in the consensus reality underwriting ordinary language. How could one explain what it's like to be outside space and time in a language generated from within space and time?

Mystics are acutely aware of this problem, yet insist that they know what they know because of their direct experience. Language be damned! To which the critic responds: "If you can't make sense of it for me, then you cannot know what it means. Without some common social matrix of understanding (usually the language of the prevailing culture) you can claim anything you like in the name of personal experience. And nobody would be the wiser!"

In defense of the mystic I propose a somewhat novel way to turn the tables. The key is the phrase "common matrix of understanding." In principle most mystics understand each other, but we do not understand them very well because they are such an isolated minority. Even if their teachings have become a part of their cultures, their specific experiences and the words used to describe them typically are not part of a common understanding.

A mystic's transcendental experience is not insurmountably more difficult to grasp than an ordinary state of consciousness, such as depression. How does one explain the actual experience of depression to people who have never been depressed (or color, to the blind person)? We are quickly reduced to metaphor and analogy. Depression is like "feeling down." But this is exactly the mystic's plight. For one who has never felt anything close to depression, "feeling blue" is no more intelligible than "falling into a pool of boundless being."

Since most of us have been depressed, however, we have something with which to link the concept of depression. With a common concept, we are then in a position to examine the causes and cures of depression. The experience is both experientially and behaviorally linked to large numbers of people under comparable kinds of circumstances. It never occurs to us, except where insincerity is suspected, to ask, "Well, what do you mean when you say you are depressed?" For the question is already answered in our common social understanding. Depression is intelligible because we have experienced it.

For the unlikely soul who has never been depressed but who seeks to understand the experience, we can provide the conditions that will cause him to be depressed. Similarly, there are available meditation practices that often bring about transcendent experiences so that those who seek to know may do so. Learning to meditate is more difficult and takes longer to implement than experiencing depression, but it can be done. Most people have not had mystical experiences, so they are more hesitant when confronted with mystical language.

I am not attempting to reduce mystical experiences to nonmystical ones or to suggest that they are qualitatively the same or equally transformative. I am proposing, however, that similar types of communication issues may be faced on different levels of the Great Chain.

The issue is not whether one type of experience is inherently intelligible and another inherently unintelligible. Rather, it's the practical challenge of determining whether critics who question it have had the experience, how many others may have undergone similar experiences, and how best to reduce the gap in our understanding when one person has had an unusual experience that another hasn't. The gap between mystical and nonmystical experiences is not that much greater than the gap between thinking and feeling. To assume otherwise is to reject the minority view for the self-serving reason that, after all, it isn't the majority view.

The question of universality. In discussions of mystical experience, it is often assumed that we are dealing with essentially the same type of experience in different cultures and spiritual traditions. A stream of twentieth-century commentators, from William James and Evelyn Underhill to W.T. Stace and Walter Pahnke, have concluded that despite major differences there is a generic core in mystical experiences.[16] With variations, this core includes the following characteristics:

1. Unity (often associated with temporarily merging with nature or dissolving the self in a universal consciousness);
2. Positive moods (joy, bliss, peace, a sense of sacredness, and unconditional love);
3. Transcendence of space and time (not the distortions that one might experience with drugs);
4. Noetic incorrigibility (an inner knowingness or wisdom that cannot be refuted by outside observers);
5. Paradoxicality (what you get when, convinced of the unity of everything, you treat different levels of the Great Chain as if they were the same, e.g., "I am everything");
6. Ineffability (the inability to fully capture the experience with words);
7. Transiency (that one generally has little control over when mystical experiences come or how long they last);
8. Positive changes in attitude and behavior (less fearful or selfish, more compassionate and peaceful).

No serious student of mysticism would argue that mystical experiences are everywhere the same in every respect. In theistic mystical traditions, for example, God is interpreted as other than the mystic, no matter how commingled they may temporarily become. In panentheistic traditions, this gap is not as formidable. The question is whether there is any element of mystical experience that is the same. In an influential series of articles and books, Stephen Katz and others have argued that there is no such element. In other words, Stace's "direct nonsensory, nonintellectual, apprehension of ultimate unity" is a fiction insofar as it is held out as a universal *core* of mystical traditions.[17]

At the bottom of this debate is a reasonable assumption which has nothing to do with religion per se. This is the assumption that *all experience is mediated* by language, culture, and mind—that there is no such thing as pure experience. This is sometimes termed the constructivist thesis and is expressed in the claim that all knowledge is socially constructed.

For Katz, "the experience of *brahman* is always a Hindu experience, the experience of *nirvana* always Buddhist, and both are fundamentally different from the Christian experience of God or the Jewish kabbalist's experience of the higher levels of reality (the Sefiroth)."[18] Perennialists appear to overlook the filters that we bring to our respective transcendent experiences. Because all knowledge is mediated, they have failed to see that mystical knowledge also must be mediated.

Katz points out that, in our tendency to read unity into mystical traditions, we gloss over important differences both among and within those traditions. He urges, instead, that we should examine mystical texts in light of our cultural conditioning.

> Our sole concern has been to try and see, recognizing the contextuality of our own understanding, what the mystical evidence will allow in the way of legitimate philosophical reflection…[Our] account neither (a) overlooks any evidence, nor (b) has any need to simplify the available evidence to make it fit into comparative or comparable categories, nor (c) does it begin with *a priori* assumptions about the nature of ultimate reality.[19]

Katz and his philosophical allies hold, in effect, that there isn't any One, much less One-without-a-Second. Only the Many exist. If true, his conclusion would undermine a critical foundation of perennialist thought. New Agers are fond of pointing out that there is one Divine Source, but different paths leading to it. If Katz is correct, then New Agers are dead wrong. For anyone attracted to the idea of a common spiritual core underlying different religions, Katz's position requires an extended response.

To begin with, Katz does not defend the assumption that there are *no* pure (unmediated) experiences. He only gives examples of how this assumption works in various disciplines. However, since such an unmediated experience of pure consciousness or ultimate unity *is* held out as a core in different traditions, Katz should provide some additional support. In the absence of further support, Katz's universal application of this assumption simply begs the issue in his favor.

All assumptions about the nature of knowledge, including Katz's constructivism, inevitably lead to certain beliefs about the nature of reality. It's inconsistent to hold, as Katz does, that one's own metaphysics is neutral, while adopting a principle of knowledge which inevitably will lead readers to a nonneutral picture of reality.

Katz boldly asserts that "there is no substantive evidence to suggest that there is any pure consciousness *per se*." Yet Franklin Merrell-Wolff's *The Philosophy of Consciousness Without an Object* and Robert Foreman's recent collection, *The Problem of Pure Consciousness*, provide abundant evidence to the contrary.[20] It would be more appropriate to put the monkey on Katz's back and require him to provide examples for the major introvertive mystical traditions which do not minimally conform to the Christian mystic Ruysbroeck's description of the highest mystical state as "so onefold that no distinction can enter into it."

Huston Smith has observed that this lack of distinction within the experience makes it impossible to draw distinctions between the Kabbalah's *en sof*, Eckhart's Godhead, Nirguna Brahman, and the Tao that cannot be spoken. Contrary to Katz, we cannot culturally peg such experience "because no culturally identifiable particulars turn up within it. It isn't culturally tinted because, as the clear light of the void, it has no tint."[21]

In a major study of Buddhist and Hindu adepts, psychologist Daniel Brown has drawn attention to important differences between these traditions. For example, the Tibetan Buddhist perspective on meditation is more "photonlike" in stressing the experiences of momentariness, discontinuity, and discrete flashes. Hindu traditions, on the other hand, stress "wavelike" perspectives where the emergence and cessation of various seeds or sense impressions are experienced as transformations of underlying substrates.

Yet photonlike and wavelike are *complementary* perspectives on light. And as we experience light, it is the perfect integration of both aspects; we don't see waves and we don't see particles. By analogy, in the advanced stages of meditative practice, wave and particle perspectives reflect progressively less duality and more integration. The differences stressed by Katz turn out to be differences of progressively converging perspectives.

Katz interprets this process not as the progressive breakdown of innate and culturally programmed structures of consciousness towards unity, but rather, as the mere substitution of one set of structures for another. "Properly understood, yoga, for example, is not an unconditioning or deconditioning of consciousness, but rather it is a reconditioning of consciousness, i.e., a substituting of one form of conditioned and/or contextual consciousness for another..."[22] Yet Brown's work establishes that, even in cross-cultural perspective, the stages are both deconstructive and progressive.

> The paths of meditation in every tradition entail progressive deconstruction of each of these structures of ordinary waking consciousness: attitudes and behavioral schemes (stage I); thinking (stage II); gross perception (stage III); self-esteem (stage IV); time-space (stage V). As a result of dismantling the coordinates of ordinary perception, the meditator gains access to a non-ordinary, or extraordinary, structure of consciousness which does not operate by ordinary psycho-physical laws. Deconstruction of even this deep structure results in enlightenment.[23]

Neither Brown nor Foreman (who, after Eckhart, terms it a special form of forgetting) would deny that the process of deconstruction carries particular cultural twists. They do argue, however, that enough of this process transcends cultural conditioning to permit our talking of the *same* experience, especially the peak freeing of awareness from psychological structures, across cultural boundaries.

If 100 people from ten distinctive cultures were to describe their experiences of joy, no doubt we would find considerable variation and context-dependency. But assuming the ability to speak a language adequately, this would hardly cause us to doubt the existence of joy or to conclude that it lacked enough internal unity of properties to justify our thinking of these experiences as being of joy, rather than of some other mental state.

So far as unity and multiplicity are concerned, we do not require exact identity in mystical experience, but enough convergence to distinguish the unity of higher states from the multiplicity of lower ones. By analogy, no two waves are identical, but their differences are inconsequential when compared to the water which is their essence.

It is tempting to compare experiences from different levels of the Great Chain of Being, as Katz appears to have done, as if they belonged to the same level. But they do not. For example, the twentieth-century sage, Paramahansa Yogananda, distinguishes between Sabikalpa and Nirbikalpa Samadhi (mystical realization). Patanjali, the second-century yoga master, distinguishes between Savitarka Samadhi and Nirvikalpa Samadhi. Maharishi Mahesh Yogi, the founder of transcendental meditation, describes four states of Transcendental, Cosmic, God, and Unity Consciousness. And Ken Wilber distinguishes five states—Low and High Subtle awakenings, Low and High Causal enlightenment, and Ultimate Unity Consciousness.[24]

Some of these mystical experiences maintain vestiges of duality, while others transcend all hints of duality. Some involve the temporary identification of consciousness with a gross object of concentration, while others do not. Some permanently transform ordinary consciousness, while others represent temporary peaks. Then, too, some provide necessary structures for the evolution of still higher states. Obviously, we are not referring to one and the same mystical state across the board. As Patanjali observes:

> When the mind achieves identity with a gross object of concentration, mixed with awareness of name, quality and knowledge, this is called Savitarka Samadhi...[whereas] when the mind achieves identity with a gross object of concentration, unmixed with awareness of name, quality and knowledge, so that the object alone remains, this is called Nirvitarka Samadhi [in which thought-waves are stilled].[25]

He goes on to distinguish two further kinds of samadhi, Savichara and Nirvichara, along similar lines except that the object of concentration is subtle, rather than gross. Both kinds still retain tiny vestiges of desire and attachment, although the mind is said to become pure and filled with a truth that transcends sensory and intellectual domains. Here, spiritual transformation takes place. The highest state, Nirvikalpa Samadhi, is totally seedless. There are no more thought waves, just the pure undifferentiated consciousness in which the identity of Brahman and Atman is fully and directly realized.

One can never return from Nirvikalpa Samadhi to ordinary consciousness. The external world is now seen as mere appearance. No personal desires or attachments remain to motivate action. The mind and the objective world "have both ended their services to the experiencer...the mind has been used to transcend the mind."[26] The power of maya is completely dissolved. Everything is as it was before—but totally different.

Patanjali represents one major tradition. But whether we are dealing with Tibetan Buddhism, Yoga, Sufism, Kabbalism or the great Christian mystics, this brief description illustrates the fact that there is no such thing as mystical experience per se. Failure to take into account the different levels of enlightenment within traditions can lead to extraordinary confusion when comparing mystical experiences among traditions.

This, plus the fact that not all mystics are masters of all levels, can make it seem that, when we compare their experiences in cross-cultural perspective, there is more divergence than convergence. Anytime we ask whether an Eckhart, a Rumi, or a Ramakrishna are reporting essentially the same type of mystical experience, we must determine on the basis of an independent analysis whether the reports are coming from the same levels in the Great Chain of Being. So far as the highest level is concerned, the experience of absolute nonduality or pure consciousness does appear to be cross-culturally instantiated.[27]

IS REALITY STRUCTURED HOLOGRAPHICALLY?

The Holographic Paradigm is one of the most interesting and fruitful models of interconnectedness to emerge in the past few decades. It may even be one of the most profound scientific developments in the past four hundred years. Still, neither New Paradigm commentators nor mainstream scientists agree upon its importance. Karl Pribram, the distinguished neuroscientist who helped put cognitive psychology on the map in the early sixties, is frequently cited as one of its godfathers. Physicist David Bohm is sometimes similarly labeled. Fritjof Capra doesn't think that the holographic paradigm does justice to the dynamic nature of reality. And Ken Wilber believes that it has only limited applicability.[28]

The Holographic Paradigm is a proposal for both small- and large-scale modeling of reality. It incorporates three critical features of hologram construction. The first is that holograms reflect interference patterns from the wave fronts of intersecting fields of energy. The fields are typically two beams of coherent laser light, one of which is reflected from a photographic plate containing a lensless collage of waveforms representing the original physical object.

The mathematics used for constructing and decoding holograms is the Fourier calculus. In its most general form, Fourier's Theorem states that any pattern can be analyzed into component sine-wave forms of different amplitudes, frequencies, and phases in relation to one another. The virtually infinite variability of intersecting waveforms described by the Fourier mathematics helps explain why holograms can store extraordinary amounts of information—up to ten billion bits in a cubic centimeter.

Another feature is their capacity to recapitulate the form of the whole image into each part. From even a tenth of the original photographic plate we can construct a complete (though somewhat fuzzier) hologram of the original object. The holographic model of part/whole relationships is boldly expressed in the observation that each part contains the whole.

There is considerable evidence for holographic modeling, especially in the neurosciences. For example, it accounts for the equipotentiality of memory storage, the fact that individual memories are not stored at particular places in the brain. Rather, they appear to be located in many or even all parts of the cortex. Destruction of half the cortex, for instance, does not result in the loss of half of one's memories.

Struck by the fact that both brains and holograms appear to spread information around equally, Karl Pribram conjectured that the principles of hologram construction must guide information processing in the brain. He set aside the fundamental assumption of locality ("To be is to be in just one place at a time") that had guided a fifty-year search for chemical memory traces. Holograms store information nonlocally.

Since then, Pribram and others have developed considerable support for viewing major neural subsystems (auditory, tactile, visual, etc.) as frequency analyzers, rather than as mere passive transmitters of discrete sense data. It has been shown, for example, that the perception of geometric form ("The box out there") is possible because alternating patterns of light and dark measured in terms of spatial frequencies (temporal frequencies for auditory stimuli) are encoded in resonance patterns in the cortex.

Even a single cell in the visual cortex, it turns out, conforms to the mathematical predictions of Fourier analysis (sometimes called Gabor functions, after the inventor of the hologram). Brain processes can be seen as quantum events describable by the same Gabor functions that Werner Heisenberg applied to quantum mechanics. This connection between brain processes, holograms, and quantum mechanics, Pribram believes, is no accident.[29]

To Pribram's pioneering work, neuroscientist E.R. John later added direct evidence for the existence of wave fronts and interference patterns emerging from sequential neural firings in the brain.[30] One of the best experimental cases for holographic modeling is laid out in Paul Pietsch's *Shufflebrain*, a book which despite Pribram's endorsement unfortunately has not found its way into New Paradigm commentary. Pietsch actually set out to disprove the holographic model in favor of a structuralist model (where structure defines function), but concluded by rejecting structuralism.

In a series of experiments, he removed, reversed, scrambled, and even transferred sections of salamander brains to frogs to determine the conditions under which feeding patterns would remain the same. Every structuralist prediction failed and every hologramic (his term of preference) prediction was confirmed. Feeding behavior (the function) survived the annihilation of structure.[31]

Some of the most astounding support for a holographic model (although this was not his intent) is found in John Lorber's provocatively titled essay "Is Your Brain Really Necessary?"[32] Lorber's studies were of patients with brains damaged by hydrocephalia. In one case the entire visual cortex was destroyed (apparently since early childhood), yet the patient exhibited normal vision. In another, only 1/45 of the entire cortex remained intact, yet the patient was normal in every respect save intelligence, which was unusually high!

The philosopher is quick to exploit this situation. If 1/45 is sufficient for normal thinking, sensing, imaging, and recall, why not in principle 1/60 or 1/90 or even some microscopically small portion? Studies such as Lorber's suggest that, far from being the seat of consciousness, the brain is more like a filtering system for the expression of consciousness. These studies support the holographic paradigm. For how else could so much structure and content be built into such a small segment of the brain?

Holographic modeling has been used to explain other unusual phenomena, such as ESP. I can read another's mind, perhaps, because we are each in some way parts of a master hologram. Reality is a sea of energy patterns out of which we unconsciously construct our local consensus version. Some commentators have even suggested that the brain itself is a hologram within the universal hologram of nature. These are but a few of the possibilities compellingly portrayed in Michael Talbot's *The Holographic Universe*. Still, some precautionary flags are in order.

To begin, there is a large gap between the principles of hologram construction, on the one hand, and the claims made for the larger Holographic Paradigm, on the other. It is tempting to move too quickly across that gap. In discussing this paradigm, we could mean only that: reality consists of a vast sea of vibrating energy-consciousness; within that interconnected whole are interference patterns that give rise to concrete images and objects; and the mind/brain in some cases interprets physical reality along lines that are consistent with hologram construction.

On this conservative interpretation, the Holographic Paradigm is not objectionable. From here, however, it is a big step to claim that the brain itself (much less consciousness!) is a hologram, or that all information in nature is holographically stored, or that reality itself is structured holographically. This is the territory where precautionary flags are in order.

One such flag takes exception to the possibility of explaining memory retention by any type of neural coding. Philosopher Stephen Braude has argued that neural coding presupposes isomorphism, a one-to-one correspondence, between an original experience and its physical trace in the brain or between its trace and its subsequent recollection.[33] According to Braude, however, such isomorphism is fundamentally incoherent. This is because any type of fixed coding appears incapable of accounting for the varied representational aspects of memory that are tied to *context-dependent* differences of interest, perspective, and ability.

Consider the picture of stairs which look reversible. I initially perceive the stairs "going up," but later recall them as "going down." Obviously, I can represent the original image from different perspectives. Yet neurologically speaking, the original experience has been encoded only once. The picture of the stairs remains unchanged. How can one and the same coding explain different representations—going up or going down? And if it cannot, what are the prospects for any explanation of memory which assumes isomorphism?

Isomorphism in memory is just the tip of a deeper mistaken assumption that nature itself divides up in only one way. And this, Braude urges, is never the case. We represent objects and their relations in many different ways, depending upon the context. Is the wine sitting on the table or is the table supporting the wine? Is the chair to the left or right of the table? Is it even important that it sit to one side or the other?

Language itself has a built-in variability. My saying "hammer" could mean "Bring me the hammer" or "Where is the hammer?" or simply "Is this the hammer?" Our current needs and perspectives dictate which reality grid we lay down over our experiences. Braude believes that such naive assumptions about one-to-one correspondences between nature, language, and memory destroy the viability of not only the Holographic Paradigm, but any type of generalized vibrational paradigm.

Braude's objections are most effective when directed at a memory trace conceived as a local neurochemical entity. However, Pribram and others specifically reject this conception in favor of a far more complex model of nonlocalized coding. Structural isomorphism, a one-to-one correspondence of neurons and memories, is not the issue Braude seems to think it is. Pribram opts instead for patterns exhibiting a common mathematical *form* described by the special mathematics of Fourier analysis. Fourier mathematics explains how form gets spread around, not locally built up out of fundamental units (whether neurons or something else)!

Braude interprets the holographic model as attempting to provide a causal analysis of memory phenomena—that some type of neural or frequency encoding causes me to have the recollection that I do. Supporting this attempt is the further mistaken assumption, he thinks, that the holographic frequency domain is logically prior to the domain of ordinary experience and must consist of patterns of vibrations that "are in principle identifiable independently of any description of the ordinary reality which the patterns compose."[34] In other words, all causes must be describable independently of their effects. Otherwise, we have circular explanations. B occurs because of A. But when we inquire into the nature of A, we are told only that it is the cause of B!

This objection appears to miss the mark. For as defenders of a holographic model would quickly point out, the memory-image *is* an interference pattern, not something independently caused by an interference pattern. The failure to obtain a one-to-one correspondence between cause and effect is not damaging, because we are not talking about cause (frequency encoding in the brain) and effect (conscious image) in the first place. No proponent of a vibratory paradigm begins by looking for vibrations behind the scenes as if ordinary phenomena didn't exist.

Our decision to interpret an object as reflecting rocklike patterns of vibrating energy does not require us first to identify the specific energetic configuration without knowing what a rock is. This is neither possible nor necessary. We may infer certain qualitative or mathematical properties of those energetic configurations which sustain, but do not causally trigger, the appearance of the rock.

Proponents of a vibratory paradigm easily can agree with Braude, at least up to a point, that nature has no preferred way to divide things. We can agree that what counts as an object is dependent on different contexts. We can even agree with the Buddhist sage Nagarjuna that, from a certain perspective, there are no things at all—just a seamless web of mutually conditioning relations and events.

What Braude seems not to stress sufficiently, however, is the dynamic *interaction* between persons and their worlds, which is continuously taking place on multiple levels. The frequency domains associated with my current needs and perspectives are continuously interacting with other frequency domains from my environment to produce the representations of the moment—my current thoughts or experiences. The representations can be as numerous and varied as the constantly shifting patterns of energy. Each aspect of the nature/persons polarity transforms the other, creating new wave patterns and representational gestalts. Nothing about a vibrational paradigm in general requires that we ascribe to a particular place, object, or relation just one and only one representation.

Ironically, Pribram and Pietsch are motivated by the same concern that fuels Braude's objections. For example, Pribram was puzzled by how perceptual constancy is possible when the neural input from a moving object is continuously changing. The ball still looks like a ball as it flies through the air. Lack of variability in standard hard-wired brain models is what initially drove him to consider the holographic model, precisely because such modeling allows infinite variability of mental representation under virtually identical stimulus conditions. Fourier mathematics permits infinitesimal variation of content while preserving a common form. No other modeling comes close!

There are other explanations of how some information gets around so fast that it appears to be in more than one place at a time. One such model derives from a feature of quantum mechanics termed "phase entanglement." All photons carry wavelike properties. And when photons or any particles carrying wave signatures meet, their vibrations become entangled. Assuming they do not cancel each other out, each continues on its way, leaving a part of itself in the slightly modified wave signature of the other. It used to be thought that such entanglements were purely mathematical fictions, part of the necessary formalism of quantum mechanics, without any counterparts in the real world.

It is probably no accident that one of the key contributors to quantum physics, Erwin Schroedinger, believed that phase entanglement was its most distinctive feature. He struggled with the question of whether mathematical waves correspond with real waves. Recent discussions in quantum physics strongly indicate that phase entanglements are a built-in feature of reality.[35] If all natural processes at the micro level conform to the principles of quantum mechanics, it is reasonable to conclude that each thing at that level carries information about all of its previous entanglements.

Notice that this line of thinking makes no reference to holograms and does not commit us to the claim that each thing in the universe contains all the information possible about every other thing (or process) in the universe. Phase entanglement provides a possible explanation, for example, of how a psychically sensitive individual can retrieve information about the history of a client's ring merely by touching it. However, it does not force us to the extreme position of supposing that a ring carries information about a distant star.

The temptation is strong to generalize from limited aspects of our experience to reality as a whole. When applied to hologram construction, this tendency can lead to a curious implication. For example, holograms require coherent light beams, mirrors, and physical objects to represent. But where are these ingredients for reality as a whole? Light in general is not coherent. How would the holograms be constructed?

Even more to the point, where are the originals to which the presumed hologram-like objects of our consensus reality conform? In some higher order reality? For Pribram, this might be the frequency domain or for Bohm, the implicate order. But to put it crudely, the frequency domain is where we obtain the stuff with which to construct our ordinary reality. Behind each chair or table there are no more originals. Even if there were, we would then have the same problem all over again. What does that original-of-the-original holographically conform to?

Consider any material object, such as a pencil. Let us think of it as a minihologram within a larger hologramic context. Now any rational account of what a pencil is and how it endures through time must at the very least invoke a principle of order and a principle of change. What holds the pencil together as a pencil and what allows it to change with use over time? In the case of holograms, we bring order out of chaos by arranging all the ingredients through our conscious intentions. We can program change into our holographic image of a pencil, for example, by causing it to grow shorter before our eyes.

However, as Braude would remind us, this still reflects our *prior intentions* to arrange the plates, mirrors, beams, etc. in a certain way. What about actual physical pencils considered independently of human intentions? What keeps the frequencies and phases all aligned properly to maintain stability and allow them to change gradually, rather than chaotically? Surely not intentions again, because we would then be in the untenable position of supposing that the pencil disappears when nobody is concerned with it. No intentions, no pencil!

We require principles of order, change, and form in order to make vibrations and phase entanglements do for us what we want in an adequate paradigm. Ultimately, these will have to come from consciousness. And this is what seems to be left out in general discussions of holographic modeling. Everything isn't just "vibrating energy." Consciousness informs energy, but is not reducible to it. Thoughts and images are not mere miniholograms. Such reductions confuse the dual aspect of energy-consciousness. Energy gets its form from consciousness, but from this it does not follow that consciousness is just energy.

Consider, once again, the case of OBEs. If people can think, perceive, feel, and remember while outside of their bodies, then what does holographic encoding in the brain have to do with success in these functions of consciousness? On the one hand, if hologramic encoding is retained by consciousness outside of the body, then appeals to neural wavefronts and the like seem irrelevant. On the other hand, if hologramic encoding is required by the brain but unnecessary for an out-of-body consciousness, then the Holographic Paradigm is not as universally applicable as we are led to believe.

One of the virtues of the Holographic Paradigm is that it allegedly provides a bridge from science to mysticism, from the brain to higher states of consciousness.[36] It's an intriguing suggestion that mystics can tap directly into domains that scientists can only infer indirectly via mathematics and experimentation. Indeed, some spiritual adepts do describe their experiences in terms of "higher frequencies" or (per Swami Rama) as distinctive patterns of energy.

This is not objectionable so long as we refrain from speaking of vibrating consciousness. Meaning and intention are not reducible to vibrational interfaces. They are what allow us to make sense of vibrational realities in the first place. Consciousness is reflected energetically. But the inside of the Great Chain cannot be reduced to the outside.

No matter how we qualify the mystic's claims, higher frequencies per se entail nothing about the holographic structuring of reality. Mystics who have made the journey to higher levels of reality do not necessarily report an overall holographic structure of reality. Rather, they invoke the principle of hierarchical interpenetration. A complete understanding of human nature at one level requires understanding of other levels. However, this does not mean that information about everything from every other level throughout the universe currently is encoded in my brain.

MAJOR LEVELS IN THE GREAT CHAIN OF BEING

While there is general agreement among the traditions of the Perennial Wisdom regarding the hierarchical structure of the Great Chain, there is as much apparent disagreement over specifics. When we consult Ken Wilber, Huston Smith, the Kabbalah, or Alice Bailey, the number of levels varies considerably, the subdivisions are not always consistent, and the terminology is not uniform. In *Forgotten Truth*, for example, Huston Smith distinguishes between what he terms terrestrial, intermediate, celestial, and infinite planes of existence, whereas popular New Age thought normally lumps everything under the umbrella of mind, body, and spirit. Still other commentators distinguish as many as thirty-three (or more) dimensions, leaving unanswered the question of who or what occupies the twenty-ninth dimension (or the twenty-seventh, thirty-first, etc.) or whether more than one dimension can be subsumed under the category of a major plane of existence.

Still, when we penetrate verbal differences, it's possible to put together a picture which does justice to the amplified core of the tradition. In my opinion, seven levels are necessary to get the job done, although the final number one arrives at depends upon how much one is willing to pack into a given level. In a recent article, "The Great Chain of Being," Wilber provides a useful overview not only of the major levels, but also of several key issues associated with their hierarchical structure and causal inter-penetration.[37]

Physical. This is the level of gross matter and energy. It includes molecules, the fundamental elements (atoms) of nature, the subatomic constituents of atoms, photons, and the four forces. It is the domain of physics and chemistry (below the level of biochemistry). In Hinduism it is termed Annamayakosa (the realm made of food), and in Buddhism it is part of the five Vijnanas (the realm of the five senses and their objects). Each primary level in the Great Chain is divided into sublevels. The lowest point in the physical dimension is field energy. The highest level involves complex molecular structures.

If the stuff of reality is energy-consciousness, then consciousness must exist even at the lowest level of the Great Chain. From the perspective of ordinary awareness, however, this stuff looks less like consciousness than physical energy. We do not think of rocks as exhibiting consciousness. But since our language is built around what is apparent to ordinary consciousness, it's more convenient to think of rocks as nothing more than inert objects or patterns of physical energy.

Bioetheric. As noted earlier, there are numerous and sometimes confusing accounts of different levels of reality.[38] I hope that my use of "bioetheric" will help to clarify matters, rather than contribute to the confusion. From the standpoint of ordinary science and common sense, we could label this simply the biological level of the Great Chain. We would include within its domain everything from the lowest forms of life up through the human body. Classical Hinduism refers to this domain as Pranamayakosa, the sheath made of biological functions.

So far, so good. But sentient matter is merely what is presented to common sense. Underlying a living thing is an etheric body, sometimes described as a look-alike double. This is the domain of life-energies described earlier. Etheric bodies are individualized expressions of prana or ch'i energy, which organize and sustain biological activity. Blockages in the flow of energy within an etheric body, or between the etheric body and other bodies (mental, emotional) which encompass it, are associated with physical disease and dysfunction. The etheric or bioenergetic body of plants occasionally manifests as a phantom image in Kirlian photography.

It leaves the (human) body sometimes during sleep and always during intentional OBEs. To clairvoyants it can appear as vivid outside the body as a hologram does to us. To healers, it appears as a colored energetic template, changes in which reflect further changes in physical well-being. When it permanently leaves, the physical body begins to deteriorate. It has no mind or will of its own, and outside the physical body (after death) it is no longer needed. New ones can be formed later. A person's etheric body is partially reflected in his or her aura.

What has all this to do with the domain of biology, of living things and processes? It seems as if we have jumped several levels ahead of ourselves. Actually, we *are* a bit ahead of ourselves, but not in the way that it first appears. We have not jumped levels, but we have jumped to the idea of hierarchical penetration. What would otherwise appear to us as nonliving, inert mass/energy, when permeated by etheric (life) energy, becomes what we normally describe as a living plant or animal. This is why the second level in the Great Chain is the *bio*etheric. As it appears to us, it's the domain of mainstream biology. Behind the scenes, it's the domain of etheric energy, a fifth force in nature. Matter plus etheric energy equals biology.

This picture also helps to explain why life is not reducible to physics and chemistry. Systems theorists see life as emerging from ever-more complex patterns of matter. For them, the picture is: matter plus progressive complexity equals biology. Irreducibility is a function of complexity. But it is left unexplained why matter arranges itself in such progressively complex patterns. "Chance" is the answer from classical evolutionary theory. The second level comes from the first.

The Perennial Wisdom, on the other hand, holds out a qualified vision of top-down causality. Etheric energy doesn't come from matter. It is precipitated from higher domains in the Great Chain. It is metaphysically prior to matter. Living matter conforms to and is, to an extent, sustained by this underlying etheric energy.

Drs. Vladimir Poponin and Glen Rein of the Institute of HeartMath, using state-of-the-art technology called laser photon correlation spectroscopy, have shown how a DNA "phantom effect" can be coaxed directly from out of subquantum vacuum space by interacting with conventional electromagnetic fields. They interpret their results as providing direct evidence for subtle energy fields, which in the context of biology I have labeled "bioetheric fields." Their results suggest that DNA, in addition to its familiar three-dimensional space, also functions at a higher dimensional level in which nonlocal interactions occur, especially with heart energy.

The irreducibility of biology to physics is not just the irreducibility of the complex to the less complex; it is the irreducibility of etheric energy to gross matter. What looks to us like evolution from the less complex realm of physics to the more complex realm of biology is the result of the interpenetration from the more fundamental etheric domains to the less fundamental domains of simple matter. The higher is already in the lower, gradually manifests there, and thus appears to have been created by the lower.

The etheric realms contain many types of beings, not just energetic doubles of humans. Devas, otherwise known as "nature spirits" or "fairies," are one example. They have a special relationship with the plant and animal kingdoms and are explicitly acknowledged and sometimes seen in the community of Findhorn on the northern coast of Scotland. Elementals are another type of etheric being. They have a special connection to the earth and to the four classical substances—earth, air, fire, and water.

We are affected by devic and elemental activities and they are affected by ours. More "homes" are lost in the destruction of our rain forests, for example, than are apparent to the naked eye. Since *our* relations with these other citizens of the planet have been based largely on ignorance and fear, interkingdom relations, so to speak, have not been altogether harmonious. A future perennialist ecology will stress more cooperative arrangements.

Astral-emotional. From the perspective of ordinary psychology and common sense, we might call the third level in the Great Chain simply the emotional. However, we need to allow for the fact that we can experience feelings in both an embodied and a disembodied state, and that the spectrum of feeling extends all the way from fear to pleasure. Hence, I am utilizing the more comprehensive notion of an astral-emotional plane. This is described in Sanskrit as kamaloka, literally "the place of desire."

The astral-emotional level is the seat of personality and character, the attitudes and traits that make us who we are. Each person's emotional body is created, built up, and modified through his or her responses to emotional programming and to perceived lacks. It encompasses the energy of our emotions and experiences from this and other lifetimes. If we carry a powerful fear of authority from a past life, for example, it may be expected to shape our personality and the issues we attract in this life.

Unconditional love is not a feeling or emotion. Its ultimate seat is with the Divine Source of all things, as manifest through our causal bodies. Hence, while it may filter through our emotional bodies and transform what's in its path, genuine love is not based in the emotional body. Rather, it is our perceived lack of love, the ways we cloak it, and our often unsuccessful attempts to get it back through sex or control, for example, that build up our emotional bodies.

The astral-emotional dimension encompasses a number of sublevels. At the very lowest level are destructive and confused energies that create a "negative drag" on everything around them. The Bible refers to this lowest level as "outer darkness," where demonic beings prey upon those too confused or depleted to resist. It also contains energies associated with such things as abusive sexual perversion, murder (especially serial killings), deeply ingrained hatred, and long-term drug abuse. Some of these spirits feed their passions by means of the physical body they currently occupy.

Those without physical bodies often attach themselves to others with physical bodies in order to partake in the baser emotional energies produced there. Fortunately, at the time of death most people avoid this hellish corner and find themselves instead at one of the intermediate astral levels.

The astral planes also contain thought forms that are projected from either incarnate or discarnate persons. "Thoughts are things," as the saying goes, and are more powerful than one might suspect. I am not referring to mere thoughts, such as "tree" or "This tree is tall." Rather, as beliefs and attitudes they may be invested with emotional energy, such as "I wish I were prettier" or "You should stay away from Harry." The power of the thought form depends upon the investment of emotional energy it carries.

The astral planes are full of such projections, some positive, some negative, and some of which may never have had any counterpart in physical reality. For example, it is possible to create a spirit simply by creating a fictional biography and investing a considerable amount of group energy in it. This process may take a while, but when complete the "spirit" seems to have an independent life. It can even produce poltergeist effects in the presence of the group which created it.[38]

Unlike real souls, however, created ones cannot survive without some investment of external energy. This is an unusual example, but the same principle is at work when meditation groups express positive energy involving, say, peace, love, or healing. Such practices can have significant effects on different levels of the Great Chain.

The astral planes are not somewhere else. They are all around us, penetrating our physical world. We are already participants in those levels as emotional beings. The difference between experiencing ourselves with bodies and experiencing ourselves as members of the astral-emotional level of the Great Chain is essentially one of perspective. This perspective is determined by the degree of our individual psychic and spiritual evolution. It is possible to access different levels of the astral planes in meditation. Most people visit there in their dream states even though they may recall little. Then again, astral planes may be directly experienced during out-of-body projections.

With the exception of sages who have mastered their emotional natures, the astral planes are where the rest of us go when we die. Those comparatively less-evolved people who die and then enter at a lower level have difficulty at first distinguishing themselves from those left behind, since our physical and etheric bodies are easily perceived from the perspective of the permanently disembodied state. To them, we may appear as real members of their continuing world. Some still behave as if they had a body and are naturally frustrated when they are unable to create the physical effects they were accustomed to producing when they were alive.

A word about terminology. "Astral" is often the preferred term in the occult wing of the Perennial Wisdom, whereas roughly the same description of emotional realms applies to the terms "subtle" or "subtle body" in spiritually oriented wings, such as Mahayana Buddhism. Ken Wilber prefers this terminology and describes the subtle (or astral) level (Sambhogakaya) as encompassing an extraordinary spectrum of images, feelings, sounds, colors, and vibrations.[39] To intend to do something in this subtle (astral) realm is tantamount to having done it. Wishes (both positive and negative) that fall within the parameters of these subtle realms can be almost instantaneously fulfilled. Moving around in subtle realms is accomplished by intention. We arrive at our destinations, as he puts it, "at the speed of thought." There is no hallucination in this domain, since there is no external reality with which to compare what one has experienced.

The upper levels of the astral plane are relevant for the transpersonal psychologist. For it's here that archetypal experiences, sacred geometry and symbolic forms, mandelic imagery, intuitive and blissful insights, experiences of interconnectedness, and sublime peace are encountered. Feeling still plays a primary role, but it is a vastly different and evolved type. These upper levels are the domain of saintly religion. They are what would otherwise be referred to as the Christian heaven.

Mental. The mental plane of the Great Chain includes language, intelligence and, at higher levels, intuitive wisdom. It extends well beyond the average human intellect into the animal kingdom, where the ability of some nonhuman primates to form simple concepts and even crude sentences is documented. In fact, together with other levels, it extends all the way down through the lowest level of inert physical matter. But from our perspective in the Great Chain it appears to manifest mainly with humans. There is intelligence in everything, as illustrated, for example, in M. Roades's *Journey into Nature*, which describes the author's identification with the consciousness of water, blackberries, crystals, and dolphins.[40]

Looking up the evolutionary ladder, the mental plane extends through scientific knowledge and philosophical understanding to the intuitive wisdom of mystics, sages, and even to angelic beings charged with maintaining energetic balance in a certain quadrant of our galaxy. Unless otherwise required, angels communicate with each other telepathically via the use of symbols, not words. The entire spectrum of mind, from the subhuman to the transhuman, is called the *manasic* plane in Sanskrit (plane of the mental functions). In the final analysis, God (and hence the entire Great Chain of Being) is infinite intelligence (as well as love and bliss).

The mental plane is intimately related to other levels. A physical sensation, for example, may give rise to an emotional reaction. Both the sensation and the emotion may then give rise to various judgments or questions. For example, what caused the sensation? Was it like others? What prompted this particular emotional reaction? Like other levels of the Great Chain, the mental plane is distinguishable but not distinct.

Beliefs sometimes have the power to produce change simply by being entertained, especially if the same ones are held in resonance by many people. But even here, beliefs or ideas are not merely floating abstractions. They are invested with a certain amount of emotional energy, which gives them their power. They are consciously and subconsciously associated with certain images, which contribute to their meaning and applicability. Even a scientific law, devoid of any obvious emotional connotations, possesses a subtle power by virtue of the fact that many people are invested in its truth.

The power of our mental body, especially as it interpenetrates our emotional and physical bodies, can be a source of considerable joy and health, on the one hand, or of illness and dissatisfaction, on the other. For if our programming causes us to believe that we are failures in school, work, or relationships, or that we should strive to please everyone, then unhappiness and ultimately ill-health are all but assured. Changing our mental programming is as important as changing our emotional programming for long-term happiness and growth. Equally important is not allowing our minds to rule our emotions and not confusing the ability to interpret our emotions (which the mind loves to do!) with the free expression of emotions.

Causal. Above gross/material, bioetheric, astral-emotive, and mental realms is the causal domain. As Arthur Powell explains in his classic text *The Causal Body,* this body derives its name from the fact that in it reside the fundamental causes that manifest in lower planes. The inner aspect of the causal body is the most direct and immediate connection with the Divine Source—the soul of Christianity or Atman of Hinduism. It may also be referred to as the ISH (for Inner Self Helper) in depth psychology, as the

Higher Self in New Age contexts, or as the Spiritual Body in general metaphysical contexts. It is the witness which observes and guides—"for whom the hour never strikes."

In its inner or divine aspect, "the causal body is only bliss; the causal mind is only empty...Everybody enters this state each night in deep sleep without dreams, and individuals *can* consciously contact it through...paths of meditation."[41] In core mystical traditions, this upper aspect of the causal (spiritual) body can be experienced as formless radiance beyond all subject-object dualisms.

If the causal body had only an inner aspect, we would have no basis for distinguishing it from other causal bodies. But every inner aspect parallels an outer one. The outer aspect of the causal body is not an individual person but is rather the basis for our understanding ourselves as individuals. The causal body has built into it certain universal capacities which, depending upon what we do with them, provide the basis for personal identity. For example, our causal bodies are conduits for experiencing and manifesting unconditional love. They are the seat of our chakra system, even though certain chakras may lie relatively dormant during certain reincarnational cycles. And they carry both masculine and feminine energies or aspects. The opportunities for exploring and using these energies over many lives are infinitely varied.

Other bodies change over time, some faster and others slower. Before we had a physical body or an astral body, however, we had a causal body, a core which endures from life to life and carries with it knowledge of the experiences from all lifetimes. The causal (spiritual) body is the basis of individuality, yet is beyond all personal identity. Through it are provided love, wisdom, and joy which our other bodies may seek out, integrate, and apply—sometimes successfully, sometimes not.

Celestial realms. Otherwise referred to as Universal or Buddhic Planes, these dimensions are beyond all subject-object dualisms, all polarities. They are populated by angels (Maitreya), archangels (Michael), lords of light (Metatron), creator-gods (Shiva and Shakti), the Elohim, Seraphim, Cherubin, and assorted Thrones, Dominions, and Powers. Events happen in the celestial realms in the sense that energy moves, intentions are formed and manifested, and consideration is given to possibilities that can shape the history of a planet or a galaxy. However, these beings exist in resonance with the Godhead or Universal Ground. They radiate unconditional love, vast powers of creation and destruction, and the corresponding wisdom to appropriately exercise these powers.

They (or an aspect of them) may choose to incarnate on a lower plane for a specific purpose but are not subject to karma (except insofar as they choose to be). They may do so because by working through issues appropriate to that dimension, their success carries great transformational power for the planet or dimension where they have incarnated. This is one way of understanding Christ's mission. The celestial realms are the first levels where the Universal Godhead becomes manifest in discernible forms. Maria Parisen's collection of authoritative interpretations, *Angels and Mortals: Their Co-Creative Power*, offers a more detailed exploration of the nature and work of angels and other beings in the celestial realms.

Ultimate Ground. The Ultimate Ground of all Being is sometimes described as Consciousness-as-such, the primordial source of all other levels. It is beyond oneness or mere unity, for even to use these terms is to imply otherness or disunity. It is the void beyond manifest creation, the highest state of realization to which a mystic might aspire. But when achieved and integrated, it encompasses in a living and indescribable fashion all other levels below it.

To achieve integrated resonance with the Ultimate Ground or Godhead is to experience the synthesis of the One and the Many which favors neither the One nor the Many. It is the complete integration of nirvana—often portrayed as otherworldly—with samsara, the world of form and flux. This transformation is indescribable, because words (especially nouns) capture what is common to events or objects over time, rather than what is unique to each. To be in a state of complete resonance with what the universe uniquely presents *at that moment* is therefore something which, by its very nature, could never be captured through language.

This level in the Great Chain is a ground state prior to all creation. However, it is also a living perspective which unites all levels in a special way. It is neither God as transcendent nor God as immanent, but the integration of both aspects. From this perspective, "everything then arises, moment to moment, in any realm, but only as one's Original Face, one's very Self. The transcendent witness turns out to be everything that is witnessed, and so itself dissolves. Then there is nothing but the universe, which is also one's own Self. It has always been just so."[42] The Ultimate Ground is thus neither emptiness nor form, but the identity of emptiness-in-form with form-in-emptiness. To experience this identity is to live in effortless grace, creating not by doing, but through the fullness of just being!

HIERARCHICAL INTERPENETRATION

So much has already been stated about the interpenetration of levels within the Great Chain that little remains but to draw out its implications and refine our understanding of how it works. Each level in the Great Chain (with the exception of the lowest) contains the level below it and (with the exception of the highest) is contained by the level(s) above it. More structured than the belief that everything contains everything else, interpenetration is asymmetric. Higher contains lower, suffuses and permeates lower, but not the reverse.

This means, for example, that consciousness is not contained in our bodies, much less in our heads, but is more akin to a field in which our physical bodies are suffused. Each cell, organ, or limb participates in this field. Each level's participation in the level above it helps sustain it and give it the characteristics it possesses. Thus, persons are physical bodies, but not mere physical bodies. They are also living, metabolizing, self-reproducing bodies. They are conscious (feeling, thinking) beings beyond that. So it goes. Higher levels sustain lower levels and when they are withdrawn in certain circumstances, such as death, the level from which they are withdrawn undergoes a change, e.g., the body decays.

But higher not only sustains lower. It also predisposes lower-level activity in certain directions, which is to say that the condition of our minds in general affects the conditions of our bodies. This should be understood in a strong pervasive sense, involving more than the simple truism that, after all, what we think or feel determines how we behave. It means, for example, that unresolved emotional and attitudinal issues can surface in the form of physical disease.

This explains why healers can work directly on a person's bioenergetic (etheric double) body, with observable effects produced on the physical body. It also explains, however, why the effects of energy work at that level may not last long if imbalances persist in the astral-emotional level above it. The bioetheric level conditions the physical, while emotional and mental levels condition the bioetheric.

Even parts of ourselves that we thought we had lost or, worse yet, were never there—like the capacity to give and receive unconditional love—have only been covered up by the accumulated activities of other dimensions. Divine *un*conditional love filtered through the fear zones of the astral planes, for example, causes us to believe that the best we can hold out for is a relatively stable *conditional* love. Higher levels not only permeate lower levels, but from the perspective of the lower levels, appear limited by them. The principle of dimensional penetration is beautifully captured in the words of Lama Govinda:

> These "worlds" [or dimensional levels] are not separate regions, spatially divided from one another, so that it would be necessary to move in space in order to pass from one to another. The higher worlds completely interpenetrate the lower worlds, which are fashioned and sustained by their activities.
>
> What divides them is that each world has a more limited and controlled level of consciousness than the world above it. The lower consciousness is unable to experience the life of the higher worlds and is even unaware of their existence, although it is interpenetrated by them.
>
> But if the beings of a lower world can raise their consciousness to a higher level, then that higher world becomes manifest to them, and they can be said to have passed to a higher world, although they have not moved in space.[43]

Metaphysical versus normative hierarchies. In an open letter to Ken Wilber some years ago Fritjof Capra formally dissociated himself with any philosophy in which the concept of hierarchy (whether interpenetrating or not) plays a pivotal role.[44] He endorsed the idea of levels of organization and of simpler and more complex levels, but disparaged use of the term "hierarchy" to describe such organization. The difference is more than terminological. Neither Capra nor many others in the Rising Culture will countenance any type of hierarchic vision of reality. Such thinking, he argues, is typical of male-dominated consciousness in particular and of the Newtonian-Cartesian paradigm in general. It implies levels of unilateral or one-way control by a few over the many and is at the root of many of our current social, economic, and environmental crises.

Capra has articulated a serious concern to everyone involved with the development of an adequate worldview, especially feminists, environmentalists, systems theorists, and writers with new economic and political agendas. The core message is this: "Don't talk to us about enlightened hierarchical leadership *or* a well-intentioned metaphysical hierarchy. The idea is so immersed in abuses of power that there is no point in holding onto it. As a guiding root metaphor, hierarchy must be replaced with more viable assumptions involving balance, integration, and mutually empowering cooperation."

With this much, all parties—from theosophists to ecofeminists—can concur. Where, then, is the issue? When properly understood, I think it pretty much dissolves, with more than a few ironic twists along the way. The concept of hierarchy has both *metaphysical* and *ethical* elements. The ontological question is this: Is reality structured so that higher levels of energy-consciousness encompass lower ones? To answer this in the affirmative, as the Perennial Philosophy does, carries no implications for intention or control, which are the bases of Capra's concerns. It does not imply that men are superior to women, that the environment is here to be raped, or that wealth ought to be in the hands of the few.

Nor does the reverse inference work. Oppression exists. And it is often linked to the abuses of institutionalized hierarchies. But from this fact it does not follow that the concept of hierarchical interpenetration is a bogus proposal. It stands or falls on its own merits. By analogy, people have committed crimes in the name of God. But this in itself does not, or at least ought not, cause us to conclude that God really doesn't exist after all.

The ethical question is whether we ought to arrange our personal and social structures hierarchically such that certain groups are given, directly or indirectly, disproportionate power over other groups. The answer is clearly no. References to top-down causality can invoke images of corporate leaders, typically men, issuing orders to subordinates. But chain-of-command models, whether in health, business, family units, or politics, clearly assume intention and control on the part of those who command or dominate. Nothing in the vision of a hierarchically structured reality, however, necessarily leads to such control.

In fact, moving up the hierarchy from a spiritually evolutionary perspective requires giving up the grasping, fearful, ego-enforcing, and controlling attitudes that underwrite the old hierarchies that feminists so strongly reject. Properly understood, hierarchical interpenetration is a great equalizer, not a covert mechanism of oppression. All wings of New Paradigm thought concur with the need to move away from institutionalized hierarchies that serve largely patriarchal interests of control. Nothing in the inclusivist and empowering metaphysics of hierarchical interpenetration stands in the way of that agenda.

RETROSPECT AND PROSPECT

The concept of hierarchical interpenetration is foundational to the emergence of any paradigm that claims adequacy. It represents a key philosophical and experiential insight that, when properly interpreted, resolves a number of long-standing philosophical disputes. Some of these have already been described; others have yet to be addressed. Here is a brief summary of the ways interpenetration fits into the worldview it inspires:

1. Hierarchical interpenetration can underwrite psychoneuroimmunology in particular and the holistic health paradigm in general. The health of our bodies is in part a function of the health of our minds and spirits. It explains, for example, why visualization can be effective in treating disease, namely, because the disease itself is a lower-level extension of energy-consciousness.

2. Interpenetration explains why yogis can perform their amazing feats of self-mastery. For it is not simply *control* of one's pulse that is at stake. The entire metabolic rate must be changed in order not to suffer brain damage from oxygen depletion. And this rate cannot be very efficiently reduced on a piecemeal basis. Reduced metabolism is only one result of a greatly calmed mind.

3. Interpenetration resolves better than any other Western theology the problem of transcendence and immanence. To what extent is God "in" us or "outside" of us? The asymmetry of hierarchical penetration allows us to say that God is in all things, but not all things are equal in their awareness of God. We grow into Godliness in our own ways only to discover somewhere near the end of the journey that God was partially reflected as us all along.

4. Interpenetration solves the problem of the One and Many. Is the universe many things or one? The answer is both, depending upon one's perspective within the Great Chain. It explains how the One can be in the Many, how the Many can appear to be distinct, and how the transcendence of both in an integrated continuum is possible.

5. Interpenetration accounts for why life, purpose, and mind are ultimately unexplainable from the perspective of gross matter, viz., because matter itself is precipitated from higher levels of energy-consciousness. It allows us to derive less from more, rather than force us to attempt to squeeze the higher qualities of life and mind from lesser stuff containing neither.

6. Interpenetration provides a very workable solution to the mind/body problem by allowing us to recognize legitimate differences between the two, while not allowing the gap to become unbridgeable. Differences between levels are of degree, not principle.

7. Interpenetration allows us to integrate the insights of Eastern spiritual traditions with those of Western psychology. It permits various schools their truth by assigning them to their appropriate level in the Great Chain and by showing how each can lead to the adoption of the next.

8. Interpenetration provides a workable basis for developing hypotheses to explain paranormal phenomena, such as spirits (or even UFOs) making sudden appearances and then disappearing. Accordingly, such entities have temporarily come from another level of energy-consciousness into resonance with our consensus consciousness. We are provisionally phase-locked.

9. Interpenetration explains why some phenomena may appear discontinuous at a certain level by inviting us to view them as reflections of continuity from another level. Electron jumps, telepathy, nonlocal causation, and Sheldrake's congruence of learning curves from shielded places all point toward the interpenetration of levels. (Sheldrake's work is examined in Chapter Eight.)

10. At virtually every juncture where we have fragmented our experience and our belief systems—whether between subject and object, cause and effect, consciousness and matter, controllers and controlled, men and women, or good and evil—the principle of hierarchical interpenetration provides an integrative model that helps to overcome fragmentation. It is not enough simply to long for unity, curse isolation, and ask others to work for the common good. One needs a vision of reality in terms of which the move away from fragmentation makes sense. Hierarchical interpenetration is that vision. It means that we all have access to inclusiveness, empowerment, and wholeness. It does not imply power over. What we need—whether an innate wisdom, the capacity to give and receive unconditional love, or the ability to balance our masculine and feminine sides—is contained within ourselves. Hierarchical interpenetration is the stage upon which we play our lives. A creative, successful, and joyous life depends upon our integrating its dynamics into the roles we choose to play.

THE SPECIAL CASE OF BELL'S THEOREM

Most of this chapter has dealt with relations between levels in the Great Chain. In this concluding section, I want to explore a special type of connection within a level, that of nonlocal causation, or instantaneous action-at-a-distance. First, a brief review of the many senses of the claim that everything is interrelated. This will be useful, since it is used to justify many points of view in New Paradigm discussions.

1. "Everything is interrelated" might mean "Everything ultimately comes from and is sustained by a common source, our Ultimate Ground of Being." In this sense, it makes a claim about identity ("Everything is one") that we explored earlier in this chapter.

2. "Everything is interrelated" also can mean "All levels in the Great Chain are asymmetrically related by means of hierarchical interpenetration." This was described in the preceding section.

3. "Everything is interrelated" sometimes expands awareness about connections we may not have acknowledged. For example, "There's more out there affecting our well-being than many suspect, e.g., florescent lighting, toxins, electromagnetic pollution, etc."

4. In some contexts, "Everything is interrelated" is an ethical principle, a prescription for certain types of action like, for example, "Our pollution is clearly affecting people in other countries, and their economy is negatively affecting our standard of living, so we had better take appropriate action." In other words, the sentence "We're polluting the environment" and the ethically charged principle "Everything's interrelated" give us the following inference: "We're harming that which sustains us, so we ought to change our ways."

5. "Everything is interconnected" sometimes means that no thing exists in its own right and every thing is constituted or defined by relations to other things. Our very essence is relatedness, not external autonomy. Our being is our becoming. To change our relations is to change ourselves. Henry Stapp describes this idea on the quantum level as follows: "An elementary particle is not an independently existing unanalyzable entity. It is, in essence, a set of relationships that reach outward to other things."[45] A word of caution. Relations logically imply the existence of things to be related. Strictly speaking, "Every object is (nothing more than) a set of relations" is as self-defeating as "Everything is up." Up is always relative to down. A relation requires something to relate.

6. Finally, "Everything is interrelated" might mean that events in one part of our environment are instantaneously connected to distantly removed events in ways that violate normal patterns of cause and effect. It might mean, for example, that someone's being murdered in China—especially if it were someone with whom you had crossed paths years earlier—will immediately affect you in some tiny imperceptible way. This is one implication of Bell's theorem, an idea which I've only alluded to in previous chapters, but which now invites a more extended exploration.

The EPR effect. In 1935 Einstein and two colleagues, Podalsky and Rosen, published the results of a thought experiment which purported to undermine the completeness of quantum mechanics by means of what is termed the EPR effect.[46] There are different ways to illustrate this effect. I will adopt one suggested by David Bohm which utilizes electron-spin states. According to his proposal, we first generate a two-particle system in which the spins of paired particles are always equal and opposite and thus, as related constituents of a single system, cancel each other out. According to quantum mechanics, if the spin of one particle ("A") in this paired system is up, then the spin of the other particle ("B") must be down.

Suppose, now, that A and B, having once been in proximity by virtue of a common origin, are sent off in opposite directions and that A's spin is artificially changed (through a magnetic field) from up to down. Quantum theory absolutely requires that B's spin simultaneously change in reverse fashion from down to up, even if the particles are widely separated. The apparent causal dependence of B upon A in this situation is the EPR effect.

In practice this effect must be determined by sending millions of electrons through variable polarizers and then noting statistical inequalities in different electron streams. But for a thought experiment, single electrons will do. Einstein's interpretation of the hypothetical EPR effect was that it was paradoxical, since it violated the assumption of local causation.

This assumption of local causation states that for any two particles (or any other states of nature) to be causally connected, the time between their respective changes cannot be less than that required for the transmission of light between them. The EPR effect is essentially a quantum-mechanical prediction that violates one of the foundations of relativity theory, the absolute speed of light. To accept the EPR effect would require accepting nonlocal causation, since any signals between the particles would have to travel faster than light in order to arrive in a manner that looks simultaneous to us. And this is tantamount to undermining relativity theory itself.

Einstein was not interested in trying to prove with this argument that all parts of the universe are one. Rather, he turned it around, urging instead that since relativity was better established than quantum mechanics, the EPR effect must demonstrate something profoundly incomplete about quantum mechanics. He went to his grave believing this.

In 1964 J.S. Bell produced a rigorous mathematical demonstration showing that *if* the statistical predictions of quantum theory are born out in fact, belief in a realistic universe independent of consciousness is incompatible with the assumption of local causation.[47] New Age partisans sometimes mistakenly take this theorem to mean that Bell proved the EPR effect. Actually, he did not demonstrate the EPR effect itself. Rather, he showed that any explanation of the EPR effect which assumes both that the particles are not causally connected and that their behavior is independent of consciousness must generate predictions which differ from those of quantum theory. In other words, when we add together the EPR effect, quantum theory, the assumption of a realistic universe independent of consciousness, and the assumption that only *local* causation is operative in the universe, there is a profound incoherence. Something has to give, but it's not clear what.

In nine experiments since 1972 the relevant predictions of quantum mechanics were put to the test. Of those involved in this work, the consensus is that quantum theory has held up and that the state of particle B must depend in an instantaneous and nonchance manner upon what an experimenter does to particle A in a separate region. Henry Stapp, a key interpreter of Bell-related work, described it as the most important discovery in the history of physics. For the quantum connectedness of distant particles is not just an experimentally produced oddity. It's happening all the time, all over the universe!

A majority of physicists still adopt Bohr's view that either there are no hidden facts behind the numbers or, if there are, we cannot know them. If the experimental predictions continue to hold up, there is therefore no point in speculating what might connect the particles in the EPR effect. For Bohr, no paradox existed. Others have attempted to get around the problem by reformulating certain portions of quantum theory, but with questionable results.[48] A growing number of physicists are facing the prospects of major conceptual revision. Bell's theorem is unshakable, but where it leads is not clear. As physicists John Clauser and Abner Shimony state:

> Because of the evidence in favor of quantum mechanics from the experiments based on Bell's Theorem, we are forced to abandon a realistic view of the physical world (perhaps an unheard tree falling in the forest makes no sound after all)—or else to accept some kind of action-at-a-distance. Either option is radical, and a comprehensive study of their philosophical consequences remains to be made.[49]

Implications of Bell's theorem. A comprehensive study, indeed! Of the many interesting questions the Bell work raises, I want to focus first upon the alleged connection between idealism and nonlocal causation. I think that the exclusive dichotomy between realism and local causation (which defines much thinking about the implications of Bell's theorem) is misleading. On the one hand, local causation (i.e., less than speed-of-light interactions) would not be preserved by adopting idealism, as Clauser and Shimony suggest. This is because even if we were to suppose that consciousness could psychokinetically and instantaneously alter the spin of a distant particle, such a feat would still involve superliminal (i.e., faster than light) action-at-a-distance.[50]

On the other hand, no physicist has shown how it is possible to preserve the boundaries of local causation without encumbering even more bizarre and problematic consequences. For example, we might preserve local causation by introducing undetectable patterns of backward time travel. But even if we adopted this proposal, it would not entail idealism. Going backward or forward in time per se does not tell us anything about whether the particles in question depend upon consciousness for their existence.

If these observations are correct, then the main issue is not realism versus locality as many commentators have assumed. That is, we are not forced into adopting idealism as the price for abandoning the universality of local causation. Rather, the issue is what becomes of realism when the principle of local causes is modified to allow instances of superliminal communication suggested by the experimental work. In other words, if there is a case to be made for the superliminal interpretation, we should not hesitate out of fear of being forced into adopting some kind of observer-created reality.

But is the superliminal interpretation to be preferred? A growing body of argument points in that direction. Stapp, Herbert, and other physicists have argued that superliminal communication is: consistent with quantum mechanics; logically presupposed by EPR effects; partially derivable from the indivisibility of Planck's quantum of action; and indirectly testable.[51] If two particles (or two clusters of events) are instantaneously correlated in a nonchance manner, then the source of their connection must lie outside of space-time as defined by the speed of light.

If so, where do we go from here? What about the objective world assumed by realism? I would submit that faster-than-light travel at the quantum level only calls into question the *complete knowability* of the world. It suggests a weaker sense of realism by virtue of running up against certain limits to scientific knowledge. We simply cannot get outside space-time in order to determine why two events are meaningfully correlated within space-time.

Instantaneous correlations within space-time require only faster-than-light travel outside space-time. How *much* faster is something we can probably never determine. Such a condition puts limits on realism but does not force us to adopt an observer-created reality. Anyone who thinks that Bell's theorem proves that we create our own reality is reading more out of it than the facts warrant.

What is the significance of the Bell work for a larger paradigm? To begin with, it clearly demonstrates the strong interconnectedness of primary elements at a physical level of reality. In Bohm's view:

> The non-local, non-causal nature of the relationships of elements distant from each other evidently violates the requirements of separateness and independence of constituents that is basic to any mechanistic approach...Thus, if all actions are in the form of discrete quanta, the interactions between different entities (e.g., electrons) constitute a single structure of indivisible links, so that the entire universe has to be thought of as an unbroken whole. In this whole, each element that we can abstract in thought shows basic properties (wave or particle, etc.) that depend on its overall environment in a way that is much more reminiscent of how the organs constituting living beings are related, than it is of how the parts of a machine interact.[52]

Bohm's "single structure of indivisible links" may be more radically monistic than his analogy suggests. For to deny separateness and independence is to suppose that there are no separate events to "cause" other events. To speak in causal terms would thus be to express a limitation of our knowledge, despite the practical benefits this still brings. From the perspective of the whole, we would describe the EPR effect simply as a meaningful correlation of events within what is perhaps a single unified field.

The abandonment of strict localization on a horizontal axis of causality brings us face to face with vertical levels in the Great Chain. It is a powerful example of why anomalous (nonlocal) interactions within a certain level require us to move to another level for a more complete understanding of how they come to be. Certain events within space-time may force us to acknowledge domains outside of space-time as we now think of it. This, at least, is what superliminalism invites us to do.

An adequate explanation of the EPR effect places us at the intersection of vertical and horizontal axes in a way that expands our conception of reality. The irony here is that the experimental evidence for EPR type effects is as strong a contributor to Systems Holism as one could hope for— a case of dynamic interrelations if ever there were one. But the explanation of the evidence propels us to other levels of reality beyond ordinary space-time. And this is more in keeping with the Perennial Wisdom.

The Bell work does not demonstrate that nature is just one whole for the simple reason that what is true of quantum reality does not automatically translate to all other levels of reality. However, it nicely illustrates the idea of radical interconnectedness within a level and, in conjunction with parallel phenomena, contributes to the plausibility of worldviews which incorporate this kind of thinking. ESP may represent one type of parallel phenomenon, given certain assumptions about how fast it works. However, this does not make the explanation of ESP dependent upon the Bell work.

Another parallel phenomenon is William Condon's discovery (described earlier) of nonlocal causation in speaker-hearer communications, where the speed of sound is the limiting parameter. You will recall that Condon filmed listeners initiating appropriate and repeatable reactions (both verbal and behavioral) to certain words as they were being uttered by the speaker before the requisite sound waves could have reached their ears. It was as if they knew what was coming before it arrived. This pattern of communication viewed in slow motion looks more like a synchronized dance than a linear cause-and-effect progression.

Examples of such synchronistic phenomena at the level of biology are a growing area of research in themselves. Cell to cell communication, not just within an organism, but between organisms spatially and physically separated from one another, seems to be a built-in feature of the biological level of the Great Chain that we are only beginning to appreciate.[53] Examples of such communication are discussed in the following chapter.

In conclusion, the Bell work does not explain anomalous synchronicities, whether of a natural or paranormal variety. It simply demonstrates that they exist. In conjunction with the growing awareness of nonlocal synchronicities in many fields, it contributes to a vision of strong intralevel connectedness throughout the Great Chain. This vision, I suspect, will continue to find exemplification in both strange and common places.

CHAPTER EIGHT

Order in the Flux

How do things change, yet remain the same? What glues together the varied processes of nature? To attempt a comprehensive explanation of all forms of change would be a staggering intellectual challenge.[1] Fortunately, such an account is beyond the scope of this book. However, there are four topics relating to change that invite controversy in New Paradigm discussions. Each provides a way of extracting order from the flux, and each deserves extended exploration. They are:

1. Interaction of opposites: Nature seems to reflect the creative interaction of complementary opposites. Is this reflection merely a cultural invention we have imposed upon nature?
2. Masculine/feminine energies: What does this distinction amount to? Is there such a thing as a masculine or feminine "nature"? Is this distinction the invention of a sexist culture?
3. Self-organization: Living systems have the capacity to organize themselves. Do the biological and social sciences adequately explain this capacity? Is a stronger metaphysical basis required?
4. Accelerated evolution: At an accelerating pace, cracks are appearing everywhere in the foundations of the old, and the new is pushing its way in. Can the social sciences adequately explain this acceleration? Is something more fundamental taking place behind the scenes?

THE CREATIVE INTERPLAY
OF OPPOSITES: DISCOVERY OR INVENTION?

Since ancient times, poets, philosophers, and scientists have been intrigued by a vision of nature in which two opposed, but complementary and creatively interacting, forces underlie all patterns of change. These primordial forces go by different names and mean different things, depending upon the context. The ancient Greek philosopher Empedocles termed them "love" (tending toward unity and order) and "strife" (tending toward fragmentation and disunity).

Historian Oswald Spengler described the rise and fall of cultures by referring to the forces of "integration" and "differentiation," the same terms used by systems holist Arthur Koestler to describe the dynamics of all systems. Every distinguishable entity (atom, cell, organ, person, country, etc.), according to Koestler, is a delicate balance between integrating tendencies toward group membership and differentiating tendencies toward individuality and autonomy. It is difficult to imagine any exceptions to this rule.

The philosopher Hegel described history as the dialectical movement from an established structure, which he termed a "thesis," to its opposite, the "antithesis," both of which are eventually unified in a "synthesis" at a higher level of organization. In science Newtonian mechanics is predicated upon the interaction of two forces: centripetal (toward) and centrifugal (away). The laws of electromagnetism and chemical bonding are expressed in terms of the interaction between positive and negative charges.

Hinduism views the cosmos in terms of expansion (Day of Brahman) and contraction, leading to the Night of Brahman. Taoism's creative inter-action of yin and yang, with all of their culturally derived meanings, is the classic example of a dynamic polarity metaphysics. "The *yang* having reached its climax retreats in favor of the *yin*; the *yin* having reached its climax retreats in favor of the *yang*."[2] Ken Carey offers an inspired vision of such polarity at a cosmic level:

> One face of the Eternal One is ever formless and beyond definition, but the other face of the Eternal One appears as Two. These Two, between them, are the source of all created things.
>
> Holy Mother, Truth: all matter is her body, the Earth is her eye.
>
> Holy Father, Love: the stars are his flesh, Spirit his I.[3]

Carey's vision suggests a distinction between dynamic polarities, on the one hand, and (seemingly) static polarities, on the other—between forces in motion and repetitive patterns that express or give rise to stable forms. Examples of such polarized patterns are form and matter, male and female, universal and particular, subject and object, and good and evil. Each of these pairs is logically complementary and represents not so much motion or action itself as an outer limit that constrains or guides change.

A number of dynamic principles are associated with the idea of inter-action between complementary opposites. Some have a distinctly Taoist flavor, but most are recognized in various esoteric schools of thought, both ancient and modern. "Every extreme bears the seeds of its opposite," for example, or "Everything has unequal portions of positive and negative energy."

The idea that every extreme bears the seed of its opposite is represented in the Taoist mandala, each side of which curves into the other and contains a small circle of the "color" of the opposite side (often black or white). This dynamic juxtaposition of opposites isn't intended to predict the outcome of any particular course of action. For example, there is some-thing of the masculine in every woman and something of the feminine in every man. But this observation in itself does not tell us which or how many men will actualize their latent feminine aspects, or when they will do this.

The creative interplay of opposites assumes that the universe is in vari-ous stages of imbalance. All things are in flux because they reflect various levels of imbalance, and all things are to some extent imbalanced because they are in flux! Change and imbalance require each other. Whether it is water seeking its own level, people fighting disease, nations competing for scarce resources, the universe expanding, or women struggling for equality, the phenomenon of imbalance striving after balance is everywhere to be found. And when balance is found, it eventually gives way to imbalance.

Sometimes a process may be pushed to a state of extreme imbalance, and, in the interests of survival, "escapes to a higher order." The stresses brought on by imbalance can be the impetus for evolutionary growth. The transformative challenges surveyed in Chapter One abundantly illustrate this idea. The institutions and ideas confronted with such challenges sur-vive, but in a different form. The institution of marriage, for example, has survived but is being defined today in quite different ways than it was in 1850.

Of course, there is no guarantee that extreme imbalance will nurture an evolutionary process in a positive way. Disintegration and destruction may also result from unsuccessfully dealing with transformational challenges. Sometimes the old must be completely let go of or, in some cases, destroyed, in order to make way for the new. And sometimes, as in the case of a possible global ecological catastrophe, the choice between transformation or destruction is up to us.

Some scientists and philosophers argue that the creative interaction of opposites may seem to be a law of nature, but is really just a projection of our own cultural biases on to nature. Is this principle a discovery of something that was already there in nature before humans came along, or only an invention that reflects our desire to make sense of an irrational universe?

It is true, of course, that many polarities are social inventions designed to advance the interests of a certain group who claim that their vision is part of the "natural order of things." This is especially evident in stereotypical gender roles. From this concession, however, it does not follow that all polarities are mere cultural conventions. The distinction between waves and particles, subjectivity and objectivity, integration and differentiation, or matter and form, for example, express real polarities appropriate to certain levels of the Great Chain. They are not merely invented, read into nature, and taught to subsequent generations. For change to exist at all, there must be some dynamic interaction between such complementary pairs of opposites.

If the interplay of opposites were merely a cultural invention rather than a universal category of nature, we should be able to find exceptions in nature where it does not apply. Yet this is precisely what the critic is hard-pressed to do. Every process in nature seems to reflect the dynamic interplay of at least two forces. Every object reflects some polarity. In describing human experience, for example, we inevitably refer to polarities such as active/passive, subjective/objective, and selfish/altruistic. Likewise, everything in the universe seems subject to competing forces of integration and differentiation. In short, we live in patterns of duality. Some we have invented. Some we have not.

It may be objected that, in covering such a wide spectrum of polarities (from wave/particle to masculine/feminine), the idea of interaction between complementary opposites does too much work; it's *too* broad a category! What covers everything in general has little relevance for anything in particular. Many examples of interaction between complementary polarities appear to have little, if anything, to do with one another. What does physics have to do with femininity? Why assume that diverse polarities are instances of the same universal principle in nature?

The answer is that the idea of interaction between complementary opposites is part description and part root metaphor. It is descriptive to the extent that it captures something very fundamental and essential in a wide variety of cases: their polarity, their complementarity, and the fact that change reflects an interaction and movement between them. Each derives its meaning, in part, by contrast with the other. However, the idea of complementary interaction is also partly metaphorical by virtue of its cross-disciplinary applicability. Its meaning is not exhausted by the territory it covers. It is partly rooted in those disciplines and partly free-floating, awaiting further application and refinement.

In the nineteenth century, it was popular to describe plants, humans, and steam engines as "machines." But scientists who thought this way did not consider throwing out this metaphor on the grounds that humans and steam engines are very different types of machine. The idea of creative interplay between complementary opposites needs to be understood in a similar manner, partly as an objective description and partly as an open-ended metaphor. We can ask no more of any fundamental category of existence.

Complementary interaction is an abstract principle, but one that has numerous practical applications. It is a great equalizer and, properly understood and applied, can be empowering. American business leaders, for example, are learning that the exercise of power is both more effective and ultimately more profitable if encouraged to flow not just from management to labor, but also from labor to management; each pole brings a distinctive contribution to the process, which is enhanced by including the complementary pole in the loop of decision-making and production. Appreciation of this fact can help to counter the excesses of hierarchical control and empower those in both upper and lower echelons of a hierarchy.

American presidents tend to see it as their duty to pack the Supreme Court with justices who, in their view, truly understand what the Constitution means and what the founding fathers intended. President Roosevelt took the liberal route. Presidents Reagan and Bush took the conservative route. Neither route, however, could possibly represent the true interpretation of the Constitution, since neither interpretation could exist without the other—a fact which most presidents tend to overlook. Any administration which packs the court to the left guarantees the eventual emergence of a right-wing court.

A liberal president who understood the principle of creative interplay between opposites would appoint at least several conservative justices to help spare the country the excesses of extreme swings to the left and to help empower the liberal appointees who would be forced to refine their views in creative and sometimes heated exchanges with their conservative colleagues. Little could do more harm to a country over the long run than a Supreme Court consisting entirely of liberal justices or of conservative justices.

Then again, sometimes extreme positions are the only way to foster change. Creative interaction between complementary opposites is as powerful as it needs to be in the cause of long-term creative evolution. Over the short-term, it may *seem* to take sides and become fixed near one end of a spectrum of possibilities. In time, however, all such illusions crumble. For every extreme bears the seeds of its own destruction and rebirth in a complementary opposite. This is especially evident in the cycles of war and peace.

A POLITICALLY CORRECT
INTEGRATION OF MASCULINE/FEMININE ARCHETYPES

Masculine and feminine energies illustrate the creative interplay between complementary opposites. However, this illustration is suspicious to those who hold that there is no such thing as an essential masculine or feminine nature apart from the inventions of a patriarchal culture. Since the distinction between the masculine and the feminine plays an important and controversial role in both the women's movement and in the Rising Culture, it deserves a more extended exploration. I suspect that readers of this book would not argue for sexism. The question I want to examine is how much of a role, if any, the distinction between the masculine and the feminine can play in New Paradigm discussions.

Divergent wings of feminist thought. Let me begin by recalling two brief encounters which illustrate a profound divergence in feminist thought. Not long ago, a feminist friend described to me another woman with whom she felt a sense of kinship. She described her as intelligent, sensual, powerful, independent, socially and ecologically aware, visionary, and sophisticated about metaphysical matters. This woman also held an upper-level management position in a Fortune 500 corporation. Significantly, she also described her friend as "the paradigm of goddess energy now coming in." She took this not as something to be debated, but as a much needed development in the larger scheme of things.

Some weeks later, I had occasion to discuss some unrelated matters with another feminist friend who has her own active connections to the women's movement. As the conversation proceeded, she mentioned that she had recently attended a "disgusting" presentation by a female healer who claimed to be an earthly connection for goddess energy. She viewed such developments as antithetical to the women's movement and punctuated her dismay with the observation that "she couldn't buy all this yin-yang sexist crap."

My two feminist friends were united in their belief that patriarchal oppression in all of its forms should be eliminated. Beyond that, however, they agreed on very little except abortion. This is a healthy and predictable development, the kind of thing we would expect in any leading-edge movement. So it should not surprise us to find at one end of the spectrum feminists whose primary agenda is ethical, social, and political.[4] They want to move women into positions of greater authority, acknowledge women's intellectual and artistic contributions (especially in textbooks), and remove male bias in the formulation, interpretation, and enforcement of the law. Ending job discrimination is only one of many goals.

This wing tends to view personal growth and development largely as a function of social conditioning, something that tends to take care of itself (and is best left to each woman) as oppression is overcome. They seek to educate both men and women about the consequences of male oppression in all of its overt and subtle forms. They do not see the need to ground social and political agendas in any metaphysics, much less that of a yin-yang variety. Injustice is injustice, with or without the interaction of complementary opposites. The lessons in Simone d' Beauvoir's *The Second Sex* or Andrea Dworkin's *Woman Hating* are still too close at hand. These feminists tend to be uncomfortable with talk about the "Earth Mother." And they prefer lobbying to meditation.

At another end of the spectrum are feminists whose views on male bias are underwritten by a strong emphasis upon the internal dynamics of personal and spiritual growth.[5] These feminists, such as Starhawk and Matthew Fox, are comfortable with "Earth Mother" talk and with meditation. Many combine their interests in spirituality (including Goddess traditions and Wicca), the environment, holistic health practices, and revisioning gender relations into the paradigm of ecofeminism described in Irene Diamond's and Gloria Ornstein's collection of essays, *Reweaving the World* and in Sallie McFague's *The Body of God: An Ecological Theology*. They also are more attracted to perennialist worldviews.

They believe that the time has come to rectify seven thousand years of prevailing male energy by acknowledging and nurturing the emergence of the complementary feminine side of things, but not the stereotypical feminine aspect men have projected. The challenge, as they see it, is to regain a sense of balance, where men acknowledge and integrate their feminine sides and women integrate both their masculine and goddess natures.

All over the country in sweat lodges, rebirthing workshops, leading-edge psychotherapy centers, and through other methods of inner transformation and spiritual growth, this challenge is being directly confronted. Carol Christ's *Laughter of Aphrodite: Reflections on a Journey to the Goddess* is one of many personal chronicles about recapturing a lost but essential nature. If this journey is successful, the outer goals of social and political equality will be enhanced. This does not mean that the more inwardly directed feminist isn't actively involved in ending oppression, or that the externally directed activist has no spiritual interests. It does mean that feminism, like any other school of thought, reflects creative polarities.

There is abundant cross-fertilization these days between many wings of feminist thought. Riane Eisler's *The Chalice and the Blade*, for example, ends with a plea for the recognition of the interdependence of all things and the importance of creative partnership. More than a call for networking, it seeks to build bridges not only within feminism but also between feminism and other agendas in the larger New Paradigm spectrum. In a similar inclusivist vein, Anne Wilson Schaef's recent *Beyond Therapy, Beyond Science* presents an integrated vision of wellness that moves beyond both philosophical and gender differences. For some feminists, the primary agenda is transforming culture; for others, it is transforming themselves. These are complementary perspectives which, in the case of particular individuals, can be creatively mixed in many ways.

The critique of essentialism. Is the concept of a feminine nature plausible? Feminists who avoid metaphysics in favor of pressing social and political agendas typically do not think so. They reject the idea of an essential masculine nature or of an essential feminine nature. Masculine and feminine natures, they urge, are merely social conventions invented by men and then read into nature as a way of solidifying their power. It suits men's interests, for example, to have us think of God as male. In fact, the very idea of a Great Chain of Being—with or without a personal God—is to these feminists a typical male notion. To them, it looks like the Great Chain of Oppression.

This critique is compelling. However, it does not so much address the question of essentialism per se as express a fear that, if it were true, men would misuse it. Perhaps they would. However, I propose to explore a related criticism which stems less from a concern with oppression than from a feminist analysis of the way men tend to think and be in the world. One summary of this analysis (of the many possible) is presented in Anne Wilson Schaef's earlier and somewhat more polarized work, *Women's Reality*. The critique with which I am concerned questions the all-too-convenient alignment of women with merely feminine energies and men with merely masculine energies.

The ideas of masculine and feminine are cluster concepts with broad historical roots. In general, the cluster concept of "masculine" has included such notions as active, ego-centered, rational, independent, competitive, and outwardly powerful, whereas the cluster concept of "feminine" has included such descriptions as passive, intuitive, emotional, nurturing, cooperative, and inwardly powerful.

I will not attempt to justify these ascriptions. It can't be done. Some of what typifies a man in one culture or historical period may apply to a woman in another culture or period. In America, for example, gender roles involving work and careers have changed considerably, thereby demonstrating a learned rather than an innate basis. For purposes of illustration, however, the above characteristics typify various historical assumptions about men's and women's natures.

Even if we do accept these complementary pairs (rational/intuitive, aggressive/passive, competitive/cooperative) as reflecting a deep structural polarity in the natural scheme of things, why do women get stuck with only the second option of each polarity? In fact, why even call the cluster of intuition, feeling, nurturing, and cooperation "feminine"? And why align masculine energy with rationality and competition? It's all too convenient, the critic charges—and too sexist!

How might we respond to this charge in a way that serves the cause of an *inclusive* paradigm? My proposal is as follows. The clusters of energies to which we have attached the labels of "masculine" and "feminine" represent deep structural polarities in nature, human and otherwise. Whether at the individual or broad-scale historical level, they are in more or less continuous fluctuation, sometimes achieving balance, but more often in imbalance.

The masculine mind-set has prevailed but shows signs of weakening. For example, in the male-dominated corporate world, some companies are actively experimenting with "feminine management styles." These styles stress consensus-building and decentralization and take into account the larger network of *relationships* (maternity leave for mothers and/or fathers, environmental impact, quality of life, personal growth, etc.) which are affected, but typically ignored, by profit-driven business decisions.

Does this mean that women are innately different from or even superior to men? (As a feminist T-shirt slogan once put it: "If you think equality is the goal, your standards are too low.") Not necessarily. It does mean that we should acknowledge a fundamental distinction in human consciousness between energies that contribute to power and isolation, on the one hand, and to mutually empowering relationships, on the other. We need not use gender terminology, such as "masculine and feminine archetypes," to denote these differences, although it's more convenient to do so. We could call them simply Energy Complex A and Energy Complex B.

Some psychologists have suggested that we substitute two fundamental personality traits for "masculine" and "feminine": *agency* (tending toward individualism and self-assertion) and *communion* (tending toward group harmony and cooperation). We could also label these the *instrumental* ("What are the steps necessary to achieve a certain goal?") and the *relational* ("Am I connected to myself and my environment in a felt, empowering way?"). Note, however, that no matter which terms are used or how their definitions are slanted, a fundamental distinction is retained.

Although there may be natural attractions within each cluster of traits—perhaps intuition is fostered by passivity or competition by independence—there is within each person the innate capacity for mixing. That is, intuition can go with competition, or emotional sensitivity with independence, and the like. Similarly, agency and communion (or instrumental and relational perspectives) are not mutually exclusive ways of being in the world. Each man and woman can incorporate these traits in variable degrees.

The most important part of my proposal, then, is that there is *no essential or fixed connection* between certain fundamental traits and men, or between other complementary traits and women. It could have transpired that women prevailed in all the characteristics which have attracted the masculine label for the last few thousand years and the same for men, in reverse. Men are not innately more competitive and women innately more cooperative, although history has conspired to make it seem that way. We can examine our current programming and redirect the course of history. We can develop a culture, for example, which encourages men to pursue more cooperative and mutually empowering relationships.

An analogy from physics may help. There is nothing about electrons per se that makes them negatively charged particles except that they behave in ways (typically as complementary opposites) that positively charged particles, such as protons, do not. Physicists didn't discover that electrons had a negative charge attached to them; they did discover that the particles circulating around the nucleus of an atom had an opposite charge from protons found within the nucleus. They discovered that some particles had to carry a negative charge and others a positive charge in order for certain basic laws of physics to work.

However, they could have decided that electrons were positively charged particles and protons negatively charged ones. To be sure, many of the laws of physics would have to be rewritten to accommodate this change, but the laws themselves would remain intact; stable atoms would still have the same number of positively and negatively charged particles balancing each other. What physicists could not do is eliminate the distinction between positive and negative charges, which is essential to the very nature of the physical universe.

A similar situation is evident, I think, between masculine and feminine energies (or archetypes). We can characterize each category as we see fit, even to label one as if it were the other, but we cannot do away with the very distinction itself. Anyone who tries to by promoting a universal gender-neutral language would be forced to tacitly reintroduce the distinction on other levels. The difference between those who adopt relational attitudes and those who adopt instrumentalist attitudes toward life, for example, would still exist, even if we were to do away with references to men and women, or to "he" and "she."

Does the influence of our genes deter our ability to balance masculine and feminine energies within each gender? Suppose that, as some research suggests, aggressive males tend to have abnormally high testosterone levels. This implies some type of innate or essential connection between having a man's body and exhibiting male behavior. Still, there are many ways to interpret this situation. For one, not all males are so disposed. Moreover, some women are equally disposed in this capacity. To the extent that there is a connection between certain types of behavior and gender, it is not an essential or a necessary one.

Once we know the determinants of a certain personality trait, we can develop strategies to change those determinants—in this case through reducing testosterone levels. Biological predispositions for both males and females will not account for a full spectrum of personality traits. But even when connections between biology and behavior are discovered, there is no compelling reason to view them as essentially fixed or as definitive of the gender.

My proposal harbors no intrinsic gender bias regarding how the energies in question will (or should!) interact in any particular culture or period of time. If there is a bias, it is in favor of each person's freedom to explore the appropriate mixture, both masculine and feminine (Jung's *anima* and *animus*). This proposal can attract women, especially those with interests in spirituality and depth psychology. And while lending itself to an archetypal metaphysics, it contains nothing contrary to the goal of eliminating patriarchy.

Polarity metaphysics is essentialist in its fundamental categories but nonessentialist in how these categories are mixed in daily life. We could raise boys to be the kind of humans that in many ways we have tradition-ally considered women to be and vice versa. Or we could strive for balanced contrast where both men and women have available to them the trans-formational possibilities of full participation in both categories. Some of us may even choose to weight our lives more on one side or the other. The important thing is to structure our social institutions to support explora-tion and informed choice in the matter.

If we happen to live in an age requiring more cooperation and less competition, or more nurturance and less control, and if cooperation and nurturance just happen to be in the cluster of properties that attract the label of feminine energy, then there is nothing wrong with the claim that the world needs more feminine energy. This claim is not sexist, because it merely seeks to rectify an imbalance, not give one gender power over the other.

Is this another proposal for androgyny? It depends on what is meant by this concept. On the one hand, the weak or neutral sense of androgyny implies sexlessness or a lack of feminine or masculine traits. Such a view, in my opinion, represents a serious misreading and implies a goal that will never be reached.

On the other hand, in its strong sense androgyny actually embraces a polarity metaphysics. It stipulates that each person—whether biologically male or female—in theory has available the entire range of masculine and feminine behaviors, as particular situations may call for them. (From a perennialist perspective, each person has literally built into his or her causal body the capacity for manifesting either orientation, depending upon the karmic agendas of that lifetime.) Research suggests that people who integrate both types of behavior into their lifestyles are more adaptive, flexible, and interpersonally competent than people with a primary masculine or a primary feminine orientation. These people may well enjoy an evolutionary advantage over their stereotyped counterparts.

Is modified essentialism still sexist? For some feminists, balance between the poles is not sufficient, even when the poles are within each woman and each man, and not as a gap between men and women in general. Any proposal which acknowledges the polarity, whether balanced or not, is still viewed as sexist. To them, it reinforces the practice of gender labeling at a time when we desperately need to move beyond fragmentation and address the transformational challenges which confront the human species. What we need, according to this point of view, is a gender-neutral language.

Retaining labels, especially when they refer to social groups and practices, can be risky business; people can be harmed when too much is made of the labels applied to them. The question is whether we should deal with the ethical issues head on, while maintaining a flexible attitude about what the labels can stand for, or whether we should do away with the labels in the hope of short-circuiting the issues.

Many readers would agree that the common challenges we face as human beings—poverty, injustice, environmental decay—override whatever distinctions we draw between feminine and masculine natures. And most would agree that many of these challenges have their origins in patriarchal mind-sets. However, we can overcome patriarchy and still maintain the categories of masculine and feminine. There is no necessary connection between a polarity metaphysics of the masculine and the feminine and social injustice.

To do away with the categories altogether, under the veil of abolishing sexism, leads to the following dilemma. Feminist thought begins with women's experience, and women's experience begins (although it does not end) with the fact of oppression. This nearly always begins at an early age—so early that it seems "natural" later on. The prime directive of all feminist thought and action is to achieve freedom from oppression in all of its varied forms.

But then what? After the shackles of oppression are lifted, women have positive and distinctive contributions to make to culture. Many are now engaged, for example, in reinterpreting history, literature, religion, and even the foundations of science.[6] Others are envisioning ways of being in the world and with each other, where the ideals of mutual empowerment and inclusiveness play critical roles. The question is where these new ways of thinking and being come from.

Presumably they didn't come from men, although the experience of patriarchy is a stimulus to their emergence. It is the ultimate sexist heresy to suppose that the only valuable ideas women have are those taken from men. For historical reasons, women appear more open to the activation of certain human capacities which, when properly nurtured, results in an overarching perspective substantially different from those developed by men over the past several thousand years. This perspective, which stresses nonhierarchical cooperative relationships with all aspects of our environment, is a powerful feature of the Rising Culture.

Can men access these same innate capacities? Surely, although they are behind women in this respect because they have not had the stimulus to do so. Women do have the stimulus precisely because men have been in positions of greater power. This does not mean that men don't have goddess energy. Nor does it mean that women don't have god energy. It is to say that women are ahead of men in acknowledging and manifesting goddess energy.

Jean Shinoda Bolen explores what this means in both history and practice in *Goddesses in Everywoman* and *Gods in Everyman*. It should be stressed, however, that just as there is no necessary connection between god energy and men, there also is none between goddess energy and women. We should guard against any interpretation suggesting that only women can access the goddess or that only men can bear god energy. Either alternative would be sexist. As a matter of current history, more women than men are closer to the goddess. But history can change.

Jean Baker Miller (*Toward a New Psychology of Women*), Carol Gilligan (*In a Different Voice*) and, indirectly, Deborah Tannen (*You Just Don't Understand*) present a modified essentialism consistent with my proposal. For example, the root metaphor of "relating" pertains more to an average woman's life than an average man's life. Women tend to use conversation to expand and understand relationships, whereas men (with their "instrumentalist" outlooks) tend to use it to solve problems, thereby ending the conversation (and returning to their newspapers)! Women tend to value caring over freedom, whereas with men it's the reverse. Women are more likely to view events in context, men to see them as isolated. But neither Miller nor Gilligan assert that only women can be this way or that men cannot access the same capacity for relationships.

In summary, women are not seeking freedom from oppression just so they can become more like men. Given prevailing power structures, the goal of a sexless society would tend to collapse the differences between men and women in favor of men anyway. Women are seeking greater freedom so that *as women* they can make contributions to culture different from those that men have made. In the eyes of many writers, these contributions must be made if we are to survive as a species. Acknowledging these contributions assumes that there is something intrinsic to the concept of the feminine that is affected by, but not merely the product of, child-bearing, hormones, or socialization in a patriarchal culture.

Feminists who criticize the polarity of masculine and feminine archetypal energies are often motivated to do so in order to escape the sexist agendas associated with such thinking. That is understandable, even though sexist agendas per se do not automatically follow from the mere acknowledgment of the polarity.

However, when they turn to the constructive task of revisioning culture (more consensus-building and cooperation, no war, more inclusivist thinking, less competition, more discernment over the role of "men's toys" in society, a less adversarial legal system, more love and less instrumentalism, etc.), they appear to be more essentialist in their thinking than the initial desire for fairness and equality suggests. Feminists who claim that, in certain critical respects, they (and women in general) can make a better world than men have been able to achieve in five thousand years strongly imply that there is something about women—or about the kind of archetypal energies that women have better access to—that is essentially different from what men have in this respect.

Unfortunately, there is a tendency for some academic feminists, especially those associated with Women's Studies departments, to focus more on issues of victimization and the politics of sisterhood than on broad cultural revisioning. As Daphne Patai and Noretta Koertge conclude in *Professing Feminism: Cautionary Tales from the Strange World of Women's Studies*, some professors stop just short of brainwashing their students into a tightly constructed ideology that includes, among other things, rejecting the literature of "dead white males" in favor of therapeutic discussions of sexual abuse and other more timely issues.

In these situations, the pain of victimhood may be too much to let go of. For others, the broader topic of, say, how women view and relate to nature cannot be seriously explored until the battle for equality has been won. For still others, the essentialist implications of broad cultural revisioning are a step in the wrong direction. Since my proposal involves deep archetypal polarities, academic feminists are therefore not likely to embrace it, despite my claims of its nonsexist character.

I can only repeat that the mere acknowledgment of such polarities does not imply the power of either gender over the other. Nor does it imply any necessary connection between masculine archetypal energies and men, or between feminine archetypal energies and women. While the mere distinction between these energies is an essential one, how the dynamic interaction between the two cashes out in any particular time, place, or gender is up to us. With that conclusion, I suspect that most men and women in the New Paradigm dialogue, with or without a feminist label, already concur.

SELF-ORGANIZING SYSTEMS: A DEFENSE OF RUPERT SHELDRAKE

Biologists and social scientists long have been aware of the capacities of open living systems to organize and maintain themselves, despite internal and external challenges to their structure and function. Up to a point, living systems are able to sustain order in the midst of chaos. When the salamander's tail is cut off, it grows a new one. This capacity for self-organization seems to be guided by unseen structures or forms, at least to the naked eye.

If so, where are these forms? Are they in the objects themselves, as Aristotle and the biologist Hans Driesch urged? Or do they exist apart from individual things in another realm where they subtly influence the organization of content, as Plato and Whitehead argued? Could it be that self-organization is determined merely by the laws of physics and chemistry? (A parallel question is whether the natural laws which govern the interactions between objects would still exist, even if there were no objects.) Self-organization involves four traits of living systems which raise questions about the existence and nature of forms (or laws) behind the scenes.[7]

The first type of self-organizing tendency in nature involves the *spontaneous evolution of novel forms* from less complex lower systems to more complex higher systems. Few scientists today would deny that random genetic mutation and environmental selection play *some* role in accounting for the evolution of species. However, the sudden emergence of major subsystems (such as the eye) and whole new species presents significant puzzles.

Explaining these emergences has led Stephen Gould and Niles Eldredge to develop their theory of "punctuated equilibrium" (sudden jumps in nature). The sudden appearance of winged reptiles, for instance, involves far more than the accidental realignment of several elements within the gene pool. It requires complex multiple realignments which defy rational expectation. Flying requires radically different visual and sensing systems and volume-to-weight ratios, not just wings. What good would under-developed wings be if they had to survive thousands of years serving no purpose at all, without accompanying morphological changes in the species?

If the adaptability of accidental mutations were all that is involved in evolution, it is difficult to understand why we evolved past plankton, which are among the most adaptable organisms on earth. Studies by John Cairns of Harvard and Barry Hall of the University of Connecticut have suggested that certain types of bacteria are capable of mutating in a "directed fashion" in order to survive.[8] In both studies the bacteria appeared capable of reprogramming themselves in order to utilize nutrients they otherwise were not capable of metabolizing. In one study the odds against chance of this happening were greater than a trillion to one.

In *Evolution: Theory in Crisis*, Michael Denton argues that punctuated equilibrium is a description of the gaps between species, not an explanation of the emergence of new species. Accidental mutations account only for evolution within species, not between them. Amino acid sequences from supposedly related species simply do not show genetic descent from one class to another. There is no trace at the molecular level, for example, of the evolution from fish to amphibian to reptile to mammal.

Neither conventional nor neo-Darwinian thinking can account statistically for the accidental emergence of the mammalian brain. Even if only one percent of the connections were specifically organized, this would still be more than all connections in the entire communications network on the planet. Indeed, there are far more specific connections in the human brain than there is information packed into the DNA code to explain them. "It is premature to claim that random processes could have assembled mosquitoes and elephants when we still have to determine the actual probability of discovery by chance of one single functional protein molecule."[9]

Perhaps, then, accidental mutations did not come first, as evolutionary theory prescribes. Rather, the sudden emergence of novel life forms, each of which paves the way for its successors, is only a part of the larger self-organizing tendency of nature as a whole. If so, then only models enabling us to derive "less from more," i.e., which allow us to interpret biological advances as reflecting higher (and prior) levels of intelligence in the Great Chain of Being, will enable us to bridge the gap from one spontaneous emergence to the next. For this fact is not explained in the "more from less" or "bottom up" approach of mainstream evolutionary theory.[10] The evolution of higher species makes considerable sense if the higher species are in some sense prefigured (perhaps externally generated) in the DNA structures of the lower species; it borders on the miraculous if they are not.

A second type of self-organization involves self-regulation and maintenance—what biologist Humberto Maturana termed "autopoisis." Autopoisis is the ability of a system to maintain the integrity of its structure and function. For example, hormone levels are continuously regulated in humans in ways that encourage consistent behavior. Nations typically regulate themselves through war, peace, and changes of leadership in ways to preserve continuity.

A machine is built to produce a certain outcome. Eventually it wears out. A cell on the other hand is principally concerned with maintaining itself. The most striking example of self-renewal is the ability of certain species to regenerate lost limbs. In such cases, the systems involved appear to obey commands from invisible blueprints, forms which guide the direction of metabolic processes.

The third type of self-organizing ability is morphogenesis, the development of characteristic form in species. Why, for example, do chimp, pig, and human fetuses go on to become chimps, pigs, and humans when in early embryogenesis they are so strikingly similar? Molecular biologists hold out the promise of explaining morphogenesis by appealing to as-yet-undiscovered patterns of DNA. But despite much progress on other fronts in molecular biology, forty years of research has not produced a solution to the riddle of morphogenesis.

It is difficult to see how it could, when the genetic codes of chimps and humans are ninety-nine percent identical. This should lead us to expect minor differences among the species, when in fact they are major. Genetic coding does tell us what type of material is needed for a certain system, how much will be needed, when it should be delivered, and even the order in which certain systems will be turned on (or off). But it does not tell us anything about the final form the completed product will take. By analogy, it does not tell us whether our brick and lumber home will have four bedrooms off the living room or none at all. Morphogenesis (from the Greek *morphe*, for "form") is still an unexplained mystery in biology.

Morphogenesis and related phenomena of self-organization led Rupert Sheldrake to the development of his widely discussed theory of formative causation. Sheldrake's ideas were first presented in his *A New Science of Life*, hailed in critical reviews as both a major breakthrough and as a pseudo-scientific candidate for burning. These ideas are refined and defended in later works, *The Presence of the Past: Morphic Resonance and the Habits of Nature, The Rebirth of Nature*, and *Seven Experiments that Could Change the World*.[11]

The basic ideas of Sheldrake's theory are straightforward. Organisms, structures, and patterns of behavior constitute morphic units exhibiting a recurring *form*. Morphic units in turn generate, reinforce, and are guided by morphogenetic fields. The explanation of morphogenesis is that the DNA sequences are supplemented by an invisible field or structural blue-print to which cells and molecules conform as they grow in number and complexity.

In the case of novel structures or learning patterns, the field strength is very small, there being so few objects to reinforce it. But once established, the field increases the likelihood of identical structures or patterns coming into existence, which in turn increase its strength, which then increases the stability of the new form in nature. This is illustrated by a phenomenon long recognized in chemistry. After the spontaneous synthesis of a novel crystalline form in a sealed jar in one part of a laboratory, there is a tendency for that form to appear spontaneously in other parts of the building.

Morphogenetic fields exist outside of space-time, do not transmit energy, and interact with other known local (physical) fields such as those of an electromagnetic nature. They operate through distinctive resonance patterns which are established among the fields, objects, and processes they guide.

Some fields are so well-established that they appear to us in the form of laws of nature. But field action should always be interpreted probabi-listically, according to Sheldrake. For unlike Plato's Forms, they are not immutable. They are subject to change and even extinction.

Sheldrake's hypothesis is testable, especially where learning is involved. For example, it explains anomalous learning curves in successive gen-erations of inbred rats trained for a specific task. (They learn the same task more readily in successive generations.) Worldwide, the hypothesis has generated much discussion, and both believers and skeptics have proposed interesting experimental formats to test it. For example, Japanese rhymes have proven easier for English-speaking children to learn than couplets of nonsense syllables, presumably because a strong morphogenetic field had already been established by generations of Japanese children reciting the rhymes.

Three other experiments completed in 1991 supported Sheldrake's prediction that the rate of learning new tasks accelerates in proportion to the expanding pool of prior subjects who have recently mastered the task. A 1994 study suggested that an M-field newly created by one group exhibits greater influence over the choices of a second group in selecting one of four defined tasks than it does over a third group whose selections from the same tasks were made before the M-field was created.[12] If Sheldrake's hypothesis is correct, we influence each other in ways that violate normal spatial and temporal parameters. His theory illuminates yet another way in which we may all be interconnected.

Psychologist Susan Blackmore has argued that, whether successful or not, such predictions could not provide evidence for Sheldrake's theory, because it is both incoherent and circular. Her reasoning relies upon Stephen Braude's earlier critique of holographic modeling. Morphic units generate morphogenetic fields. But what counts as a morphic unit? One's whole body? The cells on one's skin? Instances of specific behavior? A heart? Chanting with one's meditation group on Sunday evenings? "There are an infinite number of ways in which nature may be divided up, or parsed. And none is the 'right' way. So there may need to be an infinite number of morphic units, which destroys the central thrust of the theory."[13]

I find this objection unpersuasive. Sheldrake's theory is intended to account for certain aspects of the underlying form of perceived structural and functional similarities. The most we are committed to on this view is an indefinitely large number of *types* of things. The fact that we have latitude in dividing up the furniture of the world does not undermine the fact that preferred parsings have in fact emerged, namely, atoms, molecules, cells, organs, people, etc. To be sure, anything may be considered a whole unto itself or a part of something else. But the fact that cells are parts of organs and composed of molecules does not cause us to wonder whether they actually exist or whether the dividing line between cells and molecules is arbitrary.

Blackmore offers a second objection as follows. Sheldrake perceives certain similarities between things and posits morphogenetic fields to account for them. These fields *act* in proportion to the similarity of the original morphic units and those yet to be influenced. Yet there are infinite ways in which any two objects can be said to be similar or dissimilar, and none of these is obviously any better than any others independent of particular contexts. Sheldrake must specify his critical notion of similarity between any two objects by appealing to the effect of the field upon them. But since he posited the field in order to account for the similarity in the first place, Blackmore concludes, his theory is circular.

This objection is equally unpersuasive. If I pick two apples from a tree, one is surely more similar to the other than to, say, my automobile, no matter what the context is. Anyone who thinks that their dissimilarities outweigh their similarities has no way to avoid the conclusion that apples could be more similar to automobiles than to other apples! Sheldrake, like any scientist, can specify the similarities between the apples by examining their properties. He is not forced to specify their similarities by circular appeals to his morphogenetic fields, because the fields are intended to help explain *why* two apple seeds *become* two apple trees. It is one thing to recognize descriptive similarity, another to propose a causal explanation of morphogenesis.

Blackmore uses a familiar strategy by arguing that unobservable domains must be describable independently of the observable patterns they are intended to explain. Earlier in this century, behaviorists unsuccessfully applied this line of reasoning to mental states. To be depressed, for example, was assumed to be nothing more than behaving in depressed ways. Logical positivists attempted it (also without success) with atomic physics, by urging that electrons are merely useful descriptions of perceived effects (like tracks in cloud chambers). In each instance, it was claimed that nothing is going on behind the scenes, so to speak.

Blackmore's critique looks very similar. She would not be satisfied with behind the scenes accounts unless a direct description of morphogenetic fields was given. An inference to such fields will not do. Unfortunately, only scientifically literate clairvoyants could give such direct verification. And Blackmore doesn't think there are any legitimate clairvoyants.

Let me now introduce a critical refinement in Sheldrake's theory. His fields are described as "nonmaterial" and "outside space-time." This is presumably because: they are invisible; they are not electromagnetic (since electromagnetic fields depend upon actual states of organisms and morphogenetic fields correspond to the potential state of a developing system); and they operate nonlocally.

I would suggest to the contrary that his fields occupy intermediate territory between the physical and the nonphysical. That is, they exhibit properties found on both sides of this dichotomy and, as such, constitute a unique level in the Great Chain of Being. Morphogenetic fields, in other words, easily lend themselves to perennialist modeling and seem too metaphysical to attract positive attention from systems thinkers.

In the case of living systems, it's not clear whether corresponding bio-energetic fields reflect the physical state of an organism, on the one hand, or constitute a semi-independent blueprint to which physical states themselves conform, on the other. That the field changes after cutting a plant in half, for example, does not in itself prove that the causal relation could not work in the other direction. Experiments in Kirlian photography suggest that plant fields are not as dependent upon physical configuration as Sheldrake supposes. Morphogenetic fields, as he describes them, look like bioetheric forms in the Great Chain, which by current standards must be conceived as partly physical and partly nonphysical.

Morphogenetic fields, we are given to believe, act nonlocally. But some of the evidence cited by Sheldrake actually suggests the existence of initially small but expanding local fields. Spontaneous duplication of novel crystalline forms, for example, takes place fairly nearby, not on the other side of the world. Actually, some strains of bacteria appear to develop a resistance to antibiotics overnight—and from different locations around the world. However, this still suggests that Earth, not Alpha Centauri, is the local seat of the appropriate field.

Given Sheldrake's account, there appears no way to distinguish between a single field outside space acting nonlocally in space, and a universal field in space enveloping, say, all the pine trees on earth (including the places where future pine trees might grow). Although either hypothesis would account for nonlocally connected phenomena, Sheldrake doesn't need to go outside space to accomplish what a field spread out in space would do as well.

A final note: Any theory with empirically testable consequences falls within the purview of an expanded scientific paradigm. If, as Sheldrake holds, morphogenetic fields act on objects by mechanisms such as resonance patterns, then it's reasonable to suppose that the fields themselves are in space, even if in unusual ways. For example, frequencies, waveforms, and resonances are spatialized processes, although we do not necessarily perceive them as such.

Moreover, since fields change, they are certainly in time. And if space is inseparable from time, then we have another reason to interpret the fields as partly physical and partly nonphysical. Whatever morphogenetic fields turn out to be, it's more fruitful to suppose that they differ in degree, but not in principle, from other types of fields.

The larger implications of Sheldrake's hypothesis and this type of field modeling in general can be staggering. For example, the oppression of African Americans over a long period of time may have led to the formation of an invisible field of negativity (poor self-image, despair, etc.) whose influence is felt long after slavery and segregation laws have been changed. In addition to the standard sociological explanations of why African Americans have not made more progress in achieving racial and economic equality, the lingering effects of this field may be retarding the process. If so, the field needs to be attacked directly by changing people's emotional makeups. Otherwise, social legislation will not have the effect that it otherwise could have.

The final type of self-organization is self-transcendence. This refers to a system's ability to respond creatively to threats to its structure and function. Self-transcendence is the result of necessity, not chance. In the exchange of energy with its environment, a system may be challenged to the point that, in order to maintain its integrity, it has to undergo dramatic internal reorganization. For instance, a government may suspend certain constitutional rights in order to mount a successful war effort necessary to its survival.

The most dramatic illustration of this self-transcending type of organization is found in Ilya Prigogine's theory of dissipative structures (for which he received the Nobel Prize in 1977).[14] Any open system which takes order (energy) from its environment and metabolizes or converts it in a way that increases its own complex order in apparent violation of the second law of thermodynamics is termed "dissipative." An evolving embryo is dissipative in this sense.

Sometimes powerful fluctuations, especially in the form of feedback loops, force an open system to a far-from-equilibrium (unstable) condition. With its internal structure threatened by an unbalanced flow of energy, the system will approach a bifurcation point whereby it spontaneously begins to decay or else "escape to a higher order" via a reorganized internal structure.

Self-organization at far-from-equilibrium conditions is a delicate balance between chance and necessity. Molecules behaving independently of each other at equilibrium conditions may suddenly wake up and assume what was an initially unpredictable collective coherence. The new structure is labeled "dissipative" because of the higher level of energy needed to support it.

Prigogine's theory has been effectively applied to ecosystems, cities, and even traffic patterns, in addition to various biochemical processes. It appears capable of illuminating a wide variety of phenomena. For example, it applies to stress-generated transformations in the psychological domain ("If you don't change, I'll leave you!"); to koan contemplation and sudden illumination in Zen (where repeated attempts to ascertain the sound of one hand clapping result in a kind of rational burnout); and even to the theory of punctuated equilibrium (where cataclysmic events in nature are assumed to have brought on sudden genetic transmutations in surviving species). It also illuminates the Kervran effect, which involves a hen's alleged ability under stressful dietary conditions to transmute potassium into calcium.[15]

The most dramatic illustrations, however, are probably those involving chemical clocks. Imagine, by analogy, a mixture of red and blue dye molecules which, instead of canceling each other out in some amorphous third color, interact so as to produce a consistent alternation of a totally red with a totally blue liquid. Such phenomena are impossible according to classical thermodynamics.

They are, however, the birthing ground of new paradigms, especially when conjoined with related phenomena in other disciplines. For example, in *Order out of Chaos*, Prigogine and Isabelle Stengers point out that even though the interactions between molecules in dissipative structures do not exceed a range of ten centimeters, such systems "are structured as though each molecule were 'informed' about the overall state of the system."[16] This is strongly reminiscent of holographic modeling, where the form of the whole is prefigured in each of its parts. Moreover, the structural transformations across space in chemical clocks are described as taking place all at once. If so, we have a situation analogous to nonlocal causation described by Bell's theorem.

Why do dissipative structures consistently exhibit the higher orders they do? Especially within the context of long-term evolving systems, how random is their emergence when in retrospect it appears that each structure sets the stage for its successor? A description of the mathematical laws and initial conditions still leaves the spontaneous emergence of a new form something of a mystery, as much a mystery as morphogenesis. That the constituents of a system can undergo spontaneous, coherent rearrangement is less an explanation of order than it is a description of it. Further research into molecular processes is unlikely to reverse this situation, as content and form are correlative categories. Neither explains the other.

The theory of dissipative structures is one of the crowning achievements of Systems Holism. Yet with other systems and holistically oriented theorists, Prigogine hesitates to move metaphysically in the direction that his account strongly suggests, namely, toward the postulation of natural but unobservable fields and forms which assist in the organization of information.

According to this larger interpretation, a dissipative structure in-the-making would constitute a necessary condition for the expression of certain types of order, but would not itself produce order. Perhaps Prigogine's bifurcation point (the stage where a stressed system either decays or moves toward self-transcendence) is a point where David Bohm's holonomic order or Sheldrake's morphogenetic fields achieve material expression.[17] A crisis in one's life (where one feels like disintegrating!) is often the stimulus for an unsuspected part of oneself, such as a new form of relating, to emerge from the background where it seems to have been waiting all along.

How far beyond material reality must we go in order to explain why it behaves the way it does? Systems theorists typically resist the reductive tendencies of their scientific colleagues. But as I observed in Chapter Three, most are hesitant to move very far beyond the level of scientifically verifiable content. Still, an adequate explanation of order seems to require that we do so. Does the behavior of what we can see depend in part upon things which we cannot see?

If we are satisfied to acknowledge merely that self-organization does take place in certain ways under certain conditions, then Systems Holism provides an adequate framework. On the other hand, if we are genuinely curious and even perplexed by certain anomalous phenomena of self-organization, and we seek to determine more fully where their order is grounded, then only the fields, frequencies, and intelligible forms of higher levels in the Great Chain will provide an adequate framework. For a complete picture, we ultimately will have to consider the roles of consciousness and intelligence in the fabric of nature itself.

A test case: cellular consciousness. The idea that cells may be guided by their own intelligence as much as by the impartial laws of physics and chemistry may be yet another candidate for burning. Nevertheless, there is a growing body of evidence for this hypothesis. Clive Backster's research with plants and polygraphs, reported in *The Secret Life of Plants,* suggests that under certain conditions, plants communicate with other plants or respond to human emotions in ways that defy standard scientific explanation. For example, when live shrimp were dumped into boiling water, plants in the room responded with an immediate energetic surge on the polygraph. This doesn't prove that plants have emotions, at least in the way we normally think of them. However, it does suggest communication at biological levels previously not recognized.

Unable to replicate his results, scientific critics declared Backster's work a failure. Yet in their research, they failed to control for the very thing he proposed affected the outcome, namely, the thoughts and attitudes of the experimenter. If one is thinking "This is just a joke or a wasted experiment," plants are being subtly instructed not to respond as they normally would during environmental stress.

The results of Backster's more recent research plus studies of related phenomena are engagingly described in Robert Stone's *The Secret Life of Your Cells.*[18] Stone describes one study, for example, in which a group of fruit trees appears to collectively decide to bear fruit at different times, even though conditions of temperature, moisture, and soil chemistry remain constant.

Inferences about cellular communication at a distance in this type of research are necessarily indirect. Observing repeated synchronous correlations in plant and animal behavior, we naturally infer that some inner link (a communal consciousness?) must connect spatially separate systems. However, it may be possible to go one step further and talk to the primary intelligence involved. Such is the approach of Carol Pate and William Baldwin.

Pate's investigation of "negative cellular consciousness" (disease) began in her work with depossession, or clearing clients of negative or unnecessary energy (sometimes attached spirits). Her method requires both the assistance of a group of doctors and spirit guides "on the other side" and a channel through which they and the attached energies can communicate. The main work is done by a spirit group termed the "Band of Mercy," which lifts the energy from the client, places it in the medium for a brief communication, and assists in necessary translations. Sometimes the attached entities are benevolent and merely wish to make their presence known. Pate's method has been effective with a wide range of client concerns.

Her healing work with physical disease eventually caused her to bring forth more fundamental entities in the Great Chain of Being until she reached the level of cellular consciousness. At this point, she found herself able to talk to the consciousness of cancer, arthritis, and even AIDS. Accordingly, she then asked: "Why did you evolve in my client's body?" "What purpose, if any, do you serve?" After further clarification regarding the lessons to be learned, and with the client's consent, she would ask the disease to leave.

Skeptics, of course, will immediately dismiss her work as a grand self-delusion—the latest New Age placebo! I discuss these charges more generally in Chapter Eleven. Obviously, the burden of her procedure rests largely upon her ability to obtain positive results. And this she appears to have done, including remission of AIDS symptoms. She encourages research and investigation by physicians whose curiosity outweighs their fear of censure.[19]

Psychologist William Baldwin and his wife, Judith, also have explored a wide spectrum of "negative spirit entities," including those at a cellular level which can be brought forth in the client through mild hypnosis, rather than through a medium. Their approach more readily lends itself to mainstream psychotherapy, since the average psychologist is more familiar with hypnosis than with channeling. Each approach has its strengths. However, only time and research can determine if the results of this work on a long-term basis are as significant as they appear to be. If they are, the idea of cellular intelligence will fuel yet another paradigm shift, require a place in the Great Chain, and strengthen the case for perennialism. By contrast, systems holists, who view consciousness as a function of increasing levels of complexity, will be hard-pressed to account for such phenomena.

Field theory and the organization of systems: a review. Since we will continue to move in directions that assume a field-theoretical orientation, a brief review of this orientation will be useful.

1. A field is a state of space, not of matter. Fields generate matter, not the reverse. Since fields are the underlying reality, the appearance of matter generating a field or a specific energy pattern is simply the field itself undergoing a transformation.
2. A field connects events in space, sometimes locally and sometimes nonlocally, across great distance.
3. A field organizes growth and determines biological form.
4. Some fields can store memories, instincts, feelings, etc.

5. A field, especially one related to (4.), can be reprogrammed through assorted release methods and psychotechnologies such as affirmations, visualizations, hypnosis, educational kinesiology, and psychotronics.

6. There is a virtually infinite number of fields, of every degree of strength and complexity, stretching horizontally throughout physical space and vertically up through higher levels and dimensions. Typically, the higher the level the more "nonlocally connected" certain events, like ESP, at lower levels may appear.

7. Fields overlap, stand in resonance or dissonance with each other, locally and nonlocally produce changes within each other, subsume each other, and create novel gestalts and part-whole relationships. No field stands in isolation and all are interconnected.

8. The stuff of all fields is energy-consciousness, which may assume greater energetic components or greater aspects of consciousness depending upon the perspective of the person.

9. Their fundamental mode of expression, from an outside perspective, is vibration. In order to perform their function, however, fields must be infused with intelligible form and principles of order. Ultimately, all fields directly or indirectly reflect degrees of intention not limited to ordinary human varieties. Consciousness in the Great Chain works through fields, but is not reducible to them.

10. Fields (or parts of fields) contain information about larger fields of which they are a part or other fields with which they appear not to be spatially connected, e.g., a picture of a person may contain unseen information about that person's health.

11. Anything that ever happened is still retained in some field or other. All fields contain information. The problem is one of access.

ACCELERATED INTERDIMENSIONAL INTEGRATION

All around, the pace of change appears to be accelerating. A few years ago, foreign policy experts could barely imagine what a reunited Germany would mean. Then the Berlin Wall came down almost overnight. Rising demands for political freedom and outright independence in former Soviet republics continues to outpace the abilities of leaders from both East and West to comprehend fully what is happening and effectively relate to it. Some Eastern European countries have fallen apart as if they had never been together.

On the home front, jails are filling faster, banks are failing more rapidly, and drug abuse is spreading like wildfire. Support groups for every conceivable issue are springing up everywhere, environmental consciousness raising and action is at an all-time high, and personal relationships are materializing and disintegrating before our very eyes. Psychics are found on almost every corner. Hospital and university administrators are spending more time determining how to avoid lawsuits. Insurance companies are increasingly faced with bankruptcy. Candidates for public office are attacking each other, rather than explaining how they will solve problems. Many policy decisions are being made on the basis of who screams the loudest.

To continue, women (and some men) are claiming to have been abducted by aliens, and psychologists are listening to them! College graduates increasingly cannot find meaningful work. Teenagers are turning to the occult. People seem to get sick or just feel bad more often, for no clear reason. Everywhere we find groups and individuals motivated by fear, trying unsuccessfully to hold on to their traditional identity by means of rules that are changing without prior notice. Meanwhile, those not in denial about the possibilities of transformation are sometimes overwhelmed by the pace at which they are forced to confront their personal issues.

What *is* happening? There are plenty of sociological explanations. Here are some examples. For one, our values may not be keeping up with the pace of technological change. Then again, cultural relativism is rampant; any behavior is OK, so long as one claims the appropriate legal or moral right. Or it may be observed that the media is simply giving us more information than we can meaningfully assimilate. Then, too, people's very life-styles are being threatened by massive trends seemingly beyond their control. Congress appears unable to come to grips with major issues, especially those relating to the economy. We are being conditioned to blame others when things don't go our way. Living without a sense of rootedness causes deep anxieties, thereby causing us to invent cosmic meanings for our lives even if they have little basis in fact. And it's not surprising that, faced with massive despair and little hope, people turn to drugs.

Put these various explanations together with the transformative challenges described in Chapter One and we have the makings of a culture struggling to survive what looks like accelerating chaos. However, according to psychological and sociological perspectives, there is nothing metaphysically significant about times of great change. Nothing is going on behind the scenes, so to speak. Social critics are convinced that our culture is simply undergoing a shakedown according to psychological, social, and economic principles. Sooner or later, all cultures do. To be sure, such rapid change is painful and confusing. But it is explainable.

There is some truth to virtually all of the above explanations. However, the question is whether they go far enough, whether they really get to the heart of the matter. I don't think they do. I believe that something quite metaphysically significant is transpiring behind the scenes. Behind what we can see, I think, are energetic shifts on a global scale that we cannot see. I call this process "accelerated interdimensional integration." This is a speculative concept, but one which provides a needed supplement to the literature of crisis and change.[20] Following is an outline of its principal features:

1. According to the Great Chain of Being, higher levels are dimensionally suffused in lower ones. Each level contains its lower neighbor, yet transcends it.

2. For convenience, let us say that higher levels involve paths of love and empowerment, a greater sense of unity and wholeness, and increased multidimensional awareness.

3. Since these levels have been with us all along, our inability to fully recognize and act upon them must have been due to blocks or limitations in our consciousness.

4. Some of these impairments we put there ourselves. Others were imposed upon us. But either way, fear, competition, alienation, and three-dimensional awareness have generally been the order of the day.

5. There have always been reminders of higher paths. However, although many have claimed to believe, few have directly seen. Religions and churches, which were supposed to keep us in touch with the most sacred parts of ourselves, often repressed us instead. In the name of our gods, we killed and enslaved one another. And if that did not work, we resorted to guilt and blame.

6. But now, something has triggered a dimensional shift so that the higher, which had been implicit in the lower, is now becoming more explicit. Its power is being felt, even if its energies cannot be seen. No king, no pope, no president can control it.

7. The trigger for this shift may have been built into the evolutionary dynamic of the cosmos itself. It may be a transformational mechanism of our collective unconscious. Or it may have been triggered

and fueled by extra-dimensional beings. Nobody really knows why it has been activated now.

8. This trigger comes in the form of a "cosmic fertilizer," which accelerates the growth of everything—the good and bad alike—in its path. The promise of a better way comes more clearly into focus, together with an enhanced awareness of what keeps us from cashing in that promise. People sensitive to shifts in energy, whether on a local or a planetary scale, often have difficulty staying grounded. The effects keep snowballing, wave after wave.

9. The shift is happening simultaneously, on many levels—geomagnetic, biological, emotional, psychic, mental, and spiritual. However, it affects each of us at different rates on different levels, depending on where we are in our individual growth patterns.

10. For these new energies to become integrated into our lives, a great deal of negativity must first be pushed to the surface, acknowledged, and let go. Current blocks must be purged. Our worst fears will be put in front of us; the difference will be in how we choose to deal with them.

11. This purging is a painful and confusing process. Many individuals refuse to participate. They cling to the old, even though the cracks in the foundations are all around them. They will use every means at their disposal to control the flow of events. Such is the path of fear.

12. The irony is that the harder one clings to the path of fear, the more catastrophic will be the changes that one faces. Denial conceals a time bomb. Things will not get better by doing nothing. In fact, they will get worse.

13. The paths of love and fear are divergent. The longer one waits to make the shift from fear to love, the longer one postpones letting go of fear, the harder it will be to make the transition. The shift will happen with or without our individual participation. Our participation determines how smoothly or chaotically the process will go.

14. For those too rigid to embrace this dimensional shift, accelerated disintegration is now on the horizon. For those willing to let go of fear and deal with their issues, accelerated growth and integration are theirs to claim.

15. Each person must decide which path to pursue. Many already have. Either way, the pace of change is accelerating.

16. For those who still cannot make up their minds, many clues are available. Teetering economies, new rules for personal

relationships, new immune system deficiencies, Satanic and other dark cult activities, the end of the American Dream, paranormal experiences, and a Rising Culture that refuses to go away are but a few examples.

17. Dimensional "leakage" is all around. Some describe this process as the birthing of, and ultimate transition to, fourth-dimensional awareness. Those who understand its dynamics and participate in its birthing will prevail. Those who do not will fail.

18. Children and teens will be among the first large groups to recognize this, however tentatively. Academicians will be among the last and will make every attempt to explain away the effects of this global shift in consciousness, even as a rising generation embraces it.

This vision predicts, within the next ten years, a dramatic move away from mainstream culture, represented in essential respects by a single Bell curve, toward a split culture stretched between twin curves. Rising Culture agendas will take up one curve. They will address the transformational challenges, both personal and social, attending a global phase-shift of energy-consciousness. Its members will thrive on the accelerated pace of awakening to the possibilities of interdimensional penetration.

The other curve represents the ways of a dying culture. The more its members refuse to change, the more painful and dramatic will be the process of disintegration. They will fight for continued control and survive for a while on the power of their own denial. Lest there be any mistake on this point, the New World Order is but a revision of a very old world order based upon control, conformity, and privilege for the few.

This divergence of rising and decaying cultures is only a transitional picture. After a suitable period of time, the Rising Culture will be represented by a single curve. The shift will be relatively complete. And we shall see things and do things we never thought likely or possible, especially in the areas of health, education, and relationships. Occupying a new perspective within the Great Chain inevitably extends the limits of the possible.

Confronted with such sweeping scenarios, critics will ask whether this is a hope for what can be, a prediction of what will be, or a declaration of what should be. The answer, I think, is "All three!"

CHAPTER NINE

Time: Leading Edge of Eternity

Time is a familiar concept of daily life. We frequently ask what time it is or comment on how quickly or slowly time seems to be passing. Physicists routinely speak of time as beginning with the Big Bang, or they define positrons as "electrons going backward in time." And most everyone is confident that time marches on (no matter what). But how do we respond when someone asks, "What is the real nature of time?" As Saint Augustine observed, we know what time is, as long as nobody asks. When asked, however, we are dumbfounded.

All worldviews, however implicitly, incorporate answers to this question. How we answer it affects our understanding of history, the laws of nature, creativity, human freedom, and even the possibility of prophetic visions of the future. In this chapter, I will attempt to illuminate the nature of time by describing four theories of time and then exploring two questions: Does the future in some sense already exist? Must time have a direction and, if so, is this direction the same on every level of the Great Chain of Being?

FOUR THEORIES OF TIME

An effective explanation of time must address two clusters of questions. One cluster invites us to examine the very stuff of time. For example, should time be conceived as pure becoming, independent of all motion or physical change? Or should we think of time as identical with physical change and its subsets used for measurement (e.g., clocks, stars, radioactive decay, etc.)?

When a scientist defines time as that which is measured by a standard chronometer, is the entity being measured something other than the changes in the chronometer—something sufficient unto itself? Or is it literally identical with the movement of clocks and other changes in the natural universe? If every process in the universe came to a complete stop, if not a single photon vibrated, would time also cease? Or would it continue to move on? If time stops on this scenario, then it must be identical with some pattern of physical or psychological change. If it continues, then time must be different from natural change.

A second cluster of questions invites us to explore how events come to have a place in time or possess temporal relationships. For example, should we think of events, such as the death of Jesus or the colonization of Mars, as being at a certain place in time (the past, the present, or the future)? Or should we think of them fundamentally as bearing a certain relationship (earlier than, concurrent with, later than) to other events? Let us call past, present, or future times "A" designators, and relationships of earlier than, concurrent with, or later than its "B" designators.

The difference between A and B designators is that an event's A designators change, but its B designators never change. For example, completing this book was in the future but now is in the past. So future, present, and past change in this case. However, its completion will always be later than my decision to write it, no matter if that completion is still in the future or is now in the past. The book's completion in the natural order of events is *eternally fixed*, relative to other events that come before or after it.

The question this distinction poses is whether the essence of time is captured by the A designators, the B designators, or equally well by both. Philosophically, much turns on how we answer this question.[1] If we assume that the B series of *fixed* designators (earlier than, concurrent with, later than) capture the real essence of time, then we must explain why change appears to be a built-in feature of the universe. For example, we ordinarily believe that future events have yet to happen; they cannot be fixed, because they have not yet taken place.

On the other hand, if we decide that the A series of *changing* designators (past, present, future) is the most fundamental aspect of time, we encounter arguments that time is reversible, which is contrary to the idea of an open future. Finally, if we adopt both accounts at face value, we may end up with a contradiction. It is not clear, for example, how the future can be both open and closed.

Here, then, are our two fundamental questions: Is time identical with natural change? Is the essence of time most accurately captured by the A series (past, present, future) or by the B series (earlier than, simultaneous with, later than)? By combining these distinctions, we can produce four perspectives on time. Philosophers and scientists from Aristotle to Einstein would emphasize different aspects of each perspective. But with few exceptions, most of what has ever been believed about time fits into one of the following four categories.

The dynamic-absolute perspective. The central tenets of this perspective are:

1. Time moves in one direction only. This is usually described as "time's arrow."
2. Past, present, and future are the fundamental temporal designators, since it's only through them that we can tie down B designators (earlier than, later than, etc.) to a particular reference point in the past or future. The fact that writing this book precedes its publication doesn't in itself tell you whether both events are future or both are past. So we cannot even conceive of time without the A series.
3. The future is a realm of open possibilities; the past, of closed facts. We take the future to be a realm where things haven't yet happened, the past to be a fixed domain. The past cannot be changed.
4. Time is independent of all physical change. In Isaac Newton's words: "Absolute, true and mathematical time, of itself and by its own nature, flows uniformly without regard to anything external…Relative, apparent and vulgar time is some sensible and external measure of absolute time (duration) estimated by the motions of bodies, whether accurate or inequable, and is commonly used instead of true time."[2]

The dynamic-relative perspective. This view of time is the same as the dynamic-absolute perspective with the exception that time is identified with physical change. Instead of thinking of time as an entity unto itself, we would say that temporal unfolding is intrinsic to all events, and that the idea of an open future refers to a realm of unrealized events. Proponents of this view include Aristotle, who conceived of time as a property of motion.

According to this view, to say that time can "speed up" or "slow down" is to imply that some particular process can increase or decrease its rate of change. The dynamic-relative perspective also incorporates cyclical accounts of time, such as those built on the metaphor of expansion (Day of Brahman) and contraction (Night of Brahman).

The static-absolute perspective. An absolute theory of time distinguishes between time and physical change; they are independent of one another. If we add to this distinction the qualification that time itself doesn't move or undergo change with respect to its past, present, and future, we have the makings of a static-absolute theory. According to this view, the past, present, and future are collapsed into a static continuum, a timeless "now" sometimes described as eternity. If the world appears to undergo change, it is just an appearance, not reality. As the Zen master Dogen states: "It is believed by most that time passes; in actual fact it stays where it is."[3]

The static-relative perspective. If we add to a simple static theory ("Time does not move") the qualification that time is identical with the order of natural events (what Newton described as the "relative" order), we come full circle to a view which stipulates that:

1. Past, present, and future are reducible to the B designators: earlier than, concurrent with, and later than, respectively. We can eliminate the idea of temporal change—of something becoming past—by simply placing events at a particular position in a static continuum of relationships. For example, "X is past" could be defined as "X is earlier than Y," where Y is a conventionally chosen point of reference, say, November 11, 1991. My idea for writing this book is thus "in the past" only in the sense that it came before November 11, 1991 (or whatever other date Y might stand for).
2. The entire B series of "befores" and "afters" is objective. All events in the continuum, whether past, present, or future, are equally real. Whatever we think is going to happen in the future, like dying, already has happened. The future already exists!
3. The experience of temporal becoming is purely subjective, since changes in past, present, or future presuppose the conscious states of memory, immediate experience, and expectation, respectively. Without consciousness, a static continuum of events would exist, but our characterizations of those events as past, present, or future would not.

In this perspective, I include relativity theorists whose views are summarized by physicist Louis de Broglie: "In space-time, everything which for us constitutes the past, the present, and the future is given en bloc...Each observer, as his time passes, discovers, so to speak, new slices of space-time which appear to him as successive aspects of the material world, although in reality the ensemble of events constituting space-time exists prior to knowledge of them".[4] Translation: The future already exists! It is only the limitations of our own consciousness that cause us to believe that it does not. Neither the future nor the past changes. If anything does, it's our awareness of what already exists.

To summarize, time can be viewed as dynamically flowing, but distinct from physical change; dynamically flowing and identical with physical change; static, but distinct from physical processes; or static and identical with a fixed and unchanging series of physical events. These are illustrated in the following figures:

Past   Future   Past and Future = Now

   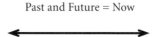

Time = Independent Moving Force   Time = Fixed Eternity
(two levels)   (two levels)

Physical change occurs and is real.   *Physical change occurs but is not real.*

FIGURE 1.   FIGURE 2.
Dynamic-Absolute   Static-Absolute

Past Closed   Future Open   Past Closed   Future Closed

Time = Creative Change   Time = Static Continuum
(one level)   (one level)

Physical events occur.   *Everything already is.*

FIGURE 3.   FIGURE 4.
Dynamic-Relative   Static-Relative

Even though they incorporate critical insights, dynamic-absolute and static-absolute accounts of time receive less attention in the New Paradigm dialogue. This is because they make time independent of experience, and in so doing, render it largely useless, if not unintelligible. A consequence of Newton's absolute theory, for example, is that time could change directions fifty times each day and make no perceptible difference in the normal flow of physical or psychological events.[5] If this is so, what purpose could time possibly serve?

On the other hand, both dynamic-relative and static-relative perspectives appear in New Paradigm discussions as well as in more traditional analyses of time. For example, readers interested in creativity, quantum fluctuations, the Dance of Shiva, personal growth, multidimensional rhythmic harmonies, and the cycles of history are already leaning toward a dynamic-relative theory. They tend to think of the future as essentially open, and time as a creative advance into that future.

If one's New Paradigm interests focus around such things as mysticism, prophecy and seeing the future, past-life regressions, and relativity physics, then a static-relative theory is more likely to fit the bill. People attracted to this theory tend to perceive time as a projection from consciousness. They are likely to believe that time has no essential direction from the future to the past. In fact, the difference between past and future is more a matter of degree than principle. According to this point of view, time does not necessarily run in one and only one direction.

No single perspective will account for all that we would like it to. Each has distinctive strengths and limitations. However, I believe that these limitations result from adopting an unnecessarily restrictive view of the Great Chain of Being. Theories that work well on one level may not work as well on other levels. And since we exist on many levels, there is ample opportunity for confusion. At the end of this chapter, I will offer a unifying explanation in which elements of each view of time have an appropriate place.

DOES THE FUTURE ALREADY EXIST?

Change is an obvious fact of life. The future seems open; the past, fixed. Yet there are three challenges to this belief which appear to support static theories of time.

The first is from clairvoyants who have visions of things to come, as if they were already in place. Actually one need not be clairvoyant per se, for precognitive dreams raise similar issues. In his classic work, *An Experiment*

With Time, J.W. Dunne noted that prophetic dreams are to be expected almost as much as dreams of the past. In *Dreams That Come True*, psychologist David Ryback concluded that one out of twelve people has had a precognitive dream. And in her analysis of 3,290 cases of precognition, Louisa Rhine reported that sixty-eight percent occurred in a dreaming state.[6] Is the source of such dreams and visions actually *in* the future? Or merely in the consciousness of the people who have them?

A second challenge to the idea of an open future comes from relativity physics, which holds that past, present, and future exist simultaneously. According to this static-relative view, what we believe will come to be in fact already exists. Past, present, and future are each parts of a static continuum. Time is the fourth dimension of space, and all events accordingly are "spread out" in space-time. Strictly speaking, we don't create anything. We just come into an awareness of what already exists.

A third challenge to an open future comes from Newtonian mechanics. The equations which describe moving objects are said to be "time reversible" and, in the case of mechanics, deterministic. According to this view, events eventually occur in an otherwise empty future, but were going to happen anyway. Our belief that the future is open merely reflects a restriction of our knowledge of all of the causes that will make something happen. Nothing really new is ever about to happen. The future in theory is as fixed as the past. And since it cannot be changed, it might as well already exist!

Precognition. Let's first consider the topic of prophetic dreams or clairvoyant visions of the future. Even in the best of circumstances, it can be difficult to distinguish between a genuine precognitive intuition about an unlikely future event—like a boating accident involving a member of one's family—and sheer coincidence or lucky guessing.[7] Let us assume, however, that on some occasions people do "see the future" in ways that defy chance. In such cases, what do they actually see? Is the future actually there, waiting, as it were, to be correctly or incorrectly seen?

When the clairvoyant correctly predicts the boating accident involving a family member, it is natural to suppose that this event was in the future at the time the clairvoyant saw it. After all, a true statement is one that we normally say corresponds to reality. So it seems that there must be a future reality for prophetic visions to bounce off, so to speak.

Suppose, however, that the clairvoyant (who otherwise has a good track record) predicts another event that does not occur. If one follows the same one-to-one correspondence thinking and believes that unusual visions or intuitions of the future are sometimes correct, it seems equally reasonable to suppose that the future was (still) there, but in this particular case was incorrectly seen. The clairvoyant didn't see what she thought she saw, just as people sometimes don't correctly see what they believe is really there.

So far, so good. Suppose, however, that both the vision that did occur as predicted and the vision that did not materialize were equally strong and clear to the clairvoyant. Suppose, moreover, that four other clairvoyants with excellent track records in this type of prediction each corroborated their colleague's two visions; all swear that, at the time they saw the events in question, they were (really) going to happen. In effect, they claim that in the case of the second event, which never did occur, they were nevertheless correct in their prediction *at the time they made it.* How is it possible for one to correctly see a future that never comes to pass, a future in which there is no event to correspond to the earlier prediction?

Granted, this type of powerful convergence of psychic opinion seldom happens. And we could still insist that, after all, this was just one of those times in which they were all wrong. But this does not do justice to the fact that both visions intrinsically seem equally clear and powerful. How could one be wrong, when it has all the same markings as the one that proved correct? If the future already exists, how is it possible for a precognitive dream or clairvoyant vision of the future to be correct, when the event foreseen never occurs? How can we reconcile the seemingly irreconcilable?

The way around this dilemma, I think, is to abandon the very assumption about the nature of time that paranormal visions of the future initially seem to support. The assumption is that there is a future "out there" waiting to be seen or otherwise accessed in the first place. This move would take care of false predictions nicely, even those that had an aura of certainty about them. The reason is simple. There isn't anything for false psychic predictions to correspond to; that is why they turn out false.

Accurate psychic predictions, however, present a different problem. Correct intuitions, prophetic visions, or precognitive dreams about unlikely events in the future lead many to assume that there must be a future to see in the first place. If we abandon this assumption, with what could a correct vision actually correspond? The answer, I think, is that the future seen in such cases is not the actual future of tangible events and objects. It is not the material future, because the material future does not yet exist.

Rather, what is seen by the clairvoyant or by the ordinary person in prophetic dreams is a complex projection of desires, fears, and thought forms within the astral and mental planes of the Great Chain of Being. Some of these will manifest on a material level in the future and some will not. As current configurations of energy-consciousness, they are real in themselves, not simply projections from out of the clairvoyant's own mind, although sometimes that happens, too!

The fact that a clairvoyant has greater access doesn't necessarily favor one vision of the future in preference to another. Each plane of the Great Chain houses many possibilities: some strong, some weak, and some in powerful competition with each other. A strong possibility may appear to the clairvoyant as clear and powerful. The clairvoyant then makes a prediction based upon the vision which, at another level, looks (or feels) the strongest.

However, there are always other possibilities. And there is always the exercise of choice and free will to take into account, right up to the moment when the original vision gains a full-bodied existence on the material plane. Strong probabilities usually materialize, but not in every case. The clairvoyant accesses multiple futures (different configurations of energy-consciousness) at other levels. Precognitive dreams are simply interdimensional leakage from those levels. Only one of several different extra-dimensional scenarios drops into our three-dimensional material reality.

This is how correct precognitive visions of nonmaterializing futures are possible. The change is never at the material level, since the material future does not yet exist! What we think of as false psychic predictions that do not materialize may still be interpreted as correct at the time they are made, insofar as they correspond to the strongest configuration of energy-consciousness on the astral and mental planes of the Great Chain. However, the strongest configuration today, as everyone knows, will not necessarily be the strongest configuration several months from now.

Regardless of whether a clairvoyant vision corresponds to something on another level of the Great Chain, we may ask why the psychic doesn't see that the strongest vision today will not be the strongest tomorrow. Why doesn't she see the influence of free will and other factors at work on the "inner planes" that would change the projected outcome? The answer is that clairvoyants, even the very best ones, make mistakes. They cannot see everything that may influence the outcome of evolving energy. Clairvoyant vision (or psychic intuition) is interdimensional in nature, and for that reason represents a practical advantage over those people whose vision is not interdimensionally aligned. But interdimensional vision is not omniscient vision; it is merely improved vision.

Suppose you and your spouse are considering divorce. In one reading, the clairvoyant may see a strong configuration of the energy of remaining together and a weak one of separating; in a later reading, a different clairvoyant may see both options in their equally powerful energetic versions and refuse to make a call. Later, divorce may be the primary vision. Since only one of these alternatives will manifest, it's tempting to conclude in retrospect that only one clairvoyant saw things correctly and others were mistaken.

However, it's also reasonable to conclude that in at least some circumstances each clairvoyant was correct to some degree of probability and none was totally wrong. Each saw on another level a possible future with varying evolutionary dynamics propelling it toward (or away from) manifestation at the physical level. The reason they saw such different futures is that you and your spouse are undergoing a complex inner evolution with the whole process, sometimes involving variables of which neither is directly aware. We need to get beyond the law of the excluded middle in supposing that the only options in thinking about the future are either complete material existence or no existence at all. In so doing, the idea of a clairvoyant seeing a prefigured future "ahead of time" which nevertheless does not materialize isn't so paradoxical.

So what is the answer to our lead question? Does the future already exist? The answer is "no" at a material level and "yes and no" at higher levels in the Great Chain (where many possible futures exist). If this analysis is correct, then a combination of Great Chain metaphysics and dynamic-relative thinking about time can best account for paranormal peeks into the future.

Relativity theory. The relativity theorist has yet to be heard, though. Einstein believed that the division of the space-time continuum into a distinct past, present, and future is an illusion. He defended a static-relative view of time (although not under that label), according to which the past still exists and the future already is! The limitations of our consciousness cause us to see a future which seems to be open—that is, yet to happen—or a past which seems to be gone. But relativity theory, Einstein and others felt, tells us that past, present, and future simultaneously coexist; no one is more fixed or real than the others.

In some circles, this is the preferred way of thinking. But its logic is not self-evident. It is true that relativity theorists have found it convenient to underwrite their mathematics with a model of space-time extending into the future. But this isn't the only model that fits the mathematics of relativity theory. It is convenient to think this way only for certain limited purposes in the area of cosmology. It's also convenient to think of electrons circling their nuclei in an orbital fashion. But they don't really move this way. The model of a future that is already materially fixed is not necessarily one that we must accept.

Moreover, it's not even clear that a preexisting future is the preferred model for relativity theory. Einstein was first and foremost a determinist, a believer (along with Bertrand Russell and others) in the equations and immutable laws which hold sway over the flux. His equations and Newton's laws of mechanics, despite their other dissimilarities, predict a future which must be as it eventually turns out. Whatever does happen has to happen.

This is rather depressing for anyone interested in free will and creativity. But a deterministic future is nonetheless distinct from a *preexisting* future. It is one thing to predict a future which has yet to happen in a rigidly determined way, quite another to describe a future which already exists! Real material change is still consistent with the equations of relativity theory.

Even careful descriptions of the space-time continuum invariably appeal to change. They speak of "successive slices" of the continuum coming into awareness, of changing consciousness, and the discovery of different parts of the continuum, all of which imply something happening. Just the presentation of a model takes time and involves some type of change.

A strict interpretation of this model ("Nothing happens because everything already exists!") and the notion of "taking time" to create and present the model involve contradictory agendas. Besides, if change is an illusion at the material level, then how can it give rise to a true theory? Relativity theory requires that we rethink the relations of space and time. However, it does not give us good reasons to deny that material change takes place. Therefore, it does not prove that the future already exists.

At least one explanation of precognition explicitly relies upon the notion of a space-time continuum and, to some extent, a B series of fixed (or at least quasi-fixed) events. This explanation violates several assumptions of common sense, but then so do a lot of theories of time. It involves the key concept of backward causation. Briefly, this theory proposes that events in the future may cause a precognitive vision in the present.

This theory has been widely discussed by philosophers and scientists, among them Russell Targ and Harold Puthoff. In their view, physics suggests or at least allows a model in which "significant events create a perturbation in the space-time in which they occur, and this disturbance propagates forward and, to some small degree, backward in time."[8]

From a God's-eye view of all of creation, the cause still precedes the effect. However, because we are locked into the present, it appears as if an effect were occurring before its cause. Hence the label "backward causation." The Targ-Puthoff version gives us more flexibility than standard relativity theory. It allows "ripples," for example. But no matter which version of the continuum is invoked, the *future is assumed to preexist our coming into direct awareness of it.*

Familiar problems surround this explanation. Belief in free choice is placed at risk. (Naturally, our choices have already been made!) Moreover, there is no independent evidence for a preexisting *material* future, a highly counter-intuitive idea to begin with. And a material future is not what clairvoyants claim to see anyway. Additionally, there is a special paradox associated with this explanation. If something in the future causes me to see my son drowning in a boating accident (perhaps as a warning), and I subsequently take steps to avert the accident, then the future event I saw never really happened. But if it didn't happen, then how could it cause me to see and to do what I did?

The only way around this paradox is to move to a different level. This is to say that the future I saw was on a different plane of reality, one of several possible ones, none of which had materialized. The perennialist vision of a Great Chain of Being permits such a move. Standard physics does not. Backward causation therefore does not appear to shed much light on precognitive phenomena, so long as we restrict ourselves to the material level of the Great Chain.

MUST TIME HAVE A DIRECTION?

Can time move only in one direction? This question makes the most sense if we think of time as being identical with natural change. Another version is as follows: Can all physical and psychological change in principle be reversed without breaking any scientific laws or lapsing into incoherence? Of course, we can't do this in fact, and it would be monstrously inconvenient if we did. The issue, however, is whether anything theoretically stands in the way of our doing so.

Before tackling this issue, let me spell out what is at stake. If time *is* universally reversible, then it will follow that:

1. free will and creativity are essentially illusions;
2. the second law of thermodynamics ("Entropy always increases") is likewise a kind of macroscale subjective phenomenon produced by our statistical calculations;
3. the future is not really open, that is, even if the future has not yet come to pass, what eventually does happen is in effect predetermined;
4. what is critical about time is the concept of ordered succession (the B series of "befores" and "afters"), not past, present, or future;
5. if reincarnation is true, we could be living all our lives simultaneously and (in principle) access both past and future lives;
6. there is a past only because we have memories, not because there is an objective past, parts of which are remembered.

On the other hand, if time is not *universally* reversible—if some processes are reversible and some are not—then one should reject the above list. So quite a bit hangs on the question of temporal reversibility. The average New Paradigm individual believes some of the above implications and denies others—with sometimes contradictory results! For the remainder of this section, I focus on the question of *physical* reversibility and reserve for later a discussion of the reversibility of our interior conscious life.

Virtually all discussions of physical reversibility begin with the Newtonian legacy. Newton's laws of mechanics apply to a universe of big billiard balls (like planets) and ideally to small billiard balls (like gas molecules). In principle, these laws allow us to predict where all things are going to be and the speed they will be traveling next week or next year. With sufficient information, these laws would enable us to predict in billiards exactly how the rack will break when the cue ball hits it.

But the equations of mechanics also allow us to "retrodict" where everything was, given a knowledge of the current state of a system (in this case the pool table). If we were to film the original game of billiards, then show it in reverse, we would see an entire series of mechanically plausible events. We might observe the 3-ball bumping the 4-ball, whereas before the 4-ball was the cause, rather than the effect. The process happens to be going one way, but it could go the other.

The equations enabling us to predict and retrodict positions and velocities are said to be "time neutral." They don't tell us that a certain physical process must move forward or backward. They merely tell us that, whichever way it is moving, events therein will have a certain determined order. Physical processes described by mechanics are said to be reversible precisely because their inherent order is rigidly determined.

Not only are the equations of mechanics reversible, so are most of those from electromagnetism, quantum mechanics, and relativity theory. In quantum theory, for example, a positron is defined as an electron going backwards in time. Many physical processes would look weird in reverse, such as people walking backwards. But they are consistent with underlying scientific accounts of what is physically possible. It appears that, so far as the physical universe is concerned, time is reversible. Many physicists, from Einstein to Stephen Hawking, believe that the laws of physics do not allow for irreversibility, even though we experience ourselves creatively evolving into the future.

However, there are six types of physical phenomena that appear to constitute an exception to temporal reversibility.[9] Most are being debated in physics today. But collectively, they constitute a strong argument for irreversibility, that is, for time's arrow. For if run in reverse, they would either disappear or become transformed into something different altogether. In certain cases their course could not be predicted, even in theory, with any certainty. These exceptions are:

Electromagnetic radiation. Although Maxwell's equations describing electromagnetic phenomena are time-reversible, nature itself seems to distinguish in an absolute and universal fashion between radio wave transmission outward and convergence of the waves backward to the source. Such a reversal would be as implausible as your smashed computer putting itself back together again.

Quantum measurement. Before the properties (spin, charge, etc.) of a particle are measured, they are treated probabilistically. Contrary to common sense, the particle itself doesn't have a determinate, actual existence. Up to that point of measurement, quantum equations are reversible. But at that point, they break down. Mysteriously, probability is transformed into actuality, there being no way to predict with certainty which state of the particle will materialize.

The act of measurement itself introduces an element of irreversibility into the total process. It is difficult, if not impossible, to imagine a physical object spontaneously and instantaneously dissolving into a mere probability wave. We can, of course, imagine it dissolving into energy; but energy still has a determinate, though fluid, status. It is substantial. Mere probability is not.

Neutral kaon decay. It is a common assumption that decay rates for various particles are the same for their time-reversed worlds. The neutral kaon appears to be the single exception to this principle. Through a process of complicated experimentation and calculation, it has been determined that this particle decays at a slightly different rate. If it were possible to film this process, a ten-second film of a neutral kaon run in reverse would not show the particle where it had been ten seconds earlier, contrary to what reversibility predicts.

Absence of white holes. Some cosmologists, most notably Stephen Hawking, argue that if there are black holes in space, there must also be white holes. This is one of the results of reversing the equations for black hole formation. However, other cosmologists, notably Roger Penrose, point out that white holes have never been found and their nature is so incomprehensible that it's impossible to see how such things could exist. If Penrose is correct, this would be another example of the irreversibility of time (change) in nature. The existence of black holes would not entail the existence of white holes. This is one of the more controversial potential exceptions to temporal reversibility.

A collapsing universe? The idea of a universe which eventually reaches the limits of expansion and begins to fall back in upon itself has been around for quite some time. Whether it will actually do this depends upon its total amount of mass-energy, and this isn't known for sure. Regarding the nature of time, the more fundamental question is whether, if the universe collapses, time would begin to run backwards at that point. Would we eventually see mountains growing rather than eroding or workable cars appearing from out of junk piles? The answer is "No." For a collapsing universe would still take time.

Quantum theory does tell us that different and sometimes new actualities would come from collapsed probability waves. With gravity collapsing gradually all around us, those of us living in such a universe would therefore require different life-styles and some revised laws of physics. But we would still grow old. Time would still be irreversible in a collapsing universe.

Entropy. This is the most difficult and long-debated argument for irreversibility and is closely related to some of the earlier arguments. The second law of thermodynamics states that in a closed system, entropy—the tendency toward disorder—always increases to the maximum, leading to a final "heat death." Thus, plants decay, mountains age, and stars burn up, scattering their parts to increasing disorder.

The evolution of humans from simple one-celled organisms to highly complex and internally organized entities looks like an exception to the second law (as biblical creationists like to point out). But temporary aberrations are permitted. Humans are not closed systems; they are systems-within-systems. We can gain order for ourselves by accelerating entropy in our environment, especially in the food chain. The whole process of sun plus earth, however, is winding down.

There are conflicting interpretations of the second law. These interpretations are rooted in contrasting philosophies of nature and in divergent metaphysical assumptions. I call these two schools the determinist and the creationist.

Consider the case of an exploded gasoline can, the contents of which are burning in small pools. At the macrolevel this is surely a one-way process. We would never expect fire and metal fragments to spontaneously reconstitute the original can of liquid gasoline. However, at the microlevel, all of the individual molecules are behaving like Newtonian units moving along on their determinate trajectories. The microprocess thus appears to be reversible. Thermodynamics appears to be moving irreversibly in one direction, but mechanics allows us to move backwards at a different level.

Defenders of both views agree that thermodynamics predicts future states of a system only on a statistical basis involving large numbers of molecules. It cannot predict the movement or place of single particles. However, defenders of a microdeterminist interpretation view this as a concession to ignorance; we cannot predict individual trajectories or collisions because we lack the necessary information to do so. Besides, there would be no point in doing so, since large-scale events are predictable in the case of the exploding gasoline cans. Irreversibility, they urge, is merely a subjective illusion reflecting the limitations of human knowledge.

Defenders of irreversibility have a different interpretation. In their view, probability needs to be built into nature, even at the very lowest levels. Chaos is more than a reflection of limited information. It's a fact of nature. Newton's laws apply to the stable systems of an idealized nature, not nature as we usually find it. If there is an illusion, it's on the part of the determinists (or time-reversalists) who like to think events are very orderly at the microlevel, even though they appear otherwise.

Such idealized reversed trajectories assume infinite information. But infinite information is not just impractical. It is impossible. Some creative advance must therefore be built into every level of nature. A piece of music played backwards is a very different piece of music, for example. Twenty years after his pioneering work on dissipative (unstable) systems, Ilya Prigogine and his colleagues have reformulated the basic laws of physics with the necessary mathematical precision to demonstrate the irreversibility of time. Even new laws of nature may be expected to emerge as the universe itself evolves. It makes no sense to suppose that there were laws of biology *before* there was organic matter.

In Prigogine's view, laws of nature are statistical probabilities (not absolutes) that may be applied to stable or unstable systems with appropriately greater or lesser predictive power. In *A Brief History of Time*, Hawking suggests that discovery of the absolute field equations governing matter and energy at the time of the Big Bang would represent the end of science; the rest would be a matter of filling in the details. By contrast, Prigogine believes that we would have arrived at a new beginning for science. Since the universe itself is unstable, we cannot predict with any certainty exactly how things will look a billion years from now. Time is fundamentally creative evolution; physically reversible trajectories are just special cases within his larger paradigm.

Of the two philosophies of nature, determinist and creationist, the creationist perspective better captures New Paradigm thinking about the nature of time. The determinist vision (Newton, Hawking) is a subset of the broader, more open-ended Creationist perspective (Prigogine, Whitehead) on the nature of time and the evolution of the universe. A comparison of the two philosophies of nature looks like this:

Determinist

1. We must rely upon probability because of limitations of human knowledge.

2. Belief in irreversibility is tied to the assumption that the future is open and the past closed.
3. The asymmetry of open future and closed past is a function of our need to rely upon probability, not strict predictability.
4. Belief in irreversibility is a subjective projection of our own limitations onto nature.
5. All physical processes, at both microlevels and macrolevels, are in principle reversible.
6. Microlevels of physics are more real than consciousness.
7. Creative advance and novelty are essentially artifacts, the rearrangement of preexisting matter and energy.
8. All events are caused, even if in principle we are precluded from knowing the causes of certain microlevel (quantum) events.
9. Since all events are caused and there is no genuine creativity, there is no freedom.
10. If there were a God, S/He would see the future as clearly as the past.

Creationist

1. We must rely upon probability because nature is itself probabilistic, both chaotic and creative.
2. Irreversibility is tied to other things in addition to an open future.
3. The future is open because it has not happened, not merely because we cannot predict it with 100 percent accuracy.
4. Reversibility is found in nature at certain levels, not merely projected there.
5. Some physical processes are reversible and some are not.
6. All levels are real.
7. Creative advance and novelty are built into nature and involve more than rearrangement of parts.
8. Since all objects and events are interconnected in diverse ways, "All events are caused" means only that "Something cannot come from nothing."
9. Since determinism fails as a comprehensive paradigm, there is room for creative advance through free choice.
10. If God saw everything in the future, there would be less reason for creation in the first place.

You may recall from Chapter Three that Systems Holism and the Perennial Philosophy each incorporate the main ideas of a creationist philosophy of nature. This in turn requires commitment to a dynamic-relative theory, which stresses creativity, some irreversibility, and an open future. So for those who adopt either or both perspectives, the answer to the question "Must time have a direction?" is "Yes" insofar as time is equated with physical change.

However, as we move into those upper levels of the Great Chain where consciousness plays a more explicit role, time gradually loses its intrinsic directionality in ways better accounted for by a perennialist vision. The possibility discussed earlier of seeing the future before it materializes, suggests such a conclusion. It is time now to explore more directly some of the issues associated with our inner sense of time's arrow.

THE PSYCHOLOGY OF TIME'S ARROW

Much has been written about human perception of time and change. For example, how long is the present? Is time perception rooted in biological rhythms? What causes people to speed up or slow down their sense of temporal flow? Is Aboriginal dream time more real than waking time? Is time less important to a culture whose language stresses gerunds rather than nouns?[10]

Interesting as they are, space does not permit me to explore these questions. I am after bigger game, so to speak. I want to probe to deeper levels of time perception, to the roots of the very ideas of succession and of the past (and, by implication, of the future). How is it possible to represent in our own minds event "A" as coming before event "B" and to place both events in a past which, although it seems to be remembered clearly, may never have existed?

How is it possible to entertain the bare notions of "pastness" or "beforeness"? This question is not about how to verify whether a certain event actually happened before some other event, or whether it even happened at all! Such an objective verification between persons already presupposes the capacity within each person to entertain the bare concept of something having a past at all. Thus, I am concerned with the logical presuppositions of inner-time sense, not with the routine application of that sense in daily living.

Consider the following thought experiment suggested by Bertrand Russell. Since there is no logically necessary connection between events at different times, it's conceivable that "the world sprang into existence five minutes ago, exactly as it was then, with a population that 'remembered' a wholly unreal past."[11] Russell didn't attach any likelihood to this hypothesis. He merely argued that it was both possible to conceive *and* impossible to disprove.

Now consider this analogy. Suppose that a person's mind deteriorates to the point of causing a misremembering of his entire past. In remembering events in his life, nothing he recalls as happening actually occurred. Now expand this to all people on the planet; everyone's false memories reinforce each other, so nobody is the wiser. It never occurs to anyone (save Bertrand Russell!) that the world is radically different from what it is remembered to be.

What these scenarios have in common is that all of the people involved feel intimately connected, from the inside as it were, to a past that never existed. Furthermore, their sense of connection is identical to ours, which is presumably grounded in a past that actually transpired.

It follows, therefore, that whatever did or did not happen in the past and whatever my memories of my past may be, they are collectively irrelevant to my sense of being connected to a past at all. In other words, my sense of having *persisted through time* from the past to the present is grounded in the present, independently of what my current memories happen to be. There seems to be something about the very structure or form of a memory-experience, something built into the structure of consciousness itself, that gives me the inner sense of being connected to an event in the past. This form must be independent of both the content of the current memory and the objective past.

I am not suggesting that there would not be a past without this structure of present consciousness. I was obviously conceived before I wrote this book. An identifiable trail of events connects my birth with my writing this book. I am suggesting, however, that my conceiving of these events as being in my past is tied to the structure of consciousness itself, not to the truth or falsity of particular memories. This structure is grounded in a recurring present, not in past events. The past *as past* is a projection from out of the present.

A necessary condition of conceiving of time, of ourselves, or even of the world in general is the ability to place experiences in successive order—to relate them as coming before or after one another. This ability is logically prior to anything else we may do as reflective, self-conscious human beings. *All* questions of science, philosophy, and daily living presuppose an inner sense of "beforeness" and "afterness." This sense of succession has nothing to do with truth; even the chronically confused or insane who reverse the true sequence of events, or place them in a time where they don't belong, still manage to place one event before or after another.

How, then, is it possible to serially order our experiences? What is needed is a frame of reference which can't be any of the contents or objects of consciousness themselves, since those contents are placed in that frame. Consider a spatial analogy. The point of view which places the chair (or any object) to the left of the sofa (or any other object) is the perceiver's own position, which is not identical with either of the objects. The point of view which determines the field of vision cannot itself be one of the objects in that field.

Now apply this analogy to time. That which allows me to place experience A before experience B cannot be either A or B or any other discrete experience. However, it could be an underlying field of awareness. Indeed, I will try to show that it must be.

According to this proposal, we are able to place one of our experiences as coming before or after another only with respect to a changeless backdrop of consciousness. Temporal succession presupposes the numerical continuity of consciousness over time. Without such a link, each of our experiences would fall into isolated worlds that don't come before or after each other, but would begin anew at each moment.

"Before" and "after" only make sense if we can answer the question "With respect to what?" The answer one gives cannot be merely "more remembered events," since the same question would then apply to them. Actual events (in the past) provide the content but do not in themselves explain the *form* in which they are cast. These events must be capable of serial ordering. Ultimately, we need to move outside the series of ordered events to the framework of consciousness itself. This framework makes it possible to recall one event as occurring before or after another event.

Consider the distinction between flashes of light emitted from a film projector and the screen upon which they are projected. Projected into empty space, the flashes themselves appear chaotic and unintelligible. The screen by itself is a changeless white backdrop devoid of content. When the flashes are projected onto the screen, however, the film unfolds in serial order before our eyes.

There are some dissimilarities between this analogy and my proposal. For one, consciousness is not white, much less sitting there like a film screen with spatial boundaries. But key parallels remain intact. Consciousness *plus* its changing contents result in an inner sense of serially ordered experiences. Consciousness by itself would be timeless. Experiences without the frame of reference provided by an underlying field of consciousness would appear to have no particular order. Together as form and content, however, they produce an inner sense of serial unfolding, just as the combination of screen and light patterns results in the sense of linear order.

The consequences of this analysis for a theory of time are significant. To begin, we cannot say that consciousness is identical with time or even that it is "in" time. For it is only the underlying field that makes seriality possible. On the other hand, the flux of experience cannot be identified with time, since the flux minus the field of awareness lacks serial structure. Nor can changing experiences be "in" time, since what they are in, viz., consciousness, is itself nontemporal.

So it must be the relationship or interplay between consciousness and its objects that results in the notion of temporal passage. Neither side of this relationship constitutes time, yet both are necessary to it. Time is a hybrid notion. It is neither change nor nonchange, but the interface between them. I am suggesting that time is nothing less than the leading edge of eternity. The leading edge is the creative advance (described in other contexts as the "Dance of Shiva") on multiple levels of the Great Chain toward an open future. But the farther up the chain we go, the closer we move toward the universal and eternal source of all change. Everything that happens between the highest and lowest levels is a matter of degree.

The past and the future are thus what you get when you run chaotic flux across an eternal backdrop. The flux is always in the present; the past is gone and the future has not arrived. *Now* is the leading edge of eternity. The ideas of past and future occupy shifting psychological space between now (the creative edge of eternity) and eternity itself (the pure consciousness or clear light of the void behind all things). Our sense of having endured through time is the offspring of both eternity *and* its creative expression in the present.

How is it possible to stretch one's personal memories into one's idealized past? By literally converting the vertical psychic distance between one's current consciousness and its object, e.g., one's last birthday party, into a horizontal psychic distance between now and then. Horizontal psychic distance is a subjective affair. It can seem like my last birthday party was a long time ago, or it can seem like just yesterday; it doesn't even matter if I had a birthday party. The vertical psychic distance between consciousness and its objects can be very flexible.

But why project one's current memory-experiences to the past rather than to the future? The fact that I remember certain events *as if* they occurred in my past doesn't mean that they actually did. What distinguishes an inner sense of "my" past from "my" future? Consider the psychological asymmetry between a seemingly determinate, expanding past and an open, personal future. For every precognitive experience an average person has—that is, every memory of the future—there are apparently thousands of retrocognitive experiences or memories of one's past.

The older you are, the greater the imbalance becomes. We remember far more about our pasts than we can see into the future. So it seems that we are moving irreversibly into the future or that time is moving in only one way—toward the past. Psychologically speaking, we reach a point where our pasts outweigh our futures, for example, when we are seventy years old. This is our sense of psychological irreversibility.

This represents how things happen to be, but not how they must be. Imagine, for example, an entire society developing remarkable precognitive powers to the extent that fifty percent of everything they remember actually happens at various points in their collective futures. For example, Smith remembers having an argument with Jones. However, the actual event takes place three months later, at which point Smith realizes that his apparent memory was in fact one of those "previews of coming attractions." In a society where this happened a great deal, the future would be no more open or closed than the past. Time would lose its arrow, and philosophers and scientists would develop theories of multidirectional time.

When the phenomena of precognition, spontaneous recall of past lives, and mystical experience are taken into account, the future and past become more balanced out. At some level, what will be already is, and what used to be still is. When clairvoyants or sages speak of time as an "illusion," they mean that time has lost its unidirectionality; it is an illusion insofar as one thinks of it as *moving* in only *one* way on *all* levels. At the highest level— that of pure consciousness or the Godhead—it doesn't move at all. At the lowest level—that of physical creation—it moves in irreversible and not altogether predictable ways.

Following is a summary of the theory of time suggested by the arguments developed in this chapter.

1. Time is not something in itself. It is neither a physical process nor a psychological one, nor a third thing behind the scenes, such as pure consciousness.

2. Time is thus neither change nor changelessness, but a hybrid idea that incorporates these otherwise incommensurable elements of experience.

3. Neither the past nor the future materially exists, although representations from each can be directly accessed at higher levels of the Great Chain through extraordinary states of consciousness.

4. Different futures with varying degrees of probability already exist on subtle levels of the Great Chain. Not all will drop into material reality. Physical manifestation takes place in the present, which is eternal. Past and future are enfolded into a higher order, as proposed by David Bohm. We create our individual and collective futures. But we do so from the perspective of the *now!* And *now* is both eternal and ever-changing.

5. Only if the relativistic space-time continuum exists could a time-traveler literally experience the material past. According to my proposal, a time traveler could experience the past only on some other level in the Great Chain. It would be as if he were in the past, although he would not actually be there. If this time traveler could travel to the future and observe his future lives, the lives he would see would not necessarily be exactly the ones that he would live when he got to that point.

6. What we think of as the past and future are essentially projections from our present consciousness. This is not to suggest that we create physical events from personal consciousness. It is to suggest that insofar as these events are recalled as being in one's past, their "pastness" is tied to present (unchanging) structures of consciousness.

7. The reversibility of time, the question of whether it has only one direction, depends upon the perspective we adopt within the Great Chain. Some physical processes are irreversible and represent a creative advance into an open future. Others are reversible. The strongest case for an open future, the asymmetry of past and future ("time's arrow"), is to be made at the physical level of the Great Chain, as demonstrated by Prigogine and others.

8. However, the higher we go in the Chain, the perceived asymmetry of future to past is reduced. When a clairvoyant sees the future, the events seen typically do not come tagged with their temporal order, much less a guarantee that they will happen on the physical level at all. The clairvoyant actually sees something other than

projections from his or her own subconscious. However, what the clairvoyant sees is only one among several possible futures, which doesn't become the (absolute) future, so to speak, until it happens in the present.

9. The upper levels of the Great Chain are closer to eternity, the lower levels to pure change. However, since higher interpenetrates lower, time must be the leading edge of eternity, the interface or point of manifestation involving both ends of this continuum.

10. From a transformational perspective, the highest state of spiritual realization is not merely the experience of Nirvana, the Godhead, or the clear light of the void. It is the perfect integration of this experience into samsara, the worlds of manifestation, form, and flux.

11. If so, we are again invited to view time not as change or nonchange, physical or nonphysical, relative or absolute. Rather, it is that point where each of these categories shades into the other, where inner translates into outer, pure consciousness gives rise to energetic manifestation, and emptiness becomes form.

12. The spiritual adept *lives* this interface, perfectly balanced on the leading edge of eternity, rising on form even while disappearing into emptiness, refusing to identify with past or future, inner or outer, seeing through all forms of duality, thereby doing something by doing nothing. How marvelous!

CHAPTER TEN

Transpersonal Psychology and Personal Growth

Today, many people seek help from psychotherapists not only for specific problems, but also for personal growth. Indeed, there has been an explosion of interest in personal growth agendas, both mainstream and alternative. The traditional goals of psychotherapy, however, have not always been so broad. They were focused instead upon helping individuals to overcome specific problems, such as impotence or psychotic hallucinations, and to adapt to the basic challenges of life, such as keeping a job. The methods to accomplish this ranged from surgery and drugs to psychoanalysis, behavior modification, and simple counseling.

Some personal growth may result from these procedures. However, the definition of success typically was, and still is, framed in terms of how well the problem is dealt with—with the elimination of symptoms. A successful outcome means that one's consciousness and behavior have been "normalized." That is still the main reason why people go for therapy. Something about their life is not working relative to what seems to work for other people. They are disturbed, sometimes to the point of being dysfunctional. They need help.

Beginning in the sixties, however, several developments have expanded this picture: greater acknowledgment of transpersonal crises; encounters with the paranormal (mystical experiences, OBEs, etc.); and a perceived lack of self-identity and meaningfulness, along with a desire to grow personally and spiritually beyond the requirements of just surviving.

On the one hand, mainstream psychology was asked to integrate certain paranormal experiences which did not fit *any* established model of reality, much less behaviorism or psychoanalysis. (This despite the fact that Freud and Jung were interested in certain types of paranormal phenomena). So the response for a while was to ignore or reject such experiences. In some circles, it still is.

On the other hand, mainstream psychology was also asked to develop models and methods for helping clients achieve levels of well-being beyond the norms of consensus reality. This transformational challenge was substantially reinforced by other elements of the cultural milieu, such as experimentation with drugs, sexual liberation, and the encounter with Eastern ideas and practices. The times were ripe for change.

New models and therapeutic strategies to address this challenge were incorporated informally under the umbrella of humanistic psychology. Gestalt, neoFreudian humanism, logotherapy, client-centered therapy, transactional analysis, and rational-emotive therapy (to mention some of the more prominent versions) each laid claim to part of the therapeutic spectrum. Some were long on technique, but short on modeling. Some were sympathetic to transpersonal experiences, others were unsympathetic. In principle, however, everyone in the humanistic camp agreed with Maslow's hierarchy of needs and with the conception of human nature as basically "good" and striving toward self-actualization. However, together with psychoanalysis and behavior modification, humanistic psychology fell short at several critical junctures.

To begin with, it never came to grips with transpersonal experiences and crises. It didn't have to. Such domains were considered marginal at best. Of course, Erich Fromm had declared as early as 1957 that Zen was the logical extension of analysis. And Maslow and later Charles Tart awakened many to the possibilities of "peak" experiences. Not coincidentally, workshops at Esalen Institute became rites of passage. But there was far more work to be done with humanistically oriented therapies and personal growth issues. As Albert Ellis (the founder of rational-emotive therapy) would put it, actualizing your full *human* potential is difficult enough without confusing the program with a lot of *trans*human mysticism.

While it held out a noble vision of human potential, humanistic psychology in 1970 was short on methods for achieving the degree of growth people had begun to clamor for. Many useful strategies did find their niche in encounter sessions, psychodrama, primal screaming, and active journaling. But the terrain between being functionally OK and fully self-actualized remained muddy. And when spiritual growth was put on the agenda—for example, experiencing the power of unconditional love—it became clear that something more was needed.

In the meantime the roots of transpersonal psychology were being nurtured by encounters with the paranormal, altered states of consciousness, Eastern ideas and practices, and the earlier works of William James, Carl

Jung, and Roberto Assagioli (a student of Freud's and the founder of psychosynthesis). By the mid-seventies transpersonalists were a recognized group, leaders in pushing the frontiers of human potential to domains seldom entertained in mainstream psychology. Many humanistically oriented psychologists went on to become transpersonalists, just as Maslow had predicted a decade earlier: "I consider Humanistic, Third Force Psychology, [the first two being psychoanalysis and behaviorism] to be transitional, a preparation for a still 'higher' Fourth psychology, trans-personal, transhuman, centered in the cosmos rather than in human needs and interests, going beyond humanness, identity, self-actualization, and the like."[1]

Transpersonalists from the beginning were actively involved in forming alliances with other transformationally oriented groups like holistic health practitioners and in contributing to the larger New Paradigm dialogue. Almost by definition, the transpersonalist's quest for the big picture ensures continuing interest in the methods and goals of humanistically oriented psychotherapy. The reverse is less often the case. Despite significant cross-fertilization, relations have sometimes been downright cool.[2]

The interdisciplinary roots and applications of transpersonalism are reflected in three general-purpose periodicals: *The Journal of Transpersonal Psychology* (perhaps the most academic of the three), *ReVision* (which maps transpersonal aspects from the entire New Paradigm spectrum), and *Common Boundary* (which stresses spiritual aspects of psychotherapy and personal growth). These are, of course, not the only transpersonally oriented journals. Many are devoted to more specialized topics, such as dreams, healing, or near death experiences.

Extensive graduate training in transpersonal psychology still is offered at only a handful of institutions which emphasize orientations such as Jungian analysis. Experts in phenomena which attract transpersonal psychologists are themselves often not psychologists, but mystics, healers, and authors of ancient texts on spiritual realization. Occult traditions, for example, have treatises available on a wide range of transpersonal phenom-ena. If your client complains of seeing colors around people, you can get more help from Annie Besant's theosophical treatise, *A Study in Human Consciousness*, than from the psychiatrist's *Diagnostic and Statistical Manual*.

Along with the rise of transpersonal psychology, there has been a grassroots evolution of thousands of growth counselors, psychic therapists, and "transformational guides" engaged in part-time and full-time practices. Some of these individuals are psychically gifted, some are not. Others have limited training in psychotherapy (not necessarily licensed or degreed), while most do not. Some are comfortable with the New Age label, others run from it.

Out of this mélange of fact, speculation, extraordinary experience, and para-professionalism, a striking folk wisdom has arisen. Typical examples are: "The Universe mirrors what you need to see," "Love is letting go of fear," and "Happiness is acknowledging your inner child." Some of this folk wisdom has clinical support. Some of it does not. However, much of it is being factored into the emergence of a transpersonal paradigm.

We are witnessing not so much the emergence of another school of psychology as a transpersonal *perspective*, which cuts across traditional disciplines and nurtures various grass roots movements. Mainstream clinical psychology will continue to play a role in the evolution of this perspective. Yet when we take note of the membership, leadership, and key speakers of the International Transpersonal Association, we see an organizational clearing house for elements of major cultural change—not just another group of clinicians.

Many gifted individuals in both spiritual disciplines and in leading-edge science have contributed to the evolution of a transpersonal perspective. Of most relevance for transpersonal psychology, however, are four giants of the field: Carl Jung, Roberto Assagioli, Ken Wilber, and Stan Grof, whose contributions diverge and complement each other in many ways.

Any summary of their respective contributions would be out of the question, especially since one can readily turn to their own works.[3] As one might expect, however, their theories harbor some underlying philosophical tensions which need to be addressed. So instead of just describing the views of any one theorist, I will focus upon a few core agenda items of relevance for the entire field.

CONTINUING AGENDAS FOR TRANSPERSONAL PSYCHOLOGY

Before getting underway, it will be useful to list some of the kinds of experiences and concerns which invite the transpersonalist's attention. I preface this list with the qualification that there is considerable debate over their legitimacy and interpretation. In no special order of importance, they include: archetypal and transformational aspects of dreams; various types of meditation; hypnosis and regression (including past-life phenomena); near-death and rebirth experiences; out-of-body experiences; drug-induced altered states of consciousness; "seeing things" (like apparitions or auras); kundalini awakenings; breaking ego boundaries; mystical experience; connecting and empowering experiences (love, letting go, etc.); transformational aspects of symbols; spirit possession and depossession; passionate, inspired creativity (as if "possessed"); and shamanic initiations and ventures.

Six challenges for contemporary transpersonal psychology cut across this spectrum of topics: Where do transpersonal experiences take place? How ought personal/spiritual growth be built into the Great Chain? How can we provide better environments to nurture and heal transpersonal awakenings and crises? How can we effectively distinguish between psychic and spiritual emergencies? How might useful esoteric diagnostic and therapeutic strategies be incorporated into a transpersonal paradigm? How might claims of false memory syndrome be effectively addressed? I will frame each challenge as an imperative.

Explain where transpersonal experiences take place. This overly simplified request may not have a precise answer. However, it highlights the issue between systems and perennialist approaches to the transpersonal. And it brings assumptions about localization ("To be is to exist at a certain place and time") to center stage. Are there levels of the Great Chain of Being which permeate our physical bodies? Do wisdom and unconditional love emanate from higher levels of reality? Or does the Great Chain reflect merely a mélange of anthropomorphism, hallucination, metaphor, and wishful thinking? Do we participate in universal archetypes with refined energetic aspects which envelope the planet? Or are archetypes merely ideas in our brain?

Transpersonalists are not reductionists, yet they often hesitate to adopt the full-blown reality of the Great Chain of Being. For example, they urge that we take past-life experiences or mystical experiences seriously for what they can tell us about the transformation of consciousness, not necessarily for what they can tell us about other levels of reality. It is frequently pointed out that archetypes are useful devices in organizing and interpreting experience, often with no further explanation of where archetypes are located or how independently real they are.

Grof, for example, entitled one of his major works *Beyond the Brain*, while leaving it an open question whether the transpersonal experiences he described in the book take place within the brain. And Capra, a systems thinker sympathetic to transpersonal psychology, devoted an entire chapter of *Turning Point* to "Journeys beyond Space and Time," while leaving it similarly unresolved whether certain individuals just *think* they are journeying beyond space and time.[4] The transpersonal vision is not reductionistic, although its central message tends to be metaphysically neutral. We are told about types of unusual and transformative experiences which *could* be limited to the edge of our skulls, even though it seems *as if* they are not. People take journeys beyond space and time in their dreams, too. A real experience is not necessarily an experience of reality. So what's going on behind the scenes?

Transpersonal therapists do not need to address this reality question, except perhaps indirectly. The client's psychological well-being is their prime concern. But developing a transpersonal *paradigm* requires that reality questions be addressed in greater depth. Transpersonalists often seem unaware that many of their observations are consistent with an open-ended materialism.

Build evolutionary growth into the entire Great Chain. Few words appear as often in transpersonal (and humanistic) literature as "growth." But are we willing to go so far as to say that everybody desires evolutionary growth—from childhood and adult consciousness to spiritual realization and bliss? If so, what are the beginning and end points of the process? What drives the whole evolutionary spiral?

If we do not build growth into the full spectrum of energy-consciousness, the raison d'être of many personal crises tends to collapse. For example, if the goal were not to move from one level to the next, then why should transpersonal crises, such as spontaneous kundalini awakenings, be interpreted as opportunities for integrating a higher level of consciousness, rather than as bad luck? How would we interpret a transpersonal crisis in the first place, if not as signaling a potential movement through the structural disintegration and reintegration of consciousness?

If we do not build the urges and opportunities for growth into the Great Chain of Being, then once we have played out the automatic part of achieving adult consciousness, transpersonalism loses its edge. For why should one want to know God, or balance her female and male sides, or properly interpret his dream symbols, if growth is simply an accidental "add on" to each stage?

Everyone, of course, wants to be happy. But given the amount of unhappiness and frustration which accompanies personal growth work, it would be hard to explain why so many people have grown as much as they have, if there were no deeper evolutionary impulses involved.

What we require is a theory which builds the higher into the lower in such a way that the impulse for growth is never permanently lost. Ken Wilber has developed such an account:

> At each point in psychological growth, we find: (1) a higher-order structure emerges in consciousness (with the help of symbolic forms); (2) the self identifies its being with that higher structure; (3) the next higher order structure eventually emerges; (4) the self disidentifies with the lower structure and shifts its identity to the higher structure; (5) consciousness thereby transcends the lower structure; (6) and becomes capable of operation on the lower structure from the higher order level; (7) such that all preceding levels can then be integrated in consciousness, and ultimately in Consciousness.[5]

But where are these higher-order structures that eventually emerge? In Wilber's view, they are "deep structures" built into the unconscious. The unconscious in his view has three aspects: the ground unconsciousness, the prepersonal, and the transpersonal unconscious. We can view these three aspects as distinguishable levels, but they are in fact interpenetrating and coexisting.

Survival instincts, the prepersonal and personal elements of ego development, and deep structures waiting manifestation in a future humanity are all contained in the unconscious as one continuous unfolding process. In other words, the unconscious contains the past, present, and future of humanity. The highest ends to which we can aspire are already built in at the beginning. The unconscious

> ...is all the deep structures existing as potentials ready to emerge, via remembrance, at some future point. All the deep structures given to a collective humanity—pertaining to every level of consciousness from the body to mind to soul to spirit, gross, subtle, and causal—are enfolded or enwrapped in the ground unconsciousness.[6]

In this way growth is built in by suffusing every aspect of the lower levels of development with elements from the higher. Each person is thus striving to become in the end what he or she already was in the beginning. The sooner this is realized, the less suffering there will be. What drives the whole process? The next higher level eventually surfaces. But why?

Part of the answer lies in the distinction between deep structures and surface structures. A deep structure defines the range of surface structures. For instance, DNA codes reflected in my physical body define the kinds of tasks I can accomplish with my body. Or once the deep structure of operational thinking emerges, I can apply it to a range of practical tasks, some of which may actually help define who I am at that stage. Or once the capacity for socialization is actualized, I may then indulge it in a wide range of activities involving, say, family, sports, or community service. And for a while, community service may help define the surface personality I present to the world.

Sooner or later, however, the surface structures begin to break down in order to make way for the emergence of still deeper-level structures. For certain levels, the process is more or less automatic, even if troubling. Just making it through adolescence is one example. In other cases, one may experience profound unhappiness with current commitments and seek out greater depth of meaning. In still other cases, a deeper structure suddenly intrudes, such as in a near death experience that causes one to reorient one's life.

Once the possibilities of surface structures are exhausted, the stage is set for another evolutionary step. Of course, we may get stuck and find ourselves unwilling to look at further growth possibilities. Only a backdrop of reincarnation gives us enough time to explore every major option at every level in the Great Chain and still get stuck along the way.

With emotional and intellectual maturity comes the realization that there are always more levels, more deep structures awaiting integration. Even after our hierarchy of needs is successfully addressed and we have actualized our authentic humanness, to use Erich Fromm's phrase, the potential for further spiritual growth is usually greater than all of the challenges we have mastered to date.

Here the question "Why go further?" can take on a special meaning. Granted, the higher is already in the lower, the end in the beginning. But a deep structure of consciousness does not automatically actualize itself without an additional ground factor built into the process.

To do what we require, this "ground" must not be dependent upon anything else. It must manifest unconditionally (whether or not it is recognized as such), and it must be intrinsically desired in and of itself. The only ground that meets these conditions is the ultimate source of all other levels in the Great Chain. The end we implicitly seek turns out to be that which we were from the beginning. If we were once integrated and joyful aspects of a divine whole but now perceive ourselves as unhappily cut off from this state of oneness, it is natural that we would seek to reintegrate ourselves with the source from which we came—no matter how many lifetimes this takes!

The closer we get, the more evident it becomes that the end is not other than the seeker. And this seeker in turn is not one among many, but pure, unbounded, and radiant consciousness itself. In our unrealized state, however, the unconditioned appears conditioned through the various deep and surface structures with which we identify. *The irony is that the reality sought is none other than the self-shining bliss behind all structures mirrored in such a way through the Great Chain so as to appear to be other than itself.* When that veil is removed, we realize it was intended from the beginning that we become cocreators with God, the prime creator, in the loving expansion of all dimensions. The desire to grow is but a faint and filtered reminder of this primordial seed.

A multidimensional growth model has important implications for therapy. It is a great equalizer, a common ground working through fundamentally similar dynamics in everyone. At the same time it's a great respecter of individual differences; no two people work through their structures in exactly the same way. Other schools of therapy, of course, also balance their principles with particular human needs and circumstances. But they are more restricted in their vision of human potential.

A model of personal evolution based upon the Great Chain implies that what counts as normal is relative to the stage from which it is viewed. Normalizing behavior to a socially acceptable level about which the client also feels good is thus a far more relative undertaking than traditionally assumed.

Transpersonalists are not the only ones to see this. For quite different reasons, Thomas Szasz pursued a similar theme to its logical end in *The Myth of Mental Illness*. R.D. Laing's *The Politics of Experience* is a sustained challenge to the idea of equating "sanity" with "normality." And the French psychoanalyst Jacques Lacan has attacked the whole ideology underlying attempts to adapt a client's behavior to accepted social norms. However, the transpersonalist has a more encompassing vision not only of the range of normal behaviors, but also of their underlying dynamics.

Perhaps the most important consequence of the transpersonal vision of growth, however, is that the goal of *normalization* is replaced by the less value-laden goal of *integration*. This is especially true for the kinds of experiences and behaviors that transpersonalists specialize in. Psychologist

Douglas Richards, for example, has shown that dissociative phenomena (especially those associated with multiple personality and channeling) normally labeled as "pathological" are often better viewed as opportunities for the breakdown and reintegration of certain personality structures that, with a nurturing environment, ultimately lead to positive transformation for the individuals involved. On the other hand, not recognizing transpersonal crises for what they are, say, in the case of a kundalini awakening, can be especially destructive. To put a person on Thorazine who has undergone such an awakening and now wonders if she is going crazy, for example, not only represses what cries out for integration into the *whole* person, but also does potentially long-term damage. It moves us toward a self-fulfilling prophecy—that of externally induced psychosis.[7]

Acknowledge and provide nurturing environments for transpersonal awakenings and crises. No one has done more to translate this dictum into a professional agenda, on a large scale, than Cristina and Stan Grof. Cristina is the founder of the Spiritual Emergencies Network, which includes a national hot line and specially trained counselors in major cities throughout America and abroad. From their mixed but complementary backgrounds, the Grofs have developed a special form of self-exploration called holotropic therapy (literally "turning toward the whole"). It combines elements of controlled breathing, evocative music, focused bodywork, and visualization.

Considered individually, these elements are not especially novel. (Rebirthers, for example, use some of the same modalities.) But the Grofs' refinements and integration of these elements into a working program merit a distinctive label. Holotropic therapy in conjunction with follow-up counseling is useful not only in treating transpersonal crises, but also for inducing them (for growth purposes) in a nurturing atmosphere.

People have been troubled by strange experiences for thousands of years. Why take them so seriously now? The answer is: Because they are all over the place in an unprecedented fashion. For anyone willing to examine the historical record, this assumption is fully justified. The National Opinion Research Center of the University of Chicago, for example, reported in 1987 that sixty-seven percent of Americans believe they have experienced some form of ESP, and forty-two percent report some form of contact with the dead.[8] This increase came with the suggestion that such phenomena would continue to increase and spill over into areas where they are least expected.

This continued growth curve is also predicted by the hypothesis of accelerated interdimensional integration described earlier. More than ordinary cultural dynamics is transpiring. Our only choice is how to relate to it, not how to control it. Levels associated with ordinary consciousness are undergoing an accelerated breakdown and reintegration resulting, for some, in a more harmonious phase-locking with higher levels in the Great Chain.

Many individuals are undergoing unusual and often transformative experiences out of proportion to what coincidence would suggest. To friends, it may look as if they are going crazy. But what they are experiencing instead is an integration crisis brought on by the accelerated phase-locking of dimensions. The process is universal, but it affects us according to our own level of development. Some are ready, some are not. The process continues with or without us.

In order to provide nurturing environments for transpersonal awakenings, we must accurately diagnose such experiences, not reduce them to standard medical and psychiatric categories. Mystical experience is not schizophrenia, for example, nor are NDEs traumatically induced instances of autoscopy.[9] The case for making such differential diagnoses has been made for the benefit of anyone willing to take the time to examine all of the nonequivalent symptoms on both sides of the skeptic's equations. *DSM IV* (1994) has begun to recognize the autonomy of some transpersonal experiences; they are not merely special cases of deviant pathology.

I have used kundalini awakenings as an example in several contexts. Let me now explain in more detail what is involved. Kundalini is "life energy" residing at the base of the spine. It has a tendency to break out and move up the spine according to the inner evolutionary dictates of each person. For many, the kundalini never breaks out (in this lifetime). One researcher suggests that in Westerners, the process is likely to begin in the left foot, proceed up through the back, across the top of the head and back down through the heart to the pelvic area.[10] Many people feel it first start to move in their lower back. However one describes the movement of kundalini energy, its effects can be dramatic but sometimes misleading. As the Grofs explain:

> The process of kundalini awakening can simulate many psychiatric disorders and medical problems. Intimate knowledge of the kundalini syndrome is essential for the clinician to make a correct differential diagnosis. The

presence of characteristic energy phenomena, sensations of heat, unusual breathing patterns, pains in the characteristic blocking sites for which there is no organic basis, visions of light, and the characteristic trajectory of the process are among the signs that distinguish the kundalini syndrome from psychosis.

The individuals involved are also typically much more objective about their condition, communicate and cooperate well, show interest in sharing their experiences with open-minded people, and seldom act out. Although hearing various sounds is quite common, intruding persecutory voices do not belong to the phenomenology of kundalini awakening...

As the kundalini purges the system, it tends to reactivate traumatic memories from the past and bring their elements to the surface. The resulting emotional kriyas can involve states of anxiety, depression, aggression, confusion, or guilt; they can thus fall under various psychiatric categories and receive a number of diagnostic labels by an uninformed clinician.

The kundalini process can also simulate a variety of medical disorders. It can be misdiagnosed as Jacksonian epilepsy, a lower back problem, incipient multiple sclerosis, a heart attack, or a pelvic inflammatory syndrome.[11]

This is only a fraction of a comprehensive description and analysis of kundalini syndrome. Yet according to knowledgeable commentators, thousands of people experience it each year. If anything, the growth curve points upward, coinciding with the curve of increased spiritual exploration. Where are these people to go? More to the point, how can they avoid the potential damage which comes from a misdiagnosis? Fortunately, there are a growing number of clinical psychologists, such as Bonnie Greenwell, capable of diagnosing and guiding the process of kundalini awakening. Her study, *Energies of Transformation*, is very useful for anyone dealing with such an awakening.

Distinguish between psychic and spiritual emergencies. Some writers place the entire spectrum of transpersonal crises under the general label of "spiritual emergency." There are some good reasons for doing this. For example, one may want to avoid the questionable connotations of the term "psychic." Moreover, one's general outlook may dictate that spiritual transformation is the most important item on the developmental agenda, with psychic awakenings to be acknowledged only as a less interesting by-product of the process. Finally, transpersonal awakenings and crises may involve such a mixture of the psychic and the spiritual that to distinguish between them seems artificial.

Still, there is an important distinction within transpersonal phenomena, and the terms "psychic" and "spiritual" seem to be the most readily available to mark it out. A clinician's diagnostic skills and interventional strategies may vary considerably, depending upon which aspect requires the most (or the most immediate) attention. Psychologist Arthur Hastings has provided much practical guidance in this regard when the client in therapy also is undergoing some paranormal experiences.[12]

A psychic awakening involves an *experiential violation* of scientific laws governing space, time, matter, and causality, as they are currently understood. By this definition, experiencing X-ray vision, being out of one's body, or feeling energy pour out of one's hands into another's body, are all essentially psychic in nature. The key question here is "How are such things possible?"

Whether they represent an awakening depends upon whether the individuals experiencing them are in the beginning stages. And whether they represent an emergency depends upon how they intrude into the person's emotional space and the extent to which failure to integrate them leads to dysfunctional behavior. Assuming they are repeated (although, strictly speaking, this is not necessary), psychic experiences tend to change a person's *belief structure*. Even after a single out-of-body experience, for example, one may conclude that materialism is not an adequate metaphysics.

A spiritual crisis, by contrast, calls into question fundamental *ego-structures*. Typically the integration issues are both difficult and profound, as would be the case of someone who experiences, say, an overwhelming divine love, while living with unloving people. One might thus experience blocks in relating effectively to others who just don't understand. The key question is "How can one best deal with challenges to an entrenched ego-structure?"

Unlike psychic experiences, a spiritual crisis is *transformationally* reflected in the potential integration of an emerging deep structure of consciousness. It may be triggered by an experience with distinctive psychic components which do not fit ordinary views of space, time, or matter. This is the case with, say, mystical union. Then again, neither the triggering experience nor the crisis itself may have any distinctly psychic components.

All spiritual crises are by definition transformational crises. However, a psychic emergency may or may not lead to a transformational crisis. For example, some people can barely remember their near death experiences and when they do, they may consider them merely as interesting. Other near death experiencers undergo a major personal transformation that proves to be the first step in a life-long spiritual quest.

In summary, a transpersonal crisis may be either of a spiritual or a psychic nature. Often it includes elements of both. Typical kundalini awakenings certainly involve both. So do shamanic initiations. When transpersonal challenges intersect with transformational ones, the result is what we normally term a "spiritual crisis." However viable my suggestions in this regard turn out to be, the fundamental distinction between the spiritual and the psychic should be acknowledged and refined. For a psychic emergency is not automatically a spiritual one, and a spiritual emergency is not necessarily psychic in nature.

Integrate useful esoteric diagnostic and therapeutic strategies into the larger transpersonal paradigm. For every licensed psychotherapist in America today, there are probably dozens of unlicensed and untrained (by any accrediting agency's standards) spiritual and personal growth counselors who work pretty much on their own. Some are personally trained, usually through a program of discipleship, in the principles and techniques of a certain tradition. Others attend different workshops and subsequently put together an eclectic program of growth. A few are extraordinarily gifted and rely more upon intuitive guidance than external training. A growing number work collaboratively with licensed clinical psychologists.

Such cross-disciplinary chaos should be expected in times of great change, together with charges of being blind, dangerous, incompetent, or opportunistic. Be that as it may, the basic challenge is to develop and refine a larger transpersonally oriented paradigm which does justice to appropriate elements of this potpourri.

This does not mean that we should believe everything we hear in this regard. It does mean that we should be prepared to struggle with the unusual and the seemingly unexplainable. An examination of alternative approaches is not possible here. However, it will be useful to describe a few examples of special relevance for a transpersonal paradigm.

First of all, a place must be made for the *body* as conducive to, and reflective of, what is troubling or transformational in consciousness. Among the questions this project must address are:

1. Exactly why is breathwork so effective in helping people to access and express underlying emotional issues? Is hyperventilation the key or is it that we are literally charging up our emotional bodies with pranic energy?

2. How is it possible for a massage therapist to give one an accurate emotional reading by touching parts of one's body? Or to rub a certain place that causes great emotional distress?

3. How is the body able to take on different physical characteristics in multiple personality and possession cases, e.g., different scars, coloration of eyes, handedness, birthmarks, acne, etc.?

4. Is it true that the body never lies? In simply asking a person to resist pressure with a certain muscle, posing a question which requires a "yes" or a "no" answer, and checking for a correspondingly sustained or reduced resistance, are there any limits to what a person might quickly and freely diagnose—from the symbolic meaning of a dream to the need for more vitamin C? Or is this technique of applied kinesiology merely an unusual type of placebo effect?

As a transpersonally oriented paradigm evolves, we will also need to integrate successful *esoteric systems* into the larger picture. Of the many possibilities in this arena, I will briefly describe only one: chakra psychology.

There are seven major chakras whose locations range from the base of the spine to the top of the head. (Others are located above the head, and we may actually be developing some additional chakras, but they need not concern us here.) Chakras take the shape of subtle pulsating or spinning energy vortexes, each with its primary distinctive color. The Chakras mediate subtle energies, especially ch'i or prana. They also correlate with specific vertebra, physical organs, and a person's aura. Their existence has long been part of Vedic and Buddhist psychology. Only more recently have they been acknowledged to any significant degree in the West.[13]

There are a variety of ways to obtain information about the state of one's chakras. The most direct approach is with well-developed clairvoyant vision. More individuals are developing such second sight these days, so this approach is not as limited as it once was. One can also gain some knowledge of the chakras through muscle testing (applied kinesiology), using a pendulum, feeling with the hands, and by using instruments that mediate their magnetic or electrical aspects.[14]

The vitality of each chakra, together with the balance of energies connecting them, reflects one's basic psychological dynamics at a particular stage of evolution. There is fairly widespread agreement concerning these correlations. For example, the solar plexus chakra is associated with issues of will and power, and the throat chakra with issues relating to communication and expression. A vital solar plexus chakra combined with a weak throat chakra thus may contribute to a variety of issues relating to holding feelings inside. The condition of one's so-called brow chakra or "third eye" is directly relevant to issues generated during a transpersonal crisis, such as seeing otherwise invisible patterns of energy.

Information relating to chakra psychology continues to grow and undergo refinement. It has been a tradition in the East and will probably become a major tradition in the West. In America alone there are thousands of growth and transpersonal counselors, including a significant number of professional psychologists, who find the chakras useful adjuncts in their work. Yet when one looks to the huge body of literature relating to human nature in the New Paradigm, one typically finds little more than a brief mention of the chakras.

Chakra psychology ought to be an integral part of any comprehensive transpersonally oriented paradigm. Understanding psychological aspects of the chakras is fueling a variety of alternative approaches to personal and spiritual growth. Nobody, of course, can address all the issues relating to the evolution of one's paradigm. However, for any psychotherapy informed by transpersonal thinking, the chakras (and subtle body anatomy in general) ought to be a standing agenda item. In some quarters they already are.

A third related agenda is how best to integrate the clairvoyant insights and healing skills of a psychic or healer into a client's diagnostic and therapeutic profile. Of course, one might not consider this a challenge at all. Why bother with charlatans? For readers who believe that psychically sensitive individuals have nothing to contribute to the therapeutic process, I can only point out that the historical record now suggests otherwise.

Psychics who work with transformational issues (which is not the same thing as reading the future) are usually naive about the range of dynamics for which clinicians have received graduate training. This is especially the case with psychopathology. Most psychics could not clearly distinguish between psychosis, schizophrenia, and multiple personality. But that is a deficit which can be overcome by working with psychotherapists.

The other side of this picture is more interesting. Skilled transformationally oriented psychic counselors often deliver more value for the money than the average clinical psychologist. For help with *certain* issues they are simply more efficient. If a psychically gifted counselor can identify a key underlying issue in ten minutes, put the client effectively in touch with its origin, say, in early childhood, in two sessions, clear it out in one more session, and deal effectively with any ensuing integration issues—all to the client's long-term satisfaction—then why refer that person to a psychoanalyst at a cost of twenty thousand dollars to reach essentially the same point?

Who would want just to freely associate if a healer can see the energetic manifestation of the client's fear wrapped around the heart chakra, and then reach in and literally dissolve it, once the client has been brought to an appropriate state of readiness? (One reason is that there are not enough good healers to go around.) There are tremendous opportunities for cooperation and cocreation in this arena.

Naturally, many questions arise. How are conflicting interpretations resolved? Who bears responsibility? What about pay scales? What kind of issues is a psychic counselor likely to be better at coping with? How should we mark out the individual specialties of psychic counselors? What should they not be permitted to do, for lack of professional training? How should we deal with the sensitive egos of both psychic and psychotherapist? Why should insurance companies pay more than necessary for certain types of counseling and therapy if alternative counseling and emotional work produce comparable results in less time?

Of special concern is the issue of whether psychic counselors and bodyworkers really understand and have the skills necessary to guide the *affective* dynamics of therapy. This is perhaps the chief concern of many clinical psychologists otherwise sympathetic to the paranormal.

These questions are on the table in America and elsewhere. The remaining question is when, not if, they will be directly confronted. For they are forcing their way into the working space of transpersonally oriented psychotherapists and many others at the leading edge of the New Paradigm dialogue. They are the very stuff of paradigm shifts and paradigm wars!

Confront the challenge of false memory syndrome. Until recently, it was generally assumed that children may have traumatic experiences, repress them beyond the point of recall, and many years later recover them in therapy. For example, instances of sexual abuse as a child may be recovered under the guidance of a clinical psychologist trained in hypnosis. This assumption is now under direct attack by the False Memory Syndrome Institute through a sophisticated public relations campaign. Money and careers are on the line as therapists are taken to court by the parents of abused children for destroying their families. A real paradigm war, in the most practical sense of the phrase, is under way.

The charge is straightforward. Biased and greedy psychotherapists are planting memories of abuse, through suggestion or leading questions, in their unsuspecting patients who are in a vulnerable frame of mind. This process may be unintentional, but the effects are the same. The client seems to recall a traumatic experience that in fact never happened. It seems all the more real, because it is often closely linked to actual events in the client's past. False memory syndrome advocates do not deny that some children have been abused. Rather, as psychologist Elizabeth Loftus points out in *The Myth of Repressed Memory*, they deny that such a terrible thing as incest or ritualistic abuse—if it really happened—would be so readily forgotten or remembered only in therapy.

Undoubtedly, some psychologists have unwittingly led their clients to believe what never happened. The therapist herself may have experienced abuse and consequently must work doubly hard at not jumping to conclusions with clients whose symptoms suggest (but do not necessarily prove) abuse. At issue, however, is the sweeping nature of the false memory syndrome thesis: virtually all of the recovered memories of abuse in this country are fabrications! As of 1994, over a thousand lawsuits are at some stage of preparation or execution against psychotherapists who have uncovered such repressed traumatic memories. A common charge is that the therapist has destroyed a parent's reputation.

Transpersonal psychologists often have clinical practices. Together with other therapists of nearly all persuasions, they have much at stake in the outcome of this debate. However, false memory syndrome also poses several additional challenges for the transpersonalist. The very core of past-life therapy, for example, consists in recovering traumatic experiences through hypnosis. (Fortunately, family members from past lives are rarely still alive to bring suit against the therapist!) Alleged alien abductees often suffer from post traumatic stress disorder (PTSD). But their memories, often recovered through hypnosis, are also challenged by the false memory hypothesis.

There are several ways to respond to the more sweeping versions of this hypothesis: cite the lack of supporting studies; point to the effectiveness of therapeutic interventions that recover traumatic memories; and provide independent confirmation, where possible, of the events in question. In *Unchained Memories: True Stories of Traumatic Memories, Lost and Found*, child psychiatrist and expert witness Lenore Terr outlines the most direct approach: show how victims of childhood abuse exhibit specific physical and emotional symptoms in adult life that collectively form an interlocking *pattern*. When such symptoms are absent, the odds increase dramatically that an isolated memory of childhood abuse has been unconsciously fabricated. It should also be pointed out that while the patient is in trance, nontraumatic memories can be altered by the therapist, whereas traumatic ones, as a rule, are so deeply embedded that they cannot be altered by hypnotic suggestion.

Few professional organizations seem concerned to rebutt these charges. Perhaps they are viewed as not worthy of rebuttal, although in view of pending court cases this is hard to understand. The extent to which false memory syndrome is or is not the case deserves more attention by transpersonalists and other psychologists than it has so far received.

SIGNIFICANT OTHERS: NEW PARADIGMS OF RELATIONSHIP

Relationships are powerful vehicles for personal growth. However, for the better part of recorded history, they have functioned more as security blankets and protection against the forces of change than as anchoring points for coevolutionary journeys. They serve this security function well and will continue to do so. But as paradigms of human potential change, so must the way we structure our relationships.

Naturally, our relationships with animals, with the planet, and with our gods and goddesses are part of the larger picture of changing relationships. In what follows, however, I will focus upon human connections (family, friends, lovers, life partners, etc.), with emphasis on adult partnerships. Consider the following cluster of Old Paradigm assumptions about human nature:

1. We are basically alone; deep friendships are rare luxuries.
2. We are basically selfish and competitive and must be taught altruism.
3. We are either locked into our bodies, or simply are our bodies.
4. We fear dying, losing loved ones, or not being cared for.
5. We need to be in control to prevent bad things from happening.
6. We possess self-images that others have defined for their benefit.

There are obvious exceptions to this picture. Each assumption applies to varying degrees to different people, and at different times in history. Christians will affirm that we are not alone, because God really cares. Atheists will insist that they do not fear dying. And altruists will point to numerous acts of human kindness. This picture is not the only one we have inherited. But it is one of the most influential. Throughout history, we have affirmed more optimistic views, but then *lived* as if we suspected that this one is closer to the truth.

The question to consider in light of this picture is: "What kind of relationship *could* one have based on these Old Paradigm assumptions?" Put differently, what type of relationship would one naturally want, given this picture of the human condition? Most of all, what type of alternative relationship does a transpersonally grounded New Paradigm offer?

The following chart answers these questions according to four primary categories. The first two, controlling and caretaking relationships, are the offspring of Old Paradigm thinking. They are aspects of what is usually described as a codependent relationship. The third category, intimate relationships, is increasingly found (or being consciously worked at) in contexts where New Paradigm thinking has made inroads. And the fourth category, spiritually integrated relationships, while rarely achieved these days, holds out an ideal for the twenty-first century and beyond.

It's possible to combine elements from different categories and create new ones. Marilyn Ferguson's "transformational relationship," for example, incorporates elements from both the third and fourth categories. And caretaking can be viewed as a subtle form of control, rather than as a separate category of relationship. Accordingly, my categories should be viewed as approximations and judged as much for their stimulus value as for their truth value.[15]

The following four types of relationship should be viewed in an evolutionary perspective. Each builds upon its less-evolved neighbor and incorporates the lessons of earlier perspectives. For example, the spiritually integrated relationship incorporates the characteristics of trust and support from the intimate relationship, but also goes beyond them. Moreover, one doesn't just skip from, say, a controlling to an intimate relationship without experiencing a caretaking relationship along the way.

OLD PARADIGM RELATIONSHIPS

	Controlling	Caretaking
Purpose:	To get controller's needs met; other merely serves; clearest reflection of patriarachal thinking	Both partners' needs are addressed out of self-interest; pain is spread around more equitably
Seeks in partner:	Someone who needs to be served or wants to serve; roles irreversible	Compensatory traits, surface attributes, validation
Guiding emotions:	Fear, control, anger	Fear, guilt, betrayal
Love seen as:	A social convenience; one-way service contract; possession	Meeting key needs, not necessarily the same for each party
Giving/receiving:	It's better for the controlling partner to receive than to give; reverse for the other	Gives in order to get; doesn't give to self; plays victim in order to receive
Mode of relating:	Issues commands; needs to be in control; assumes role of teacher, superior wisdom	Caretaking; identifies with role of nurturer or of one who needs to be nurtured
Sexuality:	Defined mainly in terms of physical effectiveness of subordinate partner	One's own needs defined in terms of other's mainly physical needs
Self-esteem:	Outwardly often strong, but inwardly weak; seeks partner with low self-esteem	Generally low, bound up with partner's successes and failures; prey to victimization roles
Center of life:	Oneself (social status, career) is center; self-validates through control, as in "I made you who you are;" intimidating	Generally can't be happy unless loved ones are; switches between victim and caretaker roles; "I did so much for you"
Spirituality:	Organized religion is a hierarchy for exercising power; guilt is used to control; little spiritual awareness; blind obedience is a virtue	Joins a church to get one's needs met or to become a caretaker on a larger scale; self-image is partly defined in terms of religious teachings
Work:	One either dominates or is dominated by others in one's workplace; works to survive	Self-concept is defined partly by successes or failures in work; makes excuses easily
Monogamy:	Dominant partner, usually the male in heterosexual relationships, does what he pleases; other is ideally monogamous	Partners tend to fear loneliness; affirm monogamy out of self-interest; affairs would be kept secret

NEW PARADIGM RELATIONSHIPS

	Intimate	Spiritually Integrated
Purpose:	Meets needs with mutual love and support; less guilt and victimization	Synergistic bonding of energies; relationship reflects spiritual quest
Seeks in partner:	Compatability, common interests and values; someone to share with; few surprises involving boundary issues	Desire to grow; often strong similarities and differences in outlooks; willingness to risk; sharing for its own sake
Guiding emotions:	Ego-level love; finds validation for who one is and what one stands for in the relationship	Soul-level love; joy in the process of growth itself; fear has been let go
Love seen as:	Support and sharing; respect for roles one's partner plays; something that must be worked at; intimate connections	Empowering energy which stimulates partner's growth; overflowing and uncondi-tional; joy in simplicity and in uniqueness
Giving/receiving:	Gives to others and to self; strives for balance and fairness in giving and receiving	Spontaneously gives and receives in ways appropriate to the circum-stances
Mode of relating:	Enjoys emotional inti-macy; shares feelings; trusting and vulnerable; values stability, but open to change; partners come from separateness but explore ways to move beyond it	Balanced resonance of "you," "me," and "we;" partners consciously create what they need to grow; joy in sharing is not used as a substitute for individual growth
Sexuality:	Makes love for emotional and physical sharing; open and trusting attitudes about sexuality; requires meaningful communication	Brings physical, mental, emotional, spiritual bodies into alignment; experiences oneness; a celebration of divinity
Self-esteem:	Good self-esteem; concern with shaping and refining identity; not easily threatened; works on particular issues	High self-esteem; few or no boundary issues; see situations that might threaten self-image as stimulating or humorous
Center of life:	Self, other, and the relationship itself; accent on balancing different roles, ideals	Transpersonal bands of love, power, and wisdom which underwrite the relationship

	Intimate	Spiritually Integrated
Spirituality:	Comfortable with diverse religious outlooks; enjoy compatible spiritual attitudes; God still tends to be "out there"	Pervasive sense of awe, devotion, and humor at shared transcendent bonding; God is outside and inside everything
Work:	Work and relationship are more compatible; career decisions are joint; career is fulfilling; greater appreciation of partner's work interests	Work expresses who one is; careers may change in response to internal shifts; what one does is less important than how one does it
Monogamy:	Committed relationships work better by providing clearer boundaries and focus; sexual intimacy outside the relationship has little attraction; lifelong relationship is ideal; infidelity is more likely to create pain and a sense of loss, rather than jealousy or a need for revenge	As a practical matter, monogamy facilitates growth; as old lessons are learned, a new partner may be attracted for a different stage of one's life; when sexual bonding is no longer appropriate, spiritually integrated partners nevertheless remain friends for life

None of these categories is pure; human nature and personal growth are always messy. Most individuals fit descriptions from several categories. Advances and retreats are found across the spectrum. Some people attempt to transcend their egos, for example, before they discover that they have one.

It should also be emphasized that nobody is superior or inferior by virtue of occupying a certain category. Nobody is a failure or should be made to feel that way because they seem stuck, for example, in a codependent relationship. Most of us have been at one time or another. The important question is not where one is, but whether one acknowledges one's present circumstances and has at least begun to act constructively on that understanding. For a friend or therapist, the agenda is not one of judgment, but rather one of facilitating change to the extent that one's friend or client is open and able to change.

Changing others versus changing ourselves. Most everyone wants to live in a happy, peaceful, and productive world. Achieving this goal, however, is directly related to our capacity to restructure our relationships, broadly conceived. This restructuring, by its very nature, must involve transforming ourselves, not merely fixing others' agendas so as to be more consistent with our own. For example, if we deal with our status as victims merely by trying to force others not to victimize us without at the same time addressing the underlying lacks which brought us to victimhood, we will eventually just find new ways to become victims. We will dress up differently to play the same role again. Gloria Steinem's *Revolution From Within (A Book of Self-Esteem)* shows the special significance of this fact for feminism.

Old Paradigm thinking often generates subtle pretenders to the throne of spiritually based (heart-centered) love. For example, if we bring our partner around to our point of view, it makes us feel more powerful. If we help our partner address their needs, it makes us feel good. If our partner creates safety for us to be vulnerable, we feel acknowledged. If our partner addresses our needs, we feel nurtured. If we experience sexual chemistry, we feel more alive. And if we experience all of the above, we may think we are in love.

All of these feelings are significant aspects of relationships. And if we are feeling lonely, such a package can look pretty good. But they do not capture the spiritual energy that pours forth from the heart in New Paradigm relationships. Such energy both empowers and transforms each partner's fullness of being. It enlivens everything in its path and, paradoxical as it may seem, actually helps one to love other people—even one's enemies. Once activated, the spiritual energy of a heart-centered relationship expands indefinitely in joyful and unforeseen ways, as Gary Zukav describes in *The Seat of the Soul.* Marianne Williamson's *A Return to Love* and Ken Keyes's *The Power of Unconditional Love* also speak profoundly to those seeking such a relationship.

The four critical differences between Old and New Paradigm relationships may be summarized as follows. In New Paradigm relationships:

1. Love, however imperfectly manifest, triumphs over fear (which has been progressively, sometimes painfully, defrocked). This is a fundamental difference in goal. Love is not based on need. It empowers the relationship. Since all love is ultimately God's love, however imperfectly apprehended, it can be progressively accessed but not created from human chemistry or psychology.

2. Transformation is built into the relationship, such that the partners don't spend a lifetime stuck in the same roles of control, caretaking, or victimization, trying out new positions in the same old game. This is the dynamic difference.

3. The relationship itself reflects a resonant interface of two healthy people who have come together to create, grow, and enjoy rather than compensate for lost or dysfunctional parts of themselves through the other person. They define a relationship of empowerment; it doesn't define them. They create a relationship with its own dynamics—a third entity—while respecting their own and their partner's individuality. This is the structural difference.

4. A fourth consideration is implied by the other three, but deserves special attention. It is that each partner has learned to love himself or herself. Each feels worthy of being loved, hence is open to receiving love and joyfully sending it back. Without self-worth, an Old Paradigm relationship is about all one could hope for. As within, so without! Those who seek loving relationships with others first need to examine their relationship with themselves.

There are many ways to characterize the differences between Old and New Paradigm relationships and many strategies in the literature of self-help to assist in making the shift from Old to New. Suitably qualified, they provide an appropriate framework for understanding *and* changing relationships—not only between individuals, but also between races, religions, and nations. Needless to say, it is imperative that these shifts begin to happen on a large scale.

PRINCIPLES OF PERSONAL GROWTH: A BRIEF COMMENTARY

There is a striking folk wisdom about personal growth emerging in America today. Some of the principles that inform this wisdom are as old as religion but with a new twist. All have roots in established traditions, although they may not always be recognized as such. Many are becoming a part of mainstream psychological counseling. And most can be interpreted in different ways.

One could select fifty books from the self-help, psychology, New Age, or religion and spirituality sections of a bookstore and find these principles illustrated in different ways. The distilled list I will present has evolved as a matter of both reading and personal interaction.[16] It aims for breadth and clarity rather than depth. However, the list is far from complete. I have simply selected the principles which seem most representative and, in some cases, in the greatest need of clarification.

Failure to acknowledge or properly understand the dynamics of our four primary bodies—physical, emotional, mental, spiritual—underlies most of the blocks to personal growth. In an ideal world, our spiritual body (which is our most direct connection with the Source of all being) provides wisdom for the mental body, love for the emotional body, and power for the physical body. However, we tend not to listen to all of our bodies with equal sensitivity, even when they knock very loudly. We leave some under-developed, mistake their individual functions, and confuse their inter-penetrating relationships. In short, we are not in optimum alignment with ourselves.

For instance, we mistakenly tend to think of love (which properly belongs to our spiritual body) as part of our emotional body: a feeling among other feelings, which competes to get its needs met from other people. Our fragmented relationships mirror this misperception. We try to sustain our inner emotional body by competing for external energy, unaware of the fact that successful relationships mirror a strong integration of each partner's own emotional and spiritual bodies. This alignment empowers the relationship.

To take a different example, we may attempt to solve a friend's problem with our mental body, when what she really needs is the support of our emotional body. We also tend to repress anger while overlooking that such actions have consequences for our physical body. And when we find a spiritually enlightened teacher—especially one with psychic gifts—we can miss the fact that he may not have dealt with all of his emotional issues.

A fundamental cause of our problems, on whatever level we encounter them, is the perception of being separate and alone. In reality, we are one. We are an expression of divine Source. But we have typically lost the feeling or sense that this is so. We have instead adopted the illusion of encapsulated ego-hood; the "ghost" is trapped in the machine. This feeling of separation is reflected in the misalignment of our primary bodies. All growth challenges reflect a misalignment of our primary bodies. And all effective growth work is implicitly an exploration of realignment and integration toward the goal of oneness.

The core fallacy: we seek unity and wholeness where they cannot be truly found. The quest for unity and wholeness is part of the human condition. At one time or another, we seek unity by identifying with our physical bodies, our parents, our families, our religions, our principles and causes, our creative endeavors, or our control dramas. We also attempt to achieve unity through destructive patterns of drug abuse, narcissism, or immersing ourselves in work. Or we may attempt to preserve what limited wholeness we have achieved through denial or control—by acknowledging only our mental and physical bodies, for example, and putting the former in charge of the latter.

All such attempts are subject to change. New circumstances eventually disrupt our fixed life-styles and expectations. Every relative institution, cause, role, or part of ourselves with which we identify has, so to speak, its day of reckoning. The sage, Wei Wu Wei, asks: "Why are you unhappy? Because 99.9 percent of everything you think and of everything you do, is for yourself—and there isn't one."[17] The final solution to the quest for wholeness is in the dissolution of false ego which seeks unity in everything except its oneness within the Great Chain itself. In the meantime, we should begin to question the programming which leads to such fixed identifications.

Many stages of identification, disintegration, and reintegration are predictable. We call this growing up. Problems begin to creep in when we get stuck. Those able to identify with the *process* of evolution acknowledge the emergence of deeper structures in consciousness and nurture the inner alignment of these structures; they typically experience greater happiness. With alignment comes a reduced need for an ego to be in charge and an increased tendency to question the fixed roles that others would like us to play.

What everyone really wants: balance, empowerment, integration, and love. The weight of this observation rests upon the term "really." People obviously want many things—sex, power, money, a comfortable home, an education, and acknowledgment, to name a few. One might simply desire to have his or her personal hierarchy of needs met, and not worry about it further. But everything people claim to want sooner or later turns out to be either a perceived means to, or some aspect of, balance, empowerment, integration, or love—which is to say, alignment reflecting the oneness of all that is. For example, one who claims to desire sex simply for itself on a continuing basis is really looking for something else, but in the wrong way.

Obviously these factors admit of degrees and should be understood in light of an individual's particular stage of evolution. Empowerment for a child is not the same as for a mature adult. Once we reach the stage of normal self-consciousness, there are few exceptions to these four fundamental categories. They are everywhere behind the dramas of daily life—even the dramas of those who behave in selfish and hurtful ways.

Each of these four factors is bound up with the others. For example, a person's masculine and feminine sides may be in a state of relative balance, where neither side overpowers the other. However, balance itself does not insure integration. Can each side call upon the other exactly at the time and to the degree that it is needed? For this, we require integration. Moreover, the fact that they can work together does not necessarily mean they are optimally empowered. They may not be able to achieve their common goal for a lack of the power to do so. And one factor that substantially contributes to empowerment is the ability to receive unconditional *love*. There are no limits to the creative synergy of these four categories.

What prevents obtaining what we really want: guilt, poor self-image, denial, and fear, all of which reflect lack of inner alignment, stemming from the perception of being separate. Many factors appear to stand in the way of our happiness and growth: lack of financial or physical resources; lack of emotional support; disease and illness; being subject to intense pressures and stress; and outright victimization. So guilt, a poor self-image, denial, and fear, must be understood as involving fundamental dynamics sometimes at an unconscious level. For example, you may not be receiving the emotional support you need. But the reason could be that you deny really needing much emotional support; a strong, silent personality may actually hide a weak self-image.

There is a potential catch–22 in this dynamic. If one is not achieving the growth or happiness one claims to want, is it because one is blocked by fear or guilt *or* because one doesn't really desire what one claims to, at least not yet? Instead of treating this as an either-or mandate, the dilemma is best viewed as a sliding scale with variable amounts of motivation and blocking involved in each person's case. If you desire a dynamic, empowered relationship, for example, but haven't found one, an unconscious fear of betrayal may be standing in the way. However, if you persist in your desire and work through the fear, the relationship can be yours.

These primary psychological blocks fuel much of the posturing and rationalizing of human existence. For example, fear lies behind patriarchy, parts of organized religion, rule-bound behavior, and even capitalism. When major boundaries (whether physical, social, or psychological) are tested or questioned, fear is often in the background. Racism, for example, is often treated as if it were exclusively a moral issue, while the fear which drives both racist attitudes and reactions to them are ignored—to the detriment of both sides!

Fear, guilt, denial, and poor self-esteem are played out in our control dramas. The individual who endures these conditions typically has to exert a considerable amount of energy not to face them directly. And if they are implicitly acknowledged, energy must then be used to prevent others from taking advantage. In other words, one has to be in control of oneself or of others. Some rely on raw power to achieve this. But the exercise of control needs to be more subtle and in keeping with the amount of energy the individual has available for the purpose. Control dramas must be successful, sometimes for many lifetimes, in order to teach us lessons. Eventually, however, they have to be exposed for what they are.

In *The Celestine Prophecy*, James Redfield describes four types of control drama: *intimidation*, the exercise of power in ways that push fear buttons; *interrogation*, the discovery and exploitation of another's flaws, thereby producing guilt or anxiety; *aloofness*, a frequent cloak for denial which causes others to come to you; *victimization*, an attitude associated with low self-esteem that prompts others to give their energy to you.

These dramas, he points out, feed upon each other in endless patterns. Aloofness invites interrogation, interrogation causes one to be aloof, intimidation breeds victimization, and so on. What they all have in common, though, is the controller's unconscious belief that he or she is lacking *energy*. It is assumed that others have to be controlled, whether overtly or subtly, in order to maintain a sufficient and steady supply of energy for oneself.

Ultimately, control dramas must be broken by overcoming the illusion that there isn't enough energy to go around. The universe has an abundance of energy which is available through our spiritual bodies. But if we are cut off from our spiritual bodies and alienated from upper levels of the Great Chain, then the perception of scarcity will drive us to experiment with different control dramas. A reintegration with our spiritual bodies will help insure a balanced and mutually empowering exchange of energies.

What was done can be undone: deprogramming and reprogramming. This principle seems obvious until it is clear just how far some visionaries go with it. To begin, it means that no matter how great the trauma, how extensive the conditioning, how universal the pattern in this life (or others), or how great the conspiracy against change seems, what one sincerely wants to change in one's life can be changed. Moreover, this can be accomplished more effectively than popular thinking suggests.

Many methods are available for identifying blocks, clearing "old programs," and integrating newer ones appropriate to each individual's journey, for example, meditation, hypnosis, breath work, advanced body-work, visualizations, clairvoyant inspection, pure energy work, rebirthing, and phase-conjugate sound.

With the assistance of a powerful and highly qualified teacher, one can even release the hold of a decision made in an earlier life—not just by past-life regression, but by direct clairvoyant inspection and subsequent ener-getic intervention at the appropriate time. Unfortunately, there are very few such qualified practitioners currently available in physical form.

Some of the tools noted above work better for particular issues. And their results are partly a function of the quality of the practitioner. But they can be very effective. If one was abused as a child, the alternatives need not be to deny it, live with it, or pay ten thousand dollars for therapy. The scarring of such traumas can be undone in several months at a cost of no more than several hundred dollars. We can work on ourselves, even if only by completing the exercises in self-help manuals.

There is an interesting procedural issue related to deprogramming and reprogramming. How much negative programming does one have to clear out at the beginning before constructive reprogramming will work? Can one get rid of destructive attitudes simply by bathing them in light, love, and positive affirmations? Or must you first deal with their origins, some-times in painful ways? Put differently, can you melt the hatred you feel with love or must you let go of the hatred before you can experience love? The answer is that you cannot melt the hatred with love you don't have, so letting go of hatred (and fear) is the primary agenda. In their boundless optimism, New Age visualization and affirmation counselors overlook the importance of this distinction.

The only absolute right we have (or why we are here): to choose what to create. Although this is my own way of stating it, this maxim seems to be in the background of many transformational agendas. I have described it as the only absolute or natural right because it's the one that nobody can take away from us. Other rights are a matter of historical conditioning, negotiation, or pressure tactics. We have only relative rights to free speech, fair housing, gender equality, a smoke-free environment, quality medical treatment, or a representative form of government. These rights all come and go with the tides of circumstance. The more we are conditioned to believe that we have them and the more widespread this belief is, the greater is the tendency to declare them sacred or absolute. However, relative rights can be replaced, as history makes abundantly clear!

Of course, those in power can repress our capacity to maintain minimal self-awareness. One could be drugged and thrown into a comatose state. But in those circumstances, we don't know what's happening anyway. Assuming self-awareness, one always has the inner right to decide what to initiate, how to react, or how much effort to expend. Stated differently, our most fundamental right is to agree or disagree with what others think our rights or their rights ought to be. In the case of disagreement, one's right is to decide what to do and how one wishes to do it—from force to conflict resolution.

To declare that God, the constitution, society, the force of history, or the planetary hierarchy is on one's side does not automatically transform personal desires, no matter how socially responsible they may be, into rights. Rights aside, the meaning of human existence resides in all that we choose to create for ourselves and with others—in relationships, art, ideas, growth (or lack thereof), and health. We are here to create how we evolve through the spectrum consciousness. We were created in order to create.

Accept responsibility for what *you* create. Here is another principle that at first appears obvious. Most people tend to accept greater responsibility for what others have created and to project more of their own responsibility onto others than circumstances warrant. This principle urges us to draw lines of responsibility in a more discerning way.

This realignment means, first of all, that there is less responsibility that falls totally on your shoulders or on someone else's. We come to see, instead, that much of life involves sliding scales of responsibility with two or more people sharing appropriate amounts. Such discoveries are the daily bread of counseling sessions involving separation and divorce. Seldom do the reasons for divorce turn out to be all one or the other person's fault.

In drawing lines between spheres of responsibility, we should consider a wider range of factors that affect our creations. Assuming responsibility only for one's verbal commitments is a comparatively small piece of the pie. Here are some more subtle ways the question of personal responsibility may arise. Do you want something you are unwilling to communicate about, then act surprised when it comes? Are you putting out subliminal or mixed messages? What is natural or not natural to expect in a given situation? To what extent might you have interpreted your inner conflicts as someone else's character flaws to deal with, because she accepted responsibility for what she didn't create in the first place? Did you allow something to happen that you could have prevented or addressed, but blame the other person anyway? What are you afraid of creating by letting go of control? Addressing such questions helps create a more discerning sense of personal responsibility.

We attract situations to mirror what we need to see. Most of us act as if this principle were not true most of the time, but then selectively apply it to whatever suits us. If you cannot maintain any relationship for more than three months, everyone would agree that you need to look at something in yourself. Your partners are mirroring something you need to acknowledge. On the other hand, only the most radical New Age partisans would hold that the rainbow appearing after the last thunderstorm has a special message for you.

For those seeking to integrate this principle into their lives, arguing its truth or falsity would be pointless without clarifying what is at issue. What does it really mean in the first place? Here are some possible interpretations:

1. Is everything you attract something you automatically need to look at carefully? (Answer: No, only if it is a major event or involves a continuing pattern of events.)

2. Is the fact that you are involved with some situation necessarily evidence that you attracted it, even unconsciously, in the first place? (Answer: I don't think so. It is a bit much to suppose that God, one's higher self, or one's unconscious—not to mention one's conscious mind—cares if the clouds over your head are fluffy or stretched out.)

3. Is the fact that you can find some significance in any situation an indication that you needed to be involved with that situation? (Answer: Sometimes. You might need to think twice about that homeless person approaching you.)

4. If you really need to look at something, will you sooner or later find a way to attract the appropriate vehicle to do so (dreams, accidents, etc.)? (Answer: Always, although you might not get the point right away. You might not even get it in this lifetime.)

5. Are you sincerely willing to examine both major events and minor clues and synchronicities for what they can contribute to your learning and growth? (Comment: One is always better off living more consciously, less habitually! Those who recognize increasing

synchronicities in their lives are better positioned for accelerated growth.)

Interestingly enough, one's car often can provide clues to the state of one's mind/body. Impatience can be manifest in frequently worn brake pads. Stress may spontaneously appear in the form of a cracked windshield. The need to stop and look at some aspect of one's life may be reflected in speeding tickets and accidents. And procrastination may be reflected in a car that frequently does not want to start. These are metaphors to be sure. But their synchronous regularity suggests that they should not be overlooked.

There are often surprises, but never any accidents. Whether there are accidents depends of course on what you mean by "accident." The present claim, accordingly, is not intended to deny the existence of accidents in the ordinary sense of unforeseen or unpredictable events. Stubbed toes, missed appointments, and plane crashes are a fact of life.

However, there are two interpretations closer to the intent of "There are no accidents." They relate to the idea, just discussed, that we attract situations to mirror what we need to look at. The strong interpretation is that *whatever* happens in your life, from the major to the seemingly inconsequential, happens for a reason which has some significance for you, even if you don't understand what it is. Not only does this strong interpretation extend well beyond what the evidence suggests, its practical significance for living is captured just as well by a softer interpretation.

The softer interpretation of "There are no accidents" implies only that, sooner or later, we will acknowledge what we need to look at. Everything that happens in our lives need not have special significance. But when accidents cause pain, bewilderment, reflection, or curiosity, especially on a recurring basis, then we should not write them off as bad luck or mere coincidence.

Rather, we should examine them for the meaning they have for one's safety, growth, or enlightenment. Accidents do not come with a built-in meaning. Each person must provide that, using the events as a stimulus. For example, is there a warning? Insight? A lesson? Part of a larger pattern or picture you have been working on? In other words, whether "There are no accidents" is a literal description of reality is not the critical issue. What is critical is how it stimulates personal growth.

For those who believe that the universe makes no mistakes and that everything that does happen is supposed to happpen, the idea of free will merits a serious second look. To say that one could have chosen not to murder his mother, even though in fact he did murder her, looks incoherent. For if one's mother is murdered, that is what was supposed to happen by this line of thinking. Thus, to assume after the fact that one could have chosen not to murder his mother is to assume that one could have contravened the universe. Yet if the universe allows no accidents or mistakes, one could not have chosen other than what the universe prescribed. So those who believe that a certain outcome could have been different if they had willed it logically should allow the universe some "slippage" as it unfolds. Everything would be just as significant a stimulus for personal growth, according to this softer interpretation, as it would have been if the universe allowed no mistakes or slippage whatsoever!

The body provides clues for what needs to be addressed. Everyone knows that when you are sick you should rest. But as with the other principles, a much wider range of clues is at stake. Here is one place where science and metaphysics overlap nicely. The scientific interpretation of this principle is that there are more connections between one's body and one's emotional and spiritual issues than are usually suspected. These correlations can be tested.

The metaphysical interpretation of this principle, on the other hand, is that the body literally reflects one's emotional and spiritual patterns and pressure points—per the Great Chain of Being. These reflections range from the general to the specific. In some cases, they form the basis of entire systems of interpretation and treatment as, for example, in neurolinguistic programming. The following is a list of physical symptoms or patterns that may be linked to one's inner life.

When you are thinking about a question, do your eyes move to the upper right or the upper left of the visual field? Why is it that L-5 in your lower back keeps "going out" for no (physical) reason (strain) at all? Do your undiagnosed pains have a way of showing up mostly on the left side of your body? Why do you start emotionally sobbing when your massage therapist works on certain muscle groups? Why have you suddenly gained thirty pounds when your caloric intake and exercise levels are constant? Are you more prone to anxiety or depression after drinking a lot of coffee? Do your hands tingle at odd times, despite excellent circulation? Do you somehow manage to get sick just before visits to the in-laws? Are you getting hot flashes in your back? These are but a few of the kinds of clues your body provides for deeper level work.

We receive according to our readiness. Of all the principles, this can be the most maddening. For it comes with no built-in criteria, save some general rules of thumb, which enable us to predict the magic moment. One can work for years on a personal growth issue to the point where everything seems poised to fall into place, then meet with apparent failure and the observation that one wasn't ready. The reason is typically that one still has some blocks to deal with, perhaps some repressed fear. As the mystic Plotinus would have put it, higher realities are received by lower realities, but only to the extent made possible by the capacity of the recipients.

Yet in retrospect, when we finally receive what we've worked for, there is often a compelling wisdom to this principle. It seems perfectly shaped to each person's path yet floats freely across all paths. A number of publishers, for example, rejected this book. In dealing with that rejection, I both improved later versions of the manuscript and came to grips with a fear of success that in turn was rooted in a core self-esteem issue.

There are two special versions of this principle: We receive according to our *desire*; We receive according to our *expectation*. Each version can be true. When they are, however, it's because the relevant desire or expectation is in alignment with one's fundamental state of readiness. For example, you may consciously desire a relationship but subconsciously expect that it will not come. Or you can expect a promotion at work on a conscious level, but unconsciously not want it. This dynamic insures a holding pattern until one is fundamentally ready for the breakthrough.

There are some questions you can ask to help determine how close to readiness you are. For example, have the issues blocking you been correctly identified? Are you truly open to receive what you have requested? Are support mechanisms in place? In your clearest moments, do you *feel* ready? In the end, however, the most fruitful application of this principle requires trusting in the innate wisdom of your own soul, of God, or of the universe itself to know exactly when you are ready to receive.

Adversity always has a potential "up" side. We grow through constructively engaging the problems of life. Even in tragedy, there can be triumph. When the challenges of life become more than we think we can handle, however, this principle undergoes its severest application. For when this point is reached, the natural inclination is to declare that this situation (divorce, severe illness, persecution, etc.) is unfair, the result of rotten luck, or utterly without redeeming value. We apply the principle up to a point, then set it aside as if it were not an integral part of evolution.

There are two ways to interpret this principle. The first is softer and more pragmatically oriented. It begins by acknowledging adversity, such as the fact that one has lost a limb as a result of an accident. With brutal consistency, however, it then requires that we ask: "What are you going to do about it?" You can make a bad situation worse by continuing to respond negatively. Or you can make it better by exploring the ways you *can* learn and grow from the experience. There need not be a single, objective lesson in it. The upside potential always provides some range of possibilities from which one can create one's own meaning.

The stronger interpretation of this principle is that in the case of major adversity there *is* always a primary objective lesson (whether you get it or not) and that since you did attract this situation, it's not just the result of bad luck. The need for a powerful challenge stems from a deeper part of yourself seeking acknowledgment. We often set ourselves up at a deeper level for a crisis at a surface level—such as losing a job—to assist a hidden part of ourselves break through to the light of day.

We may need to play the role of victim until we are so tired we choose not to play anymore. Nobody consciously wants to end up in the hospital as the result of an automobile accident that was not their fault. But from a deeper level within, such an accident may have been self-arranged to force us to look at aspects of our lives that we otherwise have refused to acknowledge. Our evolutionary agendas do not always conform to who we think we are or to what we think we can do!

We have to decide, and then clearly ask for, what we want. This maxim appears self-evident, but has a different twist in the New Paradigm dialogue. It is a useful reminder for all of us who forget to decide or ask for what we want. And it covers more territory than the average person often suspects. For it is a prescription to live the most intentional and aware life that we can—what is sometimes described as "living consciously."

Much of our lives is given over to following routines, accepting ideas, or falling into situations that are more of others' making than our own. So at one level this principle says: Decide what you really want (or need) to eat. Decide whether to spend some time with the homeless. Choose whether to protest toxic pollution. Pay attention to the nuances of daily living and choose accordingly. Decide whether you will allow another person to rob you of your power. Don't just talk about what you *might* do!

Deciding and asking are the focusing of intent. Many factors can affect the power of intent. Are there unconscious self-sabotaging blocks to what you want? Are you appropriately using affirmations? Have you brought others to join you in a community of intent, all of whom are involved by choice? When these factors are aligned, the power of intention can be directly felt at great distance as, for example, in long-distance healing. Intent is not necessarily restricted to the inside of our skulls.

Even if others do not hear your public words, powerfully intended requests begun on the inside, so to speak, have a way of invisibly rippling through other levels of energy-consciousness. Quietly lusting in one's heart for sexual favors, for example, is not necessarily the secret one thinks it is. Above all, be clear in what you put out. For as the thinking goes, the universe would like to address your scarcity with abundance. If you send out mixed messages, some consciously and others unconsciously, the results will be correspondingly confused.

Optimize the arrangement of vertical and horizontal issues. By "horizontal" I mean surface issues that relate to one's current personality and are discernible with relative ease. For example, you may have a strong need to be in control. Even though you mask it behind a lot of caretaking and nurturing, it is clearly your agenda which sets the stage and serves as a standard of evaluation in your dealings with others. You may find yourself getting very anxious when things begin to get out of control. So you decide to work on this issue.

It turns out, however, that progress is slow. Certain kinds of control issues dissolve while others remain. Then it's time to consider the vertical dimension. Here you may have deep-seated issues, buried in the subconscious, which nobody (least of all, you) suspects. Our subconscious tapes are always running and always open to change, if that is our sincere intent. Taking charge of one's life requires a willingness to explore what was formerly hidden.

Let us say that you were abused as a very young child, a painful period that you have repressed. (Actually, the perception of abuse would be sufficient to generate fear, since the subconscious does not distinguish between truth and falsity.) At any rate, your present need to control others may be rooted in the need to insure that there will be no more abuse. Accordingly, you find yourself blocked at a horizontal surface level until you are willing to address the vertically deeper issue.

The optimal arrangement of vertical and horizontal challenges does not follow a prescribed pattern. A particular issue may require deep work immediately just to bring enough stability at the surface to accomplish something. Or a vertical issue might only surface after enough clearing has been done of horizontal issues. Sometimes what seems to be a pressing issue will have to be set aside until other horizontal and vertical challenges are addressed. Keeping an open mind as to what might be an optimal progression for you is always in order. Working with a gifted intuitive counselor or clairvoyant can reduce the guesswork.

Access love by letting go of fear. The topic of love occupies a foundational place in New Paradigm literature. Briefly, the message is this: Love exists absolutely and unconditionally at the core of our being. Both its presence and its perceived absence fuel our evolution. Our emotional bodies largely are built up by how we deal with the lack of love, whether actual or perceived. Love is empowering. Through it, things considered impossible or miraculous are possible. Everybody has had at least a minimal taste of love. Everyone wants more, even though they may deny it. Unconditional love is something we can grow into. We do not possess or control it. It is not a feeling. It is a part of our being.

Love is not merely an accidental emotion that some experience more than others. It is not simply one more emotion to add or subtract from the stockpile of fear, guilt, anger, or jealousy. It is primary. The reason we fail to experience this is that we have bought into the various negative emotions—especially fear—which cover it up. Fear of failure, fear of persecution, fear of success (for other things it may bring), fear of losing something or someone, fear of being found out, and fear of loneliness and death are but a few instances.

We go to great lengths to avoid dealing with these fears. Institutions (marriage), ideologies (socialism), laws to protect us from each other, continuing threats of accountability and responsibility, control (early childhood conditioning), and projection ("They're the bad guys") are a few examples. That is why so many workshops and books deal in one way or another with the topic of identifying the roots of our fears and letting the fears go. The more we let go, the more we find love waiting. Fighting fear with fear is a prescription for failure.

Give and receive love as unconditionally as you can. The fewer restrictions placed upon the expression of love, the better its quality is likely to be. Parent-child relationships, together with other hotbeds of codependency, often harbor substantial violations of this precept. The classic instance is: "I've done so much for you, how can you be so ungrateful?"

In the Rising Culture, we are encouraged to continue actualizing the capacity for unconditional love far beyond traditional levels. On any given weekend, for example, there are several hundred individuals, from their late teens to their eighties, taking the loving relationships training or related workshops. Having a mid-life crisis may be viewed as an opportunity to break through the chains of codependent love.

This principle also urges us to extend the unconditional umbrella to as many kinds of people and situations as possible. The line does not stop at the comfort zone of family, friends, God, and country. Spend the weekend with a parentless AIDS child of another race, for example, and then see where the "lines" fall!

Another interesting twist given to this principle is the stress placed upon the reciprocity of giving and receiving. It is not necessarily better to give love than to receive it. For the quality of what you have to give can be seriously eroded by the inability to receive love until the imbalance burns you out. To be able to receive love in turn requires that you value yourself enough to merit it. "Love yourself" is not a prescription for narcissism, as critics of the New Age insist. It is the acknowledgment of a potentially dynamic circle: Love yourself in order to better love others, that they might better love you, so that all parties move toward empowerment.

Do not just interpret your issues, deal with them! Believing that one has dealt successfully with his or her issues just by understanding them is one of the top five client fallacies in personal growth work. After the standard hugs and salutations at personal growth workshops and seminars, the most common probe is, "So, what's coming up for you these days?" Translation: What is moving center stage in your emotional or spiritual life? If you are growth-oriented, there is always a good supply of issues stockpiled in the wings—from acknowledging your inner child to the challenges of advanced spiritual practice.

Most importantly, growth-oriented individuals have learned how to talk *from* their feelings, not just *about* their feelings. They have learned to acknowledge and, where appropriate, nurture the expression of feelings, whether their own or someone else's, simply for what they are, without immediately judging or interpreting them.

There is often a general uneasiness which comes from not dealing directly with one's challenges like, for example, the repressed anger left over from a perfectly "reasonable" divorce. Any number of consequences may result from not dealing with this uneasiness. One is that spiritual growth also may be retarded insofar as it interpenetrates the emotional body. Deeper emerging structures may not see the light of day. For example, trying to overcome the limitations of one's ego (a lofty spiritual goal) before seeing that one has an ego (in the form of an emotional need to be appreciated) does not foster personal growth.

Failure to deal constructively with one's (potentially hidden) emotional issues also can result in negative consequences for one's physical body. Determining the physical effects of long-term emotional stress is becoming a major research field in itself. If you continue to deny certain impulses because they seem childish, or conclude that your control issues are fixable by learning how to be nice to everyone, or address grief as if the only issue were acknowledging God's will, or rationalize recurring fears as normal, your body pays a price.

There is typically a dialectic that we must work through in order to deal successfully with emotional issues. First, we need to move out of denial, since otherwise there is nothing to work with and, hence, nowhere to grow. Next, we may experience a tendency either to be victimized by feelings and attitudes (such as low self-esteem) that attract unhealthy situations to our space; or we may project those feelings and attitudes onto someone else so we don't have to deal with them. These tendencies to feel victimized or to blame someone else also must be acknowledged.

Then we are in a position to own them. But as just explained, owning them means more than simply figuring out how they work in your life. The sentence "Yes, I'm angry" is a poor substitute for *being* angry. The final step in this process is learning how to be angry in a heart-centered way that does not disempower others, but stimulates their growth, too. If we don't break through our emotional filters, speaking our truth will be less than abundantly received.

Distinguish the players in your current drama, the form of the drama, and the (negative) emotions this drama brings up for you. This is an easy distinction to grasp intellectually. When we feel angry, victimized, or anxious, however, the parts of this distinction tend to run together. We tend to make the other person(s) in the drama responsible for our emotions and forget that the form or pattern—for example, "Why am I not receiving more acknowledgment in my life?"—is what needs to be looked at.

In particular, the players are not the important thing. To be sure, others may need to be told, sometimes forcefully, how you feel about something. But if they were not playing the role of, say, seeming to control your happiness, someone else would, until you own your emotions, recognize the drama, and take steps to reduce its power over you.

And what steps should these be? Obviously, they will vary with each reader. But *A Course in Miracles* suggests one direction in which to look: "You are never upset for the reasons you think you are." Whether or not this is true in every situation, it's always a good idea to look deeper inside oneself. For example, one may feel angry over being victimized by someone else's control drama ("Why are you doing this to me?"). The apparent power to make something happen has been put outside oneself.

The energy spent fighting with that person is better spent examining why one is being taken advantage of. It might be, for example, that underlying this recurring pattern are hidden doubts about one's own self-esteem. Until that condition is addressed, one will continue to get upset, so to speak, for the "wrong" reasons. And that condition is more likely to be constructively addressed by first distinguishing between the players, the form, and the emotions associated with one's current drama.

Trust your own feelings and intuitions. Most everyone claims to accept this advice. Yet three factors conspire against it. The first is a lack of time. Getting in touch with one's feelings or determining what one's intuitions really are do not lend themselves to immediate closure. In a hurry-up world, these tasks often lose out to our demand for immediate and tangible results.

A second factor is the value which our culture places on reason. Despite such antirationalist movements as romanticism and existentialism, we are still the children of the Enlightenment, where reason is supposed to prevail. By the time we have rationalized our feelings and intuitions to a socially acceptable form, they may not bear much resemblance to their original form.

A third factor is the control dramas we participate in. With so much energy spent in controlling others or in protecting ourselves from being controlled, owning our personal feelings and intuitions is a daunting task. For example, we may not acknowledge our own tendency to feel victimized if others convince us not to because doing so (in their control drama) would make them look bad.

A good way to trust your own feelings and intuitions with greater conviction is to reverse the influence of these three factors. Step back from the control dramas you may be involved in, allow that what seems right might not make sense or be justifiable, and allow time for your feelings and intuitions to break into the light of awareness. It is also helpful to specifically ask your Higher Self for guidance or assistance. Progress occurs when you feel more empowered, when decisions come with greater ease, and when the actions based upon those decisions produce not just the results you want, but also a more balanced exchange of energies.

A universal prescription: meditate! There is no single prescription that better takes into account the universal goals of personal and spiritual growth, on the one hand, and the distinctiveness of each person's evolutionary path, on the other. This fact is not widely acted upon partly because of the misconceptions surrounding the idea of meditation. For example, it may be assumed that meditation is merely an odd type of mind game; that its main purpose is to rid the body of stress; that having the correct mantra matters supremely or doesn't matter at all; that the secret is in the breathing; that going into a trance can be dangerous; that high-amplitude alpha waves indicate a superior form of meditation; that meditation is just paying attention to what one is doing; or that making one's mind a blank is impossible.

There are many kinds of meditation. Some stress focused breathing, concentrating on a special symbol, or chanting a mantra. Others encourage you to become a witness to your own thought processes. Some are difficult. Others are relatively easy. Their effects are not uniform. Some may be better suited for a person at a particular stage of his or her life, only to be replaced by another form at a different stage.

Behind this pluralistic outlook is a single goal which accounts for meditation's universal applicability. That goal is alignment. Meditation helps clear blocks to alignment and nurtures its emergence. The alignment of one's emotional body with the physical body, for example, is nurtured by allowing the Source which penetrates both to reach optimum expression via a guided program of meditation. Therein lies our oneness and bond of power, to borrow Joseph Chilton Pearce's phrase, leading to vitality, joy, clear vision, and, in time, spiritual radiance—the wholeness which we all seek.

CHAPTER ELEVEN

Health and Healing at the Crossroads

Three developments are profoundly and irrevocably changing our concepts of health and the way medicine is practiced: the emergence of alternative medicine; an increasing acknowledgment of the role of consciousness and personal responsibility in achieving health; and the political and economic quagmire in which conventional medicine finds itself. These developments overlap and fuel each other on multiple levels. Yet each cluster of concerns also is driven by its own internal dynamics.

The rising tide of alternative diagnostic and therapeutic methods is of such significance that the editors of *Time* (November 4, 1991) felt obliged to assess its scope and credibility in the cover story. A pioneering study published in *The New England Journal of Medicine* (January 28, 1993) concluded that in 1990 Americans spent approximately $14 billion for unconventional therapy and paid for three-fourths of it out-of-pocket! In no particular order of importance, this therapy includes practices relating to herbs, homeopathy, nutritional therapy, psychic diagnosis, chromotherapy, toning, music therapy, flower essences, pulse diagnosis, applied kinesiology, psychic and spiritual healing, affirmation, massage and bodywork, ozone therapy, emotional release work, visualization, acupuncture, medical astrology, radionics, meridian analyses, and chiropractic.

Some of these practices may slowly disappear from the scene. Many appear destined to remain and eventually become integrated into mainstream health care delivery. A number are widely and openly practiced here and in Europe. All can complement mainstream medicine. Standardized programs of study, competence evaluations, and licensing would be a welcome development for most of these practices. However, any attempt to significantly repress or outlaw them as dangerous would generate an underground swell dwarfing the days of Prohibition by comparison.

A second revolutionary development involves our growing understanding of the roles of consciousness and personal responsibility, together with preventive medicine, in achieving health. The connecting link in this arena is what we can do for ourselves, both individually and collectively.

Here are some examples: detoxify the environment; learn how to effectively combat the effects of long-term stress; adopt healthy life-styles; practice relaxation (especially meditation); work on emotional issues which undermine physical health; seek out empowering relationships with health professionals who both listen and care. Such are a few of the strategies which constitute a conspiracy for health that, even in its more extreme forms (such as visiting a spiritual healer), has assumed landslide proportions.

A third cluster of related concerns involves the legal, economic, political, and ethical quagmire that many traditionally trained physicians, nurses, and public health administrators view as pushing the health care system toward disintegration. If "disintegration" is too strong a term, then what many see coming is nonetheless a very depressing scenario.

It is by now a familiar story: annual total expenditures on health over $800 billion and rising; hospital costs out of control despite yearly measures to bring them under control (aspirin tablets in some hospitals cost over three dollars each); duplication of equipment and inefficient use of space that, in metropolitan areas, is scandalous; malpractice suits and premiums that are losing their connection with reality; a practice of defensive medicine that orders thirty percent more tests than are necessary; abominable infant mortality rates; mountains of paperwork, justifications, peer reviews, and more justifications—mainly for insurance, Medicare, and legal purposes—that turn dedicated physicians into robots and their office staffs into major bureaucracies. Paperwork alone takes $40 billion of total annual health care expenditures.

Gerontological and AIDS populations threaten to bankrupt the system. It could cost as much as $5 million just to die of AIDS by the year 2000. We stand a fair chance of getting worse, especially in hospitals, as the result of others trying to help us get better. Major population segments are unable to afford insurance premiums and are turned away by for-profit hospitals. Even corporate America is at the breaking point; in 1990 General Motors paid $3.2 billion in insurance premiums alone. The public appears outraged to discover that its main health care providers are not miracle workers, but demands that they produce miracles anyway. Ours is a system in which increases in health expenditures are progressively less related to the overall quality of life. It is a system paralyzed by special interest groups.

There are many pressure points in the transition to a new worldview. In fewer places, however, are all of the key guiding assumptions of the old order simultaneously both so public and precarious as in the health care delivery system. Here are a few examples: a reductionist view of humans as purely physical machines which sometimes break down; competition between hospitals for patients or between individuals for scarce resources; fear of dying, of being left out of the system, of being put at an unfair disadvantage; a male-dominated community of physicians bent on insuring that (mostly female) nurses remain in their proper place; a fragmented social and political environment that pits doctors against attorneys and/or patients, and those who cannot pay against those who can, and insurance companies against everybody.

By a vote of 38–0, the California Senate once attempted to outlaw any form of treatment not sanctioned by the American Medical Association. And in North Carolina, the state medical board revoked the license of George Guess, a board-certified M.D., merely because he prescribed homeopathic remedies. At the other end of the spectrum, Alaska passed a law preventing anyone from being arrested for practicing alternative health care.

Meanwhile, the FDA appears determined to undermine, if not erradicate, the use of supplements and herbs by overrating their potentially toxic effects—a pure exercise in the politics of fear—and by insisting that small companies (who cannot own the rights to substances found in nature) conduct the same $300 million clinical trials as the major drug companies. It outlawed the amino acid L-tryptophan altogether merely because a single contaminated batch reached the shelves. Vitamin C would not have suffered the same fate. In its ideal world, the FDA envisages that virtually nothing in health food stores would be available except by prescription. Talk about paradigm wars!

The 1992 presidential election made adequate health care for all citizens a national priority. Yet all of the candidates, including President Clinton, as well as Congress and the AMA, were guided in their otherwise diverse proposals by a single assumption: the way to insure better value for health care dollars spent is to find the optimum combination of changed regulations (e.g., put caps on how much doctors can charge for certain procedures) and funding sources (e.g., require small businesses to institute health care plans for their employees).

Some of the proposals had merit. And most made vague concessions to the importance of preventive medicine. But none spoke to the most fundamental assumption of all, that health is a matter of *personal responsibility*. For example, if you smoke, drink to excess, consume too much junk food, don't exercise, allow yourself to be constantly stressed, pay no attention to risk factors, run to the doctor for antibiotics every time a head cold strikes, overload your kidneys with animal protein, practice unsafe sex, fail to take proper precautions against ultraviolet radiation, endure heavy or nearly constant exposure to extra-low frequency (ELF) electromagnetic fields, and don't seek help for your depression, then why should it be someone else's responsibility—either the government's or other insurance premium payers'—to rescue you from the consequences of *your* actions? It has been estimated, for example, that ceasing to smoke, adopting a low-fat diet, and practicing relaxation could have reduced by half the $12 billion spent on heart bypass surgery in 1990.

Naturally, we need to be educated about the consequences of our actions before we can be held accountable for them. And there is a natural pool of compassion upon which most persons can draw to some degree. But education and compassion have limits. More compassion, more money, more technological fixes, and, ultimately, even more education about the negative consequences of one's actions will relieve symptoms, provide temporary cures, and keep the system going up to a point. But they will not rescue us from the inner self-destructive impulses of fear-based consciousness. What drives us, both individually and collectively, to self-destructive health habits?

When it comes to health care reform, virtually no political leader appears willing to address this question, except in relatively safe, socially validated contexts of national concern, such as addiction or teen suicide. For the most part, national leaders are either unable or unwilling to address the complex web of emotional energies that connect couch potatoes with suicide victims, or homelessness with the high cost of hospitalization.

Any health care reform package that does not address the dynamics of fear-based consciousness will be unable to deliver what it promises. We might begin, for example, with the fear of dying, which forces us to take extraordinary measures, at astronomical expense, to prolong an individual's life when circumstances strongly suggest otherwise.

BIOMEDICAL AND HOLISTIC MODELS OF HEALTH

Some writers and practitioners avoid the adversarial connotations of "versus" by describing holistic ideals and practices more positively as "complementary." Thus the holistic practitioner, who may or may not be medically trained, is characterized as someone who ideally can work with physicians in obtaining optimum health for the client. There is substantial truth in this observation; most nontraditional therapies can be simply added on to conventional therapies. I fully endorse the spirit of cooperation implied by the complementary description, together with the caveat that a true holistic paradigm must generally be inclusive of medical practices that it superficially may appear to exclude. However, characterizing holistic health practices as complementary can mask some foggy thinking and even political motivation.

If those in power have the capacity to suppress holistic practices, it makes sense to describe these practices in nonthreatening ways. Hence the proclamation that there is room for everybody. But how much room there is depends upon how broadly or narrowly holistic and biomedical paradigms are defined. Depending upon these definitions, some aspects of each paradigm may converge or overlap, others may contradict each other, and still others may be essentially unrelated. The total picture is far more complex than portrayed in the popular press.

Historical background. Before comparing the two outlooks, some historical background is needed. The biomedical model is today a loosely knit convergence of assumptions, goals, procedures, and values regarding health and healing. It affects, and is affected by, everything from gene splicing to malpractice insurance premiums. It is a paradigm in the truest sense that Thomas Kuhn envisaged. And it is still the prevailing paradigm of the total health care delivery system.

The biomedical model is a clear and natural extension of the Cartesian-Newtonian worldview. It received early support through the advances of late eighteenth- and nineteenth-century biology (especially the germ theory of disease) when mechanistic outlooks prevailed. Its story is one of small beginnings and slow but steady progress and expansion into the twentieth century, where advances in diagnostic instrumentation, molecular biology and genetics, surgical techniques, and synthetic drugs have produced spectacular results in many areas.

The successes of the biomedical model are a matter of public record. Among the better known are the eradication of major forms of communicable disease (whooping cough, typhoid, smallpox, etc.) in countries with strong immunization programs; early detection techniques; microsurgical techniques that are able to correct problems formerly thought to be untreatable; major advances in rehabilitative medicine; prescription drugs without which many people would suffer marked decreases in their quality of life or even death; and steadily improving trauma care. Each day modern medicine improves the quality of life, from the gift of sight to the repair of broken bones, for millions of people around the world. About this there is no question.

The deficiencies of the biomedical model as it is practiced are also getting to be a matter of public record. Among the more notable examples are: too much surgery prescribed too quickly (coronary bypasses where drugs would suffice); over-reliance upon drugs where simple changes in diet and life-style would be as effective; a small but growing national debate over whether vaccines are really as effective and safe as they are claimed to be; misprescribed medications (one study put the figure as high as eighty percent for the elderly)[1]; a poor record on chronic diseases, apart from providing symptom relief or replacing worn out body parts (despite what we are told, overall cancer cure rates appear to be no better now than thirty years ago)[2]; nutritional illiteracy (internists, for example, are generally not aware of the documented beneficial effects of primrose oil)[3]; and an attitude of fix it, rather than prevent it, that is only now beginning to shift significantly.

Finally, there is a built-in myopia that refuses to consider approaches other than those sanctioned by the AMA, the National Institutes of Health, or the FDA. Here's the stock catch–22: "We won't prescribe these alternatives because they are unproven, and we won't waste precious resources studying them because they cannot work anyway."

The National Institutes of Health, under a congressional mandate, is evaluating various forms of alternative medicine, among them: the use of acupuncture to treat depression; biofeedback to treat pain and diabetes; music therapy for brain injuries; yoga to treat heroin addiction; and prayer to assist healing. However, the small budget ($5 million for 1995–1996) set aside for this purpose is largely symbolic, given the amount of research that would have to be undertaken by major research institutions to generate much interest in the medical community. Changing one's mind about preferred treatments that fall within the scope of the accepted paradigm is far easier than changing one's mind about the assumptions of the paradigm itself. Still, NIH's involvement, however minimal, is a step in the right direction.

There are also a host of ethical challenges that traditional medicine, in its current cultural setting, is poorly equipped to deal with. Among them are the right to die (not to mention associated metaphysical questions like "Why keep the body going when its owner has exited?"), reproductive liberty, genetic counseling, treatment of handicapped newborns, conflicts between mothers and fetuses, involuntary sterilization, surrogate motherhood, and informed consent.

Unlike the steady progression and expansion of the biomedical model, practices which are today often labeled as holistic have a checkered evolution going back to antiquity. The Aesculapian healing temples of early Greece, for example, used such methods as psychic diagnosis, herbs, dream therapy, and spiritual healing. The Renaissance physician Paracelsus borrowed elements from both models (such as they were in his time!), e.g., a mixture of crude surgery and alchemy. Mesmer, the father of hypnosis, also practiced a form of psychic healing through magnetic passes. And Samuel Hahnemann (1755–1843), the developer of homeopathy, was a brilliant physician in his own right.

The two-hundred-year-old distinction between homeopathic and allopathic medicine contains many of the elements of what eventually evolved into the full-blown distinction between holistic and biomedical models. Homeopathy works according to the Law of Similars—like cures like. It treats illness with tinctures which reproduce the symptoms, typically at a subclinical level, thereby bringing the body's own natural resources and immune system into play. In this respect, it partly parallels the strategy of giving vaccinations.

Allopathic medicine, by contrast, works partly on the principle of directly killing the organisms which cause the symptoms (as in antibiotics). However, it has evolved today into a broader umbrella of approaches linked by the use of synthetic drugs.

The homeopathic/allopathic distinction illustrates a number of issues in today's paradigm war. For one, the active ingredients in homeopathic remedies are typically so diluted as to be ineffective, invisible, or even non-existent from the standpoint of biochemistry. By contrast, one can literally watch penicillin attack germs under a microscope. The question of whether and how homeopathic tinctures are effective has been the subject of recent major studies, critiques, and counter-critiques in the scientific literature. From controlled studies published in mainstream medical journals, the evidence is steadily growing that homeopathic remedies are effective for certain illnesses.[4] In fact, forty-two percent of British medical doctors refer patients to homeopathic practitioners. And twenty-five percent of German physicians prescribe such remedies.

The dilution ratios have led some commentators to conclude that, if it works, it does so energetically, rather than by the movement of discrete particles. But to the average biochemist, this appears to be little more than self-serving, occult speculation. As a distinguished pharmacologist at a major medical school confided to me: "A health practitioner who prescribes homeopathic solutions, as is widely done in Europe, is relying upon the fact that *any* placebo (inert substance) will get you *some* results." And so we have a powerful distinction—visible and particulate versus invisible and energetic—from which different types of health research and practice can follow.

The metaphysical assumptions of holistic medicine are incorporated into paradigms which stress fields, frequencies, subtle energies, the importance of consciousness, and (apparent) action-at-a-distance. It connects practices as divergent as psychotronics, psychic healing, Bach flower remedies, and homeopathy. The underlying paradigm of the biomedical approach, on the other hand, is materialism. With the exception of a few nonsubtle energies, such as X-rays or magnetic fields used in resonance scanning, it stresses what is visible, tangible, and discrete. It connects divergent areas such as environmental medicine, microsurgery, and psychopharmacology.

The philosophical basis of the divergence between homeopathic and allopathic medicine (affective, invisible, and semicontinuous versus the passive, visible, and discrete) is found in many scientific and philosophical contexts. The debate between nineteenth-century vitalists and mechanists in biology, for example, is one illustration. Both sides in the current debate would profit from a more extensive knowledge of the ground that has already been covered.

A number of alternative therapies coexisted with the rise of mainstream medicine into the twentieth century. In the 1920s, however, the medical community banded together and effectively declared what would count as acceptable medical practice. It refused accreditation to any medical school or physician who taught or practiced otherwise. The most notable casualty of this decision was homeopathy, despite the fact that only two decades earlier, more than half of all physicians had some training in homeopathic practices. From 1930 to 1970, one didn't hear much about alternatives in

America unless one visited a Native American reservation, a religious healing revival, a semi-secret occult group, or an anthropology class. Since then, the picture has dramatically expanded.

Logical comparison of the paradigms. What does a comparison of biomedical and holistic paradigms look like? There are a number of good comparisons which stress themes similar to those I summarize in the following lists. Marilyn Ferguson and Larry Dossey, for example, have developed two very useful and accessible versions.[5] I have developed my version with an eye to stressing the logical relationships which connect different kinds of thinking about health and healing. Given the preliminary assumptions, each perspective unfolds naturally from out of itself.

It is important to realize that each side of this chart represents an ideal limit. The average health practitioner, whether or not medically trained, may agree with different points on each side. The *net* attraction for most physicians is closer to the biomedical model, and for most naturopaths, for instance, to the holistic model. However, there is a lot of movement between different categories, and the categories themselves are undergoing refinement.

Many practitioners in either list still adopt condescending, know-it-all attitudes about their counterparts. Physicians are generally ignorant of alternative methods (although more are interested in learning about them) and tend to view holistic practitioners as not altogether harmless frauds. For their part, holistic practitioners who are not medically trained are only slightly less ignorant of medicine, especially its diagnostic aspects, and tend to preach the benefits of their specialties out of proportion to what they are capable of delivering. Such adversarial attitudes will not survive in the Rising Culture. Each side in this paradigm war has much to learn from the other. Harvard Medical School, for example, recently (in May, 1995) took a giant step forward in offering the first continuing education credits in alternative medicine for physicians.

Biomedical model	Holistic model
1. Assumption: Health is the absence of disease.	1. Assumption: Health is a systemic disposition which includes the absence of disease.
2. Assumption: Disease is defined by its symptoms and underlying pathology.	2. Assumption: Disease reflects imbalances in the entire system; symptom is only a reflection.

3. Therefore, termination of symptoms is tantamount to restoring health.
4. Assumption: Medicine ought to be practiced as efficiently as possible.
5. Efficiency requires authority, detachment, and passive interaction of patient with physician, as well as identification of local symptoms and causes.
6. In a localizationist approach, *diagnosis* is tied to physical causes; the molecular level is stressed; psychological causes are minimized. *Treatment* is viewed as elimination of symptoms and, where possible, their linear causes. *Prevention* is undertaken on a type-by-type approach, not parallel to treatment procedures.
7. Repeat only as necessary, that is, when sickness occurs.
8. Process is underwritten by the metaphysics of Scientific Materialism.

3. Therefore, termination of symptoms is only part of the larger goal of restoring health.
4. Assumption: efficiency requires both comprehensive and long-term perspectives.
5. Comprehensive, long-term health goals require consultation, involvement, and active interaction of patient with physician—a system-wide multilevel approach.
6. Systems approach views *diagnosis* as reflecting multiple interactions, including psychological and environmental factors. *Treatment* requires changing many variables (nutrition, stress, etc.), often with complex interactions. *Prevention* requires a comprehensive approach that parallels treatment.
7. Health promotion is a daily part of life on many levels.
8. Process is underwritten by the perennialist metaphysics of interpenetrating levels of energy-consciousness.

Each side of this comparison represents an idealized abstraction. To make the comparison more realistic, some further explanation and illustration of the main categories is necessary.

In the first place, it should be stressed that traditional medicine is to some degree aware of the wider range of factors that dispose one toward health or disease. This is especially true in light of recent advances in our understanding of the immune system. Still, traditional medicine tends to view health and disease as ideas of a similar logical type. One is either sick or well. If one is not ill, one must be healthy. To be cured of all disease symptoms is to be in a state of health. Health is seen merely as what is left over when the machine is repaired and remains something of a mystery.

By contrast, the holistic paradigm conceives health as an enduring and system-wide disposition which manifests on multiple levels. Strictly speaking, a virus is not a disease which attacks an organism, but is simply another living substance which is empowered by various imbalances (e.g., immune system deficiencies and their causes) within the organism as it comes into contact with it. To cure a person of disease does not automatically result in a state of health any more than curing depression results in a state of joy. Either-or thinking does not apply to health and disease.

Health prevents disease but, as the World Health Organization definition makes clear, "…is not merely the absence of disease or infirmity." Rather, it is "the ability of a system (for example, cell, family, society) to respond adaptively to a wide range of environmental challenges (for example, physical, chemical, psychological, etc.)," while disease is a failure of adaptive response "…resulting in disruption of the equilibrium of the system."[6] From this perspective, the biomedical model's assumption of health as the absence of disease is essentially a subset of the holistic model's more encompassing assumption regarding the nature of health.

From a holistic perspective which stresses *optimum* health, not just getting by, disease does not occupy only the lower end of *manifest* symptoms and pathology. Rather, disease has already begun when we slip away from the upper end of optimum health toward the "intermediate zone," where we are neither happy nor depressed, neither bedridden nor vibrant, but where toxic buildup, sluggish organs, and various emotional imbalances (such as a lack of love) quietly take their toll.

Accordingly, when disease strikes, the holistic practitioner treats multiple subsystems necessary for regaining optimum health, such as strengthening the immune system, rather than merely fighting the disease per se, which the traditional physician typically does with drugs and surgery. Holistic practitioners also address the symptoms of disease. However, they approach this task from a more encompassing conception of health, which may include everything from cleaning out impacted fecal material to freely expressing negative emotions. From a holistic perspective, each frontal attack on a particular disease may require a half-dozen rearguard actions, which medical schools are just beginning to recognize.

Physicians are free to abandon the initial guiding assumptions of the biomedical model and to adopt their counterparts under the holistic model, while still rejecting parts of the specific diagnostic and treatment methods, such as homeopathy or spiritual healing. Having done so, they may or may not describe themselves as holistically oriented. As noted earlier, the parts of each paradigm are themselves in flux.

It is easy to see the deeply rooted (Cartesian/Newtonian) assumptions involving fragmentation, reductionism, and linear causation which predispose mainstream medicine toward the biomedical model. Other social factors, especially those relating to economics and psychology, also conspire to validate the biomedical model. For example, there is a deeply ingrained set of instincts and attitudes which tells us that the primary business of life is to survive and react successfully to what life presents us with. Whatever is "left over" from this agenda can then be used to create whatever seems appropriate. The idea that health care is and ought to be primarily a process of reacting to the most immediately threatening symptoms, rather than creating a larger context of health, is thus a very natural one.

What about efficiency in health care delivery? Everyone, of course, is for it. The question is whether it should be achieved from a fragmented, hierarchical, one-on-one perspective which stresses reaction to symptoms on the one hand, or from an integrated, mutually empowering, systemic perspective which stresses prevention and health creation, on the other. Until fairly recently, the first approach has been the overwhelming favorite. After all, it achieves results which are in certain respects more timely and more dramatic, which is how many of us like to think about efficiency.

This model is filled with the production line metaphors of the Industrial Revolution. How many patients can a physician see in a day? So long as the system supports it, almost everyone goes along. But how long can our culture afford this view of efficiency? The insurance industry straddles the fence. On the one hand, it supports the biomedical model with minimum attention to the importance of prevention, such as reduced rates for non-smokers. On the other hand, it strives for greater cost efficiency in one of the few ways it can, by continuing to lower its estimate of what constitutes reasonable and customary fees, diagnoses, and hospital stays. The government and insurance industry still address skyrocketing costs in a piecemeal fashion—by paying for less.

Consider the following example which reflects traditional thinking in this area. Suppose that you are a cardiologist with the usual number of hypertensive patients. You would probably prescribe an antihypertensive drug which had the least number of undesirable side effects for your patients. However, diuretics place general long-term strain on anybody's system, which most researchers agree is not good. Still, the more immediate effects are dramatic—a ten- to thirty-percent reduction in blood pressure levels.

The pattern is set. You see each person on an individual basis during his or her fifteen-minute office visit. The power of life and death—or reduced likelihood of stroke—is in your hands. You have the magic potion. And your patients expect you to prescribe it for them. Your peers would hold you accountable if you did not. Meanwhile, more and more patients are showing up with hypertension, placing progressively heavier demands on the health care system. Is there any other way?

Well, you might prescribe diuretics on a short-term basis, depending upon the severity of each case, but then insist that your patients attend a personal health and fitness class that you or a trained assistant teach one evening a week. You would show them how to bring their blood pressure down (as well as decrease stress and improve cardiovascular function) through a combination of diet, exercise, and some meditation/visualization exercises.

Naturally, your patients would resist at first. After all, they came to you for a quick fix. But you patiently explain to them the downside factors associated with diuretics and the benefits of this alternative approach. You also firmly point out that you are part of the new breed of physicians interested in cocreating with your patients a sense of health consciousness. You do not wish to merely validate their dependence on you when they get in trouble. Prevention is the new password.

You, too, may have to look at some resistance issues. After all, you were trained to diagnose and prescribe, not to create health consciousness in your patients. And if you push this holistic perspective too much, some patients may find another physician willing to cater to their fears. Then you will have difficulty paying your insurance premiums and supporting your family in the manner to which all are accustomed! More fear and scarcity issues. It looks as if the health system itself has conspired to render both you and your patients powerless.

You may choose to act out of fear. Before you do, however, take a careful look around. Examine the numbers, the trends, the attitudes of younger physicians just graduating, patients experimenting with alternatives, the cracks in the system. Talk to your peers, the very ones who just last week exclaimed that things cannot go on like they are. Look at the direction of history. Decide whether you and others beginning to consider such matters are really as powerless as you might believe. For the power of the M.D. degree itself creates a structure through which many things can be changed.

But this is to get ahead of ourselves. Why is the type of alternative approach just described potentially more efficient in the first place? What are the sanctions for change? To begin with, there are no negative side-effects or long-term strains to factor into the equation. Second, the benefits of proper diet, exercise, and meditation spill over into many other areas of health. Third, it is less expensive. Fourth, the examples these reoriented patients set for others create positive trickle-down effects for the larger system. Fifth, with this type of increased doctor/patient trust and mutual participation, malpractice suits are likely to decline. Finally, working with small groups of similarly challenged people can make better use of physicians' time for more serious and complex cases. *This* is efficiency in a holistic (long-term, comprehensive) perspective. And it is not mere wishful thinking. In a widely publicized study that many cardiologists still cannot quite believe, physician Dean Ornish showed how a regime of yoga, improved diet, exercise, and visualization—when carefully followed for several years—not only reversed heart disease, but also left patients far healthier than they had been using drugs and surgery.

The topic of efficiency leads to a third cluster of contrasting assumptions involving localization and systems approaches to diagnosis and treatment procedures. Health professionals are generally aware, of course, that many factors on different levels interact in ways which can promote health or promote disease. It is intellectually dishonest to portray traditional health care providers as ignorant of wide-ranging interactions. The *Physician's Desk Reference*, for example, is an encyclopedia of interactions, indications, and contraindications for medications, and a very good illustration of systems thinking.

Still, the preferred mode of thinking under the biomedical model is localizationist. This is because when disease does finally surface, it typically does so in particular places—a tumor in the lung, arthritis in the hip, a cold in the head, and so on. This focus upon local effects leads naturally to a concern with local causes. What specific causes are most directly related to the disease symptoms and where are they located?

The germ theory of disease is one notable result of this type of thinking. If the effects are localized, then so are the causes. The tendency, then, is to determine *the* cause which stands in a direct linear relationship to the symptoms, when in fact there may be a half dozen factors on multiple levels which indirectly fuel the process in a nonlinear fashion.

These other factors may be recognized in traditional medicine, but only on a case-by-case basis after years of research and sometimes major paradigm wars. And when they are, they are often simply added on to other programs of research, with little integrated modeling to accompany them. They are so interconnected that clinical practice is often reduced to guess-work or to the simplest procedures that connect the fewest number of causes to the disease.

By contrast, a holistic or systems-theoretical approach *begins* with the assumption that the presence or absence of many factors may be inter-related in each person's health challenge, sometimes on levels traditional medicine claims not to have anything to do with (like emotional or spiritual concerns). Instead of starting only with symptoms plus a bio-chemical core and working out from there, it starts with the big picture (including the symptoms) and progressively refines the patterns of relationship between the symptoms and the whole person.

The complexity of these relationships requires the kind of systems approach that Laurence Foss and Kenneth Rothenberg have developed in *The Second Medical Revolution.* Of special interest is the attention they give to mapping both diagnostic strategies and predisposing conditions that are not of a linear cause-and-effect variety.

With suspected cancer under a biomedical model, you first obtain a biopsy, then (if the tests are positive) chemotherapy and/or surgery. Under the holistic model, you would obtain the biopsy and maybe chemotherapy or surgery, depending upon the severity of the cancer. But along the way, other interventions might come into play, for example, macrobiotics, re-ducing free radicals, spiritual healing or other forms of direct energy work, visualization, emotional release work, etc.

With more factors to take into account, and more levels to work on, the holistic model is a comprehensive paradigm that includes the best of what the biomedical model has to offer. It is not the purely top-down, cure-your-body-with-your-mind model that critics jump on. The presence or absence of love in one's life, for example, is only one of dozens of factors that can predispose one toward health or illness. Holism is *not* the logical opposite of the biomedical model; it includes relevant parts.

The divergence of localizationist and systems approaches is also reflected in treatment and prevention procedures. In the biomedical model, there is an asymmetry between treatment and prevention, whereas in the holistic model there is a symmetry of these procedures. For example, under the biomedical model one attempts to prevent lung cancer by not smoking or otherwise inhaling carcinogenic substances. But once one develops lung cancer, the treatment procedure is quite unrelated. You may have a piece of your lung removed or you may undergo chemotherapy.

Depending upon the severity and uniqueness of your condition, you might choose to include chemotherapy under the care of a holistically oriented physician. Either way, however, you would also immediately engage a range of alternative treatments that parallel those used to prevent cancer in the first place. With variations to suit each case, antioxidant therapy, visualization, psychotherapy, meditation, ozone injections, dietary changes, and spiritual healing all can be used either to fight cancer or to prevent it. The working principle here is that what cures disease in the final analysis is the same kind of thing that prevents disease.

The goal of a holistic model is to restore the whole person to optimum health. Disease and illness will then have the best opportunity for healing. They will either fade away (unless the patient is past the point of reversibility, perhaps close to death) or not develop in the first place. If the health practitioner does not help restore the patient to as much overall wellness as possible and focuses instead upon a piecemeal approach to each symptom, the chances of recurrence are greater.

Most holistic practitioners work with the following metaphysical assumption. Within each of us is a blueprint of perfect health from which we need only strip away the illusions, imbalances, and accumulated blocks of daily living to enjoy. In the final analysis, optimum health is not so much created from an accidental convergence of psychological and physical processes, but is progressively accessed with the assistance of professionals who know where to look, what to do, and when to get out of the way. Deepak Chopra describes this perspective in *Creating Health*, which carries the provocative subtitle "Beyond Prevention, Toward Perfection." He further refines it through the use of many examples in *Ageless Body, Timeless Mind.*[7]

Suppose, however, that you are born with a missing limb or a genetic predisposition to alcoholism or diabetes. Is this a "perfect blueprint" for health? Chopra is a Western-trained physician who also practices ayurvedic medicine, a system of diagnosis (such as pulse analysis) and natural healing based upon the Vedas of ancient India. (He is also a member of the NIH evaluation panel for alternative practices.) The Vedas contain a perennialist philosophy of nature. And a perennialist philosophy of nature doesn't stop at the genetic level.

This means that the "blueprint" for perfection is found in higher-order templates, like bioetheric levels of energy-consciousness up to and including the causal body itself. In principle, these levels can trigger subtle genetic changes or even override predispositions. In *Meaning and Medicine: A Doctor's Tales of Breakthrough and Healing,* for example, physician Larry Dossey describes cases illustrating how the meaning we attribute both to our lives in general and to specific situations can cause not so much a change in genetic configuration, but a change in the way our genes express themselves—even to the point of reversing some genetically inherited diseases. How far we wish to align our bodies, minds, and spirits is up to us.

Anyone who attempts to understand why some people are so vibrantly healthy that they virtually never suffer from chronic, degenerative, or communicable disease (including AIDS exposure) leans toward a holistic perspective. On the other hand, someone primarily interested in developing new drugs to combat or arrest AIDS (or other diseases) is working within a biomedical perspective.

Both perspectives have their place. But we should not make the mistake of thinking that they are logically parallel perspectives on the same reality—the same continuum of health and disease. For they are not. From the holistic viewpoint, understanding all the factors involved in health is the key to understanding why some people fall into disease and the better ways to deal with disease when it does emerge. Given this range of factors, some alternative therapies are bound to produce positive results. On the other hand, developing a new drug to fight disease will not produce optimum overall health. All the prescriptions in the world will not do that.

It is fair to say that the holistic model stresses prevention more than the biomedical model does. However, there are many health professionals who share a biomedical perspective and who understand very well the need for prevention on a large scale. This fact might lead one to conclude that as soon as traditional medicine catches up on this score, holism will simply fade away.

To draw such a conclusion, however, reveals a limited understanding of the qualitative factors—especially emotional and spiritual ones—that holists typically pack into their model of optimum health. To stop smoking and begin exercising is a good beginning. But when the holist thinks prevention in ways that, say, require deep-level emotional release, spiritual exercises, or major attitudinal changes, we are moving well beyond the "vitamins and aerobics" approach of popular culture.

When holists urge us to rethink our assumptions about health and healing, they are recommending far more than prevention plus some alternative therapies. Holistic health practice involves such things as listening to the patient for critical clues; integrating compassion into healing contexts; helping patients form new attitudes about life and death; and discovering what sickness tells us about other parts of ourselves.

Holists stress the importance of learning what we can do to mobilize all the forces of *self*-regulation and *self*-healing. Their concept of healing expressly acknowledges its Anglo-Saxon root *haelen*, which means "to make whole." These and other revisionings are the topic of Richard Carlson's and Benjamin Shield's remarkable *Healers on Healing*, a compilation of original essays by some of this country's most distinguished health professionals.

In *The Galileo of the Microscope*, which chronicles the life and trials of Canadian physician Gaston Naessens, Christopher Bird frames an excellent case study not only of holistic versus biomedical approaches to cancer, but also of the fear, rigidity, and politics in which much mainstream medical thinking is embedded. Inspired by the possibilities of the earlier Rife microscope, Naessens developed a device that allowed him to observe a fundamental element (termed a "somatide") in all living systems not visible through either standard laboratory microscopes *or* through much more powerful electron microscopes.

Somatides assume a variety of shapes depending upon their medium and vary in size from a few angstroms to .01 microns. According to Naessens, they are necessary for cell division. If their shapes are not held in check by immune system inhibitors in the bloodstream, disorders in cellular metabolism result. "All degenerative diseases are a consequence of these disorders."[8] So far as communicable diseases are concerned, germs are not direct causes of disease but are empowered by these underlying shifts to produce the ill effects.

Naessens went on to develop a solution (714-X) of camphorminium chloride with additional nitrogen compounds which, when injected, had the effect not of killing cancerous cells, but of restoring the natural order of cell metabolism, thereby reversing the degenerative process. Nitrogen had the effect of supressing a secretion that paralyzed the immune system.

Naessens's cure worked for many types of cancer, but when he applied for permission to conduct large clinical trials he was turned down on the grounds that his procedure was incompatible with known scientific principles. When he continued to dispense 714-X to his patients, including other physicians whose lives he saved, he was brought to trial and threatened with the loss of his license and even life imprisonment. The government's chief witness falsely claimed that Naessens was prescribing nothing more than a placebo.

Like Galileo, Naessens asked those charged with "protecting the public health" simply to consider the evidence—to look with their own eyes! The case was hotly debated in the Canadian press and eventually Naessens was acquitted. The future status of 714-X in this country, given the wisdom of the FDA, is unclear. In the meantime, however, Bird's account of Naessen's research and trial should be mandatory reading in medical schools.

Richard Thomas's *The Essiac Report* develops a stunningly parallel case for the effectiveness of the herbal remedy Essiac in successfully treating thousands of Candians for cancer, as well as for the politics of repression by medical establishment. Dr. Charles Brusch, a highly regarded physician and personal doctor to President Kennedy, declared flatly that, on the basis of laboratory studies and extensive clinical use, Essiac is "a cure for cancer."

Of course, one needn't go to Canada for a public airing of the nastier side of this paradigm war. In the case of Therapeutic Touch (a form of energetic healing), William Jarvis, president of the National Council Against Health Fraud and Professor of Preventive Medicine at Loma Linda University, in 1992 stated: "There's no published research in medical or scientific journals showing that [Therapeutic Touch] has any basis in scientific fact. What you have here is mysticism parading as science."

To which Janet Quinn, an associate professor and senior scholar at the University of Colorado School of Nursing and a leading authority on Therapeutic Touch, replied in a widely circulated letter to Dr. Jarvis: "The circulation of this kind of misinformation and abusive, sarcastic and ignorant discrediting of nursing...is absolutely antithetical to the public good. It is clear that [you] are completely ignorant of the published research on Therapeutic Touch."

Which he apparently was. For there are over 130 scientific studies of the effectiveness of spiritual and energetic healing (including Therapeutic Touch). These are reviewed in psychiatrist Daniel Benor's *Healing Research, Holistic Energy Medicine and Spirituality*. Benor's work is easily the most comprehensive study of its kind and should be required reading for anyone—both critic and healer alike—with an interest in this field.

The dark side of traditional medicine is further brought to light in the case of ozone therapy. Ozone is made from pure oxygen mixed with electrical or ultraviolet energy. In simple terms, it's an oxygen molecule and a half. Ozone is used to purify the water systems of Moscow, Paris, and Los Angeles. There is abundant scientific evidence that ozone selectively attacks viral matter and selectively inhibits the growth of cancer. It has also been used effectively for chronic pain, burns, strokes, and dozens of other medical conditions. Millions of Germans and Canadians have benefited from its intravenous application, especially those suffering from cancer and AIDS.

A recent study by the Canadian military in association with the International Red Cross found that monkeys injected with SIV (the monkey equivalent of HIV) died within fourteen days. However, all monkeys treated with ozone remained healthy and unaffected by the virus. An American company, Medizone, has conducted successful preliminary studies with ozone therapy on humans but lacks the financial backing to carry out the kind of large-scale studies required by the FDA. There are no dangerous side-effects.[9]

Still, the FDA refuses to sanction the use of ozone therapy or to support further testing. In fact, it cited ozone therapy as an example of medical fraud in testimony before a congressional subcommittee. Doctors who use it have been harassed, ozone generators have been seized, and desperate patients have had to seek treatment abroad. Ozone therapy is illegal in America despite massive evidence indicating that it is one of the closest things to an all-purpose healing agent on the horizon. How can the agency that approved aspartame turn a blind eye to ozone therapy?

The answer, I think, rests with the extraordinary financial and political power of the pharmaceutical industry. You cannot patent ozone. The healing properties of ozone are so numerous that some drug companies could be brought to financial ruin. The case for ozone therapy is so strong that a conspiracy to prevent its use in America is the only hypothesis capable of explaining the indefensible decisions on the part of those entrusted not just to protect, but also to promote, public health.

Despite these setbacks, alternative remedies are making their way into the mainstream. Physicians increasingly are allowing and even encouraging patients to supplement their health care with some of the more conservative therapies, such as biofeedback and hypnosis. Two new journals, *Alternative Therapies in Health and Medicine* and *The Journal of Alternative and Complementary Medicine,* report on the effectiveness of alternative therapies and explore timely issues relating to health paradigms and policies. Fundamental change is clearly in the air. As of this writing, twenty medical schools in the U.S. offer courses in alternative medicine. And a few, such as Columbia University's College of Physicians and Surgeons, even have centers devoted to the hands-on exploration of alternative and complementary medicine.

The holistic model of health is underwritten by a systems-oriented perennialism, which stresses not only intralevel networks of relations, but also interpenetrating fields of energy-consciousness. This paradigm of fields and frequencies, including the power and compassion of evolved consciousness, supports the alternative diagnostic and therapeutic methods of what has come to be called "energy medicine." Physician Richard Gerber illustrates the many applications of this way of thinking in *Vibrational Medicine*, which may well become a standard textbook for health and healing in the twenty-first century.

Gerber weaves together most of the new (or rediscovered) alternative treatments into a comprehensive paradigm that is firmly grounded in the Perennial Philosophy. Magnetic and spiritual healing, herbs, homeopathy, flower essences, gem elixirs and chromotherapy, radionics, connections between the principal chakras, the nervous system, spinal alignment, self-healing and the power of intent, the leading edge of diagnostic technology (which is taking us beyond magnetic resonance imaging to more subtle frequencies), toning, and crystal work all gain in both intelligibility and plausibility by virtue of finding interconnected places in an overarching vibratory paradigm.

The physics and metaphysics of energy medicine. Energy medicine is based on two fundamental principles. One is the principle of top-down influence, whereby spiritual, mental, and emotional levels of energy-consciousness affect denser bioetheric and purely physical levels in ways which dispose one toward, but do not directly cause, health or disease. I will explore this idea further in connection with the question of whether we create our own illnesses.

The second foundation of energy medicine is the belief that each type of tissue, each fluid, each organ, each emotional state or deeper character trait, the physical body as a whole, and the person as a whole all have distinctive vibrational signatures. Some are of an electromagnetic nature, while others fall into a subtle category outside the EM range. These signatures are determined by form, function, and the larger matrices of harmonics (and disharmonies) in which they nest. A healthy kidney, for example, will vibrate at certain frequencies, and it will both affect and respond to harmonics above and below it, just as certain upper-end chords on a piano will cause harmonic lower-end resonances. Gerber describes some of the implications of this way of thinking as follows:

> The atoms that form each cell contain electrons that are in constant motion and which therefore radiate electromagnetic waves. These waves are measurable as frequencies, the rate of which vary according to the particular form of matter...Cells whose natural frequency rates are the same combine to form the various structures and systems that are an integral feature of our physical existence. Each structure is a harmonic of the cells through which it is formed and maintained. It may be said, then, that [inaudible] sound creates the structures of our bodies.[10]

Every technology carries potential downside risks. Vibrations per se are not the panacea that pop holism portrays. Consider the example of sonically pulverized kidney stones. Were the power and frequencies not appropriately determined and used, it could easily be the kidney itself which is pulverized. The same goes for other parts of the body and even our minds. The long-term exposure to an ever-expanding range of artificially induced fields and frequencies involving, for example, sound (rock music), infrared dominant fluorescence, strong electrical fields, and other assorted extra-low-frequencies (ELFs) in many cases carry a stronger potential for disease than for health.

ELF exposure is a special case in point. ELFs are extremely low frequency electromagnetic fields (1–100 cycles per second) that can affect biological systems in different ways. (They may also be described as EMFs.) ELF effects have been discovered on pineal melatonin production, which may reduce immune system efficiency. This is one reason not to use electric blankets! ELFs tend to be self-organizing, can penetrate almost anything, and are less susceptible to diffusion over distance. Beneficial frequencies in the 7–9 Hz range correlate with the 8 Hz frequency (Schumann resonance) of the earth. ELFs can interact with DNA molecules and at the correct frequency can turn a gene "on" or "off." Knowledge of the correct frequencies in principle puts one in a position of considerable power—for better or worse. As physician Andrija Puharich explains:

> One frequency can cause cancer in rats in two days.

Another can reverse the process. One frequency can cause depression in humans by causing the release of cholinergic neuropeptides in the brain. Still another can cause anxiety; a third can motivate mob behavior. This can be done from as far away as the other side of the planet.[11]

Other documented effects include inducing sleep, changing time perception, inhibiting or enhancing bone growth, and altering sensitivity to pain. Paul Brodeur, author of *Currents of Death: Power Lines, Computer Terminals, and the Attempt to Cover Up Their Threat to Your Health* and a three- part series in *The New Yorker*, "Annals of Radiation: The Hazards of Electromagnetic Radiation," has chronicled the hazards of ELF pollution in three areas: high power lines, radar, and video/computer display terminals. The 60 Hz (cycles per second) emissions from power lines are potentially implicated in higher rates of cancer in those who work with or live around them.[12] Power companies have in some instances been ordered to reduce ELF emissions and, if requested, to conduct surveys in homes that may be affected. A 16 Hz microwave field has been shown both to suppress immune function and increase the likelihood of cancer. This also happens to be the frequency range of certain radar systems.

Computer terminals are yet another source of ELF pollution. The Kaiser Permanente Medical Group in Oakland, California did a study of 1,583 pregnant women. It found twice as many miscarriages during the first twelve weeks of pregnancy among women who worked at a video display terminal for more than twenty hours per week.

In *Cross Currents* (appropriately subtitled "The Promise of Electromedicine, The Perils of Electropollution"), Robert Becker, a pioneer researcher in both areas, draws our attention to both "the rapid rise of electromedicine, which promises to unlock the secrets of healing, and the parallel rise of electropollution, which poses a pressing environmental danger."[13] Becker reviews forty years of research dealing with the potentially harmful effects of ELF radiation, for example, the 45 Hz or 70 Hz of the Navy's SANGUINE communication system.

ELFs can work for or against you. The success of a vibrational paradigm over the long term will depend in large part upon how these claims about correct frequencies shake down, both in personal application and laboratory research. There is currently a great deal of interest in the theory of biological resonance, which studies the effects of extremely low intensity electromagnetic coupling to biological molecules. Becker and others have argued that this effect may help to explain hands-on healing phenomena and the spontaneous onset of certain degenerative diseases.

The typical New Age expo or publication carries advertisements for a variety of light and sound devices which claim health-promoting correlations between these devices and various chakras, states of mind, or physical states. Some may be correct. ELF blockers in the 7.83 Hz range, for example, seem to be a useful antidote to visual display radiation. Other devices may be neutral. And some may be positively harmful. One could actually weaken his or her immune responses under the guise of relaxation with some of these devices.

There are several common sense rules of thumb to use in this regard. Talk to other users of the product. Ask the company for names of customers willing to be contacted. Inquire how they came about the particular frequencies and wave forms they are using. How much research did they conduct with these frequencies? What is the theoretical basis for the claims put forth? Obviously, nobody is going to have an airtight case. One can, however, sift through a lot of posturing with such questions.

Whatever the final determination may be on specific health claims regarding ELFs, we do know this. Some ELFs can help, some can harm, and the difference depends in part on factors within each individual that are currently not well understood. Each of us tends to have sensitivities to specific ELF frequencies that others do not.

Having described some of the potentially negative implications associated with the technologies of energy medicine, let me conclude by describing three promising developments in this arena (of the dozens available). The individuals involved are committed to exploring the implications of a vibrational paradigm for healing, to refining its theoretical foundations, and to documenting the results of their explorations in research clinics and hospitals.

Tom Kenyon is a psychotherapist and founder of Acoustic Brain Research. He has developed a large base of information on exact sound frequencies, harmonics, and waveforms which stimulate various parts of the brain, with often dramatic results on both psychological and physical levels. The information is encoded via what can only be described as an unusual medium of music made available to the public in cassette tapes. There are frequencies and waveforms for everything from dyslexia and thymic stimulation to working through patterns of emotional self-sabotage.

Kenyon works from the belief that there are precise discoverable relationships between specific musical ratios and electrochemical events in the nervous system. He is convinced that someday there will be a health-promoting union between acoustic engineering and psychoneuroimmunology. He is especially interested, for example, in the healing properties of the perfect harmonic fifth, which is incorporated into many of his tapes.

There are many tapes on the market today for relaxation and stress reduction. Some fall into the New Age genre and some do not. But Kenyon's music is not New Age and his continuing research has carried him far beyond the claims of stress reduction which accompany most tapes. He has taken direct aim at such challenges as cancer and drug addiction. And he works with respected medical researchers and clinics to refine his frequencies, so to speak, and document the results. In one major study of the effectiveness of certain tapes for drug addiction, the results were nothing short of extraordinary.[14]

Another implication of a vibrational paradigm for healing is found in the therapeutic application of phase-conjugate sound and scalar detection systems developed by Peter Kelly, an electrical engineer and founder of Interdimensional Sciences in Lakemont, Georgia. Phase-conjugate sound is an application of the physics of time-reversed electromagnetic wave propagation (described in Chapter Five). Until quite recently in the West, there were few applications outside of nonlinear optics.

A time-reversed wave precisely retraces the path of the ordinary electromagnetic (EM) wave which caused it to be formed. In effect, it possesses an invisible wire through space back to whatever emitted its stimulus wave. It continually converges upon its own backtracking path and does not diverge or spread its energy, unlike normal electromagnetic waves. The net result is the creation of a standing virtual field, a bubble of scalar potential as it is sometimes described, through which information can be sent and retrieved. Such bubbles are not invasive per se, although they can be created in empty space or in and around human bodies. Conjoined with the power of focused intent, such a field may be conducive to collapsing at a quantum level the superposed waveforms associated with unhealthy physical and emotional states.

Building upon this theoretical base, Kelly has developed a technology for literally bathing every cell, organ, and bone in the body in complex scalar fields which scavenge for excess stress or energetic imbalances and allow them to be continually radiated away as time-reversed sound waves. By its very nature, it cannot invade or break down cell walls or tissues in a linear fashion. Rather, it creates a field whereby what is neither wanted nor needed by healthy tissue is automatically expunged. As one speaker pulses a vibration into the body, another aligned in phase conjugation pulls it through the body. Kelly has developed computer programming which continually scans the body's energy field in the 4–16 Hz range, gives graphed field readings on a screen, and stores the primary information going in or coming out.

His patented technology is integrated under the label of BETAR (for Bio-Energetically Transducer Aided Resonance). As of this writing, he claims only that BETAR relieves deep-level physical and emotional stress. However, clinical trials have shown it to be effective in the elimination of pain. One study at the Shealy Institute for Comprehensive Health Care and Pain Management indicated that medical expenses for pain were reduced by eighty percent, and pain intensity was reduced by seventy percent, out of a sample of eight hundred patients. Another study suggested that the BETAR could be very effective for depression. Additional studies have been undertaken at Children's Hospital in St. Petersburg, Michigan State University, and University of Washington. At one small clinic in south Florida, the BETAR has proved very beneficial for children suffering long-term adverse reactions to required immunizations. Mounting anecdotal evidence suggests that the BETAR can be a powerful ally in emotional release work and is effective for a wide spectrum of health challenges.[15]

Sherry Edwards is a pioneer in the development of methods for exact frequency toning to restore the body to optimum health. A gifted clairaudient, Edwards hears different sounds in the energy field around living things, including dominant tones for the organism as a whole. She also can tell if certain sounds are missing in comparison to the spectrum of the average healthy person. Her ability to correlate particular sounds with particular states of emotional and physical health and disease, as well as to provide missing tones with perfect pitch, has been the subject of several studies.

Edwards is primarily involved in research to develop standard procedures, which the average person can learn, to access tonal deficiencies and provide the appropriate missing links. For example, a standard chromatic analyzer can illustrate which tones are stressed or missing in a person's speech patterns. A specially designed synthesizer capable of integrating both square and sine wave oscillations at variable frequencies then produces the exact tone (or tones), which are taped for use on a cassette player.

Thus far, Edwards has established that health-promoting frequencies are significantly correlated with brain dominance; that the octave of the frequencies utilized determines which bodily system will be affected; and that the appropriate frequencies for promoting health in an individual case are determined by the person's overall tonal signature and by the type of disease being considered. In other words, the sound that reduces Smith's blood pressure is not necessarily the same one that will reduce Jones's.

Along with her work in sound (reminiscent of Dr. Guy Manners's earlier work in this area), Edwards is also investigating the appropriate color analogs (pigment and light) for specific tones. Thus, for example, red pigment or green light supplement the note "C" at 130/261/522 cycles-per-second. Obviously, much research remains to be done. To date, her therapy has proven effective for a variety of illnesses, especially those of a respiratory nature.[16] For those accustomed to thinking in terms of a vibrational paradigm, her work is one of many developments in this arena, but certainly no surprise!

DO OUR MINDS MAKE US PHYSICALLY SICK?

Like so many boldly worded questions encountered on the road to a new worldview, this one can only be answered "yes and no," depending upon what you mean. This question in particular causes volatile reactions in the holistic health community, in the larger New Paradigm discussion, and to some extent in mainstream medicine. It demands clarification and much more research.

Let us first dispose of some obvious interpretations. Do we make ourselves sick through poor diets, lack of exercise, and general ignorance about health matters? Of course. Do we make ourselves sick through poisoning the environment, breathing foul air, and ingesting carcinogenic substances? Yes, again. Do we sometimes work too hard and run ourselves into the ground, both physically and emotionally, thus making ourselves more vulnerable to a range of illnesses? Of course. Expert opinion varies on matters of degree. How much lead in one's blood, for example, is too much? But only a fool would argue that in these relatively noncontroversial areas we do not have an individual and collective responsibility for the sickness we experience.

A more complex level of interpretation is found at the leading edge of medical science which investigates the connections between emotions, brain states, and the immune system—the field of psychoneuro-immunology. Here, the research is promising and the results mixed. But our understanding of those mind-body connections which affect health is rapidly expanding.

For example, we know that the nervous system carries direct signals from the brain to immune system organs, such as the spleen, which in turn affect the number of fighting cells dispatched to a particular infection. Furthermore, the brain stimulates the pituitary gland to make certain hormones which then regulate immune cell activity or cause other hormones to do so.

However, it is the neuropeptides explored in the pioneering research of Candace Pert and others which point the way to a major reconceptualization of the relationship between emotions and immune system response. "When we document the key role that the emotions, expressed through neuropeptide molecules, play in affecting the body, it will become clear how emotions can be a key to the understanding of disease."[17] In *The Psychobiology of Mind-Body Healing*, Ernest Rossi elaborates upon the larger implications of this paradigm shift:

> Neuropeptides, then, are a previously unrecognized form of information transduction between mind and body that may be the basis of many hypnotherapeutic, psychosocial, and placebo responses. From a broader perspective, the neuropeptide system also may be the psychobiological basis of the folk, shamanistic, and spiritual forms of healing that share many of the characteristics of hypnotic healing currently returning to vogue under the banner of "holistic medicine."[18]

Not long ago the *New England Journal of Medicine*, in connection with a study suggesting no connection between cancer and attitudes, took a strong editorial position against the sort of mind-healing connection made popular by Norman Cousins, Carl Simonton, and Stephanie Matthews Simonton.[19] Although medical science is typically very conservative in drawing conclusions in this arena, the general direction of research does suggest that recurring negative or unhealthy emotions are implicated in physical disease.

Depression, stress, feelings of helplessness, fear, and insecurity have all been linked to reduced immune function. For example, depression causes the amount of cortisone to increase, thereby decreasing the number of (helper) T-cells in the bloodstream. On the other hand, feelings of helplessness are implicated in reducing the effectiveness, although not necessarily the number, of white blood cells. Harvard physician Steven Locke and Douglas Colligan further explore the scientific basis and practical applications of these connections, including the relationship between personality and cancer, in *The Healer Within: The New Medicine of Mind and Body*.[20]

These mind-body connections have not yet been demonstrated to everyone's satisfaction. The question we should be asking, however, is whether in light of current research a rational person presented with a related health challenge should assume responsibility for examining his or her emotional life and respond appropriately.

If stress or depression were implicated in your health challenge, surely it would be irresponsible not to work directly on these predisposing factors. We sometimes hold physicians responsible for not ordering certain tests which are critical only three percent of the time. Yet mind-body connections are implicated in more than this.

Controversies within psychoneuroimmunology tend to revolve around research designs, judgment calls, differences of degree, how much evidence is necessary, which states of mind are more implicated than others, and so on. At this level of the debate, there are not the profound philosophical differences that there might have been several decades ago.

There are, however, some profound philosophical differences in a stronger interpretation of the mind-body connection found in certain metaphysical or New Age circles. This stronger version has several parts. Most are stated or implied in the following passages taken from an interview with Ken Wilber in *New Age Journal*:

> At issue is the notion that, unless something is spiritually wrong with you, you should be able to [visualize disease away] all the time. And that if you can't, you should feel profound guilt. You have brought this disease on yourself, you see, to teach yourself some sort of lesson, and if you get the lesson, then in all cases you should be able to cure the disease by thinking it away…
>
> New Age types [ask]… 'What are you trying to teach yourself with this disease?' You might have, say, eye cancer, and they'll say 'What are you trying to avoid seeing?' Or you might have a broken leg, and they'll say 'Why are you avoiding standing up for yourself?' Or you might have a headache, and they'll say 'Guess whose sixth chakra isn't opened?' Or you might have some heart problems, and

they'll say 'Why are you avoiding God's love?' And all of this is completely magical, narcissistic, infantile, new age nonsense…

[This position] kills people. I mean that literally. By thinking that all disease has its origins solely or exclusively on the spiritual level, you actually and completely cease looking for causes on the physical. And therefore you give up or bypass or fail to take advantage of physical level cures, which are, in fact, the only ones that are going to work for genuinely physical level diseases…

This whole new age position can be historically demonstrated to be an unconscious offshoot…of such movements as Christian Science, which itself was a misinterpretation of the New England transcendentalists, Thoreau and Emerson. It mistakes the correct notion, "Godhead creates all," for the narcissistic notion "Since I am one with God, I create all." That's very wrong.[21]

These passages illustrate very clearly why those attracted to the Rising Culture often put as much distance as possible between themselves and the New Age. Wilber is not alone in criticizing the New Age tendency to "blame the victim." In *Healing Words*, for example, Larry Dossey also rejects this tendency, even though his constructive observations about psychological factors implicated in physical disease still draw attention to the area that Wilber thinks is overworked. The issues associated with this phrase and with Wilber's concerns clearly deserve a more extended examination.

It is certainly possible to find extremists in any movement, and Wilber no doubt had good reason to recoil from New Age types who converged upon his life under the most difficult of circumstances (his wife Treya's courageous and deeply transformational battle with cancer). Still, when all is said and done, three questions remain. First, exactly what type of connection is implied by the strong thesis to which Wilber takes exception? Second, which parts of this thesis are testable? Third, do New Age people actually subscribe to what Wilber rejects? New Agers I have questioned closely on this matter typically refuse to be backed into such a tight corner.

What is at issue: necessity or probability? Let's set aside upset stomachs or head colds, which are not worth debating. The first question is whether, for every major disease, there is some underlying psycho-spiritual factor without which the disease would never occur. Such a view is more than strong. It's extreme! I don't know anybody who holds it.

Note that this leaves open the further question of whether, if such emotional or attitudinal factors do exist, their impact is direct (like anger bringing on angina) or indirect in the sense of merely predisposing one toward an illness which may or may not materialize.

Note, too, the availability of weaker versions of this thesis. For example, perhaps only *half* of all major diseases have an underlying psycho-spiritual component. This would still be a fairly strong and controversial thesis, even if the influence of the emotion or attitude were indirect.

Who holds any of the above beliefs? A powerful version seems to be implied by a passage from *A Course in Miracles*: "All disease comes from a state of unforgiveness." Louise Hay in *You Can Heal Your Life* amplifies this root premise: "Regret, sadness, hurt, fear or guilt, blame, anger, resentment, and sometimes even the desire for revenge…come from a space of unforgiveness, a refusal to let go and come into the present moment."[22]

She then describes the role of these more specific emotional or attitudinal causes. Arthritis, she suggests, "comes from a constant pattern of criticism," cancer from hopelessness and resentment, and obesity from a "need for protection." She then provides the most comprehensive list of probable causes for physical diseases in print today, covering everything from Addison's Disease to impacted wisdom teeth.[23]

The problem here is Hay's use of the phrase "probable cause." For a probable cause indicates some degree of correlation—what might be termed a contributing factor—but not a necessary connection. Nowhere does she say that you cannot get cancer unless you suffer from hopelessness and resentment.

Tired of these distinctions, the frustrated reader might complain as follows: Who cares if the relationship is one of necessity or mere correlation? The important thing about Hay's work (and others like it) is that it's a stimulus for personal transformation. If you have arthritis, then look at your issues involving criticism. See what works for you. We will all be dead before the gap between mere correlation and absolute necessity is nailed down to the satisfaction of everyone in the medical establishment.

Very well, let's move to the level of correlation. Are such claimed correlations empirically testable? Yes and no. With $5 billion and a decade of research we could put each mind-body connection to a fair test. We could, for example, take a thousand arthritis patients, get them to dredge up their issues involving criticism and deal with them, and see if the arthritis improves to a marked degree. But there is a catch–22. If by all reasonable standards of assessment it is agreed that these patients have no more issues involving criticism and yet some show no improvement at the physical level, how do we account for the differential?

Rather than abandon the thesis, some New Age partisans will move into even muddier waters and insist that, on some level, issues involving criticism are not being dealt with. And since we have exhausted all of the possible causes in *this* life, we may have to go back and look at other lives, where the issues are very deeply buried. On pragmatic grounds, there is no reason why we should not take this proposal at face value. Try it and see what happens.

However, if one still has arthritis after exploring a dozen past lives with three of the best past-life therapists in the country, then it would be fair to say that one's day of reckoning has arrived. It would be neither scientifically nor philosophically meaningful to continue insisting, for reasons other than simple faith, that issues involving the giving or receiving of criticism are the real cause of arthritis.

I am not necessarily disagreeing with Hay's general recommendations. I would try them myself. I am urging, however, that if one intends them to be more than articles of faith, there are boundaries within which one should be prepared to work. Failure to achieve positive results cannot be explained away forever. This is one of CSICOP's constructive messages in dealing with the paranormal.

Some physical diseases may have no underlying psycho-spiritual factors. However, this still leaves open the question of whether—*if* such connections exist with some types of disease—the contributing elements *necessarily* lead to the appropriate disease. I would respond in the negative. Any kind of alleged cause-and-effect will turn out to be nothing more than some degree of correlation. Yet a strong correlation (or even a weak one) is usually all that is needed to justify taking action. The connection between obesity and self-protection issues, for example, only needs *some* evidence in its favor before one should look at such issues, especially after discovering that diet and exercise aren't working.

A final word of caution. To suppose that emotional or spiritual imbalance will eventually manifest on a physical level may put you in the driver's seat forever. For if they do not manifest, it can always be claimed that sooner or later they will. Unless the term "eventually" is tied down to a fair time frame, this claim is guaranteed to be true, no matter what. Such a guarantee, however, would lack substance.

The question of physical causes. There are numerous physical causes implicated in physical diseases. Viruses are implicated in AIDS, carcinogenic substances in cancer, and drug abuse in birth defects. Only fools would ignore such obvious facts. With considerable justification, therefore, many commentators find it morally objectionable to push the "you-can-cure-disease-with-your-mind" theme to the exclusion of physical remedies for physical conditions.

I would, too. But this is not the New Age issue it is sometimes made out to be. I have seen Christian faith healers tell very sick people that they did not need to see a physician because they were healed. And there are hard-core Christian Scientists who have withheld medical treatment from their spouses or children with tragic results. But I have never observed a New Ager claim that nobody should have their tumors surgically removed, or their diabetes medically diagnosed and treated with insulin.

Certainly Louise Hay doesn't take that line. She does urge that you fight for all you are worth on emotional and spiritual levels which complement whatever else you are doing on a physical level. Perhaps you can wean yourself gradually from insulin, or keep cancer from recurring, by changing certain attitudes and thought patterns. What she and others recommend in this regard is not the same issue that Wilber rejects.

The healing power of imagery is probably stronger than what he concedes. Recent controlled studies at Michigan State University, for example, have shown a clear connection between guided imagery and improved adherence levels of neutrophils, a type of white blood cell that enhances immunity.[24] What Wilber objects to in this regard is the belief in "psycho-kinetic magic" whereby one is encouraged to visualize cancer away over the next few weeks and found guilty if the visualization is not successful. Thus stated, most New Agers would agree.

The topic of physical causes is problematic in discussions of self-healing, not because emotional or spiritual ones are the only factors involved, but because the whole arena of physical causes and physical diseases is itself a collection of stronger and weaker correlations. Many people who smoke do not contract lung cancer. Many who consume pacific red snapper do not suffer mercury poisoning. And many who eat plenty of red meat do not die of heart disease. Why not? Partly because there are other physically predisposing conditions which must be factored into the total picture. A dozen physical factors alone, beginning with one's DNA, may figure into susceptibility to lung cancer, for example. The complex interactions of these factors are the working agenda for a systems and holistically oriented medical science.

What is frustrating about this picture, however, is that for virtually every major physical disease, no matter how complex or exhaustive our knowledge of the physical causes becomes, there are always exceptions—people who don't get sick or die when statistically they should. For cancer, heart disease, arthritis, gout, glaucoma, renal failure, and so on, the best we have are profiles which indicate greater or lesser susceptibility to a particular disease. Only in the most extreme cases, like swallowing cyanide pills, do we have clear-cut physically sufficient conditions for death or severe illness.

For less clear-cut cases, appeals to emotional or spiritual factors make perfect sense, as Bernie Siegel so amply illustrates in *Love, Medicine, and Miracles*.[25] The net result of this acknowledgment is a *sliding scale* of factors that include the purely physical, the biological, the mental, the emotional or attitudinal, and the spiritual. The relative impact of these factors varies greatly in any given case.

If you've been chronically depressed or insecure for a long time, it probably would not take much at the level of physical causality to put you into a state of serious illness. On the other hand, if you are free of these negative states and enjoy an enhanced capacity for loving and forgiving, you might well find yourself going through life virtually immune to the principal chronic and degenerative diseases. There is no reason why Wilber, or anyone else coming to grips with the mind-body relationship, should not adopt a multilevel, sliding scale approach to health and disease. It accommodates all of the empirical evidence and is consistent with the farther reaches of human potential.

A statement such as "All disease comes from a state of unforgiveness (or fear, or lack of love, etc.)" doesn't rule out physical factors; they can be implicated as well, and frequently are. Nor does it say how much unforgiveness is involved or for how long. Nor does it say that we should work only on our forgiveness issues and forget about proper diet or exercise. Nor does it say that you should not have your tumor surgically removed because there is a forgiveness workshop coming up soon, although unthinking people could twist such an interpretation out of it.

Finally, it does not imply, nor does anything in the work of Ken Keyes, Sondra Ray, or Louise Hay imply, that if you sincerely work on your forgiveness or related ego issues your cancer will always disappear. Or that if it doesn't, you must be defective. That unforgiveness is involved in some physical diseases may be a false assumption, but not outrageously so. At the least, it can stimulate personal transformation, even if one eventually sets it aside in favor of another perspective.

If your body succumbs to the ravages of cancer despite much emotional clearing, it does not mean that you have "failed" in any sense that implies a character defect. It means that certain forces were set in motion that, by the time they were fully addressed, were too powerful to reverse, even though part of what caused them in the recesses of consciousness has been cleansed and healed. Far from implying the existence of a spiritual disease, it means that one is now more radiant at the core. I can see why a materialist would reject this explanation out of hand. But I cannot see why anyone attracted to the interpenetration of the body by the mind would be so inclined.

Thus far, I have offered only some suggestions about what it may or may not be reasonable to believe about health and the mind-body connection, given certain assumptions. This, of course, is not to provide evidence, of which there is precious little anyway. The whole field cries out for extensive scientific investigation. I would hasten to add, however, that the current deficiency is not due to a lack of volunteer subjects. I would look instead to the ranks of those with the means to conduct investigations, but who fail to do so because they believe they already know the results.

The question of guilt and responsibility. Critics both in and out of the New Age have raised important questions about where the responsibility for disease rests. A typical version ascribed to New Age thought is that one unconsciously brings illness upon oneself in order to learn certain lessons. Therefore, one must ultimately accept responsibility for his or her illness, including the failure to eradicate it. And as critics are quick to point out, unnecessary guilt may result from that failure.

It is easy to find critics of this idea, but much harder to find defenders— whether in or out of the New Age ranks. There is enough ambiguity over the terms "guilt" and "responsibility" alone to justify quite different interpretations. Like many arguments in this arena, it is based upon taking several wrong forks in the road, each one taking us farther away from a more plausible or constructive path.

In the first place, the charge of producing unnecessary guilt in the sick person is a strange one. Very few people in or out of the New Age appear to feel guilt over feeling sick. If they now are a burden to loved ones, they may feel guilty over not having done more to prevent their illness. But that is a different matter. Moreover, I have yet to find a New Age person who, after working hard on his or her issues, experienced guilt or shame over the fact that the illness was not responding favorably. Anxiety, yes. Bewilderment, yes. Depression, yes. All understandable. But not guilt or shame.

Furthermore, New Age and transpersonally oriented individuals are opposed to guilt anyway. They work hard at getting out from under its grip when they do experience it, and it's part of their credo not to instill it in others. The guilt seems to be more in the eyes of the external critic. If they were to experience guilt over their illness, their friends ideally would present them with a picture of human evolution in which such guilt has no place.

Finally, if you have chosen a path which leads to physical illness in order to learn certain lessons, and if in fact you believe this, then why would you experience guilt at all when such events come to pass? Where is the shame supposed to be in a self-chosen path? Critics do not like to hear of karmic agendas which involve losing one's right arm at the age of three or a kidney at the age of twelve. However, their objection should not be that this loss inspires guilt, but rather, that reincarnation is false or is being misinterpreted. That is a different charge not directly concerning guilt or shame for illness.

We *can* experience guilt over many things, including some aspect of a health challenge. My mother once felt some guilt over the fact that her heart medications didn't work as they were supposed to. But this was not New Age guilt. The question is whether guilt is one of those things we all encounter in many contexts of living and deal with accordingly, or whether a higher-than-normal incidence of such encounters is systematically built into a New Age perspective.

In the widely discussed Simonton cancer program, for example, it was discovered that certain patients unnecessarily set themselves up for failure (and potential guilt) by establishing unrealistic goals for the limited time spent on meditation and visualization. So the program was altered and more realistic goals stressed. Here is one of the alleged guilt-producing strategies of the New Age being handled in a perfectly sane and responsible manner. In the healing arena, guilt need not carry a New Age label anymore than a humanist one.

Are we supposed to assume responsibility for taking the path leading to illness in the first place, success or failure in dealing with it after the fact, or a combination of both? I have already addressed the first option. What about the second? Using Wilber's earlier example, ought one assume responsibility for one's heart problems because one is avoiding God's love?

Along with many others, I take exception to popular New Age types playing psychologist with their smug certainty about what your issues really are. That, however, is another matter. Let us assume for the sake of the discussion that the connection in your case really is between heart disease and avoiding God's love. Now, there are two critical senses of "responsibility" in this context. One is to be (morally) blameworthy or praiseworthy. The other is to be in a position to undertake certain actions which might make a difference.

Wilber's phrasing lends itself to the first interpretation. "Why are you avoiding God's love?" *looks* like some blame and judgment are being shoveled your way. That could be true in a particular case. Every movement in history has its less-evolved members. However, there are equally plausible readings which bring out the second sense of responsibility. Some examples: "Have you considered that God is trying to speak to you in a special way?" or "Let me help you overcome some of your fear of betrayal so that you can experience more love in your life" or "Look at all the daily reminders God is giving you of the power of love." "Why are you avoiding God's love?" is simply a way of speaking which need not carry the implications of judgment, blame, or guilt that critics read into it.

In summary, I am suggesting that many New Agers and their critics may be confused over the relationship between guilt and responsibility. There is a tendency to assume that if someone is responsible for an outcome, potential guilt in the case of failure cannot be far away. But there is no logical inference from "I am responsible for X" to "I am guilty in case X does not work," given the meanings of responsibility just described. Nor is there even a logical transition from "I am blameworthy for X" to "I am now guilty over X." Guilt may or may not follow.

I am not recommending assigning blame as one of the preferable guides in interpersonal relations. However, if you accept blame for something and express your regret, there is still no presumption that guilt is the ultimate outcome. Many individuals in the larger New Paradigm dialogue, New Agers included, stress responsibility. But the inevitable trail that critics see from there to guilt simply does not exist.

Health and disease in the Great Chain. Wilber notes that three of the most evolved sages of our time—Sri Ramana Maharshi, Suzuki Roshi, and the Karmapa—all died of cancer. This must mean, he infers, either that these three suffered from a "spiritual rottenness" (his phrase) or that cancer has a lot less to do with our emotional and spiritual condition than New Agers believe. And since these sages were not spiritually rotten, the New Age partisan is impaled on the horns of a dilemma. That someone like Ramana Maharshi could die of cancer is, in Wilber's eyes, the reductio ad absurdum of the whole position.

Wilber is certainly more learned than I concerning the lives and teachings of the great sages. It strikes me, however, that alternative readings of this case are quite possible. Why not suppose that their cancer was a by-product from earlier struggles on the path of enlightenment or perhaps the result of unselfishly taking on extra karma in order to raise human consciousness. Great sages, indeed, are realized and radiant in their core, but in reaching that point, forces may be set in motion which eventually culminate in terminal illness.

Who says enlightenment is supposed to psychokinetically and instantaneously transform all material stuff in its presence? Vibrational transductions take time, even a long time. Perhaps this process was aided by certain physical factors. Perhaps not. Certainly we may presume that they saw it coming and did not seek to blame anyone for it, least of all themselves.

This interpretation is perfectly consistent with a stronger version of the spirit-mind-body-health connection and especially with the perennialist doctrine of interdimensional penetration. The biological encompasses, yet transcends, the purely physical. The emotional and mental levels encompass, yet transcend, the biological. Spiritual planes encompass all of the preceding. Here is the direct implication of such a view. If one's emotional body pervades and subsumes one's physical body, then there is no way that the condition of the physical body could fail to be affected by the condition of the emotional body.

We are not dealing with linear event causality here, such as a sudden pain causing me to recoil. We are dealing with the type of effect that a field has upon its contents, in this case the cells and tissues of my body. Some effect is virtually guaranteed, depending upon the quality, strength, and duration of the underlying emotional conditions. Consequently, the effects will vary to a considerable degree.

Specific physical manifestations may take months, years, or perhaps will never surface in this lifetime. But interdimensional penetration assures that our emotional bodies (as well as our mental and spiritual ones, too) are continuously expressing subtle, omnidirectional stimuli that, for better or worse, affect everything in their path. Such effects are not directly measurable except in terms of gross correlations. However, they can be detected by experienced clairvoyants.

Working backwards from the current results of psychoneuroimmunology, critics of you-can-heal-your-body-with-your-mind appear to think that such prescriptions are only valid in isolated circumstances and would not work more than, say, ten percent of the time. From a scientific perspective, this is a reasonable inference at the current time. But if one adopts the perspective of the Perennial Wisdom, the influence of mind upon physical health is far more pervasive. By the very nature of the modeling involved, it must be. Not only is the Great Chain a workable metaphysics for psychoneuroimmunology; if one is serious about interdimensional penetration, it also clearly predicts both the successful growth of related fields and mind-to-physical-health connections that many scientists have yet to imagine.

With abundant justification, many critics of the New Age see far too much arrogance and far too little humility in the glib assignments of creating reality (or disease, etc.). Indeed, it can get to be a preppie little game. If we are going to have continuous creation, then at least let us align ourselves, *sans ego*, with the Godhead from which it ultimately comes. To do this involves accepting more mystery into our lives, along with less certainty and less control. It involves often not knowing where the lessons lie. For all we know, an accident may happen through you in order that other people learn something. Less arrogant assignment of responsibility and more humble acceptance of the unfolding mystery of daily living is always in order.

PSYCHIC AND SPIRITUAL HEALING: PLACEBOS OR ENERGY TRANSFERS?

Near the top of everyone's list of questions about psychic or spiritual healing are those involving truth and evidence. Does it really work? How do we know? How often? Scientific curiosity about healing is not new. Mesmer, the father of hypnosis, was himself a magnetic healer, and reports of healings are not uncommon while conducting research into other paranormal phenomena.

The question of evidence. Modern laboratory tests are generally taken to have begun in the sixties with the pioneering work of Dr. Bernard Grad, a biochemist at McGill University in Canada. Grad used mice and seedlings as test objects and, with the participation of the healer, Oskar Estabany, was able to demonstrate significant effects. His work inspired another bio-chemist, Sister Justa Smith, to demonstrate healers' abilities to alter enzyme activity at levels well above chance. In the seventies, Dr. Dolores Krieger of New York University showed that a variant of traditional laying-on-of-hands, Therapeutic Touch, could alter hemoglobin levels. One of her graduate nursing students, Dr. Janet Quinn, continued researching the effects of Therapeutic Touch on stress and anxiety levels in presurgical patients.[26] It was the first project of its kind funded by the U.S. government.

Dan Wirth has conducted one of the most powerful recent tests of Therapeutic Touch. Wirth had forty-four subjects with minor surgical wounds on their shoulders put their arms through a special opening into another room. Twenty-three received Therapeutic Touch, while twenty-one served as a control group. The healer in the adjoining room did not physically touch any of the subjects, and neither the healer nor the subjects could see each other. The students believed they were participating in a study on the body's electrical conductivity, not healing. Hence, the results could not be attributed to a placebo effect.

After eight days the treated group's wounds showed approximately forty percent greater improvement over the untreated group. Measurements of the wounds were done by a physician unaware of the purpose of the study. A double-blind study with a forty percent differential between experi-mental and control groups not attributable to a placebo effect *is* a major step forward.[27]

Dr. Robert Miller, a chemical engineer in Atlanta, earlier conducted a variety of fascinating experiments with America's most-tested healer, Olga Worrall. These included such formats as altering the surface tension of water, inducing electron changes at a distance, and affecting the growth of rye seeds. Miller also conducted the only controlled study on long-distance healing (four healers working on hypertensive patients in other states) ever published in a mainstream medical journal.[28]

Electrical engineer Dr. Douglas Dean further demonstrated a nationally prominent healer's (Etel DeLoach) ability to produce distinctive Kirlian photographs.[29] The first issue of the journal *Subtle Energies* (1990), published by the International Society for the Study of Subtle Energies and Energy Medicine (ISSSEEM), is a veritable collector's item of well-designed experiments and commentaries on healers' abilities to accelerate wound healing, bacterial growth, and the molecular composition of water re-flected in infrared spectroscopy. Subsequent issues have carried equally compelling experimental studies, such as physicist Elmer Green's demon-stration of healers' abilities to produce weak, uniform electrical fields in copper walls without touching them.

Daniel Benor's *Healing Research*, noted earlier, is so exhaustive in its critical reviews of healing studies that it deserves a place in the library of virtually anyone with an interest in the field. Together with Benor's work should be a copy of *The Spindrift Papers*, a collection of well-designed experiments conducted between 1975 and 1993 on the effectiveness of prayer and healing directed at yeast cultures and germinating seeds. Inter-laced between experimental protocols are illuminating discussions of the potential roles of character, faith, and intention on the positive outcomes of the research.

Any neutral observer reviewing all the evidence would conclude that in many instances we have good reasons for believing that healers can alter the surface tension of water, enhance seedling growth, speed healing in surgi-cal wounds, alter enzyme activity, affect red-to-white blood cell ratios, re-duce stress, produce assorted effects at a distance, reduce goiters, produce Kirlian patterns unlike those of nonhealers, and generate weak electrical fields.

Is there absolute proof, suitable for God's review, in any of this? No. Is every healing experiment perfectly constructed and flawlessly carried out? No, again. Very few scientific experiments are. Can healers consistently produce complete cures on demand, as skeptics would like to see? No. Do healers fail to produce the results their clients desire? Naturally. I am suggesting merely that it's reasonable to believe, in light of existing evidence, that healers can produce beneficial physical effects.

What do skeptics say? Quite a bit, some of which I shall review shortly. Worth noting here, however, is that CSICOP's leading debunker, James Randi, makes his most persuasive case primarily against traveling faith healers and Phillipine psychic surgeons.[30] He does not directly take on the most responsible scientific research in this area or the best representatives of healing traditions outside of those he attacks.

Like so many items on the New Paradigm agenda, the pace of evolution has increased to the point where the legitimacy of psychic or spiritual healing, given current trends, is probably going to take hold in mass consciousness before scientists reach a conclusion about it. Such practices are, so to speak, all over the place. For anyone willing to take the time to talk to prominent healers (not the television variety) in this country and abroad and to some of their clients, the spontaneous evidence is far stronger than the laboratory evidence.

Average people do not reach a conclusion about healing based upon a careful examination of what an unknown healer produced or failed to produce in a laboratory. Nor do they base it upon whether the experimental controls were airtight, or whether the scientists in charge could document that a security guard was on duty at all times to prevent tampering with the evidence. They do base their decision, for example, upon whether a loved one with chronic pain obtains major relief for the first time in ten years after visiting a spiritual healer. And when that person's son or daughter later pursues a career in science, the *a priori* implausibility of such healing is greatly reduced.

This is not to suggest that we set science aside. There are dozens of critically important questions to be answered in this arena. Most healers welcome the opportunity to work in major research projects and in clinical collaboration with physicians. In their wisdom, however, the American Medical Association, CSICOP, and National Research Council decline to support such research with serious commitments of time and money. For they just know on the basis of a well-entrenched paradigm, not on the basis of evidence, that this would be a waste of time!

Is energy actually transferred? In a recent issue of *Subtle Energies* (1995), Larry Dossey marshals a variety of arguments designed to show that implicit or explicit references to "energy transfers" in healing contexts reflect an outmoded kind of dualistic Newtonian thinking and ought to be replaced by a model of *nonlocal consciousness.* Dossey's arguments reflect a growing point of view in the field of healing research and, accordingly, invite a response.

Three concerns motivate Dossey's position. The first is that energy-talk implies locality and thus the ability to measure some energetic movement across space or energetic effect at the point of healing, presumably of an electromagnetic nature. However, we have not been able to clearly measure any such energetic effects, lending credence to the skeptic's charge that, without a mechanism, healing effects cannot reflect anything but the power of the placebo or flaws in experimental design.

Dossey is aware that weak electrical or magnetic fields, or physical changes that might reasonably be construed as the *effects* of electrical or magnetic energy, have been identified in or around some healers and the objects of their healing activity. His concern seems to be that when we look for some type of traceable energetic lines (through space) connecting cause with effect, we can find none. Therefore, we are better advised to abandon talk of energy in healing contexts as well as other paranormal arenas, such as precognition, where physics is equally at a loss to shed much light.

This position invites several responses. In the first place, from the fact that we have found little of an electromegnetic nature that lends itself to *current* instrumentation, it does not follow that there may not be other types or levels of energy involved. Healing energy might very well signal a fifth force in nature, operating outside the known laws of physics, but which at key junctures is dimensionally transduced into one or more of the currently recognized four forces of nature. (Interested readers may wish to review my account of how this modeling works in the case of Kirlian photography in Chapter Six.)

Unless Dossey can provide an *a priori* argument showing that all energy in our reality grid must conform to one of those forces, his jump between the exclusive (and, I must add, dualistic) alternatives—"It can't be energy, therefore it must be consciousness"—does not follow. We would also need an additional argument to show that consciousness itself has no energetic aspects.

Dossey's second major concern is that energy-talk is in conflict with nonlocal models of consciousness necessary for explaining empirical success in distant healing, especially where, say, prayer is involved. Let us suppose that Sarah prays over John's tumor three thousand miles away, and that the tumor disappears within twenty-four hours. Nothing of an electrical or magnetic nature is measured (or measurable) around either Sarah or John, and nothing (save surgery) known to science is capable of making a tumor disappear in this brief period while leaving the patient biologically intact. Let us assume, finally, that several features of consciousness involving Sarah's clarity and sincerity of *intent* and John's *readiness* to let go and receive appear to be key ingredients in the successful outcome. So Sarah prays and, nonlocally, John heals.

What does energy-talk have to do with this unusual phenomenology of consciousness? On the surface of it, nothing. But what Dossey is implicitly drawing attention to is the mind-body problem itself. Superficially, energy-talk has nothing to do with thoughts, expectations, or memories, either. We understand these things quite independently of scientific theories about their electromagnetic, quantum, or neurological correlates.

But where is the *conflict* between energy-talk and consciousness? From the fact that consciousness (nonlocal or otherwise) is a necessary feature of an adequate theory of healing, it does not follow that energy (electromagnetic or otherwise) must be excluded. They may very well be different levels or ways of describing the same phenomena, just as theories of perception involve reference both to angstroms and to colors. Finding a way to make energy and consciousness fit together in a comprehensive paradigm is a challenge. But the perceived lack of such a paradigm is not a good reason to conclude that energy-talk and consciousness-talk are mutually exclusive.

At a deeper level, Dossey may have unwittingly traded on an ambiguity in the concept of nonlocality as the term is used in discussions of the EPR effect and Bell's theorem (described in Chapter Seven). A nonlocal connection between A and B means that the connection, first of all, is instantaneous, and secondly, for that reason is without *causal* mediation (since the jump from any cause to its effect takes time).

Now, if a scientist doing healing research could show that the connection between, say, prayerful intent and distant tumor elimination were instantaneous, we could more readily move to the conclusion that no mediating causal mechanisms were involved. To the best of my knowledge, however, no one has ever shown that any healing connections are literally instantaneous. Hence, the inference that healing connections are not causally mediated does not necessarily follow. Indeed, since any effect between healer and healee does appear to take time, the reverse inference is warranted; healing connections *are* causally mediated, although perhaps in ways and through dimensions that we do not understand.

In conclusion, if healing connections are both causally mediated and not instantaneous, we have less reason to describe the consciousness involved as "nonlocal," except in the *loose* sense that, beginning with someone's intent, anomalous distant effects are recorded. And if we have no reason to describe the consciousness involved in healing phenomena as *strictly* nonlocal, then we cannot claim, as Dossey does, that local energy-talk is in conflict with presumably nonlocal consciousness-talk in healing and other paranormal contexts. If Dossey's thesis were just that distant healing effects are causally mediated by elements of consciousness that, at transpersonal levels in the Great Chain of Being may have undetected energetic correlates, I would agree. But he seems to have something stronger in mind, namely, that distant healing effects are not *causally* mediated at all.

Third, Dossey also objects to energy-talk in healing contexts because it covertly implies a *dualistic* contrast with consciousness, involves *Newtonian* cause-and-effect relations, and finally, conflicts with both *quantum* physics and nondualistic spiritual traditions. I think this may be a case of pinning not altogether fair labels on the opposition.

One can talk about energy in many ways on many levels, both within and outside of healing contexts. In this book I have for the most part adopted the language of frequencies, waveforms, interference patterns, and phase coherence, all of which are grounded in quantum physics, not the mechanistic causal chains of Newton's worldview. These can be applied to all types of contexts, paranormal and otherwise. There are equally many ways of thinking about causal relations, including the fact that we are all interconnected at transpersonal levels of the Great Chain of Being. The mere fact that one thinks events are in *some* way causally related does not commit one to any particular conception of causality, much less a mechanistic one. As I explained in Chapter Six, the higher we go in the Great Chain, in this case to instances of distant spiritual healing, the more natural it is to describe events in terms of consciousness, rather than of energy— much less physical energy. But energy is still an aspect of consciousness, just as consciousnes is of energy.

Finally, it seems to me that the spectre of some type of dualism—not necessarily a Cartesian or Newtonian one—is still knocking at Dossey's door. Presumably Dossey believes that both consciousness and (physical) energy exist. How exactly does he put them together? Is consciousness reducible to energy? Presumably not. Is energy a subset of consciousness? Is consciousness something other than energy? If so, why is this not a kind of dualism? The fact that energy-talk in healing contexts is partly metaphorical, and that consciousness plays a stronger role than some researchers assume, hardly allows one to escape dualism.

If Dossey were clairvoyant and could see the sometimes "yucky" stuff that healers pull out of people, what would he call it, especially when it is correlated with the release of a thought-form relating to some aspect of consciousness, say, low self-esteem? "Energy" seems a reasonable term, even if not a type reducible to the four forces of nature. "Energy-consciousness" is perhaps even better, since only one thing is happening, but from two different perspectives.

Such considerations are what partly moved me in the direction of the dual-aspect theory of energy-consciousness defended in earlier chapters. Each is an irreducible aspect of the other, one inner, the other outer. This theory may ultimately fall to cogent criticism. But it avoids the problems of classical dualism that Dossey is concerned with, and is consistent with phenomena on many levels of the Great Chain of Being, from quantum to transpersonal. For readers of Chapter Seven, it will be evident that this multidimensional view of the stuff of reality is also consistent with the *non-dualistic* conceptions of Source that inform major spiritual traditions.

Types and levels of healing. When it comes to clarity regarding types of healing, the entire field is a terminological mess. This confusion is fueled by underlying philosophical controversy. For reasons of convenience, some healers allow themselves to be pictured in the public's eye in a manner that is not fully integrated with their actual practices. Other healers simply "do" it without knowing what is transpiring behind the scenes.

Some healers view themselves as conduits for divine energy and place themselves in loving relationships with their clients. Some do little themselves except call in spirit guides and doctors. Others move their hands in precise ways as if they were performing surgery on an invisible body. Many practice more than one type of healing. As Stanley Krippner explains in *Healing States* and more recently in *Spiritual Dimensions of Healing* (with special attention given to shamanistic practices), healing is a far more complex picture than the public stereotype implies.[31]

It is not even clear to what extent there is a transfer of anything between healer and client or, if there is, how it should be understood. For example, does the energy transferred directly affect the client's condition? Or does it simply empower one to heal oneself via some hidden dynamic? Despite this complexity and the inevitable political sensitivity over how one's practice is portrayed, certain critical distinctions should be kept in mind. All healing is not the same.

In general, we may say that psychic (or "magnetic") healers address such tasks as balancing chakras, clearing auras, and revitalizing the flow of ch'i or "life" energy throughout the body. They usually possess some degree of clairvoyance or clairsentience. In principle, you could clear an aura without seeing or feeling what you were doing, but it would be difficult to know how successful you were. Psychic healers typically have a spiritual orientation, but it's unlikely to enter directly into their practices. They do not pray over you or with you and ask nothing from you by way of such commitment.

Other than simply sending energy, they generally do not work directly on specific or local physical problems, such as cancer of the pancreas. If they do, they are actually practicing etheric surgery but for their own reasons have allowed the label of psychic healer to prevail. (In truth, few healers are entirely comfortable with any label, partly because where they started out is not where they are now.) While there are some exceptions, such as Ro-Hun therapy, psychic healers typically do not work directly with emotional release and reintegration or with spiritual imbalances, although they may share insights from these levels with the client.

Most forms of psychic healing are to some degree teachable. This is the premise of established programs such as Reiki, Polarity, Meridian therapy, and Therapeutic Touch. Naturally, these schools prefer their own labels and some, especially Therapeutic Touch, integrate strong spiritual components as well. But the literature and workshops associated with these schools strongly suggest that their primary focus is with forms of energy not far removed from the physical level—what I have termed the "bioetheric" but which may also be termed "bioplasmic," "biomagnetic," "life energy," or "ch'i." Whenever analogies are drawn between healing energy and electromagnetic energy (warmth, flow, buzzing, the capacity to alter biological processes), psychic healing is often the type involved. A different label for one's favorite therapy does not automatically imply a different kind of healing energy.

From the perspective of the Great Chain, psychic healing is a lower-end approach. Of course, virtually nobody connected with healing will warm to this portrayal of matters. So you will find plenty of other labels attached to the practice of magnetic healing. The distinction between upper- and lower-end approaches, however, need not imply any political judgments or relations of superiority and inferiority. Healing at the psychic or biomagnetic level can produce results which are both more immediate and more dramatic. Moreover, psychic healing is often incorporated within higher echelons of spiritual healing and etheric surgery.

As the name implies, spiritual healing is primarily concerned with healing the spirit. It also integrates more of a religious or spiritual framework into the practice itself. A session may begin, for example, with some version of the following prayer: "Dear Lord (Great Spirit, Father/Mother God, etc.), make me an instrument of your healing power in helping to make this spirit whole and channeling your energy to where it is needed, for the highest good of all concerned." Coincident with this prayer, the healer will lay hands on various parts of the body.

An evangelical Christian healer will typically want to align you with Jesus in this endeavor and will make success or failure turn on considerations of grace and worthiness. A nondenominational spiritual healer, by contrast, is less concerned with your specific religious commitments and is inclined to translate the language of grace and sin into the psychological parameters of removing or holding on to the blocks to healing, whatever they may be. There is no reason to believe that either approach is intrinsically more effective than the other.

Spiritual healers may experience unusual feelings or perceptions in their work. But as a group they are not especially clairvoyant. They don't need to be, since they are primarily conduits and the work is being done by someone or something else. They are critical facilitators of the healing process. All spiritual healers are united in the belief that healing the "upper levels" of spirit and mind is necessary for effective long-term healing of the body.

You might experience a dramatic remission of a malignant tumor at the hands of either a psychic or spiritual healer. But unless you deal with the misperceptions, negative attitudes, emotional traumas, or fractured soul which underlie physical deterioration, you can expect a recurrence sooner or later. Many of the factors which affect the success of spiritual healing are described in Dora Kunz's compilation of major practitioners and commentators in *Spiritual Aspects of the Healing Arts*.

The Mahikari School of spiritual healing emphasizes the importance of top down healing—from the level of Spirit. After several lectures and demonstrations at the local Mahikari Center, I came away with the belief that, despite the theoretical overlay, what was actually being shown and taught had more to do with psychic than with spiritual healing. Readers interested in exploring this issue further should consult A.K. Tebecis's *Mahikari*, which contains interesting case studies and practical tips for healers-in-training. Whether genuine spiritual healing can be taught to the many, as opposed to awakened in the few, is not at all clear.

It is ironic that many schools or individuals who carry the spiritual label will produce lower-end phenomena as evidence of upper-end changes. With Mahikari, for example, it is food which should have decayed but, after a healing treatment, remained comparatively fresh for weeks or even months. I am sympathetic to the need to do this as a means of giving the skeptic something tangible. However, we should be cautious in deriving any theoretical interpretation from such phenomena.

A third type of healing, etheric surgery, is one of the most interesting and problematic. As the label implies, etheric surgeons are the technicians of the group. They add and subtract energies, split them, refine them, reintegrate them, and move them in sometimes very delicate ways. They may specifically work on your optic nerve, your pancreas, or a childhood emotional trauma. Etheric surgeons must be strongly clairvoyant for the obvious reason that they have to see what they are doing!

They are not psychic surgeons, a phrase usually reserved for Phillipine (and some Brazilian) healers who claim to open and close the client's flesh. From an etheric surgeon's standpoint, the sheer energy requirements of such continued feats of psychokinesis would be very disruptive to the healer's own emotional and physical condition. Besides, such feats are unnecessary when you can work at a more refined biomagnetic level and produce comparable results.

If this in-house debate strains your credulity, aspects of etheric surgery will push you over the edge. For we are given to believe that better etheric surgeons may work in their bodies or out of their bodies! When they are without a physical body of their own, etheric surgeons are spirit doctors who assist other embodied healers and physicians. Sometimes they will work through another person's body while that person is in trance. However, unless there is a karmic relationship between the channel and the (disembodied) spirit doctor, there is little advantage in conducting matters thusly, save certain refinements of perspective and producing phenomena for unbelievers.

Why take on a lifetime body when you can pursue your life's work, so to speak, out of body? Well, for the same reason everyone else does. Even spirit doctors get the blues. Which is a roundabout way of reminding ourselves that they have other issues to work on—fear, scarcity, sexuality— which are easily magnified on a physical level. Most healers do holy work. But holy healers are in short supply.

Some etheric surgeons specialize in physical disease and illness, while others work primarily on emotional and spiritual-level issues. But whatever their level of specialization, the better surgeons "see" by refocusing their consciousness on the interdimensional spectrum constituting the individual person. Each level is as distinctive and objective to them as successive levels under a powerful microscope would appear to us. (Imagine, for example, five levels, each of which is distinguished from its neighbor by a power of one thousand.)

No matter what the terminology, I cannot stress too much the importance of perspective within the Great Chain as a fruitful way of understanding the kind of healing you may be seeking. A psychic healer, spiritual healer, and etheric surgeon may each work on your heart chakra from different levels. However, what each sees or experiences, what you personally experience, and the overall results of the work will vary accordingly. Just as all religions are not the same, all healing is not the same.

Is it teachable? Most forms of psychic healing can be learned to some degree by the average person. At one time, for example, I became fairly proficient in relieving pain. Etheric surgery and most forms of spiritual healing, however, cannot be effectively taught without presuming some highly advanced capacities which are unfolding according to their own dynamics. They can be awakened, if they are already there. But they exist in a realistically birthable form, so to speak, in far fewer individuals than the more common skills needed for general "balancing of energies."

There are a number of excellent training programs for healing in America, among them those directed by Robert Jaffe and by Barbara Brennan. Brennan's *Hands of Light* and *Light Emerging* are widely recommended in healing contexts. (Notably, both Brennan and Jaffe are clairvoyant.) Students in such programs become more sensitive to human energy fields and learn quasi-standard procedures for identifying and clearing energy blocks and for channeling healing energy. They learn to feel energy to varying degrees. And most graduates use these skills as adjuncts in their personal lives and health professions.

The training is effective and vital. But few graduates become full-time practicing healers, capable of supporting themselves with this work alone. This is partly because few are strongly interdimensionally clairvoyant (seeing auras is barely the tip of the iceberg). And few have the inherent power to reach through the dimensions, as it were, and produce the kind of sophisticated energetic changes necessary for major physical and emotional healing. They can, of course, call for assistance from spirit doctors or even from angels, but so could anyone without extensive training in healing.

While major world-class healers typically have attended some workshops on healing and read widely on the subject, most were not trained by someone else. Their abilities unfolded essentially from the inside. This latent unfolding appears to be accelerating on a global scale. Training programs for healers seem best suited to nurturing and structuring this evolutionary leap forward.

How much is attributable to the placebo effect? How one responds to this question greatly depends upon the context in which it is asked. For example, if you are interested in the general nature of healing and in healing relationships, a constructive inquiry into the patient's power of belief or expectation in the process is vital. In this arena, we have to deal with a wide range of factors that bear upon how we make ourselves healthy or sick in the first place.

For example, there are fascinating studies indicating that even the physician's own expectations and relationship to the patient can influence the outcome of a treatment. And through hypnosis, people can reverse the symptoms, if not the underlying pathology, of a variety of diseases, thus suggesting that there is a powerful "healer within" that can be accessed in a variety of ways. Since the placebo effect cuts across all healing contexts, we should assume that it's operative to some extent in psychic and spiritual healing, too.[32]

The atmosphere, however, is not always this constructive. In drug trials, for example, the placebo effect is ideally to be gotten rid of. And in clinical practice, physicians tend to view it as undermining their own control of the healing process—a qualitative intangible which can mean the difference between success and failure. Finally, it may be used as a convenient scapegoat to explain away all instances of psychic or spiritual healing that appear to be effective. This attitude itself deserves to be dismissed. Here are four reasons why.

To begin, let us agree that some type of placebo is effective in spiritual or energetic healing contexts. Beyond that, nobody knows how much or has a clear grasp of all the factors which turn it on or off. It is not entirely honest, therefore, to presume that all seemingly effective spiritual healing is nothing but a mobilization of the patient's own belief system. For all we know, healing energy could be the factor in triggering that mobilization. This need not be an either-or situation.

Second, it does not account for the fact that nonbelievers or outright skeptics may be the beneficiaries of psychic or spiritual healing. If correct, skeptics could greatly strengthen their case in this regard, by designing and funding some experiments using first-rate healers and multiple controls for the power of skeptical belief. But they appear uninterested in putting the matter to a fair test, even on their own behalf.

Third, the skeptical hypothesis involving placebos does not account for the demonstrable effects that healers have been able to achieve on nonhuman subjects, such as mice, enzymes, or the surface tension of liquids. Presumably none of these have belief systems to influence the outcome of the experiments.

Fourth, it is widely conceded that the practice of medicine itself involves a fairly strong reliance upon the placebo effect. It has even been observed that the history of medicine *is* the history of the placebo effect. Some current medical prescriptions are not much more than ten to fifteen percent more effective than placebos! If so, where is the fairness in a physician's charging a patient for his own reliance upon the placebo effect, but dismissing an etheric surgeon on the grounds that she is merely dispensing placebos in those cases where the patient improves?

There are legitimate concerns about would-be healers who claim to diagnose and cure major diseases independently of medical analysis and treatment. However, I am suggesting only that we factor the healer into the total picture (including medicine). Few would pretend that such alternative practices are the only picture. The question is not whether healers who advise you not to see a doctor are dangerous. They surely are. It is whether effective healers who work in conjunction with traditional medicine are merely dispensing expensive placebos and whether, if they were, such a practice would be any more unjustified than the practices of physicians who rely upon the same effect.

Were the clients going to improve anyway? It is a standard statistic that, if left untreated, most diseases or illness would either self-correct or not get any worse. I have seen this figure given as high as seventy percent. This fact can be used to dismiss psychic and spiritual healing on the grounds that any improvements were destined to occur anyway, with or without the healer. However, we may just as easily turn this statistic around. How many physicians do you know who turn away patients on the grounds that they will probably get better anyway? Put differently, if only twelve percent of all illnesses are curable by drugs or surgery, and many of these are made worse by such strategies, then who should be pointing the finger at whom?

As physician Norman Shealy observes, to reject alternative healing in favor of biological determinism aided by drugs or surgery fails to grasp the significance of this statistic. It also underestimates the critical importance of self-regulation which may be aided by almost anything, including spiritual healing. The issue isn't spiritual versus biological curing. It is how best to mobilize the mechanisms of self-regulation and self-healing. Shealy sees the real role of medicine as one of ruling out the ten to fifteen percent of all life-threatening illnesses which can be medically cured.

> Once we know that no such [life-threatening] problem exists, then the critical need is to...mobilize the belief

system of the patient—to reduce every conceivable stress and to teach self-regulation to control the malfunctioning autonomic nervous system that is responsible for most illnesses. Indeed, biofeedback and self-regulation training bring under control 80% of illness.[33]

The healer-patient continuum: a sliding scale of responsibility. It is common in holistic health circles to stress the importance of shared responsibility between the health care provider and patient. However, this approach can run up against a "heads-I-win, tails-you-lose" logic with psychic or spiritual healing in particular. The reasoning occurs frequently enough to merit separate attention.

Suppose you go to a healer who, as the saying goes, gives it her best shot. You experience some symptom relief, nothing else. Frustrated, you inquire why it doesn't seem to be working after several weeks. The healer explains that you are blocking the energy by holding on to something that you are not prepared to let go of. Exactly what the block is, however, remains a mystery. Note that in such scenarios, the failure is made essentially your responsibility. Had it been successful, you often would have found the healer taking more credit.

Were we to let the matter drop here, a simple standoff might be the result. Let us assume, however, that with no further changes in your attitudes or physical symptoms you seek out another healer whom the grapevine describes as "really powerful." You are skeptical, but you make the plunge. Sure enough, your symptoms dramatically disappear in two days, and lab tests indicate no remaining pathology. What happened to your blocks? Did they just disappear on their own, even though you never knew what they were? Or was the second healer truly more powerfully able to break through those blocks?

It is possible that in the intervening two weeks you crossed into the point of critical readiness, making it possible for the second healer of equal ability to trigger an effect where the first could not. But common sense tells us that this is more likely to happen over a longer period, when you have consciously dealt with your underlying blocks. It is far less likely to happen in several days. The fact that this can happen even sometimes means that there are real differences between healers. Some are more powerful with certain illnesses. Some are not.

If we do not assume some power differential between healers, then anybody can set up shop and put his lack of results on your shoulders. Besides, there are some people in such a terrible condition that to begin by telling them to work on their issues is tantamount to telling them to jump off a bridge, which may be what they feel like doing anyway. In such situations, only a powerful healer with great love and compassion may be effective.

This is not to suggest that we do not have responsibility for looking at blocks to our healing. It is to suggest that healers who too quickly account for all lack of results by appealing to *your* blocks in all probability have some issues of their own to look at. It is to suggest that, if we are going to adopt the duality of success or failure, then the relative proportion of healing power to healing blocks will occupy a sliding scale of values between different healers and their clients. It is to suggest that in the healing relationship, there is often much to be given and received by the healer *and* the patient.

Does healing ever fail? There is a perspective on healing which suggests that success or failure in curing illness is not the primary agenda. Any health care practitioner can adopt this perspective, and perhaps someday most will. For now, however, the questions it raises are most likely to be encountered in the domain of spiritual healing.[34]

According to this perspective, the fundamental goal in life is to become whole in as many ways as we can. One of the critical facilitators of this process is learning to give and receive unconditional love. And as Larry Dossey describes in *Healing Words*, the person sending you the love through prayer does not need to physically touch you or even be in the same geographical area in order to be effective.

Without love, we eventually die of broken hearts or withering bodies or alienated souls. The irony is that, at our very deepest and transpersonal levels, unconditional love is eternally ours for the asking. However, we have lost the experience of that connection. We don't know what to ask for or how to ask for the kind of love we want. We receive reminders that it exists, but the fully integrated connection is left unfulfilled.

Enter the spiritual healer who, on this view of things, has the primary task of helping to open the primary channels to our deepest levels through the power and example of unconditional love. Studies at the Institute of HeartMath suggest that a loving emotional state actually renders the electrical patterns of the heart more orderly and coherent. And this coherence in turn is linked to increased levels of salivary immunoglobin-A, a key player in healthy immune system response.[35] Over and above such physical effects, however, *unconditional love never fails to promote wholeness on some level.* According to this perspective, healing to some degree can occur on levels with which one was not in touch or, for that matter, still may not be. Physical cure may accompany the journey toward wholeness. Or it may not. One can die of cancer far more whole than one was six months earlier.

One of the most difficult lessons of life is to accept a healing on the inside that does not translate into a miracle of physical healing on the outside. Perhaps the greatest inner healing that can occur is the removal of blocks to loving oneself—the realization that one is worthy of unconditional love, whether by oneself or by others.

Even if death is on the horizon, it is perhaps better to be loved and substantially healed on the inside than to be physically cured on the outside, while still feeling fragmented and worthless on the inside. Sometimes a dramatic physical reversal may be evidenced. At other times, this realization is the last lesson before moving on. In either case, however, the journey toward wholeness will always be nurtured by a spiritual healer whose powers are grounded in compassion and unconditional love.

CHAPTER TWELVE

Paradigm Wars:
Abortion, Education, and the Environment

Paradigm wars are all around us. Few are as widespread or as profound in their potential implications for the average citizen as those found in the areas of abortion, education, and the environment. In this chapter, we will explore how reincarnation sheds light upon the standoff between pro-life and pro-choice advocates, how holistic education honors the magical child/student, and how perennialism complements the systems thinking that dominates the environmental movement.

REINCARNATION AND ABORTION:
WHEN DOES A FETUS BECOME A PERSON?

Imagine moderating a debate between pro-choice and pro-life advocates, when a reincarnationist enters the scene with a whole different way of casting the issue. "Interesting," "explosive," and "confusing" are three terms which come to mind in describing such a situation. I realize that some readers will feel that I am treading unnecessarily where informed writers have already carved out the territory. Being in favor of holistic health is relatively safe. Even appearing to take sides in the abortion debate, however, automatically gets one into trouble with a major segment of the population.

My intent is not to argue pro-choice or pro-life. However, we need some enlightenment—some semblance of a position on hard moral questions—from those who count themselves a part of the Rising Culture. Simply projecting "love and light" on all parties in this dispute will not take us very far.

My thoughts on this issue obviously do not represent any official New Paradigm position, for there isn't any such thing. One can belong to the Rising Culture and not have a position on either abortion or reincarnation (although this is unlikely). My intent, therefore, is merely to examine the implications of reincarnation for abortion. Those who already have strong positions on abortion will read this section with the reverse implication in mind. For them, metaphysics must first pass the test of political correctness. In contrast, I believe that insisting upon either a fetus's or a woman's right in this arena already assumes one of several underlying conceptions of human nature.

Why the metaphysics of personhood is still important. Abortion is often discussed as if it were mainly, if not exclusively, a question of rights.[1] Pro-choice groups typically stress the absolute right of a woman to control her own body. Personal autonomy is, and ought to be, inviolable. Pro-life groups, by contrast, point to the fetus's right to life and conclude that terminating this right is tantamount to murder. Yet pro-choice defenders do not see it as a question of murder; when they think "fetus" they think of a biological form, not of a "miniature person." To them, it's inconceivable that such an entity should have rights that take precedence over those of the woman.

The critical question then is this. By virtue of what characteristic does a fetus possess or fail to possess the requisite rights? This question cuts across both schools of thought. On the one hand, the pro-choice position is absolutely committed to the assumption—which many of its defenders do not discuss—that the fetus *crosses a threshold* into miniature personhood, after which time abortion is not morally justified. Anyone who believes that termination at seven and a half months is morally wrong—which the great majority of pro-choice advocates do—must assume that this threshold has been crossed, even if it cannot be identified. There comes a point where a fetus *does* have a right to continue. Pro-choice advocates typically concede this.

What about this threshold, or "magical moment," as I have heard it described? Actually, it might be a day, several days, or even a week. However, it does occur at some point. It's just that there are no objective criteria for making the determination. Functional kidneys, livers, hearts, and brains are all equally necessary for continued life. Why should a more developed heart at the second month, rather than a less developed brain, be made the standard of miniature personhood?

To continue, why should six months be the legal cutoff point when assisted viability outside the womb has already been established at four months? And if unassisted viability is the criterion, then we would have a fairly large number of newborn babies who could not meet the test and who thus would be candidates, in principle, for termination if other considerations dictated. Nobody on the pro-choice side will argue that newborns on respirators can be terminated if their mothers decide they should be. Medical science can declare a threshold, but that is not the same thing as discovering it. The Supreme Court (*Roe* v.*Wade*) can create an artificial line of viability by decree, but that is not the same thing as finding the difference between a fetus with a right to life and a fetus without that right.

The pro-choice position is therefore implicitly committed to the thesis that determining whether unjustified killing has taken place depends upon criteria (viability, brain waves, heart development, etc.) which can only be subjectively or arbitrarily applied at many different stages of development. To make life and death turn on a hypothetical "maybe" is not an enviable position. Pro-choice advocates thus hang an important moral position in metaphysical limbo. Abortion is permissible so long as the fetus is not a miniature person, but they cannot objectively say when that would be.

The implications of pro-life are also more strained than its proponents (especially those with a strong religious grounding) typically concede. Unable to draw an objective line for personhood during pregnancy, they urge that it begins at conception. But once conceived, why does an embryo have the right to continue? What is it about this unrecognizable person that makes it so special?

From a religious perspective, it must be essentially the same thing that makes children and adults special, namely, the existence of a soul. If a fetus didn't have a soul until it was born and God "breathed" life into it, then it is hard to see why abortion should be labeled as murder. For all we would have, indeed, is protoplasm minus the critical ingredient of person-hood, a soul.

Now souls have to come from somewhere. And if God creates souls at the appropriate time to match each conception, then we are faced with some unpleasant moral questions. Why would He create a soul that He knew, since He is omniscient, would be cast out through abortion two months later? Why would He put souls into future thirteen-year-old victims of rape? And why, if He is any kind of caring God at all, should we not assume that He would look after these young two-month-old souls and take them directly to Heaven or see that they receive another suitable body? Since the souls would have no time to grow and learn to love their creator in the same testing ground as their peers, why go through this diversionary process anyway? He could simply destroy them after they were aborted, but this would make no sense whatsoever.

It appears, then, that we are faced with the following situation. Either fetuses do not have souls until they are born, in which case it is impossible to morally differentiate in principle between aborted chimp and human fetuses. Or if they do have souls from the time of conception, then either God is immoral (assuming God is omniscient) or God is engaged in meaningless diversions. So far as the morality of abortion is concerned, the religious right does not have a coherent theology of incarnation.

Now one could be both a materialist and an atheist and still be pro-life; conservative Christianity has not co-opted all the territory. But one would then face problems similar to those already raised. Why should conception serve as the line of demarcation, rather than, say, three months? Why is a three-month human fetus any more or less deserving of abortion than a chimp fetus?

Suppose we could manufacture (with no natural sperm or egg) tiny protoplasmic fetuses, DNA and all, by the thousands. If you argue that the human fetus has a *greater potential* than the chimp's, then you need to explain how it possesses this potential, since the genetic codes are ninety-nine percent identical. It is also important for the (nonreligious) pro-life materialist to explain why six-month fetuses do not have greater potential than freshly conceived ones, since, if they do, the argument for drawing the line at conception is considerably weakened.

Both pro-life and pro-choice proponents, of course, believe that their positions are self-evident and that the opposition is a moral abomination. This intractability is possible, I believe, because both positions share a deeply rooted assumption so pervasive that few would ever think to call it into question. The assumption is this: *Whatever it is about fetuses that merits a right to continue must itself have a local beginning in time.* However, when we look for that beginning on either physical or spiritual levels, we are faced with the logical dead-ends just described.

The assumption of "local beginnings" is so much a part of Western thought that for many it's a matter of simple common sense. A corollary of this assumption is the belief that we are fundamentally distinct from one another, not one in spirit or anything else. What has a local beginning, so the thinking goes, must also have a local place in which to begin.

New Paradigm thinking, whether informed more by the Perennial Wisdom or by Systems Holism, questions this kind of localizationist or atomistic outlook. So does reincarnation. And while reincarnation is not an essential aspect of all that qualifies as New Paradigm thought, it is an increasingly widespread and independently supportable theme with profound implications for abortion. It is certainly one of the clearest alternatives to the assumption of local (personal) beginnings. For a reincarnated soul has been around a long time. It neither begins at conception nor ends with abortion.

The question of rights. Before describing the dynamics of incarnation vis-à-vis abortion, let me return briefly to the question of rights. How do we view, in light of the doctrine of reincarnation, the rights of women to control their bodies and of fetuses to continue living? From a larger perspective of spiritual evolution, rights do not occupy the absolute foundational place that they do for most schools of thought. They ebb and flow with the forces of history and culture.

Convincing those in power to agree—whether by force or negotiation—that you have certain rights is not the same thing as demonstrating that God has put the Holy Seal on them. The only absolute right we have is the right to decide what we are to do within the parameters of the circumstances we find ourselves in, which includes the right to attempt to convince others that we have the rights we think we do.

The expansion of human rights over the past several thousand years is not a discovery of what has been waiting all along. Rather, it is a series of gradually integrated desires for greater contextual *freedom*—for representative government, free speech, speedy trials, religious tolerance, etc. More rights mean less restriction. The history of rights movements is the story of how the quest for more contextual freedom is faring. Rights are the "placemarkers" along the way.

The question now becomes, "Freedom for what?" One can always choose merely to hold on to what one has, or to stagnate. Or one can devote one's energies to establishing greater freedom from oppressive restriction so that others may profit. Overall, however, the answer to that question is, "To grow or evolve." From a reincarnational perspective, personal transformation and spiritual evolution are the reasons we are here. Within this larger perspective, rights are *transformational tools, not absolute ends in themselves.* Once one has the right of free association, walking safe streets, worshiping as one pleases, and so forth, the critical question in the background is always, "What are these rights to be used for?"

With these observations in mind, the question of fetal versus women's rights undergoes a radical transformation. On the one hand, women (and men) have only a relative right to control their own bodies to the extent that this idea can be integrated in communal consciousness. Their absolute right, so to speak, is to decide what they want to do or attempt to do (if abortions are proscribed) in light of all of the factors which bear upon the past, present, and future of their pregnancy. For practical purposes, this absolute right to personal choice in general may be translated into the absolute right to control one's body in particular. But there is a difference. The latter can be taken away, the former cannot. Pro-choice means first and foremost pro-*choice*, and only secondarily pro-body.

Women ideally will make this decision with compassion, information, and sensitivity to the full range of transformational agendas and possibilities of all the beings concerned. It is a very important decision, not a routine backup to birth control. But no two situations are ever identical, and a decision regarding abortion can justifiably go either way.

The right to life, on the other hand, undergoes an even more radical reinterpretation under a reincarnational perspective. Very simply, a fetus doesn't have an absolute right to life either. One reason is that without a soul, an incarnate mind, it is merely a complex form of protoplasm, although worthy of respect and even awe. The accomplishments of biological evolution are not to be taken lightly. It is a potential vehicle for an "old" new mind. Abortion is therefore the denial of the use of the vehicle, but not murder.

Moreover, the soul itself cannot be killed. Nor does it have an inalienable right to a particular embryo. It does have the right to try to obtain what it thinks is best for its own evolution. However, that has to be worked out in light of the particular interests of the potential mother (and father) and those closely associated with her, whether now or later. Neither party has an absolute claim on the other.

I am not suggesting that fetuses do not have a right to life. Rather, I am suggesting that, from a reincarnational perspective, this idea collapses into incoherence. The reason is that the entity which merits the right already has *eternal life*, which cannot be taken away. And the physical body per se, while it merits our profound respect, doesn't merit an absolute right to continue in the first place.

My intent is not to argue pro-choice. Indeed, I have tried to show that, from a reincarnational perspective, the statement "Women have an absolute right to control their own body, which supersedes a fetus's right to life" is potentially as questionable as "Fetuses have an absolute right to life, which supersedes a woman's right to control her own body." Both sides, I believe, misconceive the nature of rights and the nature of personhood in ways that lead to the intractable debate we are faced with today.

The dynamics of incarnation. I close with a few observations about the timing of incarnation as it relates to the question of abortion. If incarnation took place universally, say, between three and a half and four months, we would have a clearer reason for preventing abortion after that point. However, the situation is more complex.

In the first place, reincarnationists generally agree that the timing of incarnation varies.[2] Everyone has their favorite candidates for upper and lower limits, ranging from conception to several days after birth. The prevailing belief is that most incarnations take place between three and eight months, conforming roughly to a Bell curve. Moreover, it's not an all-or-nothing proposition. We are given to believe that incarnation typically takes place by stages which progressively converge upon a relative point of no return. Fortunately, we do not need to come to any conclusions about either of these beliefs.

Within such a perspective, the range of factors which bear upon the decision to incarnate are more varied than might be supposed. In a typical situation, the abortion is foreseen and the soul/mind never enters in the first place. Or it may be well into the process but decide that the vehicle is not developing in a way suited to its life goals. Accordingly, it might pull back, thus triggering a miscarriage. Some souls might wish incarnation only for specialized purposes lasting for a few months and would enter knowing what the outcome would be.

Then, too, the would-be mother may change her mind after originally agreeing at an unconscious level to the arrangement; the freedom to choose is stressed on both sides of the equation. Sometimes a desperate "lower" spirit willing to take its chances might slip in during a period of vulnerability, through drug or alcohol abuse by the woman. And sometimes karmic priorities may undergo rearrangement.

Each of these scenarios, of course, raises numerous other questions and concerns. How does one determine whether a soul has incarnated and, if so, what its main goals are? (A variety of methods are available, but they in turn raise more questions than I can deal with here.) What I wish to stress is that, in all of these incarnational scenarios, questions about rights are not the only ones being asked.

Rather, the stage is a framework of negotiation where all affected parties put their interests and agendas on the table and attempt to arrive at the most optimal arrangement for the overarching purpose of growth and transformation. Sometimes the final outcome conforms to what we, from both transpersonal and limited perspectives, might label as optimal. And sometimes not; there will always be an element of mystery. But from a reincarnational perspective, working through this process is never wasted!

The farther reaches of prevention. Birth control, abstinence, and education are recommended ways of preventing pregnancy. However, another revolutionary proposal appears to be gaining limited acceptance among women. Briefly, the proposal is this: If you don't wish to become pregnant, then *will* yourself not to. (Men should participate in this process, too.) State clearly to yourself, the universe, your body, and to any lingering souls waiting for a vehicle that now is not the time, that you do not want a child, and that you are choosing not to become pregnant. You should then fully expect that you will not conceive.

This is clearly an exercise in the power of conscious intent to manifest physical differences. While in a class by itself, this proposal is related to the same kind of thinking that connects attitudes with physical disease, or loving "peace vibrations" with reduced crime rates. It's a very practical application of the dynamic laws of Great Chain metaphysics. There is, of course, no clear evidence that such a strategy works in the case of pregnancy. There are, however, women who believe that it works and who manage the sexual aspect of their relationships accordingly. Like so many unusual practices on the horizon of a Rising Culture, this one bears watching!

HONORING THE MAGICAL CHILD:
A MANIFESTO FOR HOLISTIC EDUCATION

The problems with the American educational system, aspects of which are reflected worldwide, are widely discussed and openly acknowledged. They are chronicled on the evening news, in numerous mainstream publications and official reports, such as *A Nation at Risk* (1983), *American Agenda: Report to the Forty-First President of the United States* (1989), and the Education Department's *America's Challenge: Accelerating Academic Achievement* (1991). They are also found in a growing number of reports and books of reform and alternative-minded organizations and individuals, including the *Holistic Education Review* and the clearinghouse and networking programs of New York City's Center for Collaborative Education and Seattle's New Horizons for Learning.

For a personal overview of this country's educational crisis, I strongly recommend reading John Gatto's (New York's 1990 Teacher of the Year) summary vision, "Our Children are Dying in Our Schools." For an equally compelling analysis combined with many constructive proposals that stress the importance of learning networks in a classroom-to-community environment, I also recommend James Moffett's *The Universal Schoolhouse: Spiritual Awakening Through Education*. The following are a few of the many challenges chronicled by those concerned with the future of education in America:[3]

1. average SAT scores seventy-five points below 1963 levels;
2. a quarter of our student population which fails even to graduate from high school, with a higher drop-out rate for African Americans and Hispanics;
3. an economy which will require seventy percent skilled service workers by the year 2000, undersupported by a fact-oriented education system that widens the gap;
4. drugs, violence, and crime; teacher alienation, demoralization, and burnout;
5. cultural illiteracy (a recent sampling of twenty-year-olds found that three out of five could not read a map or total a lunch bill);
6. a "chain of command" from school board to classroom that is hierarchical, often sexist, and almost always adversarial;
7. school boards more concerned with political and economic pressure than with empowering teachers and students;
8. pedagogy which assumes academic learning is qualitatively the same, just faster or slower;
9. fragmented curricula which do not connect students with the world, their culture, each other, or even with themselves;
10. high school and even college graduates who have no real skill in thinking, as opposed to merely citing statistics or repeating popular clichés;
11. a wasteland of colleges of education largely devoted to preserving the status quo, especially their role in the certification process;
12. a system in which half of all public school students in America cannot demonstrate competency in challenging material in english, mathematics, science, history, and geography;
13. a system in which few wish to claim responsibility for the completed product;

14. finally, a system which perpetuates the very assumptions of a dying worldview that have brought us to this time of crisis—especially competition, hierarchical control, fear, and nationalism.

The limitations of current responses. How do educational and political leaders perceive the problem? If the extraordinary national conference on the future of American education called by President Bush in 1990 is any indication, we are in trouble. The trouble stems not so much from flaws in the goals we hear proposed, as from a failure to ascertain real causes, question fundamental assumptions, and appreciate the wide range of systemic factors which bear upon the crisis.

The real work of the conference was conducted by subcommittees. So there is hope for a greater degree of enlightenment. The governors in attendance, however, seemed to believe that the main problem is that the United States is losing its competitive edge in the world. So we need more math, science, and computer skills to maintain our standard of living and not get "beat out" by the Japanese and Europeans.

What kinds of mainstream proposals have been floated from the governor's conference and elsewhere for dealing with the challenges just described? It is a familiar story. Teach more math and science. Teach more geography, since the average tenth grader apparently cannot locate Greece on a map. Teach more days of the year. Start teaching children earlier. Pay teachers more and offer good teachers more incentives. Graduate more minority students. Prepare more students for college entrance. Get parents more involved. Teach more communications skills. Establish national competency levels. Obtain tangible results, such as improved SAT scores, more quickly in order to prove to parents and taxpayers that administrators know what they are doing. Make teachers more accountable in ways that can be quickly demonstrated with more numbers and more paper. And, oh yes, lots more money!

These are the ways we are typically urged to save American education—with the accent on "more and more." Certainly, these proposals have some merit. However, if you look at the kinds of problems with which we are faced, the ways our leaders tend to conceptualize and interpret them, and the more-is-better assumption which underwrites the proposed solutions, you will see once again the dying root metaphors and assumptions of Western thought playing themselves out. Examples are easily come by:

1. Fear ("If you don't learn this, you will fail," "If we don't accept more accountability, we will lose our jobs");

2. Competition ("If I make a C, I won't get into law school," "You better pad your budget requests, otherwise the scientists will take it all for their labs");
3. Reductionism and linear causality ("The earlier we start teaching children, the bigger the jump we get on the whole process," "Smith has been determined to be a 14.2 percent more effective teacher than Jones");
4. Fragmentation ("What does American history have to do with getting a job?" "What does art have to do with anything?");
5. Hierarchy and control ("I'm here to teach and you are here to learn," "Men are better able to make the necessary tough board decisions").

National curricular standards should be implemented. However, it will turn into a tragicomedy if other questions are not addressed. What happens to those who don't meet the standards? Are we still in a win-lose modality? How do we guarantee better quality education to achieve those standards? Surely not by requiring more education courses of our teachers. And how are nationally standardized tests supposed to measure many of the skills necessary for success in the nineties and beyond? Surely not just more math problems and logic puzzles. And are we to assume, in spite of massive evidence to the contrary, that all types of learning take place at the same rate in all individuals? National curricular goals very easily can become just fragmented Old Age goals dressed up for the millennium!

The need for deep structural changes. Responses to these challenges which hold onto fragmentation, hierarchy, and competition at best postpone the darker implications a little longer. At worst, they accelerate the already documented decline. By contrast, those proposals which reflect an awareness of shifting worldviews and new guiding assumptions—compassion, holism and larger systemic interconnectedness, mutually empowering cooperation—stand a greater chance of success.

My proposals reflect the values of a Rising Culture. A few are mildly novel. Most have been described by others in more detail than space allows me to develop. Carol Flake's collection of readings, *Holistic Education: Principles, Perspectives, and Practices,* is a comprehensive introduction to the philosophy of holistic education. Many holistic practices are already in effect in certain private schools (among them Atlanta's Paideia School), a very few public ones, and various systems of alternative education such as Montessori. The brightest light on the North American continent, so far as major public school systems are concerned, radiates from Ontario public schools in Canada. They model what education can be in the twenty-first century. They implement the theme of relatedness that educator Ron Miller, the founder of *Holistic Education Review*, describes as follows.

> The focus of holistic education is on relationships—the relationship between thinking and intuition, the relationship between mind and body, the relationships between various domains of knowledge, the relationship between individual and community, and the relationship between self and [cosmic] Self. In the holistic curriculum, the student examines these relationships so that he/she gains both an awareness of them and the skills necessary to transform [them] where appropriate.[4]

Most parents, teachers, and knowledgeable commentators realize that such a focus, together with specific methods of implementation, can work. Yet the problems they face are so interconnected that no single special interest group by itself seems capable of making much difference without the cooperation of the others. Because Systems Holism stresses so powerfully the connections of current social ills, it has a major role to play in the restructuring of American education, if not education globally. We cannot change just some assumptions of education without addressing all the others to which they are connected. Anything less is a prescription for stagnation.

1. The first proposal for change requires that we honor the magical child/student as a fundamental cornerstone of a new vision. It requires that we take human potential seriously for art, cognitive skills, insight, emotional and physical health and well-being, creative expression, memorization, and even unfolding psychic abilities! It invites us to develop a model of human potential that incorporates the insights of Systems Holism and the Perennial Philosophy such that courses not directly linked to getting a job and succeeding make sense. This is an invitation to base the teaching of art, music, literature, and philosophy on something other than cultural validation. After all, it doesn't make much sense to talk about nurturing spiritual or aesthetic potential if we are just machines. Any new vision of human potential in this arena must take into account the fact that children are not here merely to mirror our own knowledge and values back to us. They have their own agendas and contributions to make within a larger evolutionary unfolding.

2. Teachers exist to empower students according to their natural developmental stages, not just to dictate to them. Principals exist to empower teachers. And school boards exist to empower principals and teachers. This goal ought to be the ultimate standard of judgment. Unfortunately, in many school systems, empowerment seems to move in the reverse direction. The following proposals directly or indirectly relate to the goal of empowerment.

3. Children/students are empowered in many ways, but among the most important is the development of a healthy self-image. Students who feel good about themselves, believe in themselves, and come to see that they can meet challenges successfully nearly always achieve more than those who do not. With a healthy self-image, little is precluded; without one, little is possible. Development of such an image should therefore be a major continuing goal, especially in elementary school where patterns are being set. School boards must acknowledge—not just in their rhetoric, but in their budgets and policies—the importance of emotional and social development as well as intellectual achievement. Failure to do so undermines the democratic institutions they claim to support. Democracy works poorly if citizens are cynical, undermotivated, and unwilling to accept responsibility for their actions.

4. Radically revise or abolish most teacher certification programs and deregulate teaching. Encourage teacher exploration and innovation. If we must require some courses, then require the following: in-depth communications skills (not just Speech 101); a course in the many facets of intelligence and learning styles; a course, with personal exposure, in true master teaching, relative to area(s) and level. The rest will take care of itself. Recent Carnegie and Mellon Foundation studies all urge the integration of more liberal arts graduates into the school systems.

5. Require student-teachers to read mind-expanding classics from the human potential movement, e.g., Pearce's *Magical Child* and George Leonard's *Education and Ecstasy,* as well as leading-edge articles from the *Holistic Education Review* and related journals. Most colleges of education are producing robots, with no alternative vision whatsoever, designed mainly to perpetuate a bureaucratic system which, with few exceptions, stifles everything in its path. Pearce's more recent *Evolution's End* is a galvanizing indictment of how we are sabotaging our children's development and our society's future. It should be read by all university administrators and especially state legislators who oversee teacher training programs.

6. To see how many alternative ideas achieve integration in a concrete school setting, a visit to the local Montessori or Waldorf school is a good place to begin. To gain a sense of what is possible when the spiritual dimensions of human potential are taken most seriously, Chris Griscom's *Nizhoni: The Higher Self in Education* is an adventure in itself. If one is serious about pursuing a teaching degree at a prominent institution of higher learning, Antioch College is a pioneer and perennial leader in the area of holistic education.

7. Give school principals the authority to hire anybody they think will best get the job done, including high school graduates and other non-degreed specialists who may work on their own or with established teachers and be paid accordingly! Make the ability to produce a certain desired result as important in evaluation as what a piece of paper says you are supposed to have learned. Give principals real authority or else abolish the position, since it is progressively turning into one of pushing paper and resolving conflicts of interest.

8. In evaluating instruction, make the stimulation of interest and the development of demonstrable skills in students as important as the transfer of information to them. Value the teacher who makes biology exciting and develops the capacity in one's son or daughter to think scientifically—as much if not more than the teacher who covers twice as much subject matter. Get serious about learning styles. Our entire system of education is based upon a paradigm of linear and verbal transmission of information (permitting only minor deviations) which is optimally suited to less than half of all students.

9. Involve parents deeply and widely up and down the line. Do not assume they are good only for raising money and discussing social problems at PTA meetings. Treat parents as if they deeply cared and give them multiple options to work with. Parents can do plenty of things that principals and school boards assume should be assigned only to professionals. For openers, many can teach a class more effectively on a given day than the typical substitute teacher. The price of achieving more autonomy must be a willingness to share power.

10. Empower teachers and let them do what they are in the best position to do regarding curriculum, loads, school policy, experimenting with different texts and styles, etc. Reverse the emphasis from holding them accountable for everything they do, to supporting them in most things they do (or want to try). Release teachers from mindless mountains of paperwork. Most would prefer an extra hour at school doing individual and

small group conferences and exploring new ideas, in return for a fifty percent reduction in paperwork. Teachers need to feel good about what they are doing, and there is a cultural conspiracy to prevent this. The fervent desire of most teachers is to be freed from bureaucratic chains so that they, together with their students, can truly "stand and deliver."

11. Decentralize the whole educational system. Value differences as much as conformity. Take advantage of opportunities in the larger community to explore new learning experiences and establish working classrooms. Magnet schools are fifty years overdue. Build on strengths, interest, quality. Allow and encourage students and their parents to become involved in the school of their choice, whether next door or across town. Move to flextime scheduling if necessary. In the places where this has been seriously pursued, racial polarities and the need for quotas have tended to become far less pronounced. The rising home school movement is the ultimate extension of decentralizing public school systems.

12. Once there is agreement on overall content and skill goals for major levels, there are many different ways to get there. This typically requires moving to smaller size schools and classes and instituting a programmatic diversity which roughly matches student diversity of interest and ability. Every high school does not need average computer and performing arts programs, but one or two within a system can have the very best programs.

13. A good way to learn a subject is to instruct others in it. And every student is good at something that he or she can tutor other students in— even if at a lower grade level. Properly structured in more democratic and less competitive settings, with the fear of failure removed, this process can be both highly efficient and empowering for both students and teachers.

14. Integrate a program of affirmative social values into the curriculum by progressive level, grades K–12. This is not mind control or a hidden religious agenda. It is reflective common sense as we stand at the crossroads of our individual and collective evolution and see what will be needed to survive and thrive into the next century. Among more frequently discussed examples are:

a) Peace, nonviolence, constructive conflict-resolution
b) Global responsibility, shared resources
c) Universal ecological awareness
d) An end to poverty, homelessness, hunger, and illiteracy
e) An end to sexism, patriarchy, and hierarchies that control, rather than empower

f) Unmasking the thousand faces of fear

g) Loving, caring, being connected with each other and with the concrete results of our beliefs and actions

h) Self-nurturance and physical and emotional health (not just sex and drug education), preventive and environmental medicine

i) Understanding of what interdependence means on many levels, from local to global contexts

15. Integrate proven psychotechnologies into pedagogy. Be willing to experiment and adjust to changing circumstances. Get both sides of the brain working together. Meditation/relaxation techniques have demonstrated potential for reducing behavior problems and improving certain kinds of test scores. Visualization exercises have a potentially wide spectrum of applications, from improvement of self-image to sports performance. Integrated programs like Superlearning, which utilizes a combination of meditation and music, have a documented capacity to facilitate memory work (especially in learning foreign languages).

16. Make the first priority the creation of an atmosphere conducive to learning, where students both want to learn and where they discover how to keep educating themselves in different contexts. School officials will tell you that is what they are trying to do. However, they conceptualize this mandate in narrow ways, like increasing PTA membership and keeping the halls clear of drugs. In some schools, issues of alienation, failure, sex, alcohol and drug abuse, racism, and simple failure to communicate in meaningful ways are so powerful that they detract from everything else that is supposed to be happening in the student's intellectual life. It is not too much to ask for a school where failure, both personal and academic, eventually is converted into success.

17. Individual counseling is typically too little and too late. It's terribly inefficient. An elective class dealing with the above issues on a daily basis would have a far more dramatic effect on learning curves. It would not be hard to find volunteers from the Rising Culture to staff such classes. Students will learn and support each other in personal growth courses, if given half a chance. They will also be freer to concentrate on their academic subjects. If we can support driver education, we can surely support serious personal growth courses at the time when they are most needed. We cannot expect to achieve peace on an international level if we do not help students find peace on an individual and peer-group level.

18. In some areas, school violence (closely followed by alcohol and drug abuse) is the most powerful front-line challenge that we face. Increased

security, mandatory search procedures, and stiff penalties for offenders are often justified as emergency stop-gap measures. But the violence and self-abuse will continue—even if the National Guard polices every classroom—until the seething anger, fear, despair, and alienation that drive school violence are directly addressed. With courage, visionary leadership, interventions that go beyond what traditionally trained psychologists and school principals are accustomed to, and with the power of unconditional love, and a willingness to reexamine, if not abandon, the numerous labels that educators have invented to maintain order and justify their hierarchical mind-sets, even so-called "lost" children can be saved.

19. Finally, the unifying visions of Systems Holism and the Perennial Philosophy suggest many ways to overcome fragmented courses of study. Science does not have to conflict with spirituality, creativity, and intuition. Reading about the history of war can be accompanied by exercises in creative conflict resolution—even in the fourth grade! Art and music can be shown to reflect our deepest aspirations, not left hanging as "add-ons" perennially subject to budgetary cuts. Learning facts and theories can be integrated with learning practical skills for living and working. The curriculum can be gradually transformed into a coherent whole, which illustrates the principle that all things truly are interconnected. Then students can be given more effective answers to the question, "Why must I take math, or history, or english, or art, etc.?" More college professors can give up the illusion that teaching their research, preparing majors for graduate school (for nonexistent jobs), and mental masturbation are what our culture really values or needs, and they can spend more time helping their students make connections not only between their courses, but also between their courses and their lives.

The farther reaches of empowerment. In earlier chapters, I suggested that accelerated interdimensional integration is a fruitful transformational metaphor for our times. Let me now describe a few predictions for education that follow from this model.

First, we might begin to see those teachers on a path of love able to accomplish more with less, bordering at times on the miraculous. For example, we might see test scores in a certain class dramatically improve in ways which seem to have no connection to time spent studying or presenting information. The connection between self-image and learning will become a primary agenda item, not something to which we merely pay lip service. Is it so hard to imagine a school where students and teachers *care* about each other?

If so, a visit to one of Marva Collins's classes at Westside Preparatory School in Chicago (of which she is the founder) would raise awareness. Collins has a demonstrated capacity, by now the stuff of legend, to transform her students, even the most wayward, through the power of love. Her commitment to her students is totally unconditional. Other educators have studied her presumably innovative methods. But they come down to the fact that, as she explains, "I will not let you fail."

On the other hand, those on a path of fear will experience greater restriction and will have to work harder just to stay even, leading to self-destruction and chaos. Adversarial relationships, say, between unions and school boards, will become progressively more difficult to manage until they are transformed into cooperative relationships. Open rebellion will probably break out over meaningless paperwork. Let teachers teach.

I think we may also see sudden and large-scale shifts in school systems pushed to conditions far from equilibrium. Some systems may adopt very strange procedures and policies, seemingly from out of the blue, in order to escape to a higher order. For example, we may see such things as teacher-run schools, voluntary attendance, meditation/visualization at the beginning of each school day, and gifted twelfth graders assisting in teaching some subjects to ninth graders.

Other systems, sensing things growing out of control, may suddenly adopt draconian measures—meaning more control—in order to maintain equilibrium. They will lose out nonetheless. These changes will come without much warning, like the crumbling of the Berlin Wall, as if they had been in the making for some time. The net result will be radical decentralization.

Curricular changes that otherwise might take decades to institute will in some places achieve rapid integration. Mandatory courses in "Learning to Learn" and "Global Interdependence" will take the place of "Study Hall," "The American Way of Life," and the emphasis upon accumulating facts. History will be rapidly rewritten. Spiritual exploration will be tolerated, if not encouraged. Students will spend unequal amounts of time in different courses. Natural interests will be encouraged, rather than always forced into the typical six-period day. The time to learn is when there is the interest and motivation to learn. Basic skills will be taught through a greater diversity of course offerings. In other schools, of course, such courses of action will be resisted.

To continue, students, parents, and teachers may form often unpredictable alliances which they happen to find empowering, even if this means going against the authorities and forming small splinter groups, inside or outside of school rooms. So much of this may occur that school boards will not know what to do. In general, authorities who know how to empower others will thrive and those who don't will not. The stakes will go up on both sides.

Accelerated interdimensional integration can be expected to push a wide range of deviant experiences and behaviors to the surface. Because younger people are usually less fixed in their ways, this process will affect them more. Key Clubs may give way to Dream Exploration Clubs. High school band members may explore new ways to "get high" with music. Biology clubs may stress reverence for life in preference to cutting up animals. Children may even start doing hands-on healing of animals.

One trend is already established: the tendency of many children and teens to sharply question authority (both parents and teachers) or to shut down in the face of what are often perceived as exercises in mandatory irrelevance. Identity issues which my generation had the time to work out gradually now assume such burning significance that, for many teens, suicide is a reasonable thing to consider—even if not ultimately acted on.

From a reincarnational perspective, some of this questioning is caused by older and wiser souls (in younger bodies) feeling frustrated with the decaying beliefs and attitudes of their parents and teachers. But you don't have to be a reincarnationist to see that neither parents nor teachers are prepared to deal with the profound changes that are taking shape all around us.

Disciplinary problems will be handled in far less repressive ways that get to the core of what a child/student is really missing. Students who exhibit a pattern of skipping class or of starting fights will be seen as crying out for help, rather than as requiring punishment and (ironically) suspension from school. Pious moralizing about unacceptable behavior will give way to early interventions that empower, rather than punish. Students will help each other in the disciplinary arena in ways that adults never dreamed possible.

A holistic paradigm for public schools? In the mid-eighties, Ron Miller and other leading educators felt that the times were ripe for a revolution that would usher in a holistic educational paradigm. This revolution would parallel the kinds of changes that Marilyn Ferguson, Fritjof Capra, Willis

Harman, and others were calling for on other fronts. By 1995, it still had not happened; prevailing interests were still entrenched.

Subsequently, Miller suggested that the ideological aspects (especially those with spiritual or New Age connotations) had retarded progress. The religious right, for example, has made meditation in the classroom an acid test for school boards. Miller now urges us to think of holism as a "critical theory" in dialogue with other perspectives, such as the liberal progressive wing of educational theory. This dialogue should be viewed as part of a larger cultural struggle where piecemeal innovations are the most one can hope for. Progress will be slower and the goals will be more open-ended than he originally hoped for.

The title of Miller's published conversion is revealing: "Holistic Education in the United States: A 'New Paradigm' or a Cultural Struggle?"[5] I think the situation is both/and, rather than either/or. Holism is a paradigm as well as a critical perspective. So is the Perennial Philosophy. The New Paradigm dialogue incorporates key elements from both. I have also stressed that much struggle and confusion will characterize attempts to integrate them into mainstream culture.

A careful analysis of current perspectives and experiments in education will reveal that the ones worth seriously pursuing are already holistic and/ or perennialist in broad outline. Such is the case, for example, with Wisconsin's "McFarland model," developed in partnership with the American Association for the Advancement of Science's Project 2061. Part of Miller's new direction, I think, stems from the realization that the holism he now embraces is broader than the holism he originally thought he had to work with. As I showed in Chapter Three, holism and systems thinking have always been evolving multidisciplinary perspectives, not fixed categories of understanding.

There is no reason to abandon the goal of implementing a New Paradigm in education because the cultural challenges are so vast and complex. Miller and others are understandably frustrated by the lack of progress, but this is because entrenched interests in education are so powerful. The average person has more freedom in deciding whether to visit a holistic health center, but less freedom over whether to send his or her children to a holistic alternative school.

I do not know exactly which of the above proposals will see the light of day, much less prevail, in the public sector. Some are evident in George Wood's *Schools That Work: America's Most Innovative Public Education Programs*. Piecemeal experimentation is underway. But I do believe that, within ten years, a perennialist and holistic New Paradigm for education will be firmly entrenched precisely because it is part of the interconnected dynamics of a Rising Culture. The coming worldview will change everything in its path.

SYSTEMS HOLISM
AND THE EARTH MOTHER: BEYOND SAVING THE PLANET

More than transformational crises in education, health care, science, or personal growth, a spectrum of global environmental crises has finally attracted the serious attention of many world leaders and governments. This follows decades of consciousness raising by hundreds of grass roots organizations, such as the Worldwatch Institute and Greenpeace, whose memberships transcend national barriers. At least once a week, network television news carries a major story relating to some aspect of this crisis. A Gallup Poll suggests that three of every four Americans consider themselves environmentalists.

What to do is not always clear. That we are facing very serious threats to life as usual—threats that affect us as a species, not just as Americans or Italians—is becoming clear. The crises are becoming familiar. However, they bear repeating at every opportunity. Among the more significant are:

1. At current growth rates, the earth's population will double between 1990 and 2025, typically in countries least able to sustain it.
2. Deforestation and fossil fuel burning annually pour approximately twenty billion tons of carbon dioxide into the atmosphere, fueling the greenhouse effect which could see average worldwide temperatures rise by 8° F. within the next sixty years.
3. In 1990 alone, thirty million acres of tropical forest were destroyed.
4. The cost of waste disposal in America in 1993 was $30 billion and growing exponentially. At the same time we are running out of space to deal with it.
5. The ozone hole over Antarctica remains large and is not going away. Another one appears to be developing over the Arctic.
6. Each one percent ozone depletion is correlated with an additional seventy-five thousand deaths from skin cancer.
7. Americans discard enough aluminum cans each year to rebuild the entire U.S. airline fleet four times over.
8. The energy saved by recycling a single glass bottle is enough to run a television for three hours.

9. It takes 9.0 pounds of feed to produce a pound of beef compared to 2.1 pounds of feed for chicken and 1.6 pounds for fish.

10. Only three percent of the world's water is fresh and seventy-five percent of that is locked into glaciers and ice caps. The remainder is progressively subject to pollution. A quarter of the world's population does not have safe drinking water.

11. With only five percent of the world's population, America disposes of 290 million tons of toxic waste each year, on or in the ground in places where it is increasingly not wanted.

12. Ten thousand children a day die of starvation or malnutrition. A mere day from the combined military budgets of the world could provide enough food to eradicate starvation for a year.

13. We are losing twice as much arable land each year as we are reclaiming on a worldwide basis.

14. Acid rain has destroyed one-third of Germany's Black Forest and currently threatens the forests and lakes of eastern Canada and the northeastern United States.

15. Pesticides and fertilizers continue to pollute food chains and groundwater sources with trace carcinogens, yet the average suburbanite uses more fertilizer for grass and shrubs on a per-acre basis than does the average farmer growing food.

16. Half of all the wood cut in the world is used for cooking or heating, at least four-fifths in Third World countries. Two billion people are cutting/gathering wood faster than it can be replenished. In many areas there will be nothing left in ten years, as local inhabitants literally eat themselves today out of a habitable place to live tomorrow.

17. Ninety-nine percent of all Americans (and most citizens of other industrialized countries) routinely carry far more PCBs and other cancer-causing substances in their bodies (PCBs like to congregate in fatty tissues) than did their grandparents. According to the American Cancer Institute, thirty-one percent will contract cancer before the age of seventy, mostly from environmental causes.[6]

Mostafa Tolba, executive director of the United Nations Environment Program, recently expressed the gravity of the problem: "Addressing the global environmental crisis requires nothing less than a radical change in the conduct of world policy and the world economy."[7] Unfortunately, it appears that the crisis will have to worsen before leaders take significant action.

How did we arrive at this point? There is no single cause or set of assumptions that uniformly fuel the crisis on a worldwide basis. Some apply more directly to the Industrial West, others to the Third World. From a global perspective, however, they form part of an interlocking mind-set, the main features of which are amply documented in many excellent books and periodicals. Third World leaders, for example, often see the road to greater prosperity paved with the same dynamics as those of the Industrial West. We should thus expect even more competition for and exploitation of natural and human resources, once their over-population and illiteracy rates are reduced. Among the ingredients of this destructive mind-set are:

1. Fragmentation: humans versus environment, countries versus countries, economic versus human costs, etc.
2. Localization: "Overpopulation is a Third World issue, so let them deal with it," "You can't prove that our sulphur dioxide is causing your forests a thousand miles away to die."
3. Reductionism: "It all comes back to the bottom line." "When people really start getting sick and dying off at three times the average for the area, then we will know there's a problem, so let's not overreact now."
4. Fear and competition: "If we don't get those offshore mineral rights, someone else will," "Why should we change our life-styles which we have worked so hard to achieve and maintain?"
5. Linear thinking: "Growth today, growth tomorrow, growth forever." The corollary to this dictum is the creation of perceived needs, which leads to more and more consumption.
6. Hierarchical control: "It's up to the World Bank to see that development funds are most appropriately used," "The solution is simple, just have Washington shut down all the industrial polluters."
7. To the preceding, we should add a special category: ignorance, since it has only been in the past few decades that the subtle interactions and long-term effects of our actions have come to light, beginning with Rachel Carson's *Silent Spring*.

There is still considerable disagreement among authorities both about the extent of various environmental issues and how best to go about addressing them. Some scientists, for example, are not convinced that the greenhouse effect is as progressive as it now seems to be. And, of course, there is the inevitable difference of opinion among political economists over how to make the most efficient use of limited funds to reverse environmental decay.

In some cases, government policies are incoherent, as reflected in former President Bush's pledge both to sustain America's growth and to work toward international solutions of environmental problems. One goal does not necessarily support the other. Thomas Berry argues convincingly in *The Dream of the Earth* that the ideal of endless material progress and growth is a progressive disaster for everyone. It can be overcome only through a revisioned mutually enhancing earth-human relationship.

There is a growing consensus even in mainstream thinking that the assumptions which fuel the environmental crisis need to be examined very carefully and, in some cases, replaced by a vision that various alternative or Rising Culture groups—New Age, New Left, Green, etc.—have been nurturing ever since the sixties.

The main categories of this newer way of thinking are increasingly found in informed discussions of the issues both here and abroad. They are:

1. Global responsibility: Every country both contributes to environmental problems and has legitimate interests that must be addressed by others in any workable overall solution. We are all in this together, and we cannot negotiate international solutions in which one nation (or group of nations) achieves more at the expense of others.

2. Sustainable culture: Resources should be used in ways that can be renewed indefinitely. Where they cannot be, as in the case of fossil fuels, alternatives must be developed. Policies that favor recycling are among the many ways to help achieve this goal. As the Earth Works Group made abundantly clear in *50 Simple Things You Can Do To Save The Earth*, local action can change the course of history even without a coherent national policy.

3. Voluntary simplicity: We need to adopt, both individually and collectively, less wasteful life-styles which address real (not artificial) human needs. We need to restructure the advertising and marketing goals of companies built upon fueling consumerism.

4. Decentralist networking: While local environmental and economic issues inevitably are connected to others in the region or nation, their most workable solutions typically cannot be mandated from a nonlocal source. Involving all locally interested parties with a stake in an issue, then forming natural alliances with like-minded groups is more effective over the long run. For example, with fifty

percent of food costs linked to costs of transportation, we should rethink the economics (not to mention the health benefits!) of increased local production.

5. Mutually empowering cooperation: A noncompetitive win-win attitude must be nurtured in conjunction with all of the preceding. The combination of decentralist and win-win perspectives gives rise to expanding networks of inclusivist relationships necessary to save ourselves and the planet. This combination also gives rise to the possibility that many political polarities, e.g., liberal versus conservative, guns versus butter, development versus environment, can be recast within a higher order in which everyone wins. While it's officially unnamed, this higher order includes resacralized empowering connections at one end and rational self-interest, on the other. "Let's help others" versus "Let's help ourselves" assumes the very us-versus-them polarity abandoned within this spectrum.

6. Interconnectedness: Environmental issues are radically interdependent not only with each other, but also with economics, politics, education, and even religion; piecemeal solutions are progressively less viable.

There are many ways this New Paradigm thinking can be translated into workable strategies for decreasing environmental destruction. They range all the way from new international accords in phasing out CFC production and limiting emissions of greenhouse gases, to recycling and using technology to achieve more efficient uses of water and electricity. Much of this is familiar to the average reader and is documented in countless books, periodicals, and position papers of major national and international institutes.[8]

Global implementation of this new way of thinking, of course, will not be smooth or easy. Different groups (New Left, Green, Radical Center, etc.) have varied perspectives and agendas to contribute to the process. To this cauldron of proposals, I should like to contribute some additional observations which seldom receive the attention they deserve.

How much reversible time is left? If you are not living next to a toxic waste dump or drinking polluted water, and if you do not read widely on the magnitude of environmental crises, it is easy to assume that time is on our side. It is easy to believe that if we just acknowledge these problems and begin to address them, after a while we will be able to reverse the patterns of destruction. What we need to do, as this assumption goes, is simply make pollution reduction and sustainable ecosystems both greater national and international priorities.

No informed person would disagree with these priorities. The question is how much time there is to make them work. The answer is that, in most cases, we don't know. We don't know how many PCBs are still making their way into the food chain on a worldwide basis or what their longer-term cancerous effects will be. We don't know how a two-degree rise in average temperature will cause shifting equatorial winds to produce dramatic climatic changes in any given area. And we don't know in many cases at exactly what point overpopulation itself undermines the very possibility of meaningful environmental reform. What we do know, however, is that on the whole these challenges are serious and becoming worse.

In some cases—as with the greenhouse effect—we may be approaching a critical threshold, after which our capacity for meaningful control of events declines rapidly. In other cases, we may have passed this threshold already, as evidenced by aquifer pollution. What I would like to suggest, however, is that each day, month, and year that meaningful reform is simply debated, studied, and window-dressed with pittances, the likelihood increases that one of the following will occur. Either draconian measures will be required to turn the tide or, if we find that too unpleasant, we may simply have to accept staggering losses and changes in our way of life. In a worst-case scenario, we will feel the full force of both alternatives.

Consider a hypothetical example. Either we can spend $1 billion dollars today to clean up a major toxic waste area which threatens an aquifer system, or $5 billion in two years (the effects are often exponential, not incremental); or allow the groundwater in a populated five-hundred square-mile area to become contaminated, and either ship water in by truck or move everybody to another part of the country. Then again, we might spend the $5 billion and still lose the area, which prompts today's budget watchers either not to do anything or perhaps deny the problem and let the local residents die of "unproven causes." Since nobody wants to spend a billion dollars today, we can instead commission a few studies and wait to see what happens.

If the preceding example is not sufficiently realistic, consider the following. Most experts agree that global efforts to preserve the biosphere will fail unless the developing nations of the Third World cooperate to an unprecedented degree. Yet cooperation in this context means they cannot repeat the development patterns of the industrial North. In the words of the United Nations' Tolba: "If they reach the North's levels of consumer goods and fuel consumption, and if they continue to clear the forests, then our mutual destruction is assured."[9] Yet a billion people a day absolutely must contribute to environmental destruction just to live to the end of the week.

So how is cooperation to be achieved? Only through a massive transfer of money and technology amounting to hundreds of billions of dollars from the approximately twenty-five percent of the world's population of the Industrial North to the seventy-five percent of the Developing South. What are the chances that this will happen in time? As Kenneth Piddington, director of the World Bank's Environment Department, asks: "Are the rich countries of a mind to organize the transfer of resources in such a way that the Thailands and Indonesias of this world are actually going to benefit materially from the way they have dealt with their environmental agenda?"[10] The logic of dissipative structures is useful here. The equations of war games are time-neutral, that is, reversible. The equations of living systems are not, especially when pushed to far-from-equilibrium conditions. The more we postpone action, the closer we move toward a bifurcation point where the options are either "escaping to a higher order" or decay. Yet the longer we wait, the higher the price will be, in both human and economic terms, to achieve the first option. Right now, we are in a race against time to lay the groundwork for a successful "escape" (massive reorganization). The problem is that many of the major players in the race, though saying one thing, still seem to believe that environmental decay is indefinitely time-neutral.

There appears to be an emerging consensus that we want the higher order to reflect eco-sustainability, global responsibility, and mutual cooperation among all the players. But such visionary cornerstones may take more time than we have to put into place. Achieving them may require a kind of self-destructing last hurrah of Old Age thinking—strict linear controls, top-down draconian leadership, and even violent confrontation—all justified in the name of integrating a very different vision for a New Age. We may have to trade food for mandatory birth control policies today in order to insure adequate nutrition for everyone tomorrow.

I have not factored into this picture many variables that play critically important roles. For example, birthrates are increasing in countries least able to accommodate them. From 1830 to 1930, the world's population doubled from one to two billion. It doubled again in just forty-five years. And it's now expected to be over six billion by the year 2000. Such a growth curve exposes the naiveté of those who think of environmental decay in time-neutral terms. How far from equilibrium must we go?

Does systems holism go far enough? The web of interdependent environmental processes, as well as the complex relationships between the environment, economics, and politics, is a breeding ground for systems thinking. Systems Holism is certainly not restricted to these domains; it has made important contributions across the spectrum of Rising Culture concerns. However, it's in the environmental arena that the power of systems thinking is perhaps most widely perceived, and deservedly so!

No country stands isolated from the economic and environmental policies and processes of its neighbors. American smokestacks pollute Canadian lakes. Radioactive fallout from Chernobyl rained down on much of Europe. Burning Brazilian forests contribute six percent of all the carbon dioxide pumped into the atmosphere each year. Drought and deforestation threaten mass migrations. Sewage and toxic waste disposal by even one or two Mediterranean countries threaten the coasts, marine life, and ultimately the public health of all countries on the rim.

Raising literacy rates requires more paper for reading and writing, which require paper mills, which without expensive technology often result in more pollution. This technology cannot be obtained, except by loans or gifts from wealthier countries, which in turn cannot be repaid if interest rates are not kept low and a more literate population can find jobs. And they may not be able to find them if international development funds are channeled into unsustainable industries for which there is little market anyway.

The implications of a beef-centered versus a vegetarian diet provide an excellent example of the importance of systems thinking. American homes and especially fast food restaurants demand more beef. This requires more cattle, which are cheaper to raise in Latin America than in the United States. Higher cattle production leads to deforestation. Deforestation extinguishes other species, and contributes to carbon dioxide pollution which is a major factor in the greenhouse effect. In the United States alone, eighty-five percent of topsoil depletion is related to livestock production. Additionally, more than half the water used in America goes for livestock production (twenty-five hundred gallons to produce a pound of meat). Production of factory-farmed livestock results in a billion tons of nonrecycled waste, much of which ends up in our water supply.

Additional strains are eventually placed upon our health delivery systems as a nation of meat-eaters begins to experience related diseases. Production of the current meat-centered diet uses approximately thirty-three percent of consumed raw materials, whereas a fully vegetarian diet would require less than five percent. Ordering a hamburger is therefore not the isolated event it appears to be. Systems thinking invites us to take a very close look at such simple practices.[11]

The lessons of fragmented thinking are finally beginning to take hold on a global scale. We must support the shift toward systems thinking on every level, from local recycling projects to global conferences on climate. And we can supplement this support in the sphere of economics by implementing the proposals in Susan Meeker-Lowry's *Economics as if the Earth Really Mattered* and Marilyn Waring's *If Women Counted: A New Feminist Economics*.

Why adopt a paradigm of radical biospheric interconnectedness? Well, we value truth to some degree, and the truth seems to be that the connections within our biosphere are more far-reaching than we had suspected. Still, the mere apprehension of truth does not explain the motivation to act accordingly. For that we need to probe further.

The motivational value of "Let's recognize the interconnectedness of the biosphere" for many readers is tied mainly to the desire to survive and maintain a certain standard of living. At bottom, the simple motive is fear supported by a *quid pro quo*: We won't send you our PCBs if you don't send us your acid rain, and we'll all be better off.

There is nothing wrong with this type of thinking per se, especially if it moves people to constructive action. But it does not stem from any deep empowering connection to other people or to the oneness of the biosphere. It says only that there are more relations in the biosphere than we anticipated, and that it is to our mutual self-interest to coordinate these relations more effectively. It is the same kind of rational egoism that Detroit applied to its production lines: "If we don't listen to our workers, we'll lose our competitive edge and the Japanese will beat us out; we need more worker involvement." This is the same Old Age thinking that underwrites calls for environmental action.

A second motive for appreciating biospheric interdependence is a deeply felt, empowering connection with all living things and with the earth itself. This is a level about which Systems Holism understandably has little to say. However, Native Americans, some New Agers, ecofeminists, and certain deep ecologists do have something to say. They invite us to feel the earth, love plants and animals (even talk to them), see the wisdom in seasonal cycles, replace what we take or destroy as if we were repaying a just debt, treat the earth as if it were a living organism with a consciousness of its own (which makes toxic waste dumping roughly the equivalent of pouring it in your neighbor's living room) and, perhaps most of all, be grateful for the opportunity to live here. They invite us to envision a more spiritually integrated relationship with the Earth Mother.

Systems thinking is compatible with this orientation and in some respects follows naturally from the attitude of loving Earth Mother. However, the implied perennialism of Earth Mother talk is more inclusive than systems thinking per se. It is one thing to understand how a forest fits into the ecosystem and how its destruction would affect life elsewhere, quite another just to love its trees for what they are. Shall we save forests out of fear of what will happen if we don't, or because we love them in the first place? Such is but one of the many faces of love and fear in times of great cultural transition.

The many faces of deep ecology. In recent years a radical critique of environmentalism has emerged from within its own ranks. This critique is frequently associated with the deep ecology movement and with a biocentrist paradigm. Its practical agendas and intellectual horizons vary from "green rage" over corporate greed to a critique of mainstream environmentalism, which has allegedly sold us out via a safe anthropocentric worldview.[12] This critique has also begun to seriously influence discussion of the environmental crisis in mainstream academic publications, such as philosopher Michael Zimmerman's recent *Contesting Earth's Future*, which lucidly explores the agendas of deep ecology vis-à-vis New Age, New Paradigm, and other postmodern perspectives.

With the arrogance of good humanists and good spiritualists alike, many environmentalists mistakenly assume that we are the superior species in a Great Chain of Being, with stewardship over lower life forms and the earth itself. By contrast, deep ecologists refrain from making value judgments and prefer to let nature take its course. It is not our job to interfere in this process—not even to protect animal rights. In a biocentric view, there are no special rights or values save nature itself: there just is what is. Activist-attorney Christopher Manes presents an extreme version of this critique of anthropocentrism.

> Taken seriously, evolution means that there is no basis for seeing humans as more advanced or developed than any other species. Homo sapiens is not the goal of evolution, for as near as we can tell evolution has no telos—it simply unfolds, life-form after life-form. Elephants are no more developed than toadstools, fish are no less advanced than

> birds, cabbages have as much ecological status as kings.
> Darwin invited humanity to face the fact that the obser-
> vation of nature has revealed not one scrap of evidence that
> humankind is superior or special, or even particularly
> more interesting than, say, lichen.[13]

In other words, there is no basis for an anthropocentric environmental policy when humankind is essentially the result of an accidental draw of the genetic lottery. The "depth" in Manes's version of deep ecology is to be read as the lowest common denominator of all life—the gene pool.

There are many levels on which to join this debate, beginning with Manes's extraordinarily reductive version of evolutionary theory. However, I will offer only a single observation. If a doctrine of common origins is what some deep ecologists require to overcome the excesses of hierarchical thinking, then Manes's version of it leaves us with no way to explain the deep connection some feel with all life-forms. How could we, if our genes are uncaringly neutral at best and selfishly programmed for our survival at worst?

By contrast, a perennialist vision provides us with a highest common denominator—the interpenetration of a Divine Source in all things—that bridges the gap between species and makes more sense of the felt connection to living things of which we are capable. It's more effective and more fulfilling to experience a spiritual depth in nature, like Francis of Assisi did, than to pursue the ethics of fragmentation to its relativistic end, namely, that we are so anthropocentrically biased that we can't appreciate the fact that cockroaches and people have an equal claim to exist. Deep ecology requires a spiritual interpenetration, not merely a biological hierarchy reduced to its lower end.

Ecofeminists have split agendas regarding deep ecology. On the one hand, many find common cause in a strong critique of anthropocentrism because of its patriarchal assumptions; a human worldview tends to be a male worldview. Other ecofeminists are involved in revisioning a Goddess theology that, from a deep ecological perspective, is simply an attempt to impose one set of human values (however well-intentioned) over another.

Moreover, it is not clear whether the emergence of "Earth Mother" language is supposed to be interpreted merely as a useful metaphor ("Let's live as if the earth were our mother") or whether it signals a deeper meta-physics ("The Earth Mother is an expression of the Divine Feminine, with a compassion, will, and intelligence of her own"). If the latter meaning is intended, ecofeminism will not have many defenders in the deep ecology camp.

By now it should be clear that merely being in favor of Gaia is unclear. It could mean that you think of the earth as a living, self-regulating organism (this was James Lovelock's original thesis). Or it could mean that you are a deep ecologist. Or a spiritually based ecofeminist. Or any of a half-dozen other possibilities.

Are we making Mother Nature unhappy? Each level in the Great Chain of Being penetrates and subsumes its lower level neighbors. The lower we go, the more distinct and "physical" things appear to be, while the higher we go, the less distinct and physical they really are. By the time we reach the subtle domains of emotions and thought forms, we are at levels that do not necessarily begin or end at the edge of our bodies. These levels are not spatially distinct. They still permeate physical levels.

Now consider the accumulated emotional states of the combined citizenry of the planet: war, hatred, injustice, greed, depression, oppression, failure, guilt, shame, belligerence, domination, and fear. To be sure there are pockets of joy, love, and sharing. But the balance sheet does not favor the latter, especially on a global basis.

Finally, recall what negative or destructive emotions and attitudes are capable of doing to the human body. They may not be directly causally linked, but the evidence grows that they indirectly predispose one toward physical disease and decay. Why should the situation be qualitatively that different for the earth? Our bodies are composed of similar elements, especially water. To be sure, rocks and minerals are more dense than our flesh and, in most cases, our skeletons. But the combined level of fear in the collective unconscious of all humankind might well be sufficient to produce material effects in dense objects over time, especially if they are disposed toward certain changes in the first place. Such a possibility differs in degree, but not in principle, from the connections explored by psychoneuro-immunology on a human level.

In this vision, Mother Earth participates in and reflects the same ultimate ground consciousness that we all do, but in ways and at levels removed from ordinary human consciousness. If so, she must be very unhappy with the extraordinarily dense, negative emotional fog in which she now finds herself. In an act of self-preservation, she might even blow up in places. This is, after all, one way to reduce stress.

Many thousands (perhaps millions) of people, both here and abroad, in their prayer or meditation groups, incorporate the Earth Mother vision in their work. They do not pray to a controlling God to save us from destruction. Nor at this stage are they overly concerned with fact versus fiction. With accelerated interdimensional integration raising the stakes of love and fear, they concede the destructive impact of human consciousness, offer gratitude to She who makes life possible, and ask for time while we race to get our collective agendas together. Some believe that we already have been granted one reprieve in 1988 and that a day of reckoning is close at hand.

The Earth Mother will support faltering paths of love, but not those of fear. Viewed thusly, the inner goal of transforming consciousness is the necessary complement of the outer goal of producing a globally sustainable environment. Paths of love are increasing. But there is still too much fear. Accordingly, the transformation that has not been undertaken voluntarily on a serious global scale may be accomplished out of the necessity of surviving the Earth Mother's legitimate defense mechanisms.

Technology and spirituality for a new earth. Several developments promise to change forever our relations with the Earth, especially in the area of agriculture. From a mainstream perspective, each would be labeled as "esoteric." From a perennialist perspective, they only relate to energies outside those recognized by physics, i.e., they occupy a different place in the Great Chain of Being.

The first two are technological in nature. Of these, I have already described the science of psychotronics in Chapter Five. Psychotronics is the science which studies the interface between consciousness and matter/ energy with reference to the vibrational signatures of both living and non-living things. Psychotronic machines currently are used in this country and abroad for agricultural (and other) purposes, among them: changing soil chemistry and composition without fertilizer or other physical substances; ridding crops of insects and disease without the use of chemical sprays; enhancing yield; enhancing the texture, flavor, or nutritional value; making crops more resistant to severe environmental changes.

Though somewhat dated, Christopher Bird's and Peter Thompkins' *The Secret Life of Plants* is still one of the best introductions to the history of psychotronics as it relates to agriculture. Psychotronics can also produce changes in weather and, in certain circumstances, neutralize toxic waste. In brief, psychotronics has profound implications for both human health and a cleaner environment. The FDA takes a dim view of such claims. But this is the same agency that describes ozone therapy as medical quackery.

The second technological development centers around so-called "free energy" devices. Any machine that produces more energy (usually electricity) than it takes to run, is by definition a free energy device. Most are designed to unlock the potential of vacuum space, which according to quantum electro-dynamics is full of unused energy. The United States Patent Office declares such machines bogus. But a neutral observer of the scientists, engineers, and inventors at the National Free Energy Conference each year would come away convinced that more is transpiring in this arena than government or electric utility companies would have us believe.

I have never seen a free energy machine, much less seen one work. However, I have reason to believe they exist and that at least some work. It is also abundantly clear why, *if* they exist, they have not seen the light of day; too many financial empires hang in the balance. One of the most accessible articles describing the features of such a device, together with the political hardball its inventor Robert Adams faced, may be found in the December-January (1993) issue of the Australian journal *Nexus*. My educated guess is that free energy machines will be both better understood and utilized within ten years. Their capacity to reduce environmental pollution, alter transportation habits, and shift economic and financial priorities is staggering.

A final revolutionary development is spiritual in nature. It relates to the progressive acknowledgment of our relationship to elementals (the spirits of earth, air, fire, and water), devas (or "fairies") and nature spirits (especially those of trees), together with their synergystic relationship with the biosphere. The devas in particular work long and hard to maintain the balance of nature. We are guests in their world as much as they are in ours.

When we think of environmental pollution, we tend to think of foul air and toxic waste. But negative emotions are also part of this pollution, and the human race has produced its share in this regard. Devas work cooperatively with elementals and the consciousness of the earth itself to transmute the effects of these negative emotions. When humans intentionally enter into this cooperative matrix, miracles of flowering fruits and vegetables can occur—even in places where soil chemistry would dictate otherwise. In other words, we can align ourselves with these energies, ask for help, and they in turn will assist in producing healthy gardens and in clearing and transmuting the emotional pollution that hangs in pockets over the planet, especially around battlefields.

The possibilities of such a cooperative relationship were first brought to attention through the work at Findhorn on the northern coast of Scotland, where tomatoes were grown under conditions totally unfit for vegetation. Machaelle Small Wright, the author of *Behaving As If The God In All Life Mattered*, has established in Virginia a comparable research center, *Perelandra*, where she offers workshops on how to integrate spiritual and ecological concerns. Clairvoyance helps in such procedures. But it is not necessary. What is necessary is loving intent, clarity about what one wishes to achieve, and a knowledge of how to work cooperatively with these other citizens. Wright pays special attention to emotional factors that may affect nature's bounty:

> Everything can be going along just fine in the garden and all of a sudden, out of nowhere, there's a horde of something eating three rows of vegetables. I have learned that when this happens, more often than not, it is because there has been a sudden and dramatic shift in thought, intent, or emotion either with the gardener himself, or with the family or community connected with the garden…Nature functions in the role of the absorber when it comes to ungrounded raw emotional energy that is released by humans.[14]

Anytime is a good time to explore both the impact of emotional field activity and the possibilities of more cooperative relationships with the invisible beings who have a vested interest in the well-being of the planet. There may come a time, however, when working directly with devas, elementals, and nature spirits will play a critical role in our survival. And, consequently, a time when their place in the Great Chain of Being is recognized as much as ours.

CHAPTER THIRTEEN

Shaping a New Religious Consciousness

L eading edges of Rising Cultures bring up personal issues. They force us to look at things we would rather ignore. Sometimes we play out the resulting dramas on the stage of rationality. We attempt to explain new developments by making them fit in old categories. At other times our emotional commitments blow out of the closet without their cloaks of rational respectability. This is especially likely to happen in discussions of religion.

Religion is such a pervasive aspect of life that whenever a major development with potentially religious implications comes along (such as near-death experiences), increased posturing, territorialism, and condemnation are likely. We saw this with Jesus, Luther, and Calvin, and with assorted contemporary movements such as existentialism and death-of-god theology. We are seeing it again in attacks upon the New Age movement even by those who have more in common with it than they suspect. Such is the stuff of change.

My purpose in this chapter is not to sort through current schools of religious thought, such as Liberation Theology. I will focus instead on the main challenges facing the Judeo-Christian tradition as it is variously presented and practiced in the mainstream. If hierarchical control, fragmentation, competition, exclusivism, and fear are being increasingly challenged in mainstream religion, then it is to our mutual interest to explore the shape of postmillennium religion and spirituality.

THREE CHALLENGES FOR CONTEMPORARY RELIGION

What are the current challenges for religious belief? My concern here is not with particular persuasions, such as Reform Judaism, Religious Science, or Native American traditions, much less the bloody disputes between Irish Catholics and Protestants, or Indian Muslims and Hindus. I want to explore instead three fundamental assumptions that underlie mainstream religious commitment. Each assumption is brought out in response to the question "What is religion supposed to do?"

The first thing traditional religion does is paint a picture and tell a story. It offers descriptions of human nature, our origins and destinies, and our relation to God or to a Godhead. It tells us about things, such as the soul, or evil, or a deity, which purportedly exist independently of our language and cultural conventions. Very few interpreters claim to be absolute literalists about all of this. There is, however, supposed to be a minimal core of fact-stating beliefs in any religious tradition. That a belief is fact-stating, e.g., "God gave Moses the Ten Commandments," doesn't necessarily mean that the belief is true. It means that it is *assumed* to be such.

For over a thousand years, religion and science mixed their fact-stating beliefs together. For example, the idea that an intelligent all-powerful being created the world was as much a part of scientific belief as of religious belief. Then with the support of Thomas Aquinas, Descartes, and other philosophers, modern science and religion began to go their separate ways. Religion got morality, the soul, God, and the afterlife, while science reserved for itself the dynamic laws of space, time, matter, and motion. Both disciplines were still essentially fact-stating, but the facts they described were assumed to belong to different worlds.

On the way to the twentieth century, however, science began to claim more factual territory for itself. This was illustrated, for example, by the theory of evolution, which conflicted with established religious teachings. It gradually became clear that religion was going to lose the race, insofar as the race was assumed to be "stating the facts." After all, science had empirical methods, whereas religion had mostly abstract argument based on faith. With nineteenth-century thinkers, such as Weber, Kierkegaard, and Nietzsche, a dawning awareness of this imbalance took root.

In the twentieth century, the fact-stating capacity of theological language continued to erode under the influence of Freud (psychoanalysis), Rudolf Bultman (the demythologizing movement), Paul Tillich (religion as the quest for a meaningful relation to the "Ground of our Being"), and, more recently, the deconstructionism of Derrida, Foucault, and Habermas.[1]

Moderate to liberal critics agree that religion tells a story. But these stories, they point out, are subject to different readings depending on the cultural perspectives of those who read them. And culture itself is continually changing. There is no core of theologically fact-stating truths awaiting our discovery. They have concluded, in effect, that theology is not supposed to be fact-stating, and never should have been in the first place! Protestant theologian Paul Tillich sums it up this way: Science tells us about the nature of existence, whereas theology tells us about the *meaning* of existence.

Ask the professors in all but the most conservative seminaries today if Jesus actually healed the sick and you will not hear a simple "yes" or "no." You will hear, for example, that healing was not necessarily the most important part of his ministry; that he probably created the perception of doing something unusual (we really don't know what); that "casting out demons" had a different meaning than it does today; that all of his so-called miracles should be interpreted as metaphors for personal transformation; that Jesus knew how to work the power of the placebo; or, finally, that we should not ask such simple-minded questions which have no clear answers in the first place. Most Christian and Jewish thinkers today will go to considerable lengths to avoid appearing to be in potential competition with science over the facts.

The most extreme version of this line of thinking is that it does not matter whether God exists. What does matter is how one *responds* to the belief that God exists. We should therefore begin with our experience, *as it is immersed in a particular cultural and confessional context*, and then shape our theology in light of how that experience squares with sacred texts and traditions. This is all that imperfect humans can do, even if we claim to be doing something else. This line of thinking rests upon an assumption also shared by many scientists. The assumption is that knowledge is limited to the lower three sections of the Great Chain of Being—gross matter, living things, and ordinary states of awareness. Science claims ownership of these domains through physics, biology, and psychology, and then, in one of the great question-begging moves of modern times, declares that *if* there is anything beyond these three levels, it must be taken on faith or speculation alone. Religion is thus placed on the defensive.

Left largely unaddressed by scientists and religious thinkers is the question of whether through established spiritual practices we can develop a more objective picture of the upper realms of the Great Chain than what faith and scripture alone suggest. There are encouraging signs that, despite the best efforts of skeptics, mainstream scientists and religious thinkers are beginning to address this question. In the meantime, most prefer the one-sided territorial division marked out by the five senses.

A second traditional goal of religion is to positively affect one's consciousness. Religion should be psychologically assuring, awaken one's capacity for love, promote a healthy self-image, and positively affect one's happiness and peace of mind (especially in troubled times). Religion should offer a constructive message about the kind of *person* one can become. Are we born in sin? Can we release unnecessary karmic baggage? To what extent can we open ourselves to the transformational possibilities of unconditional love? How should we face death?

Mainstream religious traditions have addressed these questions for thousands of years. Religion obviously has made a huge difference in our consciousness, sometimes for the better and sometimes not. However, with the rise of self-help groups, the human potential movement, the progressive integration of psychotherapy (not to mention psychic counseling) into the mainstream, workshops on everything your priest or rabbi never told you, and the secularization of meditation, one might reasonably ask, "Who needs religion?" In self-improvement and dealing with life's problems, religion used to be the only game in town (and still is in some areas). Now it is one among many.

Mainstream religious traditions in the West have dealt with this challenge in one of two ways. Conservative traditions have tightened their belts, so to speak, and declared exploration into unauthorized domains (NDEs, meditation, self-help, etc.) either unnecessary, heretical, or dangerous—and maybe all three! More fear, more control.

Liberal Protestantism, kabbalistically informed Judaic traditions, and Sufism, on the other hand, have cautiously welcomed these developments and found a limited place for them in their "religious education" classes. Of course, the more they do this, in some respects the less *traditional* they become. The Unity Church reflects a more extended version of such psycho-spiritual outreach programs. There, one might experience a reading of Sufi poetry on Sunday morning, an exploration of *A Course in Miracles* Sunday evening, and a workshop by James Redfield, Matthew Fox, or Scott Peck on Saturday.

The third primary function of traditional religion is one of providing ethical and social guidance—of telling us how we ought to treat one another. Of course, this goes much further than just inheriting the Ten Commandments and the Golden Rule. Religion offers social cohesion in times of great change (like war) or oppression (in dictatorships). It has played a leading role in helping the poor. And in the United States the response to homelessness by many churches has literally kept many from dying on the streets. There are whole theological schools, such as Liberation Theology, which are built on the premise that the meaning of what one professes to believe is captured by what one does in helping those who are oppressed or less fortunate. I recently heard it put this way: "Feeding the hungry *is* my religion."

Few would disagree with feeding the hungry or freeing the oppressed under almost any label—be it Christianity, secular humanism, Krishna consciousness, or the New Age. But this fact must be counterbalanced by three other considerations.

First of all, if religious commitment is predominately translated via social involvement and social involvement in principle can originate from any belief-system, how can a particular religious tradition claim to be privileged on grounds other than the fact that one was born into it? Without a theology of something distinctively spiritual, what is the point of feeding the poor in the name of Jesus rather than Marx? Perhaps the point is to express God's love. But then a similar question emerges. Why is this God's love, rather than the love that a person (even an atheist!) can feel for others?

Increasing criticism of hierarchical control also threatens to undermine the traditional moral role of religion. Feminists are not interested in hearing sermons from sexists; many American Catholics are not interested in the Pope's pronouncements on their sex lives; thinking people in general are not interested in hearing that hell awaits their sinful lives; New Agers are not interested in being told that the source of their spirituality is in another part of the universe; and liberal Jews believe pretty much what they want to believe. With some notable exceptions, religious sects built upon control of their members, whether by decree or more subtle psychology, are being progressively challenged.

Finally, many commentators have pointed out that Judeo-Christian traditions in some instances have guided our behavior in mistaken ways. Whether directly or by implication, they have supported the domination and unnecessary killing of animals ("God put them here for us"), an indifference toward the environment, the oppression of women, war, social fragmentation, ethnic exclusivity, competition, guilt, and fear. Historically, it's not an especially uplifting picture. Paths of genuine love have been in a distinct minority. Demands to change these agendas are striking at the very heart of what religion is supposed to be. Demands for including race, class, and multiple theological outlooks are eroding the claims of historical exclusivity.[2]

Religion serves other functions than the three I have described. Some people attend church, for example, because of the ceremonial value of the services. Participation in a ritual can help one to express feelings and attitudes otherwise difficult to express. (I personally like to attend evangelical services once in a while just to *sing* about the "old time religion.") Churches also serve the important function of providing a community for sharing values and supporting one another, especially in times of social turmoil. Most people feel a need for community. But without the three main functions described earlier, there wouldn't be much to build a community around in the first place. I am not suggesting that the fact-stating, consciousness-changing, and socially guiding functions of religion have disappeared. Obviously, in many quarters they are alive and well. A few traditions in America, especially Mormon and Muslim, are growing quite rapidly. Millions of people clearly derive great satisfaction from traditional religion. I am suggesting, however, that these three functions are progressively coming under powerful challenges that threaten to take away much of what is distinctive about traditional religious commitment per se, whether or not this is recognized at the local church level.

We are at the point in history where much of what religion has done in the past can be done as well by some other institutions. The transformational question is what distinctive major function(s) might be left for religion to perform. Can religion escape to a higher order? A great yearning for spiritual meaning and experience is transforming many churches from the inside and starting new religions on the outside. And contrary to how social scientists view matters, this yearning involves more than mid-life crises, economic despair, and millennium fever. Creation Spirituality is one proposal for a higher-order religious consciousness.

CREATION SPIRITUALITY: A SYMPATHETIC CRITIQUE

In his voluminous writings, theologian Matthew Fox has described much of mainstream Christianity, especially Catholicism, as "sexist, ethnocentric, anthropocentric, undemocratic, and, perhaps the worst sin of all, boring."[3] His unrelenting criticism of Fall-from-Grace theologies and espousal of heretical ideas, especially feminism, at his Institute for Culture and Creation Spirituality even earned him a one-year gag order from the Vatican. He has since left the Catholic Church and is now an Episcopal priest.

Fox has been described as a New Age priest, a label which he resists. He is certainly, however, a New Paradigm revolutionary. For anyone interested in the integration of spiritual concerns with other major developments on the New Paradigm front, such as the New Biology and environmentalism, his *Original Blessing, The Coming of the Cosmic Christ,* and *Creation*

Spirituality are required reading. He is studied by theologians of many persuasions and has struck a deeply resonant chord in major sections of the Rising Culture. When he speaks at conferences, individuals of vastly different religious orientations step forth to announce that at last someone has articulated what they have felt all along but had difficulty expressing.

Fox is so inclusivist in his spiritual outreach that substantive questions arise regarding who is a part of whose paradigm. Ecologically and spiritually oriented feminists claim Fox as one of their own—as a theological contributor to *their* emerging worldview. Yet Fox's own worldview encompasses ecofeminism and touches base with all kinds of other developments, especially in the arts. D.T. Suzuki once declared Meister Eckhart, one of Fox's favorite Catholic mystics and a precursor of Creation Spirituality, a Zen Buddhist. Could this mean that Zen Buddhists are in principle ecofeminists?

There are convergences and divergences of interest within the Rising Culture. But all are interconnected. Clear lines are neither possible nor desirable when cross-fertilization is the order of the day. Fox both subsumes and is a part of many leading-edge developments. His articulate and compassionate analysis of a wide spectrum of transformational challenges for an equally broad spectrum of audiences qualifies him as a national treasure.

Fox's perennialism. Fox's Creation Spirituality is a synthesis and extension of the perennialist spirit. He seeks not so much to start a new tradition as to *recapture* and revitalize a long-standing and largely neglected tradition in the West. His sympathy to mysticism (including a refreshing emphasis upon Western mystics), his universalism ("The Holy Spirit works in different ways through the world's religions"), his panentheism ("God is in us and we are in God"), and his desire to read human and earthly affairs in light of a larger cosmic picture, all commend him to the Perennial Wisdom. What distinguishes Fox's particular version of the Perennial Wisdom are:

1. the attempt to integrate the higher domains of Spirit into constructive resolutions of current transformational challenges. For example, he proposes that we relate to the earth as our spiritual Mother, not merely as something we need to treat better for our own benefit.

2. his emphasis upon feeling, passion, pleasure, present-centeredness, vulnerability, playfulness, and letting go as key ingredients in the creative evolution of Spirit through biological and psychological

levels of the Great Chain. God is continuously expressed through *dabhar*, creative energy, with which we can collaborate in many ways—including science, sexuality, and especially art.
3. the recovery of matriarchal/feminine values, experiences, and perspectives.
4. his interpretation of incarnation as a blessing, not as the cause for suffering as stressed in traditional "Fall" theology.

Fox has inspired many individuals who seek to integrate their personal growth with a viable worldview. However, there are places where Creation Spirituality does not go far enough, or where it leaves us still facing several different avenues of interpretation. The following observations are intended to pick up at those places. There is so much in his work which richly deserves extended commentary that I am able to select only a few foundational questions for attention.

Concerning panentheism. Worldviews based upon fragmentation and separation have generated their own crises and transformative challenges. Western theism, including mainstream Christianity, Judaism, and Islam, separates God from humankind. Once you posit an essentially all-knowing and omnipotent male God who can be reached only through petitionary prayer, it is only a matter of time until a sufficiently large number of questioning persons begin to qualify this belief to the vanishing point.

There is reason to believe, for example, that the classical theistic God, not to mention selective scriptural inclusion and the establishment of a protective church hierarchy, was essentially a projection and subsequent rationalization of male values, fears, and philosophical assumptions.[4] A growing body of literature documents this imbalance, for example, Elaine Pagels's widely respected *Gnostic Gospels*. Fox considers atheistic criticisms of classical theism to be reasonable, and the average Sunday morning service a kind of well-intentioned, if not humorous, charade. It is hard to be touched by an abstract deity "out there."

Fox cites numerous sources and inspirations for his panentheistic alternative. From Meister Eckhart: "God created all things such that they are not outside himself, as ignorant people falsely imagine." From Julian of Norwich: "We are in God and God, whom we do not see, is in us." From John 15: "Whoever remains in me, with me in him, bears plentiful fruit." And from another perennialist who fell upon hard times with the Catholic Church, Teilhard de Chardin: "Matter is transparent and malleable in relation to spirit."[5]

Panentheism states that God permeates everything and everything is *in* God. Pantheism, on the other hand, states that God *is* nature and nature *is* God with nothing left over on either side of the equation. The difference is crucial. The former cosmology retains God's transcendence, whereas the latter does not. If from your picture of reality you subtract out the entire physical universe (including us), panentheism has something left—God or Spirit—whereas pantheism does not. With panentheism, the higher includes the lower but is not reducible to it.

Panentheism has been a minority tradition in the West. But it does at least two things required for a new religious consciousness. First, because God is in us, panentheism can be an empowering outlook, to the extent that we choose to awaken inwardly to that source. Second, because God is in everybody, not just Christians or Muslims, it is inclusivist and unifying. Different religions thus may be interpreted as different ways to acknowledge and celebrate that fact.

Panentheism also helps us through certain tricky theological issues. How could God create a universe out of nothing? Answer: God did not have to, since the universe is created from out of God. Next, if God is infinite yet different from us, don't we have an oxymoron, namely, "bounded infinity"? Answer: Since God is not separate from us, we don't need to draw boundary lines. Finally, the classical problem of evil: Why did God create us in such a way that so much suffering and injustice has resulted? Partial answer: If we are not other than God, then our suffering is God's suffering, and evil is not something done to us.

Fox's panentheism is a good theological beginning. Yet there are a number of outstanding metaphysical issues which require more critical attention. I describe them as follows.

One can be a panentheist by merging spirit and nature, and then making nature a subset of spirit. God can create the world and then enter into every part of it, just as we might plant our garden and then suffuse it with electromagnetic energy (which might cause strange and wonderful things to occur). This kind of panentheism can be both inclusivist and empowering. But it stops short of asserting that we *are* God. It says, rather, that we all in principle have equal access to God within ourselves. So far as meeting the conditions of inclusivism and empowerment, we need to go at least this far for an adequate spiritually based paradigm.

Furthermore, this kind of qualified panentheism is consistent with many of the sources and precursors of creation-centered spirituality that Fox cites. When Jesus says "Whoever remains in me, with me in him, bears plentiful fruit," he is not necessarily saying that those "in him" are made of the very stuff of which he is transcendently begotten. Because Fox has only two categories with which to work, spirit and nature, it appears in places that he is adopting this "fusion" version of panentheism. He believes, for example, that an ecological spirituality (or spiritually based ecofeminism) is the bridge between science and religion as they are traditionally understood. Take a passive earth and suffuse it with the energy of the mother side of God, and spiritually based ecofeminism is one interesting result.

Yet when all is said and done, Fox is attracted to the stronger (monistic) version of panentheism. We are all expressions of the creative energy, the dabhar, of God. To quote his revision from *John 1*: "In the beginning was the Creative Energy: The Creative Energy was with God and the Creative Energy was God...Through it all things came to be, not one thing had its being but through it." Vedic creation stories involving Brahman, Vishnu, Shiva, and Shakti in certain ways parallel very nicely Fox's emphasis upon continuing, playful creation versus the notion of just a single event that happened long ago. Or as Shankara put it in his commentary on the *Brahma Sutra*: "The activity of the Lord...may be supposed to be mere sport (lila), proceeding from his own nature, without reference to any purpose."[6]

There is a curious tension between Fox's antianthropomorphism, on the one hand, and his personalized conception of the motherhood (as well as fatherhood and childhood) of God, on the other. His feminist stance is unswerving, but its ultimate grounding is not altogether clear. Patriarchal religion has contributed to a point of extreme imbalance. We had best rectify this imbalance, in Fox's opinion, by beginning to think of God (and the earth) *as if* She were our mother.

So far, so good. But here is the critical question. Should we bring our theology into line with what our culture needs, or should we base our culture in some part upon what spirit is? In other words, is there an irreducibly feminine side to the creative energy from which we all come? Do we build masculine/feminine aspects into our core metaphysics? Or do we construct our God out of an essentially neutral energy plus current cultural needs? There is support for both interpretations in Fox's works, although I think that in the end he wants to build the feminine (creative, nurturing, playful, passionate) side into the very nature of the divine.

If this is the case, however, then the polarity of the masculine and feminine needs to be taken seriously, since these adjectives (or whatever other convergence one thinks best captures the "feminine") all require opposites in order to make any sense. God (or creative energy) must then have a masculine as well as a feminine side. If so, the polarity metaphysics of Fox's creation-centered spirituality would be more Taoist or Hindu than feminist.

Fox's creation-centered perennialism does not incorporate a full-blown version of the Great Chain as I have described it. This leaves him in principle without any intermediate territory between the Godhead, on the one hand, and nature, on the other. And without intermediate territory we are hard-pressed to ground substantial differences between various kinds of mystical experience. The transcendent experiences of Saint Theresa, Ramakrishna, Rumi, the Buddha, and Van Ruysbroek virtually cry out for different levels of reality.

The problem is not restricted to mystical experiences per se. Other intermediate level experiences include out-of-body shamanic ventures to other worlds, near-death experiences, visions of the Virgin Mary, and ordinary apparitions, all of which are now becoming quite widespread. Unless we dismiss these as dreams, hallucinations, or instances of mass hysteria, we are hard-pressed to make a place for them in Fox's reality grid.

On a recent NBC television special, Fox seemed to express a belief in real angels who watch over us. If so, this would expand his reality grid. However, his phrasing left open the interpretation that it is merely the culturally ingrained *belief* in angelic intervention that produces such apparent assistance and stimulates personal growth as well.

When one is advancing an ecofeminist, creation-centered, spiritual tradition, it is understandable that most paranormal domains will be set aside. Given the increasingly widespread occurrence and evolution of various types of paranormal experience, however, an adequate religious paradigm will have to take such experiences into account. *Failure to do so will virtually guarantee a slow death of irrelevance for the religion that does not rise to the occasion.*

Taking paranormal experiences seriously does not mean that we should take them all at face value. For they are not always what they appear to be. There will always be self-centered and naive individuals who want to make them far more than what they are, especially if the experiences are their own. Once we sort through the rubbish, however, only the multilevel, interpenetrating Great Chain of Being will provide an appropriate home for diverse paranormal experiences. For this reason, the Great Chain would be a suitable addition to Fox's creation-centered spirituality.

Critique of the New Age. Matthew Fox does not dismiss the New Age. He is aware that there are so many possible meanings for the phrase that almost anyone could be in or out of the New Age, depending upon the context. Fox fairly and fruitfully carries on a dialogue with many different traditions and current outlooks, from World Bank perspectives on Third World development to Buddhism.

Fox believes the New Age has some useful perspectives to contribute, especially its attempt to move us beyond guilt, fear, and a one-sided patriarchy. On the other hand, he has some serious reservations regarding reincarnation and New Age responses to suffering and injustice. These misgivings are not unique to Fox. And they do not apply equally to all New Agers. All New Agers are not necessarily reincarnationists. Not all reincarnationists are New Agers. And there is certainly no single New Age position on suffering and injustice.

Fox's concern about reincarnation is not about rebirth per se, but rather, with more human considerations. Who would want to incarnate as, say, a Jew in Hitler's Germany or a blind person in Peoria? And isn't our explanation of these events as something these individuals chose for themselves a convenient excuse to do nothing? I have discussed these issues earlier. But since they are so pivotal, some response is called for.

From a physically embodied perspective of having only one life to live, nobody would want to be born into oppression or with one eye. But from a reincarnational perspective, this aversion would be turned inside out. I very well might want to be born into an oppressive situation, if I had certain karmic issues to deal with and I had to learn an important lesson about the use of power—perhaps from another life when I was the oppressor!

Within the perspective of this lifetime, I might choose to experience some very difficult situations, such as applying to a military academy, in order to grow in certain ways. Then again, I might not. It depends upon my perception of myself, what I want in life, what is possible, and *how much time I have.* If I have hundreds or even thousands of lifetimes, then the experience of slavery in one of them is less significant than if I have only one life to live. The idea of selecting a certain type of life—even one with suffering—makes sense within a reincarnational perspective.

It can be argued on practical grounds that a belief in reincarnation ought not be adopted, because it fosters insensitivity towards injustice. But what a doctrine could lead to in the social arena is independent of the question of whether there are grounds for believing it to be true. By analogy, nuclear power has led us to some very difficult situations which bear directly on the question of whether we should have used it in the ways we have. But the terrible possibility of a nuclear explosion in a populated area does not constitute a reason for denying the existence of nuclear power.

Consider Fox's critique of reincarnation at face value. Does it foster insensitivity towards social injustice? The answer is that it can in the hands of insensitive people, just as the Catholic Church fostered the Inquisition. *But there is nothing in the doctrine itself which necessarily leads to this effect.* Reincarnation does not override free choice, and it encourages people to work on their issues to the extent they are capable of acknowledging them.

One's chosen agenda just as easily can be fighting injustice, poverty, racism, homelessness, or disease. If reincarnation is true, it includes all liberation theologians, all social activists, all feminists, everybody in Greenpeace, the entire Green movement, Gandhi, Martin Luther King, Jesus Christ, and also all critics of the doctrine. It doesn't lead to inaction any more than it leads to action. Each of us still must choose what we shall do with our life. Each of us is free to attempt to convince others that they should be more sensitive to the needs of others. Reincarnation does not change any of that.

We would not reject democracy on the grounds that some people have misused their voting rights. Or medicine on the grounds that some doctors are guilty of malpractice. By the same token, we ought not reject reincarnation on the grounds that some superficial individuals have used it as an excuse to do nothing with their lives. A narrowly conceived moral critique of reincarnation can be met by a more broadly conceived and equally respectable response!

Reincarnation aside, is the New Age indifferent to suffering and evil? In Fox's words:

> I find that a lot of new agers don't deal with the shadow. They don't deal with the shadow of society, which is the injustice issue, and they don't deal with their own personal shadow. A lot of new agers are just running from their shadow into light. So their Christ is all light with no wounds. What I like about the Christian interpretation of Christ is that the Cosmic Christ has wounds. The Cosmic Christ is on the side of the oppressed. We have to pay attention to that and go into that darkness and suffering.[7]

It is ironic that diametrically opposed interpretations can be found in the Christian critique of the New Age. Fox sees New Agers spending too much time in the "light, light, light," when they are not driving in their BMWs to speak with archangels.

The conservative Christian right, on the other hand, sees the New Age as conspiring with darkness. When the New Age healer attempts to relieve a person's suffering, fundamentalists see Satan at work. In *New World Order*, Pat Robertson sees Fritjof Capra as a leader in the one-world New Age movement. This puts Capra in league with the forces of darkness, which is surely news to Capra! Even near-death experiences allegedly represent Satan's attempt to lead us away from the truth. This is doubly ironic, since many New Age spiritual groups open their meetings with "The Great Invocation" which, among other things, requests that Christ return to earth so that the door to evil will be forever sealed.

For anyone willing to do some serious sociological analysis of what New Age–oriented people do in their spare time (bearing in mind that some use the label and others do not), the picture is far more mixed and broadly based than most critics know. What is being insensitive to the "shadow of social injustice" supposed to mean? Is there some particular area of social injustice that Fox thinks everybody ought to put their full energy into? What counts and what does not?

Those who at one time or another adopted the labels of New Age Judaism or Aquarian Judaism (after the teachings of Rabbis Zalman Schachter-Shalomi, Schlomo Carlebach, William Blank, and others) have often combined their perennialist metaphysics with strong social justice agendas, such as a nuclear freeze, environmentalism, prisoner rights, and gender equality. They see no incompatibility between social justice issues and the New Age.

New Age Journal regularly runs major articles on social issues, as do other magazines and newsletters in the genre. San Francisco's New Age newspaper *Common Ground* and Atlanta's *Aquarius* have done lead articles on the destruction of the environment, loving relationships, nutrition, and global peace initiatives. Many of the same people who attend Lazaris workshops also do volunteer work in church kitchens for the homeless. They also write checks to the Sierra Club and to *New Options*, which (when it was in print) was one of the most socially aware newsletters in the country.

Those trained in psychic or spiritual healing often volunteer their services for AIDs patients. And they finish their sessions with a good long hug, something many physicians are often afraid to do. The New Age honored feminist political agendas and, in some cases, even offered prayers to a Father/Mother God well before such ideas gained currency on other fronts. And it has honored Native American traditions and practices for as long as the New Age label has been around. Does none of this count because New Agers also invoke "love and light" in their meditations?

When it comes to examining one's shadow side, what does Fox think takes place at New Age workshops and seminars? Most New Agers take seriously personal and spiritual growth agendas. Bantam Paperbacks even defines its New Age genre as a "search for meaning, growth, and change." And personal growth means you have to look at your issues, including your "shadow." Almost all forms of emotional release work, no matter what label they are practiced under—from rebirthing to holotropic therapy—involve facing one's shadow.

A Lazaris workshop may draw people from all over the country to explore ways of releasing guilt and fear. The participants typically find that Lazaris, legitimate channeled entity or not, helps them deal with their shadow. What's wrong with that? To take a different example, why should dealing with your issues on sexual domination at a Loving Relationships seminar not count as facing your shadow? And speaking of the need to go into darkness and suffering: who does Fox think is doing most of the exorcisms and casting out of demons (or "negative energy" as it is more neutrally put)? Certainly not the Catholic Church.

One can define the New Age narrowly, as a group of wealthy, crystal-gazing groupies or broadly, as intersecting with the entire spectrum of New Paradigm interests and agendas. *Publishers Weekly* (November, 1989) declared the end of the New Age because it is now such a part of the main-stream. Until we have an adequate definition of "New Ager" and a fair explanation of what counts as being sensitive to issues of social justice and personal shadows, discussions of where the New Age stands on such matters can lapse into incoherence.

THE SHAPE OF A NEW RELIGIOUS CONSCIOUSNESS

Taking into account Creation Spirituality, ecofeminism, liberation theologies, major spiritual traditions, the great axial sages, challenges to traditional religion, and accelerated interdimensional integration, what shape will a new religious consciousness take? Following are twelve proposals. In presenting these proposals, I vary my language between what I think *should* transpire and what I think *will* take place. These are, of course, not the same thing. To clarify matters, I believe that all of the proposals are worthy of implementation and that, in one form or another, most will come to pass.

1. A new religious consciousness should integrate absolute oneness with the creative interplay of complementary opposites along the Taoist lines suggested by Ken Carey: "One face of the Eternal One is ever formless and beyond definition, but the other face of the Eternal One appears as Two. These Two, between them, are the source of all created things."[8] In other words, God, Yahweh, or Brahman is most appropriately understood as a boundless and transcendent (nondual) radiance which gives rise to a fundamental polarity variously termed yin and yang, the masculine and feminine, Shiva and Shakti, or the forces of expansion and contraction. In their creative interplay, these polarities cause the worlds of form to come into being. This vision is balanced, nonsexist, process-oriented, and does justice to important mystical insights from different traditions.

2. Correlatively, a new religious paradigm should avoid a simple dualism of matter and spirit and adopt instead the polarity of complementary perspectives on the Great Chain of Being, which at some levels appears more as mass/energy and at other levels more as consciousness. Energy-consciousness is a dual-aspect continuum. The outside of consciousness looks like energy, and the inside of energy appears as consciousness. Beyond this polarity is the transcendent, nameless, and nondual Source. Whether our worlds of experience appear more as energy/mass or as projections of consciousness depends upon the *perspective* we adopt within the Great Chain.

If science and religion are to achieve complementarity, the desired integration must be based upon a metaphysics which makes it possible. Simply offering a blessing like "Let's all live together in the name of holism" over a mixture of Eastern mysticism and Western science won't achieve the desired result. The metaphysics of the Great Chain of Being is at least a good place to begin.

3. A new religious paradigm should incorporate a spiritually based ecological awareness. Fearful warnings that we must take care of the environment before we kill ourselves are a belated beginning, but still treat the Earth Mother as if she were an object. A spiritually based ecological awareness will promote the sacred value that the Earth Mother must be treated as if She were a valued, nurturing friend who has made herself *conditionally* available for our individual growth and evolution as a species. I should think that Jesus Christ would be most pleased if the leaders of all denominations founded in His name would declare a one-day Sunday moratorium

on homilies and requests for help. Instead of listening to a sermon, we would retreat to wooded areas to express gratitude to the earth for continuing to support us despite all the negativity we have dumped upon her.

4. A new religious perspective should incorporate the ideal of a relative balance between the masculine and the feminine, by whatever *complementary* means we choose. This balance should be nurtured within men and within women in ways that move beyond traditional social programming. Any religious outlook which continues to align itself with the preservation of patriarchy will experience progressive deterioration. But the answer to patriarchy isn't matriarchy any more than the answer to black slavery is white slavery. A matriarchally dominated religious consciousness would simply set up the conditions for yet another cyclical swing. Goddess talk, I believe, will become commonplace, but God talk will not disappear.

5. A new religious perspective should stress the progressive *transformation* of consciousness by whatever sacred and secular tools are appropriate, from meditation to the discerning use of color and sound frequencies. The challenges and ideals of this transformation must gradually be acknowledged and dealt with in daily living, not just intermittent communal rituals. Rituals that reinforce old habits, publicly espousing certain ideals of living while implicitly validating the status quo, will become irrelevant.

If you are in a position of spiritual leadership, ask not how your flock is growing, contributing, or supporting safe causes, but how many hearts you have touched and how much real difference you have made. If there is a day of judgment, then you will surely be judged by how earnestly and well you have *empowered* your church members and inspired them to grow. To accomplish this, I believe, will require fewer large buildings and many smaller consecrated centers, where the lines between spiritual alignment, personal growth, and holistic health are radically blurred. It will also require that members work through programs such as the *A Course in Miracles*, rather than merely listen to sermons.

6. A new religious consciousness should be inclusivist and non-adversarial. Its cosmology and practical guides will be broad enough to incorporate diversity without exclusivity. If you have adopted the way of Zen, your roshi may recommend certain lessons in Christ Consciousness. If you follow Christ, your priest may have you calm your mind through a program of zazen at the local monastery. If your path is service, it can expand your capacity for love. And if your path is love, it can be enhanced through

service. If your path is meditation, then you may be encouraged also to look seriously at oppression and social injustice.

So far as moral prescriptions are concerned, being a better Christian or Jew also will translate into being a better Muslim or Buddhist. Atheism will be treated as a stage of growth. Prayers will seek and express common ground. I suspect that many cross-cultural alliances will emerge that blur the lines between traditional religions. The path you are on will matter more than the name you give it. You will guide by example as much as by word, and certainly not by judgment, fear, or guilt.

If your path is fundamentally fear-based, thereby resulting in oppression and control, competition, greed, lack of forgiveness, or fragmentation, then you will not find yourself part of an inclusivist scenario. Those who continue to love and reach out to you may wish it were otherwise and for a while devise schemes to change your ways. But in the end, they will have to let go of their need to save you, and you will have to decide whether your path shall be one of love or fear. For the two do not go together.

7. A new spiritual consciousness should address social injustice through the awakening of an overflowing compassion which empowers those it touches and those from whom it emanates. The current method might be described as mixing whatever compassion you can muster with some guilt and fear in ways that result in "action at a distance." Fifty years ago the received wisdom was: "Yes, it's too bad about the Negroes, but we still can't let them in here." In 1995 the received wisdom is: "Write a check to support the church's kitchen for the homeless, but God forbid that congregation members would have to meet them and invite them to their homes for dinner."

Any orientation which attempts to deal with social injustice through moral persuasion, while leaving untouched the fear in people's hearts, will not succeed. A rising spiritual consciousness will stress empowerment from the inside, rather than control from the outside. Religious liberals explain why the poor need money for food, clothing, medicine, or shelter, although even the residents of Berkeley, California appear to be growing weary of this agenda. But when the root causes which lead to this impoverished state are not addressed, conservatives may justifiably complain that their money really isn't making much difference. Liberals and conservatives then have a holier-than-thou debate while the poor go hungry, children are molested, and the homeless sink into despair.

This is why decentralization is every bit as important in religion as it is in politics and economics. We need to be able to touch, to feel, to deal directly with those whom we wish to help. Religion must transform its own so that they may genuinely assist in the transformation of others. The problems of social injustice are too large for centralized governments to effectively deal with by themselves, especially when those governments themselves reflect attitudes and thinking which have been fueling the problems.

8. A spiritually based religious consciousness should mold its beliefs about survival of death around some suitable version of reincarnation. I have shown why belief in reincarnation is rational. Moreover, once the mistaken stereotypes of reincarnation are removed, there are no good reasons for rejecting it on moral, social, or psychological grounds. Beyond this, reincarnation cannot be conclusively proven. However, it continues to make headway in the general population. And if current trends continue, over half the population of America will be leaning toward acceptance of reincarnation by the turn of the century!

One can curse this trend, hold out for something else, work around it, or integrate it into a general worldview. Taken at face value, reincarnation is not any stranger or more difficult an idea to integrate into mainstream religious attitudes and practices than other challenges Western religion has faced. Reincarnation, more than any other perspective, will prove to be the great equalizer among mainstream religious traditions. Those traditions with exclusivist claims will fight it accordingly.

9. A new religious consciousness should not only acknowledge the paranormal but integrate it as well. I do not mean that each and every fantasy should be honored as the Gospel. Indeed, one of the major practical issues of the paranormal is how to distinguish legitimate from bogus phenomena. But if one's worldview cannot make some place for such things as near-death experiences, spiritual healing, and past-life phenomena, then it will become progressively less relevant. Far too much is happening in this arena to ignore.

I want to stress that, as the dimensions associated with normal waking consciousness and transcendental consciousness continue to become integrated (remembering that they already interpenetrate), today's *paranormal* experience will become tommorow's normal experience—especially where matters of spirit are concerned. For the most part, however, social scientists, journalists, and even many religious leaders fail to grasp this fact.

When confronted, for example, with the phenomenal rise of interest in angels evidenced in books, television, and even a new journal, *Angel Times*, they fall back upon standard psychological explanations—social angst, millennium fever, and hallucinations born of the need to believe in "something greater." The most difficult explanation for them to accept is that angels actually exist as part of a greater reality and that as more people awaken to dimensional overlays, they will see quite literally more of what the Great Chain of Being is all about.

Religion will have to incorporate this expanded awareness (as well as greater heart-centeredness) into its teachings, or risk irrelevance. Never has such a dense planet been cut off from its spiritual roots for so long. Now that the reconnection is underway, scientists and religious leaders alike should *celebrate*, rather than attempt to explain away, this fact in all of its forms. Many aspects of the paranormal, especially in spiritual contexts, are becoming normal.

10. A new religious paradigm should incorporate a progressive understanding of subtle energies informed by sacred geometry. Subtle energy gridlines in and around the earth will assume a prime importance in constructing houses of worship. Religious symbols will come to have deeper metaphysical meanings not typically appreciated in their current contexts. Why candles should be lit at certain times and where they should be placed, for example, will be dictated more by an appreciation of the energetic forms behind the scenes, so to speak, than by traditional aesthetics.

Linear, toroidal and logarithmic spiral forms will probably come to be studied and incorporated for their empowering effects as much as for their natural beauty which is amply illustrated in the physical universe and in Dan Winter's *Alphabet of the Heart*. The Platonic solids, sine wave forms, the phi ratio or Golden Section (1.618), and Fibonacci series (illustrated in everything from healthy dental curvatures to certain crop circle formations), will be more consciously integrated into places of worship and of healing—not to mention living! The power of the tetrahedron in particular will become more recognized. The precise geometry of waveforms underlying various types of experience, from depression to mystical rapture, will be explored.

Ceremonial and transformational rooms, such as those found in the Great Pyramid, will reflect precise proportions and numerical ratios in order to facilitate growth. Our understanding of the differences between the sacred and the profane, the holy and the mundane, will be deepened by an awareness of energy configurations not always recognized in traditional religion. Geometry also may come to be seen as the basis for the Hebrew (and other) alphabet(s), as argued by Stan Tenen in publications of the Meru Foundation. Noted scientists have confirmed many of the connections Tenen has uncovered between the Torah and hyperspace physics, and rabbinical scholars have suggested that his work is comparable in significance to the discovery of the Dead Sea Scrolls. In his pioneering *Keys of Enoch* and in publications of the Institute for Future Science, J.J. Hurtak explores related topics, especially the geometry underlying profound changes in DNA and cell structure, subtle body anatomy, and geomagnetic grids.

After twenty years of intensive exploration, researcher Fred Mills explains in the Appendix why one of the most important things the Creative Intelligence of the universe ever expressed was: "Let ø = 1+1/ø." In time, geometry will be understood not only as the basis for defining dimensional limits within the Great Chain of Being, but also as a basis for connecting different dimensions—in short, as one of God's primary tools of creation. And sacred geometry will become a required course in theological training. Indeed, the comprehensive course on sacred geometry (among other things) offered by Drunvalo Melchizedek through workshops and videos has already become important training for students all over the world who are seriously exploring the interface of science and spirituality.

Arguably the most formidable application of sacred geometry to an edifice of spiritual tranformation will be the Templar, a multi-level pyramidal structure only slightly smaller than the one at Giza, currently being designed by Norma Milanovich and her colleagues. The Templar will incorporate sacred geometry from all of the world's major religions. Through the precise integration of form, proportion, substance, and frequency, it will facilitate spiritual transformation in a way not seen on this planet, if ever, for thousands of years. The Templar is projected to be complete by 2012.

11. A new religious consciousness, as Fox reminds us, should nurture our capacity to hope, to play, to enjoy pleasure, to live in the moment, to be less afraid of the unpredictable, to let go, and most of all, to create (whether through art, science, or religion). Living on earth, having a body, and being in relationship will not be albatrosses around our necks, responsibilities pulling us to the grave, or dense fogs permeating our consciousness. Most of all, experiencing love's many avenues, growing in love, and being love will assume center stage in the multiple agendas of the new spiritual consciousness.

12. A new religious paradigm should give us a revitalized cosmology, including a sense of our origins, our patterns of evolution, and our possible destinies. It will place the encounter with darkness in a meaningful

perspective. It will connect us with other parts of the universe and other levels of the Great Chain of Being. It will make us unafraid to greet and interact with extraterrestrial visitors, when they manifest in a widespread and unequivocal fashion. This cosmology will spill over into and be affected by other leading edges of a Rising Culture, including education, health, science, human relations.

In summary, a new religious paradigm should assist us in the transition from a dying worldview predicated upon fragmentation, fear, competition, hierarchical control, reductionism, and localization toward wholeness, love, mutually empowering cooperation, and an expanded awareness of the many dimensions of reality. This new religious consciousness already is being birthed in the matrix of accelerated interdimensional integration. It is part of a global shift in consciousness.

APOCALYPTIC CREATION:
EARTH CHANGES AND MILLENNIUM FEVER

Beginning this last section with an oxymoron at first sight does not bode well for a sense of completion. Apocalypses represent ends, whereas creations represent beginnings. Still, there are ways to smooth over this dissonance. After all, the myth of a rising phoenix represents creating a new order from the ashes of an earlier one. And mythology can generate some predictions that, if they do not come to pass, still leave the main story intact.

This much is certain. There is a great deal of concern, speculation, research, and humorous dismissal about the approaching millennium, especially the period between 1994 and 2012. As psychologist Kenneth Ring, author of *Heading Toward Omega*, notes: "Apocalyptic thinking is in the air. As we approach that subjective date, 2000, images stored in the collective unconscious begin to populate our dreams and visions."[9] What sort of images? Floods, famine, earthquakes, strange flying objects, holocaustic (nuclear) war, angels and beings of light, and dark Antichrist-like figures.

Philosopher Michael Grosso, author of *Millennium Myth*, goes a step further in suggesting that these prophetic symbols "percolating in the collective unconscious of the West are now assuming an objective content they never had before."[10] Indeed, the worldwide poisoning of land, air, and water, ozone depletion and greenhouse effects, holy wars and terrorism, and, especially in America, higher crime rates, drugs, greed, and budgetary deficits are enough to convince some that, if anything is left, it would not be worth living for anyway. Grosso goes so far as to suggest that the mere subliminal belief in certain things, such as UFOs or the Virgin Mary, can become so strong that they appear, not merely as mirages, but as physically real—a case of collective psychokinesis!

Of course, the belief that the end is near is hardly new. Some saw it as imminent in A.D. 33, just after the crucifixion. Despite Saint Augustine's earlier (fifth century A.D.) warning against literal reading of prophecy and Christ's own warning in *Acts* 1:7 that "it is not for you to know the times or the seasons" (of his return), specific dates continued to surface. Many in Europe prepared for it on a massive scale in A.D. 999, partly because certain signs were in the air, such as visions of Saint Peter, and partly because it *was* the millennium. "So great was the millenarian fervor, according to legend, that on the stroke of midnight on January 1, 1000, [a large segment of the population of] Iceland converted en masse to Christianity, apparently as a spiritual prophylactic against the coming apocalypse."[11] Hildegard of Bingen (1098–1179) later weighed in with a vision of cataclysm by comet.

Many parishioners joined fundamentalist William Miller, who foretold the end as coming on April 3, 1843, based upon his study of *Revelation* and especially of *Daniel* 8:1–13. The prophecy failed, but a number of conservative Christian denominations like, for example, Seventh-Day Adventists still trace their roots to or through Miller's apocalyptic thinking. It was also assumed that the 1917 Fatima prophecies (when the Virgin Mary appeared to three girls) signified the beginning of the end. And in 1962, the same year Jeanne Dixon foresaw the birth of the Antichrist, an ominous astrological conjunction according to Hindu charts caused widespread panic in India. It seems as if the end is always near!

And so it is again in the nineties. A recent *U.S. News and World Report* survey (December 19, 1994) indicates that sixty percent of Americans believe in a literal judgement day and end of the world. And one-third of those believe that they will occur in less than twenty years. However, this time there appears to be a significant difference. Earlier fears of impending doom were derived from interpretations of specific individuals, based upon sources cited largely in isolation from each other. Education, the media, technology, and increased interest and research into apocalyptic scenarios have changed all this.

The Hopi may share primitive cultural roots with the Mayans and Aztecs, but they were not aware of Nostradamus or Edgar Cayce. And while Cayce read his Bible, there is little to suggest that he read *Nostradamus*. Hal Lindsey, author of *The Late, Great Planet Earth*, is vaguely aware of other prophetic traditions. But he also bases his scenario (nuclear war, China marching into Israel, and the Second Coming) primarily upon biblical scripture.

What appears to be different about this millennium watch is the *convergence* of different traditions or specific prophecies. In *Pole Shift*, for example, John White carefully develops these convergences from his investigation of many different traditions or sources, including geophysics. Kirk Nelson adopts a similar convergence approach (Nostradamus, the Hopi, Edgar Cayce, etc.) in *The Second Coming*.[12]

It requires careful historical and biographical research, of course, to determine whether we have a genuine independent convergence, or merely one prophet borrowing from another. Independent or not, belief in a massive prophetic convergence is exhibiting a powerful influence. New Age conferences are running on overdrive with "cleansing the planet" metaphors and stories of the "Let me tell you about my mission for these exciting times" variety.

However, there are also many literate, discerning and serious-minded people (many a part of the larger New Paradigm dialogue) who publicly pooh-pooh Nostradamus fever, Christian fundamentalism, and New Age groupies, while privately looking over their shoulders and behaving as if they would not be terribly surprised if some conjunction of the paranormal and the cataclysmic were to unfold. To like-minded colleagues they cloak acknowledgment of such scenarios with humor, such as "Are you strapped in for the nineties?" while their tone of voice conveys something like "Are these *really* just transformational metaphors?" Even the skeptical authors of a recent review of apocalyptic visions at times had to pinch themselves.

> We must admit that…we sometimes fell into an apocalyptic malaise ourselves. Badly printed religious tracts began to assume a weird kind of logic, and we began noticing eerie coincidences between Ezekiel and the UFO people, the Hopi and Edgar Cayce, Nostradamus, Our Lady of Fatima, the Mayan calendar stone, Jerry Falwell, and the National Academy of Sciences, all of whom agree we're in perilous times.[13]

To focus this kind of thinking in more detail I have prepared the following list. It is far from complete, but does convey most of the key claims. I have made no attempt to determine the truth of particular claims. Rather, I offer observations on the logical status of each scenario in light of the larger spectrum of interpretations. What would it take to show that we are actually living out a particular vision? Massive earthquakes and wars per se are probably not sufficient to do the trick, even if we assume that different prophets really had the 1990s in mind.

Earthquakes and volcanic eruptions. Cayce and Nostradamus (who may have been one and the same soul), Hopi legend, and conservative biblical commentators, not to mention countless practicing psychics, have predicted rather massive earth changes. Jeffrey Goodman's *We are the Earthquake Generation* integrates some of this material, although central predictions for the eighties did not come to pass.[14] The problem for the nineties is that it would take a lot of major earthquakes to provide evidence after the fact for a prediction in this arena.

To varying degrees, earthquakes and volcanic eruptions happen all the time all over the world. In themselves they are neither necessary nor sufficient for either cataclysmic or paranormal scenarios. New York, San Francisco, and Tokyo could be leveled in successive years, but the geophysicists at CSICOP would argue that this is just one of the freak coincidences that happen every ten thousand years or so. Only massive earthquakes in conjunction with other predicted phenomena would begin to count as confirming evidence for the larger apocalyptic vision. The most directly related events are described in the following sections.

Massive sinking and flooding (with or without a pole shift). We have heard it before. California (together with other Western real estate) will fall into the sea, Atlanta will become a seaport, Atlantis (or parts thereof) will rise off the Bimini coast, Northern Europe will become very "swampy" in places, and New York City and Tokyo will disappear into the ocean. Goodman's *We Are the Earthquake Generation* and White's *Pole Shift* describe such predictions from multiple sources and traditions.

Presumably, these developments might occur independently of each other and of any pole shift. But a pole shift, which Cayce foresaw as coming in 1998 in the "twinkling of an eye" and which would shift the earth's rotational axis in order to compensate for massive imbalance in the polar ice caps, is certainly the simplest explanation. For were this to happen, the forces exerted on the earth's plate structures and oceans would render the preceding cataclysms mild by comparison.

Be that as it may, this kind of geological event, e.g., California and South Florida sinking into the ocean within the next twenty years, would provide far more dramatic evidence for the prophecies with cataclysmic components. Were they not to occur in this time period, one of two things would happen. Either prophecies necessarily linked to major "earth changes" would fade into falsified irrelevance, or noncataclysmic components of the prophecy would be stressed together with after-the-fact reinterpretations stating that cataclysms were not part of the core meaning anyway.

Not only do cataclysms not have to occur, but they also need not be part of a sudden worldwide transformational vision. The Second Coming, World War III, or publicly verified exchanges with UFOs and alien civilizations would, individually or collectively, produce massive changes without cataclysms.

It is also worth noting that John White revised his earlier probability estimates of a pole shift based upon new evidence for the nonexistence of earlier shifts. For example, we now have less cataclysmic explanations of those seemingly flash-frozen woolly mammoths we've heard about. White took seriously the convergence of prophetic opinion, but his earlier case in *Pole Shift* was made on scientific grounds as well. As such, it was at least partly falsifiable. Now he believes that a pole shift will *not* occur in our lifetimes. White thus joins John Perry, Kenneth Ring, and others in urging that prophetic visions of doom should not be regarded as literal precognitions of a future-in-waiting. They should be seen instead as reflections of the collective psyche of our time generating its own images of planetary death and regeneration which psychically sensitive individuals can access. These images are neither truths nor falsehoods, but profound reminders of the necessity for global transformation.[15]

Some combination of conventional or nuclear war on varying scales. The Hopi (gourds of disease-causing ashes falling from the sky), Nostradamus (metallic objects launched from ships which vaporize a city), Fatima (those who survive vaporized oceans and fires from heaven "will envy the dead"), and Cayce prophecies all point to war on an unprecedented scale somewhere near the end of the twentieth century. Fundamentalists are convinced that, no matter what the scope or means, Israel and the Middle East will be critically involved. For many the countdown began in 1948 when Israel came into being.

However, the above predictions plus others I have seen do not require all-out total nuclear annihilation. They are consistent with either limited nuclear war involving, say, Europe and the Middle East, or an expanded conventional war. Recent arms reductions and peace initiatives between

America and Russia coupled with Glasnost and Eastern European demo-cratic reforms have rendered far less probable the likelihood of mutual nuclear destruction. Whatever Nostradamus, the Fatima girls, and Cayce saw seems not to be the American-Soviet conflagration in the background of world politics for the past forty years.

Trump card: Is the future what it used to be? Here is the grand version of a problem raised in an earlier chapter. With all of these individuals predict-ing similar scenarios, if only a few occur over the next ten years, shall we say that they were *mistaken* in what they saw? On the other hand, could it be that certain events, such as nuclear war or major geological upheavals, were going to occur in this time frame, but have been narrowly reduced or avoided? Some in the New Age and Native American communities inter-pret the recent birth of an extremely rare white buffalo in Janesville, Wisconsin as a sign of hope and reconciliation in keeping with Native American legend.

Should we now be more hopeful about what we used to fear? According to this line of thinking, "light workers" have helped to raise consciousness to the point where extreme elements are no longer necessary to force de-sired changes. We are still in a race to raise consciousness and take our des-tinies into our own hands. But we have avoided the worst-case scenario. This is an underlying theme of Ken Carey's *Starseed: Millennium*. No matter what happens in this period, it was going to be worse than what we will actually experience.

This is one interpretation of the nonevent of May, 1988: California slip-ping into the sea (Cayce had predicted 1964). Metaphysicians inform us that the Earth Mother gave her children a reprieve because there is considerably more hope for the species than there was, say, in 1960. The vibrations of planetary consciousness had risen enough to forestall this day of reckoning.

Of course, this is a bit too convenient for social critics. The light worker interpretation angers those who have been laboring long and hard for peace, arms reduction, and environmental sanity. How dare these light workers take credit for anything! New Agers, of course, simply co-opt the territory and point out that the folks in Beyond War, Physicians for Social Responsibility, and Greenpeace are all part of the shift in consciousness and deserve credit for their light work, even if they do not label themselves accordingly.

There is a catch–22 that has split New Age opinion over the relationship of reducing negative emotions, especially fear, and reducing the catastrophic elements of prophecy. Many in the New Age community worry about the right time to cash in their mutual funds and move to "safe" territory. Others, however, accuse them of buying into fear and actually contributing to the energy that will trigger dark events. (Even discussing apocalyptic scenarios or reading about them is considered taboo!) Members of the first group respond that since some of these challenging events appear destined to happen (even if we don't know exactly which ones), it is only prudent to store extra food and keep a watchful eye for some secluded property near water.

Part of the answer to this debate, I suspect, turns on being able to draw a clear line between fear-based behavior, on the one hand, and prudent behavior, on the other. Wearing a seatbelt is prudent, for example, whereas locking the door each time you walk to the mailbox is fearful. At the core of the debate, however, is some hardened opinion that refuses to budge. For any given major earth change, some will say: "I'm glad I moved away from there." Others will respond: "But if you had stayed there and anchored more light, maybe the quake would not have been so severe."

This same fuzzy logic works in reverse. If nothing untoward happens in a certain area, some will argue after the fact that the more evolved consciousness of people living there kept it safe, whereas others will point out that in all probability nothing was going to happen anyway. The solution to this impossible exchange, I think, is not to argue the truth or falsity of either point of view. Rather, it consists in reminding the disputants to practice discernment, not take themselves too seriously, trust the universe, and to unconditionally let go of fear—no matter what the outcome may be.

Still, being forewarned about certain elements of a potentially dark future strikes a powerful chord with many, both in and out of the New Age community. Even prophets from the past sometimes channel themselves on the current scene to help prevent our future being what it was when they originally saw it. The most notable example of such intervention is Nostradamus, who has allegedly returned in spirit not only to clarify the quatrains his critics misinterpreted, but also to warn us about the Antichrist. As Dolores Cannon explains in *Conversations with Nostradamus*, the Antichrist (a former philosophy and computer science major) is now a power broker behind the scenes in the Middle East. (Both Jeanne Dixon and Cannon/Nostradamus agree that he was born in 1962.)

He will allegedly surface in the mid-to-late nineties with charisma, respect, and a plan to help the world economy, which by then Nostradamus predicts will be in terrible condition. However, implementing his plan (including a universal I.D. imprint for each person) could result in a serious loss of personal freedom. There is a very real danger that we could pass the point of no return and adopt what looks like a positive proposal that will move us instead toward a world government and massive control.

Nostradamus believes that, with his warning, we are better prepared to avoid a worst case scenario. Whether we believe this warning is really from him rather than from Dolores Cannon's subconscious mind, or whether we believe the Antichrist is fictional or real, this warning should not be altogether ignored. For the seeds of dissent and the signs of revolutionary change are all around. And historically, they have been the spawning ground for Antichrist-like individuals to surface and seize control.

Another voice from the past concerned about the profound changes we face is the mother of Jesus. In addition to her numerous appearances at Fatima, Medjugorje, Conyers, and elsewhere, Mary has channeled herself clairaudiently through Annie Kirkwood, as chronicled in *Mary's Message to the World*. She predicts major famine, earthquakes, and violent weather patterns for the nineties. Of particular note are two predictions relating to UFOs and to our solar system that lend themselves to clear verification. Not only will we see more UFOs (which has been going on for several decades), we will also interact with representatives of alien cultures in a publicly acknowledged fashion. Furthermore, by the turn of the century we will become part of a binary star system. Earth will have two suns.

Of most significance in Mary's message, however, is the compassion that pours from her heart to all people of earth. She asks that we pray for each other and for the Earth Mother and most importantly that we align ourselves with God in a direct, unconditional manner. This connection will be our strongest ally in the changes to come. Her urgent pleas in this regard are as clear an expression of the divine aspects of motherhood that we could ask for.

Two contemporary prophets: Gordon-Michael Scallion and Mary Summer Rain. After an illness when he temporarily lost his voice, Gordon-Michael Scallion began receiving a wide array of clairvoyant visions, some of which related to health, but most of which related to earth changes. He sees earthquakes, tidal waves, and radical shifts in weather patterns. What distinguishes Scallion is the straightforward, unassuming, not-for-profit, and balanced manner in which he sets forth in each month's newsletter fairly specific times and places for future events. And he grades himself on misses that do not turn out as he had predicted.

Thus far, he appears to be no less than fifty percent correct, depending upon how carefully one defines a hit. He correctly predicted the devastation by Hurricane Andrew, for example, and, more recently, an 8.0 earthquake in the Indian Ocean near Sri Lanka and the devastating January, 1995 earthquake in Japan. His August, 1993 prediction of an 8.0–9.0 earthquake near Japan for 1994 was born out on October 4, 1994. What drew much attention in the spring of 1993 was his long-standing prediction that, by no later than May 9 of that year, a "mega-quake" above 8.0 with multiple epicenters would devastate California. The prediction failed so far as mass devastation occurring by that date. Since then, however, two quakes in the 8.0 range have been registered in Southern California. He predicts a 9.0 (plus or minus .5) quake will hit the Palm Springs area in 1995 and also one of the same magnitude will occur along the New Madrid fault line in 1995–'96.

According to Scallion, by 2001 much of the Western United States will be under water, Atlanta will be a seaport, and much of the rest of the coast of the country will be under water, sometimes as much as fifty to a hundred miles inland. Similar cataclysms are seen for other parts of the world. A very large island (which he believes to be Atlantis, with a retrievable technology) will rise off the coast of Florida. Strange weather patterns will continue to be the order of the day, such as a record warm February in 1995 and record-breaking rains in the spring. Food and water shortages will be rampant, and the economy will be in collapse by 1996–97. America will become a series of colonies, split by a widened Mississippi River into two subcontinents. New diseases will manifest, although AIDS will have disappeared shortly after the turn of the century.[16] With Mary, he also sees the earth as having *two* suns by shortly after the turn of the century.

Scallion calls this time period, 1993–2001, that of tribulation. And he believes that the essential overall pattern is set and can be modified only in detail, depending upon shifts in consciousness by local populations. He also believes that much of this, especially the breakup of California, was originally slated to begin in 1988, but that we were granted a reprieve. Scallion's predictions have drawn considerable attention because of his past record. No prophets have been as detailed in their geological predictions. It remains to be seen who is more correct in the big calls.

Mary Summer Rain is the friend, student, and literary intermediary of a Native American medicine woman and prophet called "No-Eyes," first introduced in *Spirit Song* and continued in a celebrated series including *Dreamwalker* and *Whispered Wisdom*. In *Phoenix Rising* (1987), Mary Summer Rain presents No-Eyes's vision of the changes to come, together with compelling insights into the relationship between the Earth Mother and all who inhabit her domain. She expresses compassion over the destruction she sees but joy over the Earth Mother's rebirth from the ashes.

In an appendix to *Phoenix Rising*, Mary Summer Rain organizes all of No-Eyes's visions. It is one of the longest and most diverse collections, based on prophetic insight, in print today. Most of the standard predictions are there, like those involving massive earth changes, in particular in the area of the New Madrid fault line. But lesser-discussed predictions are also included. Among them are increased relocation of industries overseas, rampant white collar crime, return of the dust bowl, freak wind gusts and accidents, liquefaction of soil beneath fault lines, insect infestation, increased plane crashes and train derailments, a greenish hue to the atmosphere, attempted oppression (through the courts) by conservative religious sects, amusement park disasters, increased UFO sightings, several catastrophic meltdowns of nuclear reactors, open tax rebellion, and biological warfare.

Levels of explanation. It is unlikely that we will establish clear lines of demarcation between different prophecies. Plagues and famine figure in Hopi legends, Nostradamus, the gospel of *Matthew* 24, and Scallion's prophecies, for example, but none by itself seems critical to the apocalyptic vision. Mary Summer Rain's collection in places is suggestive of biblical prophecy, yet makes no mention of the return of Christ. No single person or tradition seems to have the market cornered, so to speak.

Any apocalyptic vision can be formulated so that AIDS does or does not play a critical role. A ten-fold increase in AIDS by itself doesn't mean the end is near, and the eradication of AIDS doesn't mean that other components (e.g., a collision with a comet or large asteroid foreseen by Hildegard of Bingen and Nostradamus) would not come to play the central role. Which is one way of saying that, unless the changes envisioned are *collectively massive*, we may never know if this is really it!

The problem is thornier than one might suspect. Suppose, for example, that a man wearing white robes and performing miracles appears near Mt. Olive in 1996. Suppose, moreover, that he claims to be the Messiah. How would we know? First of all, we don't really know what Jesus is supposed to look like. Many other biblical prophecies would have to fall into place before anybody would take this man seriously. But suppose instead that the man in question really is Jesus Christ with an important message: Armageddon is canceled because the state of the world is not as hopeless as John (in *Revelation*) thought it would be. How many followers could he attract?

In this potpourri of claims, there is a strong contextual dependence. A pole shift, for example, would confirm Cayce, be consistent with Nostradamus, and tend to rule out the biblical forecast. Who wants (or needs) war when their crops are ten feet under water and the antagonists are freezing to death? You might say that if Jesus appeared this would still clinch the biblical account. The problem, however, is that the real Jesus is not supposed to appear in conjunction with a pole shift, which many in the New Age community declare is not going to happen after all. Where you end up in terms of verifying these scenarios very much depends upon where you begin.

Inevitably, simple predictions of what will happen force us to explain why they are supposed to occur in the first place. Needless to say, such proposed explanations come in many varieties and are developed on several different levels. I shall begin by summarizing the simplest and most straightforward explanations and then move to the more controversial.

First are what I shall call psychological, historical, or geophysical *tension models*. All represent forms of naturalistic explanation. They can be adapted to fit a wide variety of circumstances. According to such models, no matter what happens in the nineties, it is explainable by the relevant tensions. If nuclear war over Europe or massive plagues and famine occur, they will be seen as reflecting natural, though in some cases poorly understood, processes with no particular religious implications.

Psychologists and sociologists use tension models to account for the widespread *belief* in dire consequences. Their argument is that, in times of great stress, people can be expected to invent fictions and to find hidden meaning in various events when none is objectively there. As British historian Norman Cohn, author of *The Pursuit of the Millennium*, notes, when historical conditions create mass distortion and anxiety, "traditional beliefs about a future golden age…serve as vehicles for social aspirations and animosities…The usual desire of the poor to improve the material conditions of their lives becomes transfused with fantasies of a world reborn into innocence through a final, apocalyptic massacre."[17] Cohn's explanation, of course, is no more logically relevant to the actual occurrence or nonoccurrence of cataclysmic events than belief in God is to the actual existence or nonexistence of God.

A special version of tension modeling is found in contemporary biblical scholarship. Both mainstream scholars and even theologians associated with millennialist think tanks, such as Dallas Theological Seminary, Moody Bible Institute, and Wheaton College, have begun to suggest that biblical prophecies—understood in light of the culture of their times—should never have been taken so literally, since they were not intended as such in the first place.

For example, apocalyptic texts were often written during times of oppression using powerful images known to the people in order to assure them of God's saving grace. The Antichrist in *Revelation* may well have been intended to signify Nero, one of the principal persecutors of Christians. And passages in *Ezekiel* that fundamentalists see foreshadowing a future Armageddon most likely refer to the invasion of Israel by Scythian armies in pre-Christian times. Such culture-bound tension models contribute significantly to our understanding of prophecy. However, they do not take seriously enough the (clairvoyant?) visionary aspects of prophecy, whether biblical or otherwise.

The second level of apocalyptic explanation may be described as *metaphysically neutral*. According to this view there are "deep cycles" built into the universe which affect both the earth's geological history and human evolution. These cycles could relate to astrological lore or to something as elementary as major magnetic field shifts on the planet.

The earth's magnetic field, for example, is now considerably reduced from where it was just twenty years ago. According to some commentators, this comparative weakness has the effect of magnifying the power of our thoughts, emotions, and even the consequences of our actions. It is easier to break through conscious or unconscious barriers when there is less magnetic force sustaining them.

Deep natural cycles may have analogs in the *I Ching* or even in our genetic code. Or they may be encoded in obscure markings in the Great Pyramid. They may have been discovered and used by the Mayans, or they may not have. Interesting arguments have been marshalled for each of these interpretations.[18]

This kind of explanation, however, does not prejudge the question of whether the cycles reflect poorly understood physical principles or spiritually oriented principles grounded in higher levels of the Great Chain. We do not know why the Mayan calendar ends at 2012, except that the Mayans believed this to be the end of a major cycle. Whatever the underlying meta-physics may be, the functional convergence of a number of major histori-cal cycles is taken to have a deep prophetic meaning. We are supposed to be "prepared" for the end of one age and the beginning of another—with details to be filled in later!

The third level of explanation I describe as one of *adversarial metaphys-ics.* This type of explanation is anything but neutral. It pits the forces of darkness against the forces of light. Various apocalyptic phenomena—famine, war, plague, psychics and channeled entities leading us astray, etc.—are the tangible effects of this deeper level battle. From *Revelation 12*: "And there was war in heaven: Michael and his angels fought against the dragon...And the great dragon was cast out into the earth...having great wrath because he knoweth that he hath but a short time." According to this scenario, Lucifer is vanquished, Christ literally descends from heaven to gather up the faithful, and a thousand years of peace follow.

There are also less literal though equally metaphysically robust versions. In a passage suggestive of Matthew Fox, Tudor Pole writes:

> It is my belief that the 'Revealer of Word' (the Christos) ...has already descended into the invisible spheres that surround our planet and that those with eyes to see and ears to hear can begin to discern the message He is bring-ing, even though the Messenger may not be clothed in form or outwardly discernible.[19]

Christianity is not the only religion with a built-in polarity in this respect. In the *Bhagavad Gita*, for example, Krishna explains to Arjuna: "Whenever there is a withering of the Law and an uprising of lawlessness on all sides, then *I* manifest Myself. For the salvation of the righteous and the destruction of such as do evil, I come to birth age after age."[20]

Christ and the New Age. There is a small section of the New Paradigm spectrum who are appropriately labeled "Christ Centered New Agers." They are not Christian in the traditional sense of the term, for they nearly all believe in some form of reincarnation, extraterrestrials, and the discerning use of channeling. But neither are they flaky caricatures of New Agers running after the guru of the week. They pray as well as meditate. And they take evil very seriously, including demonic beings. For the most part they believe that Christ is about to return in a clearly recognizable form.

Such literalism makes other New Agers, who like to talk about Christ Consciousness rather than Christ, rather uneasy!

This should warm the hearts of evangelical Christians (and some Jews!), were it not for the fact that New Age Christians base their beliefs on more than the *New Testament*. They believe, additionally, that Christ has been channeling himself through a number of sources over the past decade or so, attempting to set the record straight and to prepare humankind for a dramatic transformation. His message is one of practical advice and techniques for personal transformation in some contexts, such as *A Course in Miracles*. His message is one of historical and moral rectification in other contexts, such as Evelyn Gordon's and Mary Joyce's *Sky Father and Son,* and Virginia Essene's *New Teachings for an Awakening Humanity*.[21]

I will not review the criticism that persons who claim to channel exhaulted beings like Jesus, even if well-intentioned, are on a self-delusional ego trip. This is likely true in many instances. In others, however, the power and quality of the message, coupled with the atmosphere of the channeling, are enough to cause one to give the message serious consideration. In what follows, I will set forth some of the more startling claims and invite readers to relate to them as they see fit.

1. In other levels of the Great Chain, Jesus is known as Lord Sananda, who incarnates and offers guidance throughout the galaxy.
2. He has had more than one incarnation on earth.
3. He is revered by many extraterrestrial groups, such as those associated with Ashtar Command.
4. The original Adam and Eve came from another star system with eleven other couples to form Twelve Tribes with enhanced genetic capabilities at a time when Neanderthals walked the planet.
5. Jesus had more than twelve apostles and many of his better ones were women. Prevailing Jewish (and later Catholic) patriarchy conspired to conceal the truth. Scripture was manipulated.
6. He is far more concerned with the presence or absence of love in people's hearts than with church attendance or being worshipped.
7. He deeply needs our help in raising consciousness and clearing negativity. Preparing the way for a better world is a joint mission.
8. He is extraordinarily upset by the atrocities committed in his name, by unending war and strife, and by the rape of the planet.
9. He is returning before the millennium in physical, although not necessarily tangible, form. He periodically shows himself for specific reasons. For example, Pope John the 23rd appears to have

written in his personal journal (which has only recently come to light) of such visitations by both Jesus and Mary in his private chambers.

10. He spent time in India.
11. Lucifer was not the culprit; rather, Jehovah (one of God's "sons") manipulated light codes so as to cast a veil over human consciousness. Nor is 666 the "number of the beast;" it is a holy number 999 turned upside down by dark forces to sow confusion in the minds of light workers hard-pressed to distinguish light from darkness in these transitional times.

Saying something is so does not make it so. However, it is worth stressing that, of nearly all the signs associated with an end-times scenario, the return of Christ is central. Other signs may come and go, but without him the core prophecy fails. Critics like to explain millennium fever away on a variety of psychological grounds. These accounts contain important truths, especially for understanding popular movements associated with this fever. However, the current convergence of predictions from such diverse sources may be unprecedented. Many I am not able to describe here.[22] I hope to have shown, however, that for those interested in prophetic overlays, the times in which we live provide enough clues to justify watching carefully.

Let me offer in conclusion that I do not believe the darker prophecies described in this chapter will materialize. The poles are not going to shift, Armageddon will not occur, and the Antichrist (if someone like him arises) will be neither as identifiable nor as powerful as he is traditionally portrayed. A number of factors have influenced my thinking on this matter.

In the first place, some of the worst-case predictions are so inherently unclear both in their content and in their timing, it's difficult to know what to make of them. It is simply not clear what many of their authors—with the exception of those we can talk to, such as Scallion—really intended to convey. Moreover, it is not evident that many of the events under consideration even merit the label of "dark," when what we witness may be simply the massive shift of one kind of energy in order to make room for another—an altogether natural process.

Finally, with many prophets there is the implication that certain dark events will happen, unless *we change our ways*. And in the last few decades we have begun to change our ways. I think we still face unprecedented challenges of the kind to which the seers in this chapter have drawn our attention. And a convergence of opinion on many of them is seriously worth taking into account.

But *if* the darker prophecies were going to occur in our lifetime, they no longer are. What was the future is no longer going to be. Even Nostradamus, who is generally credited with some of these darker predictions, remarked to his son: "The future is *not* fixed." And one reason it is not fixed is that when prophets bring negative thought-forms to the surface on a masssive scale, these thought forms then can be acknowledged and transmuted.

We will probably see earth changes, especially relating to the weather, on an *unexpected* scale, but not to the degreee earlier predicted. Humanity is beginning to wake up. Consciousness is transforming. And one of the key elements of this transformation, I believe, will be our officially acknowledged contact with extraterrestrials.

CHAPTER FOURTEEN

Galactic Destiny:
A Transformational Vision for Our Times

I considered several titles for this chapter, among them "Things Stephen Spielberg Never Dreamed Of" and "The Greatest Story Ever Told." For it integrates aspects of biblical prophecy, government cover-ups, the Perennial Wisdom, UFOs and alien encounters, the CIA and NASA, the clash between light and darkness, and the hopes and fears of persons in positions to know things they are not supposed to know. In other words, a potentially good piece of metaphysical science fiction. There's only one qualification. In my opinion, this account on the whole is closer to truth than fiction.

Elements have been told by others, with variable amounts of fact and speculation.[1] Indeed, television and print media are carrying so many dramatizations and investigative reports on the topic of UFOs, aliens, and goverment cover-ups that parts of this chapter are becoming common knowledge. Many persons already have integrated *parts* of this account (or some version thereof) into their worldview. If there is originality in my presentation, it's in the way I piece the materials together.

Substantial evidence has been developed for some of the main claims of this chapter. The existence of alien races, for example, may already be widely acknowledged by the time you read this book. Other claims, lacking direct evidence, may indirectly gain or lose credibility merely by their association with more *or* with less substantiated assertions. Truth value is always important. Given the nature of the subject matter, stimulus value is equally important. Like it or not, this vision is emerging on the horizons of our culture. And it promises to transform many of our most cherished beliefs. For many, it already has!

LIGHT AND DARKNESS: EARTH'S PLACE IN THE GALAXY

In the mists of time, there came from Boundless Radiance, the Source of all things, both endless worlds of form and substance and every conceivable degree and type of feeling and intelligence. We may assign to this primordial awakening a beginning comparable to that of the current physical universe, approximately 15 billion years ago. However, the Great Chain of Being is not restricted to creative evolution at just the physical levels. It embodies the emergence and evolution of all levels of consciousness, some vastly more evolved than we and some less evolved. It could not be otherwise.

All of creation did not take place at once. Just as galaxies may birth anything from gaseous clouds to delicately balanced solar systems, levels of intelligence, feeling, and form quite alien to ourselves also emerge from the primordial Source. Creation and evolution are perennially in process on many levels. It shouldn't surprise us that both visible and invisible sentient beings of diverse energetic configurations come into existence.

Some have physical bodies, others plasmic or light bodies. Still others can shift their dimensional appearance, for example, from translucent to solid and back again. Some may have lived in unity for eons, others in fear. Some have evolved primarily in mental ways unaffected by the transformational possibilities of feeling, except as an abstract possibility for other races. Some exist primarily to serve without the benefit of free will, while others were allowed to disagree and go their own way—for better or for worse!

As aspects of their long-term evolution, many may have experienced life on different worlds intermittently or in connection with stellar migrations. Extraterrestrial or extra-dimensional races more technically advanced than humans have long since conquered the limitations of space-time and move freely across our galaxy to affect in sometimes unpredictable ways the evolutionary patterns of other alien races. Certain groups, we should expect, will have formed major alliances and governing councils, while some planets may be little more than colonial outposts. Galactic war is no less likely than galactic peace.

If one takes seriously the virtually limitless possibilities of creation and evolution not only within a given level of the Great Chain, such as our own galaxy, but also within *and* between other less physical domains, then to suppose that all of the interesting action is restricted just to this planet is to lapse into myopic incoherence.

From out of this vast spectrum of creative evolution, the idea of a special new world, an experiment, took shape. The conditions of this particular experiment were set hundreds of millions of years ago when the earth's natural conditions were favorable, and additional life-forms were "seeded" into the biosphere—far more forms than would have spontaneously arisen on their own.

The evolution of species is a fact, but it would not have come to the point of such incredible complexity and diversity, and in such a brief period of time, without intelligent external assistance. Because of their inability to explain the evolution of essential genetic material within known *terrestrial* conditions, highly respected molecular biologists considered variations of the "intrusion" hypothesis, such as organically seeded meteors, at their 1986 Conference on the Origins of Life at Berkeley, California. They didn't invoke extraterrestrial intervention, but they did concede a huge problem in explaining evolution without something intervening.

Not only the fact of evolution, but also the timing of human origins and the earliest migrations are increasingly up for fundamental reconsideration. As Michael Cremo and Richard Thompson argue in *The Hidden History of the Human Race,* largely overlooked or suppressed findings, such as human bones completely immersed within coal deposits discovered by miners, are pushing back the dates which humans—or human-like beings—walked the earth by as much as ten million years.

Former Yale professor Arthur Horn argues in *Humanity's Extraterrestrial Origins: ET Influences on Humankind's Biological and Social Evolution* that genetic engineering was performed on various human prototypes to enhance evolutionary progress. The human body has been refined countless times, both here and on other planets, in order to accommodate various levels of soul infusion. Alien/human cross-breeding was part of this process as well as human/animal breeding, sometimes with questionable results that have survived in our mythology. At different times, various stellar groups, each with their distinctive agendas, overlapped with each other. To some extent, we are all aliens.

In *We, the Arcturians,* Norma Milanovich proposes that Arcturians may have been the first group to establish a small outpost on Earth, which was then as it is today overseen by a spiritual hierarchy. However, this outpost was soon destroyed and replaced by more negative warring reptoids and dinoids from Draconis and Bellatrix who fully colonized the planet, together with a more peaceful pre-cetacean group, approximately twenty-six million years ago (long before the birth of Atlantis or Lemuria). Reptoids believed then, and still do, that this planet belongs to them. In *You Are Becoming a Galactic Human*, Sheldon Nidle and Virginia Essene propose that the pre-cetacean group eventually went underwater as whales and dolphins, whereas the reptoid/dinoid alliance was defeated and retreated to the planet Maldek in our solar system, remnants of which today comprise the asteroid belt.

Since then, Sirians, Vegans, Pleiadians, and Reticulins, among others, have played significant roles in earth's history. Nidle and Essene, as well as Lyssa Royal and Keith Priest in *The Prism of Lyra*, propose that the first fully developed humans to "seed" our planet, as well as others in the Sirian and Pleiadian systems, came from the Lyran constellation.

How do extraterrestrial races make such claims? How do they transmit information to humans? In some instances, it may be through direct physical contact, whether in the form of a landing or through "on-board" exchanges with contactees. In other instances, it may be through direct voice transmission on "secure" radio channels of NASA or the Air Force—as once happened with a small group of generals from the Pentagon. In still other cases, it may be via telepathic transmission through human receivers, such as Lyssa Royal, Yvonne Cole, Barbara Marciniak, Norma Milanovich, Virginia Essene, or Sheldon Nidle—all specialists in such matters.

If we have independent evidence for extraterrestrials who have mastered the space-time continuum in ways we can barely imagine, then the idea of telepathic transmissions should not strike us as terribly problematic. However, we should keep in mind that both extraterrestrials and humans can be mistaken or biased. The pictures different groups eagerly paint are not altogether consistent. It is our responsibility to evaluate their information as we best see fit.

To return to our brief historical tour, a few early "outposts" have remained in the background, either underground or underwater, to this very day. Others were intentionally destroyed because of what they were doing to the planet—and to themselves! (In *Alien Identities* Richard Thompson, a mathematician with a scholarly knowledge of Vedic literature, argues that the epic *Ramayana* describes one such battle in quite literal terms.) Still other groups destroyed themselves. Some survivors of the Atlantean cataclysms, for example, returned to the Pleiades, while others migrated both East and West to preserve what they could and start anew.

The idea of periodic visitations by stellar beings—often termed "Gods" by local inhabitants—for purposes of genetic experimentation, enslavement, spiritual enlightenment, or technical assistance is not improbable when one's cosmology incorporates a robust galactic pluralism. But such an idea need not remain pure speculation. The plausibility of such extra-terrestrial visitations, particularly with respect to ancient Sumeria, has been persuasively argued on scholarly grounds by Zecharia Sitchin in *Genesis Revisited* and *The 12th Planet*.[2]

In the distant past, newly arriving stellar migrants had the option of "fitting" in the earth's biosphere either through direct incarnation of a physical body or by means of a bioluminescent body which would attract material particles along natural lines of force. Becoming adjusted to the earth's chemical makeup and gravitational, electrical, and magnetic fields was an extended process. Developing genetically appropriate bodies for migrant souls of varied energetic configurations was itself a major challenge. Many stellar souls experimented with different life-forms here with sometimes unpredictable results, while civilizations rose and fell. Sentient beings came to earth for different reasons, but all were attracted by the opportunities for long-term soul advancement. Properly under-stood, physical embodiment is a karmic accelerator that forces us to look at issues, such as sexuality and scarcity, about which we otherwise might only guess. Earth was an experimental outpost; many humans here now were among its pioneers.

The story of Adam and Eve is perhaps best understood as one among many such alien visitations that helped pioneer, both genetically and spiri-tually, the modern period of human development—the so-called "Adamic race." The entire evolutionary process was to some extent guided by galactic councils and cultures. Earth is a small but very significant piece of a larger evolutionary matrix.

One of the conditions of occupation in the early days was that both individually and collectively we were to remain in touch with our higher selves, our spiritual guardians, and stellar families. Information, guidance, and nurturing energy were ours for the asking, so long as we kept the communication lines open and remembered our purpose. What we would today term "psychic feats" were relatively commonplace.

Several developments undermined this arrangement. One was that we found it progressively easier to identify with our bodies and to become immersed in earth's own natural energies. This in turn had two effects. We began to forget and even deny our spiritual origins or why we had come here. We also experienced the growing sense of scarcity, fear, and compe-tition which comes from identification with perishable physical forms. These effects took place gradually over thousands of years. In some places, such as remote regions of Tibet, interdimensional linkages remained clearly and powerfully intact. (This is evidenced, for example, in Baird Spalding's *Life and Teaching of the Masters of the Far East*, especially volume one.)

Were embodiment our only major challenge, it could have been more easily overcome by appropriate outside reminders—avatars who incarnate to get us back on track. But it was not our only major challenge. For also buried in the mists of galactic history a rebellion took place that gradually affected many civilizations. And our spiritual progress became even more entwined within a larger evolutionary spiral.

The leaders of this rebellion were not *then* what we would today term evil. They simply had a strong difference of opinion about the way the show was being run, so to speak. In particular, they denied the existence of a deity or Divine Source from which everything comes; they rejected higher authorities; and they rejected the idea of long-term moral evolution as being either indigenous to all sentient beings or as ultimately bringing us closer to a mythical God. They argued instead for individual autonomy and the right of self-assertion for whatever we take our interests to be. Some alien cultures adopted this agenda. Others did not.

In biblical thought this rebellion is associated with the fallen angel Lucifer, who was cast out of heaven by Archangel Michael to lower planes of "outer darkness" in the Great Chain of Being. In Buddhist thought, a moderately parallel role is assumed by the demonic entity Mara. A modified version of this account interprets the "rebellion" in transformational terms. It suggests that those who participated in the rebellion unconsciously knew what they consciously denied, namely, that they were part of a grand experiment in *duality*. Their role was to be the "bad guys" and to set the stage for others to experience the opportunities for growth that duality affords. In fact, the Earth Mother herself had to agree to support this struggle until it played itself out. And she is now quite weary!

Still another account suggests that powerful creator-gods, some associated with negative alien cultures, laid down a negative grid upon the planet and directly altered our genetic code. The original "Adamic" plan for humans called for twelve strands of coded material. As a result of intervention by negatively oriented extraterrestrials we were left with only the double helix, with perhaps the other ten buried as subsets of the two we currently recognize. Or perhaps their intervention resulted in what is today still a mystery, namely, why more than ninety percent of our genes are shut off and have no recognized function.

They did this to keep us warring, fearful, and ignorant of our own true natures, thereby controlling us and feeding off of our emotions. They love our negativity. They believed then, and still do, that they own both us and the planet. And while some have remained in or around the planet, a larger expeditionary force may have come back to look after its interests. There has been "war in the heavens" for some time now. Fortunately, earth has it protectors.

Whatever the explanation of the origins of darkness may be, a convergence of accounts suggests that something of a negative and global significance occurred in earth's distant past. This event (or series of events) has powerfully restricted the capacity of future generations to move beyond the politics of scarcity and fear. I describe this scenario as "casting a veil" upon the planet.

Once we deny our spiritual origins, identify strongly with our bodies, and insist upon the right of exploring whatever pleases us, we encounter a long slope *down* which it is easy to slide. It is then possible to become addicted to promiscuity, slavery, power and control (especially through sophisticated technology), mind-altering drugs, and the ignorance or weakness of others. These results are not necessarily part of the original intent of the veil. And everybody doesn't slide in the same direction at the same rate, or to the same extent. But such consequences can result from claiming an unrestricted right of self-assertion oblivious to the common greater good.

Had we been approached at a different stage of our evolution, we might not have been such easy prey. But prey we were. A few alien races, acting in concert through mind-control and/or genetic technology, caused much of the human race to forget its divine origins. They manipulated our belief systems in ways which ultimately served their motives of power and control.

However, not everyone bought into this program. Compassionate and enlightened beings were concerned that those who had chosen to come here as part of an original experiment for accelerated spiritual growth, but who now found themselves trapped through no particular fault of their own, would be given periodically a beacon, a sign of light and guidance, a reminder of higher things.

And so for thousands of years an avatar in the form of a Krishna, a Buddha, or a Christ, periodically would penetrate this veil of restricted consciousness in order to give earth the opportunity to rise out of darkness. The Garden of Eden was but one of several major attempts to lift the veil and turn the tide of darkness. Although darkness has prevailed, as human history attests, it has never completely won out. There has always been light for those who sought it.

And what of those who opted for the original program of personal power and pleasure? Almost everyone in different lifetimes has experimented with a program leading to darkness. We cannot appreciate light unless we have experienced darkness. Some learn what they need to and return to the light. Others succumb and are unable to turn back the tide. A major karmic pattern sets in. Some who publicly fight evil in this lifetime themselves performed black magic in earlier lives. Everyone learns, but not at the same rate.

What does one do for nourishment if cut off from one's original source of light? The alternative is to make do with the limited light available. Darkness both attacks and is repelled by light that is powerful and clear. On the other hand, it is attracted to, and often permeates, light in borderline situations where there is potential *weakness* or *fear*. It will manipulate vulnerability in whatever ways it can. It can influence decisions from a distance, take over a body (especially if invited to), cause some people to become insane, hear voices, or manifest serious personality disturbances, push others to extremes of war and crime, and even fuel conspiracies.

This is not the devil tempting us. It is darkness doing what comes naturally. If one harbors strong fears, one will reflect this through power and control (to cloak the fears), competition and adversarial relationships (designed to assure that one does not lose power and control), guilt (in which one becomes convinced that one has misused his or her power) and, finally, denial (that none of the preceding exists). *Everyone* has a dark (or "shadow") side and has paid some price. Some just go further with it than others. The rest is human history.

It is claimed in some quarters that darkness (or evil) is an independently real force. In others, it is urged that evil does not exist, or that it is merely a matter of human perspective, or that it is something we ourselves create. There is something to be said for all of these interpretations. But the total picture is more complex than many seem to realize.

These conflicting interpretations can be reconciled, I believe, by acknowledging that darkness is *metaphysically* unreal (having no independent status in its own right), though *functionally* real (in that it produces actual effects). To say that darkness is not metaphysically real is to say that it's simply the absence of light. But the perceived absence of something can itself become a motive for action, sometimes of a harmful, greedy, selfish, and ritualistic variety.

If this process goes unchecked, some rather negative entities or thought-forms can be built up over time. But they are built up with what power we allow them to have, or they succeed in wresting from us during times of vulnerability. Those who drink to excess, do drugs, walk around clinically depressed, join hate groups, or work around accident scenes are more likely to attract dark energies. Indeed, one can pick up fear just by being around fearful people who otherwise intend no harm.

Actual physical possession by a demonic personality is rare. However, as former Jesuit Malachi Martin explains in *Hostage to the Devil*, when it does occur it confounds psychiatry and sorely taxes those charged with performing an exorcism.[3] (A careful comparison of the characteristics of possession states with the range of dissociative disorders described in the *Diagnostic and Statistical Manual IV* indicates that, while possession states exhibit some of the characteristics of dissociation, they are not reducible to mere dissociative disorders.) The tendency to confuse these two states is partly fueled by the failure to distinguish between creating negativity within one-self, such as repressed anger, and creating the conditions, such as emotional vulnerability, that attract negative energies from the outside.

It is usually *fragments* (not demons) of darkness, whether of our own creation or someone else's, that become lodged in the recesses of our consciousness. Such fragments cause us to do things we otherwise might not. Or they may influence us from a distance, through another personality, in ways that *seem* within the boundaries of normal human consciousness as, for example, in decisions which promote the selfish abuse of power. That is a source of their vitality. In this respect, negative attachments are just doing what comes naturally.

Darkness comes in all degrees, is often cleverly cloaked, and where possible feeds upon light. Mind control or blood sacrifices are only the more extreme degrees on the road to darkness, other parts of which we have all—even good Christians or Buddhists—dabbled with. Fear and hatred in otherwise good people are merely aspects of darkness. A so-called light worker who gets caught up in fighting evil is unconsciously playing the very game dark beings like to drink from—struggle, fear, and anger.

Even demonic beings were once "of the light" and, as such, still have a core of light left. But it has been covered up by the negative excesses of free will. Traditional exorcists attempt to banish demons to hell. Enlightened exorcists offer demonic beings the opportunity to return to the light.

Sensing collapse and feeling somewhat betrayed after millennia of service to dark lords, with little to show, many now are returning to the light. With humility born of awe, I have been present during some of these final conversions.

It may be useful to treat dark phenomena and the forces behind them *as if* they are independently (metaphysically) real, when they become functionally real and make an impact on one's life. However, evil is the presence of an absence, not a primordial presence in itself. Evil is functionally real in the same way that physical objects are functionally real. Both create constraints. We cannot, for example, walk through walls nor walk safely through high crime neighborhoods. But matter *is* energy. Energy is the underlying reality of matter. And light is the underlying reality that makes possible the absence of light—which is to say, darkness.

Darkness can prevail over individuals, groups, and presumably whole planets. But this is always relative to the larger whole of light which, in effect, sustains it, reflects it, and allows evolutionary exploration. By the very nature of the case, darkness could never take over the whole universe. The *consequences* of the original excesses of free will—whether in the form of an angelic rebellion or powerful alien creator-gods who interfered with our evolution—have been multiplied a billion times in as many unforeseen ways. But the original intent was not necessarily evil as we now tend to think of it. Only now, as far as *this* planet is concerned, things have gotten so far out of hand that a resolution is necessary, with everybody's stakes raised accordingly.

Before turning to the current scene, let me review the rather complex and fragile status of earth's place in the galaxy. Earth is, first of all, a planet of incredible geological and biological diversity. It is a living library of creation. Many souls are attracted for that reason alone. Nature spirits and devas have labored long and hard to support the biosphere. From the time of Adam and Eve, if not before, the plan was to make earth itself a permanent garden where *all* species lived in harmony.

Second, the "Terran experiment" was originally conceived to make possible the integration of our souls with a certain type of biological vehicle. The marriage would eventually produce not only some distinctively advanced soul patterns, but also some genetically and electromagnetically advanced bodies. The plan was to unite the full development of both wisdom and love in a physical body with advanced genetic capability. (Other species may be very intelligent, but not loving, or loving and not especially suited for biological vehicles, and so on.)

Third, most extraterrestrial cultures are homogeneous. Ours is not. The interactions between races have provided transformative challenges in their own right. Earth is a large scale version of the wild west.

Fourth, darkness has been *allowed* to coexist with light in order to give everyone the opportunity to experience its evolutionary possibilities and to decide where they stand in the larger scheme of things. Some individuals grow more rapidly through certain types of duality, and some do not.

Fifth, earth contains interdimensional portals that facilitate space-time jumps as well as influence in this part of the galaxy. To blow ourselves up would have extraordinarily adverse intragalactic consequences. For this reason, we will *not* be permitted to annihilate ourselves with nuclear war. The sanction for this claim is partly the threat of force and partly the desire to restore the original plan.

Sixth, at various stages of its evolution, earth has been viewed simply as an interesting planet *available* for colonizing no matter who else's experiment may be under way on the surface. War between planets is no more or less likely than war on this planet. Thus in certain quarters, the earth's current and relatively underdeveloped civilization(s) may be viewed as expendable. Humans make decent slaves, because we cannot conceive that any intelligent species would do to us what we do to others.

Finally, more advanced races are very concerned about the chemical, radiational, electromagnetic, and emotional pollution we project through the ethers to other star-systems and leave in our trail as we spin through space. Any long-range experiments being run here have consequences for the larger galactic picture. The slow progress of Earth's evolution retards progress elsewhere in the galaxy. Those who stress our mutual interconnections in the biosphere of this planet should consider our interconnections with life elsewhere in the universe. We are not alone.

This is the status of our planet in a larger galactic community as we move, however falteringly, toward peaceful membership in that community. How or when we will earn this membership is not clear. The methods are varied and largely up to us. This much is clear, however. The preceding seven factors combined with current levels of environmental destruction, precarious economics, religious and race wars, alien/human interaction, and the generally higher stakes of light and darkness, mean that earth is currently one of the most interesting and educational planets in the galaxy.

Earth is a powerful attraction for different extraterrestrial races whose stake in the outcome ranges from compassionate and helpful to controlling and selfish. In some instances, we are registered as little more than a colonial outpost at best and a quasi-mythical experiment at worst. In other instances, extraterrestrial races have come not only to witness history, but also to play a part in it. A few groups have been here all along. And a few others have returned to rectify the negative karma they took on through questionable interventions in human affairs thousands of years ago.

The total picture of extraterrestrial involvement is far more complex than standard treatments of the subject acknowledge. But it is unified by the fact that *many* alien races in our galaxy, and a few from beyond, have sent representatives to monitor the concluding chapters of our struggle with the duality of light and darkness.

GOVERNMENT COVER-UP: WHAT DO ETS WANT?

There are countless ways to illustrate darkness on our planet by reference to war, fear, greed, injustice, crime, oppression, and self-destruction. The recent events in Bosnia and Rowanda are grim reminders of how much we still have to overcome in this regard. However, I want to develop a special contemporary version which is linked to our encounters with UFOs and extraterrestrials.

UFOs have been around for thousands of years. This is reflected not only in written and oral traditions, but also in art (clearly illustrated on the walls of Renaissance churches and in one picture of the Madonna) and even in coins (such as Roman and French pieces from A.D. 150 and the seventeenth century respectively).

Our story, however, begins in the 1940s and 1950s with the massive number of reported sightings during and since World War II, which by 1993 numbered approximately 150 per day on a worldwide basis; thousands of air force pursuits from a dozen different countries (not to mention civilian and commercial pilot reports); growing awareness in the intelligence and defense communities from the early fifties on that the "best cases" (approximately 20 percent) could not be explained away; strong circumstantial evidence for the crashes and retrievals of alien beings and their craft beginning in the late 1940s, among them the famous "Roswell Incident," compellingly documented by Kevin Randle and Donald Schmitt in *UFO Crash at Roswell* and in their more recent work, *The Truth About the Crash at Roswell* (1994); hundreds of independently converging abduction and contactee accounts which stand up under hypnosis, intensive interrogation, lie detector tests, and depth psychological analysis; unexplained chemical differences between soil samples where craft allegedly have landed and immediately adjacent ground; frequent encounters of UFOs by NASA mission personnel which, according to Astronaut Gordon Cooper, was common knowledge among his peers.

The case for all of this has been made in numerous publications, public conferences and seminars given by physicians, independent researchers, academic scientists, and former military and intelligence personnel. There also has been sustained criticism of different aspects of this case by individuals such as Jacques Valle, Carl Sagan, and Philip Klass (a highly visible member of CSICOP and a former editor of *Aviation Week and Space Technology*). This skeptical critique occasionally points to inconsistencies and fabrications in some UFO-related claims.[4] And it provides reasonable alternative explanations for others. But it does not begin to account for all that a comprehensive explanation in this arena requires.

Many highly qualified and conscientious investigators in the UFO community themselves have come to vastly different conclusions. Some even debunk each other, not always with professional courtesy, prompting charges that one's adversary is a government mole. To ask what Linda Howe, Bruce Maccabee, Steven Greer, Rima Laibow, John Mack, David Jacobs, John Lear, Stanton Friedman, Bill Cooper, Barry Greenwood, Jacques Valle, Dennis Stacy, Walt Andrus, Budd Hopkins, Raymond Fowler, and Leo Sprinkle—all major players on the UFO scene—think about Alternative Three, MJ-12, the Billy Meier photographs of UFOs, the Roswell crash, the Gulf Breeze sightings, cattle mutilations, and alien abductions (not to mention what they think of each other!) is an invitation to a riot.

Personalities aside, there are also philosophical differences over how best to approach the entire field. One school holds that all or most UFOs are *not* necessarily of extraterrestrial origin, thus leaving open the possibility that they are secret government craft or possibly from an undiscovered subterranean civilization. The fact that UFOs exist does not in itself tell us where they are from—or even that they are piloted!

Guided by Carl Jung's reflections on the topic, especially in *Flying Saucers: A Modern Myth of Things Seen in the Skies*, another school of thought views them as *tangible* psychic projections, not piloted by anyone, from our own collective unconscious. Variations of this theme are considered in Keith Thompson's *Angels and Aliens: UFOs and the Mythic Imagination*. For example, UFOs might be a mixture of psychological projections and physical phenomena beyond current human comprehension.

Closely related to the Jungian approach is a third line of thinking which suggests that we set aside the question of evidence, at least temporarily, and focus instead on the meaning of extraterrestrial contact, if and when it ever happens. Should we respond hopefully or fearfully to the possibility of such contact? What would it mean for the human race? Such is the approach adopted by the Human Potential Foundation in convening its historic conference, "When Cosmic Cultures Meet" in May of 1995.

A fourth school doggedly searches for *hard* evidence (pieces of craft, credible witnesses whose sightings are corroborated by radar, Air Force film footage, etc.), while dismissing stories of alien abductions or treaties with alien nations as pure fantasy.

A fifth approach examines *indirect* evidence in the form of contactee accounts, electromagnetic anomalies, unusual soil chemisty from alleged landing sites, and even crop circles. But how much evidence is enough? If UFOs are real, asks Carl Sagan, tongue in cheek, where can he go to examine one? For him, nothing less will suffice.

A sixth school, typified by highly respected researcher Jacques Valle, combines elements from other approaches. In *Revelations*, Valle argues for a middle way that, on the basis of hard evidence, takes UFO sightings seriously, but rejects extreme claims regarding abductions, underground bases, and alien retrievals. After thirty years of research, Valle has concluded that many sightings are complex hoaxes that may well involve metallic UFOs, but that have been carefully engineered for our benefit.

We are being deceived. The questions are "By whom?" and "For what purpose?" The military, he believes, is obviously not explaining all that it could or should in this arena. But from this fact, we should not infer a gigantic behind-the-scenes conspiracy. In some places, Valle writes like a true believer, in others like a committed skeptic who almost wants to throw the reader off the trail when it heats up in certain ways.

Crop circles in some respects reflect a parallel microcosm of the larger UFO debate. Their geometric forms have defied rational explanation. They appear suddenly, typically during the night, in as little as fifteen seconds. In the great majority of cases, they are not produced by humans (with which even many skeptics now agree). They show clear evidence of sometimes striking design, with increasing complexity that no farmer has ever been able to duplicate. The stalks are bent with no damage such that they appear to have been growing parallel to the ground all along. In some instances, the formations are "screened" at their edges such that underlying grasses grow straight up through the bent wheat or barley stalks. In other instances, the stalks themselves are braided in remarkably neat and symmetrical patterns, which is again something that no hoaxer has been able to explain.

Confessions by two farmers that they were the perpetrators of the "hoax" explains very little, especially the third through sixth circumstance just noted. The farmers in question refused to be interviewed by serious scientists and appeared incapable of explaining how they produced anything but a crude circle which in critical respects was very unlike the genuine article. Nor did they succeed in explaining how they could produce such phenomena in less than a minute, leave utterly no trail through the field to the circle's location, or generate a variety of electromagnetic anomalies.

The most viable scientific explanation, that they are the result of unusual atmospheric vortexes, is patently weak. Even a neutral observer who has seen their crisp and progressively complex outlines, if forced to choose between this explanation and that of alien or spiritual intelligences at work, would be forced in the direction of the latter.[5] The logic of the larger UFO debate is similar. In light of the evidence, simple scientific explanations, like "The pilot experienced a glare on his windshield, not a UFO," simply don't work.

Some researchers believe major governments are involved in a cover-up of UFO activity, but don't understand (and cannot control) what they are covering up. Others suggest that governments are both covering up what they do know and collaborating with one or more alien cultures. A variety of approaches to the UFO question are examined in Richard Hall's authoritative *Uninvited Guests: A Documented History of UFO Sightings, Alien Encounters and Cover-ups*. On the topic of sightings alone, the breadth of Hall's summaries of official records—especially his more recent study, *The UFO Evidence From 1964 Through 1993*—could not fail to convince all but hardened skeptics that something very strange, and still unexplained, is going on.

The case for a cover-up is partly supported by documents released under the Freedom of Information Act, although less by their actual content and more by the unhelpful and defensive way the requests were handled and the documents eventually presented. Many additional disclosures by persons in positions to know make it abundantly clear that over the past forty years a major cover-up has been perpetuated. Even the *New York Times* has concluded that, no matter what the facts about UFOs and aliens turn out to be, our own government has seriously misrepresented its continuing involvement in the arena. The big question now is why.

Before addressing this question, I want to summarize a small amount of the information now available on the overall dimensions of both the evidence and the cover-up. Many of the following claims are discussed and referenced in Chapters 14–17 of Timothy Good's excellent work *Above Top Secret*, and are further examined in his more recent *Alien Contact*. While somewhat dated, Major Donald Keyhoe's *Aliens From Space...The Real Story of Unidentified Flying Objects* (1973) is also an authoritative and detailed account of the early days of the cover-up in its scientific, military, intelligence, and congressional aspects. (Additional sources are referenced in the footnotes.) If the government is officially convinced that UFOs of extraterrestrial origin do not exist, then:

1. Why did the National Security Council state that it "does not have any interest in UFOs in any manner," then release classified documents (under court order), yet withhold many more on the same topic for the reason that their declassification would pose a threat to national security?

2. Why did former director of the CIA, Vice-Admiral R.H. Hillenkoetter, state to Congress that: "It is time for the truth to be brought out...Behind the scenes high-ranking Air Force officers are soberly concerned about the UFOs. But through official secrecy and ridicule, many citizens are led to believe the unknown flying objects are nonsense."

3. Why did Air Force Lt. General Nathan Twining state: "The reported phenomenon is something real and not imagined or fictitious. There are objects, approximately the shape of a disc, of such appreciable size as to appear to be as large as man-made aircraft."

4. Why did the CIA go to such lengths to infiltrate major citizen groups, such as the National Investigations Committee on Aerial Phenomena (NICAP), if its members were merely chasing weather balloons?

5. Why did Apollo 11 astronaut, Neil Armstrong, upon his moon landing state: "Oh, God, you wouldn't believe it. I'm telling you there are other spacecraft out there...lined up on the far side of the crater edge...they're on the moon watching us." This was picked up and recorded by ham operators and Soviet monitors, though blanked out on NASA's own public transmissions. Armstrong now officially denies that he said this, although he confided the account to friends thereafter. Moreover, in 1979 Maurice Chatelain, former

chief of NASA Communications Specialists, confirmed that Armstrong had reported seeing two UFOs on the rim of a crater.

6. Why did U. Thant, secretary general of the United Nations, ten years *before* its historic debate on worldwide UFO research, confide that next to Vietnam, UFOs were the greatest problem facing the planet?

7. Why were UFO cases with "implications for national security" shunted around the Air Force's Project Blue Book to a higher level of secrecy, leaving the more easily explainable cases for Blue Book officers?

8. Why was General George C. Marshall, U.S. Army chief of staff in World War II and later secretary of state, reported to have confided to a respected researcher that in fact authorities had recovered UFOs and their occupants on several occasions? (This was not made public until both Marshall and the researcher had died.)

9. Why was Barry Goldwater, even as a general in the Air Force Reserve, and chairman of the Senate Armed Forces Committee, repeatedly denied access to the "Blue Room" at Wright-Patterson Air Force Base, which by all accounts is (or at least was) one of the principal centers in the United States for UFO retrieval studies? (Wright-Patterson also was probably the ultimate destination of many of Nikola Tesla's research notes, despite decades of denial by various government agencies that they knew anything of their whereabouts. Given that Tesla is one of the acknowledged geniuses of this century, and had a powerful interest in both "cosmic intelligence" and psychotronics, this convergence at Wright-Patterson is probably no accident.)[6]

10. Why is NASA officially so dismissive of the so-called "Face on Mars," when careful studies by highly credible scientists (reviewed in *The McDaniel Report*) have decreased to the vanishing point the probability of its being an accident of nature? As Richard Hoagland (*The Monuments of Mars*) and other researchers have observed, the geometry linking various shapes in the Cydonia region of Mars (not to mention the face itself) is enough to convince rational minds that more than chance is involved.

11. Why would Congress pass a law (Title 14, Section 1211, Code of Federal Regulations) allowing the director of NASA to assess a $5,000 penalty and to quarantine indefinitely, with or without a

hearing, any person who has been "extraterrestrially exposed?" (This quarantine cannot be broken by a court order.)

12. Why would a former British chief of defense, Lord Hill-Norton, urge publicly that there is little question about the reality of UFOs, although there remains considerable mystery and controversy over why their existence has been covered up so carefully for so long?

13. Why would Lt. Col (USAF) Wendelle Stevens, of the Air Technical Intelligence Center, state that his team of specially trained technicians "…reported such things as seeing disc-shaped craft close to an aircraft in flight [near the Arctic], incidences such as changes in the magnetic field and changes in the electrical potential in the airplane, [and] crafts land on the water and submerge or shoot out of the sea"?[7]

14. While it does not directly relate to a government cover-up, why would the *Fire Officer's Guide to Disaster Control*, a nationally adopted text for fire-fighters (including government officers), include an entire chapter on how to handle crashed UFOs?

15. Why would a renowned Soviet test pilot and member of the Academy of Science, Dr. Marina Popovich, state: "Many of our pilots have seen UFOs. I have gotten more than 4,000 such reports."

16. Why would Major Virgil Armstrong, formerly of the CIA and Army Intelligence, state: "On duty across my desk I received documents which said that a UFO had crashed in the middle of White Sands, New Mexico Proving Grounds. Aboard they found five bodies, each of them [between three and four] feet tall. The records and the bodies were transported to Wright-Patterson Air Force Base for further examination."

17. Why would our spy satellites record objects flying curved trajectories from (outer) space and back to space at less than escape velocity?

18. Why does our own government treat us like ignorant children when, for example, the Belgian military establishment (June, 1990) has freely acknowledged its pursuit and study of tangible UFOs?

19. Why does the government not offer a *credible* alternative explanation for the most extensively researched UFO crash (near Roswell, New Mexico) in history, for which there is enough documented evidence to convict a person many times over, if we were in a court of law? Why use a B-29 with a squadron of security officers merely to transfer a crashed weather balloon (the official explanation)?

Why accuse your own intelligence officer, Maj. Jesse Marcel, of not knowing the difference between a weather balloon and a crashed vehicle the remnants of which he had seen and touched at the site?

20. Why would our government make it a crime for active military personnel to discuss their experiences and conclusions regarding UFOs, if they all have "perfectly natural explanations"? Why face up to ten years in prison if one is only chasing swamp gas? Even civil airline pilots are subject to serious sanctions, *if* they formally report a UFO sighting and subsequently talk about it.

21. As revealed on NASA's own transmission from the space shuttle *Discovery* (Sept. 15, 1991) while in orbit and captured on tape by a Florida cable television station, why would we (or some country) fire what appear to be particle beam weapons (SDI?) from earth toward objects in position above the planet that escaped being hit in ways that defied the laws of physics? NASA's own explanation is that the objects were ice crystals and/or space debris. But since when can "space debris" rapidly accelerate at right angles to its trajectory in less than one second? (A critique of the space debris hypothesis in favor of the UFO hypothesis has been provided by Dr. Jack Kasher, professor of physics and astronomy at the University of Nebraska and a NASA consultant.)

22. Why would FBI director J. Edgar Hoover state: "I must insist upon full access to discs recovered…the Army grabbed [one] and would not let us have it for cursory examination."?

23. Why would our government, or at least our major television networks, be supremely uninterested in what are arguably the most massive sightings in history over and near Mexico City, especially July ll, 1991 (the day of a solar eclipse), as captured on film by seventeen amateur and professional cameramen? When the lead anchor for the Mexican version of "Sixty Minutes" (Jaime Maussan) put out a national call for filmed sightings (now collated in the video documentary *Messengers of Destiny*), why didn't our own "Sixty Minutes" follow up? Indeed, where was Peter Jennings when Gulf Breeze first broke, as described in *The Gulf Breeze Sightings* by Ed and Frances Walters? Where was CNN when triangular craft appeared all over Belgium?

24. Why will NASA and the astronomers and geophysicists it supports not provide a plausible explanation of the numerous anomalies associated with the moon that strongly point to intelligent

involvement there? These include flashing lights (noted by astronomers for more than a hundred years), cloudlike formations moving above the landscape, disappearing crater walls, structures that appear to be engineered, UFO citings, and a wealth of hard data that imply the impossible, namely, that the interior of the Moon is hollow. (These and other anomalies, including the lack of a satisfactory explanation of how it got to its present location, are compellingly described and documented in Don Wilson's *Secrets of our Spaceship Moon.*)

25. Finally, why would a former high ranking CIA official actually make a public case for a cover-up?

We have, indeed, been contacted—perhaps even visited—by extraterrestrial beings, and the U.S. Government, in collusion with the other national powers of the Earth, is determined to keep this information from the general public. The purpose of the international conspiracy is to maintain a workable stability among the nations of the world and for them, in turn, to retain institutional control over their respective populations. Thus, for these governments to admit that there are beings from outer space ...could...erode the Earth's traditional power structure. Political and legal systems, religions, economic and social institutions could all soon become meaningless in the mind of the public. The national oligarchical establishments...could collapse into anarchy.[8]

This last passage nicely describes traditional government thinking about why the public should not be told certain things, namely, to prevent an Orson Welles "War of the Worlds" type panic. It is the customary view of those in power. Don't let citizens know what they would have trouble dealing with. Government officials who knew the truth in the 1950s and 1960s may have been genuinely concerned about the safety and welfare of the population. This is evident in a Brookings Institute report to Congress in 1960 that examined the implications of extraterrestrial contact. It suggested that religious fundamentalists would find such contact "electrifying," scientists would find it "anxiety-producing," and that other social groups might "disintegrate."

In the nineties, however, this policy makes far less sense. The recent massive sightings in Mexico proved that UFOs do not cause panic in the streets or social decay. Suppose that we possessed a few crashed saucers, some bodies, and some film footage of Air Force chases and UFO landings. Why not just announce that the government had been secretly debating what to do for years, and has finally decided to go public, put everything in a museum, run television documentaries, and start collecting millions of dollars for the greatest show on earth? The scientists I know certainly would not let any anxiety stand in the way of their examining UFO propulsion drives or alien bodies. And the fundamentalists I know might *talk* about the "work of the devil," but otherwise would not become suicidal.

A public announcement would stimulate massive support for NASA and related space programs. For a while, of course, there would be considerable controversy. Theologians would ask if the aliens' God, if they believe in one, is the same as ours. No doubt we would have to suffer through endless congressional hearings. And the United Nations would have to establish a special blue ribbon committee to oversee "foreign relations." Acknowledged contact with alien cultures would indeed be of monumentally historic significance. But why should it cause revolution and anarchy in the streets, when the average citizen today is more inclined to greet such visitors with curiosity, even if mixed with anxiety? Hollywood has been preparing us for this for decades!

Taken at face value, darker scenarios than this have come to light. So why aren't major governments, especially our own, offering more credible explanations? Philosopher Michael Zimmerman suggests that "establishment elites" (including many in government) who reject the idea of superior nonhuman intelligence suffer the constraints of "anthropocentric and patriarchal humanism." Their sense of personal identity is so bound up with this worldview that to concede the existence of extraterrestrials would trigger serious personal crises. So they explain away the evidence for a cover-up. This done, they conclude that there is no cover-up to explain.

Zimmerman's thesis seems to me correct as far as it goes. However, it does not go far enough. The only hypothesis capable of explaining the *extent* and *complexity* of this evidence is that a Pandora's box of interrelated and questionable activities must be involved, which a hidden power structure in our own government (and probably others) has gone to great lengths to hide. For our government to officially admit some activities would automatically raise questions about others of an even darker nature. So the official response has been to publicly deny everything, on the one hand, while to privately prepare for contact, on the other. Those in the know are still patriarchal in their thinking, but they are definitely *not* anthropocentric.

Before describing some of these darker activities, let me sketch what I believe are the historical dynamics of the unfolding drama. In the late forties to early fifties, if not before, leaders of various governments, but especially our own, encountered essentially two types of aliens. One group warned us about nuclear war and a deteriorating environment, and urged us to set aside our differences and work in concert for the spiritual upliftment of humankind. This theme was developed in the classic science fiction film *The Day the Earth Stood Still.*

They were very concerned about what we are doing to ourselves as well as how our actions are affecting the larger galactic picture. They were especially concerned about our use of nuclear power. They offered help and positive technical assistance, e.g., devices to reduce pollution, but refused to intervene (with the possible exception of preventing a global nuclear catastrophe) unless they were officially invited. They never were.

The other alien group was interested in power, control, and furthering its own ends. It needed humans for genetic experiments and protected land for underground bases, preferring to work incognito rather than by overt invasion. This group basically does not respect the human species. But it was willing to trade some of its technology and cater to the fear and greed of elements within our own government in order to reach its goals.

Our government secretly decided to go with the second group. The interests it represented, a few of which stretched all the way back to Nazi intelligence circles, wanted to remain in power. Inviting a spiritually and technologically advanced race to share their resources for the good of humankind was not perceived as contributing to that end. Deals were struck (possibly even a treaty), and understandings reached. In the meantime, the first group decided that it would *gradually* announce its presence and issue its "wake up calls" through special contacts with average citizens. This contact has been escalating since the late seventies.

For a while, the original understandings between the government and the second group of aliens proceeded as planned. Gradually, however, the government realized what a huge problem it had on its hands. As more individuals became involved with various aspects of behind-the-scenes activities involving the alien presence, progressively higher levels of threats, intimidation, mind-control, and even termination became necessary—in some cases, to the point of mutiny in the ranks.

The government could not control the activities of the first group of peaceful aliens, who were appearing all over the globe and getting their message out to interested citizens. (A notable example of peaceful exchange is the alleged contact between Swiss farmer Billy Meier and a Pleiadian scout group, a subject of considerable controversy in UFO circles.) The government came to realize that it could not perpetuate the cover-up indefinitely. Yet some factions have attempted to anyway. Those who know about such matters do not necessarily share the same view about how best to handle the situation. One researcher has gone so far as to argue that the Office of Naval Intelligence currently is struggling behind the scenes with the CIA over constitutional questions raised by the cover-up.

Early on, elements within our government developed contingency plans to gradually prepare the population for some astounding revelations. However, a compromise between hard- and soft-liners was accomplished by deciding to do this in a tightly controlled fashion. They planted moles in major UFO investigation groups and put out disinformation aimed at discrediting anyone who was not "with the program." They recruited some prominent individuals and used others (probably without their knowledge) to represent both sides of key issues involving UFOs and aliens. Essentially, they have attempted to open up our *attitudes* about aliens, mainly through the media, while keeping the wraps on matters of empirical *fact*.

At some point in the 1970s, the government realized that the intentions of the second group were far darker than they had suspected. This was evidenced in the excessive number of abductions taking place, the nature of the genetic experimentation undertaken, and the extent that "implants" (arguably for purposes of control) were appearing in the general population. Naturally, nobody wants to be remotely associated with condoning such activities.

Publicly, the government's response has been to dismiss such scenarios as not even deserving a response. Privately, it has been investigating ways to take a more forceful stand. The Strategic Defense Initiative (SDI) was one result.

The government's quandary, then, is this. It will have to confess to alien involvement in the near future, and must do this in a way that will minimize negative reactions. It must subtly prepare the public for a number of scenarios, without knowing which one will unfold. Increased television coverage is one way this appears to be happening. Carl Sagan may be one of several high profile individuals charged with this task. (See, for example, his article about aliens and abductions in the March 7th, 1993 issue of *Parade*.) Above all, the government must remain in control and pretend that nothing is going on—even as events beyond its control begin to spill over into the public arena. What, then, should those in power do?

Let me turn now to a more detailed discussion of the events that have helped shape the dynamics of the cover-up. In probing darker influences within the government, I will not discuss sources, weigh evidence, or otherwise engage in a priori analyses of credibility. Additional reading is referenced at the end of this chapter. One might, of course, simply dismiss what follows. I am suggesting merely that, as the cover-up is exposed, these are the kinds of activities readers will hear about in connection with it—if they have not already.

Horrifically unethical experimentation with human subjects? Whoever is running the show may have agreed, perhaps in return for certain technical information, to a range of questionable agendas—some involving human subjects and taking place on (or under) protected land. These include genetic engineering, artificial insemination for breeding purposes, possible programs of cattle mutilation for select parts (usually eyes, blood, and genitalia), transplantation of two- to three-month-old fetuses, and insertion of various miniature devices (both physical and nonphysical) commonly termed "implants" to gather information about us as a species and to exert some control.

Some of these devices are relatively benign; they may be used, for example, to monitor our responses to environmental pollution. Others may literally sap our life energy, or protect us, in ways that elude medical science. It depends upon the extraterrestrial groups involved. As I will argue later, it is useful to distinguish between horrible abduction scenarios, on the one hand, versus dubious ones, on the other.

Subjects who recall these traumas, sometimes consciously and sometimes under hypnosis, are a growing concern for mental health professionals who are beginning to share information and hold conferences on the effects of such encounters. C.C.B. Bryan's *Alien Abductions, UFOs, and the Conference at M.I.T.* impartially reviews the proceedings of one such major conference. And David Jacobs's *Secret Life* is a good sourcebook of abduction case histories. As Harvard psychiatrist John Mack bluntly states in his introduction to a recent detailed national survey conducted by the Roper Organization: "This survey...suggests that hundreds of thousands, if not millions, of American men, women and children may have experienced UFO abductions, or abduction related phenomena."[9]

Mack and other mental health workers concerned with the issue conservatively put this figure at 2 percent of the American population (not counting, of course, other countries). Many appear to have experienced multiple abductions beginning in childhood. In a significant number of cases, a family history of abductions is indicated even though they were not discussed at the time. In his own practice, Mack has seen over ninety clients who exhibit a strong probability of having had such an experience.

Why should clients with ostensible abduction experiences be believed, if at all? In his recent (1994) book, *Abduction*, Mack explains why.

1. The emotional impact and clear signs of post traumatic stress disorder are among the most powerful that mental health workers have observed. The fear, grieving, embarrassment, and anxiety are clearly based on real events. This does not necessarily mean that they were abducted. It does mean that "something" very traumatic happened.

2. Of the abductees who have undergone intensive counseling and psychotherapy, and batteries of diagnostic tests, virtually none qualify as psychotic, schizophrenic, dissociative (including multiple personality), egocentric, sociopathic, or prone to perceptual hallucinations by virtue of a neurological disorder or drug abuse. Nor is there any independent evidence to suggest that they suffer from false or confabulated memories. In short, their symptoms cannot be adequately explained by known psychiatric categories.

3. Of those who have made it to therapy, there is no evidence to suggest that as a group they suffered childhood emotional or sexual abuse in numbers greater than any other randomly selected group. In other words, abductees do not appear to be "screening" trauma caused by family relatives in the form of sexual intrusions by aliens.

4. Many have completely unaccounted for physical markings in the form of bruises, scars, and holes in their skin that appear overnight. Some women test positive over several months for pregnancy without having had sexual intercourse and lose their fetuses just as mysteriously. A significant percentage of women diagnosed at fifteen weeks as carrying twins deliver only one child, with no evidence of miscarriage.

5. There is sometimes independent corroboration for UFO activity in the same area for the same period of time, especially in those cases

where the recall is not too far removed from the ostensible events themselves.

6. The accounts themselves are remarkably consistent about the patterns of events that took place "on board." They include descriptions of instruments, means of communication, symbols engraved on the walls, and details of physical mannerisms and appearances never discussed in the media. Therapists who attempt to (constructively) trick their clients with questions such as "What do you see in the corner of the room?" get consistent answers such as "There are no corners, they are all rounded."

7. In a few instances, clients who otherwise had never met each other have since recognized another as having participated in the same experience at the same time.

8. Abductees generally run from the press and fear for their reputations. They will often never mention their experience to even their closest friends. When they finally seek the services of a therapist they wish that they would be diagnosed as "crazy" instead. They are not. Anyone who has attended a support group for abductees will immediately see that ego-gratification is the least likely explanation.

It should be stressed that not all abductees are traumatized, nor are their experiences necessarily related to breeding schemes. Many individuals have reported dramatic physical and emotional healings. Many others have had friendly contacts with quite different alien races for purposes of historical and spiritual enlightenment. Still others have reported that their abductions were in different ways related to our destruction of the planet, and to alien attempts to understand and reverse this process by working behind the scenes through abductees. More abduction than contactee cases have surfaced, although some abductees eventually come to see the negative aspects of their experiences in a positive light.

Critics who reject abduction accounts out of hand typically do so on the basis of weak arguments. Most have simply not taken the time to thoroughly investigate the cases. A distinguished neuroscientist once claimed on national television to be able to stimulate a person's nervous system in ways that would produce vague impressions of something dark and foreboding around that person's bed. From this, he concluded that abductions were little more than fantasy projections for which our culture unfortunately provided an all-too-convenient label—"alien abduction."

He seemed unaware of the fact that the ability to artifically reproduce an externalized experience—and a poor replication at that—is itself no basis for concluding that the external object either does or does not exist in other contexts. We can neurologically stimulate the impression of a tree even where none exists in the subject's perceptual field. From this, however, we would hardly conclude that trees do not exist!

Three alien agendas. Contactee and government intelligence accounts suggest that there are many different alien cultures represented in and around the planet. Only a few, however, are playing major roles. Rather than attempt to map specific alien types, I will focus instead upon three basic goals around which alien civilizations can be grouped so far as inter-action with the earth is concerned.

To attempt a delineation according to race, origin, or technology would take us too far afield. For example, as a race the much discussed Greys break down into a number of subspecies depending upon such factors as size, the shape of their heads, and the way they process information. They are associated with several different alien cultures with quite different inten-tions. I will take as placemarkers the Pleiadians and Arcturians as examples of Group I. (The so-called "Nordics" would probably also belong to Group I.) The Draconians (sometimes referred to as "Reptoids") and Rigelian Greys are representative of Group II. And the Reticulins (who are also "Grey") are representative of Group III. (Where the so-called "Insectoid" aliens fit in this division is not clear, although they appear closer to Group III than to Groups I or II.)

The extraterrestrial cultures represented in Group I exhibit significant variations in form, but appear more human than anything else. Some are taller, others shorter. Some are interstellar, others interdimensional. A few are both. Some are more energetic than solidly physical. But all are aligned with what we would describe as a positive spiritual intent. For example, they acknowledge Christ Consciousness as a worthy evolutionary goal. They would like to help and guide us, and will defend us from external attack, as indicated earlier, but they will not impose their goals upon us.

Some Group I types have been here before and have now returned from very far away. A few sub-groups appeared as "Gods" to the ancients. Some assisted in speeding up our evolution as a species, genetically and other-wise, under what is described as the Law of One. They have evolved through mistakes in their history similar to the kinds we are now making, and would give us the benefit of their experience. Ashtar Command (a federation of extraterrestrial groups with a positive interest in earth's well-being), Lord Maitreya, and Christ are associated with Group I. Barbara Marciniak's *Bringers of the Dawn*, a Pleiadian account of human history, and Norma Milanovich's *We, The Arcturians* are good examples of the perspectives from Group I.

Group II includes quasi-humanoid forms, in the sense that they have arms and legs. However, none really look human in their natural state. Some are reptilian in appearance (with slanted pupils) and are sometimes referred to as the Draconians, although there is no generally agreed-upon label for them. This group also includes a subspecies of Grey from the Rigelian star system who are associated with some of the worst excesses of abduction and covert control. These Greys operate through group consciousness. Some appear to be under the control of the more powerful reptilian species. The ultimate agenda of Group II is power and control.

If there is a link between a secret government and an extraterrestrial race, Group II is the place to look. And if a formal treaty was signed , it was in all probability with the Rigelians, a Group II race. Some of our own military and/or intelligence personnel appear to have participated in placing implants in drugged subjects who later recalled fragments of their experience. Draconians find human greed, fear, and death stimulating. And they may have done a great deal throughout history to indirectly infiltrate and control our religions and governments in order to achieve this. They have a vested interest in holding the human race back.

The best slaves are those who, even as they toil for what they take to be their own freedom and happiness, actually contribute to their masters' pre-arranged ends. This is the primary, though not the only, reason why Group II hasn't overtly taken over the planet—or at least attempted to do so. For the long term, the best slaves are the ones who believe they are in charge of their own destinies. By some accounts, most of the human race unknowingly has been in slavery for a long time. William Bramley presents an interesting and extensive case for this thesis in *The Gods of Eden*.

Group III includes the Reticulins, who are a part of the Grey species. I cannot stress too much the fact that Greys are a generic type, with many variations, found in different parts of the galaxy. There are positively, neutrally, and negatively oriented Greys *in general*, and positively, neutrally, and negatively oriented Reticulins in particular—just as we would expect with humans. All Reticulins are some type of Grey, but not all Greys belong to the Reticulin race. To speak of what *the Greys* have or have not done, without further qualification, is to invite massive confusion. It is as misleading as "Look at what the humans have done in Bosnia." For convenience, I am stipulating that only extraterrestrials between the extremes of negative control and positive assistance should be included in Group III.

Members of Group III appear mainly interested in acquiring knowledge. Some have made a religion of science and technology. Other races are here mainly for collecting samples and learning more about the human species. A few may abduct or contact humans for informational purposes. Most do not. One small group may be involved in mining operations which our government is powerless to stop, but which it nevertheless wishes to keep out of public view. Still other races in Group III believe that there are lessons about Earth's transition that would be useful to take back to their own planets. On the whole, the *intent* of extraterrestrials associated with Group III is neither to help us nor to harm us. As the saying goes, they are here to "do their own thing."

The Reticulins in particular, however, are a special case. They may need us. On the one hand, they seem to be experiencing a "downhill genetic slide" involving both digestion and the ability to reproduce. This may have been caused by their own nuclear catastrophe. In their quest for knowledge, the Reticulins intentionally gave up feeling and emotion. They're now attempting to get it back through the creation of a new Reticulin/human species. (They have already engineered one new species, the Essassani, from two earlier ones.) Positively oriented Reticulins are learning what nurturing and play are about, sometimes by observing the interactions of human mothers with their Reticulin offspring. They have been observing human behavior for a long time.

When they implant devices in a person or take skin samples, it is primarily for the purposes of learning about and keeping track of that person, not controlling that person's behavior. Since they attempt to make the whole process as painless and forgotten as possible, they do not view their intentions as blameworthy. In fact, they only vaguely understand the concept of moral worth. From their perspective, their endeavors not only will help to preserve their species, but also will produce a major evolutionary advance within the galaxy.

Of course, *we* are not about to describe breeding schemes unwillingly foisted upon us as neutral. We would be more likely to use a term like horrific. They would remind us, however, that since they originally contributed to the gene pool from which we evolved, it's only fair (by our standards) that they retrieve some in their time of need.

They would also point out that neutrality depends upon where one is standing. From their vantage point, we should be far more concerned about the manipulation and control from Group II, or from negatively oriented splinter groups, which are the primary source of the government cover-up. For it is the reptoid-like Draconians, their slave Greys, and/or Rigelians who, in collaboration with elements of our government, appear to have participated in the most terrible abuses of power and scientific experimentation (including time travel) for reasons we can only guess at.

Finally, it should be stressed that much of the research being conducted by positively oriented Reticulins in some instances has nothing to do with sexual invasion or species enhancement. Sometimes, for example, prisoners are abducted from jail merely to determine the effects of long-term confinement on their genetic structures. Reticulins are also interested in the long-term genetic effects of human exposure to toxic environments. In other situations, humans may be taken on board simply to observe their reactions to artificially constructed, though emotionally charged, situations. This is one way a race with little emotional capacity can learn what they are missing, so to speak. Some abductees have even suggested that their alien abductors, not necessarily Reticulin, were finding their way back to God through their interactions with humans.

Is abduction for a debatable cause (preserving one's own, or even another, species by producing a more advanced one) preferable to abduction for a horrible cause (producing slaves or engaging in mind control through drugs to preserve secrets)? For some it is. In *Lost was the Key*, author/abductee Leah Haley finds the threats, abduction, and drugged mind control she suffered at the hands of our own military and government agents, in some instances with reptilian-looking creatures looking on, more reprehensible than having her eggs taken by (presumably Reticulin) Greys who both explained to her what was happening and took measures to protect her from their common enemies in Group II. Other critics, however, are unwilling to draw such a distinction; they consider taking women (and some men) against their will as immoral no matter what the intent.

Here we encounter an issue that shakes the metaphysical foundations of the entire abduction debate. What does "against one's will" mean? In their telepathic transmissions, positively oriented Reticulins from Group III point out that the humans they abduct *agreed* on a soul level to this process before they incarnated. The problem, of course, is that very few humans recall their agreements to anything—much less to work with any alien group—prior to incarnating. By contrast, humans abducted for oppression in Group II agendas allegedly did *not* agree.

Would prior agreement make abduction OK? Many argue that it does not. The problem, however, is that many who believe in alien abductions are also strong reincarnationists. And reincarnationists believe that all kinds of seemingly negative scenarios may be agreed to before (or after) incarnating. These scenarios serve the purpose of growth by forcing personal issues to be confronted. In this respect, incarnating with the prior knowledge that one is going to be abducted is no better or worse than the knowledge that one is going to lose one's legs. If the prior choice principle in reincarnationism is correct, then it is arbitrary to suspend it for just one type of negative experience.

Of relevance to this debate is the fact that some abductees report that they are the better for having had to go through the process of recalling and dealing with the experience. For a few, it seems to be a way of claiming their own power. And ironically, when that point is reached the abductions appear to cease and with them the *fear* of further alien intrusion. Then, too, some have faced the possibility of further abductions and *consciously* refused. At this point, when they refused the role of victim, they were left alone. The abduction experience apparently can be changed.

None of this justifies abductions by Reticulins in the sense of excusing their behavior. It is to point out, however, that abduction phenomena are vastly more complex than commonly supposed. If we are the result of cross-breeding, it is not evident that cross-breeding for yet another race is inherently wrong. As just noted, this depends upon how we interpret abductions for such purposes as "against one's will." I have attempted to show that, in forming an opinion on this topic, it is wise to keep one's other metaphysical commitments in mind. Consistency is always a virtue, no matter what the final verdict on abductions may be.

Alternative three? On June 20, 1977 the British television series *Science Reports* broadcast a special program entitled "Alternative 3."[10] Its producer later claimed that this particular broadcast was originally intended as an April Fools Day joke which for scheduling reasons had to be aired at the later date. However, it *looked* like straight investigative journalism, even if poorly done in places. It succeeded in convincing many viewers that some horrifically secret agenda had been kept from the public. In retrospect, it became clear that the investigation was highly fictionalized, although pieces had a ring of truth to them.

The secret agenda the producers claimed to have uncovered unfolded as follows. In the 1960s, persons of considerable power and wealth concluded that the planet would not be hospitable for more than a few decades. Whether on the basis of radical shifts in weather, related greenhouse effects, or overpopulation, earth would soon be a very bad place to live. And so they conspired to build space ships and establish a colony on Mars for the "best and the brightest."

Naturally, this would require workers whose minds were altered to prevent the kind of total recall portrayed in the movie of the same name. It would also entail a fair number of people (both scientists and drones) suddenly disappearing from off the planet. (An investigation of the British brain drain was the initial focus of the televised program.) And it would require anti-gravitational technology that made rocket science obsolete.

The project supposedly made a mockery of the public space programs of both America and the Soviet Union—a deeply troubling discovery for many of our astronauts. These programs were for public consumption and certain technological advances. Of course, some of the leaders in both countries didn't know what was happening anyway. By the time we officially accomplished manned landings on the moon, somebody else already had been there—mostly on the dark side. Remember, Neil Armstrong had a waiting party upon his arrival.

It is not clear whether the producers of the television program accidentally stumbled across some hidden agendas and, not appreciating their full significance, built them into a fictionalized piece of investigative reporting partly as a joke. Or whether they did appreciate their larger significance but, in order to get them out to the public, had to weave them into a format that later would be easy to debunk.

As matters stand, it's easy both to dismiss the program out of hand and to appreciate some of the facts that may have given rise to it. It is as if Alternative 3 never existed, but something like it actually did. This is the conclusion that Jim Keith reaches in his compelling analysis *Casebook on Alternative 3: UFOS, Secret Societies and World Control.*

For example, significant photographic evidence is beginning to converge in the direction of something like an Alternative 3 scenario. A few NASA pictures of the moon show evidence of what—were it seen on Earth— would be described as mining operations. Moreover, there is strong circumstantial evidence for the claim that the 1988 Soviet Mars probe, Phobos II, was either destroyed or otherwise rendered inoperable by an object (a picture of which was televised to Earth) coming at it when its cameras began televising other provocative material on the face of Mars.[11]

The connection of something like an Alternative 3 scenario to the same inner circle which made contact with alien intelligence and mandated a cover-up is a natural one. If there is any credence to be given to this scenario, it also follows that the technology made available to certain parties would result in a small number of UFO type craft being researched, maintained, and flown by several governments or by one governing council pulling strings within different countries. All the more reason for a cover-up, if we have been doing the very thing we officially claim has no connection to reality.

A drug connection? If one is going to undertake such expensive operations which cannot be supported from the public till, a long-term source is needed for many billions of dollars that can be laundered completely out of sight. Such a source by its very nature requires multinational cooperation, but not necessarily by those in positions of public power. The more nameless and faceless you are, the better equipped you are to control the flow of drugs and money behind the scenes.

There are many *independent* drug producers and distributors all over the world. But the combined interdiction efforts of many countries appear not to affect much more than 10–15 percent of the total which reaches the streets. Were a cover-up to become completely unraveled, many questions of how various projects were funded could lead to forbidden territory. Why has the U.S. government failed so miserably to make significant progress with the drug problem?

The case for such a scenario is not entirely speculative. Colonel Bo Gritz, a decorated former Special Forces officer and a person with extensive knowledge and participation in clandestine paramilitary operations, claims to have stumbled across a connection between the U.S. government and Asian drug lords. He has made a detailed public case for this connection based upon his investigation. Critics have countered with the charge that he has merely planted disinformation in order to fuel popular anti-government sentiments which indirectly will help pave the way for a New World Order.

Of course, a government-implicated drug connection assumes that there is a secret need for billions of dollars in the first place. In this regard, Timothy Weiner has argued in *Blank Check* that the Pentagon has access to as much as $35 billion each year for which it does not have to account. Has

Congress written a blank check for this amount, or have some of the funds been channeled from other outside sources? *If* drug money were used to fund some black projects, CIA complicity would enter at some point. Alfred McCoy argues this thesis in *The Politics of Heroin: CIA Complicity in the Global Drug Trade.* That President Bush pardoned a convicted major drug smuggler several days before the end of his term only adds to the intrigue of this theory.

I want to stress that the average government official (even most cabinet positions), the average senator, the average military officer (including generals), and the average intelligence operative do *not* know anything about the kinds of dark activities I am describing. Hence, it is misleading to claim that the government per se is playing a role in these arenas. Only a comparatively few persons in our government, or in other governments, know the whole story; most of the individuals needed to get a certain job done (e.g., pilot a UFO, experiment with mind-control techniques, etc.) simply follow their compartmentalized orders and collect their paychecks. Our government per se does not support any of these scenarios. But some individuals in the government do. Which brings us to the next topic.

A secret government? Much of what I have described so far implies the existence of a hidden power structure whose lines of influence extend both to and from key individuals in major governments around the world. While powerful enough to issue orders to the head of any country, this secret government would normally operate through individuals—some publicly known, some permanently hidden—with security clearances above top secret whose activities are planned by committees which operate outside the law. To protect and further its interests, it would have its own "black ops" officers whose loyalty is to a cause, not to a country, and technology ranging from psychotronic mind-control devices to its own UFO's.

This web of influence would require complex segregated levels of activity in the fields of banking, intelligence, science, and politics with only a comparatively few individuals near the top who know the whole picture. At times it might have to enlist various regular military, intelligence, and security forces to carry out unusual, if not unconstitutional, orders in the name of national security. To admit to a cover-up on the seemingly isolated question of UFOs would likely point to other elements in this global government within a government.

To entertain such a possibility, of course, immediately casts one into the raging fires of contemporary conspiracy theory where confusion, paranoia, guilt by association, disinformation, and even intellectual suicide all come with the territory. Nevertheless, a wide spectrum of information strongly suggests that some conspiracy theories contain more truth than falsity. One can enter the ring, so to speak, through any of several avenues, including: the political and economic influence of secret societies (Freemasons, Illuminati, etc.) and international associations (Council on Foreign Relations, Bilderbergers, etc.), elements of which allegedly will lead to a New World Order; mind control experiments and other high-tech achievements kept largely beyond public scrutiny; or investigations of certain high-profile events, such as the assassination of President Kennedy or the recent bailout of the Mexican Peso, for which satisfactory explanations have not been given. For brief "openers," interested readers may wish to explore Noam Chomsky's *The Prosperous Few and the Restless Many* or Jim Keith's *Black Helicopters Over America: Strike Force for the New World Order.*

One can be a conspiratorialist in a limited arena, such as the origin of AIDS, or on a grand scale which attempts to link, at least indirectly, everything from the large number of former Nazis employed by our government after World War II to the mysterious existence of essentially unused detention camps across America. If believing that there is a tightly controlled international cover-up on UFOs and aliens, together with the means to make it work, makes one a conspiratorialist for a narrow to intermediate range of events, then I will own the label. I am neutral to negative on various grand-scale conspiracy theories (e.g., that the New World Order has been planned for as much as two-hundred years), although James Harder's *Unholy Alliances: The Planned Destruction of America* may cause one to at least consider such a possibility.

However, I am intrigued, if not troubled, by the range of other seemingly disconnected events suggesting that more is going on behind the scenes than just a cover-up on UFOs. Logically, there is no necessary connection between these developments and a UFO cover-up. Psychologically, however, there is a reciprocal impact. If elements within the government can keep the lid on UFO/alien involvement for forty years, it is not difficult to imagine how this power structure, such as it is, could and *would* exercise its power in other areas. By the same token, if independent cases can be made for other deeply hidden agendas, then the cover-up on UFOs and aliens would be less difficult to believe.

Mainstream researchers associated with the Mutual UFO Network (MUFON), the Center for UFO Studies (CUFOS), and the Fund for UFO Research (FUFOR), become understandably angry when the subject matter of their scientific research becomes clouded by alleged conspiracies. Whether such muddying of the waters helps or hurts, I think, depends upon one's goal. If you are mainly interested in just trying to prove that UFOs exist, then conspiracy theory is largely irrelevant. On the other hand, if you are interested in why the government would go to such extraordinary lengths to cover up its knowledge of the UFO scene, then in the spirit of Systems Holism you should be prepared not to dismiss out of hand claims that lead beyond the boundaries of your current research toward a bigger picture. Here are some examples.[12]

1. The CIA and Department of Defense have developed mind control technology capable of transmitting "inner voices" to individuals, erasing their memories, hypnotizing them from a distance, and disrupting entire populations via satellite transmissions. It can also cause symptoms similar in some respects to those reported by alien abductees.

2. America has had its own UFOs for decades, which in turn made a mockery of our space program. Why build rockets if there is a better way and tax dollars can be better spent?

3. The Sixteenth Amendment to the Constitution requiring citizens to pay income taxes may never have been legally ratified by the required number of states.

4. Our own government undertook research to produce the retrovirus that subsequently came to be called HIV.

5. There is probably a stronger cause-and-effect relation between the drug AZT and HIV than between HIV and AIDS. There are some prominent virologists, such as Peter Duesberg of U.C. Berkeley, who now deny that HIV without other cofactors *could* be the cause of AIDS. Duesberg declared HIV in itself "relatively harmless."

6. The Federal Emergency Management Agency's (FEMA) prime directive appears to have less to do with helping disaster victims than with keeping the government secure and functioning in the event of a national emergency. Executive orders passed through the National Security Council give the President broad powers to suspend constitutional rights, and FEMA to take over private homes and automobiles in times of national emergency.

7. Marines were recently asked if they would fire on American citizens in support of gun laws and how they felt both about being a "United Nations fighting person" and about the President of the

United States ceding his position as Commander-in-Chief to the U.N. Secretary-General. Deputy Secretary of State Strobe Talbot had earlier written: "Nationhood as we know it will be obsolete. All states will recognize a single, global authority" (*Time*, July 20, 1992). In a September 21, 1992 speech to the United Nations, President Bush stated that foreign troops would occupy America to train for a New World Order Army. They subsequently have, together with trainloads of military equipment, which the Pentagon initially saw fit to deny. In a Presidential Decision Directive (PPD-25) President Clinton effectively abolished the law limiting the number of troops that could be placed under U.N. command without approval of Congress.

8. Transponder chips small enough to be inserted with a needle are available to identify and track animals. There are no laws governing use with humans. With data enhancement, they could easily be used in lieu of national identification cards.

9. If the inept handling, inconsistencies, concealed evidence, and largely unreported expert testimony regarding the Oklahoma bombing ever penetrate the mainstream media, "conspiracy" will be on the minds of many irate citizens.

The preceding developments are subject to different interpretations, not necessarily of a negative variety. However, it is the secrecy and lack of national dialogue on their potential implications together with their interlocking theme of behind-the-scenes control that can, and perhaps should, cause thinking people to ask what is going on. When enough information becomes public on such matters, raising the specter of various conspiratorial scenarios is not the simple exercise in paranoia it is often made out to be.

Perhaps the most controversial conspiracy theorist on the scene today is Bill Cooper who, together with his book, *Behold a Pale Horse*, has been denounced even by critics otherwise sympathetic to some of his claims. I don't believe everything Cooper says about UFOs, secret governments, and conspiracies. I draw attention to him, however, partly because he *is* so controversial. Whether you are for him or against him, he and his critics exemplify what can go wrong when undertaking a rational discussion of such sensitive topics.

Cooper may bring many of these denunciations upon himself; he has certainly denounced other researchers in the field. He may be a bit paranoid (perhaps with reason, if his accounts of harassment are true). If the two-part investigation conducted by the journal *UFO* (Issues #4 and #5, 1990) is correct, he may have misrepresented a few of his sources. He even may have been unknowingly manipulated.

These are interesting questions for further exploration. The answers in themselves, however, do not determine the truth or falsity of his substantive claims. At times the criticism leveled against him seems to me a bit *too* urgent, a bit *too* wrapped up with arguments he has had with various individuals, a bit *too* ad hominem regarding his life-style, and a bit *too* uninterested in the evidence he does present.

To take a simple example, I once attended a lecture by Cooper that included slides of NASA photographs of the moon taken by orbiting satellites approximately over a five-year period. His point was that a section of the side of a certain crater seemed to be missing in the later photographs and that this anomaly could not be explained as the result of meteor impact. He attributed the difference to "mining operations."

When I later attempted to convey Cooper's point to a former intelligence officer at a conference we were attending, the response I received went roughly as follows: "You can't possibly believe such a paranoid personality; his only friends are in para-military patriot groups and his work has been discredited." What I was waiting for, of course, was a plausible alternative explanation based upon an elementary knowledge of high resolution photography and lunar geophysics—which I never received.

Let me turn now to what could be one of the most suitable candidates for a "smoking gun" in all of conspiracy theory—if it stands up under analysis. This is Cooper's upgraded version (color enhanced, slowed down, sharper picture) of the Zapruder film of President Kennedy's assassination, which he obtained from John Lear, who in turn obtained his copy from Lars Hansson, who narrates a heavily contrasted black-and-white version. Hansson received his copy from Robert Grodin, an author of two books on the assassination and a specialist on the Zapruder film who made his copy directly from the original.

Hansson subsequently disavowed Cooper's interpretation and asked Cooper to return the tape or at least to leave him (Hansson) out of it. Cooper did neither. However, the more fundamental debate seems to be between Grodin (whom Cooper thinks is a government mole posing as an independent researcher) and Cooper (whom Grodin thinks loses all credibility by pushing such extreme views, including the view that Kennedy was killed partly because he threatened to go public with the UFO cover-up).

Cooper believes that the Zapruder film (brought into clearer focus) shows William Greer (now deceased), the Secret Service agent driving the car, turning around and firing a fatal shot into Kennedy at point blank range. The frames in question are easy to miss because Kennedy has already been shot from the back and attention is easily directed to everyone but the driver. While the color of the gun and the brake lights may have been doctored prior to Grodin's first copy, no expert to date has suggested that the frames in question have been fundamentally altered so as to make Greer appear to be doing something he wasn't; the physical movements and dimensions are authentic.

Any citizen, myself included, would prefer not to believe what the frames suggest and, indeed, when first given the opportunity to view Cooper's upgraded version, I rejected his interpretation out of hand. My first reaction was: "How could someone do that in broad daylight, in front of so many people, and escape detection?" The alternative horn of this dilemma was even darker. For if the film does show what Cooper claims, the level of conspiratorial cooperation both before and after Greer's act would have to extend widely and deeply.

On the surface, the Greer hypothesis explains three things: why blood spurts out of the front of Kennedy's head the moment his body jerks backward, neurophysiological speculation to the contrary; why Jackie Kennedy, against all instincts to remain with her husband down in the seat or on the floor, tries to crawl out the back; why the car slows down at the point that Greer turns around. The main objections to the Greer hypothesis raised by Grodin and conveyed by Hansson in the second *UFO* issue referenced earlier are as follows.

First, it does not account for the lack of muzzle blast. In response, it should be noted that Cooper later discovered the gun was gas powered and fired pellets filled with fish toxin, not bullets. Hence, there was no "blast."

Second, there is no visible recoil. This is a strange objection from anyone who thinks Greer never took his hands off the wheel. It should also be noted that the gun (or a version thereof) that Cooper thinks was used for the assassination was discussed and shown in Senate hearings. It was specially designed to minimize noise and recoil.

Third, Greer's hands never left the steering wheel. However, the upgraded version of the film clearly shows Greer turning around and his left arm coming back up over his right shoulder, with an object in his hand. Virtually every person I have shown this film to acknowledges that movement, even those who disagree with Cooper's interpretation.

Fourth, the reflection, ostensibly off the barrel of the gun, is actually off Agent Kellerman's head, who is sitting on the passenger side next to Greer. In response, I would point out that anyone who slowly freezes these frames will clearly see a white object pointing beyond the limits of Kellerman's head. If it were a reflection from the sun, we would expect it to change in some way as Greer's arm moves toward Kennedy. The main problem is that the "object" Greer is holding is not clearly discernible as a gun. It has the rough *outline* of a gun. However, the object appears so amorphous relative to its immediate context that, if there is a case to be made for tampering with the film, this would be one place to look together with the missing brake lights at the time the car slowed down.

The most one can conclude from Cooper's film is that the visual evidence suggests that Greer played a role in the assassination. It does not prove it. I have gone into some detail on this topic, however, partly because I think skeptics about Cooper's methods and personality in particular and conspiracy theories in general often devote too much energy to contextual matters and not enough to the principal claim being advanced.

In the final analysis, we will not be able to prove or disprove much in the murky waters of conspiracy theory and secret government agendas. We will have to be content with which version makes the most overall sense, not which one has been conclusively proven. Where one ultimately stands on such matters, I think, will depend on two factors. The first is whether one is willing to look at larger patterns that may connect seemingly unrelated events, rather than apply standards of proof so high to particular events that virtually nothing passes muster and no pattern is allowed to emerge. Conspiracy theory is a vast interconnected genre that neither stands nor falls with one writer.

The second determining factor is whether the plausible nuggets one does mine are permitted to create a modest halo effect for related, though less evident, claims; or whether the confusion and lack of evidence surrounding certain key claims creates a negative halo for all the others that may be related.

The question of who ultimately is working for whom in the UFO arena often cannot be satisfactorily answered. That some of the major players on the UFO scene might be government agents carefully injecting limited amounts of disinformation into the public pot should not surprise us. The scenarios I am describing are so incredible that it would take only a few false stories carefully planted in the larger truth which, if exposed, would cause massive confusion and doubt about that larger truth. This larger truth is that far too many strings are being pulled from behind the scenes on matters of utmost significance. And the cover-up on UFOs seems connected to many of these strings. This is, in part, why there is a cover-up.

The question of who is working for whom becomes especially focused in the case of Robert Lazar, a physicist who worked at the top secret Groom Lake facilities in Nevada. Lazar went public in part, he claims, because of the crimes against science being perpetrated there. Presumably our government owns, flies, and rather incompetently researches the anti-gravitational technology of a few small UFO craft there. The larger scientific community ought to be involved in this research, he believes. It is not clear how we came by these craft, although he points out that their seats were not designed for the average adult human.

Circumstantially, Lazar made a plausible case. Respected researcher Timothy Good in *Alien Contact* finds Lazar's story credible. However, questions about his personal life and business dealings have caused some in the UFO community to have serious doubts. Lazar says his life was threatened after he went public. The question is, *if* Lazar's account is essentially true, why is he still alive? Is it because if he had an unfortunate accident, his story would gain credibility? Or because the government is planting disinformation, partly through having manipulated his memories? Or because the government wants to let the truth out gradually, but maintain control in the process?

Preparation for contact? Former Vice President Quayle once called for a more effective means to deal with potentially dangerous asteroids or comets headed our way, such as the recent comet Machholz 2 (named MYRVA in some esoteric circles) which mysteriously broke up shortly after having been discovered. A few respected astronomers have detected the possible existence of a tenth planet beyond Pluto with very irregular movement, based upon indirect evidence. The orbiting Hubble telescope can detect incoming UFOs as well as distant stars. Clairvoyants also have seen a variety of objects headed toward the planet. In his last years in office, President Reagan made repeated references, in public contexts which otherwise would not suggest them, to hypothetical external alien threats as a way of bringing the nations of the world together. When asked about this, President Gorbachev said he "would not dispute the hypothesis," but that it's too early to worry about such an intrusion.

There is circumstantial evidence to suggest that we are preparing for some type of contact. Our mutual disarmament, the sudden withdrawal from Eastern Europe, the destruction of Phobos II, the stepped-up pace of SDI testing and firing at mysterious objects in orbit around the planet, and President Reagan's repeated remarks about a common enemy, make more sense in light of such a hypothesis.

In addition, television commercials have rather dramatically increased their references to aliens. For example, Camel cigarettes, Amoco gasoline, Miller beer, Payday candy bars, and Chevrolet automobiles all have been hyped with the help of extraterrestrial images. "The X-Files" on Fox television makes reference to the Reticulins. And prime time news programs are investigating topics, such as alien abductions, that formerly they would not touch. Sociologists will point out that this is simply Madison Avenue taking advantage of the UFO craze. Readers familiar with the extent of the government cover-up of UFOs, however, may not be so certain that these connections are as innocent as they appear. Then again, it could be that most of the veiled references to extraterrestrial intrusion are intended to throw us off track, by whom or for what is not clear.

This much, however, is clear. We already have fired beam weapons at some extraterrestrial objects, most assuredly not meteors or "space ice." Astrophysicist and NASA consultant Dr. Jack Kasher has shown that the photographic evidence from the *Discovery* is convincing. This claim is also supported by the fact that year in and year out the Star Wars laser gun (FEL) survives budget cuts, ostensibly for its medical applications. What is its real purpose? Who is firing upon whom? Is the secret government taking practice shots? Or firing on craft it believes to contain negative extraterrestrials? Or firing on members of Ashtar Command because it does not wish their presence to be known to the public?

The whole story may never come out. Besides, punishing the guilty, even if possible, would not accomplish much. Victimization and retribution are not the point. As David Icke observes in ...*and the Truth Shall Set You Free* (one of the most comprehensive, recent works in conspiracy theory), on an unconscious level a secret government of global elites was our creation, too. Our goal now should be to move beyond the fragmented mind-set of adversarial relationships that has brought us to the brink of destruction. We must face darkness, but not dwell upon it, to stimulate the transformation necessary to preserve both ourselves as a species and earth as our home.

The need to move beyond an adversarial mind-set is the driving force behind CSETI, the Center for the Study of Extraterrestrial Intelligence, and its physician-founder, Steven Greer. Greer and his colleagues have moved the UFO debate to another level, close encounters of the fifth kind. In these encounters, specially trained groups reach out to extraterrestrials both with coded signals and coherent positive thought fields derived from meditative practice. By demonstrating peaceful intent, the CSETI organization hopes to show alien visitors that some humans are both ready and worthy of face-to-face contact. There are even special protocols in the event a ship lands. Thus far, CSETI seems to have attracted some significant UFO activity.

But who or what is being attracted? Group I, II, III, or some combination thereof? Suppose contact is made with the wrong group. Greer argues that this is fear-based thinking. In the first place, we have no direct evidence of any negative alien intent, although this may depend on what one means by "direct" and how public such evidence would have to be. However, even if negative aliens exist, Greer argues, we are not in a position to do much about them.

Finally, by demonstrating peaceful intent, we can attract aliens of similar intent. Of CSETI's working assumptions, this is perhaps the most well founded. CSETI is performing an important function. However, CSETI members have a tendency to align themselves with whoever responds to their peaceful overtures without necessarily having the discernment to determine who the beings inside the craft really are.

CSETI is also based on the assumption that it's up to us to initiate contact with them, rather than up to them to initiate contact with us. As Lyssa Royal and Keith Priest point out in *Preparing for Contact*, alien groups may view the timing of contact as essentially up to them. They know who is ready for contact and who is not, better than we ourselves in most cases. They don't need to be summoned.

Besides, they are *already* interacting with humans on a subconscious level in preparation for more conscious contact. The situation may be one where ETs plant the suggestion for contact-readiness with appropriate groups or individuals who then, seemingly of their own free will, take steps to initiate the contact. From an interdimensional ET perspective, the difference between our subconscious and conscious minds does not appear that great. Hence, they are sometimes surprised when we claim not to know what is going on. It looks to them as if we should.

CSETI urges its members to overcome any residual fear of aliens and to understand that there is little to lose by adopting a positive orientation toward extraterrestrials in general. The suggestion should be well taken. For fear simply attracts the very things we are fearful of. However, overcoming fear should not be the same as throwing caution to the wind. Advanced technology does not automatically translate into advanced spiritual development.[13]

THE PROMISE OF LIGHT

No account of the cosmic drama I am sketching would be complete, if ever it could be, without reference to the converging visions of Michael Grosso (*Frontiers of the Soul*), and especially Kenneth Ring (*The Omega Project*). Both Ring and Grosso are intrigued by the parallels between accounts of near-death experiences and UFO abductions and of the transformational possibilities that accompany such experiences.

Ring's research, for example, suggests that near-death experiencers and abductees may be as much as four times more likely than the general population to: be very sensitive to electrical fields, light, and sound; have unusual sleep patterns; undergo powerful mood swings; and evidence paranormal abilities, such as telepathy or the ability to heal others. There may also be significant connections between NDEs, abductions, and childhood trauma. (Research by psychologist Nicholas Spanos indicates that UFO *sighters* are no more prone to fantasy, suggestibility, and psychopathology than are non-sighters.)

Ring, Grosso, and other researchers have also drawn attention to the many *positive* changes in attitude, lifestyle, and belief-system that abductees and near-death experiencers often undergo. There may be some type of evolutionary benefit to be derived from such experiences.

Ring and Grosso are transpersonalists in the fullest sense of the term. They take seriously a broad range of spiritual, psychic, and transcendental experiences. Most importantly, they believe that such experiences do not for the most part take place just within our heads, although many of their effects, as well as their predisposing conditions, may be found there and in other parts of human anatomy. Paranormal experiences, including UFO contacts and abductions, are not mere artifacts of modified brain chemistry. They are not hallucinations in the usual sense of the term, i.e., seeing something that is not there.

However, Ring and Grosso share a Jungian perspective on the paranormal. Both subscribe to the existence of a collective unconscious—what Grosso terms "mind-at-large." While they arrive at this view for somewhat different reasons and qualify it in different ways, this basic stance allows them to draw two inferences of considerable importance for any worldview.

The first is that the entities involved in such experiences, e.g., extraterrestrials performing physical examinations, tunnels, ghosts, etc., are for the most part neither subjectively internal (inside one's head) nor objectively external (independent of one's consciousness). Rather, they occupy a third category, the collective unconscious or mind-at-large, which we might characterize as subjectively external.

On this view, aliens are real but only archetypally so. People access this archetype in different ways according to their cultural programming and individual personality traits. They have real experiences of seemingly external objects when a connection is established between their individual consciousness and the collective unconscious. Jung himself believed that UFOs were projections from the collective unconscious. They may well be out there, he surmised, but not in the physically real way that the average person thinks.

Jungians are typically very liberal about paranormal phenomena. They can explain them by pushing them under the umbrella of the collective unconscious. This is a difficult position to refute. However, as Jung himself pointed out, physical readings from radar, actual metallic craft, and touchable aliens would force him to abandon such an interpretation of UFOs. The same can be said in response to Ring and Grosso.

Contactee and abductee experiences certainly have archetypal components. We are immersed in our culture and in a sea of consciousness that extends both horizontally and vertically beyond the limits of consensus reality. However, it would take only one Reticulin/human hybrid at the front door, so to speak, to burst the paradigm. I disagree with Ring and Grosso on empirical grounds and am content to let the case for or against the existence of aliens develop as it will. I don't think we will have long to wait for some definitive answers.

The other inference that Ring's and Grosso's Jungian stance allows them to draw is that the entire end-times scenario—from apocalyptic visions to UFO encounters—is serving a vital human need, a species-wide need to heal and transform ourselves. The collective unconscious is literally mirroring back to us danger signals that we should take very seriously if we are to survive as a species. As Grosso explains:

> The latest development in UFO symbolism (i.e., the abduction narrative) contains a message about healing ourselves…Taken symbolically, the idea of hybrids would be about our need to be revitalized; the need to enhance our gene pool. It certainly makes sense to say that we need to embark on evolutionary experiments to mutate ourselves. In other words, if we interpret the symbolism of the

abduction experience as a strange kind of species dream, the message is that our world, symbolized by the otherworld, is a dying wasteland and that we have to evolve into a higher (and hence much more adaptable) species.[14]

We desperately *need* to heal ourselves as a species and claim our higher potential. Other writers especially knowledgeable about UFO contact, notably Whitley Strieber in *Transformation* and John White in *The Meeting of Science and Spirit,* have also linked this contact with a larger evolutionary impulse. Carl Raschke, the ultimate New Age critic (see Chapter Two), even sees UFO contact experiences as a profound clearing mechanism—a tool for dismantling some of our most cherished beliefs and institutional structures—so that humankind will be free to follow that impulse.

The question, however, is whether as a species we are unconsciously inventing—projecting from out of mind-at-large—the whole UFO drama, including abductions, in order to address this evolutionary impulse. Or whether external and objectively real UFOs and extraterrestrials are *attracted* to our evolutionary turning point in order to play their respective roles, both positive and negative, within a larger galactic unfolding. Are we subtly deconstructing ourselves, or are we being deconstructed by something of far greater import than Raschke can integrate into his human-centered universe?

I believe that the latter alternative more accurately captures the truth of the matter. It is easier to believe that physically real aliens carry symbolic significance than it is to believe that we have created aliens from out of the collective unconscious. Here, as elsewhere in the New Paradigm dialogue, the distinction between *creating* something from out of our own consciousness, on the one hand, versus *attracting* it into our consciousness, on the other, is critical. Grosso's symbolic reading of the UFO drama, I think, is on the mark as far as it goes. However, I believe that the facts upon which his symbolism is based are more than the projection of transformational needs.

From the perspective of positively oriented extraterrestrials, there is a reverse symbolism to our transformational needs. It is not that we have created them in order to better understand ourselves, but rather that our consciousness needs to make a giant evolutionary leap in order to enter into constructive relationships with them. We need to transcend duality, overcome negative emotions, live at peace with each other, and clean up the planet in order to find our place in the larger galactic community. This is the larger evolutionary mandate.

In their telepathic transmissions, the Pleiadians have described a similar evolutionary turning point in their past and would like to help us with ours now. Other alien cultures, as well as some of our own visionaries, have pointed out that human consciousness itself, by virtue of a built-in evolutionary dynamic, is shifting from a "third" to "fourth" density level (whether we like it or not). This suggests that there will be something akin to a new human species (dubbed *Homo Noeticus* by John White) on the planet after the millennium manifesting greater wisdom, love, empowerment, and psychic awareness.

Ring further observes that a global shift in consciousness may be mediated by kundalini. Certainly, kundalini awakenings are on the rise and their symptoms are some of the most tangible evidence of a major shift. Clairvoyants also are seeing new chakras take shape in our subtle body anatomy—one, for example, between the heart and throat chakras. Robyn Quail's and Caryl Dennis's extensive work with contactees, especially siblings of "vanishing twins" (detected, but never born), even suggests direct extraterrestrial intervention for purposes of awakening childhood prodigies, transmitting blueprints for advanced technology needed for the planet, and reviving latent gifts of healing.[15] Major evolutionary change is clearly on the horizon.

The unresolved questions relate to how painful or peaceful this transition will be, and how each individual will relate to the challenges it brings. Old attitudes and beliefs must be flushed out on a profound and massive scale in order to make room for the new. Extraterrestrial contact in different ways will contribute to this breakdown and preparation. Those who do not make the shift in their consciousness, as reflected in the enhanced vibrational patterns of their energy field, will find it increasingly impossible to live on the planet. They will not be able to reincarnate here, not because they are inferior or bad people, but because they are still dancing to the old AM frequency when the planet has shifted to FM.

So with every writer who sees profound evolutionary significance in UFO and contactee experiences, I am in agreement. Even negative experiences have a role to play. Undoubtedly, a great deal that we otherwise might not acknowledge is being mirrored back to us via such extraordinary encounters. However, I am a philosophical realist at bottom. I believe there are UFO experiences *because* there are UFOs, not the reverse. We have not conjured up such experiences in order to address our transformational needs.

These needs, I think, are partly addressed by the dynamic *interface* of two relatively independent centers of reality, human and extraterrestrial. As many as a dozen extraterrestrial cultures have had their karmic fingers in our pie, so to speak. We are a part of their transformation as much as they are a part of ours. As Lyssa Royal and Keith Priest point out:

> It is not just humans on this small planet earth who are transforming. Humans are part of a vast galactic network. When one portion of the network transforms, so does the network itself. Creation is a never-ending interlocking puzzle, with the picture constantly changing.[16]

The ultimate significance of extraterrestrial contact is spiritual. Our assumptions about who we really are, what we can become, how we fit into the larger scope of creation and, most importantly, how we can respond to the foregoing, will undergo a profound revision.

It is said that God has promised light. However, I suspect that God enjoys not knowing *exactly* how the concluding chapters of this galactic drama will play out. This much we do know. Love radiates light. Darkness feeds on fear. As light from higher dimensions penetrates and becomes integrated with lower dimensions, it pushes darkness and fear out. But darkness and fear do not want to leave. Without light, darkness and fear would be nothing. On the other hand, they can remain only by becoming transformed into that which attract them. Either way, however, once light and love begin to move, darkness and fear lose ground.

The promise of light is being fulfilled, sometimes in ways that we would not expect or think to acknowledge. Here are but a few:

1. A veritable explosion of therapists and counselors are working to help us accept responsibility for our actions, acknowledge our fear-generated issues (guilt, control, denial, etc.), and let them go.

2. In the same vein, holistic and alternative health practitioners are helping us to live healthier, more balanced lives, to understand deeper causes of disease, and to promote the positive integration of spiritual, mental, emotional, and physical concerns.

3. Hundreds of major national and international groups are working to raise consciousness about the environment and take direct action on behalf of the planet. This is progressively a global agenda,

and it reflects light and love at work, no matter what other labels may come into play.

4. Various extraterrestrial groups, to a very limited degree, are assisting in holding the planet together until we can take greater direct action on our own behalf. For example, they drain off excess pressure on major fault and grid lines to reduce their potentially more cataclysmic effects. Others compensate for ozone damage. Still others assist with healing. But they cannot do it all and they would not attempt to do so. In a sense, they are praying that we face reality before it is too late. When we officially ask for assistance, undreamed of technology (pollution-free energy production, for example) will become ours.

5. Still other intelligences plead our case in galactic councils and directly intervene on our behalf against others who would do us harm. Some of these intelligences currently have human bodies, while others are members of recognized alien groups. On rare instances they may intervene to prevent our doing extraordinary harm to one another as a species.

6. Thousands of religious organizations, prayer circles, and meditation groups the world over aid the cause through their invocations of peace, protection, love, and constructive empowerment. The power of intent, especially when collectively focused, should never be underestimated.

7. Average people, with virtually no cosmology to speak of, but who spend their lives extending compassion to animals, children, the homeless, and those in need, contribute powerfully to the cause. The world is a little better off if we simply take time to talk to a homeless person, rather than turn in fear—all the more so, if we take that person in.

8. Dozens of alternative publications, among them *Nexus* and *The SpotLight*, continue to uncover information of vital public significance and to expose abuses of power behind the scenes.

9. A reawakening appreciation for animal rights and animal consciousness is very much in evidence. Living in harmony with other citizens of the planet here long before we were is another way to live in light.

10. Finally, we have the promised authority, power, and love of the legions of light and numerous angelic beings from levels above those of alien populations—Metatron, Maitreya, Christ, Gabriel,

Hilarion, Michael, Pheadrea, Raphael, Uriel, Auriel, and others. For the purpose of restoring this planet, these legions are led by Christ. Specially designed waves of energy are showering upon the planet, pushing darkness to the surface and transforming it in the process.

It is not especially important which aspects of this transformational vision are literally accepted or rejected. If you don't care for angelic hierarchies or extraterrestrials, but are concerned instead with personal growth and environmental sanity, then you should keep on doing exactly what you are doing. It is easy for those who work within this larger cosmic vision to cooperate with those who do not. And at this stage, *actions* on behalf of our species and our planet are more important than particular belief-systems. One does not have to believe in reincarnation to be a part of the solution.

Spiritually advanced beings have no personal investment in being acknowledged; they are far more concerned that we look within, embrace love and light over darkness and fear, see ourselves as parts of a greater interconnected whole, and transform the world accordingly. They are here to assist in our awakening, to help us recall what our journeys on earth are about, and to understand how we became cut off from our spiritual roots. Each of us will relate to this inclusivist vision in the ways that we are capable. Light will prevail, I believe, but only after the conflict with crooked paths of darkness is played out on the current level of human history. It is an old, old story, especially for those who long for the light and who have positioned themselves now, on this planet, for the final ascent. Light versus darkness is the ultimate transformational metaphor. It is also a fundamental evolutionary fact. To insist that darkness is merely our own creation, on the one hand, embodies an important truth. It tells us about how we have fallen away from light and how we can choose to move closer to light. On the other hand, such insistence is hopelessly naive when it comes to understanding the ways darkness actually can function in attempting to validate itself.

Doors of evolutionary opportunity are opening all around us in virtually every area of human endeavor. In some cases, the other side is only dimly perceived; in other instances, the opportunities are clear. *Paradigm Wars* is about the kind of thinking that informs movement in the vicinity of these opportunities. Yet they are of such a nature that, in order to reach and take advantage of them, we must transform ourselves in the process. We cannot take advantage of these openings merely by sliding along on the efforts of others.

Some will choose to take maximum advantage of these unprecedented challenges and opportunities. Others may stagnate with indecision. Still others will turn away and encourage us not to make the journey. So far as each person is concerned, accelerated interdimensional integration does not favor one course over another. It simply predicts that the factors inclining us to one or the other direction will accelerate along the paths we have chosen. The effects of doing nothing will be raised accordingly. The energy infusion upon the planet is currently so great that those who dwell upon their negative emotions are far more likely to attract their unpleasant physical counterparts.

Finally, accelerated dimensional integration (also described as a shift from third to fourth and fifth density consiousness) predicts that individuals whose paths are fueled by the power of love will enjoy a greater range of opportunities and a greater likelihood of being able to integrate them into their lives. It means that those who finally walk through these doors, not merely as believers in a new worldview but as shapers of a new world, will have unmasked the many faces of fear. Those who choose not to participate in this process of unmasking will find it done for them in ways which accelerate the dynamics of their dark side, restrict their options, and drive them to acts of desperation.

The whole show is coming unraveled. Those who think they will control the course of history for their own selfish ends will disintegrate into chaos, even as they attempt to insert more fear, greed, and control into the process. Even as darkness attempts to control light, it is being penetrated by light.

In a larger sense, the only lesson of life is love. The decision behind all decisions is what we choose to do with that lesson. As it is so often observed, that choice is up to us. If it is not already, it will become abundantly clear in the coming years that it always has been. For love brings up *all* things unlike itself for healing.

Final wakeup call: official contact 1996–'97? It is out of a great compassion for the earth and her children, as well as a profound respect for the cycles of galactic destiny, that Ashtar Command, representing the Galactic Federation, in early 1994 announced through Yvonne Cole and others its intent to make formal public contact by the end of the year.[17]

Unforeseen circumstances, notably the effects of electing a Republican controlled congress, caused the original contact date (November 11, 1994) to be pushed back, while our government waffled on its earlier decision to participate in the process. Our leaders were deeply divided about the role America should play in a world conference with Ashtar. However, Ashtar wants the peaceful involvement of America. Thus, a formal announcement will not be made until perhaps as late as 1996–'97.

In the meantime, the media is on overdrive with investigative reports of UFOs and aliens—almost as if by design. The August, 1995 Fox Television documentary on an alleged alien autopsy performed in connection with the 1947 Roswell crash, while presenting some plausible evidence, actually raised more questions than it addressed. It may even have been a clever and costly piece of disinformation ultimately designed either to test public reaction or to sow confusion about Roswell and ETs in general in the mind of the average citizen. Still, it raised the consciousness of those not otherwise inclined to serious study of the topic.

Currently, Ashtar Command and earth-based energy workers continue to prepare subtle grid lines not only for this planet's own evolutionary advances, but also to help insure an energetically hospitable environment for the dimensional descension of extraterrestrials and their craft. Sheldon Nidle's prediction in *You Are Becoming a Galactic Human* (representing a Sirian/Federation point view) that we are close to entering a photon belt, the dramatic effects of which will require extraterrestrial assistance, continues to draw attention. At issue from the perspective of higher dimensional beings is whether such immersion is necessary to accomplish much needed transformation on the planet, or whether less dramatic stimuli already at work will suffice.

An Ashtar- or Federation-affiliated landing probably will be preceded by extended hovering over a few population centers. Live images of alien leaders will be televised from their own ships. Any attempt to prevent this contact or to negatively manipulate public opinion about it, while causing unnecessary confusion, ultimately would backfire. The heads of major governments around the world have been invited to participate. A joint announcement by government representatives and Ashtar will precede a landing. Unlike negative extraterrestrials, Ashtar will stress that the source of our power is within ourselves—not with any alien group playing up to our victimization and control dramas.

Ashtar normally follows the principle of nonintervention. In our case, an exception has been made because a sufficient number of citizens have asked that this happen—subject to the following condition. Ashtar will land, make its existence indisputable, and offer assistance for spiritual growth, world peace, and environmental sanity. It will be up to the *people* of the planet, *not* their leaders (who have kept the truth hidden from them), to manifest in their consciousness whether Ashtar should remain.

If we decide to accept their offer, they will work with us but not for us. We will not be passively saved from the consequences of our own actions by those not responsible for them. A joint effort will require a massive change in *human* consciousness, including whole new ways of relating to each other and a whole new conception of who we are and what we are doing here. If we decide not to accept their offer, they will leave and not attempt to interfere with our free will. But they are reasonably convinced that, over the past few years and continuing as I write, there have been enough constructive changes on the planet to ensure that, after the initial shock, their overtures eventually will be accepted and integrated into our worldview.

Prior to that time, we may see public and covert attempts to unduly influence our attitudes about the contact—possibly even large-scale staged paranormal events. Discernment is, of course, always in order. There are obviously many questions to be answered. Where do they come from? What do they have to offer? Why now? But simple-minded attacks by those who fear that their myopic worldviews or selfish abuses of power will be exposed are not in order. Ashtar Command is a spiritually based group from whom we have nothing to fear and much to gain. Major portions of the population are both curious and ready. Formal contact is one of many ways the promise of light is being delivered. What we do with the delivery is up to us.

PREDICTIONS: WHAT ARE WE TO DO?

When I lay out the cosmic drama of this chapter, I am often asked for a summary of predictions and practical recommendations. Part of my response in this respect is reasonable advice for any period in history. Still, in keeping with the vision of this book, the consequences of not acting on them are greater now than in times past. So they bear repeating. Formal contact with extraterrestrial civilizations may change the timing, but not the substance, of some of these recommendations.

1. The paradigm wars currently under way will increase in scope and intensity to a level unparalleled since the shift from the medieval mind-set to the Enlightenment.
2. Whether in science, religion, health, politics, education, or economics, those identified with the root metaphors of a dying worldview—fragmentation, reductionism, hierarchical control,

patriarchy, competition, and fear—will find themselves pushing harder and achieving less.

3. Those identified with the guiding metaphors of a Rising Culture—holism, multidimensional realities, gender complementarity, relations of mutual empowerment, decentralized authority, and love—will push harder and achieve more, despite major setbacks along the way.

4. Abstract moral arguments about what is right or fair will not be effective unless they take into account concrete psychological realities. People will have to face their shadow sides.

5. Old institutions and ways of conducting business will break up at faster rates, often for surface reasons which don't make much sense. Splinter groups, acting on inwardly apprehended imperatives, will push for rapid change in many directions.

6. Businesses that introduce their employees to metaphysical and spiritual principles of integrity and growth will survive; the "bottom line" mentality will not.

7. Strange new alliances will form between groups, or parts of groups, that formerly appeared to have little in common. For example: "Feminists for Alternative Health Care."

8. Investments in ideas, technology, or practices that address real human needs will prove to be both safer in the short run and more rewarding in the long run than those generated out of greed and artificially induced desires. Those who take the former route will have to forge a vision of history capable of nurturing their courage through difficult times.

9. The existence of extraterrestrials will become undeniable, but not before those who speak to this point endure more ridicule, debunkings, and threats. The human race will have to prepare itself, one way or another, for membership in a larger galactic community.

10. More people will treat the earth as a trusted friend. They will thank the Earth Mother for her crops, but not before they have experienced hunger. And they will acknowledge the role of devas, elementals, and nature spirits in making the planet habitable.

11. Transformationally oriented "flashpoints" will continue to surface all over the cultural landscape. It should not surprise us, for example, if half the population of a school district turns out to demand the resignation of the school board while the other half

forms a "protected" zone for pursuing alternative education. Businesses will develop management and marketing structures that are self-transformational in order to remain viable.

12. Synchronicities will increase dramatically in both number and variety. Those able to recognize and act upon them will be at an advantage. For example: Your son has just been diagnosed with attention deficit disorder (ADD) when a friend in another part of the country sends you a book on holistic health that happens to have a chapter devoted to this disorder. You decide to try the recommended biofeedback, but don't have the money for the training. At which point you receive a hefty check from a completely unexpected source. Implication: Your son needs biofeedback, not Ritalin, for his attention deficit disorder.

13. For a while, Old Age attempts to control and suppress rising agendas may be somewhat effective. For example, congressional efforts will be undertaken to outlaw various holistic health practices in the name of public safety. The FDA has already raided a number of health food stores. However, such attempts ultimately will not succeed, because their proponents do not understand the real nature of what they fear.

14. Real differences will slowly prevail over names, labels, mere seniority, and arbitrary judgments about what cannot or should not be. For example, it should not surprise us if a government spy, posing as a client and gathering evidence about illegal holistic health practices, becomes so impressed with the help he receives that he lies to his superiors and quits his job. Many people in positions of power and authority will turn out to be quiet members of Ferguson's Aquarian Conspiracy—waiting for the right time to make their move.

15. By the time we take the guilt, control, and fear out of traditional religion, and factor in encounters with the paranormal and the yearning for genuine spiritual connectedness, it is not clear what will survive by way of mainstream religious institutions. Institutions that nurture genuine spirituality will flourish.

16. The gap between science and spirituality will be bridged by a perennialist worldview and the metaphysics of the Great Chain of Being.

17. A holistically based paradigm of vibrational medicine will subsume the biomedical model. Physicians who fail to take advantage of

additional training in areas their mentors never told them about will be able to maintain only marginal practices at best. History is simply moving in a different direction.

18. A fairly wide range of paranormal experiences will progressively unfold, including out-of-body experiences, prophetic dreams, clairvoyance, and various forms of energy and healing work—especially with children. Parents will fear their children are going crazy, teachers will tend to view it as a control issue disruptive of classroom activities, mainstream psychologists and physicians will try to write it off or suppress it, and politicians will adopt multiple personalities trying not to offend anyone in the ensuing paradigm wars.

19. Strange and unpredictable violent weather patterns, a greater number of high intensity earthquakes near population centers, and re-defined coastlines will take place in this decade, although *not* on the cataclysmic scale envisioned by some prophets.

20. A great deal of what happens at a social, economic, or political level should be understood in light of more deeply interconnected structural dynamics playing themselves out. Just as the causes and cures of major physical health challenges are not addressed by prescribing more medicine, the causes of and corrections for a major economic collapse necessarily involve a wide range of factors, such as fear, greed, and insecurity, that traditional economists and politicians do not like to examine. All things are interconnected.

21. Activities relating to the most extreme forms of darkness, such as gang wars, Satanic cults, psychic attacks, possessions, child abuse, and ethnic "cleansings" will continue to rise for a while. Drug abusers and children can be especially vulnerable. The behavior will often baffle already overworked clinical specialists in the field.

22. Where possible, people will move away from cities to form smaller self-supporting communities. Law and order in some places will tend to be either draconian or nonexistent.

23. Free energy technology for agriculture, transportation, and healing will finally see the light of day. Gravity will be mastered. (Secretly, it already has been.)

24. Reincarnation, together with all that it implies, will become a fundamental tenet of most everyone's worldview.

25. Clear evidence of prior lost civilizations, such as Atlantis and Lemuria, will surface. History will have to be rewritten. It already is in the case of the Sphinx.

26. So much sudden and dramatic change, on so many fronts, will cause many persons to experience destablizing anxiety, mental confusion, and/or emotional meltdown. What we desire will manifest faster. What we fear will also manifest faster.

27. Long-term personal relationships will have to pass progressively more stringent tests that speak to the question of love. They should be joyful, mutually empowering, and growth-oriented. Relationships built only upon common interests and codependent security needs will neither last nor prosper. Old Paradigm relationships will collapse rapidly; spiritually based relationships will bring partners together quickly.

28. Whether in business, government, the family, or society at large, relationships built mainly upon exercising power over others will progressively fail. Those who view their power as vested in other people or institutions outside of themselves will fall by the wayside.

29. Everywhere, people will continue to "wake up" in increasing numbers. Children already are calling their parents on their issues in amazing ways. This means more than acknowledging problems or changing beliefs. It means growing into a whole new way of relating to ourselves and to the world. Yearning for a sense of community, for revitalized spiritual commitment and empowerment, and for a multidimensional exploration of personal growth will threaten the status quo and redefine the boundaries of what it means to be human.

30. Currently, men and women are providing co-visionary leadership through massive evolutionary change. However, in sheer numbers it is women who will lead the way—in some cases dragging their men kicking and screaming into a new way of being.

31. New Paradigm literature will flood higher education where distinguished professors will make last ditch efforts to stem the rising tide of "irrationality." Smart scientists will begin studying Pleiadian hyper-space physics, even as scientific materialism collapses.

32. If Christ returns, his first order of business will not be to punish the wicked or resurrect the faithful dead. Rather, it will be to complete the lifting of the veil of ignorance and darkness that has covered the

planet for thousands of years. In other words, he will set the record straight about our true nature and place in the universe.

33. Attempts to systematically control certain political, economic, and technological agendas from behind the scenes will face progressive exposure and failure. *The New World Order will fail.*

34. Apart from the need to address the special contingencies of one's own life, my general recommendations for everyone (in no particular order of importance) are:

a) Reduce debt as much as possible and invest only in those areas which address real human needs.

b) Pick at least one area, if you have not already, where you can make a positive contribution in helping the planet and other humans. Support the development of free-energy devices, visit nursing homes, or plant trees—but do it!

c) If you have not done so already, find a teacher, a school, or a set of self-help books, with which you can seriously work on your emotional and spiritual challenges. Pay attention to letting go of habits and attitudes that no longer serve your growth, and to moving from reactive to proactive emotions. Learn to see the source of your power as within yourself, not in what other people do or fail to do.

d) Bring your work or career as much as possible into alignment with your values and core identity (which itself may be shifting).

e) Work on adopting a healthy, balanced lifestyle of voluntary simplicity. What you are is more important than what you do. And what you are is more than the sum of your programs.

f) Learn to see lessons and opportunities in chaos and pain. Do not dwell upon the latter. Let go of your victimization dramas. Accept responsibility for what you have attracted into your life.

g) Be prepared to experience the unexpected and, at times, the unbelievable. Reality will not always conform to common sense. Extraterrestrials are only part of a much larger picture. Indeed, what we can do for ourselves, especially in the area of healing, will at times seem miraculous.

h) By the same token, develop a healthy skepticism about extraordinary persons and claims. Probe and question. Do not confuse an individual's "persona" with his or her core identity. In times of rapid evolutionary advance, this gap can be very significant.

Those who claim leadership in God's name will not always be who they say they are.

i) Befriend yourself, learn to trust your feelings and intuitions. Practice manifesting what you need to survive and to grow, not just to support old habits. Pay attention to control dramas, whether your own or someone else's, in order to move beyond them. Consider letting go of partners who cannot move beyond such dramas; learn to love yourself enough to attract a partner who will grow with you, not just fill up empty spaces.

j) Above all, meditate! Reconnect with yourself, your environment, and the Source from which you came. And in so doing, move from the metaphysics of fragmentation toward the metaphysics of oneness.

I remain realistic about the challenges we face, but optimistic about the final outcome. Things will get worse before they get better. But they will get better. I expect to see in the next ten years not just a new world*view*, but a new and much improved world. Each of us will choose our own routes in getting from here to there. I hope that in some small way this book will help readers to understand and to successfully move through the territory. To live, here and now, on this planet is both a gift and an unprecedented opportunity. With our renewed commitment, the dream of the earth shall once again radiate throughout the galaxy.

Message from Mars: Sacred Geometry and the Evolution of Consciousness

by Frederick O. Mills

There is geometry in the humming of the strings.
There is music in the spacing of the spheres.

Pythagoras, 500 BCE

The so-called planetary science community has generally dismissed a body of astounding conclusions reached by independent digital imaging experts after meticulous examination of computerized data transmitted from the Viking Orbiters that photographed Mars in 1976. Since 1986, however, a few technical engineers and science-oriented scholars have been promoting public awareness of what they believe are gigantic constructed artifacts left by a nonhuman civilization hundreds of thousands of years ago upon Gaia's solar system sibling, the Red Planet.

They claim that a five-sided pyramid with three sides approximately one mile long, and two others about 1.4 miles, is situated in the region of Mars called Cydonia, apparently carved from what was once a mountain. The major axis of this symmetric, pentagonal monolith points toward a nearby "head" or "face," about 2.5 kilometers long by 2 km wide and 400 meters high, apparently sculpted from another mountain.

Most scientists have categorized all theorizing regarding the possibility that Intelligent Beings once created these ancient artifacts as "pseudo-science" or "science fiction." Tabloid media have printed outrageous stories about a "Face on Mars." So many conflicting, unverifiable scenarios involving "extraterrestrials" and "channeled messages from disembodied entities" have appeared in print that this whole topic has become indelibly linked with freak-show journalism. Regrettably, the stigma of tabloid sensationalism has been associated with quite plausible theories from serious researchers.

In 1987, science writer Richard C. Hoagland published *The Monuments of Mars: A City on the Edge of Forever,* which has sold over sixty thousand copies. By means of radio interviews, public lectures, and the distribution of video programs, he has generated considerable public interest in the

Face, the Pyramid, and other anomalous objects in their vicinity. Recently, other investigators have clarified the complex techniques of photographic analysis which support the argument that huge objects were constructed on Mars, and they have examined the scientific, political, and psychological implications from different perspectives. All of them conclude that the analysis, discovery, and speculation which began with a very small number of people now justifies serious attention by academic institutions.

Satellite telemetry analysts Vincent DiPietro and Gregory Molenaar were the first imaging experts to claim that a huge pentagonal shape near the sensationalized Face was not a natural formation; so this shape is generally called the D&M Pyramid. Cartographer and physical scientist Erol Torun analyzed the available images. No internal angle could be accurately determined by measurement of the fuzzy photos. The camera was a thousand miles away and its image resolution was limited. Definition of the structure's outline is far from clear. Its edges have obviously been eroded and concealed by sandstorms across millennia, and the structure appears to have been damaged by meteor impacts.

The basis for Hoagland's claim that "scientific evidence" supports his speculations rests primarily upon a highly sophisticated conceptual model developed by mathematician Torun. This model supposedly identifies the fifteen angles seen in a bird's-eye view of a pyramid with five triangular sides rising from a bi-symmetrical pentagonal base. Torun first assumed the two top interior triangles were equilateral; then he calculated the remaining angles so as to make his arithmetical model approximate specific roots and the ratios of selected geometric constants. Geometric analysis has legitimate merit, but Torun's approach is seriously undermined by conceptual flaws.

A fundamental assumption underlying the human Search for Extra-Terrestrial Intelligence (SETI) is that Mathematics is the only "language" in which a recognizable message could be initially communicated at a distance between separately evolved species. By encoding scientific data which reflects the structure of matter and energy, assumed to be universally identical at a fundamental level, the presence of Intelligent Beings could be communicated. The language of Geometry is considered the most universal basis for calculation because the ratios of distances between the vertices which define all regular geometric figures are always the same, regardless of size or the number base employed.

However, the entire body of mathematical argumentation which leads to Hoagland's interpretation of a "mathematical message" at Cydonia is dependent upon the validity of the initial assumption that two equilateral triangles determine the remainder of the D&M Pyramid. That assumption was derived from a composite geometric design, a hexagon/pentagon synthesis inspired by Leonardo da Vinci's canon of human proportion, the famous sketch of a man in a square and a circle. If Torun's initial supposition is false, the entire body of complex geometric analysis built upon that foundation must collapse.

Remarkably, that hypothetical shape does appear to correlate quite well when superimposed upon a digitized photo of the D&M Pyramid. However, other logically derived pentagonal designs with angles that differ by several degrees from Torun's model can be matched to the poorly defined image with a similar degree of confidence in the visual correspondence. Although the arithmetic by which nine angles were calculated to fit the initial premise is mathematically correct, I contend the geometric reasoning behind the Torun Model is fundamentally flawed.

It might seem that ratios of the numerical values which Torun assigned to adjacent internal angles might convey some meaning associated with the Laws of Geometry because these ratios approximate the square roots of 2, 3 and 5, and the value of Logarithmic "e" divided by Pi (2.72 ÷ 3.1416 = .865). However, attaching significance to a set of "approximations" of geometric constants is semantically equivalent to claiming a specific "woman" is a "mother" because she is "almost" pregnant.

A shape may be described as "round" or "oval," but there is a technical difference between a circle, an ellipsoid, and an ellipse. Johannes Kepler would not have been credited with discovering the natural laws that govern planetary motion had he been satisfied with claiming "their orbits are similar to a somewhat flattened circle." Torun's set of approximations of geometric ratios and constants doesn't convey information that meets the stringent criteria of valid scientific statements.

Even if human scientists relaxed the criterion of mathematical precision, Intelligent Beings capable of traveling galactic distances and engineering massive constructions on an alien planet would not likely attempt to communicate a universally valid message to a different species using what amounts to Geometric Pig Latin. The universal language of Geometry is based upon the irrational values $\sqrt{2}$, $\sqrt{3}$, $\sqrt{5}$, π, and $\varnothing$, specifically because they are derived from a precise set of proportional linear relationships. A unique set of equilateral, equiangular, two dimensional polygons which can be inscribed within a circle (triangle, square, pentagon, hexagon, and octagon), and a related set of three-dimensional polyhedrons whose vertices all touch the interior of a sphere (tetrahedron, hexahedron, octahedron, icosahedron and dodecahedron), commonly known as the Platonic Solids, mutually generate the grammar of Geometry.

Certain transcendental values are identified as Universal Geometric Constants specifically because they are directly derived from ratios of line lengths which comprise this set of figures, not from ratios of angle values within those figures. By attributing significance to "angle ratios" within one unique figure specifically contrived to produce approximations of $\sqrt{2}$, $\sqrt{3}$ and $\sqrt{5}$, and e/π, Torun confuses the language of Arithmetic with the language of Geometry. The two are not equivalent just because both involve numbers. The contrived mathematical parameters of the Torun Model are logically irrelevant; the only meanings conveyed by the pentagonal shape Torun has devised are those that may be read into it, which is what has transpired.

In an effort to support a claim of validity on the basis of redundant self-reference, Hoagland subsequently drew multiple lines between various anomalous objects, noting that the triangles thus formed are congruent with the equilateral angles assumed at the outset to control the design. More objective analysts have concluded that the selection of the terminal points on a large scale map was biased by Hoagland's desire to "match" the predetermined numerical values Torun had calculated, and that Torun's version of a hexagon/pentagon synthesis is insufficient to support the monumental proportions of Hoagland's speculations.

Regardless, Torun and Hoagland deserve accolades for focusing attention on Mars' mysterious monoliths. Even though the correct key to the code was not identified, the evidence of the imaging experts still supports the hypothesis that a geometric cryptogram was embodied within artificial constructions. It need not be concluded that all speculations these monoliths might inspire must remain without foundation until better photographs are obtained. Several of Hoagland's arguments regarding the relevance of Tetrahedral Geometry appear sound and need not be thrown out just because the angles Torun contrived for the D&M Pyramid are logically irrelevant.

Certain facts developed in the course of analysis by other researchers can be used to support a solution firmly associated with the ancient traditions of symbolic, or sacred geometry. A set of angles has been identified which accurately and redundently encode geometric relationships with valid scientific meanings and with symbolic meanings associated with ancient cultures. For instance, highly significant relationships between music and geometry in ancient Egyptian and Greek cultures have been thrust into prominence due to the modern phenomena called "crop circles" or "crop glyphs."

Before developing these correlations, I will briefly recap the motivating experience that resulted in my developing a hyperdimensional alternative to the Torun Model, based upon a mathematical grid that perfectly encodes the building blocks of regular polygons and polyhedrons which are so significant within the sacred science of symbolic geometry. Contemplation of specific geometric ratios has long been associated with the evocation of modes of consciousness reported by spiritually evolved religious mystics. That state of heightened perception of Unity is also reported by persons who have survived a brief period of "clinical death," usually due to a traumatic accident or to heart failure.

Over twenty years ago, when I was completing a Masters degree in Public Address and Group Communication at Texas Tech University, I attempted to create a conceptual model depicting the complex thought processes involved in the generation of human speech, one which would reflect the specificity of the flowchart of a computer program. On March 6, 1973, while mentally configuring a group of concepts within a series of geometric shapes, I experienced a spontaneous "scientific vision." In the process of visualizing and manipulating some specific textual material, black print on a white page, those images abruptly disappeared and were replaced by two points of light against a black background.

After interpreting them as a higher level abstraction of the concepts I had been verbally manipulating, I intentionally decided to rearrange the two dots to represent a newly perceived personal meaning. I projected a mental command at them and the dots moved accordingly, but this action triggered a profoundly transformative experience referred to in the Eastern religious traditions as "mystical illumination." The emotional and intellectual content of that experience inspired a prolonged quest for a scientific explication of this event—a theory subject to verification by repeated tests.

In March, 1990, I finally discovered within the branches of knowledge I'd studied across many years—cognitive science and altered states of consciousness—a concept which integrated the theory of quantum physics, the biology of neural networks in the brain, and computation procedures related to "artificial intelligence." This "synthesis" can be codified as a set of geometric designs or mandalas.

By mid-1991, I realized that a specific mathematical equation had been imbedded within the thought process that had evoked the vision of "two dots" and the profound out-of-body experience that followed. The foundational concepts for a Universal Visual Language were subsequently identified within four related sources: Ancient, Sacred, Tetrahedral, and Hyper-Dimensional Geometries. Consequently I have discovered exactly how contemplation upon specific linear relationships, including those codified by the dimensions of the D&M Pyramid, can initiate a mental process with the capacity to volitionally trigger an episode of "mystical illumination." After studying the mathematical meanings encoded by the geometric symbolism enshrined within ancient religious temples and mythologies, particularly those of ancient Egypt, I finally identified, in October, 1993, what I believed to be the Equation of Higher Consciousness.

Eight weeks later, that Equation was further confirmed by a set of angle values suggested by an Atlanta architect. In August, 1993, after viewing one of Hoagland's videos about anomalous structures on Mars, supposedly linked by geometric design, Richard A. Kilmer independently discovered a logical structure within the hypothesized pyramidal construction. The following January, after discussing our diverse perspectives, we both tested the potentials of his set of numbers through geometric analysis of a published photograph of the Cydonia region, using a computer aided design program accurate to microscopic scales. We mutually deciphered how a brilliant geometer could have used a precisely calculated plan to specify the size, the site, and the polar orientation of a penta-pyramid, based upon the internal angles which determine its unique shape.

By sharing and refining our individual insights, we discovered a geometric plan upon which the entire Cydonia complex could have been designed. Furthermore, within the perspectives of higher-dimensional geometry and its relation to quantum physics, I have independently confirmed the validity of the conceptual origin of this set of angles as determined by a Golden Rectangle. All parameters solidly confirm that the monoliths on Mars were constructed by a very advanced culture so as to redundantly encode the operative mathematical factor at the quantum level which is the root of all consciousness, the Phi Ratio.

Recognizing that the scientific community has yet to be convinced that any kind of message from an extraterrestrial culture is encoded at Cydonia, my goal became a rigorously geometric explication which offers a scientific rationale for more closely examining speculations being promoted by various researchers of anomalous physical and psychological phenomena. The 4–D geometric foundation of the D&M Pyramid design strongly implies that highly evolved Beings have acquired mental mastery of hyperconsciousness and have routinely traveled vast distances through manipulation of hyperspace. Did such Beings from another solar system, galaxy, or physical dimension once place enormous monoliths in various cosmological environments where they might eventually be discovered and decoded by the progeny of life-forms they had genetically modified?

A pragmatic consequence of my Cydonia Solution is a scientifically designed, semantically structured, 4–D Meditation. It entrains the neural frequencies generated by the dual hemispheres, leading to volitionally induced hyperconscious perception. My research has revealed that evocation of a mental image of Two Points of Light was ritually practiced in the Pyramid of Giza, probably taught to the Pharaonic Priesthood by an Interdimensional Being whose ancestors engraved the relevant equation upon the surface of Mars.

I've drawn this conclusion because the geometric structure of my consciousness theory has decoded their metaphysical mandala, defined by a grid linking five anomalous features that digital imaging analysts contend are artificial constructions. Only four values comprise the fifteen internal angles within the five-sided pyramid that points to the Face, a solution validated not only by redundant self-reference, but by simultaneous cross-references.

With only five symbolic elements and two clues relating them to the polar axis and to each other, an advanced culture quite familiar with hyperdimensional geometric theory was able to precisely encode the five mutually embedded "Platonic solids," the "Pythagorean" musical ratios, and the parameters of three geometric figures imbued with scientific meaning from dimensional perspectives greater than three. Juxtaposition of these elements in the same context reveals philosophical and cosmological messages somewhat more profound than Mr. Hoagland's statement, "Look to your tetrahedrons."

To defy Time, and to remain detectable across Space, their extraordinary message required embodiment on an extraordinary scale. Independent confirmations of a Cosmic Blueprint at Cydonia, by geometricians, cartographers, and physicists, will revolutionize current paradigms of human science and philosophy. Because its brilliant formulation can be comprehended by average human beings, subjective confirmations by millions of people may well initiate a Global Mind Shift.

I firmly believe that Hyperdimensional Travelers embodied their philosophy of Cosmic Oneness within a 3–D calling card, a pointer toward a higher stage in the evolution of Cosmic Mind. Induction of a 4–D mode of consciousness upon a global scale may be a requirement that Humankind must meet before these Visitors officially welcome the peoples of Gaia within an immortal brotherhood of Hyperconscious Beings. The purported evidence for extraterrestrial visitations upon Earth across thousands of years gains enormous credibility from the congruence between the geometric and astrological foundations of ancient religions, the geometric knowledge attributed to Pythagoras as a consequence of his tutelage by Egyptian priests, the phenomenon of "crop circles," and the shifting scientific paradigms which are steadily gaining favor.

The sequence of illustrations that follows is but a cursory introduction to a collection of concepts that will lead directly to Humankind being rapidly ushered into the next millennium with radically altered paradigms in science, medicine, religion, communication technologies and social relationships. The significance of the PentaPyramid extends far beyond its being a proof that a civilization once existed on Mars. As portentous as that recognition seems, and the consequent rethinking of human history that is now required, the PentaPyramid, purely as a geometric shape, bridges the disparity between quantum theory and relativity theory.

Einstein discovered that the "force of gravity" is a consequence of curved space acting upon itself and he sought in vain for a Unified Field Theory that would explain all "physical forces" in terms of pure geometry. His intellectual successors still strive to codify a "Theory of Everything." The fundamental premise behind Sacred Geometry, the most ancient science and philosophy of Ultimate Being, is that the Transcendental Other is continually made manifest and, within limits, can become perceptible to Human Beings as a direct consequence of precise geometric relationships within and between hierarchal levels of physical dimension. Both mystics and "new physics" theorists highly value the functional role of Geometry.

Within the recorded precepts and ritualistic meditations associated with "mystical" traditions across more than five thousand years, the Phi Ratio, the Golden Mean, the Divine Proportion, has played a prominent role. Its exalted status may be better understood as a result of the unique PentaPyramid being discovered on Mars. The mathematics encoded by the 2–D image reflect the parameters of a Phi Cuboid of unit volume within a sphere. I believe this totally Phi-based polygon, the wire-frame shadow of a 3–D polyhedron, provides the final key to Human comprehension of the geometric laws which determine all configurations within the Universe— a Theory of Everything mutually acceptable to scientists and to religious philosophers.

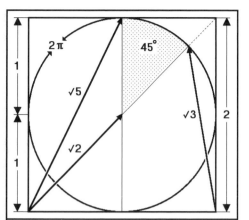

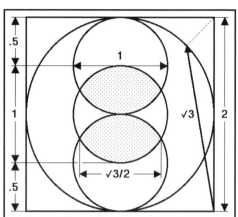

Figure 1. A SQUARE AND A CIRCLE
Sacred Geometry defines relationships between Energy, Matter, and Spirit. These basic shapes symbolize Manifestation and Source. The roots of **2**, **3**, & **5** are undefinable in decimal numbers; their values are called *transcendental*, as is the value of π. Both Diameter and Circumference of a Circle are related to **Pi:** $(C = D \times \pi)$. Therefore, *the two cannot be simultaneously measured in whole numbers based upon the same unit value.*

Figure 2. MEDITATION OF OPPOSITES
Division of a UNITY CIRCLE into smaller, equal Circles, provides an image of Duality or Polarity. A third equal-size Circle, touching the center of both, symbolizes *reconciliation of opposites by mediation,* a principle the ancient Greeks called LOGOS. A union of three Circles in this manner creates two "fish bladder" shapes, *vesica piscis.* These "two fish" are the origin of the symbol for Pisces, one of the Twelve Houses of the Zodiac.

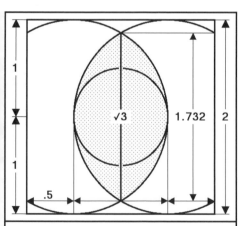

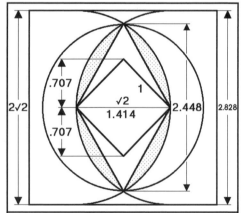

Figure 3. THE VESICA PISCIS
Drawn so that each touches the other's center, two equal Circles produce this almond shaped space, an opening to the *womb* from which are born the geometric shapes and patterns of the Universe. The first three to emerge are Triangle, Square, and Pentagon, containers of the ratios and relationships required to generate all regular shapes and forms that can be constructed using a geometer's compass, straight edge and pencil.

Figure 4. PLATO'S WORLD SOUL
Greek cosmology used the language of Number to symbolize the process of emanation through which a whole Universe comes into being. This process begins with UNITY, or **1**, representing THE ONE. A divine son, Apollo, THE LOGOS, a Mediator between Unity and Multiplicity, is born via the *vesica piscis* portal. Symbolic Generation *crosses the diagonals* of both Square and Cube: THE WORLD SOUL = **1 x $\sqrt{2}$ x $\sqrt{3}$ = 2.448.**

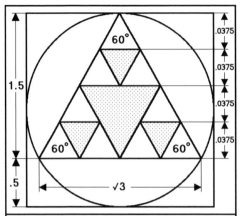

Figure 5. THE INSCRIBED TRIANGLE
An equilateral Triangle divides a circumscribing Circle into three equal segments. This *regular,* equiangular Triangle may be repeatedly divided into four equiangular Triangles. Neither curved not straight line segments reflect whole number values. However, the ratio between the height of the large Triangle and the Circle's diameter can be expressed as a whole number fraction, **3/4,** or equivalent decimal value, regardless of scale.

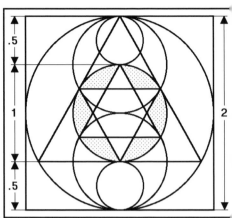

Figure 6. TRIANGLE TO CIRCLE RATIOS
Whole number ratios between the largest Circle and Triangle and the smaller figures are 2:1, 3:2 and 4:3, or the inverse. Over three millennia ago, geometers of Earth turned geometric ratios into a visual language more precise than the spoken word. Eons earlier, the same symbolic alphabet was used to spell out a message on Mars, by the placement of five gigantic constructed Markers. This geometric language can be read by anyone.

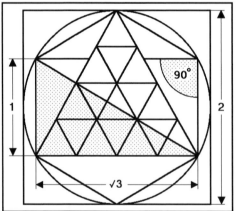

Figure 7. THE 1-√3-2 RIGHT TRIANGLE
A Hexagon inscribed in a Circle with a diameter of **2** contains three rectangles. The diagonal of any one divides it into two Triangles considered by Pythagoras to be as important as equilateral Triangles. The Right Angle allows calculation by the famous formula named after him, equating the length of the diagonal to the square root of the sum of the squares of the other two sides: $(1 \times 1) + (\sqrt{3} \times \sqrt{3}) = 1 + 3 = 4$, and $\sqrt{4} = 2$; *Q.E.D.*

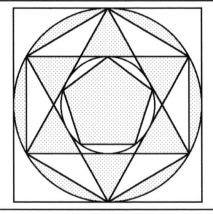

Figure 8. THE HEXAGONAL STAR
Numerical relationships among these opposed Triangles, Circles, and Pentagon were deemed so important by cosmologists that they embued this figure with major religious significance. Few of its geometric properties are generally known, even by persons familiar with *The Star of David.* The policy of ancient guilds and priesthoods was to keep their mathematical secrets hidden from persons outside their professional organizations.

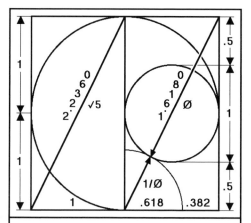

Figure 9. CIRCLE SQUARE RATIO
The diagonal of a **1x2** rectangle may be divided so that the ratio between Short and Long pieces is the same as between the Long and the Whole. If only four decimal places are used in geometric calculations, any error is less than the width of a pencil line. The √**5** is **2.2360**. A value for **Phi** of **1.6180** is quite accurate; 1 ÷ **1.6180** = **.6180**. Their sum is **2.2360**. Ancient geometers used Greek letter **Ø** to symbolize this *Golden Mean.*

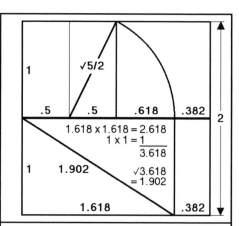

Figure 10. GOLDEN MEAN RECTANGLE
A simple construction which adds to a line **1** unit long, the length required to generate a Golden Rectangle, reveals how the Phi Ratio is directly related to the transcendental values √**5** and **Pi**. Within a Circle of any magnitude, the unique √**5** relationship between a Square and Pi is present. The diagonal length of this Golden Rectangle is identical to the diagonal of a Pentagon inscribed in a Circle with a **1** unit radius, or diameter = **2**.

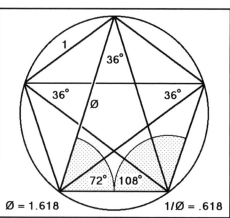

Figure 11. THE PENTAGONAL STAR
Regardless of size, the ratio between the side of a Pentagon and its diagonal is always the same, **1** to **Ø.** Each leg of the Star is a diagonal and is therefore cut by another leg in two places. When the side length of **1** unit is subtracted from **Ø**, it leaves **.618,** or **1/Ø**. The mathematical beauty of the Phi Ratio is perfectly demonstrated within a 5-pointed Star. Pythagoras made it the symbol of his school, but hid its secrets from outsiders.

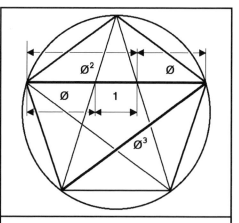

Figure 12. THE DIVINE PROPORTION
The geometric secrets of this simple figure were forbidden to all except those trained to utilize the "occult" knowledge in religious rituals prescribed for spiritual communication with Deity. Symbolic aspects of a pentacle/pentagram have obscured the significance of the Pentagon's mathematical properties. Symbolic of regeneration, **Ø** guides growth by accumulation, and by part/whole self-similarity. By some, it is even considered Divine.

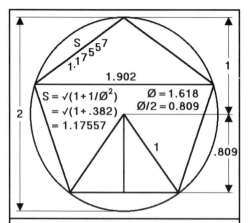

Figure 13. THE SIDE TO DIAGONAL RATIO
The side of a regular Pentagon is always related to its diagonal in the ratio **1:Ø**. If the radius is **1**, the side is ≈ 1.17557... . Thus, the diagonal has to be Ø x 1.17557 = **1.9020**. The diagonal of a Pentagon is the Geometric Mean between the enclosing Circle's diameter and its own height: G.M. = √(d x h) = √(2 x 1.809) = √3.618 = 1.902. 1.902 ÷ 1.809 =1.051. The canon of proportion used by Egyptian artists was a ratio of **19 to 18**.

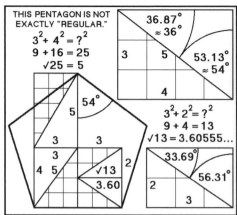

Figure 14. PENTAGON'S "3-4-5" TRIANGLE
Bisecting the angle formed between the center of a Pentagon and two vertices will produce two Right Triangles whose sides are not quite whole numbers. Ancient geometers believed that only whole numbers or their ratios should be used in measuring; they called a **3-4-5** Right Triangle a *Sacred Triangle*. A Grid of Squares is a tool with which to *measure* a Pentagon, Pentagram, and Sacred Triangle, as linked by the Phi Proportion.

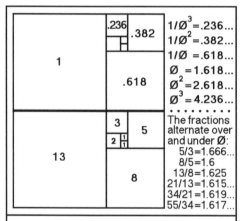

Figure 15. FIBONACCI SERIES GRID
The Phi Spiral governs a pattern of accumulative growth in plant life, sea shells and animal horns. These numbers structure the alternate spirals of seeds and petals, plus stem and leaf placement: 1, 1, 2, 3, 5, 8, 13, 21, 34, 55, 89, 144, 233, etc. Fractions, or ratios of this whole number series approaches Ø: 55/34, 89/55 & 144/89 ≈ **1.6180**. Continuing this additive series generates ratios closer and closer to Ø. *Humanity embodies Phi.*

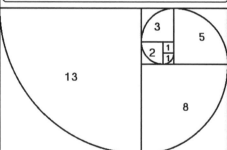

Figure 16. A FIBONACCI — PHI SPIRAL
A Golden Rectangle whose long and short sides are in a Ø relationship contains Nature's Spiral coiled within it. A Phi Spiral can be approximated by a succession of arcs drawn within a sequence of Squares, as shown. Like the Fibonacci series, a Golden Spiral grows from within itself. Both are physical representations of "self-accumulation." Egyptologist Schwaller de Lubicz found that the Ø ratio dominated the art in Pharaonic temples.

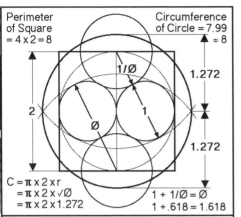

Perimeter of Square = 4 x 2 = 8

Circumference of Circle = 7.99 ≈ 8

1/Ø

1.272

2

1

Ø

1.272

$C = \pi \times 2 \times r$
$= \pi \times 2 \times \sqrt{Ø}$
$= \pi \times 2 \times 1.272$

$1 + 1/Ø = Ø$
$1 + .618 = 1.618$

Figure 17. SQUARING THE CIRCLE
Because the Circle is an incommensurable figure based on Pi, with a straight edge and compass it is only possible to *approximate* a Circle equal in circumference to any given Square's perimeter. The concept of *Squaring the Circle* is important to the geometer-cosmologist because the Circle represents pure, unmanifest Spirit-space, while the Square represents a comprehensible world he sees manifested; he seeks to reconcile them.

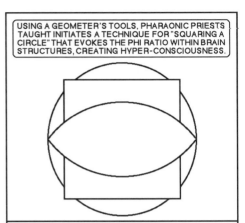

USING A GEOMETER'S TOOLS, PHARAONIC PRIESTS TAUGHT INITIATES A TECHNIQUE FOR "SQUARING A CIRCLE" THAT EVOKES THE PHI RATIO WITHIN BRAIN STRUCTURES, CREATING HYPER-CONSCIOUSNESS.

Figure 18. THE MOUTH OF RA
This image shows the quintessential relationship between **Circle** and **Square** after the two have been *harmonized* by the binding Principle of the Ø Ratio. This almond looks like a v*esica piscis,* but its Ø parameters differ from a √3 almond's. As the symbol of Ra, the Egyptian Sun God, it is the Mouth which speaks the **Creative Word** — Fractions, the Names of the Gods. It resembles the moving shape seen around a vibrating string.

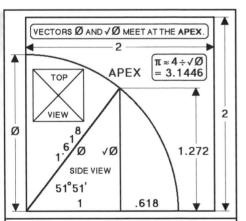

VECTORS Ø AND √Ø MEET AT THE **APEX.**

2

TOP VIEW

$\pi \approx 4 \div \sqrt{Ø}$
$= 3.1446$

APEX

Ø

2

8
1.6
1
Ø √Ø

1.272

SIDE VIEW

51°51'

1

.618

Figure 19. PHI AND THE GIZA PYRAMID
It is claimed that a temple priest told the ancient historian Herodotus that the area of each face of The Great Pyramid is equal to the square of its height, which reflects knowledge of both Pi and Phi. It is known that geometers of Ancient Egypt approximated π with $4 \div \sqrt{Ø}$. Archeologists have confirmed that the Phi Proportion is also present in the Triangle made by the height, half base and apothem (cross section) of The Great Pyramid.

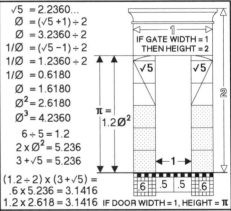

$\sqrt{5} = 2.2360...$
$Ø = (\sqrt{5} + 1) \div 2$
$Ø = 3.2360 \div 2$
$1/Ø = (\sqrt{5} - 1) \div 2$
$1/Ø = 1.2360 \div 2$
$1/Ø = 0.6180$
$Ø = 1.6180$
$Ø^2 = 2.6180$
$Ø^3 = 4.2360$
$6 \div 5 = 1.2$
$2 \times Ø^2 = 5.236$
$3 + \sqrt{5} = 5.236$
$(1.2 \div 2) \times (3 + \sqrt{5}) =$
$.6 \times 5.236 = 3.1416$
$1.2 \times 2.618 = 3.1416$

IF GATE WIDTH = 1 THEN HEIGHT = 2

√5

√5

$\pi = 1.2 Ø^2$

2

6 .5 .5 6

IF DOOR WIDTH = 1, HEIGHT = π

Figure 20. A PI AND PHI RELATIONSHIP
When calculating the circumference of a Circle, Greek geometers used the whole number ratio **22/7** for Pi. A more accurate value can be found within the gate of the Egyptian Temple of Amon at Karnak. A whole number ratio, **6/5**, multiplied by the square of **Ø,** produces the generally used π value. **6/5** implies Hexagon/Pentagon, as well as Icosahedron/Dodecahedron, both correlated with Ø-based, **6-D**, Complexified Hyperplanes.

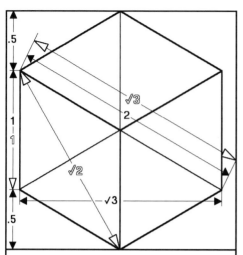

Figure 21. A 3-D CUBE IN TWO DIMENSIONS
Recognition of **3-D** forms in **2-D** drawings is due to unconscious conventions of perspective that binocular vision generates in human brains. The diagonal between opposite corners of this 1x1x1 Cube is √3, and the diagonal of any face is √2. But, in this **2-D** perspective, they are **2** and √3.

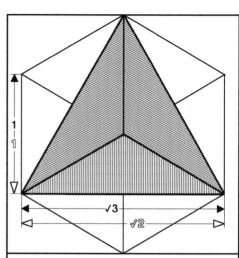

Figure 22. TETRAHEDRON IN CUBE
Viewed as the diagonal of a **2-D** Hexagon, each side of the shaded Triangle will be √3. All edges of this **3-D** Tetrahedron's four identical faces are really √2. The vertex perspective in such a **2-D** representational drawing foreshortens the faces, but **2-D** *images can accurately encode volumes.*

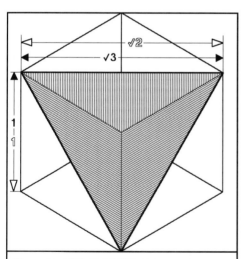

Figure 23. THE OPPOSITE TETRAHEDRON
Looking through its transparent base, a second Tetrahedron's vertex is located at the far corner of the Cube. The shaded interior sides promotes an illusion of three dimensions on a **2-D** surface. A combination of **2-D**, **3-D**, and **4-D** concepts mutually relate the Ø Ratio to **6-D** Hyperplanes.

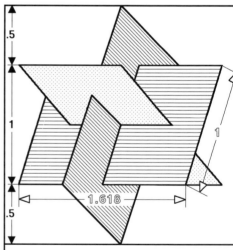

Figure 24. INTERLOCKED HYPERPLANES
Physical theorists now claim that three identical Golden Rectangles, combined at right angles as shown, have mathematical properties that place **3-D** Ø relationships within a **6-D** context. All the **3-D** edges are either 1 or Ø; the **2-D**, wire-frame shadow image appears proportionally modified.

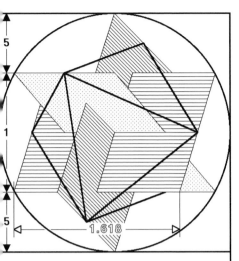

Figure 25. OCTAHEDRON ON PHI MATRIX
The third of the so-called *Platonic Solids* bonds to this Matrix of three interlocked Hyperplanes at the middle of each short side. All the diagonals of this Octahedron must be Ø because the sides of the Cube containing it are Ø by Ø. Each edge is the hypotenuse of a Right Triangle, or √2 x Ø/2.

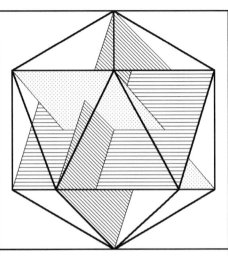

Figure 26. AN ICOSAHEDRON'S VERTICES
This fourth regular polyhedron is bonded to the 12 corners of a Hyperplane Matrix, thus forming its vertices. Its 30 edges create 20 faces, each a regular Triangle. The *Five Regular Solids* are the volumetric expressions of the Triangle, Square and Pentagon, the sole elements of their faces.

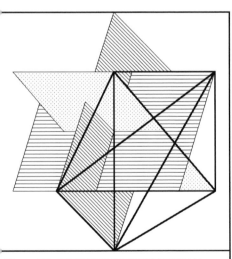

Figure 27. PYTHAGOREAN PENTAGRAM
A Pentacle, the Star drawn within this Pentagon by means of a continuous line, is bound in yet a third manner to the Hyperplane Matrix. The fifth regular solid also fits on this Matrix and is called a *Dodecahedron* because its thirty edges join at twenty vertices to form *twelve* pentagonal *faces*.

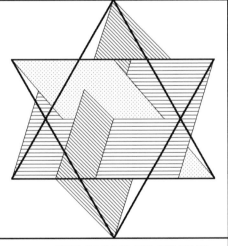

Figure 28. STAR OF DAVID RELATIONSHIP
Geometers are well aware of the Ø relationships among the Platonic Solids, but **3-D** simulations in *this* perspective do not appear in the general literature. Might the ancient religious symbolism associated with this **2-D** Star be correlated with Hyper-Dimensional Geometry encoded on Mars?

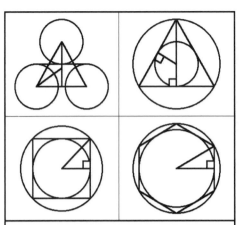

Figure 29. CROP CIRCLE RATIOS
Archaeoastronomer Dr. Gerald S. Hawkins has published numerous scholarly analyses offering geometrical proofs that formations which appear worldwide in grain fields as "crop circles" exhibit internal ratios that parallel those of the *diatonic musical scale*. His basic illustrations, above, are explicated using references to musical intervals, the way ancient philosophers linked geometry to natural science, to cosmology and to a theology.

	NOTE	H. M. FOURTH	A. M. FIFTH	OCTAVE
VIBRATION 1		$\frac{4}{3}$	$\frac{3}{2}$	2
6		8	9	12
STRING LENGTH 12		9	8	6
1		$\frac{3}{4}$	$\frac{2}{3}$	$\frac{1}{2}$
	NOTE	A. M. FOURTH	H. M. FIFTH	OCTAVE

Figure 30. GEOMETRIC RATIOS IN MUSIC
"The geometric proportion is called the *perfect* proportion because it is a *direct proportional* relationship, an equality of proportion bound by one mean term. The arithmetic and harmonic medians work out this perfection through an interchange of differences in a play of alternation and inversion." — Diagram and comment by the scholar, historian, and geometer, Robert Lawlor, in *Sacred Geometry: Philosophy and Practice.*

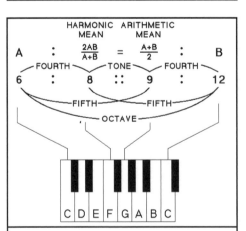

Figure 31. THE PYTHAGOREAN RATIOS
A major scale on a piano is played on white keynotes. The ineffable "Music of the Spheres" is derived from these ratios of frequencies in the diatonic scale: 1, 9/8, 5/4. 4/3. 3/2, 5/3, 15/8, 2. These fractions give the perfect major intervals of 2nd, 3rd, 4th, 5th, 6th, 7th, and octave. David Fideler explores the many connections between ancient cosmology, early Christian symbolism, and musical ratios, in *Jesus Christ, Sun of God.*

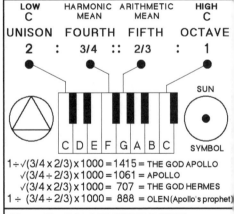

$1 \div \sqrt{(3/4 \times 2/3)} \times 1000 = 1415 =$ THE GOD APOLLO
$\sqrt{(3/4 \div 2/3)} \times 1000 = 1061 =$ APOLLO
$\sqrt{(3/4 \times 2/3)} \times 1000 = 707 =$ THE GOD HERMES
$1 \div (3/4 \div 2/3) \times 1000 = 888 =$ OLEN (Apollo's prophet)

Figure 32. SUN GOD MUSIC RATIOS
Ratios and relations shown above are in terms of the relative lengths of a musical instrument's strings, which are plucked to produce vibrations of a particular frequency. The pillars of harmony are the *perfect fourth* and the *perfect fifth*. Their ratio defines the interval of the whole tone. The gematria of Apollo was based on *Mediation of the Extremes,* the principle of *Logos,* geometric proportion, which thereby produced *harmonia.*

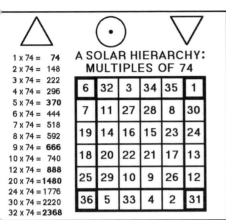

$$1 \times 74 = \ 74$$
$$2 \times 74 = \ 148$$
$$3 \times 74 = \ 222$$
$$4 \times 74 = \ 296$$
$$5 \times 74 = \ 370$$
$$6 \times 74 = \ 444$$
$$7 \times 74 = \ 518$$
$$8 \times 74 = \ 592$$
$$9 \times 74 = \ 666$$
$$10 \times 74 = \ 740$$
$$12 \times 74 = \ 888$$
$$20 \times 74 = 1480$$
$$24 \times 74 = 1776$$
$$30 \times 74 = 2220$$
$$32 \times 74 = 2368$$

A SOLAR HIERARCHY:
MULTIPLES OF 74

6	32	3	34	35	1
7	11	27	28	8	30
19	14	16	15	23	24
18	20	22	21	17	13
25	29	10	9	26	12
36	5	33	4	2	31

Figure 33. MUSIC OF THE SPHERES
The Pythagorean explanations of the harmonic ratios of music formed a foundation for Platonic cosmology and philosophy. The *Magic Square of the Sun* encodes the geometric ratio between the circumference of a Circle and a segment cut by an inscribed Triangle: 222 ÷ 3 = 74. Circles of musical ratios correlate with Plato's geometry of THE WORLD SOUL. The decimal place was not relevant in the Greek use of number symbolism.

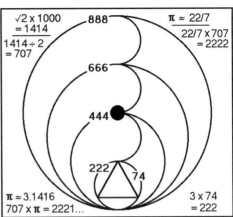

Figure 34. MAGIC SQUARE OF THE SUN
Gematria is based on number values assigned to Hebrew, Greek, Arabic, and other alphabets. The Torah and the Bible encode knowledge of cosmology and geometry using this technique. This 6x6 Solar Square exhibits KEY ratios: any symmetrical group of four numbers equals 74; perimeter numbers total 370; the total square is 666; *Solar Logos* is 888; *Illuminating Knowledge* is 1480; the total value of these words is 2368.

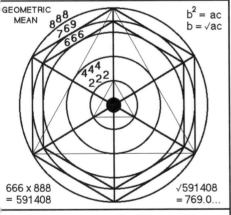

Figure 35. THE HARMONY OF THE SUN
666 & 888 are multiples of 74 in a Magic Square. 666 is the string ratio of the *perfect fifth* and 888 is the string ratio of the *tone*. The ratio 666:888 (3/4), is the harmonic relationship known as the *perfect fourth*. The square root of their product is 769, their Geometric Mean, shown above. 769 is the gematria value of PYTHIOS, another name given APOLLO, the Greek's God of Music, who personified the Solar Logos thirty centuries ago.

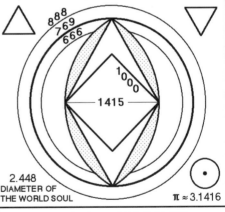

Figure 36. GEOMETRY OF A SUN GOD
Gematria for "The God Apollo" is 1415, ≈ 1.414 times 1000. THE WORLD SOUL times π equals 7.690, times 1000 equals the Geometric Mean. The *vesica piscis* is symbolically associated with the concept of a Cosmic Man or a Divine Savior. In paintings and bas-relief sculptures from many religious traditions, a personified Deity is shown within an almond-shaped frame, often reaching or stepping through this unique geometric portal.

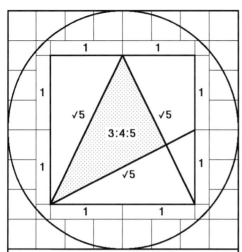

Figure 37. THE SACRED TRIANGLE
Both *reason* and *measure* are derived from the Latin root, *ratio*. Whole numbers were related to manifestation and calculation, while irrational, or incommensurable root numbers referred to that which could not be precisely measured, defined, or known. √5 *evokes* a Whole Number Triangle.

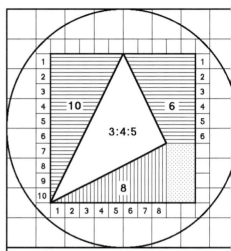

Figure 38. A PROJECTED RATIO
This Right Angle Triangle with three sides equal to whole numbers, is *projected* from vertical and horizontal lines that are 6, 8, & 10 units in length. These *square* values are thereby proportionally transformed into *tri-angular* whole numbers by an action of a *supra-rational root,* √5, upon itself.

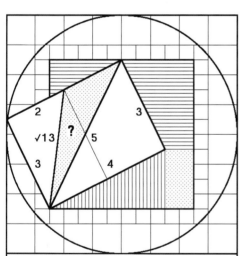

Figure 39. MUSICAL FOURTH AND FIFTH
After doubling a 3-4-5 Triangle into a rectangle, that figure is divided into a pair of 3x2 rectangles. By subtracting a 3-4-5 Triangle and one 2-3-√13 Triangle from this rectangle, the "?" angle in the remaining Triangle correlates quite well with the concept and value called the *Tetrahedral Angle.*

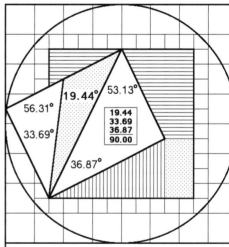

Figure 40. THE "TETRAHEDRAL ANGLE"
Richard Hoagland argues that the groove in the artificial Cliff encodes an angle of *approximately* 19.5 degrees and is correlated with the latitudes 19.47, where three vertices of a Tetrahedron will touch the inner surface of a Sphere if the fourth vertex is placed at the North Pole or South Pole.

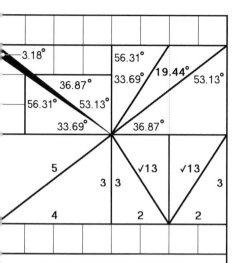

Figure 41. THE REDUNDANT RATIOS
3-4-5 rectangles are drawn on an 8x8 grid to see if geometric ratios 2:3 and 3:4 can be correlated with the "D&M" pyramid. The Arithmetical Model contrived by Erol Torun is based on assumptions many scientists reject. A *true* Geometrical Model should reflect *more precise* ratios and constants.

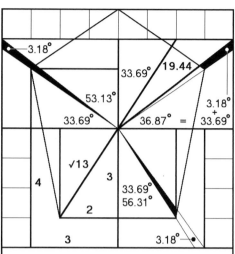

Figure 42. DEFINING THE PYRAMID
Without measurement, there is no science.
Each vertex of this pentagonal shape falls at an intersection on a Grid of Squares determined by the scientifically established Geometry of Music. Ideally, the design should also be related to both **4-D** Geometry and Hyper-Dimensional Physics.

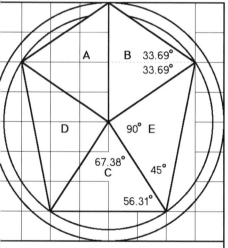

Figure 43. KEY ANGLES ON GRID
The factor of *redundancy* contributes credibility to this design; Triangles, **A, B** and **C** are identical and contain only two different angles. Four of the five vertices in this polygon define a Circle. Two Right Triangles, **D** and **E**, comprise one Square. In **3-D**, *Square* implies Cube and Tetrahedrons.

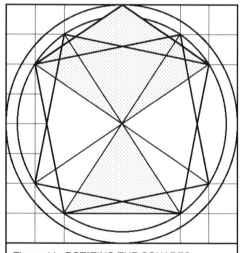

Figure 44. ROTATING THE SQUARES
Clearly, angles in this polygon can be generated by rotation of a Square within a Circle. The Giza Pyramid and the *Hyper-Tetrahedron* are related by their mutual embodiment of the Ø Ratio. Is a Penta-Pyramid on Mars similarly related to *two* **4-D** Tetrahedrons, or perhaps to a Hyper-Cube?

BECAUSE A POINT HAS NO DIMENSION, IN SOME ANCIENT CULTURES THE NUMERAL 1 WAS NOT CONSIDERED A **NUMBER**.

THIS SECOND POINT DEFINES A LINE WHICH HAS NO THICKNESS, MERELY LENGTH, SO NEITHER WAS NUMERAL 2 CONSIDERED A **NUMBER**. MONAD AND DYAD WERE CONSIDERED THE PARENTS OF NUMBERS. THE FUSION OF THE PRINCIPLES OF POINT—LINE, ONE — TWO, UNITY— DIFFERENCE, GIVES BIRTH TO **NUMBERS: 3, 4, 5, 6, 7, 8, 9**. THE DYAD IS THE DOORWAY BETWEEN THE ONE AND THE MANY.

Figure 45. DIMENSIONAL SYMBOLISM
The ancient language of Number Symbolism is denigrated by modern scientists as meaningless superstition. Symbolism is actually an effective way to communicate sophisticated concepts by non-verbal means an average person can grasp. The following Hyper-Dimensional concepts were gleaned from a scientific reference book printed in 1973, *Regular Polytopes,* by H.S.M. Coxeter. The drawings transcend the technical language.

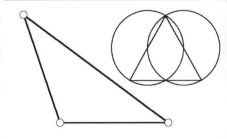

THE GEOMETRIC EXPRESSION OF **3**, THE FIRSTBORN OF MONAD AND DYAD, IS AN EQUILATERAL TRIANGLE, THE INITIAL SHAPE TO EMERGE FROM THE PORTAL OF THE *VESICA PISCIS*. BELOW IS ITS *SKEWED SHADOW.*

Figure 46. TWO DIMENSIONAL TRIANGLE
To gain a second dimension, a *third* point must be chosen, *off* the plane upon which lies the first dimension. From this point, any line is *projected* from the higher dimension onto the plane upon which it is drawn. A *second* line defines an angle but the first 2-D surface requires yet a *third* line. The *line shadow* cast by any wire-frame Triangle that is not parallel to the page will be somewhat skewed, as is the equiangular Triangle depicted.

DUE TO PERSPECTIVE FACTORS, THE LINE-SHADOWS CAST BY FOUR FACES THAT ARE TRIANGLES CAN LOOK JUST LIKE A SQUARE AND ITS DIAGONALS.

Figure 47. A SKEWED TETRAHEDRON
A *fourth* point, not on the same plane, is added. Four triangular planes form the first **3-D** solid, a Tetrahedron, which can be perceived by viewing a **2-D**, wire-frame shadow from different angles. This view is skewed; each plane is equiangular. Each face may serve as a *base* and the opposite vertex as the *Apex of a pyramid*. In space, a 4th dimension can be obtained by adding a *fifth* point beyond the four immediate planes of reference.

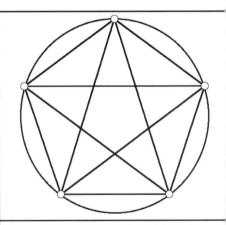

Figure 48. SHADOW OF A PENTATOPE
By adding a *fifth* vertex at a right angle to, and equidistant from each of four others, an *Apex* is formed within a Fourth Dimension. A Pentatope contains five Tetrahedrons; each triangular face serves as a base. We find the Ø ratio embodied in: 1) a **2-D** Pentacle/Pentagram, 2) the design of the **3-D** Giza Pyramid; 3) a **4-D** Pentatope's **2-D** shadow; and 4) a Penta-Pyramid on Mars. The Giza Pyramid encodes a **4-D** Tetrahedron.

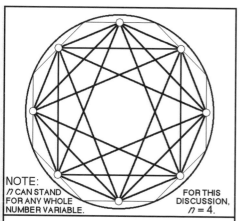

NOTE:
n CAN STAND FOR THIS
FOR ANY WHOLE DISCUSSION,
NUMBER VARIABLE. *n* = 4.

Figure 49. CROSS POLYTOPE
A fundamental property of *n* - Dimensional space is the possibility of drawing through any point **O**, *n* lines that are mutually perpendicular. *n* points equidistant from **O** along such lines are vertices of a finite region of *n* - space enclosed by *n* + 1 *hyperplanes.* By extending these perpendicular lines beyond **O**, a Cartesian frame or *cross* is produced. Points equidistant from **O** in opposite directions are the vertices of a *Cross Polytope.*

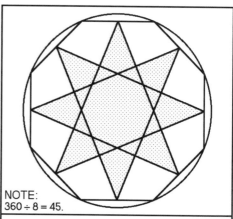

NOTE:
360 ÷ 8 = 45.

Figure 50. EGYPTIAN STAR OF ISIS
The Cross Polytope and the Octagon have eight vertices. An Octahedron looks like two pyramids pointing in opposite directions. The *Apices* of a Cross Polytope do the same, *along a line in the 4th Dimension.* The specialized language used in discussing higher dimensional geometry need not be comprehended just to recognize the **4-D** figure's **2-D** line-shadow defines an eight-point Star, a symbol of an ancient Egyptian goddess.

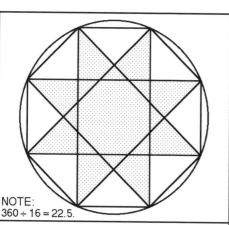

NOTE:
360 ÷ 16 = 22.5.

Figure 51. EGYPTIAN STAR OF SET
Isis is a Greek and English name given to *Aset,* an Egyptian goddess. As a prefix, "a" can mean *not,* in the sense *the opposite of.* The Egyptian god Set was imbued with *negative* personality traits, but Aset imbued *positive* characteristics. Having linked two higher dimensional geometric shapes to Ancient Egypt, the Giza Pyramid, and the worship of Sun Gods, consider this result of merely rotating the Star of Isis by *22.5 degrees.*

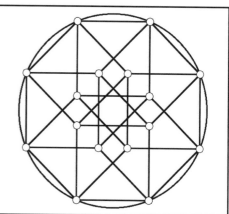

Figure 52. THE MEASURE POLYTOPE
The Star of Isis — Cross Polytope connection is paralleled by a Star of Set connection to this 4th Dimensional geometric figure, the Hyper-Cube. This mathematical matrix, a *lattice,* is also called a *cubic honeycomb.* The *measure* aspect comes from using a Hyper-Cube with edge **1** as a unit of *content,* just as a Square is a unit of *area* and a Cube is a unit of *volume.* All eight Cubes within a Hyper-Cube lie at right angles to all of the others.

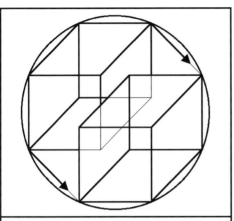

Figure 53. WIRE-FRAME MODEL
To grasp the idea of eight Cubes simultaneously being at a right angle to each other, we can look at them two at a time. The most important thing to understand is that all sides of these two boxes are the same length. These diagrams are the **2-D** shadows of what appear to be **3-D** models, but are actually geometrical constructs that exist in a higher dimension, one that the mechanisms of human perception cannot visualize physically.

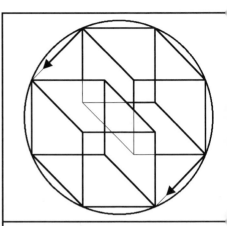

Figure 54. ORTHOGONAL MOVEMENT
Rather than distort the edge measurements by forcing the perspective, as is common when **2-D** images of **3-D** objects are created, all sides are drawn the correct length. A standard convention used to depict the movement of a **3-D** Cube into the **4th Dimension** is the representation of a 90 degree movement by a 45 degree angle. *Four mutually perpendicular vectors can meet at each vertex of eight Cubes within a Higher Dimension*

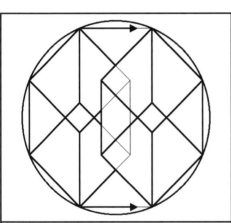

Figure 55. HORIZONTAL SHIFT
One can gain an understanding of how a fourth dimension functions in relation to just three, by considering how a **2-D** creature would perceive a **3-D** object that penetrated the plane of its flat world. Clarification of these concepts is provided by Dr. Rudy Rucker in *The Fourth Dimension: A Guided Tour of the Higher Universes.* Relevant correlations with the paranormal are offered by John Ralphs in *Exploring the Fourth Dimension.*

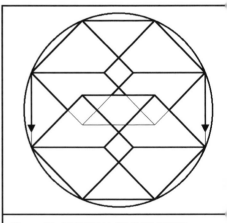

Figure 56. VERTICAL TRANSLATION
The scientists who claim to be leading a **S**earch for **E**xtra-**T**errestrial **I**ntelligence have made no effort to link the universal language of Geometry to the obvious constructions on Mars. Caustic, but cogent, criticism of these "experts" and of NASA's failure to pursue their own data can be found in *The McDaniel Report,* by Dr. Stanley V. McDaniel, Professor Emeritus, Department of Philosophy, Sonoma State University, California

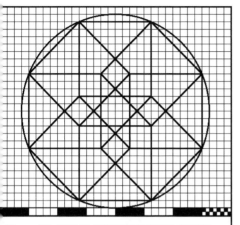

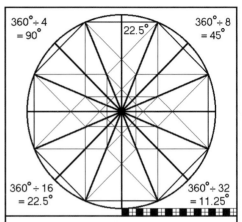

Figure 57. EIGHT SUPERIMPOSED CUBES
Assuming there is some connection between the geometry of Cydonia and the Pharaonic culture of ancient Egypt, with "tetrahedral" and "hyper-dimensional" factors supposedly involved, logic suggests that **4-D** Geometry might hold the key to the "D&M" pyramid identified by DiPietro and Molenaar in 1980. One KEY to Cydonia is a grid of intersections upon which the line-shadows of significant Hyper-Dimensional figures terminate.

Figure 58. SIXTEEN EQUAL SEGMENTS
This octagonal wire-frame shadow outline of the Hyper-Cube lends itself to division by 8 and 16. It correlates with a Circle cut into 16 segments. A NORTH line which appears to run between a Mound and a Tetrahedron on the rim of a crater is 22.5 degrees off a *vertical line* from the Mound along the left side of a Grooved Cliff. The angle between NORTH and the *mid-line* of the Face is also 22.5 (See Fig. 90). *Those lines are parallel.*

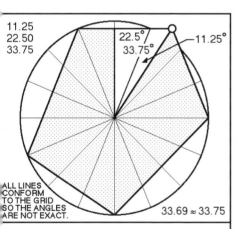

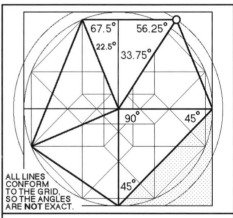

Figure 59. A FIVE-SIDED POLYGON
This polygon matches the Grid at four points on the Circle, at segment marks. The fifth vertex is on a larger Circle, which correlates with a larger Sphere. The fifth vertex symbolizes *projection* of *two* Tetrahedrons into yet a higher realm, just as the *Apex* of the Giza Pyramid is the fifth vertex of a Hyper-Tetrahedron—the Pentatope—which casts downward ten shadowlines as a **2-D** wire-frame Pentagram, the symbol of all the Ø ratios.

Figure 60. A HYPER-CUBE PYRAMID
The fact that a five-sided Penta-Pyramid can be drawn in relationship to a Circle which contains a Hyper-Cube's shadow, with the vertices of both matching Grid Points generated by a computer, seems a lot more like *science* than *numerology* or *metaphysics*. The specific ratios linking *music* and *geometry* can be encoded on superimposed grids in proportional scale by means of identical figures respectively rotated ≈ 3 x 11.25 degrees.

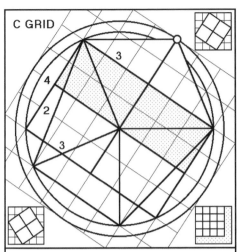

Figure 61. THE CIRCUMFERENCE GRID
Horizontal and Vertical legs of a Right Triangle thus oriented produce a whole number ratio with respect to the legs on a Horizontal-Vertical Grid. Because the PentaPyramid's internal angles are multiples of 11.25, a 5:4 ratio is generated when this Grid is enlarged and rotated 33.75 degrees.

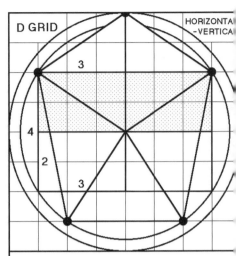

Figure 62. THE H-V DIAMETER GRID
Figs. 44 & 60 show the significance of rotating a square 8 times in increments of 11.25 degrees. Circumference and Diameter of a Circle can't be measured *simultaneously* in whole numbers with the same ruled scale, but *geometric ratios* give whole number values and they survive rotation.

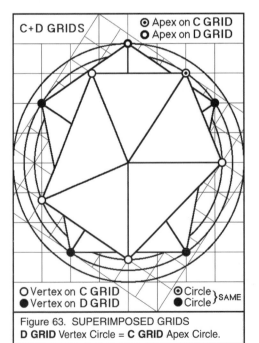

Figure 63. SUPERIMPOSED GRIDS
D GRID Vertex Circle = **C GRID** Apex Circle.

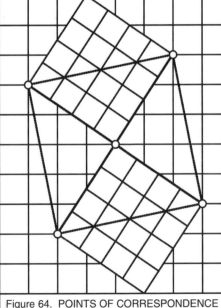

Figure 64. POINTS OF CORRESPONDENCE
Note the square that links these two grid scales.

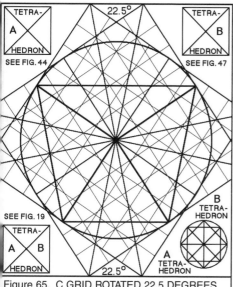

Figure 65. C GRID ROTATED 22.5 DEGREES
Spokes of PentaPyramid on a 16 point clockface.

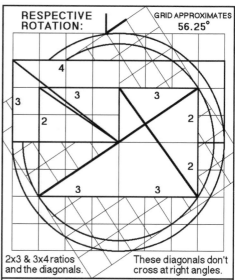

Figure 66. TWO GRIDS ARE COMBINED
A ratio between two different ratios is shown here.

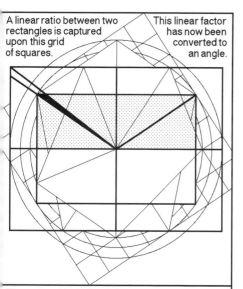

Figure 67. AN ANGLE OF 3.18 DEGREES
This angle can now be transferred to the other grid.

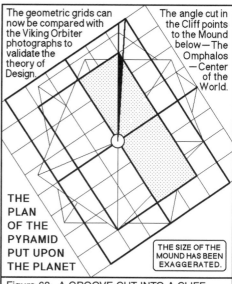

Figure 68. A GROOVE CUT INTO A CLIFF
At Cydonia, a Grooved Cliff encodes this angle.

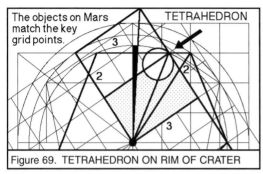

The objects on Mars match the key grid points.

TETRAHEDRON

Figure 69. TETRAHEDRON ON RIM OF CRATER

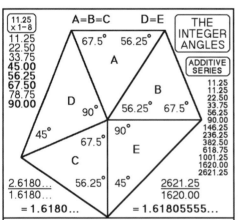

This is not a trick of light and shadow.

FACE

MARKERS NOT DRAWN TO SCALE

Figure 70. A MONUMENTAL MESSAGE ON MARS

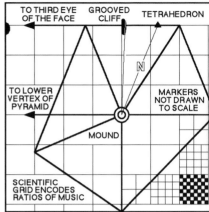

TO THIRD EYE OF THE FACE   GROOVED CLIFF   TETRAHEDRON

TO LOWER VERTEX OF PYRAMID

MARKERS NOT DRAWN TO SCALE

MOUND

SCIENTIFIC GRID ENCODES RATIOS OF MUSIC

Figure 71. KEY MARKERS ON GRID
70 illustrations have introduced many ideas relating matter and music to mathematics; juxtaposed geometric principles, historical facts and religious/metaphysical symbolism; and visualized abstract parameters of Higher Dimensions. Mutually supportive aspects of this combination of data produce this simple map which relates five gigantic Markers on Mars to each other and to Intelligent Design.

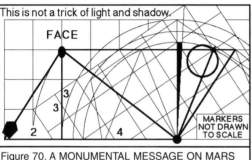

THE INTEGER ANGLES

ADDITIVE SERIES

A=B=C   D=E

$11.25 \times 1-8$

11.25
22.50
33.75
45.00
56.25
67.50
78.75
90.00

11.25
11.25
22.50
33.75
56.25
90.00
146.25
236.25
382.50
618.75
1001.25
1620.00
2621.25

2.6180...
1.6180...
= 1.6180...

2621.25
1620.00
= 1.61805555...

Figure 72. THE PHI RATIO NUMBERS
Scientific verification of the geometry of Cydonia required mathematical analysis and the use of computer generated grids to specify angles with trigonometric accuracy. Division of 360 degrees by 32 produces a factor which, multiplied only by integers, specifies the internal angles and site of the Pyramid, without reference to musical ratios or hyperdimensions. These numbers produce an easily perceived structure and Ø additive series.

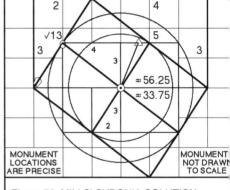

MONUMENT LOCATIONS ARE PRECISE

MONUMENT NOT DRAWN TO SCALE

Figure 73. MILLS' CYDONIA SOLUTION
In this format, no effort was made to analyze the photo images, to show any significant calculated distances, or to include all the data. The primary goal was to identify the conceptual bases from which scientific messages could be formulated for visual encoding in the Universal Language of Geometry, by means of artifacts that would not simply be interpreted as random consequences of natural forces, but recognized as products of Intelligence. Did Extra-Terrestrials build a huge Face on Mars? Grid + Objects = Design; Q.E.D.

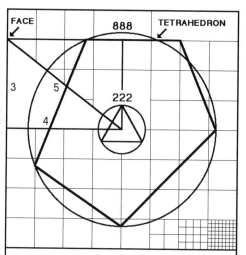

Figure 74. A SIGNIFICANT 3:4:5 TRIANGLE
The *ratio* between a 222 Circle's diameter and an inscribed Triangle's height defines the KEY *ratio* between the legs of a rectangle whose diagonal links the Spiral Mound with the Third Eye of the Face. The fact that these *Sacred Triangle ratios* control this configuration isn't *just a coincidence.*

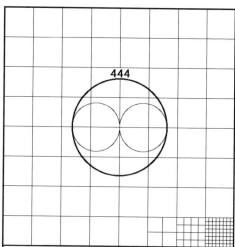

Figure 75. SYMBOL OF DUALITY/POLARITY
The religious symbolism of Sacred Geometry is based upon ratios of vibrating string lengths that produce frequencies of vibration heard as music. Geometric ratios depicted upon this grid produce mathematical values encoded by the letters that comprised the names given to Greek Sun Gods.

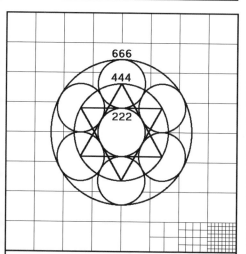

Figure 76. TWELVE DISCIPLES IMAGERY
The **Hexagon** linking the centers of six Circles mutually tangent to a seventh is reflected in the **Star of David**. In **3-D**, the central orb touches six others in two parallel layers of three identical spheres. Ancient religious symbolism is derived from *a uniform core of geometric relationships.*

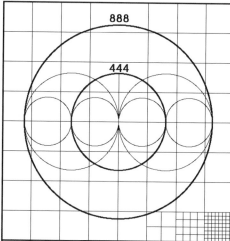

Figure 77. SYMBOLIC NUMBER OF LOGOS
Gematria encoded the fundamental ratios of the diatonic musical scale as the god-names Apollo, Hermes and Zeus, centuries before 888 and 666 became associated with a Jesus/Satan polarity. The geometric foundations of ancient religions are reflected in symbols that encode *Phi Ratios.*

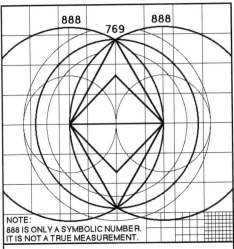

Figure 78. THE WORLD SOUL GRID
The significance of these diagrams with respect to the geometry of Cydonia is that these figures conform to intersection points or to an exact line boundary; they encode significant mathematical values, thereby establishing scientific credibility. A Magic Square of the Sun is based on 32 x 74.

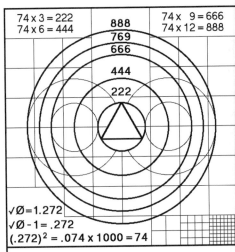

Figure 79. A MUSICAL GEOMETRIC MEAN
This grid is composed of 64x64 unit squares and the small Circles are 13 units in diameter. All the *symbolic* meanings of the figures can be thought of as an aid to memory; the major significance is the *numerical* values they encode. Logarithmic constant *e*, when squared (2.72 x 2.72), is *7.4*.

Figure 80. SUN GOD RATIOS ON MARS
The fact that the mythology of a Greek Sun God and an Egyptian Sun God are based upon ratios and numerical values that decode the geometric design on Mars suggests a Universal Language was once used to convey scientific messages in a pictograph composed of five related Markers.

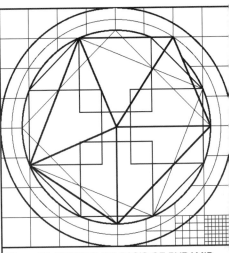

Figure 81. HYPERCUBE BASIS OF PYRAMID
The five-sided pyramid on Mars can be perfectly correlated with a Fourth Dimensional Hyper-Cube and with a Circle that defines the vertex points of the eight **3-D** Cubes which comprise that figure. This Circle is correlated with frequency ratios of the Diatonic Scale. *This is not just a coincidence.*

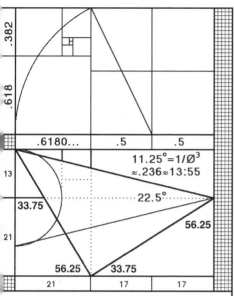

.382
.618

| .6180... | .5 | .5 |

$11.25° = 1/\emptyset^3$
$\approx .236 \approx 13{:}55$

13

33.75

22.5°

21

56.25

56.25 33.75

| 21 | 17 | 17 |

Figure 82. PHI CUTS CREATE KEY ANGLES
A Circle with the radius of Fibonacci number **13**
recalls the multiples of **13** in my World Soul Grid

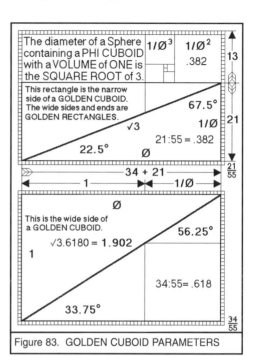

The diameter of a Sphere containing a PHI CUBOID with a VOLUME of ONE is the SQUARE ROOT of 3. $1/\emptyset^3$ $1/\emptyset^2$ .382 13

This rectangle is the narrow side of a GOLDEN CUBOID. The wide sides and ends are GOLDEN RECTANGLES.

67.5°
$\sqrt{3}$ $1/\emptyset$ 21
21:55 = .382
22.5° $\emptyset$

34 + 21
1 $1/\emptyset$
$\frac{21}{55}$

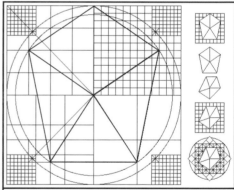

$\emptyset$
This is the wide side of a GOLDEN CUBOID.
$\sqrt{3.6180} = 1.902$
1
56.25°
34:55= .618
33.75°
$\frac{34}{55}$

Figure 83. GOLDEN CUBOID PARAMETERS

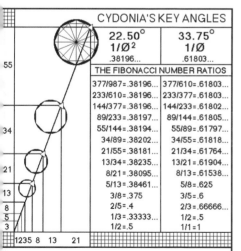

CYDONIA'S KEY ANGLES	
22.50° $1/\emptyset^2$ .38196...	**33.75°** $1/\emptyset$ .61803...
THE FIBONACCI NUMBER RATIOS	
377/987 = .38196...	377/610 = .61803...
233/610 = .38196...	233/377 = .61803...
144/377 = .38196...	144/233 = .61802...
89/233 = .38197...	89/144 = .61805...
55/144 = .38194...	55/89 = .61797...
34/89 = .38202...	34/55 = .61818...
21/55 = .38181...	21/34 = .61764...
13/34 = .38235...	13/21 = .61904...
8/21 = .38095...	8/13 = .61538...
5/13 = .38461...	5/8 = .625
3/8 = .375	3/5 = .6
2/5 = .4	2/3 = .66666...
1/3 = .33333...	1/2 = .5
1/2 = .5	1/1 = 1

Figure 84. 22.5 DEGREE CORRELATIONS
Fibonacci number ratios successively fluctuate
greater and smaller than the "ideal" Infinity Limit.
A series of Phi Rectangles generates diagonals
that approach the perfect **33.75** & **22.5** degree
angles. The scale of the Markers at Cydonia can
be precisely calculated because **Phi** is the basis.

Figure 85. TWELVE AS THE KEY TO A PLAN
It should now be evident that precise linear and
angular values can be encoded by means of key
geometric figures drawn on a uniform grid. The
Builders on Mars used nothing more than the Ø
Ratio to provide the key to Hyperconsciousness
by means of symbolic Markers at precise points
on a Grid. Physicists who desire comprehension
of the Universe will discover a mathematical key
engraved upon Mars. I believe the Cydonia Face
is inviting Humanity to know the Absolute via the
one Universal language—**G**eometry **O**f **D**ivinity.

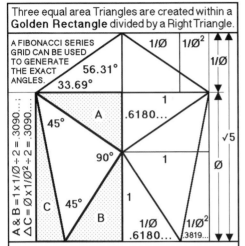

Three equal area Triangles are created within a **Golden Rectangle** divided by a Right Triangle.

A FIBONACCI SERIES GRID CAN BE USED TO GENERATE THE EXACT ANGLES.

56.31°
33.69°
45°
90°
C 45°
B
A
1
.6180...
1
1
1/Ø
1/Ø²
1/Ø
√5
Ø
1/Ø
.6180...
1/Ø²
.3819...

A & B = 1 × 1/Ø ÷ 2 = .3090...
△C = Ø × 1/Ø² ÷ 2 = .3090...

Figure 86. PHI CUTS DEFINE A PYRAMID
The significance of the data in Fig. 82 is doubled by creating a mirror image of the twin Phi Cuts of a Golden Rectangle's sides. The approximations of the Infinity Limit angles appear valid when the Fibonacci numbers are in ratio 2:3. The Diatonic Scale Ratios are linked to Ø as noted in Fig. 88.

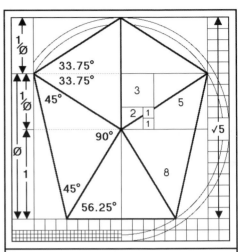

1/Ø
1/Ø
33.75°
33.75°
45°
1/Ø
90°
Ø
1
45°
56.25°
3
2 1
1
5
√5
8

Figure 87. FIBONACCI GRID—PHI PYRAMID
The larger the Fibonacci numbers, the more perfect the Ø angle becomes. A key insight into the Markers' scale is related to a **12x12 square**. The core concepts in this APPENDIX, expanded and clarified with 200 new, definitive illustrations, will soon be published as *Geometry Of Divinity*.

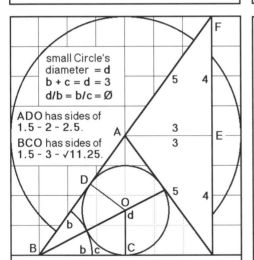

small Circle's diameter = **d**
b + c = d = 3
d/b = b/c = Ø

ADO has sides of 1.5 - 2 - 2.5.

BCO has sides of 1.5 - 3 - √11.25.

F
5 4
A
3
3
E
D
O
d
b
B
b c
C
5 4

Figure 88. 3:4:5 TRIANGLES & PHI RATIOS
A **6:8:10** Triangle offers a Phi Cut Construction. A Circle in opposed **3:4:5** Triangles leads to Ø. The arc from **B** to the Circle cuts **BC** so that the ratio b:c is another **PHI** proportion–**1.6180...** . The Sacred Triangle–Diatonic Scale correlations are encoded differently than previously depicted.

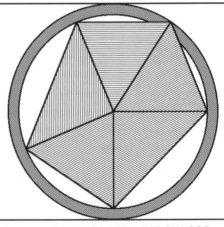

Figure 89. PENTATOPE FOUNDATION LOGO
An Educational Foundation has been formed to aid Seekers of Truth understand and master the multiple insights and transformational meditative techniques derived from Mills' Cydonia Solution. To receive additional Instructional Material about Mills' *Geometry Of Divinity on Mars: Blueprint of Cosmic Consciousness*, send address and $2 to: PENTATOPE; P.O. BOX 467312; ATLANTA, GA 31146.

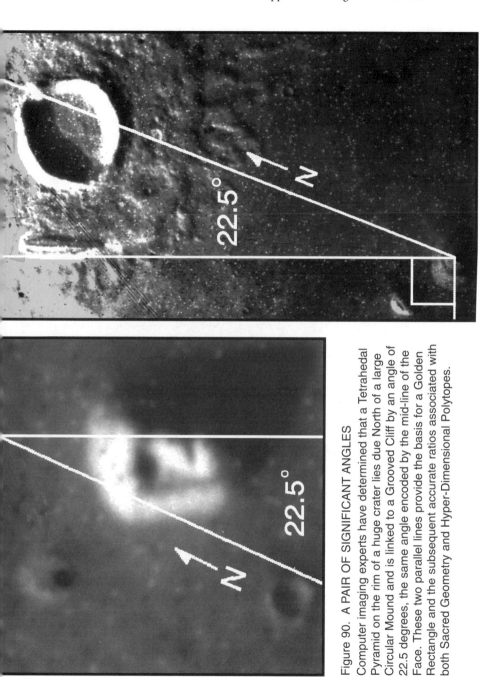

Figure 90. A PAIR OF SIGNIFICANT ANGLES
Computer imaging experts have determined that a Tetrahedal Pyramid on the rim of a huge crater lies due North of a large Circular Mound and is linked to a Grooved Cliff by an angle of 22.5 degrees, the same angle encoded by the mid-line of the Face. These two parallel lines provide the basis for a Golden Rectangle and the subsequent accurate ratios associated with both Sacred Geometry and Hyper-Dimensional Polytopes.

Figure 91.   A PORTION OF THE REGION OF MARS NAMED CYDONIA

The Geometric Grid concept developed in the diagrams reveals how only five Markers can encode mathematical data by means of standard values for √2, √3, √5, π, and Ø. This composite photo is not sufficiently accurate to validate this solution. Unenhanced digitized images, frames 35A72, 73, 74, from Viking Orbiter, courtesy of National Space Science Data Center.

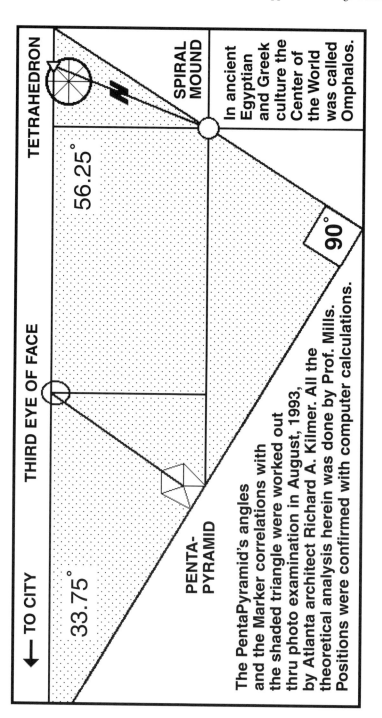

Figure 92.   A simple diagram contains the Geometric Key to the Message from Mars. This Triangle can be created by drawing the diagonal of any Golden Mean Rectangle, an embodiment of the abstract Divine Proportion. All Markers are so tightly interlocked by the Phi Ratio that a Computer Assisted Drawing program verifies their geometrically exact placement at the Infinity Level of accuracy. No approximations of the Universal Constants are involved. The concepts introduced will be totally integrated and illustrated in subsequent presentations of a *work in progress*. You may well complete the solution from the clues provided.

RECOMMENDED RESOURCES

Anomalies on Mars

Mark J. Carlotto, *The Martian Enigmas: A Closer Look* (North Atlantic Books, 1991).

Richard C. Hoagland, *The Monuments of Mars: A City on the Edge of Forever* (North Atlantic Books, 1987).

Stanley V. McDaniel, *The McDaniel Report: On The Failure of Executive, Congressional and Scientific Responsibility in Investigating Possible Evidence of Artificial Structures on the Surface of Mars and in Setting Mission Priorities for NASA's Mars Exploration Program* (North Atlantic Books, 1993).

Randolfo Rafael Pozos, *The Face on Mars: Evidence for a Lost Civilization?* (Chicago Review Press, 1986).

Symbolic Geometry

Christopher Bamford, ed., *Homage to Pythagoras: Rediscovering Sacred Science* (Lindisfarne Press, 1994).

Tons Brunés, (*The Secrets of Ancient Geometry—and its Use,* 2 vols. (Rhodos, 1967).

György Doczi, *The Power of Limits: Proportional Harmonics in Nature, Art & Architecture* (Shambhala, 1981).

David Fideler, *Jesus Christ, Sun of God: Ancient Cosmology and Early Christian Symbolism* (Quest Books,1993).

H. E. Huntley, *The Divine Proportion: A Study in Mathematical Beauty* (Dover, 1970).

Robert Lawlor, *Sacred Geometry: Philosophy and Practice* (Thames & Hudson, 1982).

John Michell, *The New View Over Atlantis* (Harper & Row,1983).

Michael S. Schneider, *A Beginner's Guide to Constructing the Universe: The Mathematical Archetypes of Nature, Art, and Science* (Harper Collins, 1994).

R. A. Schwaller de Lubicz, *The Egyptian Miracle: An Introduction to the Wisdom of the Temple* (Inner Traditions International, Ltd., 1985).

Peter Tompkins, *Secrets of the Great Pyramid* (Harper & Row, 1971).

Notes

CHAPTER ONE

1   Marilyn Ferguson, *The Aquarian Conspiracy* (Los Angeles, CA: J.P. Tarcher, 1980), p. 23.

2   Theodore White, "The Spirit of Our Times," *The Atlanta Constitution* (February 12, 1984). For further comment on the effects of scientism, technology, fragmentation, and the need for a larger vision, E.F. Schumacher's *A Guide For the Perplexed* (New York: Harper & Row, 1977) repays careful reading.

3   Corinne McLaughlin and Gordon Davidson, *Spiritual Politics* (New York: Ballantine Books, 1994), p. 7.

4   James Redfield, *The Celestine Prophecy* (Hoover, AL: Satori Publishing, 1993), from the Author's Note.

5   See Thomas Kuhn, *The Structure of Scientific Revolutions* (Chicago, IL: University of Chicago Press, 1970) and Joel Barker, *Discovering the Future: The Business of Paradigms* (Lake Elmo, MN: ILI Press, 1985).

6   William James, "What Psychical Research Has Accomplished," *William James on Psychical Research*, Gardner Murphey and Robert O. Ballou, eds. (New York: Viking Press, 1960), p. 46.

7   Fritjof Capra, *The Turning Point* (New York: Bantam Books, 1982).

8   Cited in "Dying Forests 'Ecological Catastrophe of Century,'" *New York Times* (February 26, 1984). However, recent results of a massive ten-year government study suggest that acid rain per se may not be the culprit in deforestation it is made out to be.

9   EPA risk assessment document cited in "U.S. Wavers on Guarding Ozone Layer," *Atlanta Constitution* (May 10, 1987).

10 James Lovelock, *GAIA* (New York: Oxford University Press, 1982), p. 9. For an encyclopedic survey of environmental challenges, see Norman Myers, *GAIA: An Atlas of Planetary Management* (New York: Anchor Books, 1984).

11 "Integrity in the College Curriculum," a report of the Association of American Colleges, 1985.

12 Theodore Sizer, *Horace's Compromise: The Dilemma of the American High School* (Boston, MA: Houghton Mifflin, 1984), p. 206.

[13] Allan Bloom, *The Closing of the American Mind* (New York: Simon and Schuster, 1987), p. 340.

[14] William A. Henry III, "Upside Down in the Groves of Academe," *Time* (April 1, 1991), p. 66. The citation from Leon Botstein is in this article.

[15] In one such instance, the cause of failure was a forty-five cent computer chip. Facts pertaining to the nuclear arms race are referenced in Ken Keyes's *The Hundredth Monkey* (Coos Bay, OR: Vision Books, 1982).

[16] *Bulletin of the Atomic Scientists*, vol. XVII, no. 3, p. 44.

[17] Fritjof Capra and Charlene Spretnak, *Green Politics* (New York: E.P. Dutton, 1984).

[18] My thinking on this controversial matter has been stimulated by Riane Eisler's *The Chalice and the Blade* (San Francisco, CA: Harper and Row, 1988), among others.

[19] Capra, *The Turning Point*, p. 212.

[20] This and other useful statistical information pertaining to the management of energy resources are detailed in Jeremy Rifkin, *Entropy* (New York: The Viking Press, 1980).

[21] Cf. Hazel Henderson, *Creating Alternative Futures* (New York: Berkley Publishing Corporation, 1978) and *The Politics of the Solar Age* (New York: Doubleday/ Anchor, 1981); and Duane Elgin, *Voluntary Simplicity* (New York: Morrow, 1981). Mark Satin reviews different non-growth-oriented economic models in "Alternatives to the Global Market Place," *New Options* (December, 1989).

[22] Donella H. Meadows, "Four Visionary Suggestions from a World Bank Heretic," *Planetary Connections* (Autumn 1994), excerpted from *Human Economy*, a publication of the Mankato State University Economics Department. *Common Good* (Boston, MA: Beacon Press, 1989) is reviewed in *New Options* (August, 1990), where it received the political book-of-the-year award.

[23] Many writers have postulated a connection between the Federal Reserve and the international banking system to a hidden "control group" centered mostly in Europe. Cf., for example, William Cooper in *Behold a Pale Horse* (Sedona, AZ: Light Technology Publishing, 1991) and Jim Keith, *Casebook on Alternative 3* (Lilburn, GA: Illuminet Press, 1993).

[24] For a survey of all the relevant categories, see Andrew Greeley, "Mysticism Goes Mainstream," *American Health* (January/February, 1987), pp. 47–56.

[25] Viktor Frankl, *The Unheard Cry for Meaning* (New York: Simon and Schuster, 1978), pp. 21–22.

[26] Most of these developments are surveyed in Gary Zukav, *Dancing Wu Li Masters* (New York: William Morrow & Company, 1979).

[27] O. Costa de Beauregard, "Is Kervran a True or a False Prophet?" Third International Congress on Transpersonal Psychology, Tokyo (1977).

[28] Studies pertaining to phenomena described in this paragraph are described in Jeffrey Mishlove's *Roots of Consciousness*, Revised Edition (Tulsa, OK: Council Oaks Books, 1993) and William George Roll's *This World or That* (Sweden: Lund Publishers, 1989).

[29] A critical review of holographic modeling is presented in Ken Wilber's *The Holographic Paradigm and Other Paradoxes* (Boulder, CO: Shambhala, 1982).

[30] See Kenneth Pelletier, *Holistic Health* (New York: Delacorte Press, 1979); Richard Gerber, *Vibrational Medicine* (Santa Fe, NM: Bear and Company, 1988); and Deepak Chopra, *Creating Health* (Boston, MA: Houghton Mifflin Company, 1987).

[31] Michael Toms, "The Vision of Joseph Campbell," *East West Journal* (April, 1989), p. 34.

[32] "At the Crossroads," a publication of the *Communications Era Task Force* (Box 2240, Wickenburg, AZ 85358), p. 5.

CHAPTER TWO

[1] Marion Long, "In Search of a Definition," *Omni* (November, 1987), p. 162.

[2] Quoted in Fergus Bordewich, "Colorado's Thriving Cults," *New York Times Magazine* (May l, 1988), p. 18.

[3] From a paper given by Prof. Phillip Lucas, "The New Age Movement and the Pentecostal/Charismatic Revival: Distinct Yet Parallel Solutions to the Socio/ Spiritual Crisis of the 1960s and 1970s," *AAR Abstracts* (1989), p. 364. For a scholarly analysis of other New Age themes, see James Lewis and Gordon Melton, eds., *Perspectives on the New Age* (Albany, NY: SUNY Press, 1992). In *Waiting for the Martian Express* (Berkeley, CA: North Atlantic Books, 1989), Richard Grossinger incisively and humorously comments on many popular ideas and trends associated with the New Age.

[4] Cf., for example, Constance Cumbey, *Hidden Dangers of the Rainbow* (New York: Huntington House, Inc., 1983). See also Karen Hoit, *The New Age Rage* (Old Tappan, NJ: Fleming Revell Co., 1987).

[5] Long, *op. cit.*

[6] For a review of experimental literature, see John S. Hagelin, "Is Consciousness the Unified Field? A Field Theorist's Perspective," *Modern Science and Vedic Science*, vol. I, no. I. (1987), pp. 29–86.

[7] Randall Balmer, "There's nothing new about the 'New Age'," *Atlanta Constitution* (July 6, 1992).

[8] Ken and Treya Wilber, "Do We Make Ourselves Sick?" *New Age Journal* (September/October 1988), p. 51.

[9] Cited in Robert Lindsey, "Spiritual Concepts Drawing A Different Breed of Adherent," *New York Times* (September 29, 1986).

CHAPTER THREE

[1] "Rock Power for Health and Wealth," *Time* (January 19, 1987), p. 66.

[2] Immanuel Kant, *Critique of Judgment* (Oxford, England: Clarendon Press, 1980), p. 18. I am indebted to Alicia Roque for this point. See her "Non-Linear Phenomena, Explanation and Action," *International Philosophical Quarterly*, vol. 28 (September, 1988) and "Self-Organization: Kant's Concept of Teleology and Modern Chemistry," *Review of Metaphysics*, vol. 39 (September, 1985).

3   For a historical and philosophical review of this anti-reductive tradition, see (among the many possible sources) David C. Hull, *Philosophy of Biological Science* (Englewood Cliffs, NJ: Prentice-Hall, 1980); Paul A. Weiss, *The Science of Life* (Mount Kisco, NY: Futura Publications, 1973); and Milan Zeleny, ed., *Autopoiesis, Dissipative Structures, and Spontaneous Social Orders* (Boulder, CO: Westview Press, 1980).

4   Bronislaw Malinowski, "Anthropology," *Encyclopedia Britannica*, 13th ed., Supp. I. For a review of the arguments for the irreducibility of wholes to their parts in social contexts, see William Dray, "Holism and Individualism in History and Social Science," *Encyclopedia of Philosophy* (New York: Macmillan, 1967).

5   Huston Smith, "The Crisis in Philosophy," *Beyond the Post-Modern Mind* (Wheaton, IL: Theosophical Publishing House, 1989), p. 137. Of course, philosophers never close shop; they always find new territory to mine. Smith sees this deconstructionist agenda in philosophy ultimately undermining itself, preparing the way in principle for a constructive resurgence along perennialist lines. For further discussion of themes relating to relativism and linguistic and social holism, see Richard Rorty, *Philosophy and the Mirror of Nature* (Princeton, NJ: Princeton University Press, 1979) and his more recent *Contingency, Irony, and Solidarity* (New York: Cambridge University Press, 1989). With reference to analytic philosophy, see Hilary Putnam's "Meaning Holism," *The Philosophy of W.V. Quine*, eds., Paul Schilpp and Lewis Hahn (LaSalle, IL: Open Court Press, 1986). With specific reference to cognitive science and the philosophy of mind, see J.A. Fodor, *Psychosemantics: The Problem of Meaning in the Philosophy of Mind* (Cambridge, MA: MIT Press, 1987) and William Bechtel and Adele Abrahamsen, *Connectionism and the Philosophy of Mind* (Cambridge, MA: Basil Blackwell, 1991). A convenient collection of articles by leading thinkers in this area is Jerry Fodor and Ernest Lepore, eds., *Holism: A Shopper's Guide* (Cambridge, MA: Blackwell, 1992). In the European tradition, see Hubert Dreyfus, "Holism and Hermeneutics," *Review of Metaphysics*, vol. 34, no. 1 (1980). For an attempt to escape the relativism of linguistic/social holism that also connects to the larger New Paradigm dialogue, see Alicia Roque, "Could Bohm's Hologram Succeed Where Rorty's Mirror Couldn't?" *Scientia*, vol. 121 (1986).

6   See, for example, Ludwig von Bertalanffy, *General System Theory* (New York: Brazziler, 1968); Mario Bunge, *Ontology II: A World of Systems* (Dordrecht, Holland: Reidel, 1979); J.G. Miller, *Living Systems* (New York: McGraw Hill, 1978); and Arthur Koestler's summary of systems theoretical and holistic principles in *Janus* (London, England: Hutchinson, 1978). Koestler's and J.R. Smythies's collection of essays by leading theorists in *Beyond Reductionism* (New York: Macmillan, 1969) is a watershed for holism and systems theory in the sciences, along with Ervin Laszlo's more recent *Evolution: The Grand Synthesis* (Boston, MA: Shambhala, 1987).

7   An illuminating description of the cross-disciplinary applications of Prigogine's theory is developed by Erich Jantsch's systems-theoretical treatise, *The Self-Organizing Universe* (Oxford, England: Pergamon Press, Ltd., 1980). James Gleick's *Chaos* (New York: Viking/Penguin, 1987) provides an excellent overview of this "new science."

8   Capra, *The Turning Point*, p. 267.

9   Koestler, *Janus*, p. 289.

10 Stephen J. Gould, "Utopia (Limited)," *New York Times Magazine* (March 3, 1983), pp. 23–25.

11 Cited in Gould, *Ibid.*

12 *Ibid.*

13 *Ibid.*

14 Capra, *The Turning Point*, p. 362.

15 *Ibid.*, p. 3.

16 Capra explicitly takes up the question of ESP in his "Can Science Explain Psychic Phenomena," *ReVision* (Winter/Spring, 1979), pp. 52–57. However, he gives us not so much an ontology but a Taoist-type approach to the question, namely, that ESP (intuition) and science (reason) are complementary aspects of the same whole, just as, for example, right and left hemispheres of the brain are complements.

17 Koestler did have a mystical experience, which he reported in *The Invisible Writing* (New York: Macmillian Co., 1954), pp. 350–54. However, apart from references to higher and lower orders of reality, he did not offer an interpretive model for the experience; he described it as an example of the kind of unusual phenomenon that scientists should more seriously look into. His excursion into physics and ESP in *The Roots of Coincidence* (New York: Vintage books, 1973) is again not so much modeling of higher realities as it is an attempt to convince the scientific community to look for expanded explanatory models.

18 Charles Tart, *States of Consciousness*, (New York: E.P. Dutton, 1975), pp. 3–10.

19 Ilya Prigogine and Isabelle Stengers, *Order out of Chaos* (New York: Bantam, 1982). In their discussion of Prigogine's theory, John Briggs and David Peat in *Looking Glass Universe* (New York: Simon & Schuster, 1984) suggest that David Bohm's implicate order provides a domain for ordering principles that guide the emergence of (novel) open systems.

20 William McDougall, *Body and Mind* (London, England: Methuen, 1911), p. 69. See also Sir John Eccles, *The Human Psyche* (Berlin, Germany: Springer-Verlag, 1980) and Wilder Penfield, *The Mystery of the Mind* (Princeton, NJ: Princeton University Press, 1975). Although Penfield endorsed dualism, he introduced the interesting qualification that while the content of consciousness does depend upon neural excitation, "awareness itself" does not (p. 55).

21 Arguments for this thesis are proposed by Michael Grosso in *Playing the Survival Game* (Walpole, NH: Stillpoint Publishing, 1985), pp. 45–79, and by Huston Smith, *op. cit.*, Chapter 8. It is also explored more fully in Chapter 7.

22 This argument is made by Teilhard de Chardin in *The Phenomenon of Man* (New York: Harper Torchbooks, 1965). His phrase 'involution-evolution' is adopted by Wilber, Smith, and other defenders of the perennial vision.

23 Aldous Huxley, *The Perennial Philosophy* (New York: Harper and Brothers, 1945), p. vii.

24 A good survey of the history and teachings of occult schools is given by Colin Wilson in *The Occult* (New York: Random House, 1971).

25 Arthur Lovejoy, *The Great Chain of Being* (Cambridge, MA: Harvard University Press, 1936), p. 59. Cited in Huston Smith, *op. cit.*, p. 53.

26 Its relevance for theology is debated by Huston Smith and David Griffin in *Primordial Truth and Post-Modern Theology* (Albany, NY: SUNY Press, 1989). Their exchange offers an excellent introduction to perennialist and process-oriented (Whiteheadian) worldviews. Its importance for both scientific and social arenas is further discussed by Anna Lemkow in *The Wholeness Principle* (Wheaton, IL: The Theosophical Publishing House, 1990).

CHAPTER FOUR

1 For a very readable survey of many of these related issues on falsifiability, truth, and conceptual relativism, see Carol Lambert and Gordon Britton, *Introduction to the Philosophy of Science* (Atascadero, CA: Ridgeview Publishing Co., 1988).

2 Aurobindo is quoted on the same page in Capra, *The Tao of Physics* (Boulder, CO: Shambhala, 1975), p. 138.

3 Ken Wilber, "Physics, Mysticism and the New Holographic Paradigm," reprinted in *Eye to Eye* (New York: Anchor Books, 1983), pp. 125–155.

4 *Ibid.*, p. 167.

5 Quoted in CSICOP's *Newsletter* (January 16, 1989).

6 See R. Kammann, "The True Disbelievers: Mars Effect Drives Skeptics to Irrationality," *Zetetic Scholar*, vol. 10 (1982) and D. Rawlins, "Starbaby," *Fate* (October, 1981).

7 As Richard Broughton reports in his authoritative work *Parapsychology: The Controversial Science* (New York: Ballantine, 1991), pp. 323–324, the National Research Council (a conservative, quasi-governmental group) asked Rosenthal to delete his highly favorable review of parapsychological research from his report to the Council; when Rosenthal refused, the Council incredibly deleted his findings in this area anyway. One of the most comprehensive examinations of the literature and underlying philosophies of science is published in the highly respected *Behavioral and Brain Sciences*, vol. 10 (1987), pp. 553–643, which contains lead articles and responses by many of the most noted parapsychologists and skeptics working today. While it focuses on psychokinesis, Stephen Braude's *The Limits of Influence* (London, England: Routledge & Kegan Paul, 1986) masterfully examines many of the assumptions, especially those relating to the necessity of laboratory experiments and repeatability, that fuel the skeptical agenda. Those interested in *repeated* experimental results of psychokinesis that CSICOP would be hard-pressed to dismiss should consult the work of Robert Jahn and Brenda Dunne of the Engineering Anomalies Research Laboratory. Independent statistical analysis of PK research conducted both there and elsewhere has shown the results too strong to be explained by flaws in design or researcher bias. See their *Margins of Reality: The Role of Consciousness in the Physical World* (New York: Harcourt Brace, 1987) as well as D.I. Radin's and R.D. Nelson's "Evidence for Consciousness-Related Anomalies in Random Physical Systems," *Foundations of Physics*, vol. 19 (1989), p. 1499.

8 For a skeptical, though not altogether unsympathetic examination of OBEs, see Susan Blackmore, *Beyond the Body* (London, England: William Heinemann, 1982)and *Dying to Live: Near-Death Experiences* (Buffalo, NY: Prometheus Books, 1993); also "A Psychological Theory of the Out-of-Body Experience,"

Journal of Parapsychology, vol 48 (September, 1984) pp. 201–18. For a review of the psychiatric literature which shows OBEs not to be explainable in terms of dysfunctional, dissociative, or hallucinatory states of mind, see Glen Gabbard and Stuart Twemlow, *With the Eyes of the Mind* (New York: Prager, 1984).

9   A review of the causes, variations, and theoretical explanations of MPD, including a discussion of its relevance for possession cases, is presented in "Multiple Personality—Mirrors of a New Model of Mind?", *Investigations*, a research bulletin of the Institute of Noetic Sciences, vol. 1, no. 3/4 (1985). For an in-depth case study, see Daniel Keyes's *The Minds of Billy Milligan* (New York: Bantam, 1982). See also Ian Wilson's critical study, *All in the Mind* (Garden City: Doubleday, 1982) and Eileen Garrett's own *Many Voices* (New York: Putnam, 1968). Braude's study appears in the *Journal of the American Society for Psychical Research*, vol. 55 (1988), pp. 177–95. See also his more extensive and probing analysis of multiple personality disorder in *First-Person Plural: Multiple Personality and the Philosophy of Mind* (London, England: Routledge & Kegan Paul, 1991). Scott Rogo's paranormalist interpretation is presented in his *Infinite Boundary* (New York: Dodd Mead, 1987). Some of the information presented in this section is derived from Alan Vaughn's "Mediumistic Controls: Unconscious Personalities or What?" *Theta*, vol. 13/14 (Winter 1986). That the psychic prone personality in general, and the trance medium in particular, are not especially susceptible to hypnosis is shown by Douglas Richards in "Hypnotic Susceptibility and Subjective Psychic Experiences," *Journal of Parapsychology*, vol. 54 (March, 1990), pp. 35–51. For differences between trance channeling and multiple personality disorder on structured interview, see Dureen Hughes's article of the same name in *Journal of Transpersonal Psychology*, vol. 21, no. 2 (1992), pp. 181–192.

10   A summary of the kinds of evidence derivable from mediumistic communication together with an examination of telepathic and clairvoyant explanations of mediumship is presented in Curt Ducasse's *A Critical Examination of the Belief in Life After Death* (Springfield, IL: Charles C. Thomas, 1961), pp. 153–203 and in Robert Almeder's *Beyond Death* (Springfield, IL: 1987), pp. 55–75. For further psychological analysis of trance personalities, see Hereward Carrington's *The Case for Psychic Survival* (New York: Citadel, 1957) and Jule Eisenbud's *Parapsychology and the Unconscious* (Berkeley, CA: North Atlantic Books, 1983). Richard Hodgson's evaluation of Leonora Piper's mediumship, especially the "George Pellew" personality, is described in the March, 1887 issue of the *Proceedings of the Society for Psychical Research*, and discussed by Nandor Fodor in the *Encyclopedia of Psychic Science* (London, England: Arthur's Press, 1933), p. 170.

11   Ronald Klimo, *Channeling* (Los Angeles, CA: J.P. Tarcher, 1988). Klimo's treatment is a good overall assessment of channeling from a relatively neutral perspective. F.W.H. Meyers's classic *Human Personality and its Survival of Bodily Death* (London, England: Longmans, Green, 1903) still repays careful reading, especially for some of its pre-Jungian themes. A very accessible and up-to-date collection of essays that address the question of personal survival from multiple New Paradigm perspectives is Gary Doore, ed., *What Survives?* (Los Angeles, CA: J. P. Tarcher, 1990).

12   Vaughn, *op. cit.*, p. 82.

13   See Joseph Head and S.L. Cranston, eds., *Reincarnation: The Phoenix Fire Mystery* (New York: Crown Publishers, 1977).

14 Stanislav Grof, *Beyond the Brain* (New York: SUNY Press, 1985), p. 129.

15 Many interrelated concerns involving reincarnation are discussed by Anna Kennedy Winner in *The Basic Ideas of Occult Wisdom* (Wheaton, IL: Theosophical Publishing House, 1973), especially chapters V–VIII.

16 Helen Wambach, *Reliving Past Lives: The Evidence Under Hypnosis* (New York: Harper & Row, 1978). For an application to the topic of "future lives," see Chet Snow, *Mass Dreams of the Future* (New York: McGraw Hill, 1990).

17 Ian Stevenson, *Twenty Cases Suggestive of Reincarnation*, second edition, (Charlottesville, VA: University Press of Virginia, 1974); *Unlearned Language: New Studies in Xenoglossy* (Charlottesville, VA: University Press of Virginia, 1984); and *Children Who Remember Past Lives* (Charlottesville, VA: University Press of Virginia, 1987).

18 Two critics of Stevenson's work in this area are Sarah Thomason in "Past Tongues Remembered?" *Skeptical Inquirer,* vol. II (Summer 1987), pp. 367–375 and Leonard Angel in "Empirical Evidence for Survival?" *Skeptical Inquirer,* vol. 18 (1994), pp. 481–487. Robert Almeder's defense of Stevenson against Thomason is presented in "Response to 'Past Tongues Remembered,'" *Skeptical Inquirer,* vol. 12 (Spring 1988), pp. 321–23.

19 See Almeder's earlier *Beyond Death*, especially Chapter One, and his more recent and expanded *Death and Personal Survival: The Evidence for Life After Death* (New York: Rowman and Littlefield, 1992). Also: C.T.K. Chari's "Reincarnation Research: Method and Interpretation," in the *Signet Handbook of Parapsychology,* ed., Martin Ebom (New York: New American Library, 1978); Martin Ebom's *Reincarnation in the Twentieth Century* (New York: Signet Books, 1969); C.J. Ducasse's *A Critical Examination of the Belief in Life After Death, op cit.,* Part V; Ruth Reyna's *Reincarnation and Science* (New Delhi, India: Sterling Publishers Private, Ltd., 1973); and Paul Edward's extensive critique "The Case Against Reincarnation," *Free Inquiry* (Spring and Fall, 1987). S. Cranston's and C. Williams's *Reincarnation: A New Horizon in Science, Religion, and Society* (New York: Julian Press, 1984) is a readable and relatively detailed treatment of the topic, with attention given to a broad range of criticisms.

20 These criteria are referenced to Stevenson's works by Robert Almeder in a summary given in his *Beyond Death*, pp. 16–17. For additional analysis of critical reactions to reincarnation (and survival) research, see his "Recent Responses to Survival Research," *Journal of Scientific Exploration,* vol. 10, no. 1 (1996).

21 E.S. Zolik, "Experimental Investigation of the Psychodynamic Implications of the Hypnotic 'Previous Existence' Fantasy," *Journal of Clinical Psychology,* vol. 14 (1958).

22 Stevenson, *Twenty Cases,* pp. 365 and 368. For Stevenson's views on why direct recall by children is preferable to hypnotic regression of adults, see *Children Who Remember Past Lives,* especially p. 41. For additional evidence, see Antonia Mills, "A Replication Study: Three Cases of Children in Northern India Who Are Said to Remember a Past Life," *Journal of Scientific Exploration,* vol. 3, no. 2 (1989), pp. 133–84.

23 Melvin Harris applies the cryptomnesia explanation to some of the best cases in "Are 'Past Life' Regressions Evidence of Reincarnation?" *Free Inquiry* (Fall 1986). The famous Bridey Murphy case, widely explained away along these lines by

critics, is examined by Curt Ducasse in *A Critical Examination of the Belief in Life After Death, op. cit.*, Chapter XXV. Stevenson discusses the failure of cryptomnesia explanations with respect to children in *Cases of the Reincarnation Type, III* (Charlottesville, VA: University of Virginia Press, 1980), pp. 346–48.

24 Roger Woolger, *Other Lives, Other Selves: A Jungian Psychotherapist Discovers Past Lives* (New York: Dolphin/Doubleday, 1988). Edith Fiore's more popular work, *You Have Been Here Before* (New York: Ballantine, 1979), similarly draws upon her experience as a clinical psychologist.

25 See especially the Introduction to Weiss's *Many Lives, Many Masters* (New York: Simon & Schuster, 1988). Gary Zukav's *The Seat of the Soul* (New York: Simon & Schuster, 1989) develops further implications of a reincarnational worldview, such as the concept of a "soul family" and the role that suffering plays in growth.

26 Many of these arguments are raised by J.G. Pratt and N. Hintze in *The Psychic Realm: What Can You Believe?* (New York: Random House, 1975) and reviewed and expanded by Almeder, in *Death and Personal Survival.*

27 David Quigley, *Alchemical Hypnotherapy* (Santa Renya, CA: Lost Coast Press, 1987).

28 Ormand McGill and Irvin Mordes, *The Many Lives of Alan Lee* (National Guild of Hypnotists, Box 308, Merrimack, NH 03054), with an introduction by Walter Phanke, M.D., one of the attending psychiatrists.

CHAPTER FIVE

* An abbreviated presentation of some of the main ideas of this chapter may be found in Mark B. Woodhouse, "Beyond Dualism and Materialism: A New Model of Survival," in Gary Doore, ed., *What Survives?* (Los Angeles, CA: J.P. Tarcher, Inc. 1990). A compatible view is defended by Christian de Quincy in "Consciousness All the Way Down?" *Journal of Consciousness Studies*, vol 1, no. 2 (1994), pp. 217–229.

1 Other differentiating features are qualitative vs. quantitative, purposive vs. mechanical, and emergent vs. compositional. For a general review of principal philosophies of mind, see Jerome Schaeffer, *Philosophy of Mind* (Englewood Cliffs, NJ: Prentice-Hall, 1982). For a more intensive examination of intentionality with special reference to questions of artificial intelligence, neural net theory, and cognitive psychology, see William Bechtel, *Philosophy of Mind, An Overview for Cognitive Science* (Hillsdale, NJ; Lawrence Erlbaum Associates, 1988). Many topics relating to consciousness (both normal and altered), brain states, and physics were reviewed and brought up to date at the 1994 international summit held at the University of Arizona. A second conference is planned for 1996.

2 E.R. John, "A Model of Consciousness," in G.E. Schwartz and D. Shapiro, eds., *Consciousness and Self-Regulation*, vol. 1 (New York: Plenum Press, 1976), p. 4.

3 Danah Zohar, *The Quantum Self* (New York: William Morrow, 1990), pp. 85–86.

4 See, for example, Richard Rorty, *Philosophy and the Mirror of Nature* (Princeton, NJ: Princeton University Press, 1979); Richard Bernstein, *Science, Hermeneutics, and Praxis* (Philadelphia, PA: University of Pennsylvania Press, 1983); and J. Habermas, *Knowledge and Human Interests*, trans. J. Shapiro (Boston, MA: Beacon Press, 1979).

[5] David Bohm, "Of Matter and Meaning: The Super-Implicate Order," (interview with Renee Weber) *Revision* (Spring 1983), p. 34.

[6] Leibniz, of course, was not aware of fields as we now think of them. Still, something very close to the argument presented is the basis of his critique of the Cartesian-Newtonian conception of material substance as inert, solid stuff. Atoms ("monads") must be energetic at their core. See Appendix 7 of the *New Essays Concerning Human Understanding* (LaSalle, IL: Open Court Publishers, 1949).

[7] Quoted in Milic Capek, *The Philosophical Impact of Contemporary Physics* (New York: Von Nostrand & Company, 1961), p. 319.

[8] H. Weyl, *Philosophy of Mathematics and Natural Science* (Princeton, NJ: Princeton University Press, 1949), p. 171.

[9] For a review and conceptual analysis of these developments, see John Hagelin, "Introduction to Unified Quantum Field Theories," *Modern Science and Vedic Science*, vol. 1, no. 1 (1987), pp. 30–56; also P. Davies and J. Brown, *Superstrings* (New York: Cambridge University Press, 1988). Paul Davies's *Superforce* is published by Simon and Schuster (1985).

[10] Fritjof Capra, *The Tao of Physics* (Boulder, CO: Shambhala, 1975), p. 138.

[11] D. Bohm and B. Hiley, "On the Intuitive Understanding of Nonlocality as Implied by Quantum Theory, *Foundations of Physics*, vol. 5 (1975), pp. 96, 102.

[12] W. Thirring, "Urbausteine der Materie," *Almanach der Osterreichischen Akademie der Wissenschaften*, vol. 118 (1968), p. 159.

[13] Nick Herbert, *Quantum Reality* (New York: Anchor Books, 1987), p. 25.

[14] Nick Herbert, "How Large is Starlight? A Brief Look at Quantum Reality," *ReVision* (Summer 1987), p. 32.

[15] Erwin Schroedinger, *Science, Theory and Man* (New York: Dover Publications, 1967), p. 59. See also: John Wheeler, *Quantum Geometrodynamics* (New York: Academic Press, 1962); Bob Toben's delightful visual representations of Wheeler's, Wolf's, and Jack Sarfatti's related ideas in *Space-Time and Beyond* (New York: E.P. Dutton, 1975); and, more recently, Kostas Lambrakis's "Unified Field and Physics—Part 14: The Crystalline Structure of Space," *The Leading Edge: An International Research Journal*, no. 79, (February, 1995), pp. 1–14. This journal also carries articles on scalar energy systems, discussed in the following section, and many other New Paradigm topics. Subscriptions are available by writing P.O. Box 7530, Yelm, WA 98597. Walter Russell's *The Secret of Light* (Waynesboro, VA: University of Science and Light, 1974) integrates the geometrical underpinnings of the New Physics with an unabashed spiritual cosmology.

[16] Thomas Bearden, *Excalibur Briefing*, 2nd ed., (Greenville, TX: Tesla Book Company & Strawberry Hill Press, 1987), from the Introduction to the Second Edition, p. 3. Bearden also provides an extensive bibliography of relevant literature from physics, including Whittaker's 1903 paper, and an updated and expanded glossary.

[17] K.C. Cole, *Sympathetic Vibrations* (New York: William Morrow, 1985).

[18] George Leonard, *The Silent Pulse* (New York: E.P. Dutton, 1978), especially Chapter One.

19 Donald Hicks, "Primordial Rhythms," *Georgia State University Review* (1984), p. 10.

20 Joseph Needham, *Science and Civilization in China,* vol. 4 (Cambridge, England: Cambridge University Press, 1956), pp. 8–9.

21 Lyall Watson, *Supernature* (New York: Bantam, 1974).

22 William S. Condon, "Multiple Response to Sound in Dysfunctional Children," *Journal of Autism and Childhood Schizophrenia,* vol. 5 (1975), p. 43.

23 Ralph Metzner, "Resonance as Metaphor and Metaphor as Resonance," *ReVision* (Summer 1987), p. 38.

24 J.C. Bose, *Growth and Tropic Movements of Plants* (New York: Longmans, Green and Company, 1929). See also the discussion of Bose's work within the larger context of botany and electrical vibrations in Peter Tomkins and Christopher Bird, *The Secret Life of Plants* (New York: Avon Books, 1973), Parts II and III.

25 Cited in Tomkins and Bird, *op. cit.,* p. 167.

26 *Ibid.,* p. 367. Quoted from William Tiller, "Radionics, Radiesthesia and Physics," *Proceedings of the Academy of Parapsychology and Medicine* (1971).

27 Jonathan Goldman, "Healing with Sound and Music," *New Frontiers* (December, 1985), p. 5.

28 Hans Jenny, *Cymatics: Structure and Dynamics of Waves and Vibrations,* vol. I (New York: Schocken Publishing Company, 1975).

29 Leonard, *Silent Pulse,* p. 9.

30 Joachim-Ernst Berendt, "Primordial Tones: Meditation on the Archetypal Energies of Celestial Bodies," *ReVision,* (Summer, 1987), p. 45. His complete work, *Nada-Brahma: The World is Sound* (New York: Destiny Books, 1987), may become a classic of its kind.

CHAPTER SIX

1 David Bohm, "Nature as Creativity," (interview with Renee Weber), *ReVision* (Fall 1982), p. 35.

2 Swami Muktananda, "The Dance of Consciousness and the Supreme Truth," (interview with Les Hixon), *ReVision* (Spring, 1980), p. 31.

3 The theme of duality as complementary perspectives weaves its way through many of Watts's writings. See, for example, *The Way of Zen* (New York: Vintage Books, 1957). In his *Laws of Form,* G. Spencer Brown shows why the most fundamental distinction we can draw is between "inside" and "outside."

4 Cited in Mikol Davis and Earle Lane, *Rainbows of Life* (New York: Harper & Row Publishers, 1978), p. 23.

5 John White and Stanley Krippner, eds., *Future Science: Life Energies and the Physics of Paranormal Phenomena* (New York: Anchor Books, 1977).

6 Carlos Castaneda, *A Separate Reality* (New York: Simon & Schuster, 1971), p. 131.

7 Cf., for example, H. Motoyama, *Science and the Evolution of Consciousness* (Brookline, MA: Autumn Press, 1978). Motoyama has developed a machine for measuring meridian energy differentials, which has been used in a number of Japanese hospitals.

8 Aubrey Westlake, "Further Wanderings in the Radiesthetic Field," *Journal of the British Society of Dowsers* (1951), p. 5. See also Brian Inglis, *A History of Medicine* (Cleveland, Ohio: World Publishing Co., 1965).

9 Cited in Davis and Lane, *Rainbows of Life*, p. 26. See also Margaret Goldsmith, *Franz Anton Mesmer* (Garden City, NY: Doubleday, 1934).

10 Davis and Lane, *Rainbows of Life*, p. 28.

11 Robert N. Miller, "Paraelectricity, A Primary Energy," *Human Dimensions*, vol. 5, nos. 1 & 2, (1975).

12 Bioenergy Fields Foundation in Malibu, California has prepared both video and audio tapes of Dr. Hunt's pioneering work. Dr. Hunt's studies, together with anecdotal material from her remarkable career, are summarized in her recent book *Infinite Mind: The Science of Human Vibrations* (Malibu, CA: Malibu Publishing Company, 1995).

13 Harold S. Burr, "Electrometrics of Atypical Growth," *Yale Journal of Biology and Medicine*, vol. 25 (1952–3). See also his *The Fields of Life* (New York: Ballantine, 1973).

14 Gary Taubes, "An Electrifying Possibility," *Discover* (April, 1986), p. 23–37. Nordenstrom's magnum opus, *Biologically Closed Circuits: Clinical, Experimental and Theoretical Evidence for an Additional Circulatory System*, is self-published (1983). It is reviewed in the journal *Investigative Radiology* (1984).

15 Robert O. Becker and Gary Sheldon, *The Body Electric* (New York: William Morrow and Company, 1985).

16 D. Kirlian and V.K. Kirlian, "Photography and Visual Observations by Means of High Frequency Currents," *Journal of Scientific and Applied Photography*, vol. 6 (1961), p. 397.

17 Many of these variables are reviewed in *The Kirlian Aura*, edited by Stanley Krippner and D. Rubin (New York: Anchor Books, 1974) and in Thelma Moss, John Hubacher and Frances Saba, "Kirlian Photography: Visual Evidence of Bioenergetic Actions Between People?" *Psychiatry and Mysticism*, ed., Stanley Dean (Chicago, IL: Nelson Hall, 1975), pp. 175–84.

18 Thelma Moss, *The Probability of the Impossible* (Los Angeles, CA: J.P. Tarcher, 1974). For interesting results with another healer see Douglas Dean and Etel DeLoach, "What is the evidence for Psychic Healing?" *The Osteopathic Physician*, (October, 1972). See also Moss's more comprehensive work, *The Body Electric* (Los Angeles, CA: J.P. Tarcher, 1979).

19 L. Konikiewicz and D. Dean, trans., "The Kirlian Effect and Medical Science," *The Medical Science Gazette*, no. 64 (August 11, 1976), official journal of the Ministry of Medical Technology, U.S.S.R.

20 Reported (with film slides) by Douglas Dean, a leading researcher in Kirlian phenomena, at a conference on "Energy Medicine" sponsored by the Aesculapian Institute for Healing Arts, Atlanta, 1987.

21 Classic first-person accounts are: Sylvan Muldoon and Hereward Carrington, *The Projection of the Astral Body* (New York: Samuel Weiser, 1970), originally published in 1929 as a collaborative effort between a gifted psychic and a researcher; Robert Crookall, *Out-of-the-Body Experiences* (New York: University Books,

1970); Robert Monroe, *Journeys Out of the Body* (New York: Doubleday, 1974); and Ingo Swann, *To Kiss Earth Good-Bye* (New York: Hawthorne, 1975). On the varieties of OBE, see Michael Grosso, "Some Varieties of Out-of-Body Experience," *The Journal of the American Society for Psychical Research*, vol. 70 (1976), pp. 181–82.

22 For a discussion of attempts to do so in the context of near-death experiences, see Kenneth Ring, *Life at Death* (New York: Coward, McCann and Geoghegan, 1980) and Michael Sabom, *Recollections of Death: A Medical Perspective* (New York: Harper & Row, 1982), especially Chapter III. For a skeptical rejoinder, see Ronald Siegel, "The Psychology of Life After Death," *American Psychologist*, vol. 5 (1981), pp. 911–931. Susan Blackmore in *Beyond the Body* (London: Grenada, 1982) and H.J. Irwin in *Flight of the Mind: A Psychological Study of the Out-of-Body Experience* (Metuchen, NJ: Scarecrow Press, 1985) argue that OBEs are consistent with known psychological and neurophysiological facts.

23 M. Morse, D. Venecia, and J. Milstein, "Near-Death Experiences: A Neurophysiologic Explanatory Model," *Journal of Near-Death Studies*, vol. 8 (1990), pp. 45–53.

24 Sabom, *op. cit.*, Chapter IV. Sabom correctly points out that, since the information is empirically verifiable, it stands on its own and the state of the patient is not especially relevant. In his words: "Hallucinations of reality are by definition not hallucinations."

25 K. Osis and D. McCormick, "Kinetic Effects on the Ostensible Location of an Out-of-Body Projection During Perceptual Testing," *Journal of the American Society for Psychical Research*, vol. 74, (1980), pp. 319–329. Julian Isaacs critiqued their conclusion on the grounds that the strain gauges were improperly set in "On Kinetic Effects During Out-of-Body Projection," *JASPR*, vol. 75 (1981), pp. 192–194. The authors reply in the following pages, 194–197. Since both Blackmore and Irwin, *op. cit.*, cite Isaacs's criticism as definitive, despite Osis's and McCormick's detailed rebuttal, this study and the resulting criticisms repay careful study. The entire debate is examined by Robert Almeder in *Death and Personal Survival*, *op. cit.*, pp. 174–198. For earlier work on OBEs, see Charles Tart's "Out-of-the-Body Experiences," *Psychic Exploration*, Edgar Mitchell and John White, eds. (New York: G.P Putnams's Sons, 1974), pp. 349–357, and Robert Morris, "PRF Research on Out-of-Body Experiences," *Theta*, No. 41, (Summer 1974). *New Ideas in Psychology*, vol. 12, no. 1 (Spring 1994), pp. 1–17, contains my lead article on the implications of OBE research, "Out-of-Body Experiences and the Mind-Body Problem," together with responses by Stephen Braude, Patrick Grim, and Susan Blackmore, and my responses to their criticisms. Braude in particular holds that the best OBE experiments to date are consistent with remote viewing plus psychokinesis.

26 In "The Physical Detection of the Astral Body," *Theta*, vol. 8 (1980), Carlos Alvarado reviews attempts to verify OBEs through direct measurement.

27 Swami Rama, "Energy of Consciousness in the Human Personality," *ReVision*, vol. 3 (Spring 1980), p. 65.

CHAPTER SEVEN

1 W.T. Stace, *Mysticism and Philosophy* (New York: Lippincott and Co., 1960) and Arthur Eddington, *The Nature of Physical Existence* (New York: MacMillan, 1927).

2 Eliot Deutsch, *Advaita Vedanta: A Philosophical Reconstruction* (Honolulu: East-West Center Press, 1969) and Ken Wilber, *The Spectrum of Consciousness* (Wheaton, IL: Theosophical Publishing Co., 1977).

3 In a parallel view, the Austrian philosopher Ludwig Wittgenstein in the *Tractatus Logico Philosophicus* (London, England: Routledge & Kegan Paul, 1961), p. 189, observes that: "Whereof one cannot speak, one must pass over in silence."

4 In this account of unity-in-difference (or "Bhedabheda" as it is termed in Vedantic thought) and of the relation of panentheism to non-duality, I am influenced by the Indian philosopher Bhaskara, who holds a metaphysical position between Ramanuja's qualified non-dualism and Shankara's unqualified or absolute non-dualism. See S. Dasgupta's "The Bhaskara School of Philosophy," *A History of Indian Philosophy* (Delhi, India: Motilal Banarsidass, 1972).

5 Marion Long, "In Search of a Definition," *Omni* (November, 1987), p. 80.

6 Cf., for example, Karen Hoyt, *The New Age Rage* (Old Tappan, NJ.: Fleming H. Revell Company, 1987).

7 Immanuel Kant, *Critique of Pure Reason*, trans. Norman Kemp Smith (New York: Macmillan & Co., 1958), especially B–303.

8 William James, *Varieties of Religious Experience* (New York: Collier Books, 1961), p. 305.

9 W.T. Stace, *The Teaching of the Mystics* (New York: New American Library), p. 14.

10 Quoted in J. Needham, *Science and Civilization in China*, vol. IV (Cambridge, England: Cambridge University Press, 1956), p. 33.

11 Translated from the Sutra by D.T. Suzuki, *On Indian Mahayana Buddhism*, E. Conze, ed. (New York: Harper & Row, 1968), p. 150.

12 Stace, *op. cit.*, p. 16.

13 A.J. Ayer, *Language, Truth, and Logic* (New York: Dover Publications, 1952), p. 118.

14 Ken Wilber, "Eye to Eye" and "The Problem of Proof," in *Eye to Eye* (New York: Anchor/Doubleday, 1982), pp. 1–83.

15 For a review of considerations bearing on this critique, see James I. Campbell, *The Language of Religion* (New York: The Bruce Publishing Company, 1971), Chapters II and III.

16 This tradition of interpretation and the ensuing "criteria" of mystical experience are summarized and critiqued, with special reference to alleged similarities with LSD experiences, by Richard Zaehner, "Mysticism and LSD," *Zen, Drugs and Mysticism* (New York: Vintage Books, 1974), pp. 66–112. For further discussion of these similarities, see Huston Smith, "Do Drugs Have Religious Import?" *The Journal of Philosophy*, vol. LXI, no. 18 (1964).

17 Stephen Katz, "Language, Epistemology, and Mysticism" in *Mysticism and Philosophical Analysis*, ed., S. Katz (New York: Oxford University Press, 1978). See also Katz's "The 'Conservative' Character of Mystical Experience," in *Mysticism and Religious Traditions*, ed., S. Katz (New York: Oxford University Press, 1983); Wayne Proudfoot, *Religious Experience* (Berkeley, CA: University of California Press, 1985; William J. Wainwright, *Mysticism: A Study of its Nature, Cognitive Value, and Moral Implications* (Madison, WI: University of Wisconsin Press, 1981). Stace's *Mysticism and Philosophy* is a principal object of criticism.

18 Donald Rothberg, "Understanding Mysticism: Transpersonal Theory and the Limits of Contemporary Epistemological Frameworks," *ReVision*, vol.12, no. 2 (Fall 1989), p. 7. Rothberg's treatment of the issues is one of the clearest and most balanced of all recent discussions.

19 Katz, "Language, Epistemology, and Mysticism," p. 65–66.

20 Franklin Merrell-Wolff, *The Philosophy of Consciousness Without an Object* (New York: The Julian Press, 1973). See also Robert Foreman, ed., *The Problem of Pure Consciousness* (New York: Oxford University Press, 1990), especially his Introduction "Mysticism, Constructivism, and Forgetting"; Stephen Bernhardt's "Are Pure Consciousness Events Unmediated?"; and Norman Prigge's and Gary Kessler's "Is Mystical Experience Everywhere the Same?" In "Wainwright on Mysticism," *Religious Studies*, vol. 20 (1985), Del Lewis and Paul Griffiths argue that pure consciousness is without cognitive import and hence cannot be the basis of any monistic worldview. However, this depends upon the questionable assumption that one can only remember an event insofar as it was an *object* of consciousness at the time. Quotations are from Katz, *op. cit.*, pp. 58 and 61.

21 Huston Smith, "Is There a Perennial Philosophy?" *Journal of the American Academy of Religion*, vol. 55, (Fall 1987), p. 555. For further discussion, see his *Forgotten Truth* (New York: Harper & Row, 1976).

22 Katz, *op. cit.*, p. 57.

23 Daniel Brown, "The Stages of Meditation in Cross-Cultural Perspective," *Transformations of Consciousness: Conventional and Contemplative Perspectives on Development*, K. Wilber, J. Engler, and D. Brown, eds. (Boston, MA: Shambhala Press, 1986), pp. 263–64.

24 Cf., for example, Ken Wilber, *Eye to Eye, op. cit*; Anthony Campbell, *Seven States of Consciousness* (New York: Harper & Row, 1974); Paramahansa Yogananda, *Autobiography of a Yogi* (Los Angeles, CA: Self Realization Fellowship, 1979); and Maharishi Mehesh Yogi, *Bhagavad Gita: A New Translation and Commentary* (London, England: International SRM Publications, 1967).

25 Swami Prabhavananda and Christopher Isherwood, trans., *How to Know God, The Yoga Aphorisms of Patanjali* (Hollywood, CA: Vedanta Press, 1953), p. 80.

26 *Ibid.*, p. 139.

27 For a parallel issue regarding individuals who clairvoyantly see things, such as auras and spirits, that others do not, consult Shafica Karagulla and Dora Kunz, *The Chakras and the Human Energy Fields* (Wheaton, IL: Theosophical Publishing House, 1989) and Barbara Brennan, *Hands of Light* (New York: Bantam Books, 1987). For a fascinating account of the Greek healer Daskolos, see Kyriacos C. Markides, *Fire in the Heart* (New York: Paragon House, 1990). For a

Native American perspective, see Wallace Black Elk and William S. Lyon, *Black Elk* (New York: Harper & Row, 1990).

28 See the multiple commentaries on the holographic paradigm by Wilber, Capra, Krippner, and others in *ReVision*, vol. 1, nos. 3/4 (Summer/Fall, 1978).

29 See Karl Pribram, "The Neurophysiology of Remembering," *Scientific American*, vol. 220 (1969), and *Languages of the Brain* (Englewood Cliffs, NJ: Prentice-Hall, 1971). Pribram does *not* attempt to overturn localizationist strategies in general. Rather, his thesis is that a complete understanding of information processing will require reference to a deeper (holographic) modeling. His demonstration that cellular reaction in the perception of geometric form is itself a function of frequency decoding illustrates the complementary nature of his modeling strategy. Pribram's more recent work appears in his *Brain and Perception: Holonomy and Structure in Figural Processing* (Hillsdale, NJ: Lawrence Erlbaum, 1993).

30 F. Bartlett and E. R. John, "Equipotentiality Quantified: The Anatomical Distribution of the Engram," *Science*, vol. 181 (1973), pp. 764–767.

31 Paul Pietsch, *Shufflebrain* (Boston, MA: Houghton Mifflin Company, 1981), especially chapters I–IV.

32 John Lorber, "Is Your Brain Really Necessary?" *Science*, vol. 210 (1980), pp. 1232–1234.

33 Stephen Braude, "Holographic Analysis of Near-Death Experience: The Perpetuation of Some Deep Mistakes," *Essence*, vol. 5 (1981), pp. 53–65.

34 *Ibid.*, p. 56. In correspondence with Braude, it became clear that we may not completely appreciate the other's position on this matter. In particular, I may not have done his criticisms justice. I have modified my analysis in light of his helpful comments. However, in order to spare the reader an extended philosophical debate, I have left it essentially intact in order to stimulate discussion on this important topic. I am in complete agreement with Braude's basic thesis that consciousness is not reducible to (physical) energy of *any* configuration.

35 Nick Herbert, *Quantum Reality* (Garden City, NY: Anchor/Doubleday, 1985), p. 168.

36 Cf., for example, Michael Talbot's *Mysticism and the New Physics* (New York: Bantam Books, 1980) and especially his more recent *The Holographic Universe* (New York: Harper/Collins, 1991).

37 Ken Wilber, "The Great Chain of Being," *Journal of Humanistic Psychology*, vol. 33, no. 3 (Summer 1993), pp. 52–65. A useful introductory survey of main levels is also found in Anna Kennedy Winner's *The Basic Ideas of Occult Wisdom* (Wheaton, IL: The Theosophical Publishing House, 1970). In addition to Wilber, Huston Smith, and others, I am guided in my description of the subtle bodies by A.E. Powell's classic series, *The Etheric Double*, *The Mental Body*, *The Astral Body*, and *The Causal Body*, all published by the Theosophical Publishing House.

38 The "Phillip Phenomena," as this type of exercise came to be labeled, was produced by members of the Toronto Society for Psychical Research who, after some early failures, were able to conjure what seemed like an autonomous spirit. However, researchers associated with the project interpreted "Phillip's" poltergeist activity merely as the expression of *group psychokinesis*, thereby suggesting that spirit phenomena may on some unconscious level be our own creations. For

further discussion, see Iris Owen and Margaret H. Sparrow, "Generation of Para-normal Physical Phenomena in Connection with an Imaginary Communicator," *New Horizons*, vol. 1, no. 3 (January, 1974), pp. 6–13.

[39] Wilber, "Spectrum Psychology," *ReVision*, vol. 1, nos. 3/4 (Summer/Fall, 1978), p. 72.

[40] Sue Savage-Rumbaugh, "Spontaneous Symbol Acquisition and Communicative Use by Pygmy Chimpanzees," *Journal of Experimental Psychology*, vol. 115 (1986), pp. 211–235. See also Susan Armstrong-Buck's "Nonhuman Experience: A Whiteheadian Analysis," *Process Studies*, vol. 18, no. 1 (Spring 1989). Michael Roads's *Journey into Nature* is published by H.J. Kramer in Tiburon, CA, 1990.

[41] Wilber, *op. cit.*, p. 79.

[42] *Ibid.*, p. 80.

[43] Quoted by Wilber in "Physics, Mysticism, and the New Holographic Paradigm," *ReVision*, vol. 2, no. 2 (Summer/Fall 1979), p. 44.

[44] Fritjof Capra, "Letter," *ReVision*, vol. 5, no. 1 (Winter 1983). He also addresses this issue in an appendix to the revised edition of *The Tao of Physics*.

[45] H.P. Stapp, "S-Matrix Interpretation of Quantum Theory," *Physical Review*, vol. D3 (March 15, 1971), p. 1310.

[46] Albert Einstein, Boris Podolsky, and Nathan Rosen, "Can Quantum-Mechanical Description of Reality be Considered Complete?" *Physical Review*, vol. 47 (1935), pp. 777–780.

[47] J.S. Bell, "On the Einstein Podolsky Rosen Paradox," *Physics*, vol. 1 (1964), pp. 195–204.

[48] Unsuccessful attempts are reviewed by Clifford Hooker in "Concerning Einstein's, Podolsky's, and Rosen's Objection to Quantum Theory," *American Journal of Physics*, vol. 38 (1970), pp. 851–857.

[49] John Clauser and Abner Shimony, "Bell's Theorem: Experimental Tests and Implications," *Reports on Progress in Physics*, vol. 41 (1978), p. 1881.

[50] For evidence against long-distance psychokinetic action at the atomic level, which is more directly relevant to any proposed connection between idealism and the EPR effect, see Joseph Hall, Christopher Kim, Brian McElroy, and Abner Shimony, "Wave Packet Reduction as a Medium of Communication," *Foundations of Physics*, vol.7 (1977), pp. 759–767.

[51] See, for example, Henry Stapp, "Are Superliminal Connections Necessary?" *Il Nuovo Cimento*, vol. 408 (1977), pp. 191–205.

[52] David Bohm, *Wholeness and the Implicate Order* (London, England: Routledge & Kegan Paul, Ltd., 1980), p. 175.

[53] See, for example, Robert Stone, *The Secret Life of Your Cells* (Westchester, PA: Whitford Press, 1989).

CHAPTER EIGHT

[1] The philosopher Alfred North Whitehead believed that thirty-six categories of explanation are necessary to do the job, considerably more than found in New Paradigm discussions. For an exposition, see his *Process and Reality* (New York:

Harper Torchbacks, 1960). For an application of Whiteheadian thought to cultural dynamics, including the order-to-disorder continuum and the concept of bipolarity described in what follows, see David Hall's *The Civilization of Experience: A Whiteheadian Theory of Culture* (New York: Fordham U. Press, 1973).

2   Wang Ch'ung, A.D. 80, quoted in J. Needham, *Science and Civilization in China*, vol. 4, (Cambridge, England: Cambridge University Press, 1956), p. 7. For a more extended analysis of various types of polarity as it relates to the explanation of change, see Gustav Mueller, *The Interplay of Opposites* (New York: Bookman Associates, 1956).

3   Ken Carey, *Vision* (Kansas City, MO: Uni-Sun Publishers, 1985), p. 1.

4   Cf., for example, Alison Jaggar, *Feminist Politics and Human Nature* (Totowa, NJ: Rowan and Allanheld, 1983). Andrea Dworkin in *Woman Hating* (New York: Dutton Paperbacks, 1974) and *Intercourse* (New York: Vintage, 1987) devotes considerable attention to the many faces of oppression, together with Marilyn French in *Beyond Power* (New York: Ballantine, 1986), Angela Davis in *Women, Race and Class* (New York: Check, 1981), and Betty Friedan in *The Second Stage* (New York: Summit, 1986). An authoritative review of feminist concerns is published in a newsletter of the American Philosophical Association. See especially, "On Feminism and Philosophy" (April 1988), edited by Nancy Tuana. A special issue of *Time* (Fall 1990) entitled "Women: The Road Ahead" carries an excellent review of practical and theoretical challenges facing the Women's Movement.

5   Cf., for example, C. Bruchac, Linda Hogan, and Judith McDanial, *The Stories We Hold Secret: Tales of Women's Spiritual Development* (Greenfield Center, NY: The Greenfield Review Press, 1986); Charlene Spretnak, ed., *The Politics of Women's Spirituality* (New York: Anchor Books, 1982); and Judith Plaskow and Carol Christ, eds., *Weaving the Visions* (New York: Harper & Row, 1989). See especially Sallie McFague's recent *The Body of God: An Ecological Theology* (Minneapolis, MN: Fortress Press, 1993). Various types of feminism, Psychoanalytic, Marxist, Radical, Existentialist, Liberal, etc., are examined by Rosemarie Tong, *Feminist Thought* (Boulder, CO: Westview Press, 1989). Riane Eisler's *The Chalice and the Blade* (San Francisco, CA: Harper & Row, 1988), which Ashley Montague described as "the most important book since Darwin's *Origin of Species*," develops a rebalanced co-evolutionary perspective on women and men. For further analysis of the psychology of gender, see S.L. Ben's "Gender Schema Theory: A Cognitive Account of Sex Typing," *Psychological Review*, vol. 88 (1981), and D.J. Hargreaves and A.M. Colley, *The Psychology of Sex Roles* (New York: Hemisphere, 1987). S.K. Williams in *The Practice of Personal Transformation* (Berkeley, CA: Journey Publications, 1985) develops a "transcendental androgyny" (my phrase) consistent with my proposal in this section. In *The Journal of Personality and Social Psychology*, no. 65 (November, 1993), pp. 1010–1022, Michele Grossman and Wendy Wood present evidence that men and women respond to emotional stimuli in fundamentally different ways that are not explainable either in terms of human physiology or social norms.

6   In the areas of science and ecology, for example, see Carolyn Merchant, *The Death of Nature: Women, Ecology and the Scientific Revolution* (San Francisco, CA: Harper & Row, 1980).

7   For an exhaustive multi-level overview of these traits, see Erich Jantsch, *The Self-Organizing Universe* (New York: Pergamon Press, 1976). For an analysis of the

many problems associated with the idea of order, see Paul Kuntz, ed., *The Concept of Order* (Seattle, WA: University of Washington Press, 1968).

8   Marilyn Ferguson, "Bacteria Show Evidence of Directed Evolution," *Brain/Mind Bulletin* (October, 1988).

9   Excerpted from Michael Denton, *Evolution: Theory in Crisis* (Burnett Books, 1985) by Marilyn Ferguson in "Molecular Biology Locates Flaws in Darwin's Theory," *Brain/Mind Bulletin* (September, 1985), p. 2. A collection of articles dealing with the problems and prospects of evolutionary theory is contained in John Maynard Smith, ed., *Evolution Now* (San Francisco, CA: W.H. Freeman & Company, 1982). See also: Paul Moorehead and Martin Kaplan, eds., *Mathematical Challenges to the Neo-Darwinian Interpretation of Evolution* (Philadelphia, PA: The Wistar Institute Press, 1967); Evan Shute's earlier *Flaws in the Theory of Evolution* (Nutley, NJ: Craig Press, 1961); Norman Macbeth, *Darwin Retried* (Boston, MA: Gambit, 1971); and Jeremy Rifkin, "The Darwinian Sunset," *Algeny* (New York: Viking Press, 1983).

10   For further discussion of this point, see Huston Smith, "Two Evolutions," *On Nature*, Leroy Rouner, ed (Notre Dame, IN: University of Notre Dame Press, 1984), reprinted in Smith's *Beyond the Post-Modern Mind*.

11   Rupert Sheldrake, *A New Science of Life: The Hypothesis of Formative Causation* (Los Angeles, CA: J.P. Tarcher, 1981) and *The Presence of the Past: Morphic Resonance and the Habits of Nature* (New York: Random House, 1988).

12   For a brief review of the supporting evidence see Susan Blackmore's review of Sheldrake's hypothesis in the *Parapsychology Review*, vol. 16 (May/June, 1985), p. 6. For a more in-depth discussion of one test, see "Formative Causation: The Hypothesis Supported," *New Scientist* (October, 1983), p. 279. The most recent work in which three students split a $5,000 prize was sponsored by the Institute of Noetic Sciences. Copies of the studies are available from the Institute. The 1994 study by Marc Mishkind appears in the *Journal of Analytical Psychology*, no. 38, pp. 257–271.

13   Blackmore, *op. cit.*, p.7. See also Stephen Braude, "Radical Provincialism in the Life Sciences," *The Journal of the American Society for Psychical Research*, vol. 77 (January, 1983).

14   Ilya Prigogine and Isabelle Stengers, *Order out of Chaos* (New York: Bantam Publishing, 1981). For a critical overview, see M. Woodhouse's review in *ReVision*, vol. 8 (Summer 1985), pp. 77–80. See also Prigogine's "A (Very) Brief History of Certainty," *Scientific and Medical Network*, no. 56 (1995), pp. 6–7.

15   This claim is sympathetically discussed by physicist Bernard D' Espagnat in "Is Kervran a True or a False Prophet?" delivered to the International Transpersonal Association meeting in July, 1976.

16   Prigogine, *op. cit.*, p. 171.

17   For a very readable discussion of the interrelationships of Prigogine's views vis-à-vis those of Bohm and Pribram, see John Briggs and David Peat, *Looking Glass Universe* (New York: MacMillan, 1982). *Brain/Mind* (June/July, 1994) samples a wide variety of reactions to Prigogine's pioneering work by New Paradigm writers such as Larry Dossey, Ingo Swann, and Willis Harman.

18   Cf., Peter Tompkins and Christopher Bird, *The Secret Life of Plants* (New York: Avon Books, 1973), which also introduces the reader to the idea of

communicating with plants and animals via psychrotronics, and Robert Stone, *The Secret Lives of Your Cells* (West Chester, PA: Whitford Press, 1989). The critical review of Backster's work is published in *Science News*, vol. 107 (February 8, 1975).

19 Pate gives a comprehensive explanation of her procedures in *A New Age Christian Depossession Manual*, P.O. Box 59, Wrightsville, AR 72183. Baldwin's comprehensive work, *Spirit Releasement Therapy: A Technique Manual* (Terra Alta, West VA: Headline Books, 1994), which places special emphasis on past-life therapy and the larger historical and philosophical contexts of depossession work, can also be obtained from his Center for Human Relations, P.O. Box 4061, Enterprise, FL 32725. This topic is explored further in Chapter Fourteen.

20 The concept of accelerated interdimensional integration is suggested by Ken Carey in *The Starseed Transmissions* (Kansas City, MO: Uni-Sun Publications, 1981) and *Return of the Bird Tribes* (Kansas City, MO: Uni-Sun Publications, 1988); by Matthew Fox in *The Coming of the Cosmic Christ* (Santa Fe, NM: Bear & Company, 1988); by George Trevelyan, *A Vision of the Aquarian Age* (Walpole, VT: Stillpoint Publishing, 1982); and by numerous articles in the journals *Connecting Link* and *Sedona Journal of Emergence.*

CHAPTER NINE

1 For an extensive review and analysis of "A" and "B" theories of time, see Richard Gale, ed., *The Philosophy of Time* (New York: Anchor Books, 1967). An excellent overview is also provided by C.D. Broad in "The Philosophical Implications of Foreknowledge," *Philosophy and Parapsychology*, ed., Jan Ludwig (Buffalo, NY: Prometheus Books, 1978).

2 Quoted from Newton's *Principia* in Paul Durbin, *Philosophy of Science* (New York: McGraw Hill, 1968), p. 136.

3 Quoted in J. Kennett, *Selling Water by the River* (New York: Vintage Books, 1972), p. 140.

4 Quoted in Fritjof Capra, *The Tao of Physics,* p. 185.

5 For further criticisms of the Newtonian view, see D.C. Williams, "The Myth of Passage," *The Journal of Philosophy*, vol. 48 (1951), and Mark B. Woodhouse, "The Reversibility of Absolute Time," *Philosophical Studies*, vol. 29 (1976), pp. 465–68.

6 David Ryback, *Dreams That Come True* (New York: Doubleday, 1988); J.W. Dunne, *An Experiment With Time* (New York: Macmillan, 1927); and L.E. Rhine, *Hidden Channels of the Mind* (New York: William Sloan Associates, 1961).

7 See, for example, Montague Ullman, Stanley Krippner, and Alan Vaughn, *Dream Telepathy* (New York: Macmillan, 1973). Also Stanley Krippner, Charles Honorton, and Montague Ullman, "A Second Precognitive Dream Study with Malcolm Bessent," *Journal of the American Society for Psychical Research*, vol. 66 (1972), pp. 269–279.

8 Harold Puthoff and Russell Targ, "Psychic Research and Modern Physics," *Psychic Exploration*, ed., Edgar Mitchell (New York: Putnam, 1974).

9 These considerations are nicely summarized by physicist Tony Rothman in "Time," *Discover* (February, 1987), pp. 65–77.

[10] Still a standard reference in multiple perspectives on time is J.T. Frazer, ed., *The Voices of Time* (New York: George Braziller, 1966), which includes major contributions on the biology, psychology, and physics of time perception.

[11] Bertrand Russell, *The Analysis of Mind* (London, England: George Allen & Unwin, Ltd., 1922), p. 159.

CHAPTER TEN

[1] Quoted from Abraham Maslow, *The Farther Reaches of Human Nature*, in Bryan Wittine's balanced overview of the background and evolution of Transpersonal Psychology, "Beyond Ego," *Yoga Journal* (September/October, 1987), p. 53.

[2] A stimulating exchange on the perceived extravagances of transpersonal psychology and shortcomings of at least one form of humanistic psychology is developed by Ken Wilber in "Let's Nuke the Transpersonalists: A Reply to Albert Ellis," Albert Ellis in "Dangers of Transpersonal Psychology: A Reply to Ken Wilber," and Roger Walsh in "Psychological Chauvinism and Nuclear Holocaust: A Response to Albert Ellis and Defense of Non-Rational Emotive Theories" all in the *Journal of Counseling and Development*, vol. 67 (February, 1989), pp. 332–340. With R. Yeager, Ellis's stance is more fully developed in *The Dangers of Transpersonal Psychology* (Buffalo, NY: Prometheus Press, 1990).

[3] Relevant *core* works by Wilber are *The Spectrum of Consciousness* (Wheaton, IL: Theosophical Publication House, 1977); *The Atman Project: A Transpersonal View of Human Development* (Wheaton, IL: Theosophical Publication House, 1980); *Up From Eden: A Transpersonal View of Human Evolution* (Garden City, NY: Anchor Press/Doubleday, 1981); a collection of key articles in *Eye to Eye: The Quest for the New Paradigm* (Garden City, NY: Anchor Press/Doubleday, 1983); *Sex, Ecology, Spirituality: The Spirit of Evolution* (Boston, MA: Shambala, 1995); and a two-part series "The Developmental Spectrum and Psychopathology," *Journal of Transpersonal Psychology*, vol. 16 (1984). Relevant *core* works by Grof include *Realms of the Human Unconsciousness: Observations From LSD Research* (New York: E.P. Dutton, 1976); *Beyond the Brain* (New York: SUNY Press, 1985); and, with Cristina Grof, *Beyond Death* (London, England: Thames and Hudson, 1980) and "Spiritual Emergency: The Understanding and Treatment of Transpersonal Crises," *ReVision* (Winter/Spring 1986). From Jung's voluminous works, see *Man and His Symbols* (New York: Dell Publishing Co., 1977); *Modern Man in Search of a Soul* (New York: Harcourt, Brace, 1933); *Memories, Dreams, Reflections* (New York: Vantage Books, 1965); and "Synchronicity: An Acausal Connecting Principle," *Collected Works*, vol. 8 (Princeton, NJ: Princeton University Press, 1980). June Singer's commentary, *Boundaries of the Soul* (Garden City, NY: Anchor Press, 1972) insightfully integrates Jung's transpersonal themes. Robert Johnson's trilogy, *He*, *She*, and *We* applies Jungian perspectives to self-identity and relationships. Selected additional works which round out the transpersonal vision include: Charles Tart's classic *States of Consciousness* (New York: E.P. Dutton, 1975); Stanley Krippner's *Human Possibilities* (New York: Anchor Press, 1980); Roger Walsh's and Francis Vaughn's edited comprehensive collection of essays, *Paths Beyond Ego* (Los Angeles, CA: J. P. Tarcher/Perigee, 1993); Kenneth Pelletier's and Charles Garfield's *Consciousness: East and West* (New York: Harper & Row, 1976).

4 Fritjof Capra, *Turning Point* (New York: Bantam, 1983), p. 359. See my discussion of this point in Chapter III.

5 Wilber, *The Atman Project*, p. 80.

6 *Ibid.*, p. 83.

7 Douglas Richards, "Dissociation and Transformation," *Journal of Humanistic Psychology*, vol. 30 (Summer 1990), pp. 54–83. For an introduction to Lacan's thought, see Jonathan Scott Lee, *Jacques Lacan* (Boston, MA: Twayne Publishers, 1990). Many people never feel the same about "insanity" after reading R.D. Laing's classic *The Politics of Experience.*

8 "Polls Indicate Paranormal Experiences Well on Their Way to Becoming Normal," *Brain-Mind Bulletin*, vol. 12 (March, 1987).

9 For discussion of attempts to force all mystical experience into a particular psychodynamic category, see especially Ken Wilber's "Pre/Trans Fallacy" in *Eye to Eye, op. cit.*, Frits Staal, *Exploring Mysticism* (Berkeley, CA: University of California Press, 1975), and Ralph Hood, "The Construction and Preliminary Validation of Reported Mystical Experience," *Journal for the Scientific Study of Religion*, vol. 14 (1975).

10 Descriptions of kundalini awakenings vary. See particularly Lee Sannella's *Kundalini: Psychosis or Transcendence?* (San Francisco, CA: H.R. Dakin, 1978) and John White's edited collection, *Kundalini: Evolution and Enlightenment* (New York: Paragon Press, 1990). Bonnie Greenwell's *Energies of Transformation* (Cupertino, CA: Shakti River Press, 1990) is a storehouse of cross-cultural descriptions and useful clinical insight.

11 Cristina and Stanislav Grof, "Spiritual Emergency: The Understanding and Treatment of Transpersonal Crises," *op. cit.*, p. 10. See also their extended analysis in *Spiritual Emergencies: When Transpersonal Challenges Become Crises* (Los Angeles, CA: J.P. Tarcher, 1989).

12 Arthur Hastings, "A Counseling Approach to Parapsychological Experience," *Journal of Transpersonal Psychology*, vol. 15 (1983).

13 A comprehensive Western psychology of the chakras has yet to be developed. However, the rudiments have been in place for some time. See C.W. Leadbeater's *The Chakras* (Wheaton, IL: The Theosophical Publication House, 1927) and Jack Schwartz's *Human Energy Systems* (New York: E.P. Dutton, 1980).

14 Cf., for example, H. Motoyama's pioneering work in electrically mediated subtle energies, *Science and the Evolution of Consciousness* (Brookline, MA: Autumn Press, 1978) and his more recent *The Chakras.*

15 While comparative charts like this are common, I owe part of the inspiration for this one to Carol Bonner, whose workshops stress the potential of the fourth category, and to Jackie Woods, who teaches ways to move from controlling and caretaking relationships to those that mutually empower. Marilyn Ferguson's "Human Connections: Relationships Changing," Chapter 12 in *The Aquarian Conspiracy*, insightfully compares Old and New Paradigm relationships. Ken Keyes' *The Power of Unconditional Love* (Coos Bay, ORn: Love Line Books, 1990) presents "21 guidelines for beginning, improving, and changing your most meaningful relationships."

16   I have found the following helpful: Sondra Ray, *Celebration of Breath* (Berkeley, CA: Celestial Arts Press, 1983); Ken Keyes, *Handbook to Higher Consciousness*, (St. Mary, KY: Living Love Publications, 1975); Louise Hay, *You Can Heal Your Life* (Santa Monica, CA: Hay House, 1984); Deepak Chopra, *Creating Health* (Boston, MA: Houghton Mifflin Co., 1987); Marilyn Ferguson, *The Aquarian Conspiracy* (Los Angeles, CA: J.P. Tarcher, 1981); almost anything by Carlos Castaneda, but especially *The Eagle's Gift* (New York: Simon & Schuster, 1981); Gerald Jampolsky, *Love is Letting Go of Fear*; Ken Carey, *Notes to My Children* (Kansas City, MO: Uni-Sun Publications, 1986); James Redfield, *The Celestine Prophecy* (Birmingham, AL: Satori Press, 1993); Nathaniel Branden, *The Art of Self Discovery* (New York: Bantam, 1993); Jon Kabat-Zinn, *Wherever You Go There You Are* (New York: Hyperion, 1994); Neil Vandegrift, *Recreating Your Life From the Core of Your Beingness* (Sherman Oaks, CA: Word Wizards, 1989). Any list such as this would be seriously lacking without acknowledging the wisdom and transformational power of *A Course in Miracles* (Glen Ellen, CA: Foundation for Inner Peace, 1975). Marianne Williamson's *A Return to Love* (New York: Harper Collins, 1993) is excellent companion reading for *A Course in Miracles*, as is Arnold Patent's *You Can Have it All* (Sylva, NC: Celebration Publishing, 1992), and Barbara Dewey's *As You Believe* (Inverness, CA: Bartholomew Books, 1990).

17   Wei Wu Wei, *Ask the Awakened* (London, England: Routledge & Kegan Paul, 1963).

CHAPTER ELEVEN

1   As reported at the American Public Health Association meeting in Chicago, October 23, 1989 by Dr. Helene Lipton, principal author. Statistics strongly suggesting that vaccines are neither as safe or effective as health officials would like us to believe are presented in Neil Miller's *Vaccines: Are They Really Safe and Effective?* (Santa Fe, NM: New Atlantean Press, 1992).

2   "Studies published in *The New England Journal of Medicine* conclude that mortality rates have not improved since the '50s: Two of three cancer patients still die of the disease or related therapy within five years. Statistical improvements in the numbers of 'cured' patients are mainly the result of earlier diagnosis." Quoted in Ken Ausubel, "The Silent Treatments," *New Age Journal*, (September/October, 1989), p. 33.

3   Copies of published clinical trials involving a wide range of therapeutic benefits of primrose oil are obtainable from Murdock Pharmaceuticals, 1400 Mountain Springs Park, Springville, UT 84663.

4   Despite charges raised by James Randi and other investigators involving poor experimental control in homeopathic trials conducted by Jacques Benveniste and published in *Nature*, resulting in something of a public stalemate, successful studies involving homeopathic remedies have been published in the *British Journal of Pharmacology*, no. 27 (1989) and *British Medical Journal* (August 5, 1989). Results are summarized in *Brain/Mind Bulletin*, vol. 14 (Sept., 1989). Improvement rates over placebos were comparable to those of synthetic drugs. A subsequent review of studies of homeopathic effectiveness in the *British Medical Journal*, no. 302, pp. 316–323, noted that positive results were found in fifteen of twenty-two of the best designed experiments to date (1993). A recent study in *The*

Lancet, no. 344 (1994), pp. 1601–1606, not only replicated earlier positive find-ings, but also caused its principal author, Scottish physician David Reilly, to con-clude that either homeopathy works or the standard clinical trials used to determine the effectiveness of all prescription drugs are inherently flawed.

5   Cf. Dossey's *Space, Time and Medicine* (Boulder, CO: Shambhala, 1982), pp. 148-49), and Ferguson's *Aquarian Conspiracy,* p. 246. See especially Dossey's later work *Beyond Illness* (Boston, MA: Shambhala, 1986) for an elaboration of cer-tain aspects of this comparison.

6   Cited in A. L. Caplan, ed., *Concepts of Health and Disease* (Reading, MA: Addison-Wesley, 1981), p. 36.

7   Deepak Chopra, *Creating Health* (Boston, MA: Houghton Mifflin Co., 1987). Also, *Ageless Body, Timeless Mind* (New York: Harmony Brothers, 1993).

8   Christopher Bird, *The Galileo of the Microscope* (Quebec, Canada: Les Presses de l'Universite de la Personne Inc., 1990), p. 323. On the home front, it should be noted that the AMA has been found guilty of conspiring to restrain the practice of chiropractic by the Seventh Circuit United States Court of Appeals, February 7, 1990, Case No. 76 C 3777. Richard Thomas's *The Essiac Report* is published by The Alternative Treatment Information Network, 1244 Ozeta Terrace, Los An-geles, CA.

9   In the case of both ozone therapy and Therapeutic Touch, there is a strong grassroots clash of paradigms. With Therapeutic Touch, this is illustrated by the fact that Jarvis is quoted in a health and fitness magazine, *Shape* (May, 1992) by a fitness expert, Betty Wieder, who felt compelled to expose the claims of Thera-peutic Touch for her readers. Quinn's letter was circulated privately to various boards of directors and health professionals concerned with this issue. Benor's *Healing Research* is published by Helix Verlag GmbH (Munchen 2, Germany, 1992). The evidence for ozone therapy, and the ensuing clash of paradigms, is summarized in a recent documentary, *Ozone and the Politics of Medicine,* pro-duced by Geoffrey Rogers, obtainable from Threshold Film #301–356 East 6th Ave., Vancouver, Canada V5T 1K1. For a discussion of the imprisonment of Ba-sil Wainwright over his gifts of oxygen-treated water, see "Oxygen Therapies Cover-Up Continues," *Nexus,* vol. 2, no.17, pp. 27–32. For a truly alternative medical perspective on a wide range of contemporary issues, see Dr. William Douglas's newsletter *Second Opinion,* which may be ordered through the busi-ness office at 1-800-728-2288.

10   Richard Gerber, M.D., *Vibrational Medicine* (Santa Fe, NM: Bear and Company, 1988), p. 39. See also John Davidson's less medically oriented, but equally de-tailed, *Subtle Energy,* (Cambridge, England: The C.W. Daniel Company, Ltd., 1987).

11   Andrija Puharich, "An ELF Fact Sheet," obtainable from his business office, Devotion, Rt. 1, Box 545, Dobson, NC 27017. Many of the cited results were obtained in research conducted by the U.S. Navy and released in 1984.

12   Paul Brodeur, "Annals of Radiation: The Hazards of Electromagnetic Fields," *The New Yorker* (June 12, 19, and 26, 1989) and *Currents of Death* (New York: Simon and Schuster, 1989). It should be stressed that sixteen corporate and government sponsored research projects on the effects of *transmission* line fields indicate a very mixed picture requiring more research to resolve. For further reading, see

Stock Number 052-003-001153-1, *A Report on ELF Effects by the Congressional Office of Technology Assessment,* May, 1989. The EPA apparently believes that there may be *some* significant correlations between EM fields and leukemia and cancer of the nervous system, but not enough to justify a cause-and-effect relation comparable to that of, say, smoking and lung cancer. In 1991–92, twenty-four studies were underway internationally. The physics of non-ionizing (ELF) radiation is carefully laid out in T.S. Tenforde and W.T. Kaune, "Interaction of Extremely Low Frequency Electric and Magnetic Fields with Humans," *Health Physics,* vol. 53 (December, 1987), pp. 585–606. The Fall 1993 issue of *Bridges,* a newsletter of the International Society for the Study of Subtle Energies and Energy Medicine, contains a review by guest editor James Beal of research on ELF (or EMF, as he terms it) effects on human health.

[13] From the prologue to Robert Becker's, *Cross Currents,* (Los Angeles, CA: J. P. Tarcher, 1990). This work, plus his earlier *The Body Electric* (New York: William Morrow, 1985), carries an extensive discussion of the electromagnetic foundations of life.

[14] Research summaries and abstracts may be obtained by writing Acoustic Brain Research, P.O. Box 2030, Shelton, WA 98584. The addiction studies were performed at Temple University's Stress and Research Biofeedback Laboratory. For a highly useful introduction and background to the entire field, see Randall McClellan's *The Healing Forces of Music* (Warwick, NY: Amity House, 1988).

[15] For an introduction to the theory and application of phase conjugation, see David M. Pepper, "Nonlinear Optical Phase Conjugation," *Optical Engineering,* vol. 21, (1982). See also Thomas Bearden, *Extraordinary Physics* (Greenville, TX: Tesla Book Company, 1988). Kelly's application of phase-conjugate technology derives extensively from Bearden, who is arguably one of the most knowledgeable individuals on all aspects of the topic. His foundational paper, "The BETAR and its Scalar Detection System," is available from Interdimensional Sciences, Box 167, Lakemont, GA 30552. Norman Shealy, M.D., has conducted successful research trials of the BETAR for relief of pain and of clinical depression. For information pertaining to this research, consult Self-Health Systems, Rt. 1, Box 127, Fair Grove, MO 65648 and *Medical World News* (August 28, 1989), p. 46. Jocelyn DeMers (295 St. Catherines East, Montreal, Canada) reports a wide range of healing effects at his clinic, when the BETAR is used in conjunction with counseling. Also worth investigating for its effects on consciousness is the "Ally," a product of The Clarus Discovery, P.O. Box G, Boulder, CO 80306, which introduces a phase coherence and amplification of energy in one's immediate environment.

[16] For a detailed description of Edward's research, contact The Esoteric Unlimited Foundation, P.O. Box 706, Athens, OH 45701.

[17] Cited by Brendan O'Regan in his introduction to an article by Pert adapted for publication in the research bulletin of the Institute of Noetic Sciences. Pert's original article appeared in *Advances,* vol. 3, no. 3 (1986).

[18] Ernest Rossi, *The Psychobiology of Mind-Body Healing* (New York: W. W. Norton, 1986), p. 46.

19 The editorial was by Dr. Marcia Angell, then deputy editor of the *Journal* (June, 1985) in connection with its concurrent publication of a study by Dr. Barrie Cassileth.

20 Steven Locke, M.D., and Douglas Colligan, *The Healer Within, The New Medicine of Mind and Body* (New York: E.P. Dutton, 1986). See also Brendan O'Regan's excellent overview "Healing: Synergies of Mind/Body/Spirit," *Institute of Noetic Sciences Newsletter*, vol. 14, no. l, (Spring 1986). O'Regan served as director of the Inner Mechanisms of the Healing Response Program for the Institute. Information about this program and the results of its sponsored research in healing may be obtained from the Institute of Noetic Sciences, 475 Gate Five Road, Sausalito, CA 94965.

21 Ken and Treya Wilber, "Do We Make Ourselves Sick?" *New Age Journal* (September/October, 1988), p. 51.

22 Louise L. Hay, *You Can Heal Your Life* (Santa Monica, CA: Hay House, 1984), p. 76.

23 *Ibid.*, pp. 150–188.

24 From a study by psychologist John Schneider and colleagues as reported by Marilyn Ferguson, "Imagery Influences Immune Cells," *New Sense Bulletin* (October, 1991), p. 1. See also Martin L. Rossman, M.D., *Healing Yourself: A Step-by-Step Program for Better Health Through Imagery* (New York: Walker and Company, 1987) and Jeanne Achterberg's, "Imagery and Medicine: Psychophysiological Speculations," *Journal of Mental Imagery*, vol. 8, no. 4 (1984). Her *Imagery in Healing: Shamanism and Modern Medicine* (Boston, MA: Shambhala, 1985) is a classic in the field of mind/body healing relationships. The interdisciplinary journal, *Mental Medicine*, also carries articles of related interest.

25 Bernie S. Siegel, *Love, Medicine and Miracles* (New York: Harper and Row, 1986). In *Cancer as a Turning Point* (New York: E.P. Dutton, 1989), Lawrence LeShan addresses a broad spectrum of related issues from the perspective of a psychologist and psychical researcher. In *Recovering the Soul* (New York: Bantam, 1989), Larry Dossey explores the psychological and metaphysical foundations of profound states of health and medical anomalies.

26 Gerber, *op. cit.*, reviews in some detail the key research of Grad, Justa Smith, Miller, and Krieger, among others. Krieger's research on the effectiveness of Therapeutic Touch on hemoglobin levels is in the *American Journal of Nursing* (May, 1975). Expanding upon her earlier *Therapeutic Touch*, Krieger's more recent *Living the Therapeutic Touch* (New York: Dodd, Mead, 1988), carries a description of extensive research with Therapeutic Touch over long distances. Bernard Grad's "Some Biological Effects of the Laying on of Hands: A Review of Experiments with Animals and Plants," appeared in *Human Dimensions*, vol. 5 (1972). See also Douglas Dean's historical survey in *The Mystery of Healing* (Buffalo, NY: Search Publications, 1986).

27 As reported in "Non-Contact Healing Speeds Recovery From Wounds," *Brain/Mind Bulletin* (May, 1990) and fully presented in the first issue of *Subtle Energies* (1990), pp. 43–72, published by ISSSEEM. Subsequent issues have continued to include high-quality, peer-reviewed articles dealing with the evidence for and dynamics of healing energy. See especially: William G. Braud and Marilyn Schlitz,

"Consciousness Interactions with Remote Biological Systems: Anomalous Intentionality Effects," *Subtle Energies*, vol 2, no. 1 (1991), pp. 1–46.

28   Robert N. Miller, "Study on the Effectiveness of Remote Mental Healing," *Medical Hypotheses*, vol. 8 (July, 1982), pp. 481–490. For a more recent controlled study of remote healing, see William Braud's "Distant Mental Influence of Rate of Hemolysis of Human Red Blood Cells," *Journal of the American Society for Psychical Research*, vol. 84 (1990), pp.1–24. For a review of the positive effects of distant transpersonal imagery, see Braud's "Human Interconnectedness: Research Indications," *ReVision*, vol. 14, no. 3 (1992), pp. 140–148.

29   Douglas Dean and Etel DeLoach, "What is the Evidence for Psychic Healing?" *The Osteopathic Physician* (October, 1972).

30   James Randi, *The Faith Healers* (Buffalo, NY: Prometheus Press, 1986). See also the special issue of *Free Inquiry* (Spring 1986) devoted entirely to the question of faith healing. It should be stressed that faith healing is not a purely fundamentalist agenda. It is found today in middle-of-the-road and liberal churches of almost every persuasion. As a counterbalance to Randi's selectivity, see Francis MacNutt's *The Power to Heal* (Notre Dame, IN: Ave Maria Press, 1977) and Morton Kelsey's extensive historical survey, *Healing and Christianity* (New York: Harper & Row, 1976). William Nolan's *Doctor in Search of a Miracle* (New York: Random House, 1975) sets very high standards for paranormal *human* healing, so high that in his search no cases satisfied them.

31   The range of healing practices is extraordinary. See Stanley Krippner and Alberto Villoldo, *The Realms of Healing* (Millbrae, CA: Celestial Arts, 1976) and Krippner's *Healing States* (New York: Simon and Schuster, 1986), which gives special attention to shamanic practices as does his more recent work with Patrick Welsh, *Spiritual Dimensions of Healing* (New York: Irvington Publishers, 1992). See especially Barbara Ann Brennan, *Hands of Light* (New York: Bantam, 1987) for one of the most extensive presentations of the theory and practice of etheric surgery. The illustrations by Joseph A. Smith accurately portray the kinds of energies seen by the clairvoyant healer. The energy dynamics of personal growth are described with equal clarity and depth in her more recent *Light Emerging* (New York: Bantam, 1993). The range of healing is also nicely documented in George Meed, ed., *Healers and the Healing Process* (Wheaton, IL: Theosophical Publishing House, 1977). Alan Young's partly autobiographical, practical, and theoretical *Spiritual Healing* (Marina Del Rey, CA: DeVorss & Co., 1981) presents a useful overview.

32   For a general review of clinical, conceptual, and ethical issues raised by placebos, see Howard Brody, M.D., *Placebos and the Philosophy of Medicine* (Chicago, IL: University of Chicago Press, 1980). The Institute of Noetic Sciences also has published a very useful research bulletin devoted to the topic, "Placebo—The Hidden Asset in Healing," vol. 2, no.1 (1985), which carries a helpful list of references and further reading. In *Clinical Psychology Review*, no. 13, pp. 375-385, Alan Roberts and his colleagues report dramatic new findings suggesting that placebo effects may be much greater in drug trials than the standard one-in-three rule stipulates. In "How Should Alternative Therapies Be Evaluated," *Alternative Therapies*, vol. 1 (May, 1995), pp. 6, 79, Larry Dossey reviews evidence for the physician's own beliefs functioning as a placebo bias in tresting drugs.

33 Norman Shealy, M.D., "The Myth of Right Diagnosis," *New Realities* (September/ October, 1987), p. 7. See also C. Norman Shealy and Caroline Myss, *The Creation of Health* (Walpole, NH: Stillpoint Publishing, 1993), a veritable encyclopedia of alternative methods used to successfully address a wide range of illness and disease derived from Shealy's front-line pioneering research at his comprehensive health care institute.

34 This perspective is further elaborated in John A. Sanford's *Healing and Wholeness* (New York: Paulist Press, 1977). It was also gently, though persistently, awakened in me by Janet Quinn, JoAnne Marnie, and Jackie Woods.

35 These results were reported in *Brain/Mind Bulletin*, vol. 19, no. 3, (December, 1993) and at several national conferences, including the June, 1993 meeting of ISSSEEM in Monterey, CA. Further information can be obtained from the Institute of HeartMath, 14700 West Park Ave., Boulder Creek, CA 95006.

CHAPTER TWELVE

1 A classic "rights-oriented" pro-choice argument is given by Judith Jarvis Thompson in her "A Defense of Abortion," *Philosophy and Public Affairs*, vol. 1, no. 1 (1971). A widely cited pro-life argument is given by John T. Noonan, Jr., "An Almost Absolute Value in History," in his edited collection *The Morality of Abortion* (Cambridge, MA: Harvard University Press, 1970). Difficulties in drawing the line and in defining "human" are discussed by Mary Anne Warren in "On the Moral and Legal Status of Abortion," *The Monist*, vol. 57, no. 1 (1973).

2 Reincarnational literature seldom directly addresses this question. The case for variable incarnation periods can be inferred from everything from *The Tibetan Book of the Dead* to the uterine "memories" of individuals regressed to a pre-birth stage described, for example, in Helen Wambach's *Life Before Life.*

3 These observations and statistics for the most part derive from two reports, *A Nation at Risk*, and the education section of *American Agenda: Report to the Forty-First President of the United States* (Los Angeles, CA: Times Mirror Foundation, 1989). John Gatto's pointed and deeply moving speech, "Our Children are Dying in our Schools," is reprinted in *New Age Journal* (September/October, 1990).

4 From the Introduction to Carol Flake's *Holistic Education: Principles, Perspectives, and Practices* (Brandon, VT: Holistic Education Press, 1993). A number of the following proposals are briefly summarized (with useful bibliographies) in Mark Satin's "Our Schools Need Imagination More Than They Need Money," *New Options*, no. 59 (May, 1989) and by Alleman Christian (citing Paul Messier, senior research analyst for the U.S. Department of Education) in "Future School Now," *Thought Trends*, vol. 4, no. 11 (September, 1989).

5 Ron Miller, "Holistic Education in the United States, A 'New Paradigm' or a Cultural Struggle," *Holistic Education Review* (December, 1993), pp. 12–19. For a description of Miller's new perspective, see his collection of leading theorists in *The Renewal of Meaning in Education* (Brandon, VT: Holistic Education Press, 1993).

6   Sources for these citations include the newsletter of the Worldwatch Institute, *GAIA: An Atlas of Planet Management* (New York: Anchor Books, 1984) and a series of special articles in *Time* (October 23 and December 18, 1989) reflecting the views of fourteen environmental experts especially convened for the purpose. Philip Elmer-Dewitt in "Rich vs. Poor," *Time* (June 1, 1992) examines the issues facing the participants of the Earth Summit conference that year. See also John McCormick, *Reclaiming Paradise: The Global Environmental Movement* (Bloomington, IN: Indiana University Press, 1989).

7   Cited in Thomas Sancton, "The Fight to Save the Planet," *Time* (December 18, 1989), p. 61. Political dimensions are explored further in Jonathan Porritt, *Seeing Green: The Politics of Ecology Explained* (New York: Basil Blackwell, 1984).

8   For example, see Cathy Spencer's *Help Wanted: An Activist's Guide to a Better Earth* (supplement to *Omni* (August, 1989)); Thomas Berry, *The Dream of the Earth* (San Franscisco, CA: Sierra Club Books, 1988); Susan Meeker-Lowery, *Economics as if the Earth Really Mattered* (Philadelphia, PA: New Society Publishers, 1988); and *The Action Linkage Networker* (5825 Telegraph Ave. #45, Oakland, CA 94609).

9   Cited in Sancton, *op. cit.* Though somewhat dated, Barry Weisberg's *Beyond Repair: The Ecology of Capitalism* (Boston, MA: Beacon Press, 1971) nicely captures the role of economics in environmental decay.

10   *Ibid.*

11   These facts are derived from a publication, "Meat—Destroying the Planet with a Knife and Fork," printed by the North American Vegetarian Society, P.O. Box 72, Dolgeville, NY 13329. See also Frances M. Lappe, *Diet For a Small Planet* (New York: Ballantine, 1982) and John Robbins, *Diet For a New America* (Walpole, NH: Stillpoint Publishing, 1987).

12   The distinction between deep ecology and other wings of the environmental movement was first drawn by Norwegian philosopher Arne Naess. See his "The Shallow and the Deep, Long-Range Ecology Movement: A Summary," *Inquiry*, vol. 16 (1973).

13   Christopher Manes, *Green Rage* (Boston, MA: Little, Brown and Co., 1990), p. 142. See also John Seed, "Beyond Anthropocentrism," *Thinking Like a Mountain*, eds., John Seed, Joanna Macy, Pat Fleming, and Arne Naess (Philadelphia, PA: New Society Publishers, 1988); Brian Tokar, "Social Ecology, Deep Ecology, and the Future of Green Political Thought," *Ecologist*, vol. 18 (1988); George Sessions, "Deep Ecology and the New Age," *Earth First*, (September, 1987); and Bill Devall and George Sessions, *Deep Ecology: Living as if Nature Mattered* (Salt Lake City, UT: Peregrine Smith, 1988). Robert Schultz's and J. Donald Hughes's, eds., *Ecological Consciousness: Essays From the Earthday X Colloquium* (University Press of America, 1980) probes a wide range of theoretical underpinnings of the ecology movement. For an analysis of related ethical issues, see Holmes Rolston, III, ed., *Philosophy Gone Wild* (Buffalo, NY: Prometheus Books, 1989) and Dale Westphal and Fred Westphal, eds, *Planet in Peril* (New York: Harcourt Brace, 1994).

14   Machaelle Small Wright, *The Perelandra Garden Workbook* (Jeffersonton, VA: Perelandra, Ltd., 1988), p. 189. *Behaving as if the God in All Life Mattered* is similarly self-published, 1983.

CHAPTER THIRTEEN

1 Cf., for example, Erich Fromm, *Psychoanalysis and Religion* (New York: Bantam Books, 1950); Paul Tillich, *Biblical Religion and the Search for Ultimate Reality* (Chicago, IL: University of Chicago Press, 1955); J. Habermas, *Knowledge and Human Interests* (Boston, MA: Beacon Press, 1971); Rudolf Bultmann, *Jesus Christ and Mythology* (New York: Charles Scribner's, 1958); Thomas J. Altizer, et. al, *Deconstruction and Theology* (New York: Crossroad Press, 1982).

2 There are many proposals for more inclusivist religious orientations apart from the perennialist approach I will defend. Cf., for example, John Hick's *God Has Many Names* (Philadelphia, PA: Westminster Press, 1982) and John Cobb's (Whiteheadian-oriented) *God and the World* (Philadelphia, PA: Westminster Press, 1969).

3 Laura Hagar, "The Sounds of Silence," *New Age Journal* (March/April, 1989), p. 53.

4 There is already an extensive critique. However, Mary Daly's *Beyond God the Father* (Boston, MA: Beacon Press, 1973) sets much of the initial stage.

5 These passages are from Fox's *Original Blessing* (Santa Fe, NM: Bear and Company, 1983). See also his more recent *Creation Spirituality* (San Francisco, CA: Harper and Row, 1991).

6 Quoted in Eliot Deutsch, *Advaita Vedanta: A Philosophical Reconstruction* (Honolulu, HI: University of Hawaii Press, 1968). p. 38.

7 Hagar, *op. cit.*, p. 105.

8 Ken Carey, *Vision* (Kansas City, MO: Uni-Sun Publications, 1985), p. 1.

9 This quotation comes from a delightful overview of millennium fever, Dick Teresi and Judith Hooper's "The Last Laugh?" *Omni* (December, 1989), p. 43. A wide range of criticisms of millennium fever is contained in a special edition of *Critique* (June-September, 1989), which covers such topics as "The Beast," "Acid Rain," the "Apocalypse," and "Nostradamus."

10 *Ibid.*

11 Bill Lawren, "Apocalypse Now," *Psychology Today* (May, 1989), p. 42.

12 John White, *Pole Shift* (New York: Doubleday and Company, 1980); Kirk Nelson, *The Second Coming* (Virginia Beach, VA: Wright Publishing Co., 1986).

13 Teresi and Hooper, *op. cit.*

14 Jeffrey Goodman, *We Are the Earthquake Generation* (New York: Berkley Publishing Corp., 1979).

15 John White, "Pole Shift Update: Consciousness Research and Planetary Transformation," *The Meeting of Science and Spirit* (New York: Paragon Press, 1990). Ring's earlier case for a convergence of prophetic visions was based upon the reports of near-death experiencers which suggested that 1988 was the critical year. His summary and revision of this interpretation is contained in "Prophetic Visions in 1988: A Critical Reappraisal," *Journal of Near-Death Studies*, vol. 7 (1988).

16 Scallion's newsletter, *The Earth Changes Report*, is the main source for these predictions. It is published by Matrix Institute, RRI Box 391, Westmoreland, NH 03467.

[17] Cited in Lawren, *op. cit.* p. 44.

[18] Consider, for example, Terence McKenna's discovery of novelty waves, which he obtains by dividing the time life began on earth (1.3 billion years ago) by sixty-four (borrowed from the *I Ching*'s series of sixty-four hexagrams), and that result again by sixty-four, etc. Not only do we hit the beginnings of some major cycles, but the process plays out exactly to 2,012 A.D., which is when the Mayan calendar ends! McKenna's work is described in Teresi and Hooper, *op. cit.*, p. 82. For an extensive review of all types of cycles, including historical ones, see Lawrence Blair's *Rhythms of Vision* (New York: Warner Books, 1975).

[19] Cited in George Trevelyan's *A Vision of the Aquarian Age* (Walpole, NH: Stillpoint Publishing, 1984), p. 129.

[20] *Ibid.*, p. 128. See also Chapter Sixteen, "Divine and Demonic Tendencies," in any standard edition of the *Bhagavad-Gita*.

[21] Evelyn Gordon and Mary Joyce, *Sky Father and Son* (Orlando, FL: EKG Press, 1990). See also Levi's *The Aquarian Gospel of Jesus the Christ* (Marina del Rey, CA: DeVorss and Co., 1964) and Holger Kersten's *Jesus Lived in India* (Saftesbury, England: Element Books, Ltd., 1986). Virginia Essene's *New Teachings* is published by Spiritual Education Endeavers, Santa Clara, CA (1986). The reference to Jehovah's dark deeds comes from Tuella (the only person to my knowledge ever to claim to channel God), *A New Book of Revelations* (New Brunswick, NJ: Inner Light Publications, 1995).

[22] Albert J. Hebert, S.M., has authored an insightful study of major Christian and Catholic prophecies, including those of the Virgin Mary, in *The Three Days' Darkness Prophecies of Saints and Seers*, P.O. Box 309, Paulina, LA 70763 (1989).

CHAPTER FOURTEEN

[1] I have found the following books useful in constructing the account in this section. *The Urantia Book* (Chicago, IL: The Urantia Foundation, 1955); Ken Carey, *The Starseed Transmissions* (Kansas City, MO: Uni-Sun Publications, 1983) and *Starseed: The Third Millennium* (Kansas City, MO: Uni-Sun Publications, 1992); J.J. Hurtak, *The Keys of Enoch* (Los Gatos, CA: Academy for Future Science, 1973); George Trevelyan, *A Vision of the Aquarian Age* (Walpole, NH: Stillpoint Publishing, 1984); William Eisen, *The Agashan Discourses* (Marina Del Rey, CA: DeVorss and Company, 1978); the gospels of *Matthew* and of *Revelation*; Anton LaVey, *The Satanic Bible* (New York: Avon Books, 1969); Judi Koteen, *UFOs and the Nature of Reality* (Eastsound, WA: Indelible Ink, 1991); Barbara Marciniak, *Bringers of the Dawn* (Santa Fe, NM: Bear and Company, 1992); Lyssa Royal and Keith Priest, *The Prism of Lyra* (Scottsdale, AZ: Royal Priest Research Press, 1990); James Redfield, *The Celestine Prophecy* (Hoover, AL: Satori Publishing, 1993); Phyllis Schlemmer and Palden Jenkins, *The Only Planet of Choice* (Bath, England: Gateway Books, 1993); Norma Milanovich, *We, The Arcturians* (Albuquerque, NM: Athena Publishing, 1990); and Virginia Essene and Sheldon Nidle, *You are Becoming a Galactic Human* (Santa Clara, CA: Spiritual Education Endeavors, 1994).

[2] Zecharia Sitchin, *The 12th Planet* (New York: Avon Books, 1978). Richard Thompson's *Alien Identities* is published by Govardan Hill, 1993. Other writers,

most notably Erich von Daniken in *Chariots of the Gods?*, have developed variations on a theme, which always include some reference to the prophet Ezekiel's vision of a cloud of fire and bronze out of which came "the likeness of four living creatures." Sitchin's "Earth Chronicle" series, however, reflects some of the most in-depth scholarship on the topic. The Ancient Astronaut Society in Highland Park, IL, investigates similar questions relating to the origins of humanity and of religion on earth. Alice Bryant's and Phyliss Galde's *The Message of the Crystal Skull* (St. Paul, MN: Llewellyn Publications, 1989), while not addressing the question of extraterrestrial visitations in ancient times, builds a powerful case for an ancient technology used in shaping the skull that modern science has been unable to explain. Richard Hoagland's *The Monuments of Mars* (Berkeley, CA: North Atlantic Books, 1987) makes a strong case for an ancient civilization on Mars. His account is visually supplemented by Mark Carlotto's *The Martian Enigmas—A Closer Look* (Berkeley, CA: North Atlantic Books, 1991).

3   Malachi Martin, *Hostage to the Devil* (New York: Bantam, 1977) includes five case studies and a manual describing the dynamics of possession and exorcism. Scott Peck's *People of the Lie* (New York: Simon Schuster, 1983) is compelling reading for persons not otherwise inclined to take the dark side of human nature seriously. Michael Perry, Archdeacon of Durham in the Church of England, compares possession to the complexities of both channeling and multiple personality in "Possession," *Parapsychology Review*, vol. 21 (1990). He concludes that possession is a possibility and exorcism a necessity in a few rare cases. In addition to the spirit releasement work of Carol Pate and William Baldwin (referenced in Chapter Eight), Carl Wickland's *30 Years Among the Dead* (Van Nuys, CA: Newcastle Publishing, 1974) and Edith Fiore's *The Unquiet Dead* (New York: Ballantine, 1987) pay special attention to the topic of "earthbound spirits." See also Irene Hickman's *Remote Depossession* (Kirksville, MO: Hickman Systems, 1994).

4   Cf., for example, Philip Klass, *UFOs: The Public Deceived* (Buffalo, NY: Prometheus Books, 1983) and his "The MJ-12 Crashed-Saucer Documents," *The Skeptical Inquirer*, vol. XII, no. 2 (Winter 1987–88). In the same volume, see Robert Baker's "The Aliens Among Us: Hypnotic Regression Revisited." Klass's more recent *UFO Abductions: A Dangerous Game* (Buffalo, NY: Prometheus, 1988) presents extended analyses of some classic abduction cases, including Travis Walton, Betty and Barney Hill, and the much discussed "Andreasson Affair." He urges that all can be explained as instances of intentional or unconscious fabrication. Baker and Klass give special attention to the fact that ordinary (non-abducted) persons can invent stories under hypnosis that sound very similar to standard abduction accounts.

5   Obviously, many explanations are possible. A quasi-mystical though still terrestrially based explanation, for example, would be that the Earth Mother herself is attempting to communicate with us via natural magnetic lines of force. A balanced overview of the crop circle phenomenon is presented by Dennis Stacy in "Graffiti of the Gods?" *New Age Journal*, (February, 1991). Of interest is the fact that Stacy is himself an editor of *The MUFON Journal*, published by the Mutual UFO Network, yet prefers explanations that do not invoke "super-subtle" intelligences. There are now several centers and conferences devoted to the phenomena, which have shown a clear progression from simple to more complex patterns resembling the pictograms of an ancient language. See also Pat Delgado and

Colin Andrews, *Circular Evidence: A Detailed Investigation of the Flattened Swirled Crops Phenomenon* (London, England: Bloomsbury, 1987) and especially Ralph Noyes, ed., *The Crop Circle Enigma* (Bath, England: Gateway Books, 1990), which contains diverse analyses of the phenomena. For more recent work, see Alick Bartholomew's *Crop Circles—Harbingers of World Change* and Beth Davis's *Ciphers and the Crops*, both published by Atrium Publishing Santa Rosa, CA, 1995.

6   The government intrigue surrounding Tesla's missing research notes is described (and largely resolved) by Margaret Cheney in Chapter 30 "The Legacy" in her *Tesla* (Greenville, TXs: Tesla Book Company, 1987).

7   This and the following two quotations are excerpted from *U.F.O.s: The Evidence,* a three-part television series produced by Royal Atlantis Film, Westerbuchberg 79, Germany.

8   There are many good books on the subject of UFOs, alien contacts, and cover-ups. However, Timothy Good's *Above Top Secret* (New York: William Morrow, 1988) and *Alien Contact* (New York: William Morrow, 1993) are among the most comprehensive, well-researched, and bibliographically inclusive in the entire field, so far as the existence of UFOs and a cover-up are concerned. Much of the information in this list is derived from Chapters 14 through 17. The passage from Marchetti is reprinted on p. 365. Good's book also contains an extensive appendix of letters and reports of various government agencies and officials now made public under the Freedom of Information Act. One of the very best single case studies is Kevin Randle's and Donald Schmitt's, *UFO Crash at Roswell* (New York: Avon Books, 1991) together with their follow-up study *The Truth About the UFO Crash at Roswell* (New York: M. Evans and Company, 1994). Stanton Friedman and Don Berliner also develop the case in *Crash at Corona* (New York: Paragon House, 1992) and defend the authenticity of the famous MJ-12 documents as well. Lawrence Fawcett and Barry Greenwood's *Clear Intent* (Englewood Cliffs, NJ: Prentice-Hall, 1984) develops a strong case for a cover-up. John White develops a useful introduction and overview of the field, with special attention to the question of origins, in "What's Out There?" *New Realities* (November/December, 1987). He further speculates on the darker religious and political implications of the cover-up and of abduction cases in "Aliens Among Us: A UFO Conspiracy Hypothesis in a Religious Mode" (invited address). Linda Moulton Howe's *An Alien Harvest* (Littleton, CO: LMH Productions, 1989) develops a strong circumstantial case for alien intrusion, especially involving cattle mutilations, and for current government cooperation with one or more alien groups. It also describes other alleged government agendas in this arena. Howard Blum's *Out There, The Government's Secret Quest for Extraterrestrials* (New York: Simon and Schuster, 1990) traces the actions of the Defense Intelligence Agency's UFO Working Group from its inception in 1987 and demonstrates that, no matter what the truth about UFOs may be, our government has misrepresented the actual extent of its involvement. Richard Hall's *Uninvited Guests* (Santa Fe, NM: Aurora Press, 1988) summarizes large amounts of information and maps the territory in as clear a fashion as I have seen. Michael Lindemann's *UFOs and the Alien Presence* (Santa Barbara, CA: The 2020 Group, 1991) is a summary of evidence and speculation by respective experts on various aspects of the topic. Jim Keith's *Casebook on Alternative 3* (Lilburn, GA: IllumiNet Press, 1994) effectively integrates the topic of UFOs within the larger dimensions of conspiracy theory. William F. Hamilton makes the case in *Cosmic Top Secret* (New Brunswick, NJ:

Inner Light Publications, 1991) that, whatever the truth about extraterrestrial UFOs may be, America has had its own UFO program for several decades. In *Extraterrestrial Friends and Foes* (Lilburn, GA: IllumiNet, 1993), George Andrews (with several chapters contributed by other researchers) is less concerned with evidence for the existence of aliens than with dark alliances between elements of our own government and one or more alien groups and with subtle technological invasions of human health and privacy including, for example, virtually instant and unauthorized remote wiretaps of almost any telephone in America. The farther reaches of a government/extraterrestrial connection are explored by Preston Nichols and Peter Moon in *Montauk Revisited* (New York: Sky Books, 1994), which with the earlier *Montauk Project* explores time travel and dimensional manipulation in the aftermath of the "Philadelphia Experiment." The third book in this series, *Pyramids of Montauk*, investigates the unusual history of this area over the past few hundred years, and develops circumstantial evidence for extraordinary events transpiring underground. Some of the most massive UFO sightings in American history are described by Ed and Francis Walters in *The Gulf Breeze Sightings* (New York: William Morrow, 1990), which carries a Foreword by optical physicist Dr. Bruce Maccabee stating that there is no evidence of fraud in the numerous photos the Walters took. The book also illustrates how, even in the comparatively rarified atmosphere of UFO investigations, political considerations can complicate matters.

9   John Mack, "Mental Health Professionals and the Roper Poll," *Unusual Personal Experiences* (Las Vegas, NV: Bigelow Holding Company, 1992), p. 7. See also Mack's "The Alien Abduction Phenomenon," *Noetic Sciences Review*, no. 23 (Autumn 1992), and *Abduction* (New York: Scribners, 1994). His views about abduction experiences and his alleged lack of objectivity in dealing with clients were the object of a specially appointed faculty review committee. This paradigm war could have resulted in Mack's dismissal. TREAT, The Center for Treatment and Research of Experienced Anomalous Trauma, brings together psychiatrists, clinical psychologists, and UFOlogists each year to examine various aspects of the anomalous (traumatic and otherwise). It is directed by Dr. Rima Laibow, P.O. Box 728, Ardsley, NY 10502. Dr. Leo Sprinkle has had extensive clinical experience with abductees. His annual conference, established before contacts became a popular topic, offers support and short-term therapy for contactees and abductees. More information is available from Sprinkle at 406 1/2 So. 21st St., Laramie, WY 82070. For more on abductee accounts, see: Whitley Strieber, *Communion* (New York: William Morrow, 1987), *Transformation* (New York: William Morrow, 1989), and *Breakthrough* (New York: Harper Collins, 1992); Elizabeth Bird, "Invasion of the Mind Snatchers," *Psychology Today* (April, 1989); Pamela Weintraub, "Secret Sharers," *Omni* (December, 1987); Raymond Fowler, *The Watchers: The Secret Design Behind UFO Abductions* (New York: Bantam Books, 1990); and Budd Hopkins, *Missing Time* (New York: Richard Marek, 1981) and *Intruders: The Incredible Visitations at Copley Woods* (New York: Random House, 1987). Hopkins's Intruders Foundation (Box 30233, NYC 10011) publishes a newsletter and supports a network of contactees, abductees, and therapists, most notably John Mack, John Carpenter, and David Jacobs, working to unravel this part of the larger picture. Jacobs's sourcebook, *Secret Life*, is published by Simon and Schuster, 1992. Carpenter is the principal therapist in author/abductee Leah Haley's (a pseudonym) *Lost was the Key* (Tuscaloosa, AL: Greenleaf Publications,

1993), notable for the fact that it implicates our own government in some abduction scenarios. Karla Turner's *Into the Fringe: A True Story of Alien Abduction* (New York: Berkley, 1992) is an autobiographical account of abduction. Her later work *Taken* (Bigelow, AZ: Kelt Works, 1994) also develops the theme of human as well as alien complicity in abductions. Of special interest for clinicians are Susan Powers's "Fantasy Proneness, Amnesia, and the UFO Abduction Phenomenon," *Dissociation*, vol. IV, no.1 (March, 1991) and "Dissociation in Alleged Extraterrestrial Abductees," *Dissociation*, vol. VII, no. 1 (March, 1994).

[10] The case for Alternative Three was put together for "Science Report," an otherwise respected British television series. The story of the making of the documentary, including alleged government efforts to suppress it, is contained in Leslie Watkins and David Ambrose, *Alternative Three* (London, England: Sphere Books, 1978), which is difficult to obtain in this country. The program claimed to attempt to explain the brain drain from England. It concluded that some of them had literally gone to the moon or to Mars. Science Report subsequently disowned the report. Jim Keith's *Casebook on Alternative 3* (Lilburn, GA: IllumiNet Press, 1993) makes the case for a parallel agenda.

[11] Zecharia Sitchin reports on this comparatively recent development (which received more attention in the European press) in the concluding chapters of *Genesis Revisited* (New York: Avon Books, 1990). He is not alone in arguing that the extraordinary thaw in Cold War relations makes better sense in light of the realization that larger challenges face us from off the planet. That there are, indeed, non-natural objects on Mars that NASA is covering up is additionally argued by Stanley McDaniel in *The McDaniel Report* (Berkeley, CA: North Atlantic Books, 1993).

[12] Jim Keith's *Black Helicopters Over America* is published by Illuminet Press, Lilburn, GA, 1994. Noam Chomsky's *The Prosperous Few and the Restless Many* (as interviewed by David Barsamian) is published by Odonian Press, Berkeley, CA, 1993. For a brief overview of mind control possibilities, see Vicki Cooper, "Abduction as Mind Control," *UFO*, vol. 5, no. 4 (1990). For a broader investigation, see Glenn Krawyczk's two-part series, "Mind Control and the New World Order," *Nexus* (December/January, 1993). C.B. Baker's "New World Order E.L.F. Psychotronic Tyranny," *Youth Action News* (December, 1994) goes into considerable detail on a variety of American and Russian projects, including unconscious programming. On America's own UFOs, see William Hamilton, *op. cit.*, and Thomas Bearden's *Excalibur Briefing*, 2nd ed., (San Francisco, CA: Strawberry Hill Press, 1987). The case for non-ratification of the Sixteenth Amendment is made by Bill Benson in *The Law that Never Was* (South Holland, IL: Constitution Research, 1990). The HIV paper trail through Congress, Fort Detric, Maryland, and later through immunization programs of the World Health Organization are discussed by Bill Cooper in *Behold a Pale Horse* (Sedona, AZ: Light Technology Publishing, 1991) and by Jim Keith in *Casebook on Alternative 3, op. cit.* In "HIV Infection—Tested to Death," *Nexus* (October/November, 1994), Jody Wells and Lynne McTaggart describe the growing body of evidence strongly suggesting that, no matter who or what produced HIV, in itself HIV cannot be the singular cause upon which most AIDS research is based. An in-depth analysis of this issue is given by Peter Duesberg in *Infectious AIDS: Stretching the Germ Theory Beyond its Limits* (Berkeley, CA: North Atlantic Books, 1995). *Mother Jones* (January, 1994) makes the case for FEMA's more

hidden role. See also, in this regard, FEMA Executive Order #10995 involving seizure of communications media, #10998 involving seizure of food supplies and farm equipment, and #10999 involving seizure of personal automobiles and control of all highways and seaports. The breaking story regarding Marine's attitudes was carried in numerous issues of *The Spotlight* (especially April 24, 1995), a populist weekly newspaper published in Washington, D.C. Related information is given in *The McAlvany Intelligence Advisor*, especially the April, 1995 issue, which goes into considerable depth on the constitutional implications of the proposed Conference of States. Information on transponder chip technology can be obtained from one of its manufacturers, Trovan Identification Systems, AEF/Telefunken in Germany. Martin Anderson's "High-Tech National Tattoo," *The Washington Times*, (October 11, 1993) offers a brief overview of this technology vis-à-vis President Clinton's early proposal for a national identity card. I have been told that these chips are used in the military on a limited basis. Jim Keith's exposé of the handling of the Oklahoma bombing, *OKBomb*, is due out in the Spring of 1996 from Illuminet Press. For a detailed overview of the entire spectrum of conspiracy issues, see David Ieke's *...and the truth shall set you free*, (Santa Fe, NM: Sovereignty Press, 1995).

13 Copies of CSETI's comprehensive assessment and policy statement may be obtained from Dr. Greer at P.O. Box 15401, Asheville, North Carolina 28813.

14 Michael Grosso, "UFOs and the Myth of the New Age," in Dennis Stillings, ed., *Cyberbiological Studies of the Imaginal Component in the UFO Contact Experience* (St. Paul, MN: Archaeus Project, 1989), pp. 97 and 62. Quoted by Kenneth Ring, *The Omega Project* (New York: William Morrow, 1992), pp. 226–227. See also Grosso's "The Symbolism of UFO Abductions," *UFO Universe* (Fall 1988) and Carl Raschke, "UFOs: Ultraterrestrial Agents of Cultural Deconstruction," in Stillings, *op cit.* Keith Thompson's *Angels and Aliens: UFOs and the Mythic Imagination* (Reading, MA: Addison-Wesley, 1991) is must reading for those who, like Ring and Grosso, resist the pull of either objectivism or subjectivism. An entire issue of *ReVision*, vol. 11, no. 3 (1989), is devoted to the topic of "Angels, Aliens, and Archetypes," with articles by Thompson, Ring, Grosso, and Terence McKenna. Nicholas Spanos's study appeared in the *Journal of Abnormal Psychology*, no. 102 (1993) pp. 624–632.

15 This evidence, as well as conferences, newsletters, and training relating to Extraterrestrial Telepathic Intelligence Phenomenon (ETIP), is developed by Robyn Andrews Quail and Caryl Dennis on the basis of their work with contactees. For further information write: ETIP, 3552 Hildon Circle, Atlanta, GA 30341.

16 Lyssa Royal and Keith Priest, *Visitors from Within* (Scottsdale, AZ: Royal Priest Research Press, 1992), p. 164. Their more recent *Preparing for Contact* (Scottsdale, AZ: Royal Priest Research Press, 1994), describes alternative perspectives on the ways contact may take place.

17 Yvonne Cole, "More From the Ashtar Command," *Connecting Link* (Spring 1994), pp. 10–17. William Alnor explores potential reactions by conservative Christians to direct contact in *UFOs in the New Age: Extraterrestrial Messages and the Truth of Scripture* (Grand Rapids, MI: Baker Book House Company, 1992). For more on the history and purpose of Ashtar Command, see Tuella, *Ashtar* (New Brunswick, NJ: Inner Light Publications, 1994).

Index

Thant, U., 492

Theosophical Society, 97

Therapeutic Touch, 367, 388, 395

therapy
    alternative *see* holistic medicine
    psychotherapy *see* psychotherapy

thermodynamics, and reversibility of time, 294, 297

Third World, and environment, 425, 426, 429–30

Thomas, Richard, 367

Thompkins, Peter, 436

Thompson, Keith, 488

Thompson, Richard, 478

thought
    forms, 233
    and nonlocal causation, 244–49

Through Time into Healing (Weiss), 150

Tillich, Paul, 441

Time, 71, 349

time
    direction of, 284, 293–300, 305
    environmental destruction and, 428–30
    and eternity, 101–02, 303
    and future, preexistence of, 287–93
    lack of, and trusting feelings, 347
    psychology of, 300–306
    theories of, 282–87, 304–06

Tolba, Mostafa, 425, 429–30

Torun, Erol, 536–38

toxic waste disposal, 18, 19

traditional medicine *see* conventional medicine (biomedical)

Tragedy and Hope (Quigley), 32

trance states, channeling *see* channeling

transcendentalism, New Age and, 68

transcendental meditation, field of energy, changing, 63

transformation
    challenges of *see* challenges
    of consciousness, as master agenda, 53
    crises of, 319–20
    and extraterrestrials, 519–26
    feedback loops and, 83
    immediate gratification and, 64
    in love relationships, 330
    of particles, mutual, 166–68
    and Perennial Philosophy, 97

pretending to, 66–67
    through religion, 441–42, 455–56
    see also change; personal growth

Transformation (Strieber), 521

transpersonal crises
    diagnosis of, correct, 316, 317–18
    nurturing environments for, 316–17
    psychic vs. spiritual, 318–20

transpersonal perspective, 309–10
    consciousness and, 157, 161–62
    crises of *see* transpersonal crises
    integration of strategies for, 320–23
    psychology of *see* transpersonal psychology

Transpersonal Psychologies (Tart), 92

transpersonal psychology
    astral planes and, 234
    concerns of, 310–11
    crises of *see* transpersonal crises
    development of, 307–10
    false memories and, 323–25
    growth as built–in, 312–16
    holotropic therapy, 316
    integration of esoteric strategies into, 320–23
    location of experiences, 311–12
    see also transpersonal perspective

Trump, Donald, 63

truth
    linguistic holism and, 77
    mystical, 212–14
    New Age relativity of, 65–66, 107–09, 114
    perspectivism and, 112–16
    see also beliefs; proof and evidence

Truth About the Crash at Roswell, The (Randle and Schmitt), 487

Turner, Ted, 56, 57

Turning Point, The (Capra), 84–89, 90, 311–12

12th Planet, The (Sitchin), 480

Twenty Cases Suggestive of Reincarnation (Stevenson), 143

Twining, Nathan, 491

U

UFO, 513

UFO Crash at Roswell (Randle and Schmitt), 487

UFO Evidence from 1964 Through 1993 (Hall), 490